MODERN RETAILING MANAGEMENT
Basic concepts and practices

DELBERT J. DUNCAN, Ph.D.
Professor of Marketing, Emeritus
University of California, Berkeley

STANLEY C. HOLLANDER, Ph.D.
Professor of Marketing
Graduate School of Business Administration
Michigan State University

NINTH EDITION   1977

RICHARD D. IRWIN, INC.   Homewood, Illinois   60430
Irwin-Dorsey Limited   Georgetown, Ontario L7G 4B3

Earlier editions of this book were published under the title
Retailing: Principles and Methods.

Ninth Edition

67890   54321

ISBN 0-256-01926-6
Library of Congress Catalog Card No. 76–47722

Printed in the United States of America

Learning Systems Company—
a division of Richard D. Irwin, Inc.—has developed a
Programmed Learning AID
to accompany texts in this subject area.
Copies can be purchased through your bookstore
or by writing PLAIDS,
1818 Ridge Road, Homewood, Illinois   60430.

To
ELIZABETH PEAIRS DUNCAN
SELMA D. J. HOLLANDER

PREFACE

Students when enter into retailing careers or who engage in other work that brings them into contact with retailing will find that it is both a highly *stable* and a rapidly *changing business*. Our belief in the importance of all three of the italicized words has influenced the preparation of this, the Ninth Edition, of *Modern Retailing Management*. Merchants who use this book for help in improving their own operations, and retail employees who use it in preparation for the assumption of greater responsibilities, will readily recognize the significance of *stability, change,* and a *business* orientation in retailing.

Since retailing is a *business* activity, retailers must meet the test of the marketplace. They must operate their businesses profitably if they are to survive, if they are to provide employment, if they are to distribute goods and services, and if they are to fulfill social responsibilities. Consequently, throughout this volume we have tried to direct the student's attention to the dollars and cents implications of managerial decisions and to the various methods used to measure the profitability of those decisions. Even more fundamentally, retailers can survive and enjoy profits only by meeting market demands. Therefore, we have tried to underline the importance of customer requirements, tastes, and expectations. Since many persons who enroll in retailing courses have already studied general marketing, our discussion emphasizes the retailing implications of market factors. The retailer must satisfy both market desires and budgetary constraints.

We note the *stability* of retailing in two ways. As outlined in Chapter 3, retailing continues to provide rewarding and stimulating executive and business ownership career opportunities for ambitious young men and women. Moreover, the fundamental challenges that these young people will face in retailing will remain unchanged from year to year. That is, their responsibilities as they advance along the career ladder will continue in the future, as in the past, to involve merchandising, store organization, store location and design, personnel, advertising, and customer service and related decisions. There would be little point in studying retailing if the "basic concepts and practices," to quote our subtitle, did not exhibit constancy.

But tremendous *change* prevails around that carrier wave of stability. Retail markets change, new types of retail institutions emerge, new governmental controls are imposed upon retailing while a few older ones are removed, new technologies modify operating methods, and merchants devise new strategies. Change has been particularly characteristic of the five years since the appearance of our previous edition. This Ninth Edition has been thoroughly updated to take advantage of the most recently published censuses of retail trade and similar reports; to provide descriptions of the new institutions, technologies, and laws; and, most importantly, to illustrate the dynamics of retailing. Some of the developments that have been noted in this edition, and some of the other changes that have been made, can best be indicated by a partial review of the revisions in individual chapters.

Chapter 1 is now entitled "Retailers and Their Markets," and has been reorganized to emphasize both the market environment and the retailing system's response to that environment. The new retail institutions discussed in this chapter include furniture warehouses, catalog appliance showrooms, and hypermarkets. Chapter 4, "Store Location," now includes discussion of relations with landlords, new material on location selection, and such new concepts as "multi-use building," "anchorless mall," and "metro concept." Chapters 5 and 6 review significant developments in store construction and layout, including changes attributable to urban redevelopment, energy-saving needs, and other environmental factors. Chapters 7, 8, and 9, devoted to store organization and personnel, now provide a more current discussion of centralization, include a nontechnical discussion of personnel planning, and have been adjusted to changes in personnel legislation. The chapters on merchandise planning, selection, procurement, and control, Chapters 10 through 15, have been substantially reorganized for teaching effectiveness. The presentation now begins with a discussion of merchandise budgeting in Chapter 10, since the budget is the logical foundation for all subsequent merchandising decisions. Instructors whose schedules do not provide time for consideration of merchandise budgeting can move directly to Chapter 11, "Planning and Selecting Item Assortments."

The pricing chapters, 16 and 17, now give more attention to additional markups, which have become an increasingly important problem in the contemporary economy. In contrast, resale price maintenance now receives much less attention than in the past because of recent legislative developments. Chapter 18, "Retail Advertising and Display," reflects the recent shifts in the importance of print and broadcast media for retailing. Numerous changes in the relevant laws have evoked changes in Chapter 22, "Retail Credit and Collections."

The accounting and expense analysis chapters have been revised as a result of the classroom experience of the authors and their colleagues to help in teaching these subjects to students who have had various degrees of exposure to previous courses in general and/or expense accounting. If the entire class has previously successfully completed at least one course in accounting, the instructor will probably want to start the discussion with the retail method of preparing the income statement. The basic concepts presented in the first portion of Chapter 23 will be needed if the students have not had any accounting preparation. The LIFO/FIFO discussion of earlier editions has been omitted, since the index methods of LIFO adjustment which are appropriate to the retail trades are usually not studied until the second or later courses in accounting.

The controversies over Universal Product Code (UPC) marking and Electronic Funds Transfer Systems (EFTS) are presented in Chapter 25. Chapter 26 is a wholly new one concerned with retail security and loss or damage prevention, currently a vexing problem in the trade. The final chapter, now Chapter 27, has also been extensively revised to pay more attention to the implications of the various control and coordination methods described therein.

These are but illustrations of the numerous changes that have been made, often in response to suggestions and comments that we have gratefully received from instructors, our associates, business people, and students.

Two other changes should be mentioned. First, the annotated bibliography of supplementary readings that was a feature of previous editions has been eliminated to conserve space. However, the extensive set of footnotes continues to provide guidance to the vast, helpful literature of the retail trades.

Second, we have included some Canadian data and more references to Canadian retail institutions than in the past, along with our continued attention to stores and retailing conditions in various parts of the United States. We think these references may have some special interest for our Canadian readers, but hope that our American audience will also be interested in comparative data and in such Canadian innovations as underground malls.

In addition to our appreciation of the valuable suggestions received from retailing faculty and students, mentioned above, we wish to express our graditude for the assistance that many business firms, retail trade associations, trade magazines, and government agencies have given us in furnishing pictures and current data.

Dr. Charles F. Phillips did not participate in this edition nor in the previous one and is not responsible for any of its shortcomings. Readers of earlier editions, of which he was coauthor, are well aware of his many contributions to the success our volume has enjoyed.

February 1977   DELBERT J. DUNCAN
                                   STANLEY C. HOLLANDER

CONTENTS

■ **PART I** Retailing in transition

1. **RETAILERS AND THEIR MARKETS**   **3**

    Market factors affecting retailing: *Demographics. Consumer economics. Consumer psychographics.* Technological advances in retailing. Government regulation. Retailing businesses. Competitive developments.

■ **PART II** Retailing opportunities and careers

2. **BASIC REQUIREMENTS FOR SUCCESSFUL STORE MANAGEMENT**   **41**

    Personal requirements of management. Financial structure. Buildings and physical facilities. Appropriate retailing policies. Competency and loyalty of retail personnel.

3. **OPPORTUNITIES AND CAREERS IN RETAILING**   **58**

    General employment aspects of retailing. Opportunities in small and medium sized stores. Prospects in department and specialty stores. Prospects in chain stores. "Pros" and "cons" of retailing careers.

■ **PART III   The retail store**

4.   STORE LOCATION   91

Location: A persistent problem. Basic factors in location: *Selecting a city or trading area. Selecting a specific site. Leasing or purchasing arrangements.* Changing retail markets. Retail structure of the metropolitan area. Probable future trends.

5.   THE STORE BUILDING, FIXTURES, AND EQUIPMENT   122

The store building as a selling instrument. The store front and exterior. The store interior. Future building and modernization prospects.

6.   ARRANGING THE STORE'S INTERIOR—LAYOUT   147

Definition of and factors influencing layout. Layout procedure. Display: A major factor in layout. Self-selection and self-service.

■ **PART IV   Retail organization**

7.   STRUCTURE OF THE RETAIL FIRM   175

The meaning of organization. Organization in the small store. Larger firm organization. Department stores. Chain store organization structure. Enlarged staff and management information services.

8.   RETAIL PERSONNEL MANAGEMENT   207

Personnel management: Objectives and function. Growing importance of personnel management. Factors causing increased emphasis on personnel management. Definite personnel policies essential. Conducting personnel activities. Personnel planning. Employment procedures. Employee training.

9.   RETAIL PERSONNEL MANAGEMENT (CONTINUED)   233

Compensation for retail personnel. Stimulating satisfactory personnel performance. Evaluating retail personnel. Retail working conditions. Retail unions.

■ **PART V   Merchandise management: Buying, handling, control, and pricing**

10.   MERCHANDISING POLICIES AND BUDGETS   261

General merchandise policies. Merchandise budgeting: Meaning and objectives. Basic elements in merchandise budgeting. Budget supervision. Limitations of the merchandise budget.

11. PLANNING AND SELECTING ITEM ASSORTMENTS   283

Buying plans: *Basic stock list. Model stock list.* Determining quantities to purchase: *Turnover: The economics of small and large inventories.* Determining what merchandise customers want.

12. BUYING: SELECTING MERCHANDISE RESOURCES   302

Choosing vendors: General considerations. Major types of merchandise resources. Vendor initiative to find buyers. Retailer initiative to find vendors. Organizing the buying function. Foreign markets as sources of supply.

13. BUYING: NEGOTIATIONS WITH MERCHANDISE RESOURCES   325

The invoice. Some basics of negotiation. Terms of sale: Discounts. Terms of sale: Datings. Other negotiations for merchandise. The purchase order. Transfer of title.

14. MERCHANDISE CONTROL   349

Goals of merchandise management. Basic types of merchandise information systems. Merchandise management and electronic data processing. The physical inventory. Stock shortages.

15. HANDLING INCOMING MERCHANDISE   370

Activities relating to incoming merchandise. Receiving room layout and equipment. Receiving procedures. Checking procedures. Marking merchandise. Distribution of merchandise within the store. Traffic management. Organization for incoming merchandise.

16. PRICING   394

General price policies: *Price lines. Competitive position.* Markup. Setting prices for individual items. Markup summary.

17. PRICING (CONTINUED)   420

Price changes: *Markdowns.Markdown cancellations and additional markups.* Retail price legislation. Other price regulations. Restraints on pricing freedom.

◼ **PART VI** Sales promotion and customer services

18. RETAIL ADVERTISING AND DISPLAY   443

Functions and goals of retail advertising. Cooperative advertising. Expenditures for retail advertising. Retail advertising strategy. Truth in advertising. Special sales events. Display. Responsibility for advertising and display.

19. OTHER NONPERSONAL METHODS OF RETAIL SALES PROMOTION   476

Telephone and mail-order selling. Packaging for modern selling conditions. Labeling to meet customers' needs. Consumer premiums to promote sales. Special events. Publicity. Some general observations.

20. PERSONAL SELLING   495

Current importance of retail salesmanship. Fundamental elements in a retail sale. The selling process. Management's responsibility for personal salesmanship.

21. CUSTOMER SERVICES   513

Service policies. Alterations. Wrapping merchandise. Delivery service. Complaints and adjustments. Returned goods. Repair service. Store hours. Some other services. Income-producing services. Public services.

22. RETAIL CREDIT AND COLLECTION   540

Volume of retail credit sales. Advantages of credit selling. Problems of selling on credit. Types of retail credit. Banks, finance companies, and credit card companies. Credit management. Collection management. Government regulation of consumer credit. Evaluating the credit department.

■ PART VII   Accounting controls

23. BASIC ACCOUNTING CONTROLS   577

Purposes of accounting. The balance sheet. The operating statement under the cost method. The operating statement under the retail inventory method. Merchandise management accounting.

24. ANALYZING AND CONTROLLING EXPENSES   596

Expense classification. Distribution (allocation) of expenses. Production unit accounting: An additional method. Expense comparisons and analysis. Taking corrective action.

25. CONTROL OF SALES TRANSACTIONS   617

Types of sales transactions. Objectives and requirements of transaction systems. Recording sales. Transaction systems equipment: *Traditional equipment. Electronic sales-recording equipment. Optical scanning and industry code marking. Electronic funds transfer systems.*

26. **RETAIL SECURITY AND LOSS PREVENTION** 636

Shrinkage: An indication of the problem. External crime. Internal theft. Carelessness and error. Fire and accident prevention. Conclusion.

■ PART VIII Coordination and management

27. **MANAGEMENT COORDINATION AND LEADERSHIP** 659

Coordination essential to profitable operation. Standards. Comparative figures. The budget. Retail research. Keeping "current." Executive leadership in retailing.

NAME INDEX 689

SUBJECT INDEX 697

Retailing in transition

RETAILERS AND
THEIR MARKETS

Retailing—the activity of selling consumer goods to ultimate consumers—is constantly changing. Retailers are particularly affected by changes in the consumer markets they serve. Variations in the number, age distribution, location, prosperity, attitudes, and desires of consumers demand appropriate responses from merchants. Retailing methods are also strongly influenced by technological innovations, government regulations, and competitive forces. Large retail organizations conduct elaborate marketing research studies to monitor some of these developments.[1] But all merchants learn much about what is happening and what is likely to happen in their markets by reading business magazines, studying government reports, analyzing their own sales trends, watching competition, and talking with customers, employees, and suppliers.

In this chapter we will briefly describe some of the major trends in the market environment in which retailers operate. We will then note the basic facts about the retailing system that has developed to serve the consumer market. Then we will examine how that system is changing in response to market, environmental, and competitive developments. We will present relatively few statistics here, since our main goal is to show how retailers must stay alert to new trends and developments.* Even

---

* The subject index at the end of this volume can guide you to additional statistics and to the definition of any unfamiliar terms.

though the fundamental task will still be to provide the right merchandise at the right price at the right time and place, retailing tomorrow will undoubtedly be quite different from retailing today. Your task, as a member of the next retailing generation, will be to recognize, or perhaps to lead, those changes.

■ MARKET FACTORS AFFECTING RETAILING

Many of the most important market characteristics that determine retail opportunities can be grouped under three headings: consumer demographics (the study of population and its major aspects), consumer economics (consumer income and spending power), and psychographics (consumer life styles, buying motives, and attitudes).

We will point out some implications of these factors for retailing today and in the future. But please remember that these market forces are complex, and that consumers cannot be easily stereotyped on the basis of a few demographic or psychographic characteristics. Consequently, retailers must study their own markets very carefully to learn how their particular customers will react to any individual merchandising, pricing, advertising, or store operating policy.

As mentioned in the preface, we will examine both U.S. and Canadian trends.

□ Demographics

The U.S. population (about 215 million people as of January 1, 1976) and the Canadian population (approximately 23 million) have been subject to strikingly similar trends.

Population growth Population grew very rapidly in both countries during the 20–25 years following World War II. The rate of increase has since slowed down, primarily due to a decline in the fertility rate. However, even if present trends continue, neither country is expected to reach zero population growth during the next 40–50 years, the period in which most of you will be active in business. Although long-run demographic prediction is very difficult, neither country is expected to have a level population (zero growth) before the year 2040 at the earliest.[2]

Since people are markets, many retailers, particularly those who sell products for infants and children, consider the birthrate decline to be disadvantageous. But others feel that it will give income-earners more discretionary spending power tor leisure goods and even increased purchases and gifts per child.[3] Perhaps the most significant short-run trend from a retailing viewpoint has been the increase in number of households and families, since they are the significant buying units for many products. Households in the U.S. increased from over 63 million in 1970 to slightly more than 71 million in 1975,[4] and are expected to reach 90–96 million by 1990.

Age distribution   A change in the relative importance of the various age groups, with a decline in the percentage of young people, is a natural result of the lower birthrate. People under 18 years of age constituted over 34 percent of the U.S. population in 1970, but only 31 percent in 1975, and will be an even smaller proportion of the total in the future. Young Canadians made up a somewhat larger share of their country's population, but also are becoming relatively less important.[5]

FIGURE 1–1   The U.S. Population, 1955 to 1985

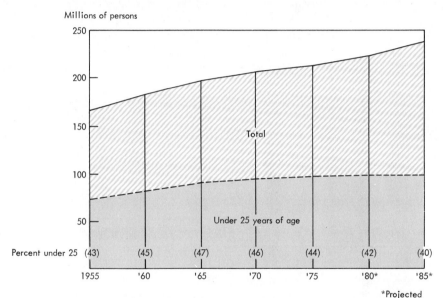

Millions of persons

Percent under 25   (43)   (45)   (47)   (46)   (44)   (42)   (40)

1955   '60   '65   '70   '75   '80*   '85*

*Projected

Reprinted with permission from the July 14, 1975 issue of Advertising Age. *Copyright 1975 by Crain Communications, Inc.*

The youth market remains significant (see Figure 1–1). Nevertheless, many retailers are beginning to place more emphasis on products, styles, and store atmosphere that will appeal to a somewhat older audience. One merchant says, "The bubble-gum junior population is shrinking and the real growth will be in the 25- to 40-year-old group."[6] Slightly more than 10 percent of the U.S. and about 8 percent of the Canadian population is over 65, and this segment will slowly increase in the future. Senior citizens often shop more frequently but buy smaller quantities than younger people, may want more geriatric foods, and often like more service and individual attention.[7] Food stores and drug stores have experimented with discounts and services, such as seminars and talks, free buses to the store, or small-sized food packages, specially designed to appeal to this market.[8]

Population mobility As *Time* magazine says, "Americans have always been a restless people," but a new locational trend has appeared since 1970 (see Figure 1–2). The standard metropolitan statistical areas with two million or more inhabitants failed to gain population between 1970 and 1974 (the last year for which figures are available) and the five largest ones actually experienced net losses, while the nonmetropolitan areas grew by 5.5 percent. This roughly means that people are moving away from the big cities; that their suburbs are not attracting substantial numbers from outside the metropolitan areas (some big suburbs also lost population), and that people are now moving to the countryside. There has also been a substantial migration to the South and Southwest —to the "Sun Belt."[9] The Canadian population movement has been in a more classic pattern: it has traveled from the rural areas to metropolitan ones, which now contain over 55 percent of the population and are becoming increasingly suburbanized.[10]

Changes in consumer location have at least three effects on retailing: (1) Stores must go where the customers are. The trend toward suburban living created the suburban shopping center movement. Currently, such

FIGURE 1–2 **Center of population, United States, 1790–1970** The center of U.S. population has moved steadily westward since 1790 and southward since 1910. The 1980 census will show a continuation of these trends. The northern states with large percentage gains in population (Alaska, Oregon, Idaho, Wyoming) are in the west; California has had a large absolute growth, and percentage growth rates have also been particularly high in Arizona, New Mexico, Arkansas, Texas, Florida, Nevada, Utah, Colorado, and Hawaii.

Source: U.S. Bureau of the Census, *U.S. Census of Population, 1970*, Washington: U.S. Government Printing Office, 1972, vol. 1, p. 14.

major chain store organizations as the S. S. Kresge Company ("K-Marts") and the J. C. Penney Company are opening experimental stores in small towns. (2) Customers who live in suburbs and in country places have different life styles and use different products than city dwellers. The very densely settled urban apartment areas, for example, provide poor markets for lawn barbecue sets or for garage-door basketball hoops. (3) Consumers who move have some tendency to patronize familiar stores at the new location. This gives large, well-known chains some advantage in attracting new arrivals.[11]

Suburbanization   The above data may indicate that the great American migration to the suburbs has finally begun to level off, at least in the largest cities. Many geographers, real estate developers, and merchants would disagree. But whatever the future rate of growth may be, retailers know that a sizable portion of the American population, and an even larger share of the total buying power, shifted to the suburbs during the 1940s, 50s, and 60s. By 1968 the suburbs held 35 percent of the U.S. population, as compared with 20 percent in 1940.[12] These new suburbanites were avid consumers, particularly of automotive and household products, and they also needed new retail facilities. Hence, they created the market for new planned shopping centers.[13] The downtown merchants in Canada were less seriously affected by the suburban trend than U.S. retailers, in part because of some very well-designed shopping complexes in the central business districts, good mass transportation in some of the largest cities, and fewer security problems. Nevertheless, the Canadian population, and Canadian retailing, also became increasingly suburbanized.

☐ Consumer economics

From an economic point of view, retailers are interested in consumer dollar income, the effects of price level changes (inflation), and the distribution of income.

Personal income   Total personal income has risen steadily in the U.S., from about $227 billion in 1950 to approximately $1,150 billion in 1974. But this does not mean that the average person could buy five times as much in 1974 as in 1950. Some of the total increase came from population growth and some was absorbed by greater taxes and related payments. Inflation, or rising prices, also reduced the purchasing power of each individual dollar. Nevertheless, real per-capita disposable income—the amount that each person could spend or save, after adjusting for price changes and taxes, rose about 73 percent between 1950 and 1974. Consumer purchases of goods and services increased about 66 percent, again after adjusting for price increases, during the same period.[14] Inflation, of course, affects shopping patterns, particularly during short periods after each price change, and makes some consumers more careful and value-conscious.[15] It also stimulates consumerism. But unless inflation becomes very serious, it does not change the way people shop nearly as much as they think it does[16] (see Figure 1–3).

FIGURE 1–3 **"How have shopping habits changed?" Same question . . . Different answers**
Shopping smart is its own reward. Both consumers and retailers agree that redeeming store and manufacturer coupons is the most popular way of shopping smart today. They also agree that the meat department is no longer treated like a minefield as it was a year or so ago. In other areas (especially store brands) consumers seem to be exaggerating how much they think they've shifted or retailers haven't yet realized some of the changes that are evolving in their aisles.

Survey A (ask a consumer)   Survey B (ask a retailer)
Thrifty, wise, rational consumers   or   Coupons and specials are big draws;
shop intelligently and save big $$$ otherwise, business as usual

Housewives reporting   Store managers/operators who observe
major change   customers making a major change

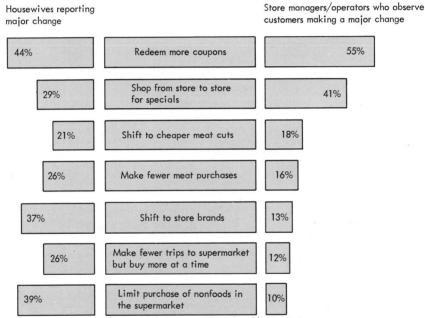

44%	Redeem more coupons	55%
29%	Shop from store to store for specials	41%
21%	Shift to cheaper meat cuts	18%
26%	Make fewer meat purchases	16%
37%	Shift to store brands	13%
26%	Make fewer trips to supermarket but buy more at a time	12%
39%	Limit purchase of nonfoods in the supermarket	10%

Source: *Progressive Grocer*, April 1975, p. 50. Reproduced by permission.

Some consumers use luxury purchases to temporarily overcome feelings of pessimism, and expenditures for convenience and pleasure remain important. But others do curtail major credit purchases, practice "little economies"—reduce shopping time to avoid impulse purchasing temptation, or try to make better buying decisions.[17]

Income distribution The way in which personal income is divided up, whether much of the money goes to a few people or whether income is distributed more evenly, also affects consumer buying. There are various ways of studying income distribution and they lead to different conclusions.[18] But the income increases discussed above have been widely distributed throughout the population. The median family income, even after adjusting for price changes, increased somewhat more than 90 percent in the U.S. and Canada during the 1950s and 1960s.[19]

Consumer credit The great growth of credit buying during the last 30 years has created new retailing opportunities and problems. Automobile and major electric appliance dealers, for example, could never have enjoyed the volume of sales they experienced if consumers had not been willing and able to buy on credit. Easily available credit has also made buying easier and more convenient for customers of many specialty and general merchandise stores. But retailers have also had to handle many difficult aspects of credit management, and have had to comply with an increasing number of federal and local laws regulating credit administration. These opportunities and problems are reviewed in Chapter 22, "Retail credit and collections."

☐ Consumer psychographics

Different researchers have used the term "psychographics" in various ways, but we will apply it to significant aspects of consumer life styles, attitudes, and retail patronage motives.

Changing role of women The changing life styles of women are reflected in a study conducted by the Newspaper Advertising Bureau:

Some time during 1971, the working woman became the retailer's number one customer . . . some time during 1971 there were more women between 18 and 64 holding jobs than staying home and keeping house.[20]

This change in employment has increased family and individual incomes and created new buying power. Women with outside jobs shop in fewer food stores, shop later in the day and purchase more "convenience" foods than women who are not employed outside the home. The trend toward multiple wage earners has left fewer people at home to interview door-to-door salespeople, and has probably contributed to the increase in mail-order shopping.[21] Recognition of women's rights has also affected retail employment and credit practices, as discussed in Chapters 8 and 22, below.

More informality but little extra leisure We can note the combined effects of several forces already mentioned. Many analysts have predicted substantially reduced working hours, and correspondingly more leisure, for the second half of the 20th century.[22] The work week has shortened slightly, and households now have more labor-saving devices, but all of this translates into little extra free time. Greater suburbanization has prevented reduction in travel time to work; working wives have very little leisure, and full-time homemakers now invest more hours in household management—family care and shopping. Television has probably absorbed much of the extra available recreation time,[23] a fact that has influenced retail advertising (see Chapter 18).

However, many consumers use or extend the available free time in ways that create new sales opportunities for merchants. Additional expenditures for sporting goods, hobby equipment, audio systems, travel-related products, and the like reflect widespread desires to "intensify" the value of each recreational hour.[24] Many consumers have chosen to reduce the formalities of life: they eat and entertain casually in preference to formal meals; they wear more "leisure-style" clothes; and they do much of their buying in informal "one-stop, self-service" outlets rather than the more elaborate, traditional department stores.[25] Yet, interestingly, the traditional department stores have also prospered greatly by adapting to their customers' suburban lifestyle. The rising costs of building and home maintenance, the changing age mix that includes more young adults, and desires to escape home care burdens, have encouraged more apartment living. The apartment dwellers tend to buy somewhat different furniture and household goods than home-owners.[26] Simultaneously, rising costs for repairs and maintenance services have augmented the market for do-it-yourself supplies.[27]

This list does not exhaust all of the changes in life styles. Moreover, none of these trends are monolithic, or uniform, throughout the market. Individual consumers vary greatly in their reactions to any specific trend: some become absorbed in it; some only partially accept it; and others move in exactly the opposite direction. The list does suggest the types of market patterns that affect retail businesses.

Store patronage motives Consumer diversity becomes most apparent when we examine patronage motives—the consumer reasons for selecting various stores—since those motives vary not only between consumers but within any one individual from time to time and depending upon the items being purchased. The same individual who rushes to the nearest convenience food store for a box of crackers or some ice cream if company is suddenly expected may go to the country club "pro shop" for expert advice and attention in buying golf clubs; to a large downtown department store for the widest selection of clothing styles; and to a self-service supermarket for efficiency in purchasing weekly supplies of food or health and beauty aids. One useful classification divides customers into: *economical shoppers* who want to obtain the best value for the time and money invested in shopping; *personalizing shoppers* who want considerable attention and personal interaction; *ethical shoppers* who feel an obligation to patronize a particular group of stores, such as small merchants or local businesses; and *apathetic shoppers* who are disinterested in the whole process.[28] Professor Tauber notes that, under various circumstances, people may go shopping to obtain diversion, to learn about new items, to meet with friends, to enjoy a sense of status, to feel skilled in buying or bargaining, or to satisfy other motives.[29] Store reputation, merchandise price/value relationships, merchandise quality, store atmosphere, convenience, parking facilities, salesclerk service, credit arrangements and other such factors influence customers' evaluations of stores.

Merchants should consider these and other aspects of consumer store selection criteria in deciding on store location, interior layout, merchandise selection, store services, and other policies.[30] To illustrate, the efficiency-oriented "economical shoppers" mentioned above want to control the time spent shopping and often plan purchases in advance.[31] In addition to attractive prices, they like stores with predictable assortments, easy access to the goods, and fast service. In contrast, the personalizing shoppers want to "kill time," browse leisurely, and chat lengthily with salespeople. Some customers enjoy store restaurants and shopping center entertainments, others are totally disinterested.

Consumerism and ecological interests Increased education, rising prices, and extensive publicity have made customers more aware of consumeristic and ecological issues.[32] The J. C. Penney Company says: "There will be more consumer action, not less, in the years to come and it will continue to be most active at the grassroots level, where the action really counts."[33] Consumerism and ecological interests have produced considerable governmental regulation, as discussed later in this chapter, but they also have stimulated stores to improve merchandise quality and customer communications.[34]

Increased crime One extremely unfortunate social change is reflected in an increased rate of shoplifting, pilferage, and store-employee theft. U.S. retailers probably lost over $6 billion to these and other crimes in 1974[35] and have to undertake extensive, expensive countermeasures described in Chapter 26.

■ TECHNOLOGICAL ADVANCES IN RETAILING

Large retailers are increasingly using electronic computers, new data-processing systems, and other technological devices and methods to improve their operating techniques and procedures. Some medium-sized merchants are also now participating in the "computer revolution."

Electronic data-processing systems have mainly been used for employee payroll records, customer credit accounts, inventory control, and accounts payable. But most authorities agree that this only scratches the surface of what EDP systems can and will do in retail stores of the future. Automated merchandise control systems that maintain balanced stocks and "spot" fast- and slow-selling items, thus helping to predict future sales, are coming into use. And the computer has great, relatively untapped, potential for use in retail research. Opportunities exist, for instance, in studying: which customers buy what merchandise and how they respond to different prices and promotional tactics; in helping schedule the use of part-time salespeople; and in forecasting. (Electronic data-processing equipment and its current and potential retail applications are discussed at several points in the chapters that follow. See especially Chapters 5, 14, and 25.)

Many other technological changes are also affecting retailing. Automation has had considerable impact in food retailing where new cashiering and check-out systems are under consideration. It is evident in automatic merchandising, in office procedures, and in handling merchandise in stores, warehouses, and distribution centers (see Chapter 15).

■ GOVERNMENT REGULATION

Retailers have become subject to an increasing volume of federal, state (in Canada, provincial), and local laws.[36] Many of these concern specific aspects of retail management, such as personnel management or buying practices, which we will consider in the chapters dealing with those topics. We cannot, in the space available here, discuss the myriad of legislative and administrative rules that govern retail operations, any more than we could possibly describe all consumer buying motives or lifestyles. We will note some major trends under the headings of (1) antitrust and competition policy, (2) consumeristic and environmental legislation, (3) anti-inflationary controls and (4) other regulations.

☐ Antitrust and competition policy

The large retail organizations have grown, in part, through *internal* expansion, i.e., the opening of additional stores and enlargement of existing ones, and in part through mergers and acquisitions. The U.S. Federal Trade Commission and Department of Justice have now tried to restrict the way these firms may grow through mergers and purchases of other stores.

The commission has announced that food-chain mergers and acquisitions that result in over $500 million food store sales per annum will "warrant attention and consideration" (which suggests they probably will be prohibited); also that food-chain mergers and amalgamations resulting in combined food store sales between $100 and $500 million will "warrant investigation."[37] The commission has also obtained agreements from several large department-store corporations to refrain for specified periods of time from any department-store mergers or acquisitions that did not have the Commission's specific prior approval. As an illustration, in 1975 the FTC accepted a settlement in which the Associated Dry Goods Corporation, a company with seventeen other major department- and specialty-store divisions, agreed to sell the Ayr-Way discount stores it had purchased in 1972.[38] During the same year the FTC allowed Arlen Realty and Development Corporation, a discount-store firm, to purchase only two of the six stores it wanted to buy from the McCrory Corporation.[39]

To date, at least, the government has mainly attempted to restrict mergers and acquisitions that involve large groups of similar stores—for example, two food chains. Amalgamations that unite different types of stores such as supermarkets and discount houses, however, have gone relatively unchallanged, resulting in important implications for the diversification policies of large retail organizations as we will note later in this chapter.

Other federal actions to foster retail competition include a Supreme Court ruling that state governments cannot prohibit price advertising for prescription drugs;[40] Federal Trade Commission and court decisions forbidding the major tenants in shopping centers from trying to prevent the rental of space to lower-priced competitors (these rulings are discussed in Chapter 4); and 1974–76 cases in which several leading New York and San Francisco fashion specialty shops paid antitrust penalties for forcing garment manufacturers to stop selling to cut-price dress shops.[41] The Canadian government has not imposed limits on chain-store growth, but the Food Prices Review Board has sponsored a study of concentration in the retail food trade in 32 urban areas. This study estimated that the share of the total business obtained by the four largest chains in each area ranged from 23.4 percent to 98.4 percent.[42]

☐ Consumeristic and environmental controls

The concern about consumer issues, mentioned earlier, has resulted in a stream of laws that now help shape retailers' pricing, labeling and packaging, advertising, and credit practices. These laws will be discussed at the appropriate points in the chapters that follow. Environmental (ecological) rules affect shopping center location and design—permission to build a new center often depends upon submission of an acceptable environmental-impact statement. The products that are available for sale in stores are increasingly subject to consumeristic or ecologically-inspired controls.

☐ Anti-inflationary controls

During 1972–74, the U.S. government experimented with official Wage and Price Guidelines in an effort to curb rapidly rising prices. These guidelines supposedly limited the wage increases that large firms (including large retailers) could pay and the price increases they could charge, but the rules necessarily included many exceptions and adjustments. Similarly, Canada established an Anti-Inflation Board in November 1975 to implement a wages and prices policy. The Board then ruled that retailers could not increase their margins (the percentage difference between merchandise cost and selling price). It also limited the wage increases that could be paid to workers in large and in unionized companies.[44] There is considerable debate, which we cannot explore here, about the effectiveness of such controls. But if inflation should persist over the long run, as some economists predict, these controls may be extended or reimposed in the future.

□ Other regulations

Many other laws also affect retailing. Various licenses and permits are required for certain types of business. Retailers may have to collect sales or excise taxes from their customers. Personnel methods, including hiring, wage, working conditions, and pension practices are increasingly subject to control, as we shall see in Chapters 8 and 9. The Robinson-Patman Act, a U.S. law designed to reduce some of the large retailers' buying strengths and advantages, affects purchasing and promotional practices. Store openings on Sundays, the use of trading stamps, and franchising arrangements are just a few of the other aspects of retailing that may be controlled by government.

□ Government assistance

It is not accurate to review the role of government in retailing solely in terms of negative controls; as simply a set of prohibitions. First, we should note that substantial numbers of retailers have wanted some of these controls. The Robinson-Patman Act, for example, was urged through Congress by groups of small grocery retailers and their wholesalers who felt threatened by large chains.[45] Second, government helps merchants through such specialized retailing-related activities as collecting and publishing census data for market research purposes; conducting distributive education classes for retail workers; and providing Small Business Administration assistance for financing and developing small stores.[46] Third, stores benefit from general public services including street and highway construction, public parking lots, water supply, and sewage and sanitation services. Fourth, and most important, however, government helps by creating a secure and dependable environment in which people can conduct their businesses without experiencing excessive risk.

▪ RETAIL BUSINESSES

A study in contrasts   There are somewhat more than 1.9 million retail establishments in the United States and about 160 thousand in Canada.* Some of these retail units are very small, with daily sales of as little as $20; others have sales of $100,000 or more each business day. Some carry small assortments of very limited lines of goods—for example, the tobacco shop and the small newsstand. In contrast, department stores carry broad assortments of many kinds of goods. Some stores extend a large number of services, such as credit and delivery, along with the goods they sell. Others sell only on a "cash-and-carry" basis and require customers to serve themselves. Certain stores are well-run; others show obvious signs of poor management. Some stores are organized as proprietorships, others as partnerships and cooperatives; still others are corporations. Alongside of the independent store, we find one controlled by an organization with a thousand or more units. Truly, a study of retail structure is a study in contrasts.

Yet if we look beneath some of the contrasting features of these retail establishments, we find that their operators have much more in common. As indicated, practically all are engaged in the final stage of the marketing of consumers' goods**: they obtain goods from various sources of supply and resell to ultimate consumers. More specifically, retailers exist to serve their customers and prospective customers by providing wanted goods and services at the proper times, places, and prices. They generally perform such marketing activities or functions as buying and selling (functions involving transfer of title), transporting, storage, and plant maintenance (functions involving physical supply), and financing, risk taking, market information, and personnel management ("facilitating functions").†

Retailing methods   Retail organizations reach their customers in one or more of four ways: through stores, mail- and telephone-order business, house-to-house selling, and automatic vending machines. Stores are the most important of these four methods of retailing, handling, according to the census, about 97 percent of all retail trade. However, the census counts mail and telephone orders received at stores and sales through vending machines located inside store buildings as part

---

* Canada does not include restaurants and other eating and drinking places in its Census of Retail Trade. Therefore for purposes of comparison, the 360,000 eating and drinking places enumerated in the 1972 U.S. Census of Retail Trade should be deducted from the 1.9 million total establishments to provide a roughly comparable figure of 1.54 million other retail locations.

** The census classifies some farm and building-supply stores that sell producers' goods as part of retail trade.

† For detailed discussions of the marketing functions, see any of the standard textbooks on marketing.

of in-store retailing rather than as mail order or automatic vending. In actuality, therefore, those latter methods probably accounted for substantially larger shares of retail business than the 1 percent and the ⅔ of 1 percent reported in the 1972 census.[47]

□ Number and sales of retail stores

Table 1–1 shows the number of retail establishments, total sales, and average sales per store in the U.S. for selected years beginning in 1929.

TABLE 1–1

Retailers and sales, United States, selected years, 1929–1975

Year	Number of establishments (000 omitted)	Total sales (000,000 omitted)	Average sales per store
1929	1,476	$ 48,330	$ 33,000
1933	1,526	25,037	16,000
1939	1,770	42,042	24,000
1948	1,770	130,521	74,000
1958	1,788	199,646	112,000
1963	1,708	244,202	143,000
1967	1,763	310,214	176,000
1972	1,912	470,800	246,000
1975	n.a.	584,423	n.a.

Source: The 1929–1972 data are from the *Census of Business*. The sales estimates for 1975 are from the *Survey of Current Business*, October 1976, p. S–12. Data for different years are not completely comparable. Figures prior to 1963 do not include sales made in Alaska and Hawaii. Military post-exchange and commissary sales are not included in any of the above figures. Some industrial, institutional, and club cafeteria, restaurant, and canteen sales are also excluded.

Changes in the price level caused some of the increase in dollar sales volume shown in this table. The actual quantity of goods sold at retail has not fluctuated as much as the dollar figures might suggest. Nevertheless, adjusting for changes in the price level indicates that physical volume probably multiplied about four-and-a-half times between 1929 and 1975. The total number of stores (retail establishments) reported in the U.S. Census remained remarkably steady from 1939 to 1967. The 1972 census showed an increase of about 150,000 establishments but much of this was probably due to improved data collection methods which covered many very small and part-time businesses that would have been omitted under earlier procedures.

□ Sales by kind of business

Table 1–2 shows the sales of different kinds (or lines) of retail businesses in the U.S. and Canada in 1972, the year of the latest U.S. Census

TABLE 1–2

Retail sales by kind of business—1972 (in billions of dollars)

United States		Canada[1]	
Kind of business	Sales	Kind of business	Sales
Total	$471	Total[2]	$33.9
Building-material, hardware, farm-equipment dealers	25	Hardware	0.4
General merchandise group[3] stores	67	General merchandise group	6.0
Food stores	101	Food stores	7.9
Automotive group[4]	94	Automotive dealers	5.7
Gasoline service stations	34	Service stations and garages	2.9
Apparel and accessory stores[5]	25	Apparel and accessories	2.0
Furniture, home-furnishings, and equipment stores	22	Furniture, TV, and appliances	1.1
Eating and drinking places[6]	37		
Drug and proprietary stores[7]	16	Drug stores	1.0
Miscellaneous retail stores	39	Miscellaneous	6.9
Nonstore retailers	11	Nonstore retailers	n.a.

[1] Kind of business classifications for the U.S. and Canada are not directly comparable.
[2] The Canadian retail trade census does not include sales of eating and drinking establishments. Some forms of nonstore retailing are also excluded, such as vending machine and direct selling business, which amounted to about $1 billion in 1972.
[3] Includes department stores, discount department stores and variety ("five-and-ten-cent" stores).
[4] Includes tire, battery, and automotive accessory stores, as well as new- and used-car dealers.
[5] Includes shoe stores.
[6] See note 2.
[7] Proprietary stores sell drugstore-type merchandise, but do not fill prescriptions.
Sources: *1972 Census of Retail Trade, Area Statistics, United States*, RC72–A–52 (Washington, D.C.: U.S. Government Printing Office, 1975).
Canada Yearbook 1973 (Ottawa: Statistics Canada, 1973), p. 729.

and very close to the latest available Canadian Retail Census. Food retailing is the largest single category in both countries, and becomes even more impressive when restaurant sales are added to those of food stores. The importance of the automotive and automotive-related, general merchandise, and apparel categories is also evident.

☐ Independent and chain stores

Both in numbers and in total sales volume, the small single-unit store is still the predominant retail institution in the United States and Canada. About 85 percent of U.S. retail establishments are operated by individuals or firms that have only one store in the same general kind of business. They handled almost 55 percent of all retail sales.[48] Canadian figures show that businesses with one to three stores accounted for about 60 percent of all retailing in 1973.[49]

Retail firms operating more than one unit accounted for about 30 percent of all U.S. retail trade in 1929, when the first census of retail distribution was compiled; by 1972 their share had grown to 45 percent. But almost all of this growth in the multiunits' share has occurred during the last 20 years. The greatest growth in market share has taken place among firms with four or more stores. Although variations in census classifications make precise comparisons difficult, chains and department-store ownership groups with four or more stores seem to have accounted for about 24 percent of all retail business in 1929; 27–28 percent in 1933; 25 percent in 1935; 23–24 percent in 1939, 1948, and 1954; 27 percent in 1958; 34 percent in 1967; and 39 percent in 1972.[50] Figure 1–4 shows the relative importance of single-unit firms, smaller multiunits (2–10 establishments) and larger multiunits (11 or more outlets) in selected lines of business. As indicated above, firms with four or more establishments handled about 40 percent of all Canadian retail trade in 1973.

Some large retail organizations Table 1–3 indicates the importance of some of our largest retail organizations; that is, for 1975 it shows the approximate average number of employees, the sales volume, and the earnings of the 20 largest U.S. firms and the seven largest Canadian ones measured by sales. Most of these companies operate primarily supermarkets, department stores, variety stores, or discount houses.

□ Small and large stores

The small size of the typical retail store often astonishes people who are unfamiliar with retailing. For example, 30 percent of all U.S. retail establishments had sales of less than $30,000 per year ($600 per week) in 1972, and they accounted for less than 1.7 percent of all sales. Only a little over 4 percent of the stores enjoyed a sales volume of $1,000,000 or more, but they did 52.5 percent of the total retail trade.[51] Another way of looking at the size distribution shows that about 58 percent of all U.S. retail establishments had only two or less paid employees. In contrast, about 30 percent of all retail workers were in stores with 50 or more employees and those stores received about 31 percent of the total retail sales volume.

■ COMPETITIVE DEVELOPMENTS

The retailing structure that we have just examined is not static. The individual companies that form the structure prosper and expand, or decline and disappear, as they succeed or fail in adjusting to the changing market environment and in meeting the rivalry of eager new competitors. The test of market performance affects large firms as well as small ones. This is illustrated by the bankruptcy of the W. T. Grant Company (previously the U.S.'s 16th largest retailer) in 1975 and the major reorganization of the Great Atlantic & Pacific Tea Company (A&P,

FIGURE 1–4 **Percent distribution of sales by firm size: 1972 (for selected kinds of business)**

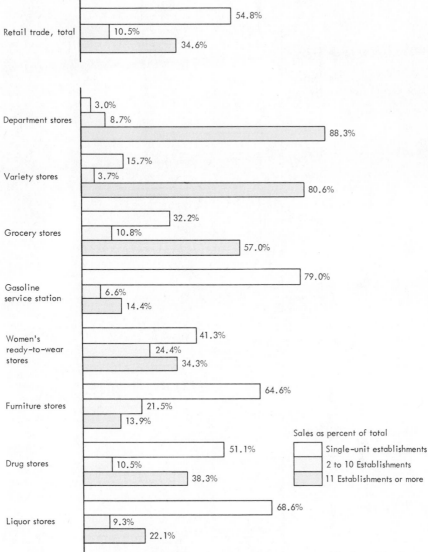

Note: Firm size is based on total number of retail establishments operated by the owning firm in the kind-of-business classification group, or total for which data are presented.
Source: 1972 Census of Retail Trade, RC72–5–1 Establishment or Firm, July 1972.

previously the country's fourth largest) in 1974–75, after substantial losses in fiscal 1973 and 1975. At the same time other retailers were increasing their sales and profits.

But competitive changes encourage or discourage *types* of stores and *methods* of retailing as well as individual companies. In the pages that follow, we will examine some of the more important developments.

TABLE 1–3

Employees, sales, and earnings of the 20 largest U.S. and 7 largest Canadian retailers, 1975

Rank	Company	Number of employees[a]	Sales[b] ($000)	Net income[c] ($000)	Net income as percent of sales
United States					
1	Sears, Roebuck (Chicago)	377,000†	13,639,887	522,591	3.8
2	Safeway Stores (Oakland)	126,964	9,716,889	148,629	1.5
3	J. C. Penney (New York)	186,000	7,678,600	189,600	2.5
4	S. S. Kresge (Troy, Mich.)	155,000	6,883,613	200,832	2.9
5	Great Atlantic & Pacific Tea (Montvale, N.J.)	92,900	6,537,897	4,314	0.1
6	Kroger (Cincinnati)	56,969	5,339,225	34,441	0.6
7	Marcor (Chicago)	145,926†	4,822,273	135,196	2.8
8	F. W. Woolworth (New York)	202,402	4,650,290	99,148	2.1
9	Federated Department Stores (Cincinnati)	88,500†	3,712,864	157,411	4.2
10	American Stores (Wilmington)	42,044	3,207,248	31,965	1.0
11	Lucky Stores (Dublin, Calif.)	42,000	3,109,406	47,940	1.5
12	Winn-Dixie Stores (Jacksonville)	39,165	2,962,165	55,552	1.9
13	Jewel Companies (Chicago)	34,985	2,817,754	28,692	1.0
14	Rapid-American (New York)	55,000	2,532,247	5,275**	0.2
15	Food Fair Stores (Philadelphia)	35,000†	2,482,539	(3,434)	—
16	City Products (Des Plaines, Ill.)[d]	47,000	2,224,968	29,117	1.3
17	May Department Stores (St. Louis)	59,000†	2,017,366	66,706	3.3
18	Southland (Dallas)	28,600	1,787,928	34,319	1.9
19	Allied Stores (New York)	55,400	1,770,635	55,451	3.1
20	Dayton Hudson (Minneapolis)	30,000†	1,692,528	51,317	3.0

Canada

1	George Weston Ltd. (Toronto)[e]	45,000	5,046,693	16,233	0.32
2	Dominion Stores Ltd. (Toronto)	24,700	1,913,986	20,437	1.03
3	Canada Safeway Ltd. (Winnipeg)[f]	n.a.	1,877,719	34,109	1.82
4	Steinberg's Lts. (Montreal)	23,000	1,420,966	11,460	0.81
5	T. Eaton Co. (Toronto)[g]	n.a.	1,400,000	n.a.	n.a.
6	Simpson-Sears Ltd. (Toronto)	n.a.	1,341,128	34,454	2.80
7	Hudson's Bay Co. (Winnipeg)[h]	20,000	1,189,330	22,004	1.85

[a] Year-end total or (if followed by dagger†) average for year. Employee figures for Canadian companies are mainly estimates.
[b] Includes sales of subsidiaries.
[c] After taxes** indicates extraordinary credit equal to at least 10 percent of income. Parentheses indicate loss.
[d] Wholly owned by Household Finance Corp.
[e] Includes processing, wholesaling, and retailing subsidiaries in Canada and the United States.
[f] Includes 156 stores in Australia and Europe.
[g] 1974 estimate. The T. Eaton Company is privately owned and does not publish its results.
[h] Includes manufacturing and wholesaling subsidiaries in Canada and for business in the United States sales were $892,766,000.

Source: U.S. data: Reprinted from the July 1976 issue of Fortune Magazine by special permission; © 1976 Time Inc.
Canadian data: *Retail Newsletter*, International Association of Department Stores, October 1975; *Fairchild's Financial Manual of Retail Stores 1976* (New York: Fairchild Books, 1976); *Moody's Industrial Manual, 1976, Standard & Poor's Listed Stock Reports*.

□ Large store development

Most, but not all, large stores are operated by large companies. A business that has one or two fairly large stores may be small in comparison to a company that operates many small units. In this section we will note some major tendencies affecting large stores.

Department store branches and planned shopping centers The traditional downtown full-service department stores were very slow in following their customers to the suburbs after World War II. Consequently, they undoubtedly lost considerable sales to the more conveniently located new discount department stores and to the store branches of the two major mail order companies, Sears, Roebuck and Company and Montgomery Ward and Company. Fortunately, most of the progressive department store companies eventually recognized the need to have stores near their customers' homes. (Also see the discussions of these topics in Chapters 4 and 7.) By 1965, U.S. department stores with sales of $1,000,000 or more per year obtained half of their business from branch stores, mostly located in planned shopping centers, and by 1974 that figure grew to almost 72 percent.[52] However, in a survey of 105 top retailing executives, two thirds predicted that these branch stores will become more specialized in the future rather than attempting to handle the full assortment of department store merchandise, as is the present practice.[53]

Discount department stores The commonly-used terms "discount department store" and "discount house" are vague and difficult to define. The most successful firm in this type of retailing, the S. S. Kresge Company, prefers to call its well-known K-Marts "promotional department stores," rather than "discount stores." But originally, discount houses were small, semi-secret stores that sold branded electrical appliances, watches, cameras, luggage, jewelry, and similar items at cut prices. Discount stores that featured apparel, rather than "hard" goods, began to appear in New England in the early 1950s and quickly attracted large numbers of price-conscious customers. Today "discount house," "discount store" and, particularly, "discount department store," are most likely to mean establishments with the following characteristics:

1. Broad merchandise assortments, including both "hard" and "soft" goods, and frequently food as well.
2. Merchandise assortments mainly limited to the most popular items, colors, and sizes in each product classification.
3. An emphasis on price as the main sales appeal. The price lines are aimed at middle- and low-income families.
4. Self-service operations with cashiers at checkout stations, except for specialized merchandise such as pharmacy and cameras.

5. Limited customer services, or extra charges for such services as credit and delivery.
6. Long hours, frequently from 10:00 a.m. to 10:00 p.m., and often including Sunday.
7. Large stores, ranging from 50,000 to 200,000 square feet or more, are common. The *Discount Merchandiser* magazine sets 10,000 square feet as a minimum, but the average size in 1975 was 71,579 square feet.[54]
8. A large, free, parking area.
9. Relatively simple, unostentatious buildings and fixtures.

The *Discount Merchandiser* magazine estimates that the 6,387 discount department stores in the U.S. achieved almost $33 billion sales in 1975.[55] There was great growth in the discount department store business from the early 1950s to about 1973, except for a troubled period about 1964 in which some weaker firms were eliminated. The industry entered another similar period in 1972, achieving dollar sales gains of only 3–5 percent per year from 1972 to 1975 or less than the rate of inflation. Much of the problem seems to have been due to over-expansion, ill-considered choice of locations, and poor internal-control methods. Several chains closed, and others suffered financial difficulties. But at the same time, the more successful firms, such as Kresge, and a number of well-managed regional chains, grew even stronger.[56]

Part of the general discount department stores' new competition has come from specialty discount outlets—chains of stores that concentrate on one major product category at low prices. Such stores may feature toys, carpets, fabrics, or some other line.[57] Other new competition comes from "combination supermarkets" which sell large quantities of health and beauty aids and general merchandise along with foods, and from "combination drug stores" that sell electric appliances, housewares, garden supplies, sporting goods, and miscellaneous merchandise in addition to traditional drugstore lines.* Finally, other competition comes from catalog showrooms, which we will discuss later in this chapter. As is evident from this discussion, many different types of discount stores have developed to cater to the variations in customers' shopping preferences.

Leased departments   Many department and discount stores have been able to expand into new merchandise departments by leasing those departments to outside individuals or firms when the store management felt unable to handle the new lines successfully. These departments, also called "licensed departments" or "concessions," are usually not iden-

---

* The *Discount Merchandiser* estimates that there were over 1,000 combination supermarkets and over 1,650 combination drug stores in 1975 ("The True Look of the Discount Industry," pp. 54, 58).

tified as being under separate control and customers generally cannot tell whether they are shopping in store-owned or leased departments.*

Leasing arrangements vary widely, but the store usually provides space, fixtures, heat and light, and bookkeeping services, plus its regular credit and delivery services if offered in the other departments. The lessee provides the merchandise and salespeople and manages the department. The lessee pays the store a flat monthly rental charge or a percentage of its sales or some combination thereof.

About 6 percent of all sales in traditional department stores in 1974 resulted from leased departments.[58] About 10 percent of discount store sales in 1974 and almost 20 percent in 1969–70 came from similar departments.[59] Although a wide variety of departments are leased in different establishments, the most frequently leased sections are shoes, millinery, jewelry, photographic studies, beauty shops, and tire, battery, and automotive-accessory departments.[60]

Leasing relieves the store from providing its own capital and staff to operate the department. Thus, it can expand much more rapidly and can experiment with new departments at minimum risk. It also benefits from the lessee's specialized management and (in the case of large lessees) buying power. The lessee gains by concentrating upon its specialized merchandise lines. It uses the store's fixtures and services. And it benefits from the customer traffic generated by the other departments and the store's overall promotion.

Nevertheless, friction may develop between the store and the lessee. Leasing increases coordination problems, and a single poorly-operated leased department can harm the entire store's image.[61] Pricing flexibility is reduced, since the store cannot cut prices in the leased department to attract customers for the other departments. And the lease limits the income that can be obtained from the department.†

Many of the advantages of leasing seem less significant as the store organization (the landlord) becomes more firmly entrenched, acquires more capital, and develops its own capable executives. As the lessor (landlord) firm grows, it often decides to operate many departments previously leased. Consequently, some observers predict a decline in leasing, especially among major discount chains, in the future. But one expert believes it will continue in some degree for departments with complicated inventory problems, such as shoes; that require considerable technical knowledge, such as watch repairs, and cameras and photo

---

* Exceptions to this rule may include travel agency branches in department stores (if the name of the national agency is an important sales tool), and in-store podiatry, optometrist, and optician's departments (when state law requires such identification).

† The lessee also experiences some disadvantages. The department develops good will for the store rather than for the lessee. The rental charge may be quite high in some cases. And, after developing a good business, the lessee may lose the lease since the landlord store may decide to operate the department or rent to someone else.

supplies; and those with service and operating problems, such as restaurants and snack bars.[62]

New types of home furnishings stores   In recent years, three new types of large stores have appeared in such "hard goods" lines as furniture, household appliances, and hardware and building supplies.

1. Furniture warehouses   These stores, pioneered by the Levitz Furniture Corporation, feature (a) a "warehouse," no-frills atmosphere, and location which give an impression of low prices; (b) a large stock of furniture, mostly still packed in factory cartons, all displayed for immediate sale. This eliminates the delays experienced when customers order from sample pieces in some conventional furniture outlet; and (c) prices that do not include delivery, since most customers take the furniture home in their own trucks or station wagons, and may not include credit. The first such stores were enormously successful, and the warehouse was hailed as the new "supermarket" of the furniture industry.[63] But the anticipated cost savings failed to develop. Moreover, many customers found the service unsatisfactory, particularly since the uninspected furniture purchased in the original carton may have been poorly made or have become damaged in transit. Consequently, the growth of such warehouse stores has slowed markedly, and many surviving companies are experimenting with additional services.[64]

2. Catalog appliance showrooms   These stores should be distinguished from mail-order company outlets. In appearance, catalog appliance showrooms resemble trading-stamp redemption centers. The items available for sale are shown both in catalogs, usually with a list price in plain numerals and the actual price in code, and in display cases. The limited number of samples on display can be closely watched, which reduces shoplifting, and also require relatively little space that is furnished and fixtured for customer service. The customers' orders are filled and sent to a cashier's desk from the adjacent "warehouse" or stockroom, where the inventory can be handled compactly and without frills. The main customer attraction is a claim of low prices for branded jewelry, watches, housewares and appliances, silver and china, luggage, sporting goods and toys. The catalog showrooms, pioneered by such firms as Consumer Distributing Company of Toronto; Best Products Company of Ashland, Virginia, Basco, Inc. of Cherry Hill, New Jersey, and Jewelco, Inc. of New York, also enjoyed considerable initial success. Sales for 1972 were estimated at $2 billion in the U.S. alone, and profits were high. But competition intensified, operating the showrooms proved more difficult than anticipated, and many companies suffered disappointing results.[65]

3. Home centers   Home centers have had a less spectacular, but more substantial growth than either furniture warehouses or catalog discount showrooms. The National Retail Hardware Association defines a home center as "a retail outlet which carries (at least) the basic hard-lines of hardware, tools, plumbing and heating equipment, and electrical supplies, as well as lumber and building materials. . . . Strong consumer appeals predominate, including how-to service and information for the do-it-yourself market, convenient shopping hours, and accessible, adequate, parking facilities."[66] The typical home center is designed for sales of $1 million or more per year. These stores seem to fill a major consumer need and now constitute an important growth sector in hardware and building supply retailing.

Hypermarkets and superstores Hypermarkets, a European innovation in retailing, are very large self-service stores (minimum 25,000 square feet, but most much larger) that sell a mixture of foods and general merchandise in a warehouse atmosphere. Many of the products are displayed in wire baskets (pentainers) and metal racks which are moved through the aisles and stacked to a height of 12–15 feet by forklift truck during selling hours. These markets spread through France, under the leadership of the Carrefour Company, and in Germany, where they were called "verbrauchermarkt" in the late 1960s and early 1970s.[67] The absence of strong supermarket competition particularly favored hypermarket growth in France.[68]

The Oshawa Group of Toronto created the first North American hypermarket, the 267,000 square foot Hypermarché Laval near Montreal, in November 1974. In part because of severe local competition, sales were unsatisfactory and expenses higher than planned.[69] Meijer, Inc. of Grand Rapids, Michigan has opened a 245,000 square foot store with 68 checkout registers in Plymouth, Michigan—the closest U.S. approximation to the hypermarket, but having somewhat less of a warehouse appearance.[70] Other U.S. and Canadian companies have also shown interest in the hypermarket concept, but executives disagree as to whether such stores can develop the necessary sales volume in countries where consumers are already supplied by large numbers of convenient supermarkets and discount department stores. Regardless of whether hypermarkets become established in the U.S. and Canada or not, many experts see a need for large combination and superstores that will sell increasing amounts of nonfoods along with foodlines.[71] Such units can permit consumers to experience "one stop shopping" for most routine purchases.

□ Small store developments

Retailing innovations do not always create large stores. We have already noted the recent growth of specialty discount stores (such as discount toy stores and discount carpet outlets) that are considerably smaller than the big discount department stores. Many very specialized nondiscount chains and specialized independent stores have also encountered a very favorable reception in recent years. A leading store designer points to the opportunities for "small stores that pre-select merchandise for certain persons, that buy with individuals' lifestyles in mind, that have a one-to-one relationship with their customers. . . ."[72]

Other small stores have developed out of two trends discussed below: the growth of franchising* and the spread of convenience stores. Again, one must carefully distinguish between establishment (store) and firm size. A company that operates only one or two small stores will naturally be quite small itself, but a company that has many small stores will be large. Franchises and convenience store companies come in both sizes.

Franchising   The term "franchising" covers a variety of arrangements under which one firm (the franchisor) licenses a number of retail or service outlets (the franchisees) to operate in accordance with a pattern it has developed. The franchisor may provide the merchandise that the franchisee sells, or may simply license the use of a name, trademark, and operating style. The franchisor's compensation may come from an initial fee charged each franchisee, from royalties imposed on the franchisees' sales, from sales of merchandise, supplies and/or services to the franchisees, or from some combination of these charges.

Franchising is really an old and well-established practice despite the present emphasis given the arrangement. Automobile dealerships (under which the independent dealer is licensed to sell only one make of car, displays the manufacturer's name, and operates at least partially under instructions from the manufacturer) are examples of franchising, as are most gasoline service stations and soft-drink bottling plants. A great many other franchise systems have emerged during the last 20 years in such fields as motels (Holiday Inns), automobile rentals (Hertz and Avis), "fast-food" restaurants and snack bars (MacDonald's, Kentucky Fried Chicken, International House of Pancakes), pet shops (Doktor's Pet Centers), dress shops (House of Nine, Bride's Showcase), and automobile equipment and repair (Midas Muffler).

The variety of franchise arrangements prohibits any precise statement of the total number of firms involved or their dollar sales. The U.S. Department of Commerce estimated 1976 retail sales of about $175 billion (including automobile and gasoline sales) and service sales at about $20 billion (income tax preparation, product rentals, etc.) for 450,000 franchise outlets in 1976.[73] (See Figure 1–5.) In Canada, approximately 2,000 franchised fast food eating places employed about 12,000 full-time and 18,000 part-time workers in 1973.[74]

Friction sometimes develops between the franchisor and franchisees. Many franchise systems have been over-optimistically promoted and have not given the franchisees the promised support and profits.

---

* Some franchised motels and restaurants are quite large, but the typical franchise establishment is relatively small.

FIGURE 1-5   **Franchising to encompass 28 percent of retail sales in 1976**

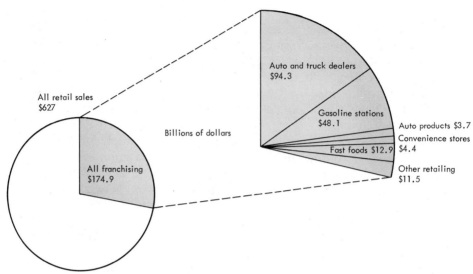

Source: U.S. Department of Commerce; *Franchising in the Economy 1974–76* (Washington, D.C.: U.S. Government Printing Office, 1976), p. 6.

But the better and more successful ones have proven very rewarding to most of their participants. However, some successful franchisors have increasingly been acquiring ownership of the best units within their systems and/or concentrating their franchises with people who will operate groups of stores.[75]

Small, convenience-type stores   These are often called "bantam stores" and are another recent development. They offer a limited selection of brand-name merchandise but usually compensate for this by convenient locations and typically long hours—frequently 7 a.m. to 11 p.m. or even 24 hours a day—seven days a week. Sunday is their busiest day. These "vest-pocket" supermarkets cater to workers whose odd hours prevent their shopping regularly elsewhere and to customers who desire fast service. They operate with a minimum of personnel and are usually somewhat higher priced than their larger namesakes. Although the average sale is only about $1.00, their careful inventory control and low labor costs often enable them to earn more per dollar-of-sales than the conventional supermarkets.

As indicated above, many convenience stores are franchised outlets, but some companies have substantial numbers of wholly-owned units. The approximately 21,000 convenience stores in the U.S. sold over $4.8 billion worth of goods in 1974, a 24 percent increase over the preceding year.[76]

☐ Other developments

Many other developments in retailing are also important.

Cooperative and voluntary chains   Membership in a cooperative or voluntary chain can give an independent retailer many of the competitive advantages of a chain while retaining much of the personal control and individualization of independent operation. These two types of affiliated retailing differ in origins. A cooperative chain is one that was established by a group of storekeepers who decided to arrange for their own wholesale supply, while a voluntary system is one created by a wholesaler or other supplier. The member stores may be either large or small, but they usually feature a common name, similar storefronts, and joint advertising. Franchised convenience stores, discussed above, are really voluntary chains. Cooperative and voluntary chains are discussed more fully in Chapter 7 and at this point we will merely note their importance. An official Canadian source concludes that the affiliated retailers probably succeeded in slowing the recent growth of the corporate (wholly owned) chains in food, drug, and hardware retailing.[77] In 1974, 57 percent of all supermarkets in the U.S. were voluntary or cooperative chain members.[78]

Diversification   Many of the largest retail firms have been expanding into highly diversified lines of business. *Chain Store Age* notes that more than half of the 50 largest supermarket corporations also own some nongrocery subsidiaries such as chains of gasoline service stations, quick-service restaurants, discount stores, drugstores, and nonretailing businesses.[79] The Dayton-Hudson Corporation, which was basically a department store firm, now owns the Target and Lechmere discount chains, the B. Dalton bookshop chain, a number of specialty jewelry stores, and the Team Central high-fidelity stores franchising operation. The Thrift Drug Company is a J. C. Penney subsidiary. Sears, Roebuck's insurance subsidiary is well-known. Numerous other examples could be cited. At least one-quarter to one-third of our largest retail firms now operate two or more different types of stores and/or engage in some business outside of retailing.[80]

Several forces are responsible for this diversification. The more vigorous firms perceived growth opportunities in new fields during the prosperous years after World War II. Government limitations on mergers within the same line of business, already noted, have stimulated mergers and acquisitions that cut across traditional retail lines. Diversification is also seen as a safety measure, since profit opportunities in new lines might offset poor competitive conditions or changing customer tastes that could reduce profits in the firm's basic business. After experimenting with new types of stores, some companies have decided to concentrate on their original line of business.[81] But diversification is a growing tendency in large-scale retailing today.[82]

Internationalization A number of U.S. retail firms have also expanded abroad. Many have Canadian subsidiaries, and some have ventured even farther afield. To mention just a few examples: Sears has numerous branches in Mexico, Central, and South America, and has also opened stores in Spain and acquired a subsidiary in Belgium; Woolworth has had a partly-owned British subsidiary for many years, has important German and Mexican divisions as well as stores in Spain. J. C. Penney now owns Sarma, an important Belgian chain. Wickes Hardware has branches in the Netherlands and Germany; Safeway operates supermarkets in Great Britain, West Germany, and Australia; and S. S. Kresge Co. is a partner in a chain of Australian K-Marts. Carter-Hawley-Hale Stores has a 20 percent interest in House of Fraser, the largest department store firm in Great Britain. Many fast food franchisers have European, Asian, or South American franchisees. Some direct-selling companies, such as Avon, Tupperware, and Singer, literally have worldwide operations. Bata, Ltd., a shoe manufacturing and retailing firm headquartered in Don Mills, Ontario, is another company with stores and plants throughout the world.

An increasing number of foreign firms are active in U.S. retailing. George Weston, Ltd., a Canadian firm with substantial holdings in Western Europe, owns the Loblaw and National Tea grocery chains in this country. The Orbach department and specialty stores in the New York and Los Angeles areas are part of C. & A. Brenninkmeyer, a very large Dutch firm. The British American Tobacco Company now controls Gimbels department stores, Saks Fifth Avenue specialty shops, and Kohl Corporation (a Milwaukee-based food and drug retailer), while Cavenham, Ltd., another English company, controls the Grand Union chain of supermarkets. Many European designers and stylists have franchised outlets in the U.S., and some foreign dealers in fine jewelry, art objects, and other luxury products also have American branches. Marks & Spencer, Ltd., the leading British apparel and soft-goods retailer, has started a chain of Canadian branches.[83] The increasing ease of communication and the growing similarity of middle-income consumer purchasing habits around the world may well encourage more such internationalization in the future.[84]

National versus private brands The larger retail firms and voluntary-cooperative groups have the option of devoting some, or even all, of their promotional and merchandising efforts to private, rather than national brands.[85] The emphasis given each type of brand has varied from company to company and even from time to time within a firm; but many retailers favor national brands because of their manufacturers' substantial advertising expenditures and aggressive merchandising tactics.

Nevertheless, large food retailers probably obtain about 15 percent of their sales (aside from fresh meat and produce) from private-brand merchandise.[86] By far the greater share of branded merchandise in Sears and Wards is sold under the stores' private labels, and private branding is also widely used in apparel, variety, and other chains. Even though most stores usually sell their private brand merchandise for less than comparable national brand items and thus receive a competitive advantage, they also usually enjoy a greater gross margin (the difference between the store's cost and selling price) on the private lines. And well-accepted private brands help build customer loyalty to the store, since the brand cannot be obtained from competitive outlets. The battle of the brands is far from over.

Additional developments   Besides the responses already mentioned, retailers have adopted numerous other measures to meet their changing environment. The number is so great, in fact, that only a sampling of them can be mentioned here, and even those must be presented in summary form. Many of these developments, however, are discussed in detail in later chapters.

1. While many merchants are continuing to relocate or place stores in suburbs and outlying areas, or in small communities, some are participating in programs to revitalize the city centers. Other locational experiments are underway in so-called "anchorless malls," enclosed shopping centers composed entirely of small stores that appeal to recreational shoppers. Major retailers are increasingly relying on marketing research techniques in selecting new locations that will promise sufficient patronage to yield a profit. (See Chapter 4.)

2. Many firms are finding that some customers prefer to purchase an increasing amount of goods outside the store premises and these firms are substantially expanding their telephone, mail-order, and in-home selling business.[87]

3. Modernization of existing stores has continued at a high rate with many improvements in design, materials, fixtures, and equipment. (See Chapter 5.)

4. Changes are being made in the organizational structure of department stores and other multiunit retailers to strengthen controls over merchandise stocks and operating activities. (See Chapter 7.)

5. Local and regional chain store companies are expanding into new districts far removed from their original base and some department stores are also establishing branches well outside their traditional market areas.

6. Shifts in store hours are being made to accommodate the needs of customers; several night openings plus Sundays—particularly for food stores—are becoming increasingly common. See discussion of "Store Hours" in Chapter 21.

7. Television has been steadily gaining in popularity as a retail advertising medium. (See Chapter 18.)

8. More store space is being given to "leisure-time" merchandise offerings and to art objects, antiques, and similar items demanded by a growing culture-conscious population.

9. While some retailers have been broadening their merchandise lines, others have been concentrating upon narrow specialties, and upon new combinations of goods. This has changed and intensified retail competition. The dealer in small electric appliances competes, not only with similar stores, but with electronics stores, discount houses, supermarkets, drug stores, variety stores, and department stores.

10. Merchants are now paying more attention to the rights of women and minorities. This has influenced personnel, credit, and advertising practices.

11. Retailers are exercising care in changing their "mix" of merchandise and operating policies and methods. Some seek a more profitable mix through store modernization programs, self-service operation, and the promotion of private brands; others place their emphasis on widespread promotional activities for bargain-price merchandise; and still others prefer to maintain "regular" prices with greater attention to improved personal salesmanship. Change in the retailing mix is still another factor intensifying competition among retailers.

12. In response to technological developments, retailers are increasingly using data-capturing and data-processing equipment for such activities as merchandise planning and control, pricing, checking credits, accounting for receivables and payables, improving turnover, payroll and sales audit and analysis. (See the discussion of "The Retailer and Electronic Equipment" in Chapter 5.)

■ REVIEW AND DISCUSSION QUESTIONS

1 Describe some of the trends that seem to be occurring in (a) size of population, (b) age distribution, and (c) location of population, and the way they will probably affect retailing in the future.

2 How has consumer spending power changed during the past 20 years, and how has this affected retailing?

3 Prepare a concise paper on one of the following topics: (a) "Changing lifestyles and the retailer of tomorrow"; (b) "Do consumers have more or less leisure and what does this mean to merchants?" or (c) "Working women and retailing."

4 Explain how you would design a store to cater to the "economical shopper," who was described on page 10. How would this store differ from one designed to cater to some of the recreational desires mentioned by Professor Tauber?

5 What are some of the major influences of government on the structure of

retailing (the number and size of retail firms) and the retailers' business practices?

6 Describe the trend in the division of retail trade between large and small businesses? What factors in your judgment are responsible for this trend?

7 Why do department and discount stores lease out some departments? Why don't they lease out more departments? How do they select the departments to be leased?

8 Briefly describe or define each of the following types of stores and report on its relative success or failure in the United States (or Canada):
   a. Hypermarket   d. Home center
   b. Furniture warehouse   e. Convenience store
   c. Catalog appliance showroom

9 As a prospective store owner, what would you gain and what would you lose by becoming a franchisee instead of being a totally unaffiliated retailer?

10 Visit some of the stores in your college or home community and examine their private branding practices. For each store, report whether it sells all, some, or none of its merchandise under private brand. What particular items, if any, are under private label? Can the customers compare prices for private and national brands? Which ones are featured in the store's advertising? What types of stores seem to give the most emphasis to private brands?

■ NOTES AND REFERENCES

1 "Making a Retail Marketing Plan—Penney's Gorman Tells How a Giant Chain Does It," *Stores*, March 1976, pp. 5, 32.

2 "The Burgeoning Benefits of a Lower Birth Rate," *Business Week*, December 15, 1973, p. 41; *Canada Yearbook 1974* (Ottawa: Information Canada, 1974), p. 139. Some social scientists think the birthrate decline may be reversing. This view is advanced by June Sklar and Beth Berkovin, "The American Birth Rate: Evidence of a Coming Rise," *Science*, vol. 189 (August 29, 1975), pp. 693–700; but most disagree. *See* "The Birth Rate Is Declining Again," *Business Week*, March 8, 1976, p. 20.

3 Ibid.

4 U.S. Bureau of the Census, *Current Population Reports*, series P–20, no. 291, February 1976).

5 U.S. Bureau of the Census, *Current Population Reports*, series P–25, no. 601 (October 1975); no. 614 (November 1975). *Canada Yearbook 1974*, pp. 142, 164.

6 "Gimbels Midwest is Up-Dating Its Goals," *Women's Wear Daily*, March 2, 1976, p. 14. Also see "How the Changing Age Mix Changes Markets," *Business Week*, January 12, 1976, p. 74.

7 "What Senior Citizens Want in Supermarkets," *Chain Store Age* (Supermarket edition), March 1972, pp. 52–60; "Independent Stresses Service in Retirement Community," *Supermarket News*, June 16, 1975, p. 33.

8 "Special Programs for Elderly Come in at Least 8 Varieties," *Supermarketing*, May 1976, pp. 1, 48–52.

9 "Americans on the Move," *Time*, March 15, 1976, pp. 54–64; U.S. Bureau of the Census, *Current Population Reports*, series P–25, no. 618 (January 1976).

10 *Canada Yearbook 1974*, p. 140; E. J. McCarthy and S. J. Shapiro, *Basic Marketing*, First Canadian ed. (Georgetown, Ont.: Irwin–Dorsey Ltd., 1975), p. 132.

11 James E. Bell, "Mobiles: A Neglected Market Segment," *Journal of*

Marketing, vol. 33 (April 1969), p. 43; James M. Carman, "Selection of Retailing Services by New Arrivals," *Journal of Retailing,* vol. 50 (Summer 1974), p. 21.

12 David L. Burch, *The Economic Future of City and Suburb* (New York: Committee for Economic Development, 1971), p. 19.

13 "Centers, Chains Boomed as Nation Went Suburban," *Chain Store Age Executive,* June 1975, p. 9.

14 *Statistical Abstract of the United States 1975* (Washington, D.C.: U.S. Government Printing Office, 1976), p. 383.

15 "The Food Shopper 1975," *Chain Store Age* (Supermarket edition), April 1975, pp. 27–29.

16 "Study Sees Only Small Shift in Long-Term Consumer Buying," *Advertising Age,* May 12, 1975, p. 60; "Shopping Smart," *Progressive Grocer,* April 19, 1975, p. 50.

17 Satenig S. St. Marie, "New Consumer Spending Patterns," *Penney News,* November-December 1975, p. 12.

18 "Study Finds Income More Unequal," *New York Times,* December 22, 1972, p. 1; Sanford Rose, "The Truth About Income Inequality in the U.S.," *Fortune,* December 1972, p. 90.

19 *Statistical Abstract,* 1975, p. 391; *Canada Yearbook 1974,* p. 244. Canadian data for 1951–1971; U.S., for 1950–1972. U.S. median family income increased further in 1973, then declined in 1974. Family income grew more than per capita income because of the greater number of families with two or more wage-earners.

20 "The Changing Role of Women Today" in *New Views of a $100 Billion Industry* (New York: Newspaper Advertising Bureau, 1973), p. 47. Howard Hayghe, "Families and the Rise of Working Wives—An Overview," *Monthly Labor Review,* vol. 99 (May 1976), pp. 12–19.

21 "The Changing Role of Women Today," in "Marketing-Eye View of Women's Lib.," *Grey Matter* (Grey Advertising Agency), February 1973; *1974 U.S. Mail Order Industry Estimates* (Chicago: Maxwell Sroge Co., Inc., 1975); "Knock," *Home Furnishings Daily,* February 22, 1973, p. 6.

22 See U.S. Department of Commerce, *Department Store Retailing in an Era of Change* (Washington, D.C.: U.S. Government Printing Office, 1975), p. 9. But *see also:* Janice N. Hedges, "Long Workweeks and Premium Pay: One Quarter of All Full-Time Workers Worked More Than 40 Hours a Week in May 1975," *Monthly Labor Review,* vol. 99 (April 1976), p. 6.

23 See "Time Use Studies Reveal Plight of Working Women: Everyday Life in 12 Countries Has Common Pattern," *ISR Newsletter* (University of Michigan), Autumn 1973, pp. 2–3; and Alexander Szalai, ed., *The Use of Time* (The Hague, Netherlands: Mouton, 1972), especially pp. 117–28.

24 "The Leisure Market," *Stores,* May 1974, pp. 6, 23.

25 See E. B. Weiss, "How New Life Styles Affect Home Goods," *Stores,* December 1975, pp. 16, 40; January 1976, pp. 10, 40.

26 Two thirds of adult Americans under 35 live in apartments. See: "The Apartment Market Means Business," *Home Furnishings Daily,* August 28, 1972, pp. 4–5; Dorothy Collins, "High Rise Profits," *Stores,* December 1973, pp. 18, 44.

27 "It's a Do-It-Yourself Boom," *Business Week,* July 6, 1974, p. 38; E. B. Weiss, "Do-It-Yourself Goes Feminine," *Advertising Age,* May 5, 1975, p. 42; "Do-It-Yourself Boosts Automotive Sales," *Discount Merchandiser,* November 1975, p. 30.

28 Gregory Stone, "City Shoppers and Urban Identification," *American Journal of Sociology,* vol. 60 (July 1954), pp. 36–45; L. E. Boone, D. L. Kurtz, J. C. Johnson, and J. A. Bonino, "City Shoppers and Urban Identification Revisited," *Journal of Marketing,* vol. 38 (July 1974), pp. 67–68.

29 Edward M. Tauber, "Why Do People Shop?" *Journal of Marketing,* vol. 36 (October 1972), pp. 46–49.

30 Yet stores that customers rank low on many of these criteria may still survive, perhaps because they rank high on one or two decisive characteristics, such as convenience, or because they are no worse than their competition. See: Marvin A. Jolson and Walter F. Spath, "Understanding and Fulfilling Shoppers'

Requirements: An Anomaly in Retailing?" *Journal of Retailing,* vol. 49 (Summer 1973), pp. 38–50.

31 For a discussion of preplanning, see J. Barry Mason and Morris L. Mayer, "Empirical Observation of Consumer Behavior as Related to Goods Classification and Retail Strategy," *Journal of Retailing,* vol. 48 (Fall 1972), pp. 17–31.

32 "The Uptight Consumer," *Progressive Grocer,* November 1975, pp. 41–57; Walter P. Gorman, "The Frightened Consumer," *Journal of Retailing,* vol. 51 (Summer 1975), pp. 31–37. *See also* Roger Dickinson, ed , "Special Issue on Consumerism," *Journal of Retailing,* vol. 48 (Winter 1972–73).

33 Satenig S. St. Marie, "Consumerism: Is It a Dead Issue?" *Penney News,* January-February 1976, p. 12.

34 Some quality control, communication, and customer information programs are described in "Seven Stores and Seven Consumer Programs," *Tempo* (Touche Ross & Co.), vol. 20, no. 1 (1974), pp. 10–13.

35 U.S. Department of Commerce, *The Cost of Crimes Against Business* (Washington, D.C.: U.S. Government Printing Office, 1974), p. 17.

36 Bob Vereen, "The Paperwork Blizzard," *Hardware Retailing,* April 1976, pp. 51–64.

37 Statement of the U.S. Federal Trade Commission, "Commission Enforcement Policy with Regard to Mergers in the Food Distribution Industry," *Commerce Clearing House Trade Regulation Reporter,* January 17, 1967, paragraph 4520.

38 "Associated Agrees to Divest Ayr-Way," *Women's Wear Daily,* April 29, 1975, p. 12.

39 "FTC Denies Arlen Four Klein Leases and Approves Two," *Women's Wear Daily,* January 23, 1975, p. 2.

40 44 *U.S. Law Week* 4686 (May 24, 1976).

41 "Another Inside Look at Retailing Case," *Women's Wear Daily,* April 14, 1976, pp. 1, 14.

42 Bruce Mallen, *A Preliminary Paper on the Levels, Causes and Effects of Economical Concentration in the Ca-* *nadian Retail Food Trade* (Ottawa: Food Prices Review Board, 1976), p. 66.

43 *See,* for example, Roger Dickinson, ed., "Special Issue on Consumerism."

44 *1976 Corpus Almanac of Canada* (Toronto, Ont.: Corpus Publishers Service Ltd., 1976), p. 10—36.

45 *See* Joseph C. Palamountain, *The Politics of Distribution* (Cambridge: Harvard University Press, 1955.)

46 *See* J. J. Boddewyn and S. C. Hollander, eds., *Public Policy Toward Retailing: An International Symposium* (Lexington, Mass.: Health-Lexington Books, 1972).

47 *U.S. 1972 Census of Retail Trade RC 72-A-52, Area Statistics, United States* (Washington, D.C.: U.S. Government Printing Office, 1975), pp. 7–8.

48 *1972 Census of Retail Trade, Establishment and Firm Size,* RC72-S-1 (Washington, D.C.: U.S. Government Printing Office, 1975), pp. 1–2, 1–66.

49 *Canada Yearbook 1974,* p. 675.

50 *1972 Census of Retail Trade, Establishment and Firm Size,* and earlier censuses.

51 *1972 Census of Retail Trade, Establishment and Firm Size,* pp. 1–5, 1–6, 1–8, 1–37.

52 Jay Scher, *Financial and Operating Results of Department Stores in 1974* (New York: Financial Executives Division, National Retail Merchants Association, 1975), p. iv. As mentioned earlier, downtown stores have retained a larger share of the retail trade in Canada, but Canadian suburban shopping centers produced 50 percent of department store sales in 1972. *Canada Yearbook 1974,* p. 676.

53 Leo Bogart, "The Future of Retailing," *Harvard Business Review,* vol. 51 (November-December 1973), pp. 16 ff.

54 "The True Look of the Discount Industry," *The Discount Merchandiser,* May 1976, p. 30.

55 Ibid.

56 The successes and the failures are discussed in Eric Aiken, "Bargain Hunting," *Barron's,* July 15, 1974, p. 11; "The Weak Sister," *Newsweek,* July 1, 1974, p. 53; "Hard Times Hit the Dis-

count Stores," *Business Week,* February 10, 1973, pp. 87–90; "Mass Merchandisers, Still Growing, But Slowly," *Nielsen Researcher,* no. 4 (1975), p. 1.

57 See "Supermarkets for Toys Get a Big Play," *New York Times,* December 9, 1973, sec. 3, p. 1. Also, Walter J. Salmon, "Can Discount Stores Continue to Prosper?" speech to Mass Retailing Institute, Spring 1974.

58 Jay Scher, *Financial and Operating Results,* p. vi.

59 Wendell Earle and Willard Hunt, *Operating Results of Self-Service Discount Department Stores 1973–74* (Ithaca: Cornell University, 1974), p. 3. The groups of firms reporting in the two periods were not identical.

60 *U.S. 1972 Census of Retail Trade, Miscellaneous Subjects* RC 72-S-3 (Washington, D.C.: U.S. Government Printing Office, 1975), pp. 3–126, 3–127.

61 For an excellent discussion of the need for communication and coordination between lessee and lessor, see Burton Elliott, "The Licensor/Licensee Relationship—A Critical Element for Success," *Retail Control,* April-May 1976, pp. 19–27.

62 *See* Robert Drew-Bear, *Mass Merchandising: Revolution & Evolution* (New York: Fairchild Publications, Inc., 1970), pp. 272–75.

63 "Great Concepts in Merchandising: Traditionalists and the Warehouse War," *Home Furnishings Daily,* September 24, 1971, pp. 4–5.

64 "Warehouse Showroom Report: Survival Struggle for Stores," *Home Furnishings Daily,* March 22, 1976, pp. 1, 4–5.

65 "Retail Discounters Face Troubled Future," *The Montreal Star,* February 28, 1976, p. C1; "Luster of Catalog Units Fading for Food Firms," *Supermarket News,* February 24, 1975, pp. 1, 23. But *see also* "Catalog Discounting Is a Small Man's Game," *Business Week,* October 13, 1973, pp. 70–76; "Catalog Showrooms Set to Grow Again, But Rate of Expansion Will Lag . . . ," *Home Furnishings Daily,* October 15, 1975, p. 28.

66 *1974 Home Center Financial Operating Results* (Indianapolis: National Retail Hardware Association, 1975), p. 4.

67 Ralph Z. Sorsenson II, "U.S. Marketers Can Learn from European Innovators," *Harvard Business Review,* vol. 50 (September-October 1972), p. 94.

68 See Eric Langeard and Robert A. Peterson, "Diffusion of Large-Scale Food Retailing in France: Supermarché et Hypermarché," *Journal of Retailing,* vol. 51 (Fall 1975), pp. 53–62.

69 "Hypermarché Laval Loss Tops Forecast," *Supermarket News,* July 14, 1975, pp. 1, 10.

70 "America's 1st Hypermarket," *Chain Store Age Executive,* March 1975, p. 25.

71 W. J. Salmon, R. D. Buzzell and S. G. Cort, "Today the Shopping Center, Tomorrow the Superstore," *Harvard Business Review,* vol. 52 (January-February 1974), pp. 89–98; "The Superstore," *Chain Store Age Executive,* February 1974, pp. 56–62; *General Merchandise in the Supermarket* (Chicago: Super Market Institute, 1975).

72 Lawrence J. Israel, quoted in Samuel Feinberg, "From Where I Sit," *Women's Wear Daily,* August 21, 1973, p. 12; *see also* "Full-Liners Face 'Twigs' Threat," *Chain Store Age* (general merchandise edition), October 1975, pp. 22–26.

73 *Franchising in the Economy 1974–76* (Washington, D.C.: U.S. Government Printing Office, 1976), pp. 1–6.

74 Statistics Canada, *Franchising in Canada's Food Serving Industry 1973* (Occasional 63–524) (Ottawa: Information Canada, 1975), p. 12.

75 See "Fast Food Franchisers Squeeze Out the Little Guy," *Business Week,* May 31, 1976, pp. 42–48.

76 "Convenience Stores," *Progressive Grocer,* July 1975, p. 58; "Oshawa Will Test Franchiser Convenience Store," *Supermarket News,* September 29, 1975, p. 1.

77 *Canada 1974* (Ottawa: Information Canada, 1973), pp. 295–96.

78 "Cooperatives and Voluntaries," *Progressive Grocer,* July 1975, p. 57.

79 "Now Retailing Conglomerates?" *Chain Store Age* (supermarket executives edition), August 1969, p. E–33.

80 For company-by-company de-

tails, see *Fairchild's Financial Manual of Retail Stores* (New York: Fairchild Publications), published annually.

81 "Food First . . . Again at Steinberg's," *Supermarket News,* September 2, 1974, p. 27; "Miller-Wohl Trims Its Style," *Business Week,* May 19, 1975, pp. 62–65.

82 Ben Gordon, "Diversity or Die?" *Chain Store Age* (Executive edition), December 1975, p. 5. Thomas Schinkel, "Multiple Concepts: An Answer to the Struggle for New Growth," *Stores,* June 1976, pp. 32–34, 40.

83 "Britain's Retail Champ Takes On the World," *Business Week,* November 3, 1973, pp. 88–90.

84 See the Special International Issue *Journal of Retailing,* Spring 1968; and S. C. Hollander, *Multinational Retailing* (East Lansing: Institute for International Business and Economic Development Studies, Michigan State University, 1970), for a further discussion of this topic.

85 As the terms are used here a "national brand" is a manufacturer's brand whereas a "private brand" is a middleman's or reseller's brand. See the discussion in Chapter 16.

86 "Finds Private Label Tapering Despite Favorable Conditions," *Supermarket News,* August 5, 1974, p. 6. Candace E. Trunzo, "Checkout Counter Lookalikes," *Money,* May 1976, pp. 70–71.

87 *See* Chapter 21. *See also* "The Awesome Potential of In-Home Selling," *Advertising Age,* April 15, 1972, pp. 27–30; Michael Granfield and Alfred Nicols, "Economic and Marketing Aspects of the Direct Selling Industry," *Journal of Retailing,* Spring 1975, pp. 33–50; "Millions by Mail," *Forbes,* March 15, 1976, pp. 82 ff.

Retailing opportunities and careers

BASIC REQUIREMENTS FOR SUCCESSFUL STORE MANAGEMENT

Successful operation of a retail business in the changing market and business conditions prevailing in the late 1970s and early 1980s, as well as in the social, political, economic, and competitive environment discussed in the previous chapter, is a very challenging task. Some of the main requirements for performance of that task can be classified into five broad groups: (1) the personal qualifications of the proprietor or of top management; (2) an adequate financial structure; (3) necessary physical facilities; (4) effective policies and procedures; and (5) competent, loyal, and productive personnel in both sales and sales-supporting activities. Effective combination and correlation of these factors will result in satisfied customers and in profit for the retailer.

■ PERSONAL REQUIREMENTS OF MANAGEMENT

Most young people who enter retailing eventually hope to become store owners or department, division, store, or area managers. We should therefore examine this goal, the executive function, at this early stage in our study of retailing. What is the retail executive's role? What personal qualifications are necessary for success as a retail executive? What is the retail executive's social contribution?

□ The executive's functions

The key executives (or the management) are the most significant single ingredient in the success of a retail business. As one writer points out, they must perform three basic functions: (1) *Giving direction* to the firm (establishing goals, framing policies, developing operating programs, initiating action and coordinating activities to achieve the goals); (2) *representing the company to the public* ("the most underrated of management's multiple responsibilities"); and (3) *evaluating results,* that is, examining the company's performance, analyzing the causes of deviations from the goals, and determining what must be done to improve operations.[1] The retail executives who perform these functions successfully are usually hard-working, self-disciplined men and women who are willing to accept significant responsibilities and to give unstintingly of themselves to serve their organizations. In the informal world of retailing, these executives are likely to be highly active and energetic people who maintain close relationships with their associates and with their firm's day-to-day operations.

Thus the retail manager may be viewed as a teacher or a coach who molds management people into an effective team by teaching them how to work together and by training them for greater responsibilities. Morale should be built within the organization, and the drive and leadership necessary for accomplishment of the organization's goals be provided. Knowledge concerning developments in one's own firm, in the entire retail field, and in the overall environment in which the store operates is essential. Otherwise, operations will not be adjusted to shifting conditions. The manager plays a significant role in long-range planning and policy formation and institutes procedures to be sure the plans and policies are put into effect. In addition, management personnel represent the company in the community, at public functions, and in community betterment activities designed to fulfill the social responsibilities of all businesses today. The breadth and time-consuming aspects of the manager's many tasks are obvious.

□ The retail executive's personal qualities

Satisfactory performance at the management level in retailing requires the same personal characteristics, in general, as are needed for good management in most lines of business.* Certain characteristics, however, should be emphasized. These include: a market orientation,

---

* Some social psychologists might disagree with this statement and claim that retail executives have greater sensitivity to short-term changes in business activity, greater aesthetic awareness, and somewhat less analytical ability than executives in other organizations.

knowledge, experience, drive, friendliness, leadership, judgment, decisiveness, vision, effective expression, and character. The need for overall administrative ability overlaps all of these characteristics.

Market orientation The retail executive must be sensitive to market demands and market opportunitiés, must understand consumer buying motives and habits, and must become skilled in developing satisfactory relations with customers.

1. The consumer is king The retailer's business and profits depend upon satisfying customers, thus ensuring their continuous patronage. The goods and services they want, when, how, and where they want them, and at the prices they are willing to pay must be offered continuously. An experienced grocery merchant once expressed the same thought in these words: A retailer must so please customers that they will "never go to another store. They might like it better there, and never come back."[2]

This requirement is illustrated by one author's explanation of the success of the J. C. Penney Company: Its executives "never lost sight of the elementary fact that without customers they could not remain in business. They looked upon their customers as their *real* board of directors. They realized that the success of their stores and the security of their own jobs were decisions completely within the keeping of the public."[3] Or, as an eminent merchant once put it:

> You'll get along fine so long as you never forget it's the *people* in our business who make it a business. Management, merchandisers, buyers, salespeople, but most of all, customers are *people,* not sales figures.[4]

2. The marketing concept Retailers and marketers in general who accept and practice this "consumer is king" philosophy are said to be using the marketing concept. Specifically, they accept "customer needs and wants . . . (as) . . . the starting point for all their efforts."[5] Consequently, they plan their merchandise assortments, the services they render, their physical facilities, and their personnel policies so as to meet these needs and wants. Everyone in the firm takes "marching orders from the market."[6]

Knowledge The retail executive needs to know a great deal about (1) human relations, including the effective leadership and direction of employees as well as for developing satisfactory customer relations, (2) retail operating methods and procedures, and (3) merchandise and sources of supply. As noted previously, the successful retailer of today must also understand the nature and structure of retailing and the current developments and trends in its environment.

Experience Large retail organizations now assign their young executives much more responsibility and authority at an earlier age than they did in the past. The major variety chains, for example, are now promoting their executive trainees to the position of store manager in about half the time required for promotion some years ago. A new urgency seems to exist in developing managers and getting them "up to speed."[7] But some years of meaningful experience in performing or dealing with the major retail activities is a necessary qualification for top management.[8] The young man or woman who wants to "reach the top" in a large retail organization should try to obtain experience in successfully handling increasingly difficult assignments in several major phases of store operations. And the individual who wants to own and run a store would be well advised to gain considerable knowledge of retailing problems and techniques as an employee before venturing on one's own.*

The successful retailer must learn the relationships involved in all of the following functions and activities, and will benefit greatly from experience in as many of them as possible:

1. Effective buying.
2. Judicious pricing.
3. Sound merchandising control methods.
4. Creative advertising and sales promotion.
5. Constructive salesmanship.
6. An adequate store system.
7. Enlightened personnel administration.
8. Customer-attracting customer services.
9. Effective expense control.

But experience must be something more than mere "time on the job." All who want to develop mature judgment and an ability to make wise decisions have to analyze their activities, determine the causes for their successes and failures, and avoid repeating their mistakes. They must learn to appraise situations systematically and deliberately, to recognize the value of assembling all relevant and pertinent data (in so far as time permits), to evaluate alternative courses of action, and to think objectively and logically.

Drive   Old fashioned ambition and hard work are usually prerequisites for success in retailing. The way to a top management post, as one merchant has expressed it, is to "forget the glamour, accept the responsibilities, and work like the devil." Drive—not the kind typified by the person who works hard for a few days and then loses enthusiasm, but the type which perseveres year after year—is a key ingredient for the progressive retailer. In this respect, retailing differs little from most other worthwhile and challenging businesses and professions that demand constant effort and devotion. But the successful retail executive must expect to deal with a wide variety of obligations in a vigorous and zestful manner.

---

*Yet some franchising organizations which train their franchises in their own highly-structured operating methods prefer to deal with people who have had no previous retailing experience.

During working hours, the executive must think constantly about a wide range of problems, meet a steady demand for new ideas, and face everlasting competition both from inside and from outside the company. Numerous conferences and meetings must be attended, travel to distant places made when necessary, and an active part taken in the life of the community. This latter obligation includes participation in such activities as Community Chest campaigns, church work, youth movements, leadership of clubs, and speaking engagements. Someone has said that "success consists not only of doing extraordinary things but of doing ordinary things extraordinarily well." Dynamic retail executives get keen satisfaction from doing the best possible job in every assigned task. Moreover, they build a reputation for doing the job right the *first* time.

Friendliness   Retail executives should sincerely try to get along well with people: their employees, superiors, and business associates. Winning the friendship and respect of staff people is not an easy task. A good supervisor leads rather than drives employees, but loses their respect if company rules and regulations are not enforced. Any necessary criticisms should be constructive, based upon careful study of the circumstances, and expressed to the employee in private. Unjust criticism, or even justified criticism made under improper conditions, can do considerable harm to the individual criticized as well as to the executive.

The typical retail executive does a great deal of work in association with other people. The major problems of the firm are frequently solved in executive conferences. Moreover, the various executives have to consult with each other very frequently to coordinate and harmonize the various aspects of their integrated operations. Most large retail organizations need a very considerable number of middle management executives, who stand between top management and the employees and who have to think in terms of both groups' needs and interests. Individuals who do not like to work with people will be at a great disadvantage in a business as humanized as retailing. Their talents probably could be used better elsewhere.

Leadership   Good managers inspire the confidence of others in their ability as leaders. They communicate assurance to their staffs and arouse their assistants' confidence in and enthusiasm for the firm's goals, policies, and procedures. They use their authority to guide the organization and motivate their associates to ever-higher levels of performance. Constant improvement is expected, but employees are shown how to achieve it, and encouraged to strive for excellence.

This emphasis on people and performance is important from the standpoints of productivity and the personal satisfaction derived from tasks well done. Moreover, increasing attention is being given by successful managers to provide the charismatic "turn on" or excitement designed to attract and retain quality personnel.[9] Retail executives do not automatically receive their leadership capacity and their authority from the titles on their doors. These must be earned through the confidence, respect, and support of the people with whom they work. Authority comes when the ability to assume it is demonstrated.

Judgment Successful executives must be able to judge the probable outcome of their own decisions. Also, they must gauge the effect of outside events on their own operations. The ability to reason, to draw valid conclusions from facts, to withstand some pressures and give way to others, and to sift good advice from bad—all these call for sound judgment. Frequently one is called upon to exercise judgment on merchandise; in such cases aesthetic taste, sense of style, and appreciation of merchandise may be important in reaching valid decisions. Of course, their judgment will not be infallible, but wise decisions must outweigh faulty ones.

Decisiveness Retail management involves a never-ending series of decisions: decisions about merchandise, prices, promotional programs, space allocations, personnel, customer relations, business policy, etc. Many of these decisions are subject to pressing time deadlines. Often at least some of the facts that the executive would like to know are unavailable, despite all the data that modern information and control systems provide. Yet procrastination and failure to reach a decision is often tantamount to making a very bad decision. For example, the merchandising executive who delays too long in selecting Christmas or Mother's Day stocks will undoubtedly have a very poor assortment of goods for a peak selling season. The capable manager learns to make sound and timely decisions, and to translate thought into action.

Executives must be willing to make unpopular decisions if their best judgment calls for such action. And they should constantly keep in mind the overall well-being of the company. The one who says, "We'll take care of our own department; let the others solve their own problems," takes far too narrow a view. Top retail positions should be filled by individuals who continuously strive to fulfill the purposes and aims of the entire organization.

Vision As we have already noted, retailing is a highly dynamic, changing industry. Tomorrow's customers are likely to live in different places, shop in different fashion, and want different merchandise than today's shoppers. Competition constantly presents new challenges. The retail executive must be able to look beyond the company's immediate problems and goals and to plan for the future. The ability to anticipate and to lead change is also important. And all current problem-solving decisions should be designed to strengthen the firm's future growth, reputation, and organization. In order to do this, a vivid picture of what is believed to be the company's ultimate goals should be developed.

The manager's vision of the future should go far beyond the confines of the business and embrace the entire environment in which the firm operates. Thus, in addition to achieving effective internal operations, continuous effort should be devoted to help maintain a free and viable economy in a healthy social system.

Effective expression   Having a vision of desirable changes is only half the battle: the retail executive must also be able to "sell" the vision to associates, customers, and the public. Consequently, effective communication—the ability to use the English language convincingly and persuasively, both orally and in writing—is important to growth and success.

Character   Good retail managers are both reliable and courageous. Obligations to the firm's customers, employees, stockholders, and sources of supply are always kept in mind. Their reputation for keeping promises is their business livelihood and their character is reflected in the actions of their companies, in the quality of the products they handle, and the services they render. Honesty in dealing with a firm's customers and employees is not just the *best* policy but it is the *only* policy upon which continued patronage and employee loyalty can be founded.

Administrative ability   Another approach to many of the characteristics already discussed is to say that the executive must have a high degree of administrative ability. One authority believes that successful administration rests upon three basic and related skills—technical, human, and conceptual—which he defines as follows:

Technical skill [which] implies an understanding of, and proficiency in, a specific kind of activity, particularly one involving methods, processes, procedures or techniques. . . . It involves specialized knowledge, analytical ability within that specialty, and facility in the use of the tools and techniques of a specific discipline.

Human skill is . . . the executive's ability to work effectively as a group member to build cooperative effort within the team he leads. As *technical skill* is primarily concerned with working with "things" (processes or physical objects) so *human skill* is primarily concerned with working with people.

Conceptual skill . . . involves the ability to see the enterprise as a whole; it includes recognizing how the various functions of the organization depend on one another, and how changes in any one part affect all the others; and it extends to visualizing the relationship of the individual business to the industry, the community, and the political, social and economic forces of the nation as a whole. Recognizing these relationships, and perceiving the significant elements in any situation, the administrator should then be able to act in a way which advances the overall welfare of the organization.[10]

In the retail field the manager who possesses such skills and utilizes them with discretion and judgment is likely to be a *good* administrator. Exercising the leadership which such skills imply and remaining in close touch with the major activities of the business should give satisfactory results both in the short and the long run.

Thus the successful retail executive is a composite of many qualities. Adequate knowledge, practical experience, and certain personal attributes are all essential. The knowledge necessary for advancement in retailing comes from a variety of sources—formal academic training, careful observation, reading and study on one's own initiative, and experience. But, there is no substitute for experience in the learning process. The actual doing of jobs, the performance of specialized tasks, personal observation of customer buying habits, and intimate contact with day-to-day problems as they arise are an important part of the executive's training.

□ The retail executive's social contribution

The retailer's most basic social contribution comes from the successful and efficient operation of the business. A prospering, continuing business in any field provides a livelihood for many people, both directly for its own employees and indirectly for the employees of its many suppliers. (See also the discussion of social responsibilities of retailers in Chapter 27.) But the well-conducted retail business also performs other functions in our complex market economy. We are so accustomed to visiting stores that we can easily forget their vital role as supply points for the necessities and amenities of life. The successful retail business, at the very heart of the marketing system, is in close touch with both consumers and suppliers. It can act as coordinator between the manufacturer's product development, merchandising and promotional activities, and the requirements and aspirations of the consumer market. Convenient, reliable, and attractive retail establishments facilitate consumer purchasing, help stimulate economic expansion and play a significant part in raising our standard of living. Moreover, through innovations dictated by our changing times and shifting competitive forces, and by providing cooperation and support to local, state, and federal programs designed to improve social welfare, they contribute to the advancement of society in many ways. In this broad area small businesses have numerous opportunities for service.[11]

Some illustrations of these services and others are instructive. The International Executive Service Corps, a private nonprofit organization that provides consultants to assist struggling businesses in the developing countries, finds that some of its most successful and helpful volunteers are retired chain store and supermarket executives. Other retailers render their contributions closer to home. A British writer has noted that American and Canadian stores have "a genuine sense of civic responsibility towards the community they serve. They tend to be leaders rather than followers in charity drives, patriotic occasions, even municipal politics."[12]

Senior store officials often play prominent roles in municipal development and rehabilitation efforts. Some stores have developed active programs for training and promoting disadvantaged workers. Department stores frequently sponsor youth groups, sometimes in cooperation with magazines and suppliers, that engage in a wide variety of civic, charitable, and educational activities. One firm that works with stores in developing these groups comments:

> Today, youth is intensely interested in people and their problems—in community service and action.
> Today, the progressive retail store is actively involved in the welfare of its community.
> Community service is the meeting place—For retailing, which wants to attract more creative and dedicated young men and women . . . For youth, seeking a challenging opportunity for community participation.[13]

■ FINANCIAL STRUCTURE

The second basic requirement of successful retail management is adequate capital. Regardless of one's personal qualifications and interest in the field, profitable operation of a retail store is impossible without sufficient funds. The need for funds permeates all phases of the business from the exploratory and planning stages up to the final payments for merchandise and employee services.

The capital needed should be very carefully estimated before establishing a new store or buying an established one. And much depends on proper timing in relation to general business conditions, particularly those prevailing in the immediate area in which the proposed store will be located. To be specific, conditions existing in 1974 and 1975 with high interest rates, limited capital available in some areas, and numerous retail failures, among other factors, required extreme caution before opening a retail store.[14] Many would-be retailers have seriously underestimated their initial expenses and overestimated their early sales and profits. Consequently, these estimates should be checked and rechecked before the business is started (or purchased). The sources from which those funds will come should then be determined. (These points are developed more fully later in "Financing Methods," pp. 69–74.) The retailer must also be prepared for unexpected demands for funds not included in these estimates. After going through the difficult opening period and first few months of operations, it should be possible to formulate reasonably accurate merchandise, expense, and overall financial budgets. (The merchandise budget is discussed in Chapter 10 and the expense and financial budgets in Chapter 24.) But certainly considerable "room for error," i.e., a reasonable safety margin, should be left in the initial plans.

■ BUILDINGS AND PHYSICAL FACILITIES

Adequate physical facilities, the third broad group of factors underlying the successful operation of a retail store, include a satisfactory building—properly located and constructed—suitable fixtures and equipment, and other devices and mechanisms necessary to provide customers with needed merchandise and services in a pleasant environment. Recent years have witnessed important advances and improvements in site selection, store construction and arrangement, merchandise handling and storage, and the use of electronic equipment—to mention but a few of the major areas. These matters are discussed in considerable detail in Chapters 4, 5, 6, and 15.

■ APPROPRIATE RETAILING POLICIES

Effective, well-maintained policies for operation of the business constitute the fourth major requirement for profitable store management. Business policies are the written or implied rules of conduct under which the firm operates. A policy establishes a definite and uniform course of action which all members of the organization must follow under substantially similar and recurrent circumstances.

In small businesses, these "rules of conduct" are often simply the ideas the proprietor keeps in mind as to the way the store will operate. Policies are adopted when it is decided to sell on credit rather than for cash only and when salespeople are paid bonuses in addition to their regular salary. Larger retailers, however, usually put their policies in writing because they must be communicated to many people, frequently at several locations. All policies should be clear and definite, workable, stable and consistent as long as circumstances are similar, and adjusted promptly when fundamental conditions change. Policies that meet these requirements can be very useful management tools for the retail store proprietor or executive.

□ Need for effective policies

We have already noted that the retail stores of today operate under trying conditions, a fact well-demonstrated during the recession years of the middle 1970s. Competition steadily intensifies, many stores are broadening their "product mix," discount houses are growing rapidly, and traditional retailers are revising their services. Population shifts, particularly the growth of suburban areas, complicate the problems of downtown stores. High taxes and tight money may make it difficult to generate internal funds for expansion purposes; and sharply increased construction, modernization, and interest costs resulting from continuing inflation tend to deter necessary or desirable changes in physical facilities. The potential growth of retail unions and the increase in government regulations place restrictions on some of the retailer's former freedoms. Shorter working hours, higher wage rates, and night and Sunday openings have raised "break-even" points and made profitable operation more difficult.

These changing and trying conditions necessitate carefully established policies and their frequent evaluation.[15] Otherwise the retailer may be swept along with the tide—merely trying one opportunistic adjustment after another without thinking through the long-run implications of those adjustments. Stated positively, the retailer who goes through the mental process of determining policies has a set of standards to guide desirable courses of action; thus drifts off the main road are prevented in spite of the superficial attractiveness of some bypaths.

At the same time, changing conditions may well call for policy adjustments. In fact, as has already been emphasized, a policy is valid only so long as the circumstances which brought it into existence remain substantially the same. But the retailer who has carefully established sound policies for a certain set of conditions, will usually be the one who is willing to make adjustments in them *after investigation* indicates changes are necessary.

Well-established policies reduce the number of decisions that key executives have to make. Comparable cases can be settled on a routine basis according to predetermined and well-understood rules. Thus, the time of major executives is conserved by allowing others in the organization to make decisions based on the company's policies. Sound policies that insure consistent and equitable treatment of similar situations will reduce the danger of improperly treating one customer, employee, or supplier more favorably than another.

□ Steps in policy formulation

Careful study of the problems to be solved is the first step in policy formation. Accurate and complete information should be secured, rather than relying upon hunches and guesswork. The business's objectives, the anticipated operating conditions, the possible alternative polices, and their potential results should be carefully analyzed. Then the policies may be properly formulated.

Considerations influencing choice of policies   While the proprietor's, management's, or the board of directors' judgment is the final determinant in each policy decision, the business policies of any firm will depend upon what is desired and what is possible. What is desired, of course, is not always possible. Like most businesspeople, the retailer must constantly make compromises to meet the situations that confront the firm and especially to meet the restrictions placed upon any choice of alternatives. These include, among other factors, legal restrictions, public opinion, cost considerations, activities of competitors, vested interests of individuals in the organization, personal preferences, the services customers expect, and the limits of the resources available.

Responsibility for policy formulation Responsibility for establishing retail policies varies with the size and type of store and with the form of business organization. Most small firms and some rather large ones are individual proprietorships or partnerships. The proprietor or the partners, sometimes along with other family members, frame the rules for conducting these businesses. The board of directors should play a major role in policy formation for the incorporated small store. Unfortunately, however, the boards of small corporations often have only a purely nominal existence to satisfy legal technicalities and do not participate in policy formation.

The boards of directors of larger retail firms, such as corporate department stores and chains, are usually responsible for major policies, but they normally give the president or possibly a management committee authority to approve other policies. In so far as possible, though, the people who will be expected to carry out a policy should play some part in its development, regardless of where the final authority lies and regardless of who drafts the actual policy statement. Their experience and insights will not only help in framing the policy but they will become committed to its successful implementation.

Many retailers become so busy with daily routine affairs that they fail to devote enough time to policy formation. Despite the constant stream of daily matters demanding attention, every retailer should reserve sufficient time and energy for consideration of policy questions. The proprietor or chief executive should never forget that formulating suitable policies (in cooperation with the board of directors, if one exists) constitutes a major responsibility.

□ Areas of policy decisions

The retailer must make policy decisions concerning numerous aspects of the business, including, for example, the kinds and quality of merchandise to be carried, forms of customer service to be rendered, types of sales promotion to be used, and personnel administration problems. Conditions prevailing in very recent years, however, have magnified the need for frequent policy evaluation in these and numerous other areas. For example, energy conservation alone has forced many changes in store design and lighting; self-service and self-selection have been adopted in specialty stores formerly looking with disdain on the practice. Moreover, some of these stores, Bergdorf-Goodman for instance, are finally opening branch stores.[16] Policies concerning the matters mentioned and others are discussed in subsequent chapters and need not be treated at this point. In passing, however, let us consider briefly two other areas in which policies should be established—participation in community activities and membership in trade associations.

Participation in community activities   Many retailers—small and large—belong to service clubs such as the Kiwanis, Lions, or Rotary. Membership is considered a mark of distinction because of the interest such organizations take in community affairs and because of the exchange of ideas on business problems. Other retailers are members of chambers of commerce, local school boards, Community Fund committees, hospital boards, and parent-teacher associations. Still others serve as scouting leaders, members of the city council, city officials, and church officers. In deciding how active a part they will play in the life of the community, retailers will be governed by their desire to serve, the time involved, and their judgment of the long-run effect such participation will have on their sales and profits.

Membership in trade associations   Sooner or later retailers are confronted with the question of whether to join an association of similar stores. The decision will be based largely upon the services the association renders, the cost involved, and the time necessary to devote to it. Recent years have witnessed a continued growth in the membership of such associations because of the increase in services provided to members. Today there exist strong associations—local, state, and national—in almost every field of retail enterprise; and their membership lists include most of the successful retailers in the country.[17]

☐ Policy enforcement and review

Policies and procedures   Once policies have been established, operating procedures must be developed to carry them out. These procedures should be as simple and clear-cut as possible so as to be easily understood and applied by the people who will be using them. Otherwise, the time spent developing procedures is wasted and the business cannot function according to plan.

A simple illustration will clarify the relationship between policies and procedures. When the owner of a supermarket decides to offer delivery service to customers, a policy is being adopted. In choosing a method of handling the goods sold so that they will be delivered to customers as promptly and as economically as possible, an operating procedure is being established.

Policy enforcement   No policy, however well conceived, can be of value to a retail store unless it is adhered to closely and consistently throughout the organization. Continual follow-up and enforcement are necessary to assure such adherence, especially in regard to the rank and file of employees.

Many store employees tend to disregard rules and regulations, not because of disagreement with those rules but because of unwillingness to spend the time and effort to become familiar with them. Others are particularly averse to making changes, to being forced to learn "something new." Consequently the employees must be educated in the purposes of the new rules as well as in the advantages of conformance to them. Employees will accept the situation more readily and adjust themselves to it more quickly, if they can be shown the new procedure is simpler in operation, that it saves time, that it achieves the firm's objectives substantially better than the old method, or it results in greater customer satisfaction.

Unfortunately many retail executives become lax about insuring compliance with the company's policies. They become so engrossed in major decisions relating to immediate profits that they neglect the essential continuous reemphasis of established policies and procedures. Their own negligence contributes significantly to the carelessness of their employees.

Coordination   Top management must also make certain that the policies and activities of the various sections of the business are coordinated and contribute to the overall objective of providing needed goods and services and thus keeping the business profitable. Departmental and divisional personnel sometimes think of a store as a number of separate parts, each of which operates in its own interest. As a result, insufficient attention is given to the necessity of integrating these parts effectively.

Adjusting policies to changing conditions   The dynamic nature of retailing necessitates continuous policy development and adjustment. Policies, like retail prices, are constantly on trial. They must constantly be examined in the light of experience and, as previously indicated, adjustments made when conditions change to a significant degree. The following excerpt from a statement of Ralph Lazarus, chairman of Federated Department Stores, is indicative of the actions helpful in policy evaluation to keep stores "in tune" with the changing conditions of today. Representatives of ". . . each division went home to conduct a [thorough] review and analysis of its business: Where it is now; where it would like to go; how it might get there; what it knows and what it needs to know. In-store task forces were formed and bright, young people joined top management in drawing a new road map to the future . . . plans are [then] analyzed by men and women from division and corporate levels for action and . . . exploratory research into unsolved problems. . . ."[18]

Policy changes and adjustments call for some caution. Occasionally a policy will be discarded as an apparent failure after a short period of trial when actually the program of implementation rather than the basic policy itself was the cause of failure. Further investigation would have revealed the true problem. All of which suggests again that the successful operation of a retail store depends to an important degree upon how closely the proprietor or chief executive officer remains in contact with the essential activities of the business. Systematic and thorough follow-up of policies and procedures substantially influences profits.

■ COMPETENCY AND LOYALTY OF RETAIL PERSONNEL

The importance of the human factor in retailing, the fifth basic requirement of success in this field, has already been stressed in previous pages. It should be emphasized further, however, that profitable store operation is impossible unless an adequate sales and sales-supporting staff is carefully selected, effectively trained, adequately compensated, and properly supervised. Competency in the particular activities in which they are engaged, loyalty to top management and their immediate supervisors through close adherence to established policies and practices, and performance of duties and responsibilities efficiently and at reasonable cost are major obligations of every employee. Likewise, it is the obligation of the proprietor or of top management to be so objective, logical, and progressive in policies and practices that employees respond with loyalty and respect. Chapters 8 and 9 are devoted to personnel management in the retail store.

■ REVIEW AND DISCUSSION QUESTIONS

1 Explain how current developments in the retail field intensify the need for the basic requirements of successful retail management?

2 What do you consider the essential personal qualifications of an effective retail executive? Defend your answer.

3 Explain the "marketing concept," and its applicability to retailing. How widely is it employed in the retail field? Why?

4 Discuss the social contributions of a retail store executive under conditions prevailing today.

5 Who, in the retail firm, should be responsible for policy formulation?

6 Define "retailing policy" in your own words and point out the characteristics of a good policy.

7 Explain why effective policies are essential to success in retailing and illustrate three areas in which they are required.

8 Based on your observation in retail stores or your recent reading, give examples of policy changes by special retail firms. Explain, where possible, the circumstances which brought about the changes.

9 Do you agree or disagree with the opinion of some social psychologists that retail executives are particularly sensitive to short-time changes in business activity and probably possess less analytical ability than executives in other kinds of business? Defend your answer.

10 Assume that your first job following graduation is in a retail store and that the controller asks you to suggest ways through which better adherence to established rules and regulations can be obtained. Prepare a brief report covering this assignment.

■ NOTES AND REFERENCES

1 W. N. Mitchell, The Business Executive in a Changing World (New York: American Management Association, 1965), pp. 48, 58, 60, 75.

2 "The Agile Man Who Built Third Avenue," Fortune, vol. 71 (May 1965), p. 146.

3 Norman Beasley, Main Street Merchant: The Story of the J. C. Penney Company (New York: Whittlesey House, McGraw-Hill Book Co., Inc., 1948), p. 80.

4 James McCreery, quoted by Margaret Dana, "Listen to What Your Customers Tell You," in Readings in Modern Retailing (New York: National Retail Merchants Association, 1969), p. 75.

5 E. H. Fram, "Application of the Marketing Concept to Retailing," Journal of Retailing, vol 41, (Summer 1965), p. 19.

6 Wroe Alderson and P. E. Green, Planning and Problem Solving in Marketing (Homewood, Ill.: Richard D. Irwin, Inc., 1964), p. 5.

7 G. J. Berkwitt, "The Big Shake-up in Management Development," Dun's March 1973, pp. 79–81 and his "The Crisis in Management Talent," February 1973, pp. 56–58.

8 The young lady who was appointed president of a 30-store shoe chain at age 26 is very definitely an exception to the general rule. See "Jane Evans: The Whiz Kid Who Fills I. Miller's Shoes," Chicago Tribune, December 6, 1970, sec. 5, p. 8.

9 See D. E. Berlew, "Leadership and Organizational Excitement," California Management Review, vol. 17, (Winter 1974), pp. 21–30.

10 R. L. Katz, Executive Skills, (Hanover, N.H.: Amos Tuck School of Business Administration, 1954), pp. 4–6. In 1974 the Harvard Business Review republished Dr. Katz's discussion of these skills as one of its "classics" under the title "Skills of an Effective Administrator," vol. 52, no. 5 (September-October), pp. 90–102. The complete article, and especially the author's "Retrospective Summary" evaluating favorably these skills in the light of the developments since its original publication, is enlightening for businesspeople as well as students.

11 See W. A. Fisher and Leonard Groeneveld, "Social Responsibility and Small Business," Journal of Small Business Management, January 1976, pp. 18–26.

12 Ann Roush, Selling to North American Stores (London: Routledge & Kegan Paul, for the British Export Council, 1969), p. 15.

13 Quoted from the Bonne Bell Community Service Citations.

14 This caution is well illustrated by an article entitled, "Is this Any Time to Start a Business?" in Changing Times, October 1975, pp. 24–28. See also "Raising Capital for Small Businesses," Business Week, November 3, 1973, pp. 96–97 and Joseph C. Schabacker, Small Business Information Sources (An Annotated Bibliography). (Tempe, Ariz. Publication Services, Inc., 1976).

15 See the excellent and concise discussion by Samuel Feinberg in his

"From Where I Sit," *Women's Wear Daily,* January 23, 1974, p. 8.

16 "Bergdorf Goes Suburban," *Chain Store Age Executive,* March 1975, p. 47.

17 For a comprehensive list of retail and nonretail trade associations, see the *Encyclopedia of Associations,* 10th ed. (Detroit: Gale Research Co., 1976).

18 In the "Ninth Annual [Financial] Report Contest," *Stores,* September 1975, p. 6.

OPPORTUNITIES AND CAREERS IN RETAILING

Retailing offers many opportunities for stimulating and reward-ing careers. It employs about as many people as the combined fields of construction, transportation, communications, public utilities, real estate, insurance, banking, and finance. Moreover, retail stores are diverse enough and positions in stores are sufficiently varied to provide opportunities for almost every kind of ability, training, ambition, need, and desire. Top management has become increasingly aware of the advantages of community college and university training for success in this field.

■ SCOPE OF THE CHAPTER

Many retail employees are unskilled and poorly trained. Often employed on a part-time basis, they hold little or no authority and executive responsibility, but yet seem reasonably satisfied with their work. Our discussion here, however, concentrates on the opportunities for students who wish to advance to responsible positions in retailing, with commensurate salaries, where their abilities will be fully used. Of course, advancement involves accepting the responsibilities along with the rewards. Many people want to avoid the obligations inherent in higher position. Some, for example, have limited opportunities in retailing—or elsewhere—because they will not accept promotions that involve supervising other people's work.

Students will find career opportunities in small, medium-sized, and large retail organizations located in communities of various sizes. We cannot safely generalize, however, as to the size of store or community that provides the greatest possibilities. The opportunities in any particular retail venture depend upon many factors: the suitability of the store's merchandise and service to its market, management's progressiveness and alertness, the owners' ultimate willingness to share control and responsibility, general business and competitive conditions, the managerial candidate's own qualifications, and to some extent, the "breaks" that the trainee receives or creates.

This chapter is divided into five parts: (1) general employment aspects of retailing; (2) prospects in small and medium-sized stores; (3) prospects in department and specialty stores; (4) prospects in chain stores; and (5) "pros" and "cons" of retailing careers.

■ GENERAL EMPLOYMENT ASPECTS OF RETAILING

□ Decentralization

Retailing offers opportunities, as an employee or proprietor, in every city, town, and village in the country. Talented and ambitious individuals can receive highly useful early experience in their hometown stores or in stores near their school community. This background will often prove helpful even in seeking employment with large retail firms elsewhere.

□ Many kinds of stores

The *1972 Census of Retail Trade* shows 82 separate classifications of stores, such as automobile dealers, drugstores, hardware stores, and millinery shops, as well as many types of "nonstore" retailers. The stores within a classification also often differ greatly in character and personnel requirements, since some may feature style, others service, and still others low prices. The different types of experience, knowledge, abilities, tastes, and desires that these various stores require furnish opportunities for people with very different interests and talents.

□ Large number employed

Retailing in the United States employed more than 13 million persons in 1975, more than twice the 1945 figure and about three million more than in 1965.[1] The U.S. Department of Labor forecasts that increased consumer expenditures, continued suburbanization, and longer store hours will raise future retail employment. Mechanization and self-service will supplant some low-level jobs, resulting in a moderate net increase throughout the mid-1980s.[2]

□ Stable employment for full-time employees

Employment is more stable in retailing than in many other industries. Some retail businesses, such as food stores, experience little seasonal fluctuation in sales. Seasonal variations are significant in other retail fields, but are not as great as the production fluctuations in many manufacturing industries. The increasing use of part-time employees in retailing permits adjustments to fluctuating conditions without altering the size of the regular staff.

□ Changing opportunities

Retailing is a stable industry, but not static. Total retail volume and employment fluctuate with, and are dependent upon, national income. Some groups of retail stores are increasing in importance, while others are decreasing. During the period between the 1967 and 1972 censuses, for example, most types of retailing in the U.S. increased employment, but a few, such as retail furriers, household appliance stores, mail-order establishments and direct-selling companies actually reduced the number of paid workers.[3] Employment and career possibilities also appear in retailing developments, such as: the growth of "bantam, convenience-type" food stores, the expansion of stores that rent rather than sell merchandise, the increased development of franchising and the emergence of various new-style boutiques.

□ Many different occupations

Mention retail employment and most people think of selling or cashiering. Yet only a fraction of the employees in many large organizations meet the customer on the sales floor. Jewel Supermarkets, for example, employs 3.12 people behind-the-scenes for every cashier the customer sees.[4] One department store lists 800 different job classifications.[5] Many retail stores need buyers, fashion experts, accountants, advertising staff, traffic and delivery experts, research directors, and personnel specialists, as well as salespeople.

□ Opportunities for women

Retailing has traditionally offered employment to a large number of women. About 47 percent of all retail employees in the U.S. in October

1974 were women.[6] The percentage of women employees varies widely with the kind of business, being low in tire and automotive-supply stores, for example, and high in dress shops.

Women in retailing have not always achieved or received full equality with men. One union study of high-earning commission salespeople in New York reported that among 35 furniture sales clerks averaging $25,000 per year, only four were women; and that among 50 shoe sales clerks averaging $15,000 per year, only 20 were women.[7] More importantly, until recently many stores paid lower rates of salary and commission to saleswomen in dress and related departments than to salesmen in men's clothing department, although the two selling jobs are often equally difficult. (See the discussion of antidiscrimination legislation in Chapter 9.) Promotion to top management and to some other executive positions has also often been difficult although not nearly so restricted as in other industries. But in general, the promotional opportunities for women in retailing have been better-than-average and are steadily improving. One report says that two out of every five buyers and merchandise managers (perhaps the most important level of middle management in many retail firms) are women.[8] Women are also often appointed as personnel and training directors and as advertising executives. Chain-store companies, including five-and-ten-cent stores, supermarket, and general-merchandise companies, are now assigning store managerships to women, and many large retail firms have now promoted women to the vice-presidential level.[9] Four of the "100 Top Corporate Women" cited by *Business Week* are retail executives.[10]

☐ Training essential for key positions

Training, through academic background, trade- or business-school education, in-store development programs, and/or experience, is essential for many retailing positions. Large retail firms recruit promotable young men and women at community colleges, universities, and graduate schools, and in some cases have sponsored employee and prospective-employee enrollment in community and senior colleges.[11] Some typical jobs offered to graduates, according to one survey, included: trainee, assistant buyer, assistant store manager, interviewer, selling-floor supervisor, department sales manager, advertising specialist, financial assistant, and many other titles.[12] Large retailers also often implement their "promotion from within" policies by establishing development programs for the academically-trained and other promotable individuals in their organizations. These programs vary in extent, format, and effectiveness, but usually involve rotating work experience in various sectors of the firm. They may also include lectures and discussions with corporate officials and selected outsiders, attendance at evening courses and short seminars, correspondence study, and other activities. Department and chain store training programs are discussed more fully at pp. 73–78 in this chapter, and in Chapter 8.

One study of franchisees' success in the fast-food business found, interestingly enough, that earnings as a franchisee were not related to previous experience, either in the food/restaurant business or as an independent businessperson, but that they were related to years of formal academic training, to participation in the franchisor's training program, and to annual income before becoming a franchisee.[13]

□ Retailing salaries

Salespeople and nonselling employees Table 3–1 shows average hourly wages, working hours and weekly wages for full-time and part-time *nonsupervisory* workers in selected retail trades. These figures do not include any executive, professional, or managerial personnel. Hardware store salespeople averaged about $2.85 per hour in 1974.[14] Salaries for beginning salespeople in small communities tend to be close to the statutory minimum of $88–92 for 40 hours.* Beginning salaries for routine saleswork in stores in larger cities are somewhat higher—one recent union contract provides a $2.50 an hour minimum. Two labor contracts with general merchandise/discount stores on the Pacific Coast established 1976 rates of $3.95 to $5.80 per hour, depending upon seniority and departmental specialization.[15] Capable, experienced specialty salespeople in shoes, clothing, and "big ticket" appliance departments may earn $150 to $400 per week or more.

Trainees' initial salaries Retail executive trainees also tend to re-

TABLE 3–1

Average hourly earnings and weekly earnings of nonsupervisory employees in selected retail trades, January 1976		
Type of store	Average hourly earnings	Average weekly earnings
Department stores	$3.44	$105.26
Food stores	4.13	133.40
Men's and boy's clothing	3.63	114.71
Women's ready-to-wear	2.90	82.65
Shoe stores	3.22	93.70
Furniture and home furnishings	4.12	149.14
Drug stores	3.41	105.37
Book and stationery	3.53	116.14
Motor vehicle dealers	4.68	184.39

Source: U.S. Department of Labor, *Employment & Earnings,* vol. 22 (March 1976), p. 98. Preliminary figures subject to minor revision.

---

* There are some minor exceptions to this minimum for very small businesses and for student workers.

ceive relatively low starting salaries, although some firms have improved their compensation substantially in recent years. For example, an analysis of several thousand job offers received by bachelor's degree candidates at 133 colleges in 1974–75 shows that "merchandising and related firms" (wholesaleing, retailing, advertising, etc.) offered about 15 percent less than the all-industry average.[16] Clearly, retail organizations should do more to meet the inducements of other industries. Beginning salaries must be raised so that qualified trainees receive adequate compensation.[17]

Top executive salaries The chief executives of the large firms earn very substantial incomes. Sears, Roebuck and Company paid its chairman $400,000 and its president $258,000 in 1975; the two senior executives in Federated Department Stores received compensation of $375,-000 and $350,000; while the two chief executives of Safeway Stores earned amounts of $235,000 and $175,000. A 1973 survey of large firms showed that, on the average, retailing companies paid their second-highest executive 81 percent of the amount paid the top executive, compared with 74 percent in manufacturing and 70–71 percent in banking and insurance.[18] In February of the same year, *Fortune* magazine published a list of 39 individuals who had become "extraordinarily wealthy" (that is, had reached an estimated net worth of $50 million to $300 million) during the preceding five years. That list included seven retailers: the chief executive-owners of Petrie Stores Corp. (women's clothing), Jack Eckard Corp. (drugstores), Arlen Realty and Development Corp. (shopping centers and discount stores), Long's Drugstores, Val-U-Mart Stores (discount and variety stores), and Fingerhut Corp. (mail order), as well as the principal officer of a trading stamp company and two restaurant owners.[19]

Obviously, only a few persons entering retailing will reach these levels. Nevertheless, in at least a few cases, career progress may be quite rapid.[20] More importantly, as indicated later in this chapter, middle-management executives in retailing are also usually very well-paid. Unfortunately, relatively low executive-trainee salaries and the prospect of some Saturday, Sunday, and evening work (often heaviest during the first few years of employment) drive many able young workers away from retailing careers. Yet those who have the necessary personalities and abilities and who can "stick out" the first hard years may eventually obtain very large financial rewards.

Other rewards Although dollar compensation is important, retailing also offers other satisfactions. An executive trainee is usually given direct operating responsibilities quite early in her or his career, and from then on can enjoy the challenge of producing measurable results. As Dean Walter Salmon of the Harvard Business School says:

Retailing is a field where you get feedback on your accomplishments pretty fast—i.e., as a buyer you get a profit-and-loss statement that is a pretty good yardstick of your contribution. . . . If you want to influence the action, you have to be willing to take on a leadership role. Retailing, because it is people intensive, offers leadership roles.[21]

Retailing executives often assume major roles in community and civic affairs; they can have a sense of satisfaction in helping create job opportunities for many people; and they make significant contributions to the modern standard of living. They also experience the stimulation and excitement of experimenting with new ways of operating their stores or departments, of constantly meeting new competitive thrusts, and of working with people in an active, vigorous, ever-changing environment.

□ Working conditions in retailing

The following discussion is in general terms since working conditions vary greatly among different types of work in a given retail firm, among firms in the same field, among fields, and among sections of the country.

Hours Retail working hours have been sharply reduced in recent years. Small-store proprietors and employees may work 48, 54, or more hours per week, but larger retail organizations generally observe a 40-hour week, with some overtime at peak periods. The five-day work-week has also become common in spite of the increase in Sunday openings. In fact, work schedules in retailing are frequently far more regular than in such fields as airline transportation, newspaper and television communications, medicine, or law. As is true in any other business or profession, rising young retail executives and proprietors tend to work longer, but more flexible and more self-determined schedules than do employees with routine jobs.

Environment Employees in nonselling departments, such as bookkeeping or warehouse operations, sometimes work in rather unattractive surroundings, since management often concentrates upon decorating and improving the portions of the store that customers see. Similarly, chain store managers (particularly in the smaller outlets) and department store buyers are often given rather small and cluttered offices. In any event, overly elaborate offices would not be appropriate in the informal atmosphere that characterizes most retail organizations. However, top retail executives, senior headquarters staff and an increasing number of middle managers work in attractive offices and are provided competent secretarial assistance.

Retailers are also recognizing the need for improving the mental and social conditions of work. Employee clubs, house organs, social events, athletic contests, and similar amenities contribute to the rank-and-file employees' *esprit de corps* and contentment. Many retail workers find the social contacts and opportunities to talk with customers and fellow employees even more pleasurable and stimulating.

Vacations   Vacations in retailing are comparable to those in most other businesses. Extra pay or compensatory time-off is often allowed if and when work is required on conventional holidays. Regular employees usually receive one, two, three, or in some stores, even five weeks paid vacation depending upon length of service. Both stores and employees have usually preferred summer vacations, when business is slow and children are out of school, but an increasing number of workers now take at least part of their vacation in winter. Executives have great flexibility in scheduling their own time-off.

Job security   Retailing is a stable business and thus provides substantial job security for most regular workers. Technological unemployment has not been a problem, as in some industries, and should not be significant in the reasonably foreseeable future. In spite of further warehouse mechanization, check-out automation, and computerization of accounting and record-keeping, retailing will continue to require large numbers of employees and executives. The employees of the larger firms especially benefit from increased personal security through expanded corporate group insurance, health insurance, and pension programs in addition to governmental provisions for medicare, old-age, and unemployment benefits.[22]

Unions   Although labor unions have less influence in retailing than in some other industries, they have become more important in recent years. See the discussion of retail labor unions in Chapter 9.

Future prospects   In spite of night and Sunday openings, overall retail working conditions will undoubtedly continue to improve in the coming years. Working hours, however, are not likely to decline for either the small-store owner who must compete on the basis of customer service and convenience or for the ambitious junior executive who is seeking to get ahead. Promotion and success in any business usually require long hours, often for additional study as well as directly on the job, and hard work along with the assumption of increased responsibilities.

■ OPPORTUNITIES IN SMALL AND MEDIUM-SIZED STORES

Some students plan careers in small and medium-sized stores because of opportunities to participate in, and ultimately manage, a family or friend's business. Others are attracted by the possibility of buying or establishing their own stores, although, of course, this alternative involves the capital and experience requirements noted in the previous chapter and amplified below. However, many students must postpone store ownership, and in some cases even entry into the family business, until they have gained experience and training through a job in someone else's store.

□ Limited opportunities as an employee

The person who seeks experience in a small or medium-sized store should hold long-run career objectives clearly in mind. He or she should recognize that employees outside the owner's family are at a disadvantage if they hope to eventually acquire the business in which they are working. Consequently, more attention should be given to training possibilities rather than to immediate pay or future promises. Establishments with out-moded methods that lack real training value should be avoided. Stated positively, the ambitious individual should seek a position in a progressive independent store that provides experience in all aspects of retailing, including knowledge of merchandise and suppliers, operating methods, sales promotion, relations with customers, and store records and controls. Store work should be supplemented by reading relevant trade magazines and textbooks, and government and commercial reports, and by careful study of other retailers' practices and policies.

□ Store ownership

Students who have thought only about "big business" overlook the possible rewards of ultimately owning their own stores.

Many possibilities Few fields offer as many opportunities as retailing does for independent business ownership. There are approximately 1.6 million single-unit independent retail establishments in the U.S. Retirement and death of store owners and other factors constantly create opportunities to purchase going businesses. Some are advertised in newspaper and trade-publication classified sections, and people in the trade, such as manufacturers and wholesalers and their salespeople, often know of others that may be available. Business brokers, who specialize in selling retail businesses, will also suggest purchase opportunities. However, as the Bank of America points out, a broker's reputation and purchase recommendations should be carefully checked, since the broker is the seller's representative in the transaction.[23]

Manufacturers, wholesalers, store designers and builders, and equipment houses are usually eager for outlets and sales. They will often provide considerable assistance, through advice and credit extension, in finding a store to buy or in establishing a new one. Many franchising companies, including automobile manufacturers and gasoline refiners, act as "management consultants" for their new (and old) dealers. Some voluntary-chain wholesalers, especially grocery firms, will find a location, erect a building, and stock it for the new owner. Even the growth of large organizations, such as chain discount houses, provides some opportunities for smaller leased-department operators.

Moreover, even though chains and other large organizations are handling an increasing portion of total retail sales, as noted in Chapter 1, opportunities for *profitable* independent store ownership remain and will persist. While alert small merchants can be quite flexible in adjusting to changing conditions, the giant organizations are often handicapped by their own size; the need to maintain very large inventories; by problems of internal communication; and by the difficulties of adjusting to local situations. One knowledgeable consultant says: ". . . the smaller stores—and particularly those with good, aggressive, active management will likely do better than the mammoth chains. . . ."[24] The rate of chain growth may be levelling off, and there will always be room for independent stores that properly serve specialized markets or that offer distinctive assortments and services at satisfactory prices. Many independent appliance-TV dealers are reported to be growing through the use of aggressive pricing and merchandising policies, in spite of a general tendency toward concentration of ownership and big-firm dominance in their trade.[25]

Of course, the small retailer who hopes to be successful must expect to work very hard. The owner who operates entirely independently must often be an innovator, with a store differentiated from competitors, and offering products, services, convenience, or an "atmosphere" that is unavailable in larger establishments. The participant in a voluntary-chain or franchise system must be willing to sacrifice some independence.

Profitability and failure   The returns from independent store ownership vary considerably, but can be quite attractive. One study, for example, found that the proprietors of small flower shops with sales of about $125,000 per year received average incomes of approximately $17,500. Proprietors of stores in the $25,000 to $60,000 class, however, only averaged about $9,000 per year.[26] The 1974 average compensation of men's clothing store owners varied from about $15,000 for stores with sales below $300,000 a year to about $50,000 in stores with sales over $3.5 million.[27]

Concerning franchises, a consultant notes that earnings will be affected by the size of the individual establishment; by the skills, effort, and capital the franchisee provides; whether the franchisee joins the system early or late in its development; and, of course, by the quality and fairness of the franchise arrangement. But he concludes that "although few franchisees can attain the fantastic profits sometimes promised . . . many of them do quite well financially."[28]

Studies which show retail profits of only 1 to 4 percent of *sales* often suggest that retailing is unprofitable. But these apparently small ratios often equal a return of 10 to 20 percent or more on *net worth* and, in small stores, are *in addition* to the proprietor's salary or drawing account.

But along with these profit possibilities, independent store ownership also involves risks, including the danger of failure.[29] There are no universally accepted figures, and the failure rate varies from field to field and from year to year, depending upon general economic conditions. But often 10 to 20 percent of the new store owners fail within the first year, and perhaps 30 to 40 percent within the first five years of operation.

While this may seem high, it certainly does not exceed the rate for new independent wholesaling, manufacturing, and service businesses. Moreover, many retail failures result from inexperience, inadequate capital, and lack of managerial ability.[30] The student who acquires adequate experience and develops capital resources and managerial talents before opening a store may enjoy considerable success.

Personal qualities Store ownership requires all of the abilities of a successful retail employee plus some additional qualities. Some highly-skilled chain-store managers who have left their firms to open stores of their own have been absolute failures while others have built very rewarding businesses. Perhaps the differences are that a storeowner must be a complete "self-starter," without a district supervisor or headquarters to monitor the work; that the storeowner must be able to deal with all phases of the business, including buying, employee relations, and customer service; and that the storeowner must make the proper mental adjustment to the strain of risking his or her own money in the venture. In addition, the National Retail Hardware Association points out that a successful hardware store owner must be patient in dealing with customers and employees, must like people, must be a decision-maker, must be prepared for long hours and hard work, and must be willing to be tied to one location for a long period of time; but the rewards are well worth the costs.[31]

Buying an established business or starting a new one The choice between buying an on-going business and starting a new store depends on many factors. These include: the availability of a business for purchase, the price the seller demands, whether a good location is available for a new store, whether the community can support an additional establishment, and which of the two propositions is easier to finance. The prospective purchaser should try to determine why the present owner wants to sell the business. Does the store suffer from new competition? Is the location deteriorating? Are customers moving away?

An entirely new business has some strong advantages. Its stock can be completely "clean" and fresh. New fixtures, equipment, and layout provide an attractive shopping atmosphere and may reduce operating expenses. There are no payments for goodwill, and the new proprietor isn't burdened with any "ill-will" the former owner might have created.

But an on-going business frequently has its own advantages. The new owner doesn't have to spend considerable time acquiring fixtures and equipment, assembling inventory, engaging personnel, and establishing record-keeping systems. Some steady customers will "stay with" the store. The purchase of a going business does not increase the total number of stores in the area, which would divide the existing trade among more retailers.

Thus the question of "whether to buy a store or start a new one" often comes down to the price the seller will accept. If it is low enough, even a poorly-equipped and ill-stocked store may be a good purchase. The appraised value of the store's assets is, however, only the starting point for all the bargaining usually involved in setting the final price. Payment of a premium over "book value" may be both necessary and profitable for a store with an attractive location and a well-developed clientele; in other cases, the reverse is true. One rule-of-thumb is that the store's "goodwill" is worth from one- to five-times the amount by which the annual return to the owner has exceeded the sum of a reasonable salary for managerial work plus a reasonable (competitive market) rate of interest or dividend on the investment. The highest figure (five "years of profit") would apply to a well-established business with a good reputation and good prospects.[32] The buyer should have the store's assets appraised carefully and its profit possibilities estimated before bargaining, so as to have a sound basis for judgment.

Financing methods   The size of the establishment and the types of merchandise handled help determine the capital requirements for an independent store. Some idea of the capital investment needed for various types of outlets can be derived from figures prepared by the *Small Business Reporter* for "typical" hypothetical stores, as shown in Table 3–2. Other types of stores can demand much greater sums: the average modern supermarket involves an investment of almost $1 million, including the building, "and the typical chain drug store opened in 1974 cost about $315,000."[33] However, the various sources discussed in later paragraphs will often supply financial support for some of these capital outlays.

TABLE 3–2

Initial investment requirements for "typical" hypothetical independent retail stores

Kind of business	Sales volume range per year (in thousands)	Approximate investment (in thousands)
Sporting goods	$150–250	$40–70
Health foods	100–250	25–45
Bicycle	75–250	17–35
Fabric	100–200	38–58
Yarn	50–100	16–25
Bookstore	75–100	25–54

Source: *Small Business Reporter*, (Bank of America) vol. 10, no. 11 (1972), p. 6; vol. 11, no. 2 (1973), p. 8; vol. 11, no. 10 (1974), p. 9; vol. 12, no. 1 (1974), p. 6.

1. Determining requirements The purchaser of an *established business* can estimate financial needs fairly easily: these include the purchase price plus rough estimates for the costs of layout changes, inventory adjustments, additional working capital requirements, living expenses, and contingencies until store revenue becomes available.

The retailer who wants to establish a *new business* should try to get information from friendly, comparable retailers in other communities concerning investments in fixtures and equipment, merchandise inventory, accounts receivable (if credit sales are contemplated), and other working capital items. Possible equipment cost increases, an allowance for unforeseen contingencies, and the cost of living and operating expenses until the store opens and develops reasonable sales volume must be added to these figures.

The resultant sums should be compared with all data available from relevant trade associations, business publications, university research bureaus, and the U.S. Small Business Administration. Then all of this information should be checked against the prospective retailer's own estimates for each major item. For example, fixture and equipment costs can be checked by obtaining bids from two or three equipment firms. Reputable franchisors also will indicate capital requirements for their franchisees, but unfortunately unscrupulous firms often understate this figure. Some typical cash requirements for various types of franchises are shown in Table 3–3.

Finally, all estimates and purchase or franchise contracts should be checked very carefully by a knowledgeable accountant and attorney. The importance of these careful reviews in avoiding future disappointment and hardship cannot be overemphasized.

2. Securing funds The new owner's own capital is usually the most important single source of funds for the venture. As a general rule, subject to many exceptions, the owner should provide at least half of the total opening investment. It may be difficult to secure additional funds from other sources without a personal investment of this size. Moreover, excessive dependence upon borrowed capital will raise interest costs to a dangerous level.

Several sources are available for the remaining 50 percent. Wholesalers or manufacturers will usually supply at least part of the inventory on 30-, 60-, or 90-day credit. The amount of trade financing (as this sort of credit is called) and its importance in the retailer's total financial picture tends to vary with the rate of merchandise turnover and the relative risks of the business. Trade credit tends to be limited in the case of grocery stores, where the merchandise is usually quickly sold, and is more significant in the slow-turnover jewelry and furniture trades.[34] The fixtures and equipment may be purchased on an installment basis. A commercial bank may provide a short-term loan if the prospective retailer can show that it will be repaid within the bank's time limits.

TABLE 3–3

Total investment and start-up cash required for a franchised retail or service business 1974[1] (thousands of dollars)

Kinds of franchised business[2]	Number reporting	Total investment			Start-up cash		
		Lowest	Highest	Median	Lowest	Highest	Median
Automotive products and services	78	10	500	35	2	100	10
Business aids and services							
Accounting, credit, collection agencies and general business systems	20	3	250	20	2	65	8
Employment services	45	3	55	20	2	40	15
Printing and copying services	10	29	45	40	5	21	16
Tax preparation services	7	1	11	3	1	5	2
Miscellaneous business services	29	3	125	14	1	85	10
Construction, home improvement, maintenance and cleaning services	82	5	500	22	2	100	10
Convenience stores	22	10	185	65	3	25	10
Educational products and services	25	5	145	25	1	75	15
Fast food restaurants (all types)	213	10	500	80	2	80	20
Hotels and motels	19	60	2,100	850	15	700	100
Campgrounds	7	125	500	250	8	200	50
Laundry and drycleaning services	12	22	80	55	8	50	16
Recreation, entertainment and travel	16	5	200	30	2	100	15
Rental services (auto-truck)	8	10	500	100	5	50	30
Rental services (equipment)	16	2	100	26	2	45	10
Retailing (non-food)	115	4	300	50	1	150	20
Retailing (food other than convenience stores)	44	5	500	50	1	125	20
Miscellaneous	16	2	800	30	2	100	10

[1] Investment and start-up cash represent averages reported by respondents.
[2] Does not include automobile and truck dealers, gasoline service stations and soft drink bottlers for which data were not collected.
Source: U.S. Department of Commerce, *Franchising in the Economy 1974–76* (Washington, D.C.: U.S. Government Printing Office, 1976), p. 44.

Friends may provide loans, or in the case of a corporation, purchase stock. In such case, the retailer must be sure to retain control of the business. If a going business is being acquired, the seller may accept a well-secured note for part of the purchase price. U.S. Small Business Administration provides loans to some retailers who cannot obtain funds elsewhere, while Canadian financial institutions may provide government-guaranteed loans to small enterprises under the Small Business Loans Act (1960).

Wholesalers and other voluntary chain sponsors (variety, food, hardware, and drug stores) will sometimes accept a note from the buyer for a substantial part of the store equipment and merchandise investment. Automobile manufacturers often give their new dealers substantial aid, a typical arrangement being that the dealer provide at least one quarter of the total investment. Many franchising companies either extend some financial assistance or help arrange loans. The major gasoline companies often help equip and stock their service stations, so that the dealer may only have to arrange working capital, which may be as little as $10,000.

Legal form of organization   The merits and disadvantages of the proprietorship, partnership, and corporate forms of organization are discussed in many business law, accounting, finance, and management texts,[35] and need not be analyzed here. Most American small retail businesses are operated as individual proprietorships because of (1) the resultant tax savings, and (2) freedom from the complications and legal problems of incorporation. However, the corporate form's limited liability, and the fact that it is not automatically terminated by the proprietor's death, make it more attractive for the retailer who is borrowing heavily or investing substantial personal savings in the business. The new retailer who begins with a proprietorship or partnership may want to convert to a corporation as soon as the business has shown some growth.

■ PROSPECTS IN DEPARTMENT AND SPECIALTY STORES

Department store employment increased by more than 20 percent between 1967 and 1972 alone.[36] The more alert and progressive department and large specialty store firms have been growing rapidly during the past thirty years and have been opening numerous branch and suburban stores. This growth has greatly increased the need for qualified managerial personnel. Many of the leading firms have instituted or expanded strong programs for recruiting and developing executive trainees, and they have maintained these programs in spite of temporary economic recessions.[37]

Again, as in other fields, the executive promotional opportunities vary considerably from company to company. Promotion will be slow in stores that have "gone to seed," or that have a full staff of seasoned, stable executives and no real growth prospects, or where management prefers to fill most executive positions from outside. In contrast, progress may be very rapid in fast-growing or expanding firms that have policies of promotion from within. Vacancies through resignation, retirement, or otherwise also create many chances for promotion. Everything considered, students can find many attractive career opportunities in department and specialty stores.

More salary information appears on the following pages in discussions of various department store divisions, but junior executives usually earn about $6,500–$10,000 yearly. College trainees were offered an average of $9,000 in 1975–76, and MBA's an average of $13,600.[38] Even though its figures are now quite outdated, due to inflation and other factors, some idea of department store executive remuneration can be gained from one of the very few comprehensive national surveys ever conducted on that subject. This survey, published in 1973 and covering 1971 earnings, showed that among relatively small department stores, buyers' annual compensation (salary and bonus) averaged $7,800, in stores with total sales of $2–$5 million, and $9,300 in stores doing $5–$15 million. Buyers in larger stores, $30 million and up, and in group headquarters averaged $12,700 and $19,500, respectively. Of course, some skilled and experienced buyers received much more than the average, with individual compensation ranging up to $40,000. The salaries and bonuses of major divisional heads in each store size-category tended to be about two- to four-times as large as the buyers' compensation.[39]

A subsequent study of 1975 compensation of 421 senior executives in 50 department stores showed that the chief merchandising officials (who might have the title executive vice president) received, on the average, $39,000 to $121,000 in salary and bonus depending on store or firm size. The smaller stores (sales from $5 million to $50 million) paid their senior financial officer $32,000; their chief operations executive $25,000; the top personnel manager $20,000; and the chief of security and protection $15,000. The median salary and bonus of the comparable executives in firms with sales over $500 million were: top financial executive, $135,000; top operations executive $110,000; top personnel executive, $94,000; and chief of security, $48,000. There was considerable dispersion of individual salaries above and below these medians, and practically all of the executives also enjoyed long-term income-accumulation plans and other fringe benefits.[40]

☐ Junior executive training programs

The growth of executive training programs is a highly favorable feature of the department-store field. Employment in the better programs is often highly competitive, and is based on interviews with store executives, evaluation of the prospective trainee's academic, extracurricular, and employment record, and perhaps personality tests. But

FIGURE 3–1 Promotional paths for merchandising executives, (A) Dayton's—Minneapolis-St. Paul and (B) Famous-Barr—St. Louis

A. Dayton's

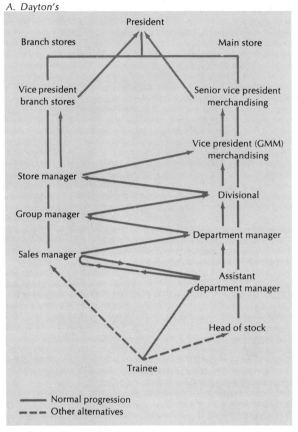

Source: Company brochure.

the people selected for participation can learn practically all aspects of the business in a relatively short period. An executive trainee can also be very certain of not being "lost in the crowd." Instead, top management will be very much concerned with his or her progress.

□ Opportunities in the merchandising division

Department stores and large specialty stores are usually organized into several main divisions, such as merchandising, operations, publicity, accounting or control, and personnel. (Figure 7–3 shows the relationships of these divisions in typical department stores.) The merchandising division buys the goods that the store handles, and in most firms, is also

FIGURE 3–1 *(continued)*
B. *Famous-Barr*

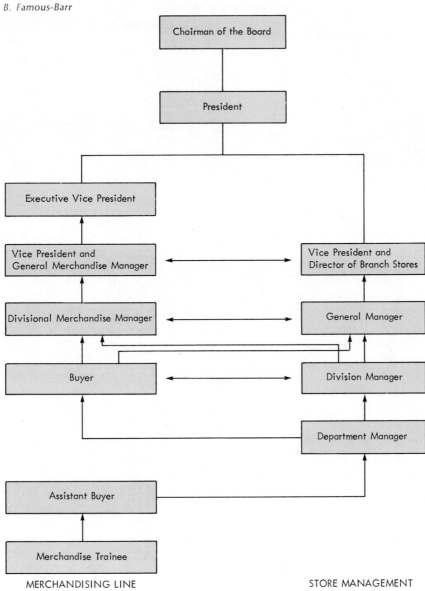

MERCHANDISING LINE   STORE MANAGEMENT

responsible for selling those goods. Even when sales responsibility is located in another division of the company, department store merchandising trainees usually obtain considerable experience as sales supervisors and sales managers. The buying and selling functions are the heart of the retail business and provide the majority of executive job opportunities.

Promotion from department store selling positions is usually fairly slow for people who have not been hired as trainees. The normal promotional path, if advancement comes, is from salesperson to head of stock, then to assistant buyer (often now called assistant department manager), to buyer (department manager), and finally to merchandise manager.

Figure 3–1 shows typical promotional paths for merchandising executives in two large department stores: Dayton's, Minneapolis-St. Paul; and Famous-Barr Co., St. Louis. You should notice two things in comparing these charts. (1) Position titles vary from store to store. Famous-Barr calls the executives who are responsible for the selling function, "department managers" and "division managers," while Dayton's calls them "sales managers" and "group managers." Dayton's uses the term "department manager" for the job that Famous-Barr calls "buyer." (2) Regardless of the titles, the two functions are closely interrelated and trainees normally move back and forth between them.

The head-of-stock usually supervises the merchandise in one of the department's sections, keeping it clean and orderly, notifying the buyer of needed items, and instructing and helping new salespeople. Another function may be to assist in departmental administrative work, such as helping prepare advertising copy (in the smaller stores); planning merchandise displays; and handling some departmental records. The head-of-stock sometimes prepares reorders for basic items, subject to the buyer's approval and normally earns $10 to $30 a week more than salespeople in the department. Executive trainees also often spend a period performing similar duties.

The assistant buyer's activities may vary from head-of-stock's work up to some of the buyer's functions, depending upon the particular buyer, the assistant's experience, the size of the department, and whether or not the buyer is in town. Salaries (depending upon store, individual, and department) range from $100 to $200 per week or more.

Traditionally, the buyer has been responsible for a department just as if it were her or his own small store. The buyer selects and purchases merchandise; supervises stock and record keeping; plans advertising and displays in cooperation with appropriate departments; and supervises actual sales to customers. The growth of branch stores has created new positions for departmental sales managers, and in some stores the buyers no longer supervise sales. A mature, capable, young trainee requires at least two or three years experience, usually longer, to qualify for and obtain a buying position. Earnings depend upon departmental sales volume and profit, but run between $10,000 and $35,000 a year. U.S. department and specialty stores employ about 120,000 buyers and merchandise managers, approximately 40 percent of whom are women.[41]

A small store may have only one merchandise manager, and the proprietor may assume that position. In larger stores, a number of divisional merchandise managers, each supervising possibly 5 to 20 buyers, report to the senior or general merchandise manager. The merchandise manager provides leadership for the buyers, helps them develop merchandise plans and programs, and exercises general financial and merchandising control over the assigned departments. Income, which varies with volume and often includes a bonus or profit-sharing arrangement, depends to a very great extent upon ability to achieve satisfactory results. But merchandise managers usually receive $20,000 to $50,000 or even more.

☐ Opportunities in the publicity division

Advertising positions call for writing and planning ability, imagination and originality, and an understanding of human nature. Some actual sales experience, to provide first-hand knowledge of customer reactions to merchandise and sales appeals, is also often required. Applicants with some advertising experience may begin as copywriters, or as window trimmers and display people, and will earn from $100 to $200 per week.

The successful advertising employee may advance to sales promotion director at $12,000 to $30,000 per year or more. There are very close ties between advertising and merchandising, and some firms also promote good copywriters to buying positions, especially in fashion departments.

☐ Opportunities in the service or operating division

The operating division's responsibilities involve merchandise receiving, warehousing, marking, and delivery; building and equipment maintenance; store security; supply procurement; and a wide variety of customer services that may include store restaurants and workrooms for custom-made merchandise. Executives in this division may supervise highly-advanced systems research, procurement, or traffic specialists; skilled workers such as plumbers, carpenters, and electricians; or large numbers of relatively unskilled workers. The operating division, however, ordinarily offers somewhat lower salaries and fewer promotional opportunities than does merchandising. Even the store superintendent or operating manager, who must have considerable ability and experience, usually earns between $30,000 and $40,000, which is less than what the successful merchandise manager will receive. An operations executive who is responsible for numerous branch stores as well as a downtown headquarters may receive considerably more as we have already noted. The promotional path for operating executives at Dayton's is shown in Figure 3–2.

FIGURE 3–2 **Promotional path for operating executives, Dayton's—Minneapolis-St. Paul**

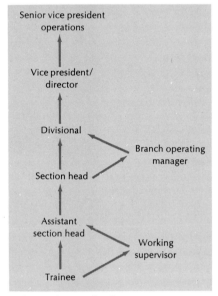

Source: Company brochure.

□ Opportunities in the accounting and control division

The controller heads the accounting and control division, and is responsible for administering the store's finances, credits, collections, and accounting records. Numerous federal and state recordkeeping requirements and new developments in electronic data processing systems have substantially increased the opportunities in this division. Advancement requires a thorough knowledge of accounting or systems, accuracy and precision in handling figures, and the ability to analyze and interpret those figures in the light of broad store policy. An accounting or control executive needs an orderly mind that can create systems for recording voluminous data and that can summarize those data for easy interpretation by other executives.

The current tendency, particularly in the larger firms, is to pay the principal financial and control officers amounts that compare satisfactorily with what merchandising executives receive. Accounting majors receive about $200 per week; head cashiers and other supervisors probably about $12,000 to $20,000. Credit managers, office managers, and statistical-information managers have higher salaries. In mid-1973, bill collectors who worked for banks, finance companies, and retail stores, received starting salaries of about $100 per week, while collection department managers were often paid $15,000 per year or more.[42] The controller in a small department store may receive $15,000 to $25,000, and the senior financial executive about $5,000 to $10,000 more, but in a very large store that executive may earn $60,000 or more.[43]

☐ Opportunities in the personnel division

The increasing opportunities in department store personnel work include training activities, where women have traditionally predominated, and various forms of personnel analysis and research, where more men have been employed. A potential personnel executive may begin as a personnel clerk, as assistant employment manager, or as a staff training worker, although some experience on the selling floor is considered essential before good work can be done in those departments. The chief personnel executive may receive about as much or somewhat more than the controller and slightly less than the operating store superintendent.

■ PROSPECTS IN CHAIN STORES

The great growth of many chain organizations in recent years has created numerous opportunities for career-minded men and women. One chain store company comments that along with store executives, it requires "buyers, merchandising managers, architects, computer programmers, fashion consultants, financial analysts, attorneys, distribution experts, accountants, advertising copywriters, catalog merchandisers, credit managers, and people with many other skills.[44]

The major variety, junior department store, department store and mail-order chains recruit executive trainees from academic institutions in their sales territories. Some important food and drug chains, such as The Kroger Co., Jewel Companies, Walgreen Co., and The Stop and Shop Companies, also have active recruiting programs. But most food and specialty chains do little campus recruiting. Consequently, anyone who wants a career with those firms must usually write to, or visit, the chain's personnel officer. Yet many of these companies offer fine employment opportunities, in part simply because only a limited number of trained people may be competing for promotion. Naturally the opportunities vary from company to company and are greatest in those firms that are engaged in soundly-financed, well-considered, vigorous expansion programs.

□ Opportunities in store management and supervision

The store operating division usually provides the largest number of managerial positions in a chain store organization. The organizational structures of representative chains are shown in Chapter 7. Store management trainees start at about $7,000 to $9,500 per year, depending upon the firm and the trainee's academic preparation. The number of steps in the training program and their duration depend upon company policy, the trainee's ability, and several other factors. These include: (1) the size of the stores used for training (promotion to assistant manager will require more experience and there will be more intermediate levels in large stores than in small ones); (2) the variety of functions performed in the stores (for example, the prospective manager has more to learn and consequently will need more time.in those firms where the stores handle part or all of their own credit activities); and (3) the merchandise lines involved (fashion merchandise may require more experience than staple products). Of course, the intermediate levels can offer quite satisfactory compensation and the financial rewards of store management can be very good in the businesses that operate very large stores.

General merchandise, discount, and variety chains. At one time most of the chains in this category primarily operated variety (5-and-10-cent) stores. Their training programs generally included one to two years of stockroom work and permitted very slow progress toward store managership. Now even though many of these firms operate large general merchandise discount stores, and the store management job has become much more complex, the training programs have become accelerated. Figure 3–3 diagrams the stages of managerial training in the S. S. Kresge Co.'s Kresge variety, Jupiter discount, and K-Mart general merchandise stores. Somewhat similar programs are used in other major discount-variety chains such as Woolworth and G. C. Murphy. The training paths within department store-general merchandise chains of the Sears Roebuck, Montgomery Ward, and J. C. Penney type tend to be somewhat different in detail because of the greater variety of staff positions to be experienced within the individual stores. (Figure 3–4 shows Montgomery Ward's store manager program.) In the discount-variety chains a short general orientation (perhaps four to six months) in sales supporting work, will be followed by assignment to another store as an assistant manager with responsibility for merchandising and supervising several selling departments. The departmental responsibilities are then

FIGURE 3-3 Career paths through Kresge management training program

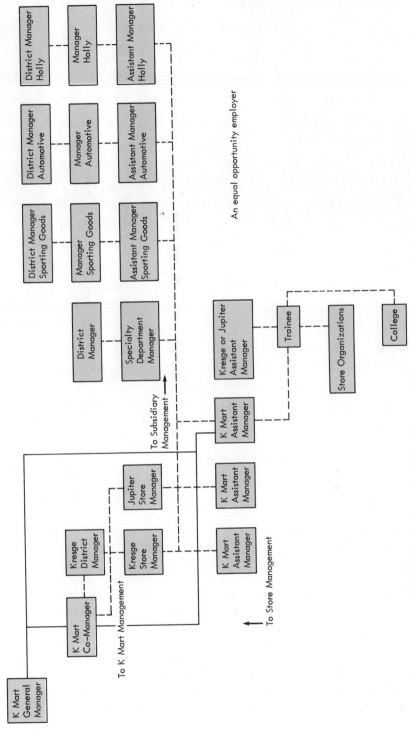

Source: S. S. Kresge Company. Holly is the K-Mart fashion merchandising division.

FIGURE 3–4 **Careers in retail store management, Montgomery Ward and Company**

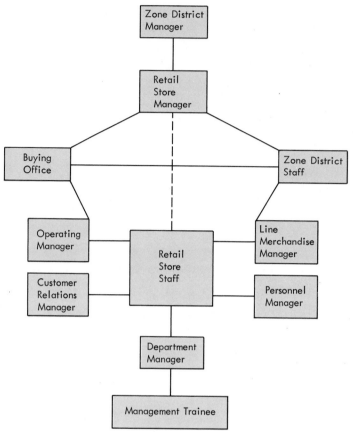

Source: Montgomery Ward and Company.

changed according to schedule, and the trainee will also usually be transferred to two or three different stores to build experience with all lines of merchandise and with a variety of personnel, operating, and market conditions. In some companies, such as Kresge, the trainees also attend a series of seminars at corporate or regional headquarters. Three to six years—depending upon the company and type of stores involved, the trainee's own rate of development, and economic conditions—will lead to appointment as a store manager, usually with assignment to a small store for a start. The store manager's compensation includes incentive payments that may be based upon store sales, expense control, or profits. Earnings range from about a $12,000 minimum in very small stores up to even $50,000–$70,000, or in a few cases more, in large establishments.

The firms that started more or less directly as discount store chains during the 1950s and 1960s (including many of the pioneers in the business) often promote junior executives much more rapidly, have much less formalized training programs and engage many managers and assistant managers from the outside. Recent help-wanted advertisements for discount store managers have offered earnings ranging from $12,000 to $15,000. One chain provides a four-week orientation program at corporate headquarters, followed by about a 1–1½ year experience as ·soft- and hard-goods department manager in a store. Then three months in a regional training store leads to appointment as assistant store manager, followed by promotion to manager. Managerial compensation is $16,000 to $22,000 plus bonus.[45] Some of the newer chains, however, tend to offer less job security than the older organizations[46]

Supermarket and drug chains   Supermarket chains have shortened the training period and now appoint many 25- to 30-year-old individuals as store managers. The average food store manager (stores of all sizes combined) earns about $13,000 to $14,000, but managers of large stores may make two or even, in some cases, three times as much.[47] Chain drug store managers (of whom only about two thirds are registered pharmacists) mainly earn between $12,000 and $17,000.[48]

☐ Area supervisors and central management positions

Some chains employ functional supervisors who oversee a particular activity in a group of stores. Some variety chains, for example, have district or regional fountain and lunch-counter supervisors who coordinate lunch-counter operations in their areas, check on the maintenance of the physical facilities, and help train new food-service managers for the stores. Many supermarket chains have traveling meat and·produce supervisors to advise store managers on the special problems of handling their particular types of merchandise. Compensation in this position varies greatly with the amount of responsibility, the requirements for technical knowledge and managerial judgment, and the total sales volume involved.

The district manager is directly responsible for several stores. This executive performs general supervisory tasks, acts as a link between the store managers and headquarters, sees that the stores conform to company policy and practices, and usually pays close attention to the management development program in the district. The district manager recommends trainees for transfer and promotion. Satisfactory experience as a store manager is a prerequisite for this position, although the managers of the largest and most profitable stores may earn almost as much as, or even more than, their district managers.

Large chains divide their district managers into regional groups, each reporting to a regional or area manager. Regional management carries great responsibility, and hence a large financial reward. Regional managers will earn at least $25,000 per year, but many will receive substantially more, in part through incentive compensation.

Headquarters' positions Buyers for discount chains earned about $15,000 to $28,000 in the mid-1970s and divisional merchandise managers averaged $20,000 to $40,000.[49] Drug chain senior buyers and purchasing managers (similar to merchandise managers in other types of retailing) received roughly comparable salaries. Other drug-chain executives whose salaries averaged about $20,000–$25,000 included advertising, accounting, warehouse, security, store planning and construction, food operations, personnel, data processing, and real estate managers or directors.[50]

Most chains have traditionally used successful store managers to fill the majority of their headquarter and top executive positions. Technical specialists, such as architects and attorneys, were once the only exception to this rule, and most chains still prefer store experience as a background for headquarter's responsibility. But an increasing number of very large organizations that need a variety of talents, including Sears, Roebuck, J. C. Penney, and Montgomery Ward, are now recruiting trainees for direct assignment to central buying, advertising, traffic, and systems analysis staffs at headquarters.

■ "PROS" AND "CONS" OF RETAILING CAREERS

In spite of the career opportunities that retailing offers, many students have a negative view of the field.[51] In some cases this view rests upon a careful self-appraisal which indicates that the individual's talents and interests fit some other business or profession more satisfactorily. In other cases, the negative impression may result from some unexciting employment as a routine part-time retail worker while in school, or from partial or erroneous information about retailing careers.

Some of the merits and limitations of careers in this broad and varied field are summarized below. In the final analysis, only the student can decide whether or not retailing should be one's field of endeavor. But this decision should be based upon a careful evaluation of all relevant facts, personal preferences and experiences, and the knowledge that the rewards for high-quality work and accomplishment in retailing—as in other trades and professions—go far beyond monetary income.

Disadvantages of retailing careers The following are some of the negative aspects of retailing as a career field:

1. Beginning salaries are frequently lower in retailing and have increased less in the past two decades than in other areas of employment. Fortunately, progressive retailers have recognized this fact and raised starting salaries.
2. While retail executive working hours are probably no greater than in other business and professional fields, they may include some Saturday, Sunday, or evening work.
3. Initial assignments, including selling duties, in stores that have poorly organized training programs may discourage the trainee.
4. Some retailing positions, but not all, involve more competitive pressure, physical strain, and nervous tension than is true of a number of other occupations.
5. Chain store personnel are sometimes required to relocate rather frequently, which is disagreeable to the person who wants "to get roots established" in a community as soon as possible.
6. Some students feel "lost" and far removed from headquarters in the widespread branches of a chain system.
7. Some people assert that retailing lacks social prestige as compared with banking and finance, for example; that it does not offer a sufficient "intellectual challenge" for those with "creative talents"; and that it gives but a limited opportunity to serve others.

Advantages of retailing careers   The disadvantages cited above do not apply to all retailing positions, however, and in many cases may be offset by some of the following advantages:

1. There is a wide range of opportunities in all parts of the country for men and women of various talents and interests.
2. The size and variety of retailing institutions provides an increasing number of executive positions for qualified people.
3. Men and women of demonstrated ability can advance to positions of responsibility with commensurate salaries more rapidly than in most other fields of employment.
4. Knowledge and experience gained in one firm may be easily transferred to another or used in creating an independent store.
5. The many personal contacts, and in some positions opportunities for extensive travel, are stimulating and enjoyable, and broaden perspectives.
6. Reasonable security results from the relatively great stability of retail sales volume from year to year. Inefficiency, however, is just as unacceptable in retailing as in any other field.
7. Progressive retail firms encourage their executives and employees to participate in their communities' public and civic organizations. In addition, satisfaction comes from building, or helping build, busi-

nesses that give customers good value and that provide employment for many people.

■ REVIEW AND DISCUSSION QUESTIONS

1 Try to outline the satisfactions you want from your career. What relative value do you assign to starting compensation, lifetime earnings, fringe benefits, job security, rapid promotion, working conditions, relative independence, etc.? How well does retailing seem to match your desires?

2 What fields of retailing (kind of business, such as clothing, hardware, or auto-supply store, and type of store, independent or chain) and what types of retailing work (merchandising, store operations, promotion, etc.) seem most suited to your interests and abilities? Why?

3 Talk with owners and managers of various retail stores in your community and summarize their opinions regarding the opportunities which retailing affords. What do they consider to be the chief limitations?

4 What are some recent developments in retailing which encourage (discourage) students to seek careers in this field?

5 Evaluate the opportunities for women in retailing? How do they compare with other fields?

6 What factors would you consider, and what information would you seek from what sources, in trying to decide whether to open a store of your own?

7 Assume that you want to own your own store in some particular line of retail business (clothing, hardware, sporting goods, etc.) in your current school or home community. What are the arguments for and against opening a wholly new business rather than trying to buy an established store?

8 Explain briefly: (a) How would you prepare for an interview with a department-store recruiter concerning possible employment with that firm upon graduation? and (b) What questions would you want answered before accepting a position if one were offered?

9 Compare the "promotional ladders" in a traditional department store and a general merchandise chain.

10 Prepare a paper of about 2,000 words on the subject: "A practical program for attracting qualified executive trainees into retailing."

■ NOTES AND REFERENCES

1 U.S. Department of Labor, *Employment and Earnings*, vol. 22 (March 1976), p. 61. Canadian employment statistics are now organized to show the type of work that people do, rather than the type of firm or organization in which they are employed. However the 1971 Census, which did include an industrial analysis, showed 1,045,000 workers employed in retail and food service establishments—the rough equivalent of the American classification, "retail trade." *1971 Census of Canada*, vol. III, part 4, bulletin 3.4–10 (Ottawa: Statistics Canada, 1975). Much more current data on the number of workers employed by "larger firms" (20 or more employees) appears in *Employment, Earnings and*

Hours (Statistics Canada, monthly) but such firms provide only about 60 percent of all employment in the trade sector.

2　U.S. Department of Labor, Bureau of Labor Statistics, *Occupational Outlook Handbook,* 1974–75 ed. (Washington, D.C.: U.S. Government Printing Office, 1974), p. 763.

3　*Census of Business 1967, Retail Trade, United States Summary* BC67-RA1 (Washington, D.C.: U.S. Government Printing Office, 1970), pp. 1–6 to 1–9; "Summary Report of the 1972 Census of Retail Trade," *U.S. Department of Commerce News,* March 17, 1975, pp. 2–3.

4　Donald S. Perkins, "The Low-Income Consumer—A Human Problem and a Selling Problem," Executive Lecture Series, University of Notre Dame, March 2, 1970.

5　Richard J. Braun, "The Retailing Specialist," in *Marketing, Business and Office Specialists,* Garland D. Wiggs, ed. (Chicago: J. G. Ferguson Publishing Co., 1970), p. 215.

6　U.S. Department of Labor, *Employment and Earnings,* vol. 22, (March 1976), p. 69. The comparable figure for Canada is about 44 percent.

7　Samuel Feinberg, "From Where I Sit," *Women's Wear Daily,* May 7, 1975, p. 36.

8　Marlene A. Carey, "Goods Well Bought are Quickly Sold," *Occupational Outlook Quarterly,* vol. 18, no. 3 (Fall 1974), p. 5.

9　An interview with a woman who has become personnel manager of the frozen food, meat and produce warehouse and distribution center—a traditional "man's job"—in the Pathmark Supermarkets division of Supermarkets General Corp. is presented in "I Asked for the Job—and Got It," *Chain Store Age* (Supermarket edition), August 1974, pp. 34–35.

10　June 21, 1976, p. 66.

11　For descriptions of several such programs in the supermarket field, see "Super People Go to College," *Chain Store Age* (Supermarket edition), March 1973, pp. 40–45 and "Alpha Beta Combines School Theory with Store Practice," *Chain Store Age,* February 1974, pp. 47–51.

12　"Retailing Has a Place for College Graduates," *Personnel News and Views,* Fall 1973, pp. 14–15.

13　Shelby Hunt, "Experiential Determinants of Franchisee Success," paper delivered to Southwestern Social Science Association annual meeting, Dallas, March 23, 1973.

14　National Retail Hardware Association, *Management Report Retail Hardware Stores 1974 Financial Operating Results* (Indianapolis, Ind.: The Association, 1975), p. 22.

15　*Retail/Services Labor Report* (Washington: Bureau of National Affairs), no 1357 (August 7, 1975), p. A1; no. 1370 (November 6, 1975), p. A9.

16　"A Study of 1975–76 Beginning Offers," *CPC Salary Survey,* no. 2 (March 1976), p. 5. Detailed breakdowns within the so-called "merchandising group" are not available but retail firms probably provided most of the offers included in the average figure.

17　See J. L. Goldstucker, "Competent Retail Trainees—Where Are They?" *Journal of Marketing,* vol. 27, no. 2 (April 1963), pp. 38–41.

18　Harland Fox, *Top Executive Compensation* (New York: The Conference Board, 1974), p. i.

19　Arthur M. Lewis, "A Cache of Multimillionaires," *Fortune,* September 1973, p. 174.

20　Samuel Feinberg, "Rise of Men in 40's or Younger to Top Retail Command Posts," *Women's Wear Daily,* October 8, 1975, p. 72.

21　"The Case for Retailing," *MBA,* December 1974, p. 40.

22　These benefits are discussed in Chapter 9, "Retail Personnel Management—Continued."

23　"How to Buy or Sell a Business," *Small Business Reporter* (Bank of America), vol. 8, no. 11 (1969) p. 2.

24　Robert Kahn, *Retailing Today,* vol. 10 (January 1975) p. 2.

25　"The Fighting Independent," special section, *Home Furnishings Daily,* March 2, 1973.

26　Paul R. Krone, *Starting and Managing a Retail Flower Shop,* Small Business Administration Starting and

Managing Series (Washington, D.C.: U.S. Government Printing Office, 1970), p. 4.

27 *1974 Annual Business Survey* (Washington, D.C.: Menswear Retailers of America, 1975), p. 20.

28 Louis M. Bernstein, "Does Franchising Create a Secure Outlet for the Small Aspiring Entrepreneur?" *Journal of Retailing*, vol. 44, no. 4 (Winter 1968–69), p. 33. For a more adverse view of franchising, see Robert M. Dias and Stanley I. Burnick, *Franchising: The Investor's Complete Handbook* (New York: Hastings House, 1969).

29 See, "Retailing: Small and Vulnerable," *Newsweek*, April 14, 1975, pp. 74–75.

30 "Business Failures," *Dun's*, September 1970, p. 101. See also "Who's Failing," *Retail Today*, December 1970, p. 3. Approximately 4,800 U.S. retail firms failed in 1975, which suggests a somewhat lower rate than indicated above. See: *Survey of Current Business*, May 1976, p. S-7.

31 *Opportunities for Careers in Hardware Stores and Home Centers* (Indianapolis, Ind.: Russell R. Mueller Retail Hardware Research Foundation), 1973, p. 22.

32 "How to Buy or Sell a Business," *Small Business Reporter* vol. 8, no. 11 (1969), p. 11.

33 *Facts about New Supermarkets Opened in 1973* (Chicago: The Super Market Institute, 1974), p. 12; "Chains Add Record Number of Stores—And Pay the Price," *Chain Store Age* (Drug edition), May 1975, p. 62.

34 Robert W. Johnson, "Trade Credit as a Source of Funds," *The Vital Majority: Small Business in the Amercian Economy*, Deane Carson, ed. (Washington: U.S. Government Printing Office, 1973), pp. 129, 131.

35 For example, Harold Koontz and Robert M. Fulmer, *Practical Introduction to Business* (Homewood, Ill.: Richard D. Irwin, Inc., 1975), Chapters 4 and 5.

36 *U.S. Department of Commerce News*, March 17, 1975, p. 2.

37 Samuel Feinberg, "Retailers Seek Top Grads in Curbed Recruitment,"

Women's Wear Daily, March 12, 1974, p. 13.

38 "A Study of 1975–76 Beginning Offers, Report no. 2," *CPC Salary Survey* (The College Placement Council), March, 1976, pp. 2, 6.

39 *Executive Compensation in Retailing* (New York: National Retail Merchants Association, 1973), pp. 15–27.

40 Harvey Braun and Herbert Sher, *Executive Compensation Study of the Retail Industry* (New York: National Retailers Merchants Association, 1975), p. B-5. This study is summarized, "Retail Executive Compensation," *Stores*, February 1976, pp. 2–3, 33–34.

41 Marlene A. Carey, "Goods Well Bought are Quickly Sold," *Occupational Outlook Quarterly*, vol. 18, no. 3 (Fall 1974) p. 5.

42 Terence Jackson and Steve Ginther "Collection Worker: A Creditable Career," *Occupational Outlook Quarterly*, vol. 18 (Fall 1974), p. 24.

43 *Executive Compensation Survey of the Retail Industry*.

J. C. Penney Co., *Annual Report*, 1967, p. 4.

45 Zayre Company, corporate booklet.

46 See Robert Drew-Bear, *Mass Merchandising: Revolution and Evolution* (New York: Fairchild Publications, 1970) pp. 412–13.

47 See "Food Store Manager," in *The Encyclopedia of Careers and Vocational Guidance*, rev. ed., William E. Hopke, ed. (Garden City, N.Y.: Doubleday & Co., Inc., 1972), p. 290. Figures quoted above adjusted for post-1972 changes.

48 *Management of Managerial Resources* (Washington, D.C.: National Association of Chain Drug Stores, 1967), p. 26; figures adjusted.

49 Positions advertised in *Discount Store News*, June through December 1975.

50 *1975 Middle Management Salary Survey* (Arlington, Va.: National Association of Chain Drug Stores, 1975).

51 "Retailers Have Difficulties Recruiting College Students," *Women's Wear Daily*, June 2, 1969, p. 14. These difficulties still persist.

The retail store

STORE LOCATION

A store's location strongly influences its profits and long-run success. Some retailers, such as those selling general merchandise and women's apparel, consider location so important that they prefer to pay larger-than-usual rents to obtain desirable sites, even if this means other expenses must be restricted. Good locations frequently offset deficiencies in management, but poor locations seriously handicap even the most skillful merchandisers. This chapter will consider (1) the importance of the location problem and its neglect by some retailers; (2) basic factors in selecting (a) a community in which to locate and (b) a specific site within that community; (3) the growth of retail markets resulting in the creation of megalopolises; (4) the retail structure of metropolitan areas; and (5) probable future trends in retail location.

■ LOCATION: A PERSISTENT PROBLEM

Most discussions of retail location concentrate on the selection of sites for new stores, but the problem is even broader. Population shifts, the emergence and departure of competitors, the improvement or deterioration of buildings, and the growth of new competitive shopping centers constantly change the value of any particular site. Consequently, existing store locations must be reevaluated frequently to determine if they are still satisfactory and likely to remain so in the foreseeable future. Furthermore, from time to time, a retailer should study the flow of customers to his or her store (using much the same techniques as in a location study for a new store) to determine whether or not it is drawing properly from all of its "natural" trading areas. If, for example, an examination of sales records or a customer survey shows a failure to attract customers from a nearby neighborhood, further investigation is warranted to determine whether local people dislike the merchandise assortment, or whether they don't receive news about the store in the form of handbills and other local advertising. Retailers, therefore, are always faced with a location problem.

□ General neglect of the location problem

Despite its significance, many retailers still decide upon a location without proper analysis. Some shopping-center developers and large-scale retailers however conduct careful studies of locations before final decisions are made. For example, one development firm will not approve a site for a proposed shopping center until it is subjected to a searching analysis, covering such factors as current population in the trading area, population trends, current and potential per-capita income of the area, competing centers or retailers, shopping loyalty of potential customers, road patterns, and expected sales by major classes of merchandise. Many leading chains conduct similar investigations before they authorize a contract for a new store.

But thousands of small stores are opened each year, with little or no analysis, in sites that simply happen to be available. This situation exists because many retailers fail to appreciate the significance of location. Moreover, most prospective retailers have the confident expectation of doing better in a particular location than their predecessors and hence fail to study the past history of a site.[1] They also consider research to be too costly. Still others are eager to start "tending the store" and do not want to take the time needed for a worthwhile site-selection investigation.

Even some retailers who recognize the importance of location research and are willing to spend money and time on it consider it too complex a problem for them to approach entirely on a scientific basis. They also point out that even the most complex location research techniques are still imprecise and subject to error. Furthermore, while these retailers may gather and analyze statistical data on a site, they believe the validity of the decision rests with the person making the final judgment—and that this judgment cannot be replaced with a computer.

The foregoing factors *explain* why some retailers neglect the location problem; but they do not *justify* this neglect. Even the criticism that research cannot "produce all the answers" is beside the point, since no one claims that it does. As two knowledgeable writers point out, the firms that use market research do not expect 100 percent accuracy, but that with the help of research, "serious mistakes will be avoided and the probability of success will be improved."[2] In brief, location plays such an important part in determining sales and profits that the retailer should assemble and evaluate as much information as possible before deciding where to place the store. And these tasks become more difficult as choice locations become scarce for individual stores and shopping centers alike.

■ BASIC FACTORS IN LOCATION

Factors governing the choice of a location for a retail store may be divided logically into two groups: (1) those that influence the choice of a city or trading area and (2) those that determine the particular site within the chosen city or trading area. They will be discussed here in terms of site selection for a new store, but they also apply to appraisal of existing store locations, and in many respects, to the location of new shopping centers and to the selection of sites within such centers. Both groups of factors are closely related. Moreover, the number of factors mentioned should not obscure the fact that potential sales and profits are the most important criteria for store location. Few, if any, available locations will score perfectly on every factor; and if any place comes close to being the "ideal spot" for a store, it is likely to involve a high rental or purchase price. The merchant who is evaluating a location must weigh the good aspects against the less desirable ones and try to find the best balance.

□ Selecting a city or trading area

The small retailer is at a serious competitive disadvantage when it comes to choosing a city in which to locate. This decision is often based on considerations of health, climate, or nearness of relatives and friends. Unlike the chain store and the shopping-center developer, the small entrepreneur has neither the financial resources nor the personnel to conduct a systematic review of cities, suburban areas, or even shopping centers. However, the chances of success will be improved by assembling and evaluating all pertinent information concerning the community under consideration. One should use any data or aid available from prospective suppliers, from bankers, and from the Chamber of Commerce in the area under consideration.[3]

Type and character of industries   The number, type, and character of the industries within a trading area influence (1) the amount and the stability of potential customer income and (2) the kind of goods customers will want. The alert retailer will attempt to locate, as far as possible, within an area where income is regular, assured, and substantial in amount. Generally speaking, income is more stable and assured in cities with diversified industries than in areas where one single industry dominates the picture. The single-industry town may be affected by peculiar seasonal business variations (for example, slow retail business when factories in that industry close for an annual model change) and it will be vulnerable to changes in the market for its industry's product.

Labor-management relationships may affect the stability of income from local industries. A poor relationship may mean constant labor strife and periodic strikes. Such strikes can have significant effects on retail sales: for the cash store, they may result in violent fluctuations in volume; for the credit store, they may encourage an overextension of credit.

The retailer will also be interested in the growth of local industries. An area with expanding and progressive industries has advantages over one where maximum development has already been attained. Towns and cities from which industries are moving have serious limitations as retail locations.

Population of the trading area The population of the city and the surrounding trading area determines the number of potential customers of the retail store.* But knowledge of those currently living in the area is not sufficient; equally important is information on the rate of growth (or decline).[4]

The pattern of growth varies widely between cities, and between regions. Some have an almost stationary population; but this alone does not necessarily mean that they are undesirable as areas in which to locate stores. However, the reasons for lack of growth and the impact of this factor on the retailers of the area should be carefully investigated.

Attention should also be given to seasonal shifts in population. Many trading areas gain people during the summer or winter vacation months and lose them the rest of the year. Thus resort areas in such states as Florida, California, Arizona, Maine, Vermont, Michigan, and Colorado have a large influx of temporary residents who substantially increase the potential customers for several months each year.

---

* Economic geographers have developed many general theories and models to predict or explain the relative drawing power of competing communities. Some of these models, which resemble the laws of gravity in physics, regard the size of a center (in terms of population or in square feet of retail floor space) as the attracting force and distance from the customers as a very powerful friction or resistance to trade. However, these general models are the subjects of considerable debate and are not very precise guides to specific locations since the individual situations can vary so greatly from the average. For a thorough review of gravity models and other theories, see Peter Scott, *Geography and Retailing* (Chicago: Aldine Publishing Co., 1969). Sophisticated models for measuring the drawing power of a community in terms of population and travel time are reviewed and recommended in R. W. McCabe, *Planning Applications of Retail Models* (Toronto: Ontario Ministry of Treasury, Economics and Intergovernmental Affairs, 1974).

Progressiveness of the city   The progressiveness of a community is closely intertwined with the type and character of its industries, its population trend, and other factors discussed in the following paragraphs. Some signs of progressiveness include: an active Chamber of Commerce or industrial development group that will attract new industries; an ongoing urban-renewal program; a good local school system that draws families to the community; efforts to attract conventions that bring additional customers into the area; well-developed sport, cultural, and recreational programs that enhance life for the residents and also serve as a magnet for visitors; local service club programs for community betterment; merchant sponsorship of periodic events—dollar days, festivals and fairs—to expand the trading area; well-designed traffic, parking, and public transportation facilities and systems. All of these factors and others must be given careful consideration in forecasting the city's future.

Buying habits of potential customers   The selection of an area in which to locate is also influenced by the buying habits or practices of the populace. Although we are steadily becoming more homogenous, people in some regions and communities are willing to drive greater distances to shop than may be the case in other communities. There are also variations in preference for downtown versus suburban shopping; in desire for clerk-service versus self-service; in interest in fashion changes; in attitudes toward buying on credit; and in demands for different types of foods and food stores. Variations in climate (whether bad weather may make travel difficult or uncomfortable at times) age distribution (college town versus retirement community), occupation and ethnic background may affect not only the merchandise people buy but where and how they shop for it. The more familiar the prospective store owner is with the customary buying habits, preferences, and prejudices of the people in the area, the greater the assurance that a location will prove satisfactory.

Purchasing power of the population   Total retail sales in an area are closely correlated with the purchasing ability of the nearby population.[5] The number of people employed, the total payrolls of the industries located in the district and the average wage, the regularity and frequency of payment of wages and salaries, social security payments to the elderly, and the amount of, and trend in, bank deposits are among the significant sources and indicators of consumer purchasing power.[6] As a matter of fact, skilled retailers can frequently use these factors as the basis for a reasonably accurate estimate of the community's potential expenditures.

Dispersion of wealth   The dispersion of wealth is another factor influencing sales and profit opportunities. A retailer who proposes to open a store dealing in gourmet groceries, high-priced dresses, or custom-made men's clothes should not seek an area populated largely by persons with low incomes. In this connection, it is important to note that the rise in earnings during the 1950s and 1960s, widely distributed among the population, brought about considerable "trading up," with people buying better quality merchandise and patronizing higher-class stores.

Some specific evidence of the relationship between (1) family income, and (2) the sales and profits of the retailer is given in Table 4–1. This table classifies the sales and profits achieved by each unit of a chain organization according to the annual income of the families which it serves. Note that the units in areas having the highest annual incomes had over three times the sales and nearly twice the profits of the units in the lowest annual-income areas.

TABLE 4–1

Sales and profits of stores in a chain classified by annual income of families served

Annual income of families served	Index of store	
	Sales	Profits
Under $3,000	100	100
$3,000–$4,999	160	112
$5,000–7,999	240	125
$8,000 and over	320	188

Source: William Applebaum, "Store Performance in Relation to Location and other Characteristics," *Chain Store Age* (Executives Edition), November 1965, p. E15.

A prospective store owner can use some of the following information to determine the dispersion of income in a trading area: the types or kinds of homes, the proportion of home owners, the educational levels of the community, the number of telephones, the number and makes of automobiles, per-capita retail sales, and the number of credit accounts. Very useful, even if slightly out-of-date, tabulations of income tax returns classified by income size, for U.S. Standard Metropolitan Statistical Areas appear in *Statistics of Income–Individual Returns* (Washington: U.S. Government Printing Office, annually).

Nature and strength of competition   The number, type, floor space, and location of competing retail stores must also be examined in the light of the community's need for stores of the type under consideration. Is the area already over-supplied with stores of that type? Will the new store meet market needs more effectively than the existing units? Competing stores must be analyzed carefully to determine the services they offer, the extent to which they are alert to the present and prospective demands of consumers, and their merchandising methods in general.

In this process the retailer should recognize the trend toward "scrambled merchandising." Today much of the competition for an electric appliance store may come from auto-supply stores, discount houses, or hardware stores, while drugstores are feeling the effects of the nonfood lines of supermarkets. And women's-wear shops face competition from variety store, mail-order and discount firms. In other words, the study of competitors must be made on a realistic basis and not just on the basis of the name given to a particular kind of retail establishment.

State and local legislation   Local and state property, income, sales, excise and business taxes, and licensure requirements—including the trend in tax rates—often influence the decision on location. Variations in sales tax rates among nearby cities and across state lines can be particularly troublesome. State credit sale laws and limits on credit charges must also be taken into account. And local or state regulations concerning hours of business are significant in view of the increasing night and Sunday openings for many stores.

Other factors influencing choice of a city   Several other factors influence the choice of a city or trading area. Practically all retailers need bank loans at some time or other to finance expansion plans, seasonal inventories, or larger-than-usual credit accounts. Hence, merchants benefit from the presence of bankers who have some understanding of the retailer's financial problems. Likewise, the attractiveness of a community is increased if suitable advertising media are available; if police and fire protection are satisfactory; if trade-union regulations are not so restrictive that profitable operation is difficult; if adequate merchandise resources are conveniently located; and if the area is served by satisfactory highways and public transportation facilities.

☐ Selecting a specific site

The selection of a particular location within the chosen city or trading area is determined by the following major considerations.

Estimated volume of business   One of the first steps in the appraisal of a possible store site is an estimate of potential sales volume, since volume is vital in determining profitability. Several methods, ranging from rough guesses to detailed studies, may be used to prepare such estimates. Prospective owners of independent stores often simply try to judge whether competitive stores are doing well, and then try to decide whether a new entrant can match those competitors. The would-be merchant may also ask wholesalers' and manufacturers' representatives who know the area for their best judgment.

1. Method of analogies Careful retailers, however, will use more rigorous methods. Chain store companies that have considerable experience often prepare sales estimates by comparing the planned store with "analogs," that is, with other company units of comparable size and situation in cities of about the same population, employment characteristics, and competitive interaction. Of course, considerable judgment is needed to insure that the proposed and comparative stores are really similar, and to adjust for any apparent differences.

2. Competitive comparisons Such "inside-the-company" forecasts are usually supplemented by estimates of sales for competitors near the site under consideration. Retailers watch the number of customers entering a competitive store at various times of the day, the number of salespeople employed, and the number of checkout registers in use to obtain an estimate of the store's sales volume.

3. Number of potential customers within reach The most basic method, however, involves finding out how many people live within a reasonable distance of the proposed site and how much spending power they have. The question of what is a reasonable distance depends upon the kind of merchandise involved, since most customers will normally drive three miles or less (usually considerably less) for groceries but will go greater distances for clothing;* upon the degree of population and highway congestion, since people will go greater distances to shop in sparsely settled areas; and upon the presence of alternative or intercepting retail facilities that will draw customers away from the proposed locations. Concentric circles may be drawn upon a map and then the number of consumers living at various distances can be counted.[7] Potential sales estimates derived from measuring the trading area must be adjusted upward if substantial business can be expected from tourists or business visitors, and reduced if area residents tend to go elsewhere to shop.

4. Long-run considerations Long-run factors must receive serious consideration when estimating potential sales. The history and the probable future of the district should be studied and the probable effects of any shifts or movements in the business sections should be weighed carefully. No business site stands still in value. The main shopping block in a city today may be several blocks removed from the one of three decades ago. And an undeveloped and outlying piece of land today may be a flourishing shopping center five years from now.

---

* One major study of 6,000 women in five cities found that 44 percent traveled five miles or more to shop for apparel and general merchandise. Distance traveled increased with consumer income, being highest among families with over $15,000 income, but decreased with age. "Shoppers on the Move: Behavior Proves Consistent," *Stores,* March 1975, p. 6. Some earlier studies, not completely comparable, have suggested somewhat greater reluctance to travel more than 15 minutes to purchase even shopping goods. See: J. A. Brunner and J. Mason, "The Influence of Driving Time on Shopping Center Preference," *Journal of Marketing,* vol. 32 (April 1968), p. 61.

5. *Accuracy of sales estimates*   The Supermarket Institute has reported in the past that about one-fourth of all new supermarkets fell below management's first-year sales estimate by 10 percent or more.[8] One marketing consultant says that only about 60–70 percent of branch store location selections work out satisfactorily.[9] The problem may not be quite as serious as these figures suggest, but vastly improved sales forecasting techniques are needed for store site-selection.

TABLE 4–2

Actual sales versus estimated sales

Year	Percentage of supermarkets		
	With sales more than 10 percent above preopening estimate	*With sales as estimated*	*With sales more than 10 percent below preopening estimate*
1966 30	45	25
1967 40	38	22
1968 29	43	28
1969 34	37	29
1970 30	34	36
1973 42	31	27

Source: *Facts about New Super Markets Opened in 1970. Facts about New Supermarkets Opened in 1973* (Chicago: Super Market Institute 1971, 1973), pp. 7, 19.

Customer buying habits in relation to types of goods sold   We have noted that customer buying habits influence the choice of a city or town. They are equally important in the selection of a site. A store handling staple groceries, for example, ordinarily will be located (1) close to the homes of the customers it hopes to serve or (2) in shopping centers or areas where parking facilities are available and which can easily be patronized when the customer is also buying other merchandise. A department store, on the other hand, should be situated close to other stores of the same type since those stores thrive best in groups. Consequently, shopping center developers usually try to bring two, three, or more department stores into a planned large-scale center. When customers are attracted on bases other than convenience and opportunity for shopping, the store proprietor has a greater degree of freedom in choosing a location. Accessibility remains important, however, with the result that stores handling goods of this type are commonly located in the chief shopping districts, either on the main thoroughfare or on a better-class side street, or in shopping centers.

Pedestrian traffic   Planned suburban or regional shopping centers received most of their customers by private automobile, and to a much lesser extent, by public transportation. Pedestrian or "walk-in" trade is not important to most such centers (this is one reason why many enclosed mall buildings are designed without exterior window displays), but the pedestrian traffic flow *within* the center is quite important in determining the relative value of different sites within the mall. Moreover, the volume, kind and distribution of pedestrian traffic will significantly affect business in downtown shopping areas and other traditional retail locations.

The number of people passing a site is measured by a traffic count. Depending upon the type of store under consideration, all passers-by may be counted or only all males or all females and/or only people in certain age brackets. A sample number may be interviewed to learn the reasons for being at that location, purchasing power and shopping habits, and the likelihood of becoming customers if the new store does open at that spot.

The significance of a flow of potential customers past a store varies widely from one retailer to another. A high traffic count may be essential for a cash-and-carry variety store which depends mainly upon small purchases from a large number of customers. In contrast, the gourmet food shop that appeals largely to the "carriage trade" through a telephone sale-credit-delivery type of service will be less interested in a high-traffic location.

Location in relation to competitors and other stores   The proximity of the store to chief competitors and to other types of retail establishments requires close study by the prospective retailer. For some types of stores, location in the central shopping district or in a large shopping center is almost essential to success; for others, successful operations may be conducted outside such areas. A retailer of automobiles, for example, may find it highly desirable to locate near competitors on "automobile row." A women's-wear store may also seek a site near other similar shops or near a department store to appeal to customers who desire to shop from one store to another. Other retailers, perhaps those selling drugs and groceries, may seek neighborhood locations which are removed from direct competitors.

Compatibility and incompatibility   Some types of stores work well together, other types can have harmful effects upon each other. For many retailers the reputation and merchandising methods of the others in the immediate area are important considerations. An exclusive dress-shop operator will not seek to locate beside a "cut-rate" drugstore or near a retailer of low-priced women's wear. A children's shop will not rent a building contiguous to a liquor store. Some areas have obtained reputations as locations for "good" merchants, and this fact is significant to the retailer who seeks to acquire a comparable designation.

Accessibility   Despite its obvious significance, accessibility is often neglected by retailers eager to find a site and "get in business." The employees' needs often receive inadequate attention. Detailed investigation should be made of the following factors, among others, affecting accessibility. Some location executives recommend examining a proposed site from a helicopter to judge some of these factors such as traffic flows and population concentrations:[10]

1. Distance of the proposed store from customers' and employees' homes.
2. Availability of public transportation, such as streetcars, buses, and subways.
3. Amount of traffic congestion prevailing in the district and the variations in this congestion during hours of the day and days of the week.
4. Parking facilities available within convenient walking distance of the proposed store and the charges therefor.
5. Side of the street upon which the site is located (in many towns and cities, one side is more popular than the other).
6. Width of the street, so that potential customers are not discouraged from visiting the store because of being jostled or by having to push through crowds. Streets with marked inclines and dead ends are also less desirable.
7. The part of the block in which the site is located, i.e., whether it is a corner location or an "inside" location and, in the case of a large store, whether entrances may be made available on two, three, or four streets.

It should be emphasized that some retailers may successfully overcome part of the inaccessibility of a particular location by means of a low-price appeal. This possibility is well-illustrated by stores which make use of basement or second-floor locations. Similarly, other retailers attempting to "build up" locations frequently sell at low prices for a time.

Site characteristics detrimental to retail outlets   Site characteristics which decrease the retailer's ability to attract customers include the following: (1) smoke, dust, disagreeable odors, and noise; (2) proximity to garages, hospitals, taverns, and similar places; (3) poor sidewalks; and (4) old and worn-out neighboring structures.

Some other factors affecting choice of site   In the case of the chain organization, or the parent store considering the establishment of a branch, certain operating factors should be carefully considered in selecting a specific site: The distance of the proposed unit from headquarters, the parent store, or from a warehouse, to permit effective supervision and servicing; the incremental advertising expense required; and the availability of qualified personnel at the firm's existing pay rates are of major concern.

"Metro" concept   Some chain-store companies believe in a "metro (or metropolitan) concept," that is the desirability of having a number

of stores in a metropolitan area to make a definite impression on the community and to support a large-scale advertising campaign in local media. Some of these chains will not build a new store in a city where they are not currently operating unless they can plan to build several stores in that city.[11]

Return on capital investment Of major concern is the retailer's return on capital invested in a specific site. The investment is determined by the cost of the equipment and fixtures to be used, the size and turnover of the merchandise inventory, and the rent to be paid, or the cost of the site and building, as discussed below, under "Leasing (or purchasing) arrangements." The return or earnings are determined by the potential sales volume and margin minus operating expenses. Although the retailer may be willing to accept a small return in the short run, over a longer period a reasonable return on the overall investment is necessary.

□ Leasing (or purchasing) arrangements

A retailer must consider the *costs* associated with any particular site, as well as the anticipated *revenues* indicated by a market study. In some instances the merchant may purchase land on which to erect a store building, or the property may come equipped with a more or less suitable structure. In such cases, the major costs to be considered are the purchase price, the costs of constructing or remodeling the building, the interest charges and amortization rate (rate of paying-off) for the mortgage(s), the extra fire, flood, and storm-damage insurance required to cover the property, anticipated maintenance costs, and current and anticipated real estate taxes and assessments.

Many retailers, particularly those in planned shopping centers, lease —rather than own—their stores. The rental may be a fixed-dollar amount per year, or it may be a specified percentage of the store's annual sales volume, usually with some guaranteed minimum amount. Retailers who had over-committed themselves to expensive fixed-dollar rentals during the economic boom of the 1920s, began to favor percentage leases during the great depression of the 1930s, since such leases provided an automatic adjustment when sales volume declined. In contrast, shopping center developers and some other landlords were the ones who insisted on percentage leases in the expanding economic climate of the 1950s and 1960s.

The rental charges (both the guaranteed minimum and the percentage of sales) in a planned shopping center will vary with the kind of business, as well as inversely with the tenant's bargaining power and ability, and with the landlord's desire to obtain the store's participation in the center. The "anchor stores" that attract customers to a mall pay much less per square foot than the "satellite stores" that profit from the big stores' traffic-building ability. Thus, department stores covered in a 1974 survey of new shopping-center leases guaranteed from $1.50 to $4.00 per square foot (with most stores in the $2.00 to $3.00 range) while women's apparel shops guaranteed $2.25 to $8.35 per square foot (with most stores in the $5.00 to $7.50 range). Percentage rentals also varied with store markup (margin) rates and the other factors indicated above. Supermarkets, which have a low markup rate signed shopping center leases calling for payment of 1 to 1½ percent of sales, while menswear stores agreed to pay about 4.0 to 7.0 percent.[12] A more comprehensive 1974 survey showed that tenants in regional shopping centers who paid high rentals per square foot included key shops (average total payment $26.00 per square foot); watch repair shops ($11.91); hosiery shops ($11.56); costume jewelry stores ($10.04); and camera stores ($9.35). Low rental (per square foot) establishments included department stores ($1.44); bowling alleys ($1.47); discount department stores ($1.53); tire, battery, and accessory outlets ($1.90); and supermarkets ($1.92).[13]

In addition, a shopping center tenant must examine what charges will be imposed for "common area maintenance" (care and lighting of parking lots; and heating, lighting, and maintaining the central mall spaces), for contributions to the merchants' association and any joint promotions, and for possible inflationary increases in the center's own insurance or tax costs. Another question is whether the landlord will deliver an almost completely finished and decorated store, or only a "shell" that needs considerable carpentry, wiring, and painting work. The prospective tenant should also carefully study, and perhaps bargain over, some lease restrictions and requirements affecting store hours, display and promotional practices, merchandise assortments, and pricing practices. But it should be remembered that at least some of these rules will probably benefit all tenants by helping to preserve the center's desired character and atmosphere. Tenants, whether in a planned center or not, are naturally concerned with the length of their leases and the number of renewal options so that they do not invest a great deal of money and effort in building a clientele without being assured of an opportunity to serve that clientele for a considerable period of years. Most retailers will want a 10- to 20-year lease with perhaps one to four five-year renewal options.

Governmental objections to restrictive leases   The U.S. Federal Trade Commission holds that shopping center lease provisions unduly restrain competition if they: (a) give the major tenants ("the anchor stores") the right to veto or approve other tenants; (b) give those tenants the right to approve the amount of space that other tenants may have; or (c) impose limits on the merchandise, price lines, or price advertising that tenants may do. The FTC has obtained several "consent orders" prohibiting the use of such clauses, but permitting tenants and developers to agree on reasonable rules to preserve the center's character and appearance.[14] The U.S. Department of Justice and some Canadian provincial governments have also attacked what they regard as excessively restrictive leases.[15]

■ CHANGING RETAIL MARKETS

Population movements greatly affect the selection of retail locations. As noted in Chapter One, our population has become increasingly urbanized, that is, domiciled in cities and suburbs. At this point we will examine some general aspects of this concentration and then we will look, in some detail, at the types of locations available in the urban areas.

□ Continued viability of small towns

The increasing urbanization of the population has by no means meant the end of small town retailing. Some small communities have suffered from increased metropolitan competition. "Outshopping"— the tendency of consumers to leave their home communities and go elsewhere for shopping goods—is a problem in such towns. But other small cities and villages that have a good collection of friendly, progressive stores with good reputations for fair value, that have good parking facilities and traffic patterns, and that have a pleasant atmosphere, have continued to do well.[16] The market potential of these communities is evidenced by the S. S. Kresge Company's decision to build "mini-markets" in towns of 8,000 to 15,000 population.[17] Similarly, Gamble-Skogmo Inc., a major diversified retailing firm, has announced its intention to "intensify its dominance in 'small-town' retailing."[18] Nevertheless, some of the current small-town growth seems to be in communities just outside metropolitan areas and which will probably some day be part of those areas.

□ Definition of metropolitan areas

During the last 30 to 40 years, however, the metropolian (urban) area has taken on new importance as a social and economic unit. Defined by the census as a "county or group of contiguous counties . . . which contains at least one city of 50,000 inhabitants or more or 'twin cities' with a combined population of at least 50,000," in practice it consists of a declining or slowly growing central city and an exploding suburban area. The U.S. Department of Commerce lists some 254 such areas with about 80 percent of all consumer income.[19] Of these areas, 66 had 500,000 or more people in 1970.[20] And a leading student of these "large conglomerations" refers to them as "the most efficient producing-consuming units that mankind has ever devised."[21]

☐ Suburbanization of retailing

Close observers of retailing trends in recent decades are well aware that the growth of suburbia has been accompanied by a relatively large gain in the retail sales of such areas. Although retail sales in many of the older downtown central shopping districts of our metropolian areas have declined, the total retail sales of these same areas have advanced.[22] It is quite clear that much retailing activity has moved to the suburbs and outer edges of the cities. This trend is due to several factors, including:

1. The pronounced shift of population to the suburbs.
2. Increasing industrial and commercial employment in the suburbs, and the development of suburban social, cultural, spectator sport, and recreational facilities have greatly reduced the suburbanite's dependence upon downtown. Visits to downtown stores were once frequently combined with trips to other downtown facilities; now the total set of needs is often satisfied in the suburbs.[23]
3. Changes in shopping habits during the last 30 years or so. The desire to compare merchandise and prices in more than one store is no longer so great, so that one-stop shopping has become increasingly common. Women are continually broadening their interests outside their homes; and have less time for shopping. Moreover, growing feelings of independence from the dictates of fashion and/or confidence in the fashion information obtained through television, magazines, newspapers and movies has probably made some consumers feel more secure in their fashion judgment. These consumers no longer feel obliged to shop for style information, but instead will go directly to a favorite, conveniently-located store for clothing and similar items.
4. Increased use of the automobile. Rising gasoline prices and shortages may eventually reverse this condition, but all during the 1950s, 1960s, and early 1970s, increased car ownership and use encouraged consumers to go to suburban shopping centers and to patronize roadside clothing, furniture, shoe, and discount outlets. Good roads also helped the suburban facilities attract customers from outlying communities, beyond the Metropolitan Area boundaries, as well as from nearby and in-town locations.[24]
5. The rapid rise in the cost of public transportation to downtown, and alternatively the congestion, cost, and difficulty of finding parking space if one drives there.
6. The excellent retail facilities which have been developed in the suburbs. Since many of our best retail buildings—containing the most

modern equipment and fixtures and stocked with both broad and deep assortments of merchandise—are now found in the newer shopping centers and as free-standing units scattered about metropolitan areas, the customer no longer finds the "pull" of downtown what it was 20 years ago.

☐ Trend toward megalopolis

Today the conglomeration is becoming even larger! As metropolitan areas expand, some of them begin to overlap to produce what we refer to as a "megalopolis": witness the coming-together of the Boston, New York, Philadelphia, Baltimore, and Washington metropolitan areas so that they—in effect—form a single stretch of urban and suburban areas.[25] Similar megalopolises are gradually taking shape elsewhere, especially along the California coast, along Puget Sound in the Northwest, in the lower Lake Michigan area, and in Canada, along the 750 miles from Quebec City to Windsor, Ontario. And there is abundant evidence that "the big retailers are zeroing in on the megalopolis and metropolitan areas."

As indicated, the growth of a megalopolis creates a market for retailers, it also presents problems. Since a megalopolis results from the overlapping of several metropolitan areas, it has no common center or nucleus. Merchants cannot rely on the newspapers or the broadcast stations of a single center to cover the market, and they often must be alert to competition from two or more centers as well as from many intermediate areas.

■ RETAIL STRUCTURE OF THE METROPOLITAN AREA

Although significant differences exist among our metropolitan areas, they also exhibit some general similarities in structure. Each area seems to contain an older central shopping district, one or more older secondary shopping districts as well as the newer shopping centers, several scattered but large free-standing stores, some neighborhood business streets, and many scattered areas with single units or clusters of small stores.[26]

☐ The older central shopping district

The central shopping district has been the heart of the retail structure of the city which, in turn, is an integral part of each metropolitan area. (For a discussion of possible future developments in the central shopping district, see pp. 115–17.) Public transportation lines converge on this district. It contains many of the area's leading shopping and specialty-goods stores—department stores, departmentized specialty stores, and limited-line independent and chain stores that sell apparel, furniture, shoes, and jewelry. These establishments have much more floor space and sales volume than the average store in the city, and draw a far greater part of their total business from nonresidents than do the other city retailers. In addition, there are a number of convenience-goods retailers—drugstores, cigar stores, and food stores. Although the area covered by this district is small, it draws customers from the entire metropolitan area, and its total sales form a substantial but declining part of the total sales of the whole metropolitan area. Some specialty-store firms that cater to a traditional clientele may obtain much more satisfactory results in downtown and small fashion-store cluster locations than in large suburban malls. This has happened to Giddings-Jenny, Inc., a Cincinnati-based quality apparel chain and to other similar merchants.[27]

□ The older secondary shopping districts

The older secondary shopping districts came into existence mainly as the city increased in population and spread over a broader area. Gradually many people began to buy at least part of their requirements outside the central shopping district, and the stores located on a neighborhood business street expanded to meet this demand. Several centers which have developed in this manner may be found in practically every large city, each well-located on a main traffic artery leading from a residential area to the central shopping district. In addition, some of these secondary shopping districts developed within the smaller towns which have gradually been absorbed by the metropolitan area. Regardless of their origin, the kinds of goods sold here are generally similar to those sold in the main shopping district; but the stores are smaller, selection is more limited, people are not attracted from such wide areas, and the sale of convenience goods predominates.

□ Neighborhood business streets

Neighborhood business streets, which are the most numerous types of locations in the metropolitan areas, consist mainly of convenience-goods stores located very close together. Here are the grocery stores, superettes, meat markets, small bakery shops, fruit and vegetable stores, small variety stores, and drugstores, as well as smaller shopping and specialty-goods stores. In the majority of cases, these streets follow the main arteries of traffic throughout both the city and its satellite communities. The stores are relatively small and attract business primarily from the immediate vicinity.

In recent years a development somewhat comparable to the controlled shopping center has taken place in neighborhood business streets. Instead of developing gradually as in the past, in some areas a large building—sometimes known as a "shopping plaza"—has been constructed and its various sections rented out to several retailers. Ample parking space is usually provided.

□ Small clusters and scattered stores

The clusters or scattered individual small stores of the metropolitan area are distinguished from the neighborhood business streets largely by the number of stores. Typically, the stores are complementary; that is, a cluster may be made up of a grocery store, a drugstore, and one or two other noncompetitive stores. Recently, such clusters are being located in a centrally-owned plaza or retail development. Sometimes, however, there may be only a single small grocery or drugstore in the area dealing mainly in convenience-type goods.

Although many neighborhood, small cluster, and scattered stores have been forced to close because of competition from merchants in more developed parts of the metropolitan areas, these locations continue to demonstrate remarkable vitality. In a few cases the stores in these locations have been able to draw trade from a considerable distance by offering unique merchandise, such as imported goods, unusual styles, distinctive handcrafted products, antiques (in some cities an "antique row" has developed in an out-of-the way location), or exotic foods. Some, such as warehouse and factory outlet stores, may charge, or give an impression of charging, unusually low prices. But most of these widely dispersed stores survive by selling convenience goods to customers who cannot or do not want to travel greater distances to search for better selections or greater values. Some neighborhood stores also offer a type of friendliness that appeals to many people and that is seldom found in larger, more impersonal establishments.

The next two facets of metropolitan retailing that we will examine, the growth of planned shopping centers and of large free-standing stores, to a very large extent result from the increased suburbanization of trade.

□ The newer shopping centers

Nature and growth One major response to (and also a factor encouraging) the decentralization of shopping areas is the rapid growth of planned or controlled outlying shopping centers. Usually the entire center is an integrated development, under single ownership, with coordinated and complete shopping facilities, and with adequate parking space. The stores in the center are leased to various retailers. Frequently, all of the stores in the center engage in joint advertising and adopt a unified public relations program. Such joint activities are usually required by or are actually carried out by the central organization which owns the center.

A few of these newer shopping centers were established earlier but the overwhelming majority have been built since the end of World War II. The number of shopping centers in the U.S. and Canada grew spectacularly, from about 1,000 at the end of 1955 to almost 19,000 by 1975.[28]

The department store and the departmentalized specialty store During the late 1920s and the 1930s, as Sears, Roebuck and Company began to develop its chain of department stores, the firm's management correctly interpreted the trend to the suburbs and began to open freestanding units in such areas. At the same time, a few downtown department and departmentalized specialty stores started to serve these areas through freestanding suburban branches or, increasingly, through units in planned shopping centers.

It was not until after World War II, however, that the number of these stores, both chain and branch, became important. Now, practically all traditional downtown department stores have one or more (usually quite a few) suburban branches. Even though the typical branch is smaller, and generates less sales volume than its downtown "parent" store, there are more branches than downtown units, so that—as a group —the branch stores provide the larger share of total company sales.[29]

Benefits and problems of branch stores Through branches, downtown stores follow their customers to the suburbs. Branches attract business because of the downtown store's prestige and also acquaint people with the firm, so that even the parent store acquires new customers. The nonmerchandising departments of the parent store are able to perform additional work, such as accounting and advertising, without a significant increase in total overhead cost. The net result is that the branch store has added substantially to the total profit of the organization.

Branch stores, however, have their problems. Sometimes they cut substantially into the sales of the parent store; some are in such poor locations that they result in losses rather than yielding additional profits. Effective management is still another problem. Some organizations attempt to solve this by assigning the merchandising function, for example, to the parent store with the branch responsible mainly for selling; others allow the branch to select merchandise from parent-store stocks; still others authorize the branch to buy directly in wholesale markets; but, increasingly, chain-store principles of organization are being adopted. (See the discussion of branch store organizational practices, Chapter 7.) Nevertheless, none of these solutions has eliminated all the friction and overlapping of responsibility between branch and parent stores.

Shopping center developers There are two main ways of sponsoring shopping centers. Most centers have been built by real estate organizations, that is, firms which expect to make a profit on their investment by leasing the units of the center to others. Many centers, however, have been developed by large retailers who sometimes dictate the kinds of stores to be located in the center. In some cases, a large chain has organized what is, in effect, a subsidiary corporation to develop centers. Examples are Food Fair Properties, Inc., sponsored by Food Fair Stores, Gamble Development Co. organized by Gamble-Skogmo, Inc., and Sears' Homart Development Co. In other instances the developer is a large department store which operates one of the anchor stores in the center and leases the remaining buildings to others. Centers developed by May Department Stores (through its subsidiary, May Realty & Investment Company) and the Broadway Department Store in southern California, and Allied Stores Corporation in Seattle through its affiliate, Bon Marche, are examples of this type. The Southdale Shopping Center, near Minneapolis, Minnesota, developed by Dayton's provides still another illustration.

Trends and problems The dynamic nature of retailing is well illustrated by shopping center developments. Continuous improvements are being made to attract customers, to make parking and shopping more convenient, and to provide merchandise and services comparable to those "downtown" or in the older central shopping districts. Some of the other major shopping centers trends and problems are as follows:

1. Currently there is a strong trend toward the fully-enclosed-mall, air-conditioned type of shopping center. Although the first of this type dates just from 1956 (Southdale, near Minneapolis), it has become the standard form of regional center. Moreover, many older centers are including these features in their modernization and expansion programs.
2. In contrast to the early large centers which included just one major department store, today's large centers usually have at least two full-line department stores, and some now with three, four, or five such stores of this type are in existence.
3. Along with the development of new centers, successful established centers are also expanding. These expansion programs give their tenants an opportunity to enlarge their stores. During lease negotiations, some retailers now seek a clause which guarantees them an area for later expansion if it proves desirable.
4. Multilevel centers are being built in locations where space is limited, or where land costs are high, or when the amount of floor space involved would require walking uncomfortable distances on a single level. Multilevel parking ramps are also being used in some centers. This type of construction plus the popularity of the air-conditioned, enclosed-mall design has raised building costs enormously in comparison to the simpler, old style centers.

5. There is growing recognition of the fact that more careful planning and research is necessary, both for the center developer and the lessees of the space occupied. Far too many centers have been built without a sufficient number of "lead in" roads; or they have generated more traffic than the nearby road system can handle, with the result that customers have difficulty entering or leaving the center. Additional marketing research data are also needed regarding customer preferences, wants, buying motives, and buying habits.

6. Improved methods are required for forecasting sales volume in new shopping centers. A variety chain found that its methods of predicting sales for new stores in established central shopping districts and smaller communities were inaccurate for shopping center units.

7. Small retailers often need outside advice when faced with the problem of choosing between the growing number of centers in their metropolitan area.

8. Discount houses are evidencing a growing interest in shopping center locations. The attitude of existing tenants is mixed. Some believe that these low-margin operators draw traffic to the center and represent a favorable development. Others either fear the competition afforded by the discount firms or believe that their presence cheapens the center and object to their entry. Government agencies oppose collusive restrictions on the admission of discount stores.

9. As real estate taxes rise, the insertion of tax escalation clauses in shopping center leases is gaining despite opposition by many center tenants.

10. Determining uniform and profitable hours of operation, including Sunday openings, constitutes a problem for operators of shopping centers. It is made more difficult because of disagreement among tenants on the number of nights (and which nights) they wish to remain open. The trend is toward as many as three to six nights per week plus Sunday.

11. General agreement now prevails on a topic that once was widely debated in retail circles—the need for merchants' associations in planned centers. Membership in such an association is now usually required as a condition of leasing space. But debate remains over how much association membership should cost and how much promotional activity should be funneled through, or controlled by, the association instead of the individual stores.

12. Many centers provide a certain amount of periodic entertainment, exhibits, craft shows, antique car displays, and the like, in the common areas to attract customers to the mall.

13. While many centers are providing attractions to draw more people, some center managements are now concerned that they have attracted too many "loungers" and individuals who discourage trade.

FIGURE 4–1 **Fairlane—a planned complex** The Fairlane development in Dearborn, Michigan includes office buildings, a health care center, a luxury hotel, a residential area, and a major regional shopping center planned for six "anchor" stores plus 170 small shops. An automated "people carrier" provides transportation for the half mile from the hotel (shown below) to the shopping center shown on p. 113.

This situation is a delicate one for developers and merchants who want to maintain a reasonably businesslike atmosphere without offending the teen-agers who have turned the center into a "hang out." Some malls have successfully developed teen centers and youth activities; others have had less happy results. General security and crime control problems have also increased.

14. Intensified concern over ecology and the environment has led to more restrictive zoning, and tighter control over the design and general appearance of new centers.[30]

15. "Anchorless malls," or relatively small centers that contain only highly individualized specialty shops and no big general line stores have become popular. Some of the first such malls, for example Ghiradelli Square in an old candy factory in San Francisco, or Larimer Square in a reconstruction of a Denver frontier trading area, or the Spanish style Quadrangle in Dallas have provided architecturally appealing uses of recycled or reproduced buildings. Others have been located in discontinued discount stores. All of these centers are designed for shopping as fun, rather than simply as a means of obtaining needed items, and tend to emphasize arts, crafts, and distinctive merchandise.[31] Some other anchorless or "mini-malls"

FIGURE 4–1 *(continued)*

are really smaller versions of conventional shopping centers, but are built without a general-line store, have a limited number of tenants, feature convenience goods, and are designed to serve smaller trading areas than the major centers.[32]

Future   Shopping center development seems likely to continue, but at a slower rate than was characteristic of the 1950s and 1960s. This growth does not insure the success of each center. As has been indicated in previous paragraphs, great care is necessary in choosing locations, studying competition, designing buildings, providing adequate parking space, selecting tenants, preparing leases, and arranging proper promotion. Many present shopping centers have suffered from a lack of careful economic appraisal prior to their development.

Some criticism has also been directed toward the roles large stores play in shopping center developments. It is sometimes alleged that department and chain stores too often assume the "self-appointed position of prime minister," without giving adequate consideration to the needs and preferences of smaller, independent tenants. Certainly there needs to be closer cooperation among tenants in shopping centers in considering each other's problems. Such cooperation is needed, also, among developers and tenants to insure the "partnership" relationship essential for mutual success. Despite these problems, and others, the continued growth of the shopping center seems assured.

□ Large free-standing stores

Another development of some significance is the large free-standing store. Normally located in the suburban parts of the metropolitan areas, this store is usually: (1) a discount store, (2) a department store, or (3) a departmentalized specialty store. If it is one of the latter two types, it is typically a unit of a chain or a branch of a downtown store.

The free-standing discount house Discount houses are not always welcomed into the newer shopping centers. As a result, some discount retailers have turned to the free-standing store as an alternative to the center or have established centers of their own. States the real estate vice president of S.S. Kresge Company: "[For our K-Marts] we favor free-standing units. . . ."[33] Back of this policy is the belief of many discount retailers that the free-standing store gives them a lower rental, complete freedom of choice on merchandise lines (merchandise restrictions have typically been included in center leases), better parking facilities (usually around a great part of the store building), and a greater flow of traffic for the types and quality of merchandise they offer for sale. By "ringing a city" with units (for example, E.J. Korvette, Inc., has used the "cluster" approach around New York, Chicago, and Baltimore), a substantial promotional program is possible at a relatively low cost per store.

■ PROBABLE FUTURE TRENDS

No one can be certain of the future, and it is always best to be prepared for the unexpected. Nevertheless, some widely-discussed actual and potential tendencies and experiments in retail location could have important implications for retailing in the future and thus warrant our attention.

☐ What will happen to the central shopping district?

Some authorities and merchants expect continued decentralization so that the central shopping district will become an insignificant element in metropolitan retail trade. Other merchants believe that the energy shortage, curtailed use of private automobiles, and disenchantment with suburban life, plus extensive and elaborate downtown rehabilitation, will draw a large portion of total trade back to the city center. These merchants are willing to spend substantial sums in remodeling and rebuilding downtown stores.[34] Perhaps the most reasonable view is that of the president of Larry Smith Associates, well-known retail location consultants, who says that downtown retail sales will improve, but in most cities primarily through increased business with people who work or live in existing or new developments near the city center rather than by serving as a magnet for suburban customers.[35] In addition to remodeling existing downtown stores, erecting new ones, and creating additional parking and transportation facilities, merchants, real estate developers, and municipal authorities are trying several approaches, discussed below, to make downtown more appealing to shoppers.

Pedestrian malls Shoppers can more easily and conveniently move from downtown store to store if those shops are connected by pedestrian areas or plazas that are closed to most or all vehicular traffic for part or all of the day. However, simply closing off the connecting streets to motor traffic will not provide a successful downtown mall. In addition, good parking and public transportation are needed as well as some type of intra-mall transport (such as an inexpensive, slow-moving, amusement-park-type motorized train) if the mall is more than 1,000 feet long. The stores, and especially their façades must be revitalized; the mall needs attractive decoration, benches, signs, and lighting; the stores must use good merchandising and promotional practices; and there should be a constant series of events to maintain a carnival atmosphere.

The most elaborate American mall has its base on Nicollet Avenue, the principal shopping street in Minneapolis, which is closed to all but bus traffic. Enclosed second-floor walkways or bridges connect the buildings for several blocks around Nicollet Avenue so that pedestrians do not have to go out into the weather. Some of the other 25 or so downtown malls built in the United States, such as Kalamazoo, Michigan and Pomona, California have had results ranging from good to very favorable, but generally these malls have stopped downtown sales declines rather than induced sales increases. Downtown malls have also attracted much attention in Canada where suburban growth has not affected sales in the center city as severely as in the United States. A very prosperous underground mall, filled with various types of specialty retailers, connects the principal points in central Montreal and is being copied elsewhere. In Ottawa, sales increased when the luxury Sparks Street shopping area was pedestrianized, but at the same time declined in the nearby Rideau Street main shopping district. Part of a major center being developed in downtown Toronto is shown in Figure 4–2. It is clear that downtown malls will not solve all center-city retail problems, but they can help do so.[36]

Vertical centers and multi-use buildings Where downtown land costs remain very high, as in the most desirable sections of large cities, developers try to maximize the return per-square-foot of land used. High rise construction, involving vertical shopping centers, multi-use ("omni-

FIGURE 4–2 View of Toronto Eaton Center in downtown Toronto   The high-rise structure at the extreme right is a 30-floor office building. It overlooks the eight-floor, 1,000,000-square-foot T. Eaton Company department store. Adjacent to this is a three-level retail store and office mall, with an enclosed central pedestrian gallery parallel to the street shown in the photograph. The mall is surmounted by parking facilities, and when completed, will connect to another office tower and to Simpson's, one of Eaton's major competitors.

Courtesy T. Eaton Company

structure") buildings, or both are advanced as the maximizing solution. Both design features are exhibited in Water Tower Place, which opened in Autumn 1975 on Michigan Avenue, a luxury shopping area adjacent to Chicago's central loop. The 13-level base building, which fills a city block, is surmounted by a 62-story tower. There are four levels of underground parking, a shopping center built around a central court with seven-floor Marshall Field and Lord & Taylor stores serving as anchors for the specialty stores on each level, a 1,200-seat theatre and two floors of office space in the base. The tower includes a 23-floor hotel and 40 floors of luxury apartments. Water Tower Place is adjacent to the 100-story John Hancock Center which also contains a large specialty store (Bonwit Teller) surmounted by office and apartment accommodations.[37] Multi-use buildings with hotel and residential space, restaurants, and theatres, in addition to offices and stores, tend to encourage shopping traffic during hours when offices alone would generate little business.

☐ Other potential developments

New towns   Some city planners, who noted the wave of construction of completely designed "new towns" in Europe after World War II have advocated the creation of similar communities here to relieve population congestion in existing cities. The new towns divide into two types: (1) *satellite cities,* with mainly residential, service, and retail facilities adjacent to existing communities, and (2) *self-supporting* with their own manufacturing and industrial activities to provide employment for their residents. The distinguishing feature of both types is the complete planning and control of transportation, housing and land use, including the location and variety of retail stores. Some satellite communities, such as Columbia, Maryland, have achieved an impressive physical development, but have encountered financial difficulties during slow real estate markets. The few attempts to implement plans for new self-supporting communities have also been generally unsuccessful.[38]

Store-less shopping   About three percent or so of all retail sales are conducted by nonstore merchants, such as direct sales (house-to-house), machine vending, mail-order and telephone selling businesses. Modern technology, including closed-circuit TV and computerized methods for order-handling and billing provide technical capabilities for "in-home" purchasing systems that would enable customers to push buttons on a household console to order merchandise for home delivery. As noted in Chapter 1, some experts believe such systems will soon greatly expand the amount of non-store retailing and thus will change or eliminate many retail location problems. Limited experiments, largely with telephone-based systems, suggest that such home-ordering and delivery arrangements are likely to be quite costly and subject to technical difficulties and limitations. Moreover, consumers who use the systems would be unable to inspect the goods, have difficulty in changing a selection after ordering an item, and would have to make arrangements to accept delivery when the goods arrive. Consequently, the substitution of electronic systems for most in-store retailing seems unlikely in the near future, although such systems may become important in the long run.

□ Conclusion

The net result of all of these trends should be a continuation of in-store shopping; some change in the relative proportion of downtown and suburban shopping, probably in favor of downtown; and increasing skill and care in the planning of retail shopping facilities.

■ REVIEW AND DISCUSSION QUESTIONS

1 Why should a merchant who has a store conduct locational analysis of the present site? What types or sources of information can be used for an existing store that would not be available to a merchant studying a potential new location?

2 How do you explain the failure of many merchants, including some large-scale firms, to give adequate attention to locational analysis and research?

3 Summarize, in sufficient detail to make your meaning clear, five of the basic factors influencing the choice of a city or *trading area* in which to locate a store. Try to gather the relevant information concerning those factors for your city or college town.

4 Suppose that you were examining an area and potential location from a helicopter, as mentioned in this chapter. Specifically what would you look for?

5 Describe six factors that you would consider important in selecting a specific site within a city. How would your answer vary if you were considering locations for: (a) a full-service drugstore, (b) a department store, (c) a retail lumberyard, and (d) a high-fashion boutique?

6 Define "method of analogies," "percentage lease," "suburbia," "metropolis," "megalopolis," "pedestrian mall."

7 Should government exercise any control over the leases that retailers (one group of businesspeople) sign with shopping center developers (another group of businesspeople)? Present the arguments "pro" and "con" on this question.

8 What are the major elements in the retail structure of a metropolitan area? What types of stores would you expect to find in each of these elements? (It may be helpful to try to identify examples of each such element in the nearest metropolitan area.)

9 Explain five current trends in shopping center development, supporting each one with specific examples or evidence.

10 What factors seem to be contributing to the possible resources of downtown shopping districts? How might those districts differ from the way they have appeared in the past?

■ NOTES AND REFERENCES

1 See "Old Chain Units: Independents' Pitfall," *Supermarket News,* October 27, 1975, pp. 2, 22.

2 Dwayne Laws with William Applebaum, *How to Evaluate Hardware Store Locations* (Indianapolis, Ind.: Russell M. Mueller Retail Hardware Research Foundation, 1971), p. 6.

3 For a list of factors influencing the choice of a trading area, *see* William Applebaum, "Guidelines for a Store-Location Strategy Study," *Journal of Marketing,* vol. 30, (October 1966), pp. 42–45. Also see Laws and Applebaum, *How to Evaluate Hardware Store Locations;* and R. A. Kerin and Michael Harvey, "Evaluation of Retail Store Locations through Profitability Analysis," *Journal of Small Business Management,* vol. 13 (January 1975), pp. 41–45.

4 *Current Population Reports, Population Estimates,* published frequently but irregularly by the Bureau of the Census of the U.S. Department of Commerce, contains a variety of information concerning population such as growth, shifts, and age groupings by regions and states. Special censuses covering numerous cities and areas are also available from the Bureau. For Canadian figures see Statistics Canada, *Quarterly Estimates of Population for Canada and Provinces,* Series 91–001.

5 The correlation between population changes and retail sales in 1958 and 1967 for each state and the country as a whole are given in R. C. Sizemore, "Census Reveals Retail Potential," *Women's Wear Daily,* September 15, 1970, pp. 1, 18. For a study in much greater depth, *see* Ben-chieh Liu, "Relationships among Population, Income and Retail Sales in SMSA's 1952–66," *Quarterly Review of Economics and Business,* vol. 10, no. 1 (Spring 1970), pp. 25–40.

6 Starting with the April 1975 issue, the *Survey of Current Business* now annually publishes estimated total personal income data for the 254 Standard Metropolitan Statistical Areas that account for about 80 percent of all American income, and for all 3,133 U.S. counties and similar local areas.

7 U.S. Department of Commerce, *Measuring Markets: A Guide to the Use of Federal and State Statistical Data,* Washington: U. S. Government Printing Office, 1974, is an excellent reference to the available official American statistical sources that are useful in retail location analysis.

8 Various annual editions of the Institute's publication, *Facts about New Supermarkets Opened in —.* But about 30 to 40 percent achieved 111 percent or more of estimated sales.

9 "Ross Urges Using Research in Branch Outlet Site Selection," *Marketing News,* January 31, 1975, pp. 9–10; See also: E. B Weiss, "Turning Off the Red Ink," *Stores,* April 1976, p. 44.

10 "Shopping Bag Helicopter Flying North for New Sites," *Supermarket News,* March 26, 1973, p. 24.

11 See "Ward's Goal: More Metros," *Women's Wear Daily,* March 21, 1973, pp. 1, 57.

12 "Abstracts of Latest Shopping Center Leases," *Chain Store Age* (executive edition), May 1974, pp. L4, L16, L25.

13 *The Dollars and Cents of Shopping Centers 1975,* Washington, Urban Land Institute, 1975, p. 71.

14 *Gimbel Brothers, Inc.,* Docket 8885, January 30, 1974, CCH Trade Regulation Reporter ¶ 20,478; *Tysons Corner Regional Center,* Dkt. 8886, June 26, 1974, CCH Trade Reg. Rep. ¶ 20,532; *The Rouse Co.,* File no. 721 0067, January 30, 1975, CCH Trade Reg. Rep., ¶ 20,818.

15 J. B. Mason, "Power and Channel Conflicts in Shopping Center Development," *Journal of Marketing,* vol. 39

(April 1975), pp. 28–35; *The Shopping Center Industry and Antitrust Laws* (New York: International Council of Shopping Centers, 1973); "Antitrust Action in the Shopping Malls," *Business Week*, December 8, 1975, p. 51.

16 See "Where We'll Live," *Changing Times*, January 1976, p. 8.

17 "Keeping Up with Kresge," *Business Week*, October 17, 1974, p. 72.

18 "Gamble-Skogmo at 50: Casting a New Mold," *Chain Store Age* (general merchandise edition), December 1975, p. 42. *See also* "Small Towns: Big Business for Sampsons," *Chain Store Age* (supermarket edition), March 1976, pp. 34–35; "Family Store in Town of 2,400 Pulls 28,000 Shoppers a Week," *Supermarket News*, January 5, 1976, sec. 2, p. 12.

19 *Survey of Current Business*, April 1975, pp. 30–35.

20 The Canadian census uses a larger minimum population figure, 100,-000, for its Census Metropolitan Areas (CMAs). Yet, in 1970, 55 percent of Canada's population lived within its 22 CMAs. E. J. McCarthy and S. J. Shapiro, *Basic Marketing*, 1st Canadian ed. (Georgetown, Ont.: Irwin-Dorsey Limited, 1975), p. 133.

21 P. M. Hauser, "Is the Market Moving away from You?" *A View to 1970* (Chicago: Super Market Institute, 1965), p. 11.

22 On the trend toward retail trade decentralization in ten *nonmetropolitan* Ohio cities in the period 1958 to 1967 see P. S. Carusone, "A Shift in the Point of Patronage," *MSU Business Topics*, Autumn 1970, pp. 61–69.

23 "Introduction," *Suburbia in Transition*, Louis H. Masotti and Jeffrey K. Hadden, eds. (New York: New Viewpoints, 1974), pp. 7–10.

24 Eli P. Cox, "SMSA's Revisited," *Michigan State Economic Record*, vol. 17, no. 2 (April 1975), pp. 1–2, 6, commets on the extent to which highway improvements have brought nonmetropolitan area consumers to Michigan SMSA suburban shopping facilities.

25 By far the best treatment of megalopolis is found in Jean Gottman, *Megalopolis* (New York: Twentieth Century Fund, 1961).

26 See J. B. Schneider, "Retail Competition Patterns in a Metropolitan Area," *Journal of Retailing*, vol. 45 (Winter 1969–70), pp. 67–74. Supermarket's place in this picture is discussed by Bryan Thompson, "Intraurban Retail Structure: The Supermarket Structure," *Journal of Retailing*, vol. 45 (Fall 1969), pp. 69–80.

27 "The Recession Balks Genesco's Turnaround," *Business Week*, July 7, 1975, p. 67; "Anatomy of Failures," *Chain Store Age* (executive edition), April 1973, pp. E19–E23.

28 See M. A. Paule and L. A. Gaines, *Directory of Shopping Centers in the United States and Canada*, 16th ed. (Burlington, Iowa: The National Research Bureau, Inc., 1975).

29 For example, in 1974, branches accounted for 72 percent of total sales of department stores reporting in the NRMA's annual survey. National Retail Merchants Association, Financial Executives Division, *Financial and Operating Results of Department and Specialty Stores* (New York: the Association, 1975, p. v

30 "Now Communities Are Resisting New Shopping Centers, Zoning is Stricter, and Design has to be Better," *Architectural Record*, vol. 155 (April 1974) pp. 150–52.

31 "Can Anchorless Malls Make It?" *Chain Store Age* (executive edition), July 1973, pp. E19–E21; "A Threat: Anchorless Malls," *Chain Store Age* (general merchandise edition), March 1975, pp. 30–31; "Shopping Malls Going Small," *New York Times*, October 5, 1975, sec. 3, p. 2.

32 Samuel Feinberg, "Mini-Malls Forecast Filling Vacuum between Regionals," *Women's Wear Daily*, March 13, 1974, p. 10.

33 "Nailing Down Locations Is the Key to Kresge's Expansion," *Chain Store Age* (executive edition), December 1965, p. E15. The first K-Mart placed inside a shopping center opened at Pyramid Mall (Syracuse, N.Y.) in November, 1973, and the first one in a regional center was opened at Richland Mall (Johnstown, Pa.) in fall, 1974. "Shopping Center News," *Chain Store Age* (executive edition), May 1974, p. E6. In contrast, practically all of the Woolco units of the F.

W. Woolworth Company are in shopping centers.

34 For example, *see* "Cleveland's [Ohio] Big 3 Invest in Downtown," *Women's Wear Daily,* July 1, 1975, pp. 1, 10.

35 Everett Steichen, "CBD's Require a Second Look," *Retail Control,* vol. 42 (February 1974), p. 9.

36 *See* David Carlson and Mary R. S. Carlson, "The Pedestrian Mall: Its Role in Revitalization of Downtown Areas," *Urban Land,* vol. 33 (May 1974), pp. 3–9 for a detailed and authoritative

discussion of topics outlined in this paragraph.

37 B. A. Brownell and C. C. Peterson, "Cities within a City," and Nory Miller, "Marble-Clad Carnival," *Architectural Forum,* vol. 140 (January-February 1974), pp. 38–43, 44–47.

38 *See* Alan Turner, "New Communities in the United States 1968–1973," *Town Planning Review,* vol. 45 (July 1974), pp. 259–73; no. 4 (October 1974), pp. 401–14; "Can 'New Towns' Survive the Economic Crunch?" *Business Week,* February 10, 1975, pp. 43–44.

THE STORE BUILDING, FIXTURES, AND EQUIPMENT

After a suitable location has been chosen, a building must be prepared for occupancy. This preparation involves the following: (1) Constructing a new building or making the necessary structural changes in an existing one to provide the space and facilities required; (2) providing adequate lighting equipment, properly colored walls and ceilings, and suitable floor coverings; (3) procuring the fixtures and equipment essential to the conduct of the business; and (4) arranging and locating the merchandise, fixtures, and equipment in such a manner that customers may be served promptly and satisfactorily at the lowest cost.

■ THE STORE BUILDING AS A SELLING INSTRUMENT

A well-designed store attracts customers and facilitates their movement inside the store, provides a pleasant environment in which they may shop, makes possible economical operations and maintenance, and has adequate space for selling and sales-supporting activities currently and in the foreseeable future. Well-designed stores are as essential to profitable operation as good assortments of merchandise at reasonable prices. Contemporary architects realize that "form follows function" and that store buildings must be effective selling instruments. Experience demonstrates that effective store planning may result in sales 10 to 100 percent higher than in the poorly-planned unit. Consequently, interest in better design permeates the whole field of retailing: through the cooperation of store executives, building architects, lighting and ventilating engineers, and specialists in store equipment and layout, marked progress has resulted.

☐ Land, building, and equipment expenditures

Building and land costs continue to be high despite a small decline in 1974 from 1973.[1] For instance, land, building, and equipment for a large supermarket may cost $1 million or more, a modern full-line drugstore $400,000 to $500,000, a large discount house may require an investment of $3–5 million, and a free-standing full-line department store may range between $8 and $12 million.[2] As a result, retailers are becoming increasingly cost-conscious in their store building programs with some delaying construction[3] and many large firms assigning to their architects and engineers the task of achieving equally efficient and impressive facilities at lower costs.

Some organizations have attempted to achieve their economy goal by reducing the construction period through more careful integration of all phases of the job, including use of the Program Evaluation and Review Technique—commonly known as PERT. Others have found that a newer and less costly material may be substituted and that less expensive fixtures may be installed. Perhaps a prefabricated structure or section of a building may be used.[4] Corporate and voluntary chains often develop a prototype or pattern store which reflects such savings and can be approximately duplicated many times.

☐ Some common features of the newer store buildings

No store building can be described as the "typical" one of today, but common features of the newer buildings may be noted. Very recent years have brought numerous changes in store design, materials, and plans designed to meet the changing economic scene and reflect the increasing sophistication of retail management, store engineers, and equipment specialists. Among these changes are the increased attention given to strengthening store security, adoption of measures to meet the perplexing energy situation,[5] provision of space to allow for greater flexibility in locating and arranging fixtures and equipment, even relocating complete departments.[6] Of special interest, perhaps, is the growing recognition by retail management and store designers of the needs of handicapped persons both in gaining access to stores and their mobility once inside. Some states and cities have already passed regulations covering this accessibility and movement factor and the trend is likely to grow. It is also evident in connection with modernization and store layout planning.

Phased construction techniques, that is, the use of carefully planned and timed efforts on related phases of the construction project to expedite its completion, thus saving time and enabling the new store to meet competition and attract customers more quickly, are often employed.

Other current developments of interest in store buildings are the use of reflective glass exteriors (for example, Bloomingdale's of New York City and Saks Fifth Avenue in Houston, Texas); the "clean sophisticated look" of the Tempo-Buckeye stores owned by Gamble-Skogmo;[7] and the contemporary building with a precast concrete exterior of Goudchaux's branch store in Baton Rouge, Louisiana. The latter store is completely carpeted with terrazzo aisles and with shades changing from area to area to meet various department themes.[8]

Among supermarkets an important trend is the enlargement of space to accommodate the increase in their marketing mix with some adjustments in layouts—but energy conservation, discussed in the next section, is a matter of vital concern.

The energy problem The perplexing energy question mentioned previously is of sufficient importance to justify additional comments about it. Few problems in recent years have received the attention from retail stores of all types as has this particular problem. And, although it is of national concern, attention here must be restricted for illustrative purposes to one type of retail establishment—the supermarket. Electrical costs among such stores increased by 24 percent in 1974 over 1973 and heating costs by 20 percent. With the energy cost squeeze continuing in 1975 and 1976 (and likely beyond) it is not surprising that a 1975 survey revealed that 72 percent of the operators ranked increases in the cost of electricity as their most serious area of concern. Moreover, since they recognized energy costs as a controllable expense and also the need for energy conservation, 86 percent of the largest companies have adopted formal energy conservation programs.[9]

Note, however, the following comments of the *Progressive Grocer:*

In spite of this awareness, even elementary conservation practices are far less than universally adopted. A logical first step—to remove overhead lighting —has been taken by only 25 percent. Similarly 26 percent have replaced or eliminated energy-consuming equipment. The lone widespread practice is to cut heating and air conditioning, but even here, only 50 percent of independents have tried even this basic approach.[10]

---

* Sears, Roebuck and Co., for example, built an anchor store in a Kansas City shopping area in half the normal time through phased construction.

In Dallas, a distinctive development in store construction that reflects contemporary design as well as awareness of the energy problem is the Sanger-Harris store, a unit of Federated Department Stores, and pictured in Figure 5–1. Its uniqueness warrants further details concerning it.

While not the largest unit in the Federated chain, this 463,000-square foot facility ranks as the most attractive. The six-story facade of the building comprises a succession of contiguous Roman arches and slender piers of white marble framing a commanding mural of Italian glass tiles. Claimed to be the largest of its type anywhere, the mosaic starts at the second level and rises four stories to the crowns of the arches. It rings all four sides of the store, which occupies most of a trapezoidal city block.

On two sides of the structure the columns are integral with the outside walls. Piers on the two remaining sides are freestanding, giving the effect of an open collonade. Outside walls within the collonade are recessed just beneath the mural to provide a sheltered walkway lined with a panorama of quartz-lighted show windows. Along one side of the portico there is a row of trees

FIGURE 5–1 Sanger-Harris department store, Dallas, Texas At night store is spectacle of illuminated Roman arches and mosaic glass tiles.

Courtesy Sanger-Harris and Electric Energy Assn.

and along the other a sunken terrace flanked by long masonry planter boxes filled with greenery.

Sanger-Harris is promoted as a "block of fashion" and in keeping with this, interiors are artfully designed to provide tasteful settings for the display of high-style clothing and home furnishings. Various architectural motifs are employed throughout the store to give each department a feeling of being an individual specialty shop. Dominating the engineering aspects of the building is an electric year-round space-conditioning system capable of recovering heat from people, lights, and equipment and using it for comfort heating.[11]

FIGURE 5–2   Artist's sketch of rebuilt Jordan-Marsh store in Boston

Courtesy Jordan-Marsh Co.

FIGURE 5–3   Bullock's store in South Coast Plaza, Costa Mesa, California The unique appearance and construction reflect the drastic changes in store design during recent years.

Courtesy Bullock's, Inc. and Chain Store Age Executive

Still other examples of the exterior (and interior) appearance of modern and unusual store buildings are given in Figures 5–2 through 5–8.

FIGURE 5–4 **Front of new Lit Brothers store in Neshaminy Mall northeast of Philadelphia** Note inviting entrance and effective lighting.

Courtesy Lit Brothers

■ THE STORE FRONT AND EXTERIOR

Since "the front often sells the store," it should give the impression of a going concern and reflect neither stagnation nor decline. Moreover, it should typify the spirit of the organization and the nature of the activity within. By suggesting stability and permanence, the front and exterior create confidence and goodwill. The massive stone columns in front of the Marshall Field and Company State Street store in Chicago and Selfridge's in London give this impression.[12] Since identification is another function of the store front and exterior, symbols and distinctive store fronts—as well as large signs—have long been used. Furthermore, a minimum maintenance cost and protection of the store's windows and interior from sun damage require attention.[13]

FIGURE 5–5   Grand entrance to the atrium shopping mall of the shopping center at Water Tower Place, Chicago   Lobby has Marshall Field and Company on the right and Lord and Taylor on the left. Amid plantings and waterfalls, escalators lead to the grand atrium with a seven-story vista. Glass-enclosed elevators are also available.

FIGURE 5–6   Dramatic design of three-story escalator court in Bullock's South Coast Plaza (California) store   Featured is a blend of wood, tiles, and bricks with lighting producing a starry effect.

Courtesy Bullock's and Chain Store Age Executive

FIGURE 5–7   The R. H. Macy and Company's department store, Queens Boulevard, Queens, New York   Opened in 1965 with over 330,000 square feet of area, this unusual structure parks 1,500 cars on its roof and ramps.

Courtesy R. H. Macy and Company, Inc.

FIGURE 5–8   Longs Drug Stores discount unit in shopping center in National City, California   Note one-floor construction and large parking area.

Courtesy Longs Drug Stores, Inc.

Still another development of some significance is the increasing construction of one-floor stores by drug organizations, supermarkets and others, although some two- and three-floor stores continue to be built in shopping centers. Figure 5–8 is an example of this trend. Moreover, as noted, some firms, Bloomingdale's of New York, for instance, are building stores with reflective glass exteriors that mirror surrounding trees to emphasize a "back to nature" trend.[14] In contrast, Bamberger's (a subsidiary of R. H. Macy and Company) unit in East Brunswick, New Jersey, has a glassless exterior. Reasons for these design changes are the desire to obtain better control of the interior environment at a lower cost, to benefit from new merchandising techniques that place greater emphasis on mass displays and impulse buying, to avoid the necessity (and cost) of constructing elevators and escalators found in multistory buildings, and to facilitate the movement of customer traffic. Figure 6–4, page 155 (Longs Drug Store) is illustrative.

But innovation in design and construction patterns is by no means limited to single-floor stores or to two- or three-floor ones. Although variety in design is legion, as even casual observation will reveal, one example—the Water Tower Place development in Chicago, Illinois and described in Chapter 4 indicates the extreme form design may take.

☐ Customer entrances

Entrances should be wide and inviting,* with doorsills preferably at the street level. To avoid congestion and concentration of customer traffic, two entrances are advisable for stores with a frontage of 75 feet or more. Entrances on two streets are preferable for corner locations. Doors should permit easy access; in fact, some retailers have replaced them with "curtains of air" (warm or cold, depending on the weather), thus eliminating them as a deterrent to entrance by the customer. Whether or not revolving doors are used depends on the size of the store, willingness of the retailer to meet the cost, and the climate.

☐ Show windows

The use of windows to display merchandise offered for sale has been an almost universal practice, with supermarkets and some discount houses the most notable exceptions. Recent years, however, have witnessed, a decline in their use by other stores, particularly chain organizations, department and specialty stores, for reasons already mentioned. Yet as the "eyes" of the store, they continue in use by most stores as a

---

*The main entrance of F. R. Lazarus and Company, Columbus, Ohio, department store, is over 33 feet wide. Open winter and summer, merchandise displays are brought close to customers. When the store is closed, folding doors protect the entrance.

desirable feature of the store exterior from the sales point of view because the impressions customers receive from the window displays largely determine whether or not they will enter the store. Consequently, even some of the so-called "windowless" stores have windows at the ground level to "show their wares."

The size and type of windows used in a particular establishment are determined by the kind of store and the goods displayed. To illustrate: Many department stores, with items varying in size from furniture suites to notions, have large and deep windows to accommodate many different types of merchandise; variety stores* frequently use large, shallow windows with no backgrounds above eye level, thus affording an unobstructed view of the store's interior; and some jewelry stores favor the so-called "invisible" window, which consists of a curved sheet of glass so formed as to cast reflections downward and away from the observer's eye, thus giving the effect of an open window.

Backgrounds   Among stores using show windows, three general types of window backgrounds are found: (a) The open background, which permits the passer-by to see into the store, as in grocery stores, candy stores, and florists' shops; (b) the semiclosed background, with a partition extending to a height below the line of vision, sometimes found in drugstores and hardware stores; and (c) the closed background, which shuts off the window completely, as in department stores and in specialty stores handling men's and women's wearing apparel. Retailers using closed or semiclosed backgrounds claim that they focus attention upon displays, provide attractive settings for the merchandise shown, and permit more effective illumination.

Visual fronts   Still found in some stores is the open or visual store front, which has no formal window; instead, the customer looks through glass directly to the store's interior displays. This front enables the customer to grasp more quickly the scope of merchandise offered for sale. It also adds selling space, reduces the time required to trim windows, permits greater use of natural light, and creates a more open and attractive shopping "atmosphere."

■ THE STORE INTERIOR

Regardless of the reasons why the customer enters the store, the impression of the interior must be favorable. Such an impression may be created by, for example, an open area inside the entrance, aisles wide

---

* As used here "variety stores" refer to those institutions handling a wide range of merchandise in low price lines and usually operating on a self-serve or self-selection basis. Formerly many such stores handled merchandise sold at 5, 10, 15 and 25 cents giving rise to the terms "limited price variety store" or "5-and-10-cent store" but increases in the general price level and changes in "product mix" have resulted in substantially higher prices and dropping of the "limited price" designation. F. W. Woolworth Co. is a good example.

enough to readily accommodate customer traffic, good light, ceilings of the proper height, and colorful displays. Also helpful in this connection are floor, wall, and ceiling finishes, store equipment and fixtures—including lighting, elevators and escalators, and air conditioning, and the proper harmonizing of these factors.

□ Floors, walls, and ceilings

The retailer may choose from among more than 50 floor finishes made of such materials as wood, marble, tile, linoleum, rubber, cork, and carpeting. Different types, of course, are required for different purposes; the finish in the receiving or marking room, for example, would be unlike that required on the second floor of a department store. Likewise, exclusive specialty shops, where wall-to-wall carpeting is quite common, require a floor different from that of a neighborhood grocery store. In general, however, the trend is toward the newer types of vinyl, glass tile, and other resilient tiles as replacements for the older masonry and wood floors because of their durability and attractiveness.[15]

Wall and ceiling finishes are dictated by considerations of attractiveness, economy, and preference of store executives. While many economy-type stores rely heavily on paint spread directly on cinder or concrete blocks for much of their wall area, even these establishments usually finish off some areas with wood panels, reclaimed brick, or some of the plastic laminates. In other stores, plastered walls finished with paint or decorative wallpaper are common. The newer vinyl fabrics, while involving a larger original cost, are preferred by many retailers because they can supply texture and color effects not possible with paint, and the increased cost is largely offset by longer life and reduced maintenance costs. The use of movable walls, modular fixturing, unistruts, and baffles instead of the conventional ceiling, is designed for flexibility and minimum customer inconvenience, the additional cost offset by fewer walls.[16]

The color of the store's interior makes the store more attractive and aids in the sale of specific merchandise. Color combinations are also employed to emphasize the individuality and character of a store and to reduce lighting costs. The new Lit Brothers store in Neshaminy Mall near Philadelphia and shown in Figure 5–4 provides a good illustration of modernized interiors. The store

focuses around a central court which contains the escalator banks and around which are grouped jewelry, handbags, hosiery, "and finishing touches that complete a coordinated fashion picture." The main aisles and central court have bleached-teak flooring. The remaining areas, divided into quadrants, are "color zoned" by wall and carpet treatment. For instance, women's apparel is in white lacquer with burnt-orange carpets and wall accents. The next quadrant, for men's wear, is in terra cotta and hunter green, with brown and beige accents. In juniors the predominating color is red. The escalators and department entrances are in white stucco finish and sisal is used on many of the walls. The ceiling is stepped and the lighting is fluorescent with incandescent spots for accents.[17]

☐ Store fixtures and equipment

The appearance of the store's interior and its effectiveness as a retail facility are determined in large measure by the fixtures and equipment used. The terms "store fixtures" and "store equipment" are often used interchangeably by students of retailing: Some retailers speak of the lights they install as "light fixtures" while others refer to their "lighting equipment." Despite such loose usage, however, the term "fixtures" is properly reserved for those durable goods which the retailer uses directly in the sale, display, storage, and protection of merchandise, such as display cabinets and cases, shelves, counters, and tables; whereas the term "equipment" refers to such other durable goods as elevators, escalators, air-conditioning units, sales registers, and delivery trucks, which are used in- or outside the store to facilitate both selling and nonselling activities.

Selecting fixtures and equipment In choosing fixtures and equipment, certain factors, in addition to cost,[18] are decisive. First is the clientele or class of trade to which the store intends to cater; second,

FIGURE 5–9 **Women's Fashion section in Gemco Discount store, Tucson, Arizona** Note intensive use of space to display merchandise.

Courtesy Lucky Stores, Inc.

FIGURE 5–10 Forecast Shop—Designer dresses and sportswear, Kaufmann's Mill Creek Mall, Erie, Pennsylvania Note sharp contrast in space utilization and display with those shown in Figure 5–11.

Courtesy Kaufmann's, Pittsburgh, Pennsylvania

those chosen should not divert customers' attention from the merchandise; third, they should be adjusted to the type of merchandise handled, including such closely related factors as size, value, need for protection from theft and deterioration or spoilage, and the methods employed to display and sell it;[19] fourth, the type of service rendered in connection with the merchandise, *i.e.,* whether the store is a self-service or full-service one; fifth, the original cost and maintenance expense; and sixth, the types and kinds of items available for use in the particular kind of store under consideration.

□ Lighting the modern store

Effective lighting is essential for the conduct of both selling and sales-supporting activities. While cost of equipment and economy in operation are basic considerations, the retailer is also interested in how the lighting—among other things—improves the store's front and interior and if it adds to the customer's shopping pleasure, steps up sales personnel productivity, makes self-selection easier, increases merchandise turnover, decreases shoplifting, ties in with the kind of merchandise sold, and adds to the effectiveness of displays. In other words, lighting is a sales tool.

One successful supermarket operator emphasizes the facts that "merchandise in a store should be alive and different types of lighting do more for it. It may be more costly to install and maintain such lighting, but it's good in terms of what it does for the merchandise."[20] Conforming to such convictions, the company's newest store features (1) mercury ceiling lights, (2) custom-built neon lights in the service meat cases, (3) perimeter lights throughout the walls of the store, and (4) lighting on the gondolas or shelving to relieve shopping monotony in the dry groceries area.

FIGURE 5–11   **A small Massachusetts store uses various lights and separate controls to save energy and reduce costs**

Courtesy Wilson's, Greenfield, Massachusetts

Diversity in lighting is also effective in creating the desired store image when adapted to the type of service the store wishes to render and the kind of illumination desired.

Typical of the questions to be answered in solving a store's lighting problems are the following:

1. Does the lighting arrangement make it easy for customers to find and identify the store during evening hours through effective use of electric signs, luminous façades, and well-lighted parking lots?

2. Does the lighting plan cause the customer to focus attention on the merchandise or the displays desired?
3. Are the lighting conditions most effective for buying decisions through providing for the best rendition of color on all types of merchandise?
4. Does the lighting add emphasis to merchandise and yield maximum results from display space?
5. Is lighting used properly to identify departments and direct customers?
6. Is the lighting used at check-out counters and sales registers of the kind that permits easy reading of prices and the writing of sales slips, yet avoiding glare reflections from surfaces on merchandise and sales registers?
7. Does the lighting plan speed stocking and order-filling in the storage areas of the store, thus improving production?
8. Is the lighting arrangement one that minimizes the maintenance and cleaning of light fixtures, replacing lamps, and similar work?
9. Are the newest types of lamps being used to save energy and deliver more light?
10. Does the complete lighting program provide an atmosphere where the customer can shop pleasantly and help build continuous patronage?
11. Are measures being adopted that will conserve energy and reduce lighting costs?

The technical nature of lighting viewed in relation to energy conservation makes it advisable for the retailer to consult a qualified lighting engineer to solve the problems in this area.*

□ Equipment for handling vertical customer traffic

Handling vertical customer traffic, especially during peak periods, is a problem for retailers who operate on more than one level. Stationary stairways are adequate for many stores with just a basement or perhaps only one floor above the street level, but other stores find they must install elevators and escalators or moving stairways. R. H. Macy and Company, New York City, to cite an extreme example, found 70 escalators and 29 passenger elevators were necessary to provide vertical transportation for its many thousands of daily customers.

The marked improvement in elevator types has increased their usefulness because large numbers of customers can be handled more

---

* A leading trade magazine comments: "Since a formal industrywide program [of energy conservation] is still only a concept, many merchants are coping on their own, and report they already have realized savings through their own innovations." *Progressive Grocer*, October 1975.

rapidly and more comfortably than formerly. Automatic stopping, microleveling, and power-operated doors have all contributed to greater speed.

Escalators were long considered as unsightly, impractical equipment but today they are a "must" in the larger stores. Improved design, "streamlined" effects, and inlaid lighting have contributed to this growth. Moreover, their advantages over elevators are increasingly being recognized including the following: elimination of waiting for elevators and reduction of congestion and crowding—thus saving the customer's time and energy; provision of fast and comfortable transportation between floors while affording a good view of adjacent merchandise offerings; and finally, in large stores which need to provide for considerable vertical transportation, they occupy far less space than elevators, require no operators, and provide continuity of motion with low power cost.

Among smaller stores the elevator is usually more advantageous than the escalator. If a single elevator is adequate, it will require but one-third as much space as an escalator and installation cost is lower. An observer of the heavy loads carried by escalators during the peak Christmas business in the larger stores, however, wonders how they operated without escalators for so many years. But even in these stores some elevators are needed, especially to provide rapid movement for customers wishing to move vertically several floors at one time, for those who are aged or infirm, and for those who prefer to ride in them.

☐ Air conditioning in retail stores

Currently, practically all major department and departmentalized specialty stores as well as chain stores are air conditioned, at least in part. In fact, most of the new stores being built today are air conditioned, regardless of their type or location. And in shopping centers even the malls are being treated in this manner by means of automated controls to provide the desired "climate."

The main advantage of air conditioning is its attractiveness to the customer. It encourages shopping on warm days and it increases impulse sales to people drawn into stores just "to cool off." It also improves employee morale, resulting in better performance as well as contributing to a cleaner store and merchandise. Finally, if a retailer's chief competitors adopt air conditioning, it may be necessary to "follow suit" to maintain competitive position.

Some limitations Despite its present popularity and advantages, air conditioning has not been adopted by some small independent stores which consider the initial, operating, and maintenance costs of various types of equipment too high. Moreover, they lose some sales or storage space. Even the fact that a competitor has installed such equipment should not cause undue alarm, unless that competitor also practices effective retailing methods. Air conditioning a store will not overcome unsound merchandising practices.

☐ Other kinds of equipment

For selling activities Service equipment, such as sales registers and devices for recording credit transactions, is discussed in Chapter 25, "Control of sales transactions." Exclusive of service equipment, various other kinds of equipment are required to facilitate the handling of sales transactions. The types and amounts of these kinds of equipment used in particular stores and departments will depend upon existing needs and conditions. In grocery stores, for example, weighing machines or scales are essential in selling bulk goods, fruits, and vegetables. In department stores, certain departments—candy, for instance—also require scales. For stores that sell yard goods or piece goods and therefore need linear measurements, there are machines available that measure such merchandise accurately.

For sales-supporting activities A wide variety of equipment is required to carry out sales-supporting functions. This equipment, which has contributed to improved performance and to reduced costs, may be classified as follows: (a) Mechanical equipment used in receiving, marking, checking, and delivery rooms, including small floor trucks, mobile marking tables, price-ticket machines, marking machines, time-stamp machines, belt conveyor systems, and wastepaper baling machines; (b) labor-saving devices used in the general offices for handling correspondence and other clerical work such as typewriters and machines used for calculating, duplicating, bookkeeping, addressing, and stamping; (c) store communication devices, such as call systems—bells, lights, or electronic—for store executives, private telephone systems, and dictographs; and (d) miscellaneous equipment, including time clocks, signature-recording machines for timekeeping purposes, and sewing and textile-repair machines in workrooms. Relatively few stores, of course, use all of these types of equipment; but retail executives should be aware of the fact that such equipment is available when, as, and if it may be used advantageously.

Electronic equipment The use of electronic data-processing systems and the equipment required for their effective functioning, is growing rapidly.[21] Frequently referred to as EDP, these systems provide a means of gathering, storing, and processing data to provide the retailer with required information.* Already so complicated that few persons

---

* In February 1971 *Chain Store Age* estimated that retailers would increase their expenditures from EDP from $500 million at that time to $800 million in 1976. Complete data for this later year are not available as this is written but expenditures are likely to exceed the estimate.

know a large computer's wiring diagram in full detail, many new electronic machines with even greater complexity continue to be developed. In fact, it may prove true that the machines now being used are Neanderthal models compared to what is coming in the relatively near future.

1. *Current uses of EDP in retailing*   In the hands of an able operator, usually referred to as the programmer, EDP equipment can provide timely information on such matters as (1) sales by classifications, departments, or stores and even by individual items broken down by price lines, sizes, colors, or other factors, (2) inventories, (3) expenses, (4) purchases, (5) accounts payable, (6) accounts receivable, (7) gross margin, and (8) returned goods. In later chapters, including our discussions of merchandise management, credit, and sales registers, some of these uses of EDP are developed at greater length. Clerical work can be minimized, and speed and accuracy maximized, by using EDP to prepare payrolls, to reorder certain items automatically, to supply open-to-buy reports, and to prepare checks for merchandise and other purchases. Some retailers now use computer models to analyze the desirability of store locations, to determine the most efficient truck routing, and to make judgments concerning the addition of new products.

2. *Limitations and probable future of EDP in retailing*   EDP systems are very costly with the prices of computers varying widely according to the capabilities they provide. Although some of the new mini-computers —"easy to use as a typewriter"—sell below $25,000, other small and medium-sized installations are in the $25,000 to $150,000 range and the larger ones are priced at $200,000 to $5 million. Perhaps 90 percent of such equipment is rented. To cite a specific example of the leading producer in the field:

The company's 3650 Retail Store System is a family of data processing tools that can link a complete large organization into an efficient, cohesive unit. That is, its various components can generate data needed by such establishments as department stores and mass merchandisers both for handling and selling their goods. These components are:

1. The IBM 3651 store controller, with its own programmable storage and disk file, controls all other devices in a store network and communicates directly with a virtual storage IBM System/370.
2. The IBM 3653 point-of-sale terminal, with built-in logic and memory, which can operate interactively with or independently from the controller . . . it has a three-station printer, customer and operator guidance displays, data entry keyboard, and can accommodate an optional "wand" for reading magnetically encoded data.
3. The IBM 3657 ticket unit, an online device that can print, encode, and read information on price tags.
4. The IBM 3659 remote communications unit, which links a remote store to the controller.

5. The IBM 3275 display station and, optionally, 3284 printer, which can be used to prepare purchase orders and receiving documents as well as for credit, administrative, and management applications.

Cost of the 3650 system depends on the size of a user's retail network. Monthly rental is $2,697 for a store system that might include a controller, four display units, two printers, one ticket unit and one remote communications unit. The system also would include 80 point-of-sale terminals purchased for $286,000 and 64 magnetic-wand readers purchased for $22,400. The total cost of the system is $412,690.[22]

Considerable expense is involved in the year or two of study leading to the selection of the proper equipment and in the comparable "breaking-in" or testing period after the equipment has been installed.[23] Consequently, the purchase or full-time lease of EDP systems is open just to the large retail organizations. Yet the medium-size retailer can still secure some of the advantages of these systems by renting their use for a few hours at a time. Both equipment manufacturers and independent firms now offer a rental service, including the aid of programmers and other skilled personnel, throughout the country.

In view of the cost involved, there is a wide range of opinion, even among large retailers, as to how rapidly they should adopt electronic equipment. Certainly the retailer should precede the purchase or "time sharing" of such equipment with a careful study of business needs, exercise great care in retraining employees to think in terms of the new machines, and not expect the new equipment to serve as a panacea for all the store's problems. Kept firmly in mind should be the facts "that these new devices are only tools" to aid judgments and that some "data refinements of the precision which these devices make possible may not be needed at all by many astute executives in making many business decisions."[24] As a matter of fact, some very successful retailers operate with a minimum of reports. For instance, note the case of the large English retailer mentioned in Chapter 24. Some discount houses also operate with a minimum of records. How to balance the gains from added information against the cost of obtaining it is not one of the retailer's easy decisions. Present indications, however, are that in the foreseeable future retailers will seek more aid from the newer electronic equipment.

Leasing fixtures and equipment Previous reference to the fact that retailers often lease electronic equipment is illustrative of a trend toward the leasing of fixtures and equipment in general. Faced with a growing need for capital in the "tight money" situation and the high interest rates prevailing as this is written, plus other factors, many retailers have found it advisable to practice leasing to ease their problems. To illustrate, some large retailers lease a complete fleet of trucks, many of their store fixtures, and their headquarters' bookkeeping and billing equipment.[25]

■ STORE MODERNIZATION

Store modernization, often termed "store development," may be defined as bringing and keeping up to date the physical appearance, the fixtures, and the equipment of a store to increase its attractiveness to customers and to aid in obtaining continuous patronage. Moreover, it is designed to minimize operating costs and improve profit possibilities by such means as increasing the flow of traffic through the store, stepping up employee productivity in both selling and sales-supporting activities, and cutting maintenance expenses.* As a continuing responsibility of the retailer, modernization involves the utilization of improved construction materials and techniques as well as the most modern equipment and fixtures suited to store requirements.

☐ Modernization expenditures

During comparatively recent years, the United States has experienced its greatest retailing modernization program in history. Progressive retailers of all types, regardless of their location, are well aware of the necessity of keeping their stores up to date. They know modernization is essential for satisfactory service to customers and for the maintenance of one's competitive position. And they spend large sums in the process: For 1976 alone, despite the business situation and rising costs of labor and materials, chain organizations in various fields and their landlords budgeted $863 million to remodel 10,954 stores, an average of about $79,000 per job. Comparable figures for 1975 were $770 million to remodel 12,720 stores, an average of over $60,000. In fact, in 1976 they modernized more old stores than they opened as new units (10,954). During the same year, department stores were expected to spend $72 million to refurnish existing units and discount stores planned expenditures averaging $246,334 on improvements.[26] In 1975 capital expenditures of the J. C. Penney Company were $298.4 million which included $21.7 million to modernize and renovate older stores with its landlords contributing an additional $145 million.[27] The average annual modernization expenditure of the Emporium-Capwell Company of San Francisco is $8 million.

The continuing nature and significance of store modernization is also illustrated by the supermarkets. Although the total number of new units planned in 1976 declined 3 percent from 1975 and total square footage by the same amount, the emphasis placed on improving existing areas is evident from the fact that remodeling expenditures increased by some $46 million or 10 percent.[28] Further increases were probable in 1977.

---

* Note, however, this comment by the executive of a supermarket chain: "We never remodel if a unit's problem is poor merchandising or operations. And we don't believe in remodeling as a curative for a poor location."

□ Modernization programs

It is reasonable to conclude from the preceding discussion that the nature and extent of modernization in retail stores of various types as well as the new construction projected will depend upon such factors as the general business situation, availability of funds at costs considered reasonable, competitive forces, and broad urbanization projects in the area in which the store is located. Moreover, company failures or sharp reductions in the number of stores by national organizations tend to create a business climate not conducive either to the building of new stores or the modernization of existing ones.

It may also be presumed that despite these factors modernization and new building projects continued to be undertaken during the recession of the 1970s because management, after analyzing the total situation, concluded that the favorable factors outweighed the unfavorable ones. Some of these projects, of course, were limited for financial reasons, among others, to new store-fronts or, perhaps, to improved interiors. Changes of this nature often result in significant sales increases. Other extensive programs such as complete renovations and rearranging departments to utilize newly-designed fixtures also have produced excellent results. Even more extensive have been some programs that have resulted in new stores. This is true, for example, in the Jordan Marsh case described in the next paragraph. Yet many large stores have centered attention on elevators, escalators, air conditioning, improved illumination, and additional selling and nonselling space; and small stores have emphasized better lighting, more attractive windows, and— to a substantially lesser degree—air conditioning.

The comprehensive renovation program of Jordan Marsh in Boston, undertaken as part of a broad urbanization program in that city, is noteworthy because of the numerous changes made in the store's structure and its accompanying facilities. Prior to its modernization moves the company occupied six downtown buildings. All but one of these structures were demolished in a consolidation move tied to a multi-use project planned for Boston. The main seven-story building was joined by a three-story addition in a complex costing $35 million. Total store space was reduced from 1.7 million square feet in a three-block area to 800,000 square feet.[29] A general view of the exterior is shown in Figure 5–2. The upper floors of the new building overhang the sidewalk to form a pedestrian arcade. The windows at the sidewalk level show the latest in display and interior viewing techniques. Entrances are defined by high sloping overhangs and glass canopies. Zion's Cooperative Mercantile Institution, widely known as ZCMI, also recently undertook a very extensive and costly remodeling and modernization program of its historic structure in Salt Lake City, and downtown merchants in other cities have also rehabilitated their buildings.

It is evident from the foregoing that large retailers can obtain the funds necessary to renovate their stores and to retain experts in layout, lighting, and other aspects of modernization, sometimes establishing their own store-planning departments. Smaller ones often find these services too expensive. The latter rely to a considerable extent on the assistance provided by their trade associations. For example, the National Retail Hardware Association not only advises its members to "Consult your association first on all store modernizations," but it also encourages modernization by the preparation and dissemination of printed material.

Other small stores—and some larger ones—are aided by wholesalers and by manufacturers of fixtures, equipment, glass, and paint.

■ FUTURE BUILDING AND MODERNIZATION PROSPECTS[30]

Despite the decline in the rate of growth of our population in recent years and the delays in the construction of new stores and in modernization programs forced by the recession of the 1970s, future prospects appear bright. Urban renewal programs, the increase in the number of shopping centers and continuing inflation indicated, however, that the delays in construction and modernization would be temporary. And competition offered by new and improved stores will further stimulate the trend toward store modernization. Despite high break-even points, narrowing profit margins, current high interest rates, and the sharp increase in modernization costs, today's merchants are convinced that improved buildings and better equipment are essential to their preservation at a satisfactory level of profit.[31] Furthermore, remodeling and renovation are encouraged by the development of new materials, equipment, and devices which tend to make those in use obsolete.

In view of these facts, it is not surprising that by 1977 chain store annual expenditures on new construction and modernization approximated $6 billion, up from $4.6 billion in 1975. Yet most small retailers will probably continue to operate as they have in the past, rationalizing their actions on the ground that they cannot afford to make extensive structural and equipment changes. The more progressive stores, however, both large and small, will modernize to increase their attractiveness to customers and their efficiency as selling instruments.

■ REVIEW AND DISCUSSION QUESTIONS

1 Account for the growing emphasis on well-designed and attractive retail store buildings despite increasing construction costs.

2 Explain some of the common features of the newer store buildings in your area and the main factors responsible for their adoption.

3 Discuss the reasons for the trend toward disappearance of traditional parts of the retail façade (principal face or front) such as glass windows and entrance ways.

4 Explain briefly the essential elements in providing an attractive, desirable store to induce regular customer patronage.

5 Summarize the decisive considerations in the choice of fixtures and equipment by the retailer. What major trends do you consider significant? Why?

6 Review some current trade magazines or visit local store engineers and determine the most recent developments in lighting equipment and methods.

7 Based on the brief treatment in this chapter, what are the major current uses of EDP (electronic data processing) in the field of retailing. What future developments do you anticipate? Why?

8 From your own observations and experiences, what differences are there in the design of retail stores in downtown areas and those in outlying shopping centers. Explain.

9 Some observers contend that many of our metropolitan areas are becoming "overstored," i.e., there are more stores than needed to meet customers' needs. How may such a situation be determined?

10 A survey of food chain executives in 1975 by the Progressive Grocer revealed that (1) the rising cost of construction including materials and equipment and (2) high interest rates were the most important factors dominating thinking about construction. What other factors, in your opinion, are decisive in arriving at construction decisions? Support your answers.

■ NOTES AND REFERENCES

1 Among food chains typical new store costs were $414,200 in 1974 and $455,000 in 1973. And equipment, regardless of its particular use or location in the store, more and more has to "pay its way by demonstrated productivity." See "1976 Equipment Guide," Progressive Grocer, December 1975, pp. 39–46; see also "Federated Program Fights Building Costs," Chain Store Age Executive, March 1976, pp. 19–20 and "Store Construction Costs: Materials Rise, Labor Holds," ibid., December 1976, pp. 20–21.

2 These figures are based on retailers' statements to the authors. Average building costs per square foot in supermarkets were $20.35 in 1975 and $16.90 in 1974. See Facts about New Super Markets Opened in 1975 (Chicago: Super Market Institute, Inc., 1976), p. 6.

3 Chain Store Age Executive reports, however, that 2,563 supermarkets were to be opened in 1975 compared with some 2,000 in recent previous years. January 1977, p. 28. And in 1977, the same source reports that "the nation's top retail builders [all chain organizations] increased their square footage by 20 percent over 1975 largely fueled by takeovers of existing stores." November 1976, p. 22.

4 In 1970 mass-produced stores of modular construction were innovated by Montgomery Ward. "Wards Stores Go 'Modular'," Business Week, November 28, 1970, p. 21. Since that time some other stores have adopted this type of construction. Supermarket News, October 6, 1975, pp. 1, 13, 29.

5 On this subject see J. H. Fulweiler, Profitable Energy Management

for Retailers and Shopping Centers (New York: Chain Store Publishing Corp., 1975).

6 See "Hudson Store Design Has Flexibility," Chain Store Age Executive, March 1975, pp. 33–34 and "The Pros and Cons of Store Design Flexibility," March 1976, pp. 22–24.

7 See "Tempo-Buckeye Giving Stores Clean, Sophisticated Look," Chain Store Age Executive, December 1975, p. 19.

8 Stores, June 1976, p. 8.

9 The Supermarket Industry Speaks 1975 (Chicago, Ill.: The Super Market Institute, Inc., 1975), p. 14. Measures adopted by other types of stores are outlined by Samuel Feinberg and D. V. Burchfield in "Retailing, the Economy, and the Energy Crisis" in Tempo, vol. 20, no. 1 (1974), a publication of Touche, Ross & Co. See also "Issues '76/Energy," Progressive Grocer, April 1976, pp. 92, 94.

10 "Energy Front: Move Faster, Grocers," April 1976, p. 21.

11 "Energy Management Program" Case Study No. 5 (New York: Electric Energy Association). Not dated.

12 One department store official, however, believes that the day of the "monument" store is over and that stores in the future will be smaller and less cluttered. See L. S. Golden, "From Quantity to Quality," Chain Store Age Executive, September 1975, p. 28. This opinion is shared by an officer of a drug chain. See Ronald Gorgano, "The Changing Drug Store: Escaping from Giantism," ibid., p. 39. Note also "Vons Shrinks Square Footage," ibid., December 1976, pp. 17–18.

13 Examples of current hardware store fronts are shown in color in "Putting Up a Good Store Front," Hardware Retailing, July 1975, pp. 36–38.

14 This movement is well described in "New Bloomingdale's Features Natural Look," Chain Store Age Executive, December 1975, p. 33.

15 "Flooring Update: Glass Tile Is Newest in Stores," Chain Store Age Executive, June 1975, p. 20.

16 The J. L. Hudson branch store in Briarwood Mall, Ann Arbor, Michigan, and described in "Hudson Store Design Has Flexibility," Chain Store Age Executive, March 1975, p. 3, is illustrative.

17 "Lits—Neshaminy Mall," Stores, December 1975, p. 7. Another excellent example of the newer trends in store interiors is the Bullock's store in the Mission Valley Shopping Center near San Diego, Calif. It is described in "Bullock's Mission Valley: Where Architecture is Sculpture," Stores, December 1975, pp. 2–3.

18 Such costs continue to be high. The J. C. Penney Co., for example, spent $111 million for fixtures and equipment in 1974 and $103.1 million in 1975. 1975 Annual Report, p. 22.

19 A large store may use some 400 different specialized display fixtures. A most unusual and costly installation of display cases or capsules in some Liberty House stores is described in "Display Cases That Really Move," Chain Store Age Executive, December 1975, p. 30.

20 "Lighting Makes Petrini's Store Different," Chain Store Age Executive, March 1975, p. 62. See, however, "Energy Front: Trade Tries Less Light, More Doors, Lower Ceilings," Progressive Grocer, October 1975, p. 14 and "Store's Plug-In Lighting System Saves Both Time and Energy," Architectural Record, April 1976, pp. 141–42.

21 This is true even among small stores. See "Much More Electronics in the Independents' Future," Progressive Grocer, September 1975, p. 100 and "Minicomputers Challenge the Big Machines," Business Week, April 26, 1976, pp. 58–63. Included in the latter article are the market shares of the 10 leading makers of minicomputers and of the seven mainframe computers.

22 Information supplied by IBM's Data Processing Division. Readers will recognize the impracticality of including details concerning operation of the system here. Such information is available from IBM's Data Processing Division in White Plains, New York 10604 or from branch offices in various areas.

23 Helpful suggestions regarding installations of one type of electronic equipment are provided in "What to Look for When You Install Electronic Front Ends," Progressive Grocer, May 1975, p. 54.

24 W. N. Mitchell, *The Business Executive in a Changing World* (New York: American Management Association, 1965), p. 77.

25 For general treatments of leasing versus purchase, see D. B. Romans, "Why Leasing Is Becoming So Popular," *Nations Business*, June 1975, pp. 74–75 and J. T. Leathan, "No Letup in Leasing," *Conference Board Record*, March 1974, pp. 61–64.

26 "New Stores Down by Four Percent in 1976," *Chain Store Age Executive*, January 1976, p. 16.

27 *1975 Annual Report*, p. 22.

28 "New Stores Down by Four Percent in 1976," and "1976 Uncertain for Food Chains," *Chain Store Age Executive*, January 1976, pp. 17–18.

29 "New Marsh Store to Anchor Downtown Boston Complex," *Chain Store Age Executive*, June 1975, p. 22.

30 On this topic see "Stores Guide to Design," an 11-page special on store planning and visual merchandising. *Stores*, June 1976, pp. 2–12.

31 Valuable suggestions on "How to Get More for Your Remodeling Dollar" during periods of high costs are given in a summary with this title in *Progressive Grocer*, May 1975, p. 56.

ARRANGING THE STORE'S INTERIOR—LAYOUT

In the previous chapter, some of the factors involved in preparing the store building for use were developed. In the present one, attention is devoted to its interior arrangement or layout; more specifically, with arranging and locating the merchandise, fixtures, and equipment to provide the desired standard of customer service at the lowest cost to the retailer. In other words, the goal is to maximize space productivity.

■ DEFINITION OF AND FACTORS INFLUENCING LAYOUT

The layout of a retail store refers to the arrangement of equipment and fixtures, merchandise, selling and sales-supporting departments, displays, aisles, and check-out stands where needed in proper relationship to each other and in accordance with a *definite plan*. According to this concept, stores that have "just grown" on a haphazard basis are not actually "laid out" despite the fact that, broadly speaking, they are arranged in a particular manner.

☐ Factors influencing layout

The layout of any retail store is affected by such factors as (1) the size and shape of the space to be occupied, including the number of floors; (2) the location of the unloading dock or area, elevators, escalators, and other permanent installations; (3) the kinds and amounts of merchandise to be handled; (4) the type of operation to be employed, such as self-service; (5) the characteristics and buying habits of the clientele to be served; (6) the nature and quantity of the fixtures and equipment to be installed; (7) the personal preferences of the retailer; and (8) general economic conditions in relation to activities of competitors.[1]

In considering the foregoing factors, the retailer will seek a layout designed: (1) To make the store as attractive, inviting, and convenient as possible to the customer; and (2) to provide the most effective and efficient utilization of the space. Special emphasis will be placed on the sales promotion aspect of layout, including maximum exposure of goods to sale. This is especially the case in discount stores and supermarkets. An important exception to this rule is exclusive specialty shops where the layout is deliberately planned to hide merchandise from the customer's view. In one store, for example, the only ready-to-wear shown is that displayed on a few mannequins; the merchandise is brought by sales personnel to customers who sit at small tables. Such personal service is possible in only a few retail stores; most retailers find it too expensive.

□ Increasing emphasis on layout

Among larger stores, the desire to gain more sales space at the expense of their nonselling areas,* the development of stores in shopping center malls, the "shop within a shop" concept and boutiques, new kinds of fixtures and equipment, and the tremendous growth of simplified selling, self-selection, and self-service, among other reasons, have outmoded old store arrangement patterns and resulted in more attention to and far-reaching changes in the layouts of stores of all types. Currently, layouts are being designed to permit easy access to merchandise by customers; to facilitate selection through grouping of related items, which permits comparison of brands and prices; to allow for future expansion of the store; to permit greater flexibility; to provide for the needs of aged and handicapped persons; and to provide sufficient checkout stands and trained cashiers to insure fast customer service in the light of current electronic developments. Moreover, retailing literature has continued to stress the importance of layout while retail trade journals, trade association literature and meetings, the obvious success of other stores which have changed their layouts, and the efforts of equipment and fixture manufacturers—all of these, and others, have made

---

* Goldblatt, Inc., a 39-store regional operation centering in Chicago, experienced a significant improvement in both sales-per-square-foot and margins after increasing sales areas 20–30 percent in a number of its stores.

both large and small retailers more conscious of the need to study layout problems.*

■ LAYOUT PROCEDURE

To accomplish the main purposes of layout we have mentioned, a logical procedure is essential. Appropriate steps include a survey of space requirements; a review of the characteristics of satisfactory layouts; visits to other stores; the securing of recommendations from equipment and fixture manufacturers, merchandise resources, store engineers, and architects; and the tentative location of selling and sales-supporting departments on paper for review. In addition, the layout should remain sufficiently flexible to allow for adaptations to the changing needs of both the customers and the retailer.

In going through these steps, it is usually desirable that the retailer be guided by a competent store architect and, in some instances, by an engineer. The large retailer may employ well-qualified architects and engineers, although on many occasions even these need to be supplemented by outside experts who can bring in a "fresh" point of view. The small retailer usually hesitates to engage an architect because of the added cost, but a competent architect can often recommend cost savings which more than offset any fee.

□ Survey space requirements

Sales forecast This step requires an estimate of sales, both immediately and in the future. (Refer back to "Estimated volume of business," pp. 97–99.) A retail firm planning a new store may estimate the sales volume that may be obtained at a particular location. This will be determined by the size of the total market, the extent to which customers may be drawn away from competitors, and the attractiveness of the firm's particular offerings for that market. Market research, the use of government statistics, and observation of both customers and competitors are helpful in making the sales forecast. Once the immediate sales forecast is at hand, the minimum square footage of the store can be determined by dividing into it what experience has indicated is a reasonable projection of sales-per-square-foot based on the merchant's previous experience (if any), cost trends, trade association data, and studies

---

* Note, however, the following statement regarding food stores made some years ago but still relevant: "Although store design and layouts change, equipment developments advance, and methods of merchandising are altered, the important reasons for store selection by shoppers—everyday low prices, convenience of location, quality and freshness of meats, variety and selection of merchandise, and friendly personnel—have remained reasonably constant over the years." "Super Markets of the 70's," *Progressive Grocer,* July 1969, p. 58.

reported in trade papers. If a substantial future sales increase seems likely, provision should be made to enlarge the area at a later date—perhaps by a new wing to the building or by adding a floor or floors. To make such a step practicable, the Macy store illustrated in Figure 5–7 was constructed strongly enough to carry one additional floor.

In estimating space requirements for a new store or in considering changes in the location or size of departments in an existing one, the retailer should avoid one error which is all too common—the idea that a high figure for sales-per-square-foot can be attained merely by constructing a large store without worrying too much about its layout. As a matter of fact, large stores frequently waste space simply because they have so much of it.

Checklist of space needs A valuable guide in analyzing space requirements is a detailed checklist of the merchandise, functions, and facilities for which space must be provided within the store. This list, naturally, will reflect store policy and procedure. Moreover, the kinds and amounts of merchandise stocked and the services rendered will depend on the type of store. But, in general, each retailer should ask if, to illustrate, space for the following has been provided:

1. Merchandise departments, including the necessary space for storing, displaying and selling goods in appropriate fixtures and on shelves.[2]
2. Sales-supporting departments of all types—receiving and marking goods, reserve stock storage space, deliveries, returns and adjustments, storage of supplies, and similar activities.
3. Comforts and conveniences for customers and employees.
4. Office space, including areas for purchase of merchandise.
5. Workroom space.
6. Heating, lighting, air conditioning, and ventilating equipment and fixtures.
7. Stairways, elevators, and escalators.
8. Aisles wide enough to permit free flow of customer traffic.
9. Window space of the form or type desired, if any.
10. Suitable areas for EDP equipment and other demands of the new technology.

In reviewing this checklist, the prospective store proprietor will find that the experiences of other retailers are very helpful. For example, the prospective supermarket retailer can benefit from the information available from the Food Marketing Institute; the department store from that furnished by the National Retail Merchants Association; and the hardware store from that supplied by the National Retail Hardware Association.

An illustration of the assistance provided by the latter organization is a suggested approach to the utilization of sales space. It begins with two basic questions: (1) Is each department in the store producing sales in proportion to the space it occupies? (2) Do you (the proprietor) really know how much space each department takes . . . what it contributes to total sales?[3] After the square footage used by each department is obtained and its percentage of the total is found, its share of total sales should be calculated. These figures may then be compared with the average for the industry as a whole (see Table 6–1) for whatever action is advisable.

TABLE 6–1

Sales dollars versus sales space—How are you doing?

Department	Percent of net sales	Your figures	Percent of sales-floor	Your figures
Hardware	11.3%		11.8%	
Hand and power tools	9.9		8.8	
Plumbing	10.2		9.1	
Electrical	8.2		7.0	
Paint and sundries	12.3		11.0	
Housewares	16.0		21.9	
Sporting goods	9.0		9.7	
Lawn and garden	12.2		11.9	
Automotive	3.2		3.0	
Lumber/building materials	11.8		7.8	
Major appliances	11.5		9.6	
Other departments	12.0		11.6	

Source: 1973 Management Report published by the Retail Hardware Association and given in *Hardware Retailing*, © September 1975, p. 109.

☐ Review characteristics of good layouts

The desirable characteristic of a good layout from the point of view of both the customer and the retailer should be reviewed carefully.

Customer point of view   A logical basis for sound layout decisions should be consumer satisfaction. In other words, the needs and expectations of potential customers together with their shopping habits, more than any other factor, should dictate the retailer's arrangement of the store's interior.

Generally speaking, customers want an attractive place in which to shop, convenient access to merchandise throughout the store, aisles wide enough to prevent crowding during normal business days, freedom from obstructions that prevent a general view of the floor, related merchandise together, similar locations of merchandise in the stores in which they concentrate their purchases, infrequent changes in the location of departments, privacy for the fitting of garments, and daylight rather than artificial light to judge the color of certain merchandise. Stores that cater primarily to customers of one sex but wishing to attract those of the other sex (for example, a men's clothing store that wants to sell tailored suits for women or a department store that operates a sizable men's wear section or "men's store" catering mainly to male customers) should design a layout that permits the latter to enter such sections directly without having to pass through areas in which they may feel uncomfortable.

Developing a layout to meet customer wishes is not always easy, a point which is illustrated by the problems encountered by department stores in bringing together related merchandise. At first thought, it may seem easy to set up a bath shop (with "everything for the bathroom," from towels and bath mats to marbletopped lavatories) and a "wilderness recreation shop" (including men's and women's hiking and camping clothing as well as equipment). But such arrangements immediately raise a number of questions (more fully discussed in Chapter 7), such as: Who buys the men's clothing for the shop—the shop personnel or the buyers in the men's clothing department? Can a seller in the shop be trained to sell both men's and women's clothing as well as equipment? Will garments on sale in the shop be duplicated in the apparel departments?

In practice, there is no single answer to any of these questions. For instance, some stores let the sport shop personnel do all of the buying for the shop, while other retailers spread that function among the regular department buyers. But each store must find its own answers since this practice of classification merchandising and selling by category continues.

Retailer point of view Although customers' preferences are vital in laying out a store, other considerations are also important. Because of the increase in night and Sunday openings, shorter working hours, and the higher rates of pay received by employees in recent years, layouts which will increase employee productivity are required. Consequently, store plans are sought which will reduce both the time required to complete sales transactions and the amount of walking necessary by customers and salespeople.

To encourage self-selection and impulse buying, layouts designed to facilitate the movement of traffic throughout the store are increasing in number. Many recently modernized stores have adopted the so-called "wandering aisle," which replaces the more or less straight aisles with a series of circular, octagonal, or oval counters around which traffic moves so that more merchandise is brought into the customer's view. Others have moved in the opposite direction, to a mall-type or wide central aisle which encourages the flow of traffic in a predetermined pattern. Under such an arrangement, each department in the store fronts on this main aisle, with two advantages: (a) The department is easily located by the customer; and (b) the department can use this front as a promotional spot.

The relation of layout to profit is suggested by the efforts of many retailers to place high-margin merchandise where it gets maximum customer exposure. One self-service retailer found that since the first two aisles near the entrance carried the most traffic, the better margin-yielding departments were moved to these areas with a resulting gain in profits. Other retailers have discovered that the amount of merchandise of a particular kind displayed on a shelf, as well as the location of the shelf in the store, is important from a sales point of view and have rearranged their stocks to take advantage of this fact. Still others, such as discount houses and supermarkets, make extensive use of gondolas, i.e. sections or units of shelving of various height, length, and depth designed to attract customers and encourage examination of the merchandise shown, and main-aisle displays to feature special offerings of seasonal merchandise often advertised.

Figures 6–1, through 6–4 illustrate layouts in various stores intended to meet the needs of both customers and the retailer. To make certain that the characteristics of good layouts are carefully considered for each new store and that existing ones are frequently reviewed to determine if changes are advisable, many retailers have developed checklists.

FIGURE 6–1   **Men's shoe department in branch store in Millcreek Mall, Erie, Pennsylvania**
Note attractive displays. Compare with Figure 6–2.

Courtesy Kaufmann's, Pittsburgh, Pennsylvania

FIGURE 6–2 Layout of shoe department in Gemco discount store in Tucson, Arizona Note wide variety of shoes displayed and space for customer circulation.

Courtesy Lucky Stores, Inc.

FIGURE 6–3 Interior view of section of Emporium-Capwell Company branch store in Salinas, California Note wide aisles and extensive use of display fixtures.

Courtesy Emporium-Capwell Company

FIGURE 6–4 **Part of the standard layout of a Long's Drug Store** Note wide aisles and numerous displays of easily accessible merchandise.

Courtesy Long's Drug Stores

Sources of information on layouts A study of available literature on store arrangement is invaluable to the retail merchant. Such action provides knowledge of the opinions of authorities on the subject concerning the desirable characteristics of good layouts and also of current developments in this field. Such sources as the United States Department of Commerce (including the Small Business Administration), trade associations and trade magazines in the retail field,[4] equipment manufacturers, and periodicals such as *Architectural Record* provide numerous services useful in solving layout problems.

☐ Visit new stores of same type

Although most written material on store arrangement includes diagrams and illustrations to facilitate understanding, many retailers find it advisable to visit new and recently-remodeled stores similar to their own and to observe the layouts and the flow of traffic. They are then in a better position to judge the wisdom of arranging their stores along similar lines.

☐ Secure recommendations from outside sources

Recommendations of manufacturers from whom equipment, fixtures, materials, and merchandise have been or may be purchased are valuable guides in deciding upon the arrangement of the store's interior. These firms are well qualified to make suggestions based upon their experience in solving such problems and upon their researches in this field. Some of them, voluntary-chain wholesalers and equipment manu-facturers, for instance, have developed prototype layouts for stores of different sizes, which are available to the retailer. And a few have con-structed small-scale model fixtures and equipment to enable the retailer to visualize exactly how the store will look. Because of their interest in selling store equipment, or in promoting the sale of the manufacturers' products, no charge is ordinarily made for these services.

□ Locate selling and sales-supporting departments

In locating each particular selling and sales-supporting department the major considerations are as follows: (1) Providing the best possible service to customers based on their known buying habits;[5] (2) establish-ing the most effective coordination of selling and sales-supporting ac-tivities; and (3) maximizing the selling area in relation to other functions. Their basic objective, of course, is to increase sales and minimize expenses.

Locating particular departments is commonly done through the preparation of diagrams or blueprints, because of the convenience af-forded in visualizing relationships of departments and the ease with which plans may possibly be changed. It should be noted, however, that regardless of the care exercised in drafting the proposed layout, unless it is based on a well-thought-out selling policy founded upon one's own experience or that of others it may be doomed to failure. It is helpful, also, both in planning the layout and in judging its effectiveness, for the retailer to obtain the ideas and opinions of associates whose judgment is valued.

A specific example How selling and sales-supporting departments in a department store may be placed in close proximity to each other is well illustrated in Figure 6–5. Designed to provide the maximum in economy and efficiency, the main feature of this arrangement is a "magic core" occupying 36,000 of the store's 297,000 square feet of floor space. Despite its size, customers are almost unaware of the core because it is partially hidden by display counters. Yet all the facilities for handling merchandise and customer traffic are present. Each of the three main shopping floors has two levels in the "magic core" and the upper one (the mezzanine) is connected with the floor on which the goods will be sold. Goods are carried by elevators to the mezzanine where they are checked and marked. Then they are sent to the appropriate stock-room on the same floor or delivered by chute to the level below.

Variations in space value within a store Wide variations in the value of space exist in different parts of the store with respect both to sections of a single floor and to floors, when more than one floor is occupied, a fact well known to management. Particularly in large stores, the equi-table assignment of values to specific areas or sections is a continuing

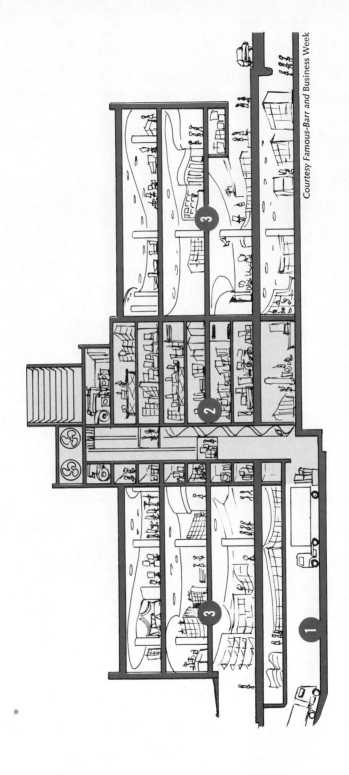

FIGURE 6–5 An illustration of the "magic core" of Famous-Barr's Southtown store in St. Louis, Missouri A truck ramp leads to the basement platform (1), where goods are unloaded and later stored on various levels of operating core (2), then fed to the various sales floors (3).

Courtesy Famous-Barr and Business Week

problem.[6] These values are based upon the management's estimate of the sales and profit possibilities of each area and thus are chiefly arbitrary in nature. Generally speaking, space charges decrease from the front to the rear of a one-story building and as one moves away from the traffic lanes. In multiple-story structures, the charges assigned to each floor decrease as the height of the floor increases; that is, space on the second floor is less valuable than space on the first, and so on.

□ Layout flexibility

Once the layout of the store has been decided, the problem is by no means permanently solved. As noted, even the original layout should give the retailer the maximum degree of flexibility to make future changes. Adjustments may also be necessary because of shifting seasonal demands, changes in buying habits and in tastes of customers, and new policies and practices of competitors. Or, it may be advisable to expand the areas where merchandise is growing in popularity and to shrink that devoted to items losing in customer acceptance. Furthermore, analysis of developments may dictate the conversion of certain departments or areas to self-service. (See also the discussion of self-service on pp. 164–69.) "Change is the order of the day" in retailing, and store layout is not exempted from this rule.

In this connection an official of the J. C. Penney Company recently commented: "Every square foot of retail space is being examined and challenged . . . steadily rising rentals, sharply increased construction costs, higher wages . . . , energy and environmental considerations plus the very high cost of money have combined to put the efficient use of space under the microscope. Sales per square foot, one good measure of store productivity, is high on the priority list of most retailers."[7]

□ Floor plans of various stores

A suggested layout for a hardware store, reflecting consideration of the steps discussed, and intended primarily to stimulate the thinking of the retailer in arranging the store and afford the necessary security against pilferage, is shown in Figure 6–6. The layout in Figure 6–7 shows the first three floors and basement of the five-floor F. W. Woolworth Company store in Boston, the company's largest. Finally, Figure 6–8 provides a detailed plan of a supermarket revealing location of selling and nonselling departments and other facilities.

A comparison of the layouts in Figures 6–6 to 6–8 with those of other retailers will suggest that there is no ideal layout which will meet the needs of all stores handling the same kinds of merchandise. Local circumstances and individual preferences markedly influence the particular arrangement adopted. Some chain-store organizations, however, have

FIGURE 6–6   A "typical" hardware salesfloor plan?

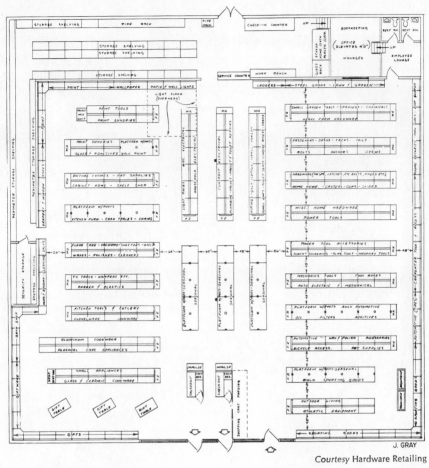

J. GRAY

Courtesy Hardware Retailing

adopted some standard layouts with a resulting economy in the cost of opening new stores. To illustrate, Colonial Stores has developed five different sizes of standardized layouts for food stores in the process of which all the steps we have mentioned were taken. Final decisions were made by a store-planning committee. These standardized arrangements are changed periodically to incorporate improvements and suggestions from store personnel.

■ DISPLAY: A MAJOR FACTOR IN LAYOUT

As already mentioned, layout may be considered a form of sales promotion. An effective layout facilitates sales from the point of view

FIGURE 6–7 **Layouts of three floors and basement of F. W. Woolworth Company's Boston store, largest in the chain with 133,400 square feet of space** The selling floors are topped by a four level 1,000 car-capacity parking garage.

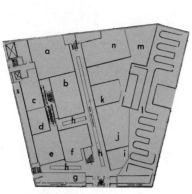

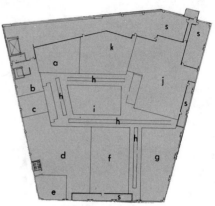

First floor. a- toiletries; b- cosmetics; c- handbags; d- hair goods; e- style accessories; f- jewelry; g- hosiery; h- promotional mdse.; i- novelties; j- candy; k- delicatessen; l- restaurant; m- stationery; n- gift shop; s- stockroom areas; *store entrance.

Second floor. a- music shop; b- plants; c- pet shop; d- toys, books, and games; e- hobby shop; f- fabric and sewing shop; g- bedding-bath-curtains; h- promotional merchandise; i- kitchen wares; j- home decor lines; k- household lines; and s- stock areas.

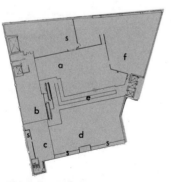

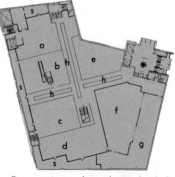

Third floor plan. a- sporting goods; b- tools and paints; c- men's and boys' shoes; d- men's and boys; e- promotion mdse.; f- offices and employees quarters; s- stockroom areas. (Main stock area located in sub-basement, not shown).

Basement. a- shoe dept.; b- ladies dept.; c- sportswear; d- infant's and toddler shop; e- intimate shop; f- restaurant; g- utilities; h- promotional merchandise; s- stockroom areas; *subway-level store entrance.

Courtesy The Merchandiser/Magazine of Mass Retailing

of both the customer and the store proprietor and display considerations are inseparable from layout. Display means simply that goods are exposed to customers to facilitate observation, examination, and selection —and the way a store displays its merchandise has much to do with its sales volume. (See also the discussion of "Interior Displays" in Chapter

FIGURE 6–8 Detailed floor plan of King's Supermarket, Forest, Virginia This was selected "store of the month" by *Progressive Grocer* in March 1976.

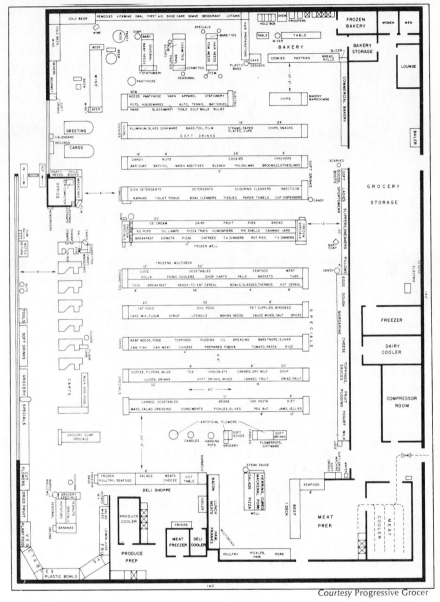

Courtesy Progressive Grocer

18.) A study of over 300 shoppers in New York City department and specialty stores some years ago revealed that about one-third of them entered these stores without any intention to buy. Attractive merchandise displays, however, induced over half of this group to make purchases.

Since most types of retail stores carry large assortments of merchandise, management is faced with problems concerning the amount of display and the kind of display to give certain items. As noted in the next section, discount houses and supermarkets display a wide variety of merchandise in considerable quantity to invite inspection and to encourage purchase. But display problems are not easy ones to solve, since, at some point, the variety of merchandise becomes confusing to the customer. In addition, many retailers must decide on the best time and the length of time to display certain merchandise. As is true in other areas of responsibility, however, certain general rules are available for guidance.

□ Types of interior display

The primary purpose of interior display is to enhance sales and profit possibilities within the store; but the type of display for any specific item or group of items depends upon such characteristics as perishability, bulk, value, risk of breakage, packaging, danger to customers, attractiveness, seasonableness, and fashion. The significance of these factors can be demonstrated with a few examples from various kinds of merchandise, as follows: While cured meats can be openly displayed without special equipment, fresh meats demand refrigeration; passenger-car tires, which are bulky, may be displayed with little thought of the danger of theft, but pilferage is a consideration for small items which can be slipped into a pocket or handbag; valuable jewelry usually requires closed display cases; mechanical toys may be damaged if they are available for everyone to handle; packaging encourages open display in that it makes the merchandise more attractive and reduces the possibility of deterioration. Special precautions should be taken for items which create hazards—poisons should be out of the reach of customers and heavy items may be dangerous if hung on display over store aisles. Unattractive items, such as bulk vinegar in a food store, may not even be placed on display. As for seasonableness and fashion, it is evident that the time factor and fashion rightness are decisive factors.

Display variations by type of store Wide differences exist among retail stores in planning their interior displays and in the frequency with which they are changed to promote the sale of specific merchandise. Discount houses, food, and drug stores, for example, make extensive use of "merchandise islands" in their layouts—that is, tables, counters, cases, or a small group of any or all of these—upon which merchandise is displayed and which are surrounded by adequate aisle space. Many of the display materials (racks, stands, signs) placed on these aisle tables are provided by merchandise sources. Shelves and racks are also used extensively to display wares with less-frequent use of closed display fixtures, such as cabinets or cases. The latter are commonly employed by department stores and specialty shops. Jewelry stores, camera stores, and others handling expensive merchandise enclose their displays to provide the necessary protection.

Food and discount stores, among others, place considerable emphasis upon displays as "silent salesclerks"; upon the merits of "talking signs" which give convincing reasons for purchase; upon "mass displays" for the purpose of impressing the customer with the quantity of items sold at a particular price;[8] upon "dining-room" displays illustrating the product(s) in use for delicatessen and dairy products; and upon the arrangement of merchandise items in a manner designed to induce customers to pick them up, as opposed to balanced symmetrical arrangements designed chiefly for decorative purposes.

Other types of retail stores are guided in their display problems by such considerations as the following: (1) The type of product, its value, size, and appeal to the buyer; (2) the purpose of the display, i.e., the actual sale of the article or the creation of prestige or "atmosphere"; (3) suitable location; (4) attractiveness; (5) timeliness as related to seasonableness; and (6) desired frequency of change.[9] Originality and distinctiveness should continually be sought by most stores in order that they may be set apart from their competitors.

☐ Exterior displays

Although some retailers have long made use of out-of-door displays —for example, food stores and the department stores of Sears, Roebuck and Company—today there is also a strong trend for many other kinds of retailers to employ exterior displays. Branch department stores, many discount houses, the so-called home and garden stores, and supermarkets typically have their own parking areas which serve as locations for displays of lawn and garden supplies and tools; plants, shrubbery, grass, seeds, and weed killers; automobile tires and tubes; Christmas trees and other seasonal items. In general, such displays are rather crude, boxes of the merchandise being placed on the parking area surface or on plain tables. Frequently the display is unprotected from the weather, although canopies—either canvas or permanent—are also being used.

Outside display offers such advantages as (1) inexpensive selling space (2) opportunity to show additional merchandise in natural settings, (3) a place for bulky and untidy goods, (4) visibility to a greater number of potential customers, and (5) customer convenience, since much of this merchandise is not suited to shopping cart usage.

☐ Aisle tables

We have noted that many retailers use "merchandise islands" in promoting the sale of certain articles. When tables are located in the main aisles of the store and used as islands, as is often done in department and specialty stores, they are referred to as "aisle tables." Many supermarkets and discount stores use such tables or similar equipment to display "specials" currently advertised.

Aisle tables may be used to display either regular or special merchandise. In a service store, they usually have a salesperson regularly assigned to each and a cash register is placed on or near the table. When tables are arranged in units of four in the form of squares and when merchandise is offered at reduced prices or at featured prices as a regular practice, they are known as "bargain squares." Some stores prefer the "Y" arrangement.

Whether or not a store uses aisle tables will depend largely upon the type or types of merchandise handled, upon the clientele to which the store caters, and upon the desire of the store management to avoid congestion in customer traffic, particularly during busy periods such as the holiday season.

■ SELF-SELECTION AND SELF-SERVICE

A major problem associated with store arrangement concerns the retailer's decision regarding the extent to which access to merchandise will be allowed customers to permit them to serve themselves, with aid being provided by sales help if needed. This decision obviously influences the entire layout of the store as well as the kind and amount of store equipment and fixtures purchased.

□ Definition of terms

When a store is operated on a *self-selection* basis, merchandise is so displayed and arranged that the customer can make a selection without the aid of a salesperson. Typically, open display shelves and tables are used, frequently supplemented by racks, stands, and islands. Once the selection is made, the merchandise is usually taken to a nearby cashier-wrapper or salesperson who takes the further steps necessary to complete the sale. This type of operation long characterized such variety stores as F. W. Woolworth and S. S. Kresge although they have turned increasingly to self-service in recent years.

Under *self-service* operation the customer not only selects the items desired, but brings them to a check-out stand where payment is made and the purchases wrapped or "sacked." Credit, delivery, and other special customer services commonly found in service stores ordinarily are not offered by the self-service store, since a low operating cost is one of its major goals. Although, technically speaking, the term "self-service store" should refer to one with all of its sales on this basis, many stores described by this name handle a substantial amount of business on a service basis. To illustrate: Many self-service discount stores provide salesperson service for jewelry, cameras and supplies, major appliances, and for bakery products, meats, and fruits and vegetables in their supermarket areas.

For some years it has become customary, especially among department and specialty store retailers, to speak of *simplified selling*. Within the scope of this term they include both self-selection and self-service—and much more, such as better fixtures, improved layouts, more effective packaging, displays which lead to increased sales, and techniques and devices to speed up sales transactions. So broad is this usage that, for present purposes, we shall limit our discussion to self-selection and self-service as defined above; however, we should recognize that where self-selection and self-service techniques are used, many of the other aspects of simplified selling are also involved. (See also the discussion of "Requirements for self-selection and self-service," later in this chapter.)

☐ Historical development

Contrary to much current opinion, neither self-selection nor self-service operations are particularly new, especially the former. As mentioned, self-selection has long been used in variety stores. Moreover, for years the trend in stores of many types has been toward open displays which encourage self-selection. Yet self-selection has been widely adopted since World War II and today it is practiced in varying degrees by stores of practically all types.

In food stores The self-service plan of operation was employed by a few grocery stores in southern California at least as early as 1912. Immediately after World War I, the Piggly-Wiggly grocery stores began to expand on this basis. Moreover, there were some early successes in the ready-to-wear and drug fields; the S. Klein store in New York City and the Pay-Less Drug Stores on the Pacific Coast are good illustrations.

Despite this earlier development, as late as 1927 only two of the major food chains in the Los Angeles market—the area in which self-service first developed to any significant degree—used the self-service method. Consequently, we may conclude that it was during the depression of the early thirties, which also saw the development of the supermarket, that self-service became popular in the food field. As retailers sought ways to reduce their costs, they were naturally attracted by any method which would lower their payments for wages—the greatest single item in the cost of operating a store. The trend was further encouraged by the personnel shortage of World War II and by the "profit squeeze" of the 1960s and early 1970s. By 1970, 79 percent of some 7,380 supermarkets surveyed by the Super Market Institute were found to be fully self-service in all four major departments—grocery, meat, produce, and dairy—an increase of 10 percent since 1964.[10] This trend has probably continued.

In other stores Following the success of self-service in food stores, and recognizing that "service" provided by the salespeople in many stores leaves much to be desired, self-service has been adopted by many kinds of stores handling a wide variety of merchandise and operating independently or as chains. Among those now offering self-service in some or all of their departments are department stores, discount houses, and stores selling drugs, variety merchandise, shoes, stationery, and home furnishings. To take a few specific illustrations: In 1975 Walgreen's, continuing its expansion and diversification program, operated 616 drug stores, most of the newer ones being self-service. Its Globe Division ("Shopping Cities") consisted of 25 full-line self-service department stores.[11] And the 1975 Annual Report of the J. C. Penney Company notes that "Making the most of our store space is a challenge approached in many ways" including two directly related to self-service: "fixturing that puts more merchandise within the customer's reach and packaging that facilitates self-service where appropriate." In the stores operated by R. H. Macy and Company the basements have been almost completely converted to self-service and self-selection operations. Moreover, while retaining personal selling for major home appliances and higher-priced fashion merchandise, the trend is still in the direction of additional stores and departments on the self-service principle.

□ Requirements for self-selection and self-service

Experience with self-selection and self-service reveals that among the factors essential to success are the following:

1. Sound merchandising decisions made in advance regarding the following: (a) the basic stocks to be carried with particular reference to styles, types, price lines, sizes, and colors; (b) the amount of space that will be required for each style, size, and price line; and (c) the extent to which feature items will be used and the importance that will be given to them.
2. Good fixturing. The merchandise to be stocked will govern the types of fixtures to be used. Sometimes good fixtures prove unsatisfactory because of improper use.
3. A layout which allows for, and encourages, the flow of customer traffic.
4. Adequate check-out facilities.
5. Well-filled stocks and appropriate signs. Unbalanced stocks, poorly designed signs, and incorrect prices irritate customers and lose sales.

6. Attractive packages. Because competition for the customer's attention is strong under self-selection and self-service arrangements, attractive packages are essential.
7. Cooperation of personnel. When a shift to a self-service plan is contemplated, resentment within the department or store will be minimized if the personnel involved are kept fully informed.
8. Training of personnel in new duties. Particular emphasis should be placed on the need for proper coverage of the floor to provide satisfactory service to customers and to prevent pilferage, currently at an all-time high.

In general, arrangement of a store for self-selection or self-service operation is motivated by the same considerations which determine the layout of any store—that is, attractiveness and convenience from the customer point of view, exposure of merchandise for sale, and satisfactory sales volume and economical operation from the point of view of the retailer. But attainment of these goals is no easy matter and, whether a new store is being opened or the conversion of a service store into one providing less service is being weighed, the favorable and unfavorable elements of the self-selection and self-service plans should be studied carefully. So far as self-service is concerned, these elements, many of which are also applicable to self-selection, are summarized in the next two sections.

Merits of self-service operation   The chief merits of self-service operation are as follows.

1. Generally speaking, stores arranged on the self-service plan have wider aisles with fewer obstructions, thus encouraging circulation of customers and minimizing congestion in customer traffic.
2. Many customers prefer self-service because it enables them to leisurely examine merchandise, make selections based upon their own judgment, and overcome their dependency on salespeople who may lack the courtesy and helpfulness expected.
3. Fewer salespeople and other personnel are required, thus reducing selling expenses and personnel problems.
4. Economies in operation make it possible to sell at lower prices than other stores and to appeal to customers on this basis.
5. Self-service arrangements permit larger and better displays of merchandise which, in turn, contribute to greater sales.
6. Customers of self-service stores purchase more at one time, both in amount and in variety, than patrons of other stores. This occurs because customers shop in a more leisurely manner and examine more merchandise and because self-service encourages impulse purchasing.

Limitations of self-service operation   The publicity given to successful stores and departments using the self-service plan frequently has resulted in failure to consider the shortcomings of this type of operation, such as the following:

1. Since self-service arrangement requires more floor space for a given sales volume than the counter-service plan, the physical makeup of the store—its size, shape, and location—may not be adaptable to self-service.
2. Many customers prefer to be served by salespeople and dislike having to locate specific merchandise and bring it to the check-out counter.
3. The large sales volume of some stores creates congestion at check-out points, especially during rush periods. The result is both inconvenience for the customer and more errors by the check-out operators.[12]
4. Since self-service arrangement and operation are most successful in stores catering to middle- and low-income groups and offering well-known brands of packaged merchandise, retailers appealing to upper-income groups and selling unadvertised goods which are not customarily packaged find it difficult to operate profitably on the self-service plan.
5. Shoplifting and common thievery are easier and more prevalent in self-service stores, and consequently losses are greater. Presently, this is a problem of some magnitude.
6 Certain types of high-priced products such as mechanical durable goods, drug prescriptions, women's hats, and many other items, require the advice and service of salespeople. Nevertheless, the experience of discount houses reveals that many customers like to serve themselves even when buying such items as shoes, dresses, and millinery.
7. An impersonal atmosphere is common in the large self-service store and the shopper may fail to develop any emotional attachment or loyalty toward it.

□ Future prospects

The recent tremendous increase in self-selection and self-service seems likely to continue in the foreseeable future. Moreover, further improvements in techniques will undoubtedly be developed. To illustrate, one of the present serious problems of self-service operations is that the shopper must bring purchases to the check-out point. In this process, pilferage takes place, merchandise is damaged, customer time is involved and fatigue results. Yet many stores are taking these risks to reduce the substantial payroll costs that service by salespeople involve. Even prestige stores have adopted it.[13] One authority, however, more than a decade ago was convinced that mechanization will eventually make it unnecessary for the shopper to bring purchases to a check-out point.[14]

All conversions to self-selection and self-service, however, are not —and will not be—successful. Despite the care with which they are planned, conditions in every case may not be suited to such methods of operation. A case in point is the experience of Famous-Barr Company in St. Louis. Some years ago check-out merchandising operations were instituted on an experimental basis in the basements of three stores. Discontinued two months later, management reported the check-out failed because of (1) the high-fashion level of much of the merchandise, (2) the large share of "big ticket" items sold, and (3) inability to handle efficiently the large number of transactions on peak days.

In general the future of self-selection and self-service will depend mainly upon (1) the continued willingness of customers to serve them-selves in return for the savings they realize on their purchases; (2) im-provements in fixtures, displays, and package design that will enable customers to locate and examine desired items more easily; (3) the in-creasing diversification and expansion in merchandise lines by such organizations as the food and drug chains; and (4) the conviction of retail store management that these methods afford excellent opportu-nities to increase sales, reduce expenses, and alleviate some of their problems in the continuing increase in operating costs.

■ REVIEW AND DISCUSSION QUESTIONS

1 Define layout in your own words and state concisely the major factors which influence the layout of a specific store.

2 How do you account for the increased emphasis given store layout in many stores during recent years?

3 What do you consider to be the major problems regarding layout facing department stores today? Compare these problems with those of super-markets.

4 Visit a branch store in or near your local community and diagram its layout. If possible, compare this layout with the main or parent store of the com-pany which owns it. If this is not feasible, compare it with another store of the same type in your vicinity. Give special attention to location of specific departments, size of space devoted to particular merchandise, width of aisles, and use of displays.

5 Outline in sufficient detail to make your meaning clear the steps in a logical layout procedure.

6 Evaluate critically the suggested approach to the utilization of sales space in hardware stores shown in Table 6–1.

7 What is the relationship of store display to layout? Explain how the type of display employed by a store depends upon each of the following: value of the item, perishability, staple or impulse character of the item, packaging, and profitability.

8 Compare and contrast the interior displays typical of self-service food stores with those of department or specialty stores.

9 Distinguish among self-selection, self-service, and simplified selling. Explain the factors responsible for the growth of these methods.

10 Discuss briefly the basic requirements of a successful self-service operation. Appraise a local self-service store in the light of these requirements.

■ NOTES AND REFERENCES

1 The significance of this latter factor among supermarkets is evident from the following comment in the *1976 Annual Report of the Grocery Industry:* "The cosmetic skills of designers and architects were applied to 3300 supers last year as an antidote to the tired blood evidenced by older stores. Among independent supers, 11.6 percent reported that they had enlarged their selling areas in 1975." See *Progressive Grocer,* April 1976, p. 131.

A significant development in this connection relates to the interior arrangement of a new 60,000 square feet store by Ralph's in Northridge, California. For details, see "Ralph's Store within a Store," *Chain Store Age Executive,* December 1976, pp. 15–17.

2 Some interesting studies on shelf position and the allocation of shelf space have been made during the past decade. Among these are R. F. Frank and W. F. Massy, "Shelf Position and Space Effects on Sales," *Journal of Marketing Research,* vol. 7 (February 1970), pp. 59–66; K. K. Cox, "The Effect of Shelf Space Upon Sales of Branded Products," *ibid.,* pp. 55–58; and J. A. Kotzman and R. V. Evanson, "Responsiveness of Drug Store Sales to Shelf-Space Allocations," *ibid.;* vol. 6 (November 1969), pp. 465–69. See also R. C. Curhan, "Shelf Space Allocation and Profit Maximization in Mass Retailing," *Journal of Marketing,* vol. 37 (July 1973), pp. 54–60.

3 The allocation of 88,375 square feet of selling space in a new Woolco store is described in "The Woolworth/ Woolco Pattern for Growth," *The Discount Merchandiser,* August 1975, pp. 25–34.

4 See, for example, "What Makes a Good Store Layout?", *Progressive Grocer,* January 1976, pp. 68–73.

5 See Part III of a report on "Consumer Behavior in the Super Market" by the *Progressive Grocer* entitled "What Makes a Good Store Layout?" in the January 1976 issue. Data on the effectiveness of some newer arrangements provided by measuring traffic patterns of customers are presented. Earlier segments of this report are given in the October and November 1975 issues.

6 The allocation of rental charges to specific departments is discussed in Chapter 24.

7 In Ben Gordon, "The Customer Isn't Always Right," *Chain Store Age Executive,* July 1974, p. E6. See also "J. C. Penney: Getting More from the Same Space," *Business Week,* August 18, 1975, pp. 80–88.

8 A recent development of interest among such stores is the increasing use of gondola ends or end-cap fixtures in high traffic locations to stimulate impulse buying. "No fixture can do more to start sales, catch the eye or draw traffic into a department. . . ." See "Are You Wasting the Sales Appeal of Gondola Ends?", *Hardware Retailing,* September 1975, p. 148; also "Attract Sales with Exciting Gondola Ends," *ibid.,* July 1975, p. 63.

9 These considerations and others are developed and illustrated in E. M. Mauger, *Modern Display Techniques* (New York: Fairchild Publications, Inc., 1965).

10 *The Super Market Industry Speaks 1970* (Chicago: The Super Market Institute, 1970), p. 22.

11 *Fairchilds Financial Manual of Retail Stores 1975,* p. 18.

12 One study some years ago disclosed that errors were made on 11.3

percent of all the items "rung up" by the check-out operators of food stores, the final result being an undercharge equal to 0.7 percent of sales. See E. M. Harwell, *Checkout Management* (New York: Chain Store Age Publishing Co., 1963), p. 7.

13   See "Prestige Store Goes Self-Service," *Chain Store Age* (executive edition), September 1968, p. 50.

14   See E. B. Weiss, "Robot Retailing Inches Along," *Advertising Age*, April 5, 1965, pp. 131–32.

Retail organization

STRUCTURE OF THE
RETAIL FIRM

Every business has to have a structure or organization to perform its work. Retailing firms often find that establishing the proper organization is particularly complex and troublesome, since such businesses usually engage in *many* separate transactions with *many* individual customers, sometimes employ *many* workers, perhaps at *many* locations, and often handle *many* different items from *many* suppliers. Consequently, coordination of all of these activities is both important and difficult. The organizational plan used will vary with such factors as size, kinds of merchandise sold, services rendered, and preferences and desires of the executives. But the plan for any retail business—a three-person company with little division of labor or a giant enterprise with thousands of specialists—must meet the company's individual requirements. Moreover, a plan that was satisfactory at one point in a firm's history may be unsuitable at a later date; the structure must be adaptable to changes in fundamental conditions.

This chapter, therefore, (1) discusses the meaning of "organization," (2) examines the various plans that retailers have developed to meet their specific needs, and (3) notes some major trends in retail organization.

■ THE MEANING OF "ORGANIZATION"

Organization has been defined in various ways.* One expert describes organization as including "a structure or network of relationships among given individuals."[1] Other authorities include personnel selection as a part of organization.

Probably the most useful approach for our purposes is to define "organization" in terms of its component parts. Using this approach, we may say that organization involves four aspects, as follows:

1. Arranging the activities that the retailer has decided to perform in convenient groups for assignment to specific individuals.**
2. Providing for the selection of the personnel to whom the activities will be assigned.
3. Assigning responsibility for each group of activities and determining the authority that is to go with the responsibility.
4. Providing for control of and harmonious adjustment among the individuals to whom responsibilities are assigned.

This chapter discusses three of these four aspects of organizational structure, while personnel selection is among the topics considered in the next chapter.

□ Organization charts

The preparation of a written or printed organization chart is an important step in planning or revising the firm's structure, since drawing the plan on paper exposes inconsistencies, forces clear thinking, and encourages logical arrangement. The organization chart shows the formal relationship within the firm and helps everyone visualize the company as a whole. Montgomery Ward and Company's organization manual aptly describes the value of carefully prepared organization charts:

A company's success and progress are in great measure related to the efficient utilization of the efforts of its management representatives. To achieve success we must adhere to a plan which clearly establishes areas of responsibility and lines of authority within the company's structure. To provide complete understanding and consistent interpretation, it is necessary that this organization plan, by which the company operates, be set forth in writing.

---

* Our discussion here is concerned with organization for *operation*, or *administrative* purposes. For detailed discussion of the concept of *legal form of organization* (in other words, use of single proprietorship, partnership, and corporate forms of ownership) consult any standard business organization or business finance textbook.

** The *selection* of the particular activities which a specific retailer will undertake —for example, credit extension, comparison shopping, and delivery service—is a matter of *policy*, not of organization.

[Our] charts and accompanying [job] descriptions mirror the plan for guiding and controlling the activities of the business. . . .

It is essential that you be completely knowledgeable about your authority and responsibility. It is also important that you know the functions, responsibility and authority vested in other management positions. . . .

You are expected to become familiar with this manual. In so doing, you will be better able to view your individual activities in relation to all Company activities. You will be better able to visualize how your specific actions affect other segments of the business and the attainment of Company objectives, and how your own areas of responsibility are affected by the actions of other managers.[2]

Although organization charts are highly useful for all types of retailers, and particularly so for the larger ones, some of their limitations must also be recognized. An organization chart should not be mistaken for an organization. A firm may have a fine-appearing chart and still fail to function effectively. A business organization is a group of human beings; attention must be paid to their individual personalities as well as to the formal relationships shown on the chart. Members of different departments must constantly work together and cooperate in handling joint problems and activities without referring every question to their individual superiors as shown on the chart. These day-to-day relationships are often called the "informal organization" and are very important to the successful conduct of the business. And, as indicated below, organization charts must be revised frequently in fast-moving, everchanging businesses such as retailing.

☐ Organization plans must be flexible

The organizational task is never completed. Different structural patterns may be required as the firm adds or drops activities, as the number of branch stores changes, or as various merchandise lines gain or lose importance. Management may discover a better way of grouping present activities, or become convinced that the business will function better if the lines of authority are shifted. The idea of a "plural" chief executive was unknown a few years ago, yet a number of firms now divide the chief executive's functions among two or three individuals who operate as a team.[3]

But the fact that the organization plan probably will have to be changed in the future never eliminates the need for careful preparation of the current structure. Good organization defines the relationships of the various departments, specifies each unit's authority and function, determines responsibility for the various objectives of the firm, encourages specialization of effort and the development of skill in particular tasks, facilities planning, reduces waste effort and increases productivity.[4]

■ ORGANIZATION IN THE SMALL STORE

The structural requirements and organizational problems of small stores differ greatly from those of the large retail businesses.

The term "small store" covers a variety of establishments that range from the individual newsstand, the gasoline service station with several attendants, and the neighborhood grocery store, to more complex businesses that employ a fairly large number of people. We will use the term to indicate stores that are too small to be divided into separate departments.*

The small retail store usually carries on fewer activities than its large competitor: It may provide fewer services; often carries a narrower variety of merchandise; may have a more limited advertising program or none at all; and probably uses less elaborate planning techniques. Consequently, it can have a much simpler organizational structure.

Moreover, there will be much less specialization of labor in the small store. In the one-person store, all aspects of organization center around the question: How can the store owner best plan *the use of his or her own time?* And even where there are several employees, each will be expected to perform a wider range of duties than is customary in the large establishment. In contrast, the large retailer must assign specific responsibilities to many different persons, determine each one's authority, and provide for harmonious adjustment of all the different parts of the business.

Figure 7–1 illustrates the restricted activities and limited specialization typically found in small stores.** It shows the organization of a store employing four persons in addition to the proprietor. Although this organizational plan is very simple in structure, it provides all three aspects of organization discussed in this chapter: It groups the firm's activities for assignment; it gives individuals authority and fixes their responsibility for carrying out activities; and it provides—in the person of the proprietor—a means of control and of making any necessary adjustments among the store's personnel.

■ LARGER FIRM ORGANIZATION

In larger firms, such as department stores and chain stores, the organizational problems result from the variety of merchandise handled, the numerous functions performed, the specialization of personnel, and the

---

* The small department store (a large establishment in comparison to the stores mentioned above) is discussed below, along with other types of departmentalized stores.

** Comparison with Figures 7–2 and 7–3 will demonstrate the way activities tend to increase with store size.

FIGURE 7–1   Organization of a small store

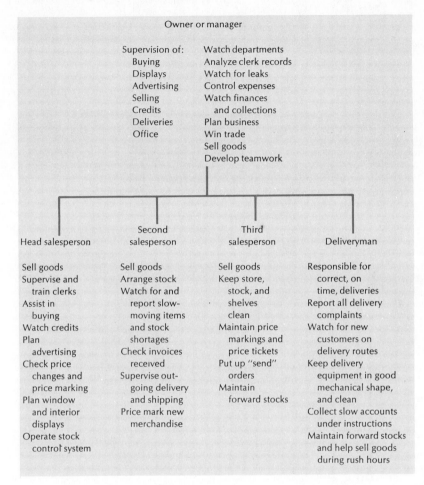

need for coordination and control of all of the firm's activities. We should particularly note two aspects of organization in the large retail business: (1) The store's merchandise is divided into groups or departments so that the buyers and sales staff can become specialists in handling particular types of goods. Departmentalization can be useful even in fairly small stores;[5] it is an absolute necessity in large ones. (2) As the firms grow in size, the owners and top executives spend less and less time performing day-to-day tasks, such as buying, selling, preparing advertisements, or designing displays. Instead, they increasingly concentrate on planning for the future and on coordination and control of the executives and workers who perform the daily tasks. Both of these topics are discussed below.

☐ Departmentalization

As stores become larger, the proprietors have increasing difficulty in maintaining close contact with each line of merchandise, and become less able to locate (and eliminate) the weak spots in their merchandising activity. Consequently, they departmentalize; that is, they divide their merchandise into a number of groups or departments, each of which operates as a more or less separate unit. Information about the store's operations becomes more meaningful when broken down on a department-by-department basis; and each department can be placed under a middle-management executive (buyer or department head) who concentrates on that merchandise line and perhaps closely-related ones.

The advantages of logical and systematic departmentalization can be summarized as follows:

1. Customers can more easily find what they are seeking.
2. Management is simplified.
3. Better control is possible over each part of the business.
4. Responsibility is more easily assigned among personnel.
5. Salespeople can be assigned by departments and specialize in selling a line of merchandise.
6. Specific assignment of responsibility to salespeople gives them a greater incentive to work and to take a greater interest in the business.
7. Any part of the business can be checked at any time.
8. Profitable lines are revealed.
9. Unprofitable lines are brought to management's attention.
10. Profitable average margin can be maintained.
11. Margins can be easily adjusted on each kind of merchandise.
12. Necessary markup can be computed for each line.
13. Inventory is more easily controlled.
14. Stock turnover is increased.
15. "Leaks" and losses are more easily located and checked.
16. Larger profits are obtained.

Steps in departmentalizing The following steps are usually followed in departmentalizing the store:

1. The merchandise is divided into well-defined and related groups. Most stores use relatively traditional and similar groupings. Consequently, even new customers are likely to know which section or department will handle any specific item they want.
2. A decision is made as to the number of departments and the groups of merchandise assigned to each department. The number depends upon the size of the store and the variety of goods handled, but each department usually handles a complete line of two or more related smaller lines. Creating too many departments is a mistake.

3. Each department is assigned a location within the store. The customers' buying habits, the types of merchandise involved, and the size and shape of the available space influence the selection of these locations.
4. Henceforth, many of the store's records are kept on a department-by-department basis and the business results of each department are analyzed separately:
   (a) Each department is charged with its direct expenses, such as the wages of its own sales staff. Indirect expenses, such as rent, light, heat, and power, are often allocated to the various departments on some reasonable and equitable basis. (Methods of allocating expenses to departments are discussed in Chapter 24.)
   (b) The gross margin—the difference between merchandise cost and net sales—that each department obtains is recorded. Different margins will be realized on various items in a department, but the department head will try to sell a satisfactory amount of high-margin merchandise in order to increase the operation's profit or minimize any loss.
   (c) Purchases, returns to vendors, sales, price reductions, and customer returns are recorded on a departmental basis.

Problems of departmentalization Although departmentalization is helpful to both customers and stores, it involves two serious problems. One is the question of borderline merchandise that might fit in two or more departments: Should ladies' fur-trimmed coat-style sweaters be sold in the coat department or in the sportswear department;[6] should tablecloths be sold in the domestics (linens, towels, etc.) department, or in the "tabletop" (china/glassware) department;[7] should digital watches, be sold in the electronic calculator department or in the jewelry department?[8] Sometimes the answer is to let both departments handle the disputed products, particularly if they sell different styles or brands obtained from different suppliers. But this tends to increase total inventory, can lead to embarrassing situations if price differences develop from department to department and also irritates some customers who wonder why the total selection is not available in one place.

The other problem arises because a customer who must assemble a set of items for a particular purpose may be forced to visit many different traditional departments to get the desired merchandise. To illustrate: A ski enthusiast may want to buy a pair of skis (normally sold in sporting goods), stretch ski pants (men's or women's sportswear), ski hose (hosiery), and an overnight case (luggage). Many stores now try to bring all these items and other related products together in ski shops, so as to provide better service and make shopping easier for the customer. Similarly, large stores have developed cruise shops, sports shops, gun shops, bath shops, junior miss shops, and many other types of specialized sections to match customer interests.

But this regrouping in terms of customer interests also has serious disadvantages. Different customers buy similar items for different purposes. Skis are very specialized, in that they are only bought for skiing, and so present no problem of classification. But some people might want the ski pants in the above example for ordinary sports or campus wear and will want to compare them with other similar clothes in the sportswear department. Similarly, the overnight case might be used by a skier on a ski trip, by a college student going back to school or by a business traveler for a sales trip. Yet the store will have difficulty in offering a good, convenient selection, even with excess inventory, if the suitcases are scattered between the ski shop, the cruise shop, the college shop, the gift shop, and the luggage department. Moreover, many customers who are used to traditional departmental groupings have considerable difficulty in trying to learn new classifications. A highly innovative clothing and home furnishing store that opened in Kansas City in 1973 with three main groupings—merchandise for leisure time and casual living on the first floor, elegant merchandise for gracious living on the second floor, and contemporary items on the third floor— found that its customers often tended to look for traditional categories rather than learn the new system.[9]

Finally, regrouping creates an organizational problem. Who should be responsible for buying the assembled items; and if the task is divided among specialists, who will coordinate them? Should there be a separate buyer for the ski shop discussed above (an extra expense) or should the regular sporting goods, clothing, hosiery and luggage buyers (each of whom is a specialist in a particular line) handle the buying? Stores are experimenting with both plans, but neither system is perfectly satisfactory. The customer, assortment, and inventory problems are even more pressing. So the best rule is to set up specialized or regrouped departments (often called "boutiques") when, and only when, they serve clearcut needs of a substantial number of customers.

□ General management

The top executives of large retail organizations must devote their time and efforts to general management's major function of providing leadership and direction for the firm, while their subordinates oversee the day-to-day operations of business. The prime obligations of general management are: (1) To formulate and announce basic policies; (2) to direct, correlate and coordinate the activities of the various divisions, so that the business operates effectively and profitably; (3) in accordance with the previous step, to approve the selection, promotion and reassignment of subordinate executives; (4) to exercise final authority over the budgets established for each major division; (5) to make decisions (subject to approval by the board of directors) concerning the firm's future growth and expansion; and (6) to represent the business in major civic, social, and public activities. The proprietor or head of a small store can give only limited time to these functions, but the chief executives and general management of a large enterprise can give these responsibilities their full attention. See the further discussion of the coordinating functions of general management in Chapter 27, "Management coordination and leadership."

■ DEPARTMENT STORES

Although the two major types of large retail businesses, (1) department and departmentalized specialty stores and (2) chain stores exhibit many organizational similarities, there are also some differences between them. Consequently, we will first study department store organization and then turn to the special characteristics of chain stores. We should note, however, that in recent years the growth of suburban branches (See the discussion of branch store organization, pp. 190–91) and other factors have caused many department store firms to adopt some of the features of chain store organization.

The larger department store businesses, which produce by far the major share of total department store sales volume, have all the elements of large-scale retailing: wide range of activities, departmentalization, many staff functions, intensive specialization of labor, and all operating duties located below the general management level. In contrast, the small department store has at least one similarity to other small establishments—the general manager often takes direct charge of either merchandising or operating activities.

□ Small department stores

Small department stores often use a two-function plan that separates such operating activities as store maintenance, adjustments, and deliveries, from the merchadising tasks of buying and selling. Figure 7–2 shows this organizational structure. The specific responsibilities of the merchandising-sales promotion director and the store operations director are discussed at greater length in connection with the description of large store organization, pp. 186–89. This plan also provides for two staff officers, a combination treasurer-controller and a personnel director, who report directly to the general manager or proprietor. These two officers have store-wide duties; placing them in staff positions permits them to carry out their activities without interfering with the line executives' day-to-day operating functions.

The organization plan shown in Figure 7–2 is well suited to the small department store. It is simple and uncomplicated, yet it establishes a desirable degree of specialization. It permits the personnel director to

FIGURE 7–2 **Two-function organization chart for a small department store**

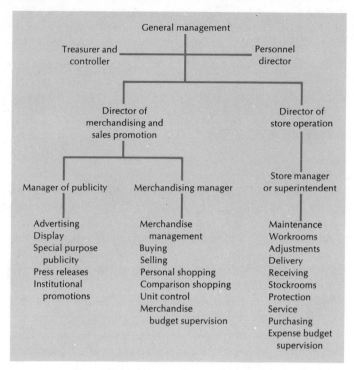

function on a store-wide basis; it centralizes responsibility for control activities in the treasurer-controller; and it unifies buying and selling activities. The specialized publicity manager reports directly to the director of merchandising and sales promotion, so that publicity work is closely integrated with the whole merchandising process.

□ Four-function or Mazur Plan

Many medium-sized and large department stores use a four-function plan, illustrated in Figure 7–3, that divides the store's activities into the following groups: (1) merchandising, (2) publicity, (3) store management or operations, and (4) accounting and control. This widely accepted organizational structure is often called the Mazur Plan in honor of its proponent, Paul Mazur, an investment banker and chairman of a National Retail Dry Goods Association special committee on store organization.[10]

The Mazur Plan is more complex than the two-function structure suggested for small department stores, but it permits greater specialization and a wider range of activities. Some weaknesses have led to

FIGURE 7-3 **The four-function organization chart of a department store**

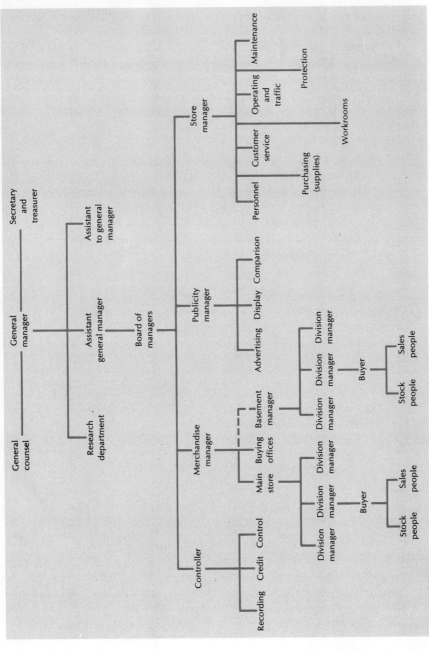

Source: Adapted from Paul M. Mazur, *Principles of Organization Applied to Modern Retailing* (New York: Harper & Bros., 1927), frontispiece.

changes and modifications in some stores, as discussed later; but first we will analyze the traditional roles of each of the four major divisions.

Merchandising division This division is responsible for all buying and selling activities. Top management usually considers it to be the "heart" of the business and gives it the greatest amount of attention.

1. *Merchandise managers* The general merchandise manager, who is in charge of this division, supervises merchandising activities in all locations, including the main store, the basement store, and buying offices.* Next are several divisional merchandise managers, their number depending on the size of the store and the number of departments, who supervise groups of related and adjacent merchandise departments. The divisional merchandise managers work closely with their buyers (or department managers), coordinating the departments, guiding the buyers' merchandising plans, and helping the buyers evaluate present and future merchandise and sales trends. More specifically, the general and divisional merchandise managers have the following functions and responsibilities:[11]

a. Interpret and execute the merchandising policies of the company.
b. Unify the efforts of all buyers or department managers so as to present a single "image" to the buying public.
c. Assist each department in planning and carrying out its individual buying plans.
d. Supervise other departmental activities and provide each buyer with an objective view of departmental needs and performance.
e. Aid buyers to get and use current information regarding business trends and market conditions.
f. Assist buyers in locating and developing new resources.[12]
g. Establish and administer a merchandise-control system.
h. In cooperation with the publicity or sales promotion division, plan sales promotions.
i. Plan and supervise comparison shopping (unless it is assigned to the publicity division).

2. *Buyers or department managers* Under the Mazur Plan, the buyers have major responsibility for buying and selling activities within their departments and consequently are very important individuals in the merchandising operation. Their buying duties generally include preparing preliminary merchandise plans or budgets under the guidance

---

* Department stores traditionally operated their basement selling floors as lower-priced "budget," "economy," or "downstairs" stores, usually with their own merchandise managers and buying staffs. Many surban branches have been built without such units, while the downtown stores have taken diverse approaches: some have extended the economy method of operation by adopting self-service checkout techniques for the basement; others no longer try to maintain a special price policy in that part of the store and simply use it as additional selling space for regular merchandise.

of the divisional merchandise manager; making contacts with manufacturers, wholesalers, and other sources of merchandise; studying fashion trends and price movements; obtaining proper qualities and grades of merchandise in styles suited to the customers' tastes, securing deliveries of merchandise at the proper times; and making purchases at prices which permit resale at a desired markup.

The buyer's responsibilities for selling activities include: Planning the number of salespeople needed for one's department; determining their qualifications; and, in cooperation with the personnel department, maintaining the proper-size selling force at all times. Buyers give the salespeople information about the department's merchandise and about fashion trends in general. They supervise the department closely; cooperate in preparing merchandise displays; and do everything possible to insure customer satisfaction and departmental profitability.

But the buyer does not have sole responsibility for sales efforts, even under the four-functional plan. Problems often arise because the selling function is actually divided among three major divisions: the merchandising division, as indicated; the publicity divison, with its advertising and display efforts; and the store management division, which has responsibilities for customer service and for recruiting and maintaining a satisfactory sales force. The growth of branch stores, which often extends the department's sales efforts to a number of remote locations, also makes it difficult for the buyer to be an effective sales manager. Consequently, as discussed later in this chapter, many stores are now moving away from the Mazur Plan and are particularly changing or reducing the buyer's responsibilities for sales activities.

Publicity division The publicity (or sales promotion and advertising) division is responsible for all selling efforts not classified as personal selling. Specifically, its responsibilities include:

1. All forms of advertising.
2. Window displays.
3. Interior displays, usually excluding counter displays.
4. The planning and executing of sales-promotion events, in cooperation with the merchandising division.
5. Special forms of sales promotion, such as fashion shows and educational exhibits.
6. Advertising research.
7. Public relations.
8. Comparison shopping (unless assigned to the merchandising division).

The publicity or advertising manager, who heads this division, works with the personnel department to recruit, train, and maintain an adequate advertising and display staff. This executive supervises the methods used in special forms of sales promotion and tries to devise special events that are more interesting and effective than competitors'. Such work requires very close cooperation with the merchandising division which generally selects the items to be featured in the store's advertising. Because of this, many stores make the publicity division virtually subordinate to the key merchandising executive.

Store management or operating division This division, headed by the store manager or store superintendent, covers a greater variety of activities than any other. In fact, it is usually responsible for all activities not directly associated with buying, selling, accounting, or financial control. Its duties have actually increased over the years as it absorbed functions the other divisions refused to assume.

The store manager is usually responsible for the following functions:

1. Store maintenance.
   a. Construction.
   b. Repairs and renovations.
   c. Maintenance of mechanical equipment.
   d. Ventilation, including air conditioning.
   e. Heat, light, and power.
   f. Janitor service.
2. Customer service.
   a. Adjustment bureaus.
   b. Service superintendents.
   c. Floor service supervisors.
   d. Personal service bureaus.
3. Operating activities.
   a. Receiving, checking, and marking.
   b. Stock rooms.
   c. Warehouses.
   d. Shipping rooms.
   e. Deliveries.
   f. Returned goods.
4. Purchasing of store supplies, equipment, and other property.
   a. Supplies needed for store use.
   b. Fixtures and equipment of all kinds.
   c. Fuel.
5. Store and merchandise protection.
   a. Special service operators.
   b. Night security personnel.
   c. Service shopping.
   d. Outside protection agencies.
   e. Insurance (in cooperation with control division or treasurer).

6. Personnel.*
   a. Employment.
   b. Training.
   c. Compensation.
   d. Health and welfare.
   e. Employment stabilization.
7. Workrooms.
   a. So-called "Cost departments," such as restaurants, soda fountains, beauty shops, and drapery workrooms. These are called cost departments because they normally use the cost method, rather than the retail inventory method, of determining profits and loses. (See Chapter 23.)
   b. Manufacturing departments, such as candy and ice-cream making, and bakeries.
   c. Expense workrooms, such as laundries and employee cafeterias.

Control division   The controller, or occasionally, the treasurer, heads this division. This officer's chief tasks are to protect the company's assets and to obtain adequate working capital to meet the needs of the business. Detailed responsibilities of this division usually include:

1. Devising and maintaining adequate accounting records.
2. Planning, taking, and calculating the physical inventory.
3. Credits and collections.
4. Merchandise budgeting and control (in cooperation with the merchandising division).
5. Expense budgeting and control.
6. Development of procedures to provide the desired control.
7. Preparing reports for general management.
8. Insurance (often the responsibility of the treasurer).
9. Safekeeping of all records prepared by or furnished to the division office.
10. Familiarity and compliance with governmental rules and regulations, city, state, and federal.
11. Preparing reports for governmental and other agencies.

Increased responsibilities   The controller's responsibilities and prestige have increased greatly in recent years. The duties have widened and many specialized assistants have been added as a result of the growth of credit transactions, the increased use of electronic data-processing and scientific control methods, and the increasing complexity

---

* There has been a definite trend in recent years toward removing the director of personnel from under the jurisdiction of the store manager and making the personnel officer a major executive reporting directly to the general manager. See p. 193 below.

of federal and local tax and other regulations. The expansion of functions and personnel is illustrated by the fact that in many stores the credit department alone now employs as many people as the entire control division did a few years ago.

□ Changes in department store organization

Since World War II particularly, many department stores have deviated from the Mazur Plan or adopted other organizational structures to meet changing conditions. Three of the major changes have been: (1) Adjustments made necessary by the growth of branch stores, (2) separation of buying and selling activities, and (3) changes in the number of divisions. A fourth change, the expansion of staff services, is discussed separately later in this chapter.

Branch organization The development of branch stores, which now account for more than two-thirds of all department store sales, presents difficult organizational problems for their parent companies. No single best method of coordinating parent and branch operations has yet emerged, but three general patterns are quite clear.

1. *"Brood hen and chick" organization* Under this plan, the parent store organization operates the branch. The parent-company publicity director advertises for the branch; the controller and store superintendent perform their functions for both parent and branch store; and parent-store buyers are responsible for all buying. Those buyers continue to have direct supervision over selling activities in the main store. They also strongly influence or even control such work in the branches, although the branch department sales supervisors are supposedly under the direction of the branch managers. The "brood hen and chick" plan is usually followed for the first few branches, especially if they are considerably smaller than the parent store.

2. *"Separate store" plan* As the number of branches increases or as they grow in size, however, the "brood hen and chick" structure soon reaches its obvious limits. The parent-store buyers cannot continue to absorb the additional work load indefinitely. At this point, a few firms—especially those with large branch units—have decided to treat each branch as a separate store with its own management and buying staffs. This plan provides maximum flexibility and adjustment to local conditions, but it involves multiplication of management and buying salaries, travel costs, and other expenses. The separate store arrangement also reduces the stores' combined buying power and interferes with efforts to build a consistent "store image" for the parent and branches. Bullock's of Los Angeles, long the best-known advocate of this plan, has now changed to more closely-coordinated operations.[13]

3. *"Equal store" structure* Most firms with numerous branches have

moved in the opposite direction and centralized major management functions, *including buying,* at a single headquarters. For reasons of economy, the executive and buying offices are usually, but not invariably, in the same building as the downtown store. However, the buyers and other central executives have no special relationship or duties in connection with the downtown selling departments. Selling responsibilities are separated from buying* and the downtown store and the various branches all become sales units with equal organizational status. As we shall see, the "equal store" structure (illustrated in Figure 7–4) follows chain-store organizational principles. Although department stores are still experimenting with various branch store structures and modifications, the "equal store" plan is becoming dominant as the number of branches increase. This central control arrangement seems the most likely to give department store organizations the economies and efficiencies of chain store systems.

Separation of buying and selling responsibilities As we have noted, department stores that use the Mazur Plan or other traditional structures give the buyer or department manager responsibility for both buying and selling activities. The major arguments for combining these functions are:

1. Separation of buying and selling will result in lack of responsibility for department profits.
2. The person who buys the merchandise should be responsible for selling it.
3. The buyer needs direct consumer contact for good information about consumer wants.
4. Only the person who buys the merchandise can convey the necessary information and enthusiasm to the salespeople.
5. Separation is too expensive, since it makes dual staffs (sales managers and buyers) necessary.

Reasons for separation Despite these arguments, department stores now tend to separate buying and selling responsibilities. The growth of branch stores has been the prime cause for this trend, since buyers cannot supervise sales activities in a number of locations and still perform their buying duties properly. But the following arguments for separation are relevant even when there are no branches:

1. Buying and selling are different jobs which require different types of ability, personality, and training.
2. Combining buying and selling has resulted in buying becoming predominant and overshadowing selling.
3. Suitable emphasis on selling can be obtained only by setting up a sales organization which is divorced from buying.

---

* See the discussion of separation of buying and selling immediately following.

FIGURE 7–4 **An organization model for department or specialty stores with four or more selling units**

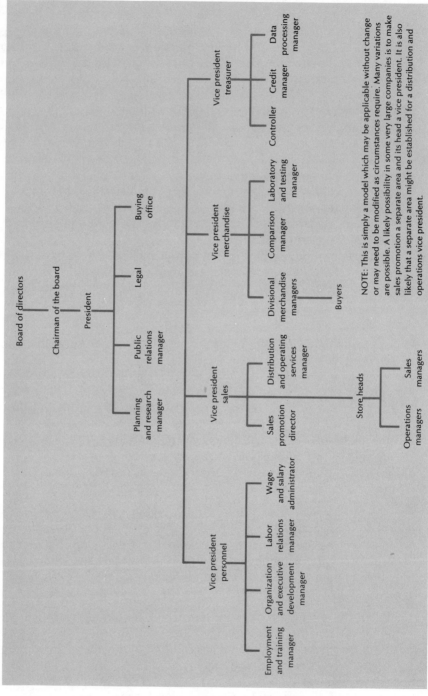

NOTE: This is simply a model which may be applicable without change or may need to be modified as circumstances require. Many variations are possible. A likely possibility in some very large companies is to make sales promotion a separate area and its head a vice president. It is also likely that a separate area might be established for a distribution and operations vice president.

Source: Milton Woll, "Store Organization: How to Build in the Capacity for Change," *Stores*, October 1961, p. 20.

4. Separation of buying and selling works well in chain stores, even those handling fashion merchandise.
5. Modern merchandise-control systems can now provide proper coordination even if different persons are responsible for buying and selling.
6. The regrouping of merchandise into such combinations as cruise shops, sport shops, gun shops, and ski shops suggest that the best combinations of goods for buying purposes are not necessarily the most strategic combinations for sales purposes. (See the discussion of departmentalization problems on pp. 181–82.)
7. Separation of buying and selling makes it easier to shift salespeople among departments according to need.
8. Frequently one person can buy efficiently for several departments, but then will have little time to handle the selling function.

Organization for separation   Various organizational plans have been used to separate buying and selling activities. In one plan, with complete separation, both a merchandise director who heads all buying and a sales director who heads all personal selling and publicity report directly to general management. Other retailers have left the merchandise manager responsible for both buying and selling, and made the separation at lower levels. Under this arrangement, one of the merchandise manager's subordinates supervises all buying and another supervises all sales work. The key executives' personal preferences, the personalities involved, the particular needs of the firm, management's willingness to experiment, and the size of the business tend to influence the decisions on how (and whether) to divide sales and buying responsibilities. In some firms junior- and middle-level executives (up to and including people at the store manager and divisional merchandise manager level) may move back and forth between sales supervisory and buying posts.

Changes in the number of divisions   Many stores have raised the personnel function to major divisional status, with the director of personnel reporting directly to top management. This change, which makes personnel a fifth division in stores that otherwise use the Mazur Plan, is due to the increasing complexity of personnel activities and problems—the result of new labor legislation, growth of labor unions, shortened working hours in spite of expanded store hours, rising wages, development of new training techniques, and the need to improve the employees' productivity.

The separation of buying and selling, discussed above, often also adds another division to the traditional pattern. Some stores, however, have reduced the number of divisions; others have simplified their organization (at least at the upper levels of the charts) by concentrating responsibility in just three or even two divisions. Publicity and sales promotion are frequently made subordinate to merchandising in the three-divisional organization. All activities are concentrated in merchandising and store operations in the two-divisional firm.

□ Ownership groups

Some leading department stores, once independently-owned and operated, have been merged into ownership groups such as Federated Department Stores, Allied Stores Corporation, Cities Stores Company, Mercantile Stores Company, Dayton Hudson Corporation, and Carter Hawley Hale Stores. These groups differ from chains of more or less uniform stores, such as Sears' and Montgomery Wards' department stores, discussed later in this chapter. Actually, they are department stores which have usually been in existence for a long time and which were gradually brought together under common ownership. The stores retain their original name, in most instances, and few customers are aware of the group ownership.* Some of these corporations now also own chains of supermarkets, discount stores, or specialty outlets and are truly retailing "conglomerates."

While management responsibilities in some ownership groups have been centralized much as is true of chain-store operation, in most of them—Federated Department Stores, for example—the stores have retained many of the management functions they had when they were individual units. Each parent store (each major division of the group) typically has its own merchandising, publicity, operations, and control divisions. The group's central management establishes basic policies and provides certain services—such as financing, research, central market-buying facilities, exchange of operating statistics. In addition, it helps each store set overall goals, thereby stimulating local management to improve its operating results. A small staff of experts at central headquarters can help the stores solve various problems. However, the central managements of these groups currently seem to be increasing their influence over basic decisions, although the individual units still have considerable autonomy.[14]

---

* For example, Federated Department Stores' 18 major divisions include The Boston Store (Milwaukee), Bloomingdale's (New York), Abraham and Straus (Brooklyn, N.Y.), Bullocks-Magnin Co. (California), and Shillito's (Cincinnati) as well as Ralph's supermarkets on the West Coast. Allied Stores Company includes Bon Marche (Washington, Oregon and Utah), Jordan Marsh (Boston and Miami), Joske's (Houston) and Donaldson's (Minneapolis-St. Paul) as well as other divisions in other cities. McAlpin's (Cincinnati), Jones (Kansas City), Gayfer's (Alabama and Florida) and Lion (Toledo, Ohio), are part of the Mercantile Stores Co. The Carter Hawley Hale Stores Inc. group include Broadway, Emporium and Capwell stores (California), Nieman Marcus (Texas, Florida and Georgia), Holt, Renfrew and Co. (eastern and central Canada), Bergdorf Goodman (New York) and Sunset House (mail order).

■ CHAIN STORE ORGANIZATION STRUCTURE

Chain store companies vary in organization because of differences in types of merchandise handled, in services performed, in size of individual retail units, and in territory covered. Company policy, past experience, and the executives' preferences and personalities also influence organization structure.

□ Some common characteristics

Most chain store companies have the following characteristics:

1. Major responsibilities are centralized in the headquarters or home office, regardless of the chain's geographic spread. Decentralized responsibility for sales is the chief exception to this rule.
2. The organization is divided into more main divisions than is typical of department stores. These often include real estate and maintenance, merchandising (buying), sales promotion, store operations, personnel, control, and, perhaps traffic, transportation and warehousing and others.
3. Trained and capable executives are employed to direct these divisions.
4. Recognition of the personnel division's importance, and appointment of the personnel director or manager as a major executive. As noted, many department stores are now following the same policy.
5. Careful supervision and follow-up of store activities.
6. An elaborate system of reports to keep headquarters informed on operations and to enable the executives to maintain effective control over all activities for which they are responsible.

□ An apparel chain

Many of the common chain store characteristics may be found in the organizational structure of a 100-store apparel chain. This company's stores are divided into 10 districts, with a manager for each store, and a field manager or supervisor for each district.

There is a clear-cut division of duties between store managers and field managers. The store manager's main function is the sale of merchandise that has been selected and purchased at the chain's headquarters. The store manager actually makes some sales personally, hires and trains a sales staff of 4 to 20 persons, arranges store displays, and reports daily sales to headquarters. The field manager, the connecting link between headquarters and the store, hires store managers, takes physical inventories, checks displays, and gives the buyers at head-quarters the store managers' requests for merchandise to meet local demand.

At headquarters, a merchandise manager, aided by five buyers and eight divisional distribution managers, supervises buying and merchandise control. Each buyer purchases a specific type of merchandise, such as dresses or hosiery. The divisional distribution managers then control the shipment of this merchandise to the stores, with each manager responsible for 10 to 20 stores. Purchases and shipments are based upon the information contained in the stores' daily sales reports (including ticket stubs for all items sold), and the buyers' and distribution managers' knowledge of styles, prices, and consumer buying trends.

□ A variety store chain

A national variety store chain has a relatively similar structure. The president is charged with the overall administration and coordination of the company's operations. Policy decisions made by the president involve close attention to analytical studies conducted by the research manager and to legal advice obtained from the general counsel. The treasurer is responsible for handling company funds, arranging for financing, and the purchase and management of insurance.

Six operating officials also report directly to the president. The controller's responsibilities are similar to those of a department store counterpart (see pp. 189–90) except (1) there are no credit and col-lection problems since this firm sells for cash, (2) the treasurer handles insurance problems, and (3) supervision of the physical inventory count is a function of the retail operations department. The advertising director prepares the basic advertising budget, subject to top management ap-proval, and then plans and initiates sales and promotional campaigns within the budgetary limits.

The merchandise manager is concerned with the buying of mer-chandise and supplies and with related activities. The merchandising division establishes retail prices and prepares merchandise bulletins for store managers. In this particular firm, it is also in charge of company-operated warehouses and supervises shipments; although in some large chains, these duties fall to other executives.

The actual operation of this chain's retail units falls to the director of retail operations, although the director of real estate and maintenance is responsible for obtaining the stores, planning layouts, installing fix-tures, and maintenance. All district managers report to the retail organi-zations director, and each store manager to the appropriate district manager. Finally, the personnel director performs duties comparable to those already outlined on page 189 for the department store.

□ Some other chains

Figure 7–5, which shows the basic organization structure of Colonial Stores, Inc., a 400-store regional food chain, and Figure 7–6, which shows part of Montgomery Ward and Company's organizational plan, illustrate other facets of chain store organization. Both show the separation of selling (store and mail-order) activities from buying and merchandising; both show the existence of a large number of staff and advisory functions; and both show more divisions reporting to the president than is customary in department store organizations. Figure 7–6 is especially interesting in showing how Montgomery Ward has faced the problem of integrating chain-store and mail-order activities.

The individual store managers in these, and other chains, are supervised by district or area managers (various titles are used in different firms) who have been successful store managers themselves. The district manager's main task is to help each store manager operate more effectively. Regional officials or vice presidents then coordinate the work of the various district managers. Figure 7–7, based on part of The Kroger Company's organization plan, shows how district product specialists work in a staff capacity to advise and assist both store managers and the respective product department heads within the stores.

□ Centralization and decentralization

Chain store companies frequently change the balances of authority and decision-making between central headquarters and the field organization. Sometimes, in view of market developments and in view of the capabilities of company personnel, it seems advisable to give more power to the store or district managers; at other times management wants to concentrate more decision-making at central headquarters.

Many years ago, most chains exercised such tight control over their stores that one could almost say: "When a store manager sneezed, the president—seated in an office hundreds of miles away—said 'Gesundheit.' " Some chains still maintain very close control; the increased information flowing to headquarters through the new data-processing system has actually increased centralization in a number of firms. Nevertheless, numerous other organizations decentralized many buying, selling, and sales promotion activities. In some cases, divisional headquarters perform or control these functions for groups of stores. Other chains especially those with large stores, have delegated more authority to the zone, district, or store managers.

Some illustrations of decentralization   Company after company illustrated this tendency toward decentralization. Sears, Roebuck and Company divided its stores into five regions supervised by regional vice

FIGURE 7-5 Organization chart of Colonial Stores, Inc., a food processing firm and regional food chain with approximately 400 stores

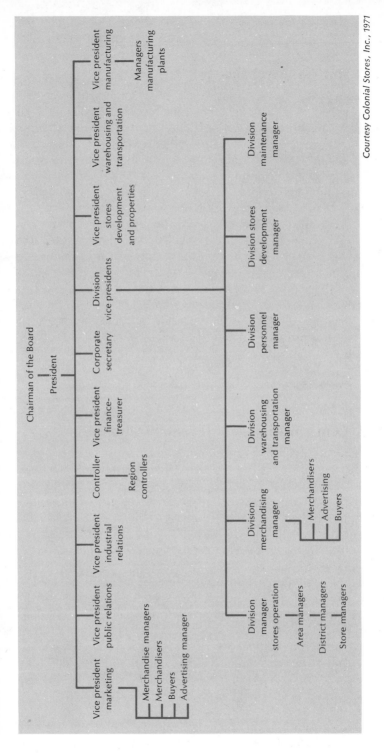

FIGURE 7-6 Organization chart, Montgomery Ward and Company, Inc., a subsidiary of Marcor, Inc. Eastern Region and Merchandising Division shown in greater detail than other regions and divisions.

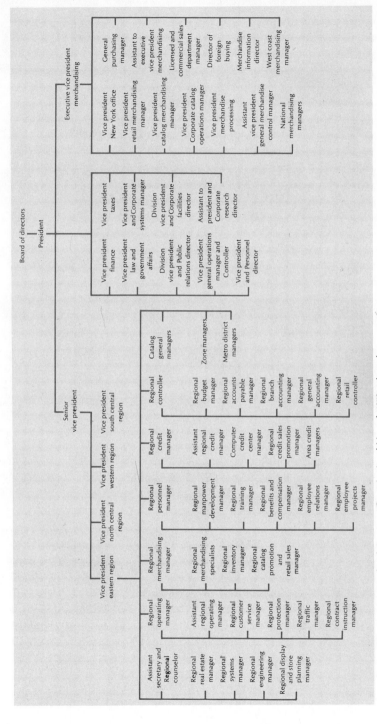

Source: Montgomery Ward and Co., Inc., *Organizational Manual*, 1970, adapted.

FIGURE 7–7 **Line and staff relationships of product supervisors and managers in Kroger Food Stores, a division of The Kroger Company.**

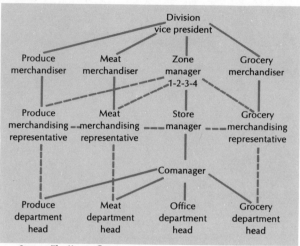

Source: The Kroger Co.

presidents. Each of these executives was given considerable autonomy within the assigned region, and also played an important role in overall policy determination as a director of the company. In spite of centralized buying, Sears' store managers were free to select many of their merchandise items from lists prepared at headquarters. Montgomery Ward and Company has revised its operating methods so that:

. . . where almost every merchandising decision of the entire chain was once made on Chicago Avenue (national headquarters), Ward now manages 115 retail stores in nineteen major urban areas through metropolitan district management staffs whose say-so extends to merchandising, distribution, advertising, warehousing, inventory, and expense controls.[15]

Even the supermarket chains, once perhaps the most highly centralized of all retail groups, became much more decentralized. Firms such as Kroger and Jewel transferred many important decisions to regional and zone managers, and also gave the store managers increased authority. The various regional divisions of The Kroger Company, for example, have the power to decide whether or not they will issue trading stamps.[16] A knowledgeable analyst says that Safeway's "decentralization of retail pricing and merchandising decisions . . . to conform more closely with local competitive supply and demand conditions" is probably fairly typical of the chain supermarket industry.[17]

Centralization trends Despite the developments mentioned, not all retail firms are decentralizing. Some chains maintain very tight central control over store advertising, pricing and markdown, and other practices.[18] Some discount, supermarket, drug, and other self-service chains now send their store managers "planograms" for at least some sections of the store. These are detailed diagrams of the way the display shelves are to be stocked and show the exact desired arrangement and quantity of each item and brand.

At the end of 1975, Sears engaged an outside consulting firm to study the duplication of decision-making within its organization, apparently to identify opportunities to re-centralize some decisions.[19] We have already noted a tendency toward some reduction of decentralization among department store ownership groups. The trend toward the "equal store" structure and away from the "separate store" plan for department store branches constitutes a centralization of buying along with decentralization of sales responsibility.[20] We also noted, in Chapter 1, that the leading discount chains have substantially reduced the proportion of their total sales handled through outside leasees.[21] Similarly, some large franchising organizations are now buying back some of their franchised outlets and operating them as parts of wholly-owned chains.

Many voluntary and cooperative chain groups are also centralizing in several ways: (1) The central headquarters or wholesaler-sponsors are purchasing and operating some of the formerly independent member stores; (2) many of these chains are placing greater emphasis on centrally-purchased private brands; and (3) the affiliated members are relying upon the central headquarters' services (store planning, financing, accounting, and supervision) to a greater degree than ever before.[22]

Balancing centralization and decentralization   The problem of balancing centralization and decentralization is to retain the advantages and economies of group purchasing and sales effort while encouraging the appropriate store and district officials to use their initiative in adjusting to local conditions.[23] Even the chains that are decentralizing retain many functions at central or regional headquarters, where they can be performed on a group basis. An experienced chain store merchant says:

"The name of the game in chain-store operation is central direction, taking full advantage of the combined power of the chain, including the immense power of good store managers . . .

The central core of chain-store effectiveness is centralization. Centralization of decision-making in marketing brings grave responsibility but great rewards."[24]

No chain ever finds the absolutely perfect point of balance between centralization and decentralization, if such a point even exists. Constant experimentation and adjustment, however, will keep the chain from becoming either excessively loose and uncoordinated or overly rigid and inflexible.

■ ENLARGED STAFF AND MANAGEMENT INFORMATION SERVICES

The larger and more progressive department and chain store firms have established many staff units within their organizations to gather, analyze, and summarize information and to furnish advice for top management and other executives responsible for decisions.

□ Management information and advice

Research units Although research findings can never replace executive judgment, top executives in retailing, as in other fields, are increasingly using research studies as an aid in making well-informed decisions. (See the discussion of research as a coordinating function in Chapter 27, "Management coordination and leadership.") The research department or unit within the large firm is responsible for conducting some of the necessary studies and for analyzing and supervising the flow of information purchased from outside organizations. The research department, which serves in a staff capacity, commonly reports directly to the general management because its investigations cover all divisions of the business as well as outside conditions.

Long-range planning Although only a few large retailers have long-range planning and development staffs, their number is steadily increasing.[25] This planning unit is normally headed by a very competent vice president for (or director of) planning and development who works with a few skilled assistants. The planner's task is to help the president or chief executive answer two critically important questions:

1. What should be this firm's position 5 (10;20) years from now?
2. What policies and actions must we adopt to reach that position?

Policy and planning committees In some companies, the board of directors and top management may also turn to a policy committee for advice and suggestions on major decisions. The policy committee usually consists of the firm's key executives plus perhaps an outside consultant and one or two board members. In a few cases, where the board of directors wants to play a very active role in long-range planning, it may set up a planning committee consisting of selected board members and the chief executive plus possibly one or two other executives or consultants.

These committees are not new to retailing, but they have assumed greater importance in recent years. Their growing significance indicates the emphasis that many firms now place upon consideration of all relevant points of view when making fundamental decisions. However, the chief executive and the board of directors as a group remain responsible for those decisions. The policy committee, the research director, the planning director, or even the planning committee cannot assume those responsibilities. But their information, insights, analyses, and opinions can be of substantial assistance to top management.

☐ Other staff services

Consumer representation   Some retail firms have had their own merchandise testing departments, or have used outside laboratories, to examine the products they sell. This results in better buying, greater customer satisfaction, and reduced return rates. Some major retailers, have gone beyond this and appointed a consumer advisor or representative to present the consumer point of view to top management. In 1970, Giant Food, a Washington, D.C. supermarket chain, appointed Mrs. Esther Peterson, former Consumer Advisor to the President of the United States, to create such a position in its organization, and since then other chains have established similar offices.[26]

Other services   Various other staff services have grown in usefulness and in personnel in the large retail organizations. Comparison shopping plays a growing role as retailers find themselves faced with an ever more-competitive market. (See p. 296.) Some retailers have established industrial engineering staffs to apply work simplification methods to repetitive activities such as merchandise handling. Fashion coordinators have been appointed to make certain that the store is in touch with current style trends and to coordinate quality and fashion position in the various departments.[27]

Place on the organization chart   Retailers disagree as to where these various staff services should be located in the organization structure. In some instances, a number are grouped together and placed under a staff vice president. Or, the activities may be distributed among various qualified personnel throughout the organization. For example, the heads of merchandise testing and comparison shopping might report to the general merchandise manager, the fashion coordinator to the advertising and sales-promotion manager or to the general merchandise manager, with the research and public relations directors responsible to the general manager. As is true with so many aspects of organization, existing personnel and management preferences play leading roles in determining exactly where these staff services will report within each company.

■ SUMMARY OF ORGANIZATIONAL CHANGES AND TRENDS

The trends and tendencies discussed in this chapter do not exhaust the list of organizational developments in retailing. Other significant organizational arrangements that apply to specific retail activities are analyzed in the chapters devoted to those activities. Buying committees, for example, are discussed in Chapter 12. But a recapitulation of some of the overall trends noted in this chapter may be helpful:

1. Merchants are experimenting with various groupings of merchandise lines and various bases for departmentalization, but have encountered difficulties in doing this.
2. Many department stores are changing their organizational structure to accommodate an increasing number of branches. Stores with a large number of branches tend to use the "equal store" (chain store) approach.
3. Department stores increasingly separate buying and selling responsibilities.
4. Many department stores have departed from or modified the traditional Mazur four-functional organization structure.
5. Some chain store firms have decentralized important functions and decision-making power to regional, district, and store levels.
6. In contrast, many firms, including department stores, ownership groups, voluntary chains, franchising organizations, and some corporate chains are increasing centralization.
7. Personnel directors and controllers have assumed increased responsibility and importance in both department and chain store firms.
8. Consumer representation is growing.
9. Staff and informational services have also grown greatly in importance and use among the large retailers.

Clearly, retail organization is in a state of flux.

■ REVIEW AND DISCUSSION QUESTIONS

1 Describe the differences between the formal and the informal organization of some retail company with which you are familiar, either as a customer or as an employee. What lines of communication seem to exist outside the formal organization chart, and who seems to have influence that is disproportionately strong or weak in relation to position on the chart?

2 Compare and contrast the organization needs of each of the following: (a) a small drug store and a large drug chain; (b) a general store and a department store; (c) a mail-order company and a chain selling similar goods.

3 What is meant by "departmentalizing"? What steps would you take in departmentalizing a general merchandise store? Concisely state some of the benefits and problems of regrouping merchandise in new, customer end-use categories?

4 Explain the traditional or orthodox organization of a department store in

sufficient detail to make clear the major duties and responsibilities of each division. What are the major weaknesses of this organization plan?

5 Explain how the "equal store" approach to department store branch organization differs from the "separate store" and "brood hen and chick" approaches? Why is it becoming the preferred approach?

6 Summarize the major disadvantages of separating buying and selling? Why, in spite of these disadvantages, are stores increasingly separating the two functions? What steps can they take to overcome the disadvantages?

7 "Chain-store companies vary in organization because of differences in types of merchandise handled, in services performed, in size of individual store, and in territory covered." Explain how each of these factors has an influence on the organization structure.

8 Compare and contrast the general characteristics of chain-store organization with the four-function department-store organization.

9 Some multi-store organizations are decentralizing while others are centralizing various activities and functions. How do you explain these apparently inconsistent trends? What do firms expect to gain by centralizing? By decentralizing?

10 Explain the term "staff services"? Why are these services being expanded in retail stores? Give examples of their expansion.

■ NOTES AND REFERENCES

1 Dalton E. McFarland, *Management Principles and Practices*, 4th ed. (New York: Macmillan Publishing Co., Inc., 1974), p. 104.

2 Montgomery Ward Organization Manual (June 1970), courtesy: Montgomery Ward & Co., Inc.

3 "Federated Will Have Another President," *Home Furnishings Daily*, July 28, 1972, p. 2, describing a corporate executive management committee plan subsequently revised in several respects; and Samuel Feinberg, "You Shouldn't Know Who's Boss of a Good Tandem Team," *Women's Wear Daily*, August 6, 1974, p. 14.

4 Wilbur B. England, *The Purchasing System* (Homewood, Ill.: Richard D. Irwin, Inc., 1967), pp. 133–34.

5 "Why Departmentalization Is a Prime Industry Need during the '70's," *Hardware Retailer*, October 1969, pp. 82–84.

6 "Focusing on the Customer," *Women's Wear Daily*, July 17, 1974, pp. 8–9.

7 "Housewares vs. China," *Home Furnishings Daily*, March 16, 1976, pp. 1, 14.

8 "Buyer Fight Builds on Digital Watches," *Home Furnishings Daily*, February 4, 1976, pp. 1, 6.

9 "Hallmark Expands and Revamps," *Stores*, January 1975, pp. 12–16.

10 See P. M. Mazur, *Principles of Organization Applied to Modern Retailing* (New York: Harper & Bros., 1927). See also the excellent discussion of the Mazur Plan and modifications of it by R. C. Bond, "Department Store Organization," in National Retail Merchants Association, *The Buyer's Manual*, 4th ed. (New York: The Association, 1965), pp. 11–22.

11 One leading Cleveland, Ohio department store has created a new supervisory level, Divisional Group Managers, between some of its buyers and their divisional merchandise managers to help coordinate their buyers' activities and to give the divisional merchandise managers a broader scope of control. The Filene store in Boston has established a similar post, group department

manager, to oversee small groups of buyers. "May Company Cleveland Revamps Merchandisers," *Women's Wear Daily,* June 24, 1974, p. 27; "Simon Shapes Filene Staff to Spot Trends Early," *Women's Wear Daily,* February 6, 1976, p. 8. Other stores have increased the number of divisional merchandise managers so that each can more effectively control a more limited number of buyers.

12 This list is based on that developed by E. J. Brown in his chapter on "The Merchandising Division" in *The Buyer's Manual,* pp. 29–30.

13 See Eleanore Carruth, "Federated Department Stores: Growing Pains at Forty," *Fortune,* vol. 79 (June 1969), p. 145. Bullock's is now a Federated subsidiary.

14 "Leading toward a Green Christmas," *Time,* December 1, 1975, p. 77.

15 "Marcor: How's It Managing," *Dun's Review,* August 1969, p. 73. Headquarters buyers, however, still retain considerable control over merchandise selection, inventory assortments, and retail prices. *See* "The Strategy That Saved Montgomery Ward," *Fortune,* vol. 81, May 1970, p. 170; "How Montgomery Ward Is Outpacing Sears," *Business Week,* January 19, 1974, pp. 38–39.

16 "Kroger Doing Overhaul in Three Sectors," *Supermarket News,* January 6, 1975, p. 4.

17 Daniel I. Padberg, *Economics of Food Retailing* (Ithaca, N.Y.: Cornell University Food Distribution Program, 1968), p. 173.

18 "All King's [Department Stores] Men Don't Make Decisions about Markdowns," *Home Furnishings Daily,* June 12, 1975, p. 15.

19 "Sears' Identity Crisis," *Business Week,* December 8, 1975, pp. 52–54.

20 For example, "Hecht (Washington, D.C. and Baltimore, Md.) Revamps Executive Lineup to Centralize Duties," *Women's Wear Daily,* August 30, 1974, p. 6.

21 *See* Robert Drew-Bear, *Mass Merchandising: Revolution & Evolution* (New York: Fairchild Publications, Inc., 1970), pp. 171–76; and "S. S. Kresge Steams Ahead," *Women's Wear Daily,* January 7, 1971, p. 13.

22 *See* Daniel Padberg, *Economics of Food Retailing,* pp. 40–41.

23 Ben Gordon, "The Year of the Short Leash," *Chain Store Age Executive,* February 1975, p. 9.

24 Robert F. Chisholm, *The Darlings: The Mystique of the Supermarket* (New York: Chain Store Age Books, 1970), pp. 14, 105.

25 *See* "Programming Tomorrow: Looking Ahead Is a Full-Time Job at Walgreen's—and a Very Serious One," *Chain Store Age* (Drug edition), December 1975, p. 140.

26 *See* "Giant Food, Consumer Aid Agree on Job's Importance," *Supermarket News,* April 7, 1975, p. 4.

27 *See* Elaine Jabenis, *The Fashion Director: What She Does and How to Be One* (New York: John Wiley & Sons, Inc., 1972).

RETAIL PERSONNEL
MANAGEMENT

The importance of personnel—the human factor—in the suc-
cess of a retail enterprise was emphasized in the previous chapter. Many
factors, as discussed below, have increased the variety and complexity
of personnel problems in all types of retail businesses today.

■ PERSONNEL MANAGEMENT
OBJECTIVES AND FUNCTIONS

Personnel management is concerned with the firm's employees. The
major retail personnel activities include: personnel planning; selecting,
training, and compensating employees; maintaining adequate performance levels; conducting service activities for employees; and handling
employees' complaints. The successful performance of these activities
requires understanding and application of the basic principles of human
relations. The personnel executives must also stay familiar with all the
complex and changing federal, and state or provincial regulations that
affect employment and labor practices.

Personnel activities are intended to develop staff that will perform
the other retail functions satisfactorily from both the retailer's and the
customer's point of view. The personnel department must cooperate
closely with the executives and other store divisions, since its basic
task is to help those divisons operate more effectively. The ultimate

aim to to help maximize the store's profits; thus, in the final analysis, personnel management is a dollar-and-cents matter.

■ GROWING IMPORTANCE OF PERSONNEL MANAGMENT

Retailing is a "humanized" business involving frequent contact between the firm's customers and its employees. It has been well said: "Any organization depends on its management and employees in carrying out its objectives. This is particularly so in retailing where, unless employees are satisfied and feel involved, they will not give satisfaction to the customer."[1] But only in recent decades have retailers recognized the need for increased attention to personnel management. In 1882 a general store owner-operator handled many personnel problems by simply posting the following:

Rules for Clerks

1. This store must be opened at Sunrise. No mistake. Open 6 o'clock A.M. Summer and Winter. Close about 8:30 or 9 P.M. the year round.
2. Store must be swept—dusted—doors and windows opened—lamps filled, trimmed and chimneys cleaned—counters, base shelves and show cases dusted—pens made—a pail of water also the coal must be brought in before breakfast, if there is time to do it and attend to all the customers who call.
3. The store is not to be opened on the Sabbath day unless absolutely necessary and then only for a few minutes.
4. Should the store be opened on Sunday the clerks must go in alone and get tobacco for customers in need.
5. The clerk who is in the habit of smoking Spanish cigars—being shaved at the barbers—going to dancing parties and other places of amusement and being out late at night—will assuredly give his employer reason to be ever suspicious of his integrity and honesty.
6. Clerks are allowed to smoke in the store provided they do not wait on women with a "stogie" in the mouth.
7. Each clerk must pay not less than $5.00 per year to the Church and must attend Sunday School regularly.
8. Men clerks are given one evening a week off for courting and two if they go to prayer meeting.
9. After the 14 hours in the store the leisure hours should be spent mostly in reading.[2]

■ FACTORS CAUSING INCREASED EMPHASIS ON PERSONNEL MANAGEMENT

The intensified personnel consciousness of businesspeople in general, and of retailers in particular, has been caused by both changes in the business environment and by factors within retailing itself.

☐ External factors

The environmental changes include: the development of new human relations concepts of management; the changing social and political climate; the growth of labor unions; employee demands for extensive "fringe" benefits; shortages of qualified workers during most of the post-World War II period; and the growth of federal and state legislation. Major labor laws include those dealing with wages and hours, social security, unemployment insurance, pension rights, occupational safety, and mandatory collective bargaining, as well as legislation banning job discrimination based on "race, color, religion, sex, national origin, or age."[3] These factors have affected all businesses, but retailers have also gradually recognized a number of other, more specifically retailing-related reasons for the growing emphasis upon personnel management. These factors require further analysis.

☐ Causal factors within retailing

Good people bring good results   Progressive retailers realize that the success of the store depends as much upon personnel as upon the store's merchandise or its fixtures and equipment. Competing stores often have similar merchandise, equipment, and sales promotion, so that the personnel becomes the distinguishing feature. Customer goodwill rests upon contact with the proprietor in the very small store. But the customer gains impressions of larger stores through experiences with all types of employees—salespeople, telephone operators, cashiers, credit interviewers, delivery workers, and complaint adjustors. The customer will feel favorably towards the store if these people are alert, friendly, and helpful; but even extensive advertising cannot overcome the ill-will that results when the employees lack these qualities. There is an old saying in big-league baseball: "If you want to be a good manager, get good ball players." This also applies to the general manager of a retail store: "If you want to run a successful store, get (and keep) good people." Dissatisfaction with employees and their attitudes probably drives far more people away from stores than does discontent with the merchandise.

Human relations in retailing   Thoughtful retailers have been worrying about the constant deterioration in the quality of selling service, about lowered employee morale, and about the number of able young people who fail to consider retailing as a career because of (what they consider to be) unsatisfactory working relationships.[4] These merchants are seeking to solve such problems through improvement of human relations within their firms. They approach their personnel situations from the point of view of the people involved, and ask why some supervisors and personnel specialists achieve so much better results than others. Why is employee morale and productivity so much higher in some departments or stores than in others with identical working conditions and compensation?

Part of the answer seems to be some human relations principles that can be applied to all relationships with people.

1. We do not like to be dominated by others.
2. We are more likely to agree with those we like personally.
3. All of us like to feel important, to be recognized as individuals, and to do work that is significant.
4. We want to be "in the know."
5. Emotions, as well as objective analysis, are important in our reactions to situations.
6. We accept change slowly.
7. In our job, we want good working conditions, a fair wage, a chance to get ahead, and to feel secure.

Yet as one executive points out, retailers often become so interested in merchandise that they overlook "the need for managing human resources."[5] Attention to "the people side" of the business is particularly important in view of the number of young, inexperienced, and part-time workers in retailing.

Young workers Young people, without previous business training, often start in routine retail jobs. Many leave after a period of time, to get married or to· seek employment elsewhere, and must be replaced by other new workers. An increasing number of inexperienced older workers, especially married women, are also entering retail employment. These people often need special training and supervision.

Large number of part-time employees Wide fluctuations in retail sales, both from hour to hour and seasonally, and night and Sunday openings that extend store hours far beyond any individual's working hours, have led to widespread use of part-time personnel. Probably half of all personnel are part-time workers. Skillful part-time employees are increasingly difficult to find and consequently retailers are hiring inexperienced people who require much more extensive training. Moreover, training and other employee communications are more difficult when workers are on a variety of different full-time and part-time schedules.

High rate of employee turnover High employee turnover rates in retailing result from many factors: business seasonality; poor supervision; poor training leading to resignations or discharges; many young and inexperienced employees; belief that better jobs are available elsewhere; employee restlessness and dissatisfaction with immediate superiors or general management; low morale, poor health, or dislike of a particular community. Turnover rates vary widely, but may rise to 50 percent or more, thereby substantially increasing the store's hiring, training, and unemployment compensation insurance costs.

Few industry-wide figures on labor turnover in retailing are available, except for a series compiled by the Supermarket Institute. The Institute reports an average 1973 turnover rate of 3 (out of 100) for executives above store level and for store managers, 8 for store department managers, 20 for cashiers, 24 for stockboy/clerks and 64 for part-time workers.[6]

Close management attention is usually essential whenever the turnover rate is above 25–35 percent. The following steps, discussed in later paragraphs, often help reduce excessive employee turnover.

1. More careful selection.
2. Better training.
3. Using a compensation plan which the employees consider fair and which is at least as generous as the plans used in similar stores throughout the community.
4. A well-conceived promotion policy.
5. Adequate employee service activities.
6. Satisfactory procedures for handling employees' complaints and grievances.
7. Pension system improvements.
8. Recognizing the importance of morale in effective performance, even to the point of employing outside agencies to conduct "morale surveys" as a step toward better human relations within the store.[7]

Executive turnover costs The labor turnover problem also extends to the management level. Some chain store managers have become very dissatisfied with the frequent city-to-city transfers that are part of the usual promotional path in that business.[8] A variety chain executive, for example, reports that over a 10-year yeriod, 70 percent of his firm's management trainees withdrew or were let out before finishing the third year of employment. This executive estimates the cost of training a manager at $8,000 or more. Department and specialty stores, supermarkets, and discount house chains have experienced similar executive turnover difficulties. This is a major problem since many retailers, department stores for example, require about one executive for every ten employees.

Expansion of many retail firms Some retailers' personnel problems come, in part, from rapid expansion. For example, between 1967 and 1975, Sears, Roebuck and Company's payroll grew by 62,000 employees, from 315,000 to 377,000; the J. C. Penney Company from 87,000 to 186,000; S. S. Kresge Company from 67,500 to 155,000; and Lucky Stores from 10,400 to 42,000.[9] And many smaller retailers are also modernizing and enlarging their establishments. Some of the smaller food chains, for example, are growing even more rapidly than the larger firms.

High wage-to-sales ratio Wages commonly represent more than one-half of a retailer's total expense, another reason for emphasis on personnel work. No retailer faced with normal competitive conditions and low profit-ratios can ignore such a large part of total operating expense.

Various kinds of ability needed Employees perform many different kinds of jobs, especially in the larger stores. Different selling and sales-supporting positions require different qualifications. Retailers need people with various skills—check-out cashiers, stock room workers, store managers, basement salespeople, fur department sales staff, heating engineers, watch repairers, garage mechanics, testing laboratory technicians, registered nurses, dieticians, accountants, pharmacists, economists, and top management people. Variations in requirements complicate the task of selecting and training qualified staff.

Employees' requirements The retailer must either satisfy the employees' many legitimate wants in varying degree or pay the penalty of bad personnel relations. The employees want good working conditions, satisfactory wages and hours; employment security; recognition for good work and suggestions; paid vacations; purchasing discounts; treatment as individuals rather than as cogs in a machine; a feeling of importance; a chance to work to their full capacities and to use their maximum abilities and aptitudes; and, in many cases, opportunity for advancement. Although such demands can be costly, failure to meet them may be even more expensive, especially if a strike should result. Personnel management must try to reconcile the employees' desires with the employer's resources.

This reconciliation is difficult, however, since many aspects of retailing work against high wages, short hours, and employment security at the submanagerial levels. The individual retailer who faces keen competition from other merchants cannot raise prices in order to pay higher wages. Many of the rank-and-file jobs do not demand unusual physical abilities or high levels of education, experience, or formalized training and thus are unlikely to command high salaries. Steadily increasing store hours already require much part-time and double-shift employment and thus tend to block any reduction in normal working hours. Seasonal fluctuations in retail sales preclude employment security for all workers. Even in the relatively stable drugstore business, December sales are normally double January's. Many retailers also experience sales peaks before Easter and during back-to-school days. Sales volume also varies among different days of the week and hours of the day. The job stability of "regular" employees has been greatly improved in recent years through increasing use of "part-time" and "extra" workers, but this has transferred the insecurity to these latter employees.

■ DEFINITE PERSONNEL POLICIES ESSENTIAL

Personnel policies should be clear and definite—which, where practicable, means they should be in writing; carefully formulated; consistently administered; stable, yet flexible enough to meet changing conditions; cover all major aspects of employee-management relationships; and widely publicized among employees. Definite, well-publicized policies are especially important in large-scale retailing where minor executives make many decisions that affect store personnel. Unless these officers know and follow the firm's policies, employee ill-will is inevitable.

Definite personnel policies should cover, among other areas:

1. The personnel division's authority and responsibilities, and its relationships with other divisions and departments, including the location of responsibility for determining the size of the workforce (i.e. staffing requirements).
2. Personnel recruitment and sources of supply.
3. Selecting personnel—number and types of interviews, use of tests, and similar devices.
4. Training methods and content of training—for new and existing personnel.
5. Compensation and compensation methods.
6. Working conditions—hours of work, number of days per week, and vacations.
7. Pensions, insurance, sick leave, and similar benefits.
8. Induction of new employees.
9. Promotions, transfers, and terminations.
10. Personnel reviews and ratings.
11. Dress codes or any other rules affecting salespeople.
12. Employee discounts on purchases.
13. Employee cafeterias and lunchrooms and other service activities.
14. Personnel complaints and methods of handling them.
15. Unions and labor organizations.

■ CONDUCTING PERSONNEL ACTIVITIES

The proprietor or manager of a small store usually conducts all personnel activities. This individual normally knows the store's few employees well and has close working relationships with them. Consequently relatively little time is needed for formal personnel work. Hiring, training, and other personnel activities require more attention in the medium-sized establishment with 15 or 20 employees. A "sponsor" may be appointed to handle some of the training work. (See pp. 220, 223.) Chain store district offices may absorb some personnel responsibilities for the units, particularly the smaller stores in their areas, but the store managers will still handle most personnel tasks.

Personnel work requires more elaborate programs in the larger retail establishments. The mere number of employees creates a hiring and training problem in the large organizations. Lack of direct association between the executives who formulate general policies and the employees can generate misunderstandings and ill-will which must be minimized. Consequently, personnel departments or divisions are needed, both to perform personnel tasks and, even more importantly, to help the operating supervisors understand and fulfill the firm's personnel policies.

Actually all the store's executives and employees, whether in the personnel department or not, are involved in personnel work. Many will have responsibilities for training new people, and executives on the promotion ladder are often expected to develop their own successors. But every individual's actions contribute to the growth of good, or poor, human relations within the store. The chain organization superintendent who ridicules or undermines the firm's manager-training plan weakens the entire personnel program. The department manager who fails to understand human relations and tries to dominate subordinates invariably increases labor turnover and complicates the personnel department's employee-selection program. In contrast, the executive who leads associates to successful performance of their tasks bolsters the firm's personnel objectives.

■ PERSONNEL PLANNING

The personnel division has two responsibilities in personnel planning. In cooperation with the top officials of the company, it should develop long-run forecasts of executive requirements, showing the number and types of middle and senior managers needed at future dates. These figures should include consideration of any probable increase in the size of the business as well as replacements for executives who retire or leave the firm. The long-run plans should also show how many trainees are "on-stream" to fill those needs, and what steps will be taken to remedy any gaps in the supply of potential executives.

In addition to such long-run planning, the personnel division should work with operating managers, such as department heads, to develop *current* workforce or labor expense budgets. The heads of selling departments, for example, must always have enough salespeople on the floor to provide coverage and prevent pilferage. Even more importantly, they must have enough salespeople on hand to insure adequate customer service. A study conducted in a shoe department found that the profits lost when customers left without buying as a result of delays in service were greater than the cost of adding extra sales staff, even though those "extras" would have been idle during some low-demand portions of the selling day.[10] Yet sales expense must be controlled, so department heads must balance the number and hours of full- and part-time workers against the anticipated volume of customer traffic.[11] One simple, short-cut method of balancing sales staff in line with anticipated customer traffic is to: (a) measure the amount of selling time and sales-supporting activity required per normal transaction. This can be done by random observation of the salesforce in a department over a period of weeks. The resultant figure, multiplied by adjustments for customers who do not buy and for salespeople's personal time indicates the number of salesclerks needed to handle a given hourly volume of traffic. Then (b) the department manager should prepare estimates, based on experience, of the number of customers likely to arrive in the department during each hour of the week. This will then indicate staffing requirements.[12]

■ EMPLOYMENT PROCEDURES

Recruitment of capable retail employees involves at least four important steps: (1) making careful job analyses and preparing adequate job specifications or descriptions; (2) developing satisfactory sources of supply; (3) using application forms, interviews, tests, and physical examinations to select employees; and (4) introducing the new employees to the store and to their jobs. Large-scale retailers frequently also have to maintain a contingent force and a file of prospective employees.

☐ Job studies

A job analysis (or study) is the basis for establishing a job specification. The analysis describes the exact nature of the work, the quantity and quality of output that is expected, organizational aspects of the job, and necessary personal qualities such as leadership, judgment, tact, and the ability to cope with emergencies. The job specification then outlines the education, experience, training, and personal attributes that are required for successful performance. This specification serves as a blueprint for employee selection; it also is useful for measuring training needs and promotional opportunities and also helps in setting wage scales.[13]

The U.S. Civil Service Commission, for example, has prepared job studies for various levels of workers in government-owned retail food stores, such as post exchanges. Part of the standard for store-workers, Grade WG-5, is shown in Figure 8–1.

☐ Sources of personnel

The retailer is ready to look for people with the desired qualifications after obtaining a more or less precise idea of the type of person needed. Some good candidates for at least some of the open positions may have already applied to the store for a job, either in person or by correspon-

FIGURE 8-1   Standard for store worker WG-5 (excerpt)

General: In addition to work described at the WG-4 level, the WG-5 store worker uses judgment in deciding the work to be done in his area on a day-to-day basis; he performs tasks such as the following:

Determining the proper display area or amount of shelf space for items and how to make room for new products or increased quantities;

Estimating needed perishable items for which there is a purchase agreement (dairy products or frozen foods) and advising vendors' salesman or deliveryman of adjustments in daily or weekly orders;

Checking incoming shipments for obvious spoiling or damage, overages, or shortages; reporting differences between amounts indicated on the receiving report and amounts received; signing receiving reports; and

Keeping supervisor advised of customer preferences, unusual turnover, or the need to increase or decrease stock of particular items.

Skill and Knowledge: The WG-5 store worker needs more knowledge of the turnover of items and how they are displayed than WG-4 store workers to plan his work so that items are available as needed and that displays are safely and neatly arranged. For example, in making decisions about how much shelf space to use or how to rearrange displays, he considers the amounts to be displayed, whether the display is to be permanent or for special holiday needs, and other factors such as whether shipments are expected for out-of-stock items. In ordering highly perishable items such as dairy products or frozen foods, he considers customary sales for the day of the week, current inventory, and capacity of display and storage areas. He checks incoming shipments, signs receiving reports, and advises supervisor when there are any problems with the shipments. In working with produce, he advises his supervisor when items show signs of spoiling so that the price may be reduced for quick sale. In recommending changes in the amount of stock carried, he uses his knowledge of requests received from customers and the turnover of particular items over a period of time. He also answers questions about the stocking or availability of items referred by the lower grade workers.

Source: U.S. Civil Service Commission, *Job Grading Standard for Store Worker* (WG–7602). Washington, D.C.: U.S. Government Printing Office, 1972, p. 5.

dence. Many stores keep availability files and hire qualified individuals in order of application. Employees and customers often recommend other desirable candidates.

However, most retailers must seek out people if they want the best available. Many different sources may be used to help locate good prospects. High schools, business schools, community colleges, and university employment and placement units are often good sources. The retailer may also use government (U.S. Employment Service and Canada Manpower) and private employment agencies; and window signs and display pieces, as well as classified or regular-space newspaper advertising. If an executive position is open, the store's own personnel should be reviewed carefully, inquiries may be made among vendors and others familiar with the organization, and specialized employment agencies may be used.

Some retailers use well-developed recruiting programs to attract graduating students.[14] A few, especially chains and department stores, have gone beyond this and established summer or part-time employment programs for college and high school students. These merchants hope that the participants will ultimately want permanent careers with their stores and also will encourage their classmates to become interested in retailing. A drug chain, in addition to offering loans and part-time jobs to pharmacy school students, also attempts to attract high school students through weekend work. Some retail trade associations—the National Retail Merchants Association, for example—have also undertaken programs to encourage more college students to enter the retail field.

☐ Selecting personnel

The next step is to acquire knowledge of the various candidates' qualifications so as to select the ones who best meet the store's requirements. Information may be obtained through (1) application forms, (2) references, (3) preliminary interviews, (4) tests, (5) physical examinations, and (6) final interviews. Although the order may vary from firm to firm, most large retailers use all six sources of information. The number of interviews and/or tests will also vary with the importance and nature of the job to be filled. In contrast, the proprietor of the small store usually only draws upon interviews and references.

Application forms and references Some retailers use a very simple one-page preliminary application form. The form, which calls for a brief description of the applicant's experience, education, type of job sought, and expected salary, provides a quick screening without imposing a lengthy form upon either the candidate or the personnel department.

Retailers' regular application forms—while not so lengthy as they once were—contain many questions. These questions concern the applicant's educational background, health, previous employment, reasons for leaving previous employers, and reasons for desiring the job under consideration. The applicant may be asked to submit a transcript of high school or college credits, and to supply the names of several references.[15]

Preliminary interviews After receiving the information described, and possibly immediately eliminating some candidates, the personnel manager—or the small store proprietor—is ready for relatively brief preliminary interviews with the prospective employees. The interviewer seeks information about basic interests and fields of proficiency, and tries to get an impression of the applicant's voice, appearance, use of English, poise, self-confidence, and attitude toward work. A good interviewer also tries to give the interviewee a candid, but favorable, picture of the job, including its requirements, opportunities, and benefits so that the interviewee can judge whether she or he is suited for, and interested in, the work. However, a skilled interviewer will let the applicant do most of the talking since that will help disclose many of the interviewee's characteristics.

Tests Retail personnel specialists hold widely differing opinions about the value of the four main types of employment tests—intelligence, aptitude, skill, and personality. Some retailers, especially department store firms, require every applicant to take an intelligence test. Some of these firms believe that there is an appropriate intelligence quotient range for every job: People with IQ's below the desired range will not be able to handle the job while those with higher IQs will get bored and quit. However, probably fewer than 15 percent of all large-scale retailers, including perhaps only 25–30 percent of the department stores, use intelligence tests.

Aptitude tests, which probably have somewhat wider use among retailers than intelligence tests, attempt to measure potential—capacity for developing skills and abilities. For example, the New York State Employment Service has developed a sales aptitude test battery which the service claims helps predict probable performance in sales jobs. Some retailers claim considerable success with aptitude tests and they are being used by a growing number of firms.[16] Yet others have been disappointed in the results and the great majority of merchants still have little faith in aptitude testing.

Many retailers use skill, job, or trade tests that measure very specific abilities in evaluating prospective employees for certain nonselling jobs. For example, a prospective stenographer may be tested on speed and accuracy in taking dictation and in typing. A deliveryworker may be given a test on local geography. Prospective salesclerks are sometimes tested for arithmetic skill and ability to prepare an accurate salescheck, but very few retailers have found any satisfactory way to test for selling skills.[17]

Personality tests assume that certain personality traits (friendliness, flexibility, sociability, stability) are essential to success and that measurement of these traits will help predict an individual's success or failure. Retailers are showing increased interest in these personality tests, but no reliable estimate of their use is currently available. Some observers believe that no available test accurately measures significant personality characteristics; others think that some firms give exceseive weight to these tests in making personnel decisions. Many other merchants have found personality measures helpful. Sears, Roebuck and Company has reported considerable success with the use of an elaborate management game as a combination personality and executive aptitude test to help screen managerial trainees.[18]

In summary, tests have been used increasingly in recent years, as psychologists have improved their measuring techniques and as retailers have recognized their value in avoiding serious selection mistakes. Some retailers also use outside testing agencies to help select executives and to assist in upgrading present employees. But, most retail personnel people still believe that the tests described above are primarily useful as supplementary tools in personnel decision making and that they should never be the sole criterion for any decision. That is, they should only be used in conjunction with interview, reference, and personal history information.

Physical examinations   Many small and medium-sized stores do not require physical examinations, and even some large retail organizations put them on a voluntary basis. This is probably unwise. Retail work is often quite demanding and may be too difficult for people in poor physical condition. Recognition of this fact is leading to greater use of mandatory physical examinations. The examinations may also help to reduce costly accidents and injuries. The growth of employee pension and health insurance plans also argues for more preemployment physicals.

Final interviews   The applicant is usually given a final interview after the test and examination results become available. At this time an effort will be made to ascertain the interviewee's knowledge and opinion of the position, and to answer any questions either party may have. The executive who will supervise the person hired for the job often conducts this interview in large stores, perhaps with some assistance from the personnel division. Chain-store firms typically have an experienced interviewer conduct the final interview, commonly at central or branch headquarters.

In view of retailers' reliance upon interviews, we may well ask: How satisfactory are they as a means of selecting employees? This is a difficult question to answer. Because of lack of care in interviewing, disagreement as to qualities desired, and divergence of opinion concerning the outward indications of those qualities, various interviewers frequently give a single individual widely-different ratings. All of these difficulties cannot be completely overcome, but some may be minimized through use of experienced, trained interviewers, and carefully drawn specifications. The interview is a useful selection tool under such conditions. In the future, the interviewers' conclusions may become even more valid when they are checked against computerized comparisons of job requirements and applicant characteristics.

☐ Job orientation

Broadly speaking, the selection process has not been completed until the new employee has been introduced to the job and to the fellow workers.[19] All too often this step is neglected. In many stores no effort is made to acquaint the new employee with the firm's history, organization, and policies, and the introduction to co-workers may be very perfunctory. Yet this indoctrination task is essential if the new employee is to begin work with a feeling of "really belonging." Moreover, many retailers and many employees regard the first month on the job as a probationary period during which both parties will decide whether they are satisfied.[20] During this period, management will obtain a better evaluation of the employee's capabilities, and the employee will obtain a better picture of the positive and negative aspects of the work if the induction is handled smoothly and without delay.

What can the retailer do to improve the employee's orientation to the store and to the job? In the small store, the proprietor should inform the employee about the store and its promotion opportunities. The owner should also take the time to introduce the new worker to the other employees, and to explain the duties, hours, and other working conditions.

Employee induction is a joint responsibility of the employment and training departments in the well-run large retail organization. The training department takes over after the applicant is employed, and uses store tours, classes, conferences, and handbooks to provide information about store organization and policy as well as about the specific job. A sponsor, the department head or the store manager, or a member of the personnel division provides introduction to immediate colleagues. The sponsor or supervisor in turn should be trained to give the new employee sympathetic and tactful guidance.[21]

□ The contingent force and prospect file

Most medium-sized and large retail organizations maintain a "contingent force" or "flying squad" of employees who can move from department to department to replace absent workers or to help handle sudden peak sales traffic. Some stores use their most experienced salespeople, who can serve successfully in new and unfamiliar departments, for this purpose. Other organizations build their contingent force from part-time workers or from inexperienced new employees who give promise of being satisfactory workers after some service in the store.

In addition, particularly when labor turnover is high, many stores maintain a "prospect file" or list of applicants who have been approved by the personnel department but who are not yet on the payroll. By keeping this list up-to-date and by steadily adding new names, the employment office seeks to be able to fill all personnel requisitions soon after they are received.

☐ Review of employment procedures

The personnel manager should carefully review all personnel practices, but particularly those concerning employment and evaluation (see pp. 244–47), to make certain that they comply with laws prohibiting discrimination and protecting employee privacy. No *unnecessary* educational or other requirements should be built into the job specification; required tests should relate directly to potential job performance so that they do not seem to be devices for screening out some qualified candidates; application blanks should not call for photographs or ask questions about race, religion, etc.; and the candidate must be notified before personal information can be gathered through interviews with neighbors or associates.[22]

▪ EMPLOYEE TRAINING

A second major responsibility of personnel management is employee training, an activity that clearly demonstrates the axiom: "Personnel work is a dollar and cents matter." Adequate training results in more effective job performance and greater productivity; it insures conformance with established rules and regulations, thus reducing errors and increasing customer satisfaction; it lowers short-run and long-run selling costs, thus enhancing profits; it increases the employees' earnings through better job performance; it reduces employee turnover, improves morale and strengthens loyalty; and it simplifies management's supervisory tasks. Consequently, in recent years, many retailers have been trying to develop more effective training programs to help improve the general quality of service.

☐ Centralized and decentralized training

The terms "centralization" and "decentralization," when used in connection with training, may refer to either the organizational unit within the company that is responsible for training or to the place where training sessions are held. Centralized responsibility means that the training department conducts the classes and provides the instruction that constitutes the training program. This has the advantage of using skilled instructors who can concentrate on training tasks. Employees may be brought to specially-equipped facilities in the training department or headquarters unit for the sessions (centralized location) or the trainers may go to where the employees work in the stores and operating departments (decentralized location).[23]

But training responsibility, which usually devolves upon proprietors and managers in small and medium-sized stores, is also being increasingly decentralized in the larger stores. Management often feels that the department heads and operating executives have more knowledge of job requirements than people in the training department and thus can more readily obtain the trainee's respect. Also, training is a constant responsibility and is more economically handled by supervisors who are in constant contact with the workers.

When training responsibility is largely decentralized, the central training department may concentrate on three major functions: (1) providing a certain amount of introductory schooling for new rank-and-file employees; (2) organizing some special courses, seminars, and other special activities; and (3) of most importance, helping the department heads and supervisors develop their training programs and abilities, or in other words, "training the trainers." Moreover, the central training staff often prepares films, other visual aids, and other materials to be used in the various units of a chain store system or in the departments of a large store. Some chains also try to assign as many new employees as possible, particularly managerial trainees, to specially designated training units where the managers are especially adept in personnel development and training.

□ Determining the extent of the training program

Executive attitudes, personnel turnover rates, the store's service objectives, and the size of the store often determine the extent of a store's training program. A minimum of formal training will be used if the store does not aim at a high service standard, if its personnel turnover is low, and if the executives do not believe strongly in training programs. A comprehensive training plan is likely to be maintained under opposite conditions.

The training problem becomes more complicated as the size of the store increases. Many more people need training for a wider variety of selling and sales-supporting jobs involving many diverse types of goods. The training of part-time employees also is more complicated. Furthermore, some of the present staff, who are candidates for promotion, must be prepared for advancement. Finally, large and growing firms are most likely to support extensive employee training programs. Such firms often spend many thousands of dollars per year on these programs. Some supermarkets budget 3/10ths of 1 percent of sales or more for training activities.[24]

□ Training different types of employees

In view of the factors mentioned in the previous section, we should note the differences in the amount of training usually offered to different kinds of employees.* Broadly speaking, they may be classified as follows: (1) new, inexperienced employees; (2) new, experienced employees; (3) current regular employees; and (4) "extras," that is, individuals employed for short intervals such as the pre-Christmas period.

☐ Training new, inexperienced employees

1. *Salespeople* New salespeople in large retail establishments often receive 15 to 20 hours of very specific instruction, sometimes concentrated in a few days and sometimes spread over the first week or two, in organized selling classes. The neophyte salespeople are given a picture of the store's organization—made more vivid, perhaps, by a trip through the store. They are taught how to prepare sales slips, use sales registers, and keep stock. Store policies are explained concerning returned goods, credit, adjustments, absences from work, dress regulations, employee discounts, and safety regulations. Methods of greeting customers, showing merchandise, and closing sales are also usually discussed.

The proprietor or manager of the small store usually supplies this instruction right on the selling floor. Some medium-sized and larger stores also provide much of this training through the "sponsor" system— an experienced salesperson who also acts as a training department representative in the selling department—since they believe this approach is more effective than the use of formal classes. Sponsors also often supplement sales classes in introducing the new employee to the other workers, in teaching selling techniques, in helping correct individual difficulties, in perhaps periodically rating each new worker, and especially in building morale through regular follow-up.

Some retailers, particularly the larger organizations, have developed extensive sets of slides, movies, posters, and other teaching materials to supplement the information provided through the sponsor systems, classroom lectures, workshop groups and role-playing demonstrations.[25] These supplementary materials may demonstrate right and wrong tactics to use with different customers, illustrate suggestion selling, or remind the staff of basic matters such as courtesy to customers and care in preparing sales slips, and explain store policies. The written material is being increasingly reorganized for programmed instruction, that is, systematically presented so that the student can absorb it individually either from a book or a teaching machine.

Several retail trade associations have also prepared helpful manuals on selling for use by their members[26] and some manufacturers will help train the clerks who sell their products. The Quaker Oats Company, for

---

* Academic recruitment and training programs have already been covered in Chapter 3, "Opportunities and careers in retailing," so they are excluded from the present discussion.

example, publishes a 13-unit "Self-Study Program for Retail Operations" for use in food stores. The Whirlpool Company holds 4½-day retail seminars for its electrical appliance dealers' staffs. In recent years, many stores and groups of stores have employed specialized outside agencies to help develop training programs for inexperienced salespeople. The smaller store can gain access to training materials and skills it could not afford to develop on its own through joint or part-time use of such agencies and even large stores find them helpful. The outside training must be supplemented, however, by some internal instruction on the systems used in the employee's own store.

Many local school systems offer distributive education programs that are supported in part through federal grants. These courses usually include basic and career-development retail-job training for students who often assume part-time positions in local stores.[27] Some school systems also provide in-service refresher and advancement distributive education courses for experienced employees and store owners. The Vocational Education Acts of 1963 and 1968 provide additional support for curriculums for youths with socio-economic or other handicaps. Many retail firms have established special programs, in some cases with government cooperation, to train disadvantaged and minority group potential employees for sales and other positions. Such programs are underway in department, discount, and variety stores, and supermarket and drug chains.[28] However, many of the programs have encountered more difficulties and have been less extensive and effective than was envisaged at the outset.[29]

Despite all the training efforts discussed above, some experts feel that retail management fails "to appreciate the real contribution that creative sales effort can have on the final sale."[30] One observer states that retailing lags far behind manufacturing in sophisticated training.[31] These opinions may be harsh, but they emphasize the need for constant attention to the sales training programs for new (and experienced) salespeople. Such programs are the best possible means for improving sales efforts and the prestige of selling positions.

2. *Sales-supporting employees* The same two general methods employed in training salespeople—class sessions for a short period and the sponsor system—are also used for new sales-supporting employees, such as delivery workers, elevator operators, and cashiers. Movies, demonstrations, group discussions, individual conferences, store manuals, and programmed instruction are also used. Much of the instruction is decentralized and delegated to operating supervisors and employee sponsors even if the program is planned by, or in cooperation with, the central training department.

But, unfortunately, many stores, including a large portion of those that do train salespeople, fail to give their sales-supporting personnel any formal training. Still others limit the programs for nonselling employees to a brief introductory period. Relatively few stores take the trouble to give new receiving clerks or markers an understanding of their place in the retail organization. This attitude has undoubtedly hurt performance standards and made the nonselling employees more receptive to unionization.[32] If these workers are to feel that they are an essential part of the organization, their training should go beyond the question: How is my job performed?

Training new, experienced employees   New employees with previous retail experience do not need as much introductory training as inexperienced employees. In the small store, such employees are usually put quite completely on their own after a minimum of instruction concerning the exact duties of the job and peculiarities of the store's system. In the large retail organization, however, some formal training in store organization, policies, and methods is necessary. A few class meetings or a brief period under sponsorship usually accomplishes this task satisfactorily.

Training regular employees   Although retail training programs still emphasize the new employees, increasing attention is being given to workers who have been on the staff for some time. Progressive retailers recognize the value of continuous training for all employees. Few people can fully absorb and remember all the material presented in the induction training for new employees. New questions, not covered during that training, arise out of actual work experience. Even veteran cashiers, salespeople, stockroom personnel, and other staff can become overconfident, careless, or forgetful and need follow-up programs. New fashion and merchandise developments must be outlined for the employees. Formal training for promotion may prod some who are slightly lethargic into seeking advancement and will help satisfy and retain the ambitious employee who looks to the firm for assistance in moving ahead. Some stores make this training a more or less implicit precondition for promotion, while other merchants believe that the best results can be obtained by putting the formal programs on a more voluntary basis.

1. *Follow-up or job training*   Follow-up training often includes private conferences to discuss ways the individual employee can improve performance. Classes are also used for large numbers of employees. Department store buyers often hold weekly meetings to give employees information about fashion trends and new merchandise. Suppliers' representatives may participate in some of these meetings to supply additional product data, and other store executives and trainers may be brought in to discuss salesmanship, the use of sales quotas, or the ways the salespeople can help reduce expenses. Chain and branch store managers and department heads hold similar meetings, often with the help of a constant flow of pamphlets, films, bulletins, selling tips, and other training aids from central headquarters.

Some firms carry out job training by switching employees from one branch of the business to another, thus providing a complete view of the firm's operations. Still another technique is sending small groups of salespeople out from time to time to observe competing or affiliated stores. This technique stimulates interest and encourages employees to notice things that will improve their performance. Such observation trips are followed by group conferences in which experiences are exchanged.

2. Promotional training The majority of successful retailers agree that a policy of promotion from the ranks is highly desirable. For example, Edison Brothers Stores, a major shoe retailing chain, has always believed in preparing its sales clerks to move up to the higher posts within the company. This recently gave the firm a supply of about 200 assistant store managers who were ready to become managers when the company began a profitable expansion and acquisitions program. Moreover, as *Forbes* magazine commented, they were good managers since they had been through a rigid training program in which "virtually every executive rises from the ranks—selling shoes."[33] Promotion from within builds employee morale, attracts forward-looking individuals, provides officers who are well-trained in the store's policies and practices, and is a relatively inexpensive method of securing executives.

A house organ can supplement the training program. News of employee promotions may stimulate other persons to greater efforts. Data on new lines of merchandise, on the use of good salesmanship, on outstanding or unusual services rendered to customers, and on certain of the store's policies may also be covered in the store paper.

For maximum effectiveness, a policy of promotion from within the firm should be accompanied by an adequate training program for promotable personnel. This may involve company-planned conferences and courses in various aspects of the business, work-study arrangements with universities, evening courses in colleges, correspondence courses, job rotation, and the use of sponsors.[34]

Unfortunately, most of the advanced training (and much of the other training as well) given by stores to nonexecutive employees is largely technical in nature and designed to explain how certain jobs are performed. This type of training is important, of course, but something broader is needed to stir the interests of retail workers effectively. The employee should receive help in developing a greater understanding of the job, its personal and interpersonal dimensions, its potentialities for change, its promotional opportunities, and its relationship to the total company objectives. Moreover, most retailers have probably been too slow in advancing those who have taken advantage of promotional training opportunities. A decrease in this time lag could be a significant factor in demonstrating the dollar-and-cents advantage of such training to retail personnel.

3. Training supervisors No retail training program can be really effective without the full support and cooperation of the supervisory force. Consequently, some large retailers have adopted various measures to involve the supervisors in the training process, to improve their training abilities, and to make them aware of training's significance. Some provide the supervisors with special self-study programs which make use of textbooks, correspondence courses, phonograph records, and (in a few instances) teaching machines. Still other retailers have rather formalized training courses, which may include lectures, films, and business games, that emphasize leadership qualities and stress the wise application of company policies and procedures. Supervisors are taught that their job is to maintain good human relationships through proper indoctrination and on-the-job training of employees, through frequent personnel reviews, and through appropriate salary, promotional, transfer, and release recommendations. Chain store supervisors may receive all or part of this training through meetings at regional or main office headquarters. The personnel division, of course, plays a key role in carrying out all of these activities within the framework of the firm's general policies.

4. *Advanced management programs*   Some progressive retail firms offer an elaborate assortment of management advancement programs. For example, Stop and Shop, a New England-based supermarket and discount chain, has used approximately 20 different management development programs, including some taught by its own staff and some conducted by universities, trade associations, and other outside organizations. Allied Supermarkets of Detroit pays travel expenses for trainees' spouses who are invited to attend the initial orientation weekend of the company's eight-week district manager seminar.[35]

In addition to encouraging attendance at formal courses and seminars, many retailing companies have adopted other, often more individualized, techniques for management development. A promising individual may be moved through a variety of assignments, so as to acquire familiarity with all phases of the business. Sometimes an executive or a small team will be given an analytical or "trouble-shooting" task, such as preparing a report on how stock shortages may be reduced or on how computerized record-keeping may be extended to some new function. In such instances, top management will be very much interested in the report as a means of helping to solve an important problem, but both top management and the individuals involved will also regard the project as valuable training. Similarly, other stores have found that assigning problems to committees composed of executives from various divisions not only produced helpful recommendations, but also broadened the committee members' perspectives and understanding.[36]

Training part-time and "extra" workers   The short period that most extras are on the payroll seldom makes intensive training worthwhile. The limited hours that part-timers may be available also creates training difficulties, yet these two groups of employees may account for one third or more of a store's sales.

The larger stores usually give the "extras" a one- (sometimes two-) day "cram" session covering, in abbreviated fashion, the material given to new inexperienced employees. Then a sponsor takes over. Some retailers, both large and small, rely practically entirely on the sponsor system, perhaps supplemented by printed material. One variety chain gives each extra employee a short manual which covers such matters as store policies and regulations, care of stock, and the manner of approaching customers. In a few cases, retailers in a city have cooperated in arranging initial general training of holiday employees through a local business school or college. Some stores also provide their own training sessions at odd hours to fit part-timers' schedules.[37]

Regardless of the training given extras before they begin work, the retailers must depend in large measure upon the aid and advice they receive from regular employees. Through its house organ "Field Glass," Marshall Field and Company appeals to its employees for this necessary cooperation as follows:

Let's Welcome Them

Christmas hiring has started. Between now and the end of November we will nearly double our number of employees. These new people come in to aid us during the greatest rush of the year—it is only through their efforts added to our own that we will be able to give our large number of holiday customers the traditional courtesy and service that spell FIELD'S.

Let's welcome them—remembering our own first days in the store, let's help them. We know the store. We know its systems, its locations, its habits and its people. And all these are strange to our new members. We can do much to help them overcome their strangeness, and to make their work here the pleasant experience we all want it to be. Let's increase our constant effort to do this during the next few weeks—let's resolve that each new member will learn of Field's courtesy and service from personal experience—will learn that these qualities are genuine and are extended to customers because they are practiced "at home."

☐ Appraising the training program

The precise value of employee training is very difficult to measure. But some checking techniques will give management a rough indication of what the training is accomplishing. Larger retailers often send professional shoppers into their stores to act as customers and then report on their experiences with specific sales personnel. These shopping-service reports, however, are expensive and are likely to be influenced by chance factors (an employee may be approached when specially tired or bothered) and by such human elements as the shopper's own training and background. Records of employee average sale and the number of errors and complaints reported have some value as indicators when used with appropriate caution. Periodic examinations sometimes afford a fairly satisfactory check.* Personnel reviews at regular intervals are also used for this purpose.

In the final analysis, however, the effectiveness of the training program is measured by the general morale of the store's employees, the opportunities for advancement and the extent of promotion from within, the quality of supervision, the number of customer complaints, the rate of employee turnover, and—most important of all—the quality of customer service and its reflection in profits.[38]

■ REVIEW AND DISCUSSION QUESTIONS

1 "Personnel management's job is to make people happy—it is not a matter of dollars and cents." Discuss.

2 How do the problems of personnel management in retailing differ, either in their nature or in their difficulty, from the problems of factory or office personnel management?

3 Do your own experiences, either at work or elsewhere, provide illustrations of any of the seven human relations principles listed on p. 210? Should any other principles be added to the list? For example, do you think people are stimulated or upset if their work requires them to shift frequently from one task to another?

4 Prepare a job analysis for some retailing occupation with which you have become familiar as an employee or as a customer. (Select some job other than the supermarket stock supervisor described on page 216.)

5 Discuss the important steps involved in recruiting an adequate force of retail employees.

6 What steps would you take and what sources would you use in recruiting a staff for a new grocery store? For a new department store branch?

7 How useful do you think each of the following selection devices might be if a retailing firm wanted to hire a new sportswear buyer: (a) an application blank, (b) preliminary interview, (c) aptitude test, (d) references, and/or (e) final interview? Explain your answer. How would your answer differ if the store was seeking a checkout cashier; a salesperson for the shirt department?

8 Define the term "orientation of employees." Indicate the significance of the orientation program from both employer and employee points of view.

9 Compare and contrast the training program of a small retailer in your home town with that of a competing large-scale retailer handling the same general types of merchandise. To what extent do large-scale retailers use

---

* These tests need not be written. The "test sale" is becoming a popular means of checking on the effectiveness of sales training programs. The employee who has finished initial training is required to demonstrate the sale of specific merchandise with another salesperson or an employee of the training department as the customer.

centralized training? What are the organization chart positions and duties of their personnel and training directors?

10 Describe what you consider the ideal training program for you in your first retailing job after graduation and explain the reasons for your recommendation.

■ NOTES AND REFERENCES

1 Adapted from Jan de Somogyi, "Human Dimensions in Retailing," *Retail and Distribution Management*, vol. 2 (May-June 1974), p. 11.

2 Carson Pirie Scott & Co., *"We" and Our Business* (Chicago, 1927), p. 20.

3 Title VII, Civil Rights Act of 1964, as amended (42 U.S.C. 2000 e) and Age Discrimination in Employment Act, 1967 (Public Law 90–202, 81 Stat. 602); Also see "Government Regulations Affecting Retailing in the Employee Relations Field," *Personnel News and Views*, vol. 4 (1974), pp. 23–25; "The Courts Reinterpret Old-Age Discrimination," *Business Week*, February 24, 1975, p. 91. Canadian labor legislation varies somewhat from province to province but generally includes extensive antidiscrimination clauses, wage and hour provisions, and rules relating to working conditions and employee rights and benefits. Annual reviews of changes in each major aspect of labor legislation appear in Canada Department of Labour, *The Labour Gazette* and *La Gazette du Travail* (Ottawa: Information Canada, monthly).

4 *The Generation Gap and Employee Effectiveness*, transcript series no. 103 (Toronto: Retail Council of Canada, 1972).

5 Ray A. Killian, Vice-President, Belk Store Services, quoted in Samuel Feinberg, "From Where I Sit," *Women's Wear Daily*, January 18, 1974, p. 9.

6 *1974 Personnel Department Research*, Special Research Report no. 7 (Chicago: Super Market Institute 1974), Table 6. The turnover rate is measured by the formula:

$$\frac{\text{all position separations, regardless of cause}}{\text{average number of position employees during year}} \times 100$$

7 For advice on conducting morale surveys and some of the problems involved, *see* R. A. Morano, E. D. Howe, and David Sirota, "Opinion Surveys," *Personnel*, vol. 51 (September-October 1974), pp. 8–31.

8 Paul Varro, "The Relocation Blues," *Chain Store Age* (general merchandise/variety store edition), February 1973, pp. 61–67.

9 "The Fifty Largest Retailing Companies," *Fortune*, July 1976, pp. 210–11; and "The Fifty Largest Merchandising Companies," *Fortune*, June 15, 1968, pp. 212–13.

10 R. Dale VonRiesen, "Toward Staffing Optimality in Retail Selling," *Journal of Retailing*, vol. 49, (Winter 1973–74), pp. 37–47.

11 For a helpful guide to sales staff planning *see* R. V. Daggett, *Optimizing Selling Floor Coverage* (New York: National Retail Merchants Associtaion, 1973). *See also* "Planning Improves Performance, Productivity," *Hardware Retailing*, December 1975, pp. 33–36.

12 Richard Furash, "Salesforce Scheduling Simplified," *Stores*, June 1975, pp. 5, 27. The use of computers in such an analysis is discussed in *Retail Store System: Manpower Management Concepts* (White Plains, N.Y.: Data Processing Division, International Business Machines Corporation, 1973) and "Sentry Finds Keen Cost-Cutting Tool in Computerized Labor Scheduling," *Supermarket News*, May 10, 1976, p. 25.

13 For a discussion of job analysis and job specification, *see* Michael J. Jucius, *Personnel Management*, 7th ed. (Homewood, Ill. Richard D. Irwin, Inc., 1971), pp. 101–13.

14 *See* Samuel Feinberg, "Retailers Seek Top Grads in Curbed Recruitment," *Women's Wear Daily*, March 12, 1974, p. 13.

15 For differences of opinion about the value of some of the informa-

tion usually requested on application blanks, see Charles N. Weaver, "An Empirical Study to Aid in the Selection of Retail Salesclerks," *Journal of Retailing*, vol. 45 (Fall 1969), pp. 22–26, which reports sales performance significantly correlated with age, education, and marital status; Robert F. Hartley, "The Weighted Application Blank Can Improve Retail Employee Selection," *ibid.*, vol. 46 (Spring 1970), pp. 32–40, which recommends a technique for giving exact weights to various items on the blank; and James C. Cotham III, "Using Personal History in Retail Salesman Selection," *ibid.*, vol. 45 (Summer 1969), pp. 31–38, which reports little correlation between personal history data and the sales records of different retail major appliance salespeople.

16 Among 348 supermarket organizations, 46 percent used "aptitude and other tests" in 1970 as compared with 22 percent in 1955. *See: The Super Market Industry Speaks*, 1970, p. 28.

17 A series of skill, aptitude, and knowledge tests relating to the hardware/home center trade, developed by the National Retail Hardware Association, are described in "NRHA Develops New Personnel Evaluation and Testing Forms," *Hardware Retailing*, August 1975, pp. 160–61.

18 "How to Spot Executives Early," *Fortune*, vol. 78 (July 1968), pp. 106–11. J. P. Muczyk, T. H. Mattheiss, and Myron Gable describe a forced-choice personality test that was successful in identifying high- and low-performers among managers in a greeting card shop chain. "Predicting Success of Store Managers," *Journal of Retailing*, vol. 50 (Summer 1974), pp. 43–49.

19 "First Week on Job Held Critical," *Supermarket News*, August 21, 1972, p. 22.

20 Edith M. Lynch, "Trial Period for Employees," *Stores*, June 1974, p. 23.

21 Charles E. Kozoll, "How to Train Supervisors to Break in New Employees—Gently," *Training in Business and Industry*, May 1973, pp. 41–42.

22 *See* Edith M. Lynch, "Hiring Procedures: Avoiding Legal Pitfalls," *Stores*, June 1976, pp. 41–42, and George Kohlik, ed., *Credit Manual of Commercial Laws 1973* (New York: National Association of Credit Management, 1972), p. 185.

23 Some chains have also established regional training centers to reduce travel costs and to permit more employees to benefit from the stimulus of attending group sessions with fellow workers from other stores of the same chain. "J. C. Penney Opens First Regional Training Center," *Penney News*, July-August 1974, p. 8.

24 "Training Budgets," *Chain Store Age* (supermarket edition), March 1972, p. 94.

25 "In-Store Audio-Visual Boom, Sales Training Cited," *Home Furnishings Daily*, July 11, 1972, p. 32; "Miller & Rhoads [Richmond, Va.] Communicates with Closed-Circuit Television," *Women's Wear Daily*, August 13, 1973, p. 20.

26 "Retail Training: Teaching the Old Salesman about the New Consumer," *Training in Business and Industry*, October 1969, pp. 33–38, outlines some of the steps in the development of the National Retail Furniture Association's selling course. An 100-hour store-developed classroom course for furniture salespeople is summarized in "How Kittle's Makes Good Furniture Salespeople," *Home Furnishings Daily*, November 11, 1974, p. 13.

27 For more information about distributive education *see* L. C. Crawford and W. G. Meyer, *Organization and Administration of Distributive Education* (Columbus, Ohio: Charles E. Merrill Publishing Co., 1972) and Carrell B. Corkley, *Distributive Education: Teacher Coordinators' Handbook* (Danville, Ill.: Interstate Printers and Publishers, Inc., 1972).

28 Allen R. Jancer, *Employing the Disadvantaged: A Company Perspective* (New York: The Conference Board, 1972).

29 *See* "Minority Hiring: Quiet Progress or Benign Neglect," *Supermarket News*, September 9, 1974, pp. 1, 32–33.

30 James C. Cotham, "The Case for Personal Selling," *Business Horizons*, vol. 11 (April 1968), pp. 75–81.

31 E. B. Weiss, "Let Me Put It This Way," *Stores*, March 1970, p. 47; *see also* Bird McCord, "The Training Department as an Aid to Management Planning,"

Journal of Retailing, vol. 44 (Fall 1968), p. 68.

32 "Training Plan Keeps Union Away," *Supermarket News,* March 13, 1972, p. 21.

33 "The Brash Young Man and the Wise Old Uncles," *Forbes,* February 15, 1975, pp. 22–23.

34 *See* "Alpha Beta Combines School Theory with Store Practice," *Chain Store Age* (supermarket edition), February 1974, pp. 47–51, for an account of a supermarket chain that has developed a joint program with a local community college.

35 "Allied Maps District Manager Training," *Chain Store Age* (supermarket executive edition), June 1973, pp. 35–36.

36 *See* Murray Abott, "Ambitious Training Policy Foretold Pathmark Growth," *Supermarket News,* March 15, 1976, p. 4; Samuel Feinberg, "Managers May Be Developed without Formal Programs," *Women's Wear Daily,* August 29, 1973, p. 10.

37 "Stores Wrestle with Problem Catch-as-Catch Can Training," *Supermarket News,* March 5, 1973, p. 28; Samuel Feinberg, "Contingency Training: You Can't Afford to Neglect It," *Women's Wear Daily,* September 18, 1973, p. 30.

38 The J. C. Penney Company evaluates some of its training programs by (a) measuring the job performance of trainees before and after participating in the programs, (b) obtaining "feedback" comments from trainees and their supervisors, and (c) studying sales records of stores where the programs have been utilized. Donald Bouton, "Evaluating the Training Program," *Personnel News and Views,* vol. 4, no. 3 (1974), pp. 1–6.

RETAIL PERSONNEL
MANAGEMENT (continued)

Developing satisfactory compensation plans for rank-and-file employees and for executives constitutes a third very important personnel responsibility. Dissatisfaction with compensation plans is a common source of complaint.

■ COMPENSATION FOR RETAIL PERSONNEL

It is very difficult to devise any payment method which is satisfactory to personnel performing a wide variety of tasks that require different skills and abilities. Some of the difficulties will become apparent if we describe the requisites of an ideal plan and then see how closely the plans in use conform to this goal.

☐ Compensation plan objectives

An ideal compensation plan, designed to meet the requirements of both the store and the employee as far as this is practicable, should:

1. Keep wage costs under control. These costs, expressed as a percentage of sales, should be compared frequently with labor costs in fairly

similar stores.* Simple comparison of the store's present rate with its past experience is not adequate, since past wage costs may have also been excessive.

2. Minimize employee discontent and help to reduce labor turnover. It should not only *be* fair but should be *considered* fair by employees.
3. Be easily understood by employees and easily administered by management.
4. Provide an incentive for better work, rewarding improved performance and penalizing inefficiency.
5. Guarantee a minimum income and regular periodic payments, so as to give the employee a sense of security.
6. In addition to the basic payment, modern compensation plans provide the staff with many benefits, such as health insurance, vacations, life insurance, and subsidized cafeterias, which the employer can arrange more effectively or economically than the employees could. These benefits add an additional 20–25 percent to the average supermarket executive's and full-time employee's compensation.[1]

□ Compensating salespeople

The four main compensation plans for salespeople are:

1. Straight salary.
2. Salary plus commission on *all* net sales.
3. Quota bonus, also known as salary-quota bonus.
4. Straight commission (usually with drawing account).

Some stores use different plans in different departments and practically all retailers employ various salary supplements to stimulate their salespeople.

Straight salary The employee is paid a definite amount each payday —for example, $120 each Friday. It is the most common method of compensating salespeople, being almost universally used in small stores and in chain stores selling convenience goods.

The straight salary plan has many advantages. It is especially suitable for the small store where each employee performs many different jobs that are difficult to measure. Adequate salaries can minimize employee discontent and hold those individuals who might be attracted to other firms. This plan is easily understood, and the fixed regular payment meets the objections of many who dislike the insecurity of a fluctuating income.

---

*Note that the employees in the stores under comparison should perform relatively similar functions. If store A operates its own delivery system while store B, otherwise similar, uses an outside package-delivery service, store A will have higher payroll costs than B. This is so since A will have to pay wages to delivery-personnel, garage-personnel, etc. not incurred by B. But B will have higher costs for purchased services. See Chapter 24, "Analyzing and controlling expenses."

These advantages are so significant that straight salary, accompanied by a well-conceived personnel-rating program to provide incentive (see pp. 244–46), is probably the best single method of compensating retail salespeople. But, when used without personnel rating, it fails to offer an immediate incentive to greater effort. Straight salary also lacks any degree of automatic flexibility so that the wage-cost ratio may get out of control. This disadvantage is especially serious if sales decline significantly, since the retailer may hesitate to reduce salary rates because of union contracts, fear of employee discontent, or hope for a reversal of the sales trend. Consequently the payroll ratio may increase sharply.

Salary plus commission on all net sales This plan, which is even more common in the very large stores than straight salary, usually calls for a salary which is somewhat less than would be paid in the absence of a commission but adds a relatively low commission rate on *all* net sales. Currently, the commission rate runs about 1 percent. Thus a person with a $95 weekly salary and weekly net sales of $1,500 would receive a total of $110 (with a 1 percent rate).

Adding a small commission to the salary helps answer some of the objections to the straight salary method. Some immediate incentive to greater effort is provided; and the wage ratio becomes somewhat more flexible since commission payments will fluctuate with sales. At the same time, the main advantages of the straight salary plan are retained by keeping the basic salary large relative to the weekly pay.

Quota bonus Increasingly, some large and small retailers selling shopping and specialty goods use a basic salary plus a commission on all net sales in excess of a certain quota. This plan involves four steps:

1. Determining the weekly (or monthly) quota for the department or unit. This is usually based on past sales, with adjustment for changed conditions and for seasonal fluctuations. If $1,500 has been the average weekly sales in the past, this figure may be used as the quota. To be a sales stimulus, the quota should remain within the reach of practically all the salespeople. Yet, it cannot be too low or everyone will reach it without much effort.
2. Establishing the basic salary. This salary is usually determined on the basis of the past wage-cost ratio adjusted in the light of competitive practices. If this ratio has been about 7 percent, the basic salary might be established at 7 percent of the quota; that is, $105 on a $1,500 quota.
3. Setting the commission rate for sales in excess of the quota. In practice this commission is usually set considerably below the store's average wage cost. Frequently, the commission is set at about 2 percent.[2] In some cases the bonus is a specific dollar amount, rather than a percentage of sales in excess of the quota.
4. Deciding whether each period involves a "fresh start" (noncumula-

tive plans) or whether salespeople who fail to make their quota in one period have to fill the deficiency before becoming eligible for a bonus in the next period (cumulative plans). Most plans today are noncumulative.

How does this plan compare with our "ideal" requirements? On the favorable side, (1) the plan does stimulate sales efforts if the quota is set properly, that is low enough to include most of the salespeople and yet high enough to require some striving for accomplishment; (2) it may reduce discontent since each salesperson has a chance to earn as much as any other; (3) the basic salary does provide a steady income. However, (1) the wage cost ratio remains relatively inflexible, since the basic salary makes up the bulk of the wage payments; (2) changes in quotas may be interpreted as attempts to reduce wages and may be resented—consequently, adjustment of the quota becomes difficult, even though necessary, in periods of rising or falling sales; (3) the plan is complicated, thereby involving extra bookkeeping costs and possibly causing some confusion and resentment among employees.

Straight commission   Under the straight commission plan, employees receive a specified percentage (commission) of their net sales figure. The commission rate may be set as low as 2 percent, or as high as 9 percent of sales depending upon the type of merchandise, the store, and in some cases, the season of the year. The most common rate is 5–6 percent with perhaps an extra 1 percent for selling private brands.[3] This payment method has its widest acceptance in stores and departments selling high unit-value merchandise, such as furniture, bedding, TV, men's clothing, and shoes. The straight commission plan is often modified somewhat through the use of a "drawing account" or flat sum paid to salespeople each week or month during slow periods as an advance against future commissions and then deducted from the commissions when they are subsequently earned.

Straight commission provides an incentive for sales efforts. Commission salespeople tend to have higher earnings than those paid in other ways. To cite an extreme example, a September 1973 U.S. Department of Labor retail salesperson earnings survey in Boston reported average weekly earnings of $132.00 for salaried shoe clerks while those on commission averaged $215.50.[4] Employees can easily understand the commission system and the payments can be computed without difficulty. A drawing account provides some stability of income. From the store's point of view, the plan is very flexible and helps keep the wage-cost ratio under control as a steady percentage of sales volume.

Paradoxical though it may seem, the incentive provided by the straight commission plan has proved to be one of its weaknesses, especially for stores that desire to build a reputation for service to all customers. Salespeople paid on commission may try to avoid persons who seem merely to be "looking," who are interested in low-priced merchandise, or who want to exchange or return merchandise. Stores sometimes minimize this disadvantage through a call system which provides a supervisor to greet each customer and to assign the salespeople in rotation. In this way each salesperson gets an equal chance to make sales and cannot "pick" customers. Even so, the salesperson who tries to increase income may exert pressure on the customer to buy. Some customers object to such tactics. Another difficulty is that new salespeople, without a "following" or experience, often find it difficult to make a sufficient number of sales to obtain what they feel is an adequate income.

Salary supplements for salespeople Some retailers also provide their salespeople with opportunities for earning extra compensation which may add 10–15 percent to their regular salary. Sometimes this is done through profit sharing. Studies over the last 10–15 years show that the percentage of retail workers and executives participating in profit-sharing plans has grown significantly and may be higher than in any other major industry group.[5] About 25 percent of the supermarket chains share profits with *all* employees.[6] In 1963, Montgomery Ward and Company adopted a general profit-sharing plan covering sales and sales-supporting personnel as well as store managers, superintendents, and major executives. The National Retail Merchants Association reports that the number of pension and profit sharing for all employees, and not merely for executives, has continued to grow and improve in benefits in medium-size and large retailing firms.[7]

Prize money (P.M.'s) or extra commissions, another kind of salary supplement, may be paid for selling certain kinds of merchandise, such as private brands.[8] Dollar awards are used to encourage courteous treatment of customers. Some retailers hold sales contests in which salespeople can win valuable prizes, such as major appliances, wardrobes, and winter trips to Florida.[9]

Many department and specialty stores allow employee discounts on all purchases made in the store—and, of late, retailers are liberalizing this arrangement. Whereas, formerly, some weeks or months of service were quite typically required, today the discount privilege is granted almost immediately. Moreover, many retailers have increased their discounts; the former 10–15 percent figures have been replaced by 15, or, in even more cases, 20 percent. With employee purchases amounting to five percent or more of department and specialty store sales, retailers consider the discount as a way to promote the store's merchandise to employees as well as an important aid in retaining personnel.[10] In contrast, just 6 percent of the food chains grant employee discounts and even in these firms the discounts are held within the 5–10 percent range. With their relatively low mark-ups and the possibility that the discount privilege might be abused (employees purchasing for friends and relatives), these chains tend to minimize this form of salary supplement.

Still other salary supplements include paid holidays, the cash award given for usable suggestions and the special bonus, based on length of service or other factors, often given at Christmas time. Finally, various insurance and pension programs provide compensation and protection in case of illness, accident, disability, or retirement (see pp. 249–50).

□ Compensating sales-supporting employees

Straight salary is the most popular way of compensating sales-supporting employees. Widespread use of the salary plan results in part from the difficulties involved in setting quotas or in finding a satisfactory basis for a commission. Yet a standard unit of output can be set for some nonselling jobs and payment could be made for the number of units produced. Department and chain store industrial engineering and "work study" bureaus have developed new methods to measure productivity in an increasing number of sales-supporting jobs. Thus, the number of units marked may serve as a basis of payment for people who mark goods; the number of packages put up as a basis for paying packers; and the number of pages or lines typed, for stenographers. But even in these instances, it is hard to get a standard unit of output. For the typist the number of lines typed depends somewhat upon the material, and this is a variable factor. Not all goods are marked in the same way, and various-sized packages have different time requirements for packing.

Incentive plans for nonselling employees are limited almost entirely to the large retail firms. However, in retail stores of all sizes, sales-supporting employees are usually eligible for most of the salary supplements given to selling employees, especially discounts on purchases, insurance and pensions, profit sharing, cash awards, and special bonuses.

□ Managerial compensation

Most compensation plans at the managerial level include an immediate incentive to greater efforts. Also see the discussion of top management compensation in Chapter 3.

Buyers Most department and specialty stores pay their buyers a bonus, in addition to salary, with the specific arrangement usually set forth in a definite written contract.[11] A few organizations, however, believe that bonus plans put too much emphasis on short-run departmental goals that may actually be contrary to the firm's long-run general welfare. Plan 3, described below, attempts to meet this objection.

Six common methods are employed for determining the bonus, as follows, but some stores use more complicated combinations of these plans:

1. Bonus based on sales—either a percentage of the total sales of the department (such as 1 percent) or a percentage of the increase in sales over a quota. A stated minimum gross margin is also often required.
2. Bonus based on increased sales plus increased gross margin or net profit. For example, a store may agree to pay "1 percent of sales increase over previous year plus 5 percent of additional net profits after income taxes."
3. Bonus based on total store operations. Such an arrangement is designed to induce buyers to "merchandise" with a storewide approach to problems. The amount the buyer receives is dependent on a management review of the department's operation during the year.
4. Bonus based on departmental net profit, either before or after federal taxes. The bonus may vary from 1 to 10 percent and it may not apply until after a stated dollar amount of net profit has been reached, e.g., $10,000.
5. Bonus based on a department's contribution. "Contribution" is usually defined as the dollar gross margin of the department minus specified controllable expenses. (For further explanation of the contribution concept, see Chapter 24, "Analyzing and controlling expenses.") The bonus is calculated as a percentage of the department's contribution and commonly ranges from 1 to 3 percent.
6. Bonus based on departmental gross margin, such as 3 percent or more of the gross margin realized.

Chain store managers Variety, discount, and junior department store chains often pay a salary and then give the manager 10–15 percent of the profits made by the store. Other firms use a drawing account and give the manager 10–20 percent of the profits minus what has already been received from the account. Such plans give the manager a direct incentive to make the store produce profits. Even when a salary is paid, it is kept relatively low, so that a large part of the manager's income results from the store's profit.

Food and drug chains, on the other hand, usually base their incentive payments on sales, a common plan being a salary plus 1–2 percent of sales. Although this arrangement encourages the manager to seek volume irrespective of profits, the chains feel that other controls will insure profitability.

Chain organizations in several other fields—auto supplies, for example—also use bonuses based on the store's contribution to company profits. Frequently, the bonus is paid only on the contribution above an established goal for the store; and it may be divided between manager and assistant manager on a 3-to-1 or some other fixed basis.

Companies frequently have to try several plans before they find the most suitable one, and after time, even that one may have to be changed to meet new conditions or variations in company objectives. For example, the McDonald's Corporation tried paying the managers of its company-owned (not franchised) hamburger shops a bonus based on sales increase. However, that increase seemed to depend upon so many factors beyond the manager's control that the company eliminated its formal incentives. Instead, it substituted salary raises based upon supervisors' judgment. That approach appeared too subjective and unstandardized, and was replaced by bonuses related to success in meeting Q.S.C. (quality, service, and cleanliness) standards plus a bonus on contribution to profit. This didn't provide enough motivation toward all company objectives, so it was changed to an overly-complicated system that included separate bonuses for labor-cost control, for control of other costs, for sales increases, and for meeting Q.S.C. standards. In 1974 the company simplified its arrangements to include base salaries that then ranged from $11,000 to $17,500 per year, depending in part on local living costs and in part on supervisor's judgment of performance, plus bonuses of up to 40 percent of salary for success in meeting Q.S.C., cost control, and staff development objectives.[12]

Senior executives Previous mention has been made of the search for executive talent. (See pp. 72–84 and 216.) An attractive compensation plan is only one major factor in attracting and retaining properly qualified retail executives. Studies indicate that the fundamental satisfactions desired by those who operate their own stores or who serve in executive positions for others are as follows:

1. Financial rewards commensurate with the responsibilities of the position.
2. Freedom of action within the individual's sphere of responsibility with commensurate authority.
3. Adequate title and prestige of position.
4. Stability of position, with adequate provision for retirement.
5. Satisfactory working quarters and conditions. Many executives report that they want comfortable offices with adequate light and ventilation and good furnishings. One company president who had recently moved into a new office was heard to say: "I'd gladly take $5,000 a year off my present salary if it were necessary to justify my present office facilities.
6. Association with an organization that is "moving ahead," so that one may take pride in being a part of it.
7. A position that offers an opportunity of public service.

Despite the fact that financial reward is by no means the only consideration important to retail executives, a fact which is currently not given sufficient attention in the retail field, dollar compensation *is* significant.

The majority of small store proprietors pay themselves a regular weekly or biweekly salary. This salary may be adjusted from year to year according to the proprietor's judgment as to the expected profits. Moreover, it may be supplemented from time to time or at the end of each year by extra withdrawals of funds if the profit position is satisfactory.

While the executives of some large retail organizations are paid by salary only, the incentive aspect is so important that most of them receive a salary plus some form of bonus or profit-sharing arrangement, all or part of which may be deferred until after retirement when the recipient will be (presumably) in a lower tax bracket. Option plans which permit the executive to benefit (by paying a capital gains tax rather than an income tax) from advances in the price of the firm's stock have also been common. Although such deferred compensation plans became very popular during the 1950s and 1960s, they have subsequently been replaced in many instances by arrangements for more immediate and current payments.[13] Still other typical elements in the executive compensation package are insurance payments and pension plans.

In some instances the firm's bonus or profit-sharing arrangement is not formalized, the amount paid being determined each year by the president or the board of directors. But most firms set aside a fixed percentage of net profits as a bonus or profit-sharing fund, to be divided among key executives in ratio to their salaries or according to some other predetermined formula.

One recent study of the 38 U.S. companies that had profit-sharing trust funds with assets in excess of $50 million included 10 retailing firms, as well as 25 manufacturers and three banks. These 10 large retailing organizations, which together employed almost a million workers, enjoyed profit rates (return on equity) substantially above the average reported for other large chain store companies.[14] A study that cites Lowe's Companies of North Wilkesboro, N.C. (paint and home supplies retail chain) as one of the "ten most responsible companies" in the U.S., in part because of its extensive profit-sharing program, comments that it enjoys the highest sales and profits-per-employee of any retail firm in the country.[15]

The long-run nature of the executive compensation plan should not, however, force the company to retain incompetent officials. The plan should include equitable separation arrangements and, in some cases, early retirement at a reduced pension.

Finally, the executive compensation plan should be reviewed frequently. In part, such a review is necessary because constantly changing taxation and inheritance laws alter the tax status of different executive remuneration techiques. But the plan also needs periodic review from the point of view of individual executives. An executive's needs change with the various stages of the career cycle. In one's thirties and early forties, one's main requirement may be for cash; from forty-five until mid-fifties, the executives may be able to forego some immediate cash in favor of stock options or a long-range incentive bonus plan; and upon approaching retirement, a deferral arrangement may be attractive.

□ Job evaluation

Job evaluation is a method of setting fair compensation rates for positions that are filled by current as well as by new or prospective workers and thus is discussed at this point in our study of retail personnel practices. But a sound job evaluation program rests upon the same sort of thorough job study mentioned in the preceding chapter as the basis for preparing meaningful job specifications. Job evaluation is simply a carefully worked out program for appraising the value of jobs and obtaining an equitable pay relationship among them. It has been carried on in a more or less formal way in industrial plants for many years, but only recently has it received the close attention it deserves from retail personnel executives.

Objectives   The objectives of job evaluation are:

1. To implement a company policy of equal pay for equal work, thereby building employee goodwill.
2. To pay all employees in proportion to their responsibilities and to the difficulty of their work.
3. To recognize monetary differentials for different quality and quantity of work, thus giving employees an incentive for improved performance.
4. To provide a basis for explaining to employees why a job is valued as it is.
5. To establish pay rates in keeping with those for similar work in the community.
6. And through the above steps, to improve morale, reduce turnover, and obtain conformity with federal wage legislation.

Job evaluation methods   A great variety of methods are employed to evaluate jobs in retail stores. One progressive store, for example, evaluates all jobs on the basis of four major groups of factors, with weights within each group assigned as follows:

1. *Skill requirement factors,* including education—10 percent; job knowledge—15 percent; customer contact—10 percent; personal contact (other than customer contact)—10 percent; special aptitudes —7 percent.
2. *Responsibility requirement factors,* including supervision—12 percent; and responsibility—15 percent.

3. *Effort requirement factors,* including mental effort—9 percent; and physical effort—6 percent.
4. *Working conditions factor*—6 percent.

A job evaluation committee composed of the appropriate executives prepares these evaluations for each division and distributes them to the divisional manager concerned. Inequities are promptly corrected, after which the personnel manager prepares a total store summary and forwards it to top management.

Steps should be taken to gain employee acceptance before any job evaluation is instituted. Unless employees understand the reasons for its adoption and how it will affect their work, the program will not produce its maximum results. Management should avoid such errors as lack of simplicity, failure to apply common sense, and general impatience for results. Job evaluation is a painstaking process, and its value will depend upon the care with which it is planned and carried out.

A survey of 98 department stores some years ago found 47 percent used some kind of job evaluation.[16] While this figure is far too high for retailing as a whole, the gains from job evaluation are so significant that some retail store executives at the 1975 National Retail Merchants Association convention predicted: "Job evaluation, tied to cost cutting, will get top priority. . . ."[17] Experience has proven it a necessary and useful tool in determining and maintaining a satisfactory compensation program.

■ STIMULATING SATISFACTORY PERSONNEL PERFORMANCE

As already emphasized, personnel management's responsibility does not end with the hiring and initial training of employees. Some of the most important personnel functions involve maintaining and improving the present staff's performance level. To a degree, achieving this goal depends upon the spirit which management injects into the firm's personnel—the birthday greetings to salespeople, the breakfast for the contest winner, and the picture of the "best manager of the week" in the weekly house organ.

More than enthusiasm, however, is needed to stimulate employees to a higher-level performance of their responsibilities. There must be a suitable compensation plan, preferably based on sound job evaluation; continuous evaluation of personnel; equitable promotion, transfer, demotion, and discharge of some workers; adequate working conditions; appropriate employee service activities; and successful handling of employees' complaints. Compensation plans and job evaluation have already been covered; the other activities will be discussed in the remaining sections of this chapter.

□ Evaluating personnel

Personnel evaluation seeks to give the retailer a carefully formed opinion as to the value of each employee to the firm* Such evaluation is important as the basis for salary adjustments, promotions, transfers, and terminations and also as a method of encouraging employees to do better work. It aids in detecting employees who are "slipping," before they have fallen to such a low performance level that termination of employment is necessary. The evaluation process brings the management into closer touch with the employee, which leads to greater mutual understanding.

Careful evaluation of personnel is difficult because an employee's services include many factors which cannot be measured objectively. Not only is the employee's production important; ability, loyalty, honesty, and work attitude are also significant. Many of these elements are matters of opinion, and various individuals may differ in rating the same employee. In spite of such difficulties, worthwhile results can be obtained if the retailer will maintain adequate up-to-date records, set up objective standards wherever possible, get opinions from a number of sources, and carry out the process on a regular schedule.

In the small store Many small store proprietors fail to use definite, objective standards in personnel evaluation; hence personal likes and dislikes excessively influence their opinions. Greater objectivity may be obtained, however, through recognition of the importance of establishing measurable criteria to use as yardsticks. A salesperson, for example, might be judged on the basis of sales, both in dollars and in number of transactions, customer complaints, errors in filling orders and recording sales, the number of times late or absent from work, and the ratio of dollar value of goods returned to sales. The proprietor may occasionally get customer reaction to certain employees by interviewing a number of patrons. Fairly similar techniques may be used to evaluate any sales-supporting employees.

In the large store A committee, frequently consisting of the personnel director and two or three other executives, supervises the systematic "personnel review" or evaluation in most large retail firms. This committee originates forms for recording the performance and ratings of each employee (see Figure 9–1). Although each individual may be rated as often as once a month or as infrequently as once a year, about every six months is usual. To minimize personal prejudice, each employee is usually rated by two to four associates. The factors appraised usually include some or all of the following: personality, attendance, sales, industry, initiative, cooperation, knowledge of the

---

* Personnel evaluation should not be confused with job evaluation. Job evaluation involves measuring the difficulty of handling a particular assignment, for instance, shoe buyer, and determining its value to the company. Personnel evaluation involves measuring how well an individual is performing as a shoe buyer.

FIGURE 9–1   Job performance form

TO: _____   DATE: ___2-/5-_____

___Duppy, Joseph___   ___Asst. Mgr.___ ___971-6___   _____
Name of Person to be Rated   Position   Department   House Number

Please check the appropriate squares below to indicate the above-named person's present job performance. Give detailed comments below, on all ratings checked Deficient or Poor. For example, if you have checked Quantity of Work as deficient, you might comment that the cause is lack of interest; or lack of stamina; a personality clash with a fellow worker; lack of knowledge of his job; or lack of planning.

	POOR	DEFIC	AVER	GOOD	EXCEL
QUANTITY OF WORK				✓	
QUALITY OF WORK					✓
LEADERSHIP (Includes training and supervision of subordinates)				✓	
INITIATIVE (Can he see things to be done?)					✓
AMOUNT OF SUPERVISION REQUIRED					✓
ATTITUDE TOWARD OTHERS (Is he pleasant, courteous, tactful, cooperative, self-confident and aggressive?)					✓
ORGANIZING ABILITY (Can he analyze a problem or a bad situation and effect a solution smoothly and easily?)					✓
OVER-ALL RATING					✓

comments: _Mr Duppy has become a valuable assistant in the department. Is learning shoe know-how rapidly. Sees his job and does it thoroughly._

PROMOTIONAL POSSIBILITIES: Is this person promotable immediately? _Yes_ What more responsible position do you think he could fill ably? _Asst - larger shoe dept_ What more responsible position does he have as a goal, if any? _Mgr - shoes_ If not immediately promotable, when do you think he will be? _6 months_

___M Manager___   ___Joe Duppy___
Signature of Department Manager   Signature of Person Rated

___D. Smith___
Signature of Divisional Manager

After discussing this rating with the Employe, please return as soon as possible to the Personnel Office

Courtesy The Emporium, San Francisco

job, loyalty to the firm, accuracy, appearance, treatment of customers, health, and willingness and ability to assume responsibility.

Another type of personnel evaluation for salespeople is the "shopping report" prepared by an outside organization. This report covers important points regarding salesmanship, the appearance of the salesperson and the department, and the extent of compliance with the store system. See the discussion of service shopping on p. 228.

The committee reviews the individual performance records and ratings and employees are divided into several groups: (1) Those who deserve promotion; (2) those who should stay where they are; (3) those who should be shifted to some other department or job in the hope that they will do better there; (4) those who should be discharged if they do not improve before the next periodic review; and (5) those who have previously been warned that they must improve, have failed to do so, and should be discharged.

□ Relocating personnel

The relocation of employees is common in retail stores, just as it is in practically every career field. Some relocations will be *promotions;* others will *transfer* the person to a job in another store or department or to a position within the same department with about the same responsibility and pay; still others, less common, will involve *demotion* because of unsatisfactory performance.

Promotions Promotion from within an organization serves both management and employees. Management gains qualified personnel to fill responsible executive positions. The able employee obtains an opportunity to advance and the satisfaction of participating in an organization that recognizes and rewards ability. One of the best ways to build employee goodwill, to offer an incentive for improved performance, and to hold valuable employees is to assure them that they have a "job with a future."

Transfers Transferring a worker to another job will often benefit both employer and employee. Some transfers are made to find an assignment for which the employee is better suited by training, ability, and temperament. Others result from the employer's desire to stimulate the employee's interest in the business or to reduce the monotony associated with the steady performance of a certain task. Sometimes transfers are designed to broaden the employees' backgrounds and to prepare them for advancement; this use of the transfer is important especially in chain and department stores.

Demotions As a general rule, no demotion should take place until the retailer is convinced that successful transfer is impossible. Demoting employees requires great skill and tact. Frequently the demoted employee takes the new job with a feeling of having been "railroaded" or unfairly treated. Unless goodwill can be retained (or soon regained), it is best to sever connection. Satisfactory demotions can sometimes be carried out—for instance, when the firm has to contract its operations, or when the employee realizes that age or physical defects preclude continuing the present assignment. But the retailer should recognize the difficulties in demoting an employee.

□ Terminations

Employers today regard terminations with increasing disfavor. This attitude is partly the result of the growth of unions, with the employer hesitating to discharge a worker for fear of being accused of antiunion activities. But other factors have also played a part. Many retailers try to stabilize employment as much as possible so an to reduce the payments they have to make to state and federal unemployment insurance programs. Merchants also realize that an excessive number of terminations may cause other employees to worry about their jobs and, as a result, lower morale. Moreover, a termination involves the loss of the firm's investment, which may be quite considerable, in the employee's training. Termination should ordinarily be considered only after serious attempts at relocation have been made and the employee has been given adequate warning.

In spite of this dislike for terminations, management should not hesitate to face the employee with its decision when one is required. Certainly the employee has a right to at least an interview with the proprietor of the small store or with someone from the personnel department in the large organization and, in most cases, to receive the reasons leading to the termination. The store will reap benefits if it can retain some of the discharged employee's goodwill, so that that person will not go into the community and spread unfavorable comments. Although not even the most carefully conducted termination procedure can always avoid this unfortunate result, much success can be achieved by a well-handled final interview. Some companies arrange counseling and placement services for executives who have been released.[18]

☐ Retail working conditions

The personnel department has the duty of reviewing and suggesting improvements in working conditions. (See also the discussion of this subject on pp. 64–65.) It must look at such matters as lighting, heating, ventilation, rest periods, working hours, safety, and vacations from both the employer's and the employee's viewpoint. Perhaps certain employees can be given somewhat reduced hours without reduction in their accomplishments. Rest periods may increase efficiency. An employees' cafeteria may provide good food at reasonable prices, and still pay its own way or at least cover its direct costs.

Working hours   The hours that retail stores are open for business have increased greatly in recent decades with the increasing trend towards night and Sunday openings. (See the discussion of store hours in Chapter 21, "Customer services.") But the individual retail employee's working hours have been progressively shortened in recent years. The 40-hour work week is fairly standard for retail workers in metropolitan areas, and the work week is only slightly longer in rural area stores. Staggered hours or a double shift of employees is used when stores are open six or seven days a week. Some stores pay substantial premiums for Sunday work.[19]

Safety Retailers are now more "safety conscious" than ever before. Safety provisions and preventive measures should receive constant attention to reduce accidents. Employee injury rates in retail stores range from about 2.0 per 100 work/years in apparel shops to 9.1 per 100 work/years in department stores, 11.2 in auto dealerships, and 11.9 in food stores.[20] Special attention should be paid, among other factors, to safeguarding mechanical and electrical equipment, providing nonslip walking and working surfaces, maintaining fire protection and proper exits, and observing safe methods of merchandise handling and stock-keeping. The increasing number of government regulations concerning working conditions, particularly the Federal Occupational Safety and Health Act of 1970, has also imposed additional safety requirements.[21]

□ Service activities for employees

Retailers increasingly provide employee benefits beyond the unemployment insurance, workmen's compensation, and old-age pensions (social security) required by law. The largest retailers spend very substantial sums every year for employee vacations, group life insurance, purchase discounts, illness allowances and medical care, profit sharing, pension funds, and other benefits. The survey of 98 department stores cited previously disclosed that 73 percent sponsor athletic and recreational activities; 62 percent aid employees to locate living quarters; 62 percent offer a fully equipped medical department; 77 percent provide group insurance; and 43 percent offer savings and loan programs.[22] Still other retailers engage in educational activities, and offer counseling services on a wide variety of subjects, including preparations for retirement.

Sometimes the service work immediately pays for itself, as when a retailer offers health services which increase productivity. It is quite impossible to say whether the costs of other services, such as pension systems, are offset by greater effort. But retailers' service activities are important in attracting and keeping employees, and competition is forcing more and more employers to undertake them. Nevertheless, at least one knowledgeable consultant believes that most retailers have failed to develop truly adequate and competitive fringe benefit programs that have kept pace with inflation.[23]

Medical and health services Large retail establishments furnish medical and health services on a formalized, continuous basis, with one or more full-time doctors and a staff of nurses. The smaller firm may use a doctor only part time, often having regular hours at the store to serve employees. A visiting nurse may be retained to aid employees confined to their homes. Some organizations have set up dental clinics

Vacations, which are steadily being liberalized, are still another way to improve the health of employees.[24]

Increasingly retail organizations have encouraged and aided their employees to take medical and hospitalization insurance, often through organizations like "Blue Shield" and "Blue Cross." Under these plans, both the store and the employee pay part of the cost, with the latter's contribution being deducted from one's paycheck. The present emphasis on medical care is also demonstrated by the frequency with which union negotiators seek greater medical and dental benefits.[25] And, of course, both employer and employee pay a compulsory payroll tax in support of the medicare hospitalization and medical programs.

Recreational and educational activities   Store-sponsored recreational activities such as orchestras, glee clubs, dramatics, athletic events, all-store picnics, costume parties, dances, and other social events can help build goodwill. Some firms provide facilities for the groups they sponsor—an auditorium where the glee club and dramatic group may entertain, an athletic field, a hall for social gatherings. Management, however, should go slowly in "pushing" recreational activities, and all signs of paternalism must be avoided. Probably the retailer's best approach is to sponsor only those activities in which the employees take some initiative. A common method of ascertaining employee interest is to establish one or more recreation clubs which are partly supported by employees' dues.

Educational activities of retailers, other than those directly connected with the training program, are not wide-spread but are steadily becoming more common. Some of the larger firms have long maintained libraries, and increasingly they are offering financial assistance, through scholarships and work-study arrangements, to encourage employees to continue their education in business schools, colleges, and universities.

Employee financial benefit plans   Retailers extend other kinds of financial aid to their employees through group insurance, mutual-aid associations, retirement pensions, and savings and loan programs.

1. Group insurance   Low-cost group life insurance plans, under which both employer and employee make a contribution, have been restricted chiefly to large stores and chain organizations, but some retail trade associations now sponsor group programs for smaller member companies and their workers. Employee contributions are deducted from pay checks. There are no age restrictions and no physical examination is required. But the insurance lapses if the employee leaves the company (although some plans permit conversion of some or all of the group insurance to another kind of policy); and, since it is term insurance, it has no cash value.

2. Mutual-aid associations   These voluntary associations provide sickness, accident, and death benefits for employees not covered by

workmen's compensation and insurance plans. They also render extensive assistance in times of financial stress. They are usually incorporated,
to have a legal existence separate from that of the store. Contributions
come from both employees and employer. The employees usually control the association, although workers and management may cooperate
in its operation. In some cases the employer underwrites the establishment of the association and then leaves it up to employee contributions
to carry on from that point.

3. *Retirement pensions* The federal Social Security pension plan
applies to retail, as well as other, employees. Both the employer and the
employee contribute at least 5.85 percent on wages up to $15,300 per
year plus additional amounts resulting from scheduled increases in the
tax rate (up to 9.45 percent in the year 2011) and inflation adjustments
to the taxable wage ceiling. Upon retiring at ages 62 to 65, a worker
receives a pension ranging between $85 to $820 plus inflation adjustments per month, depending upon age and date of retirement, average
earnings subject to social security, and number of dependents. The plan
also provides disability income benefits and partial benefits for widows,
and other surviving dependents. In addition, an increasing number of
firms have their own retirement plans to supplment these payments.[28]

4. *Savings and loan plans* Some large retailers provide savings
plans. Employees usually make periodic cash deposits, which are then
supplemented through contributions from the employer. For example,
employees of one large retailer may deposit 3 percent of their annual
pay in the savings plan and the company—depending upon its annual
earnings—will contribute an amount equal to 25 to 50 percent of each
employee's deposit. In a recent year, this firm contributed over $1.7
million to this plan. Many retailers, both large and small, encourage
the purchase of government savings bonds through deduction of agreed
amounts from the employee's regular pay check. Others offer emergency loan services through which a worker may secure funds to be
repaid by wage deductions. Management may encourage the establishment of a credit union to handle such loans.

□ Handling employee complaints

Employee complaints cover a wide range of subjects—hours, wages,
promotions, working conditions, "fringe" benefits, and tactics of other
salespeople. Many retailers go to great lengths to minimize or eliminate
such complaints. Practically all of the work of the personnel division, as
well as the employee-service activities discussed in the previous section,
are helpful in reducing complaints. Many retailers use an "exit interview" to try to learn the causes of dissatisfaction when an employee
resigns and to undertake remedial action. Figure 9–2 shows the exit
interview checklist used in one retail firm. Still other companies

FIGURE 9–2 Exit interview checklist

		Date
Name	Department	
Date Employed	Last Day Worked	Salary or Rate

Why is employee leaving? _____
What, if anything, was especially disliked about work? _____
Were working conditions satsfactory? (light, heat, atmosphere, etc.) _____
Was equipment for your job satisfactory? _____
Were rest periods—eating periods satisfactory? _____
Was salary satisfactory? (increase?) _____
Does employee have any unfinished financial business with the company?
  (Credit Union, etc.) _____
Was treatment received from this office satisfactory? _____
How was the treatment from the other employees? _____
Does employee think a person has opportunity for advancement in this firm? _____
Does employee have any suggestions for improvement on anything
  within organization? _____
Does employee think management is interested in employee? _____
Was ample training given on job? _____
Would employee be interested in working again for the company? _____
Other comments:_____

_____   _____
Signature of Interviewer   Signature of Employee

encourage their employees to elect representatives to meet with management and discuss problems of mutual interest. Employer-employee committees are established to consider especially difficult problems, such as improving working conditions and the more advantageous planning of vacations.

Nevertheless, complaints continue to develop and provision should be made to handle them promptly and effectively. The proprietor of the small store usually handles them directly and informally; but the large operation needs a definite procedure for dealing with them. Such a procedure has been made imperative by the growth of retail trade unions, since the union demands that there be some responsible executive with whom it can negotiate and from whom it can expect action when agreements have been reached. The personnel director, or a special assistant well versed in personnel relations, is usually given the duty of dealing with complaints.

☐ Retail unions

Growth of labor organizations Unions are not a new development in the retail field. Several unions of store employees existed as early as 1882.[27] Their main aim of seeking shorter hours earned them the name of "early closing societies." Although these early unions had some successes and experienced some growth, most of the limited development of retail workers' unions has occurred since the early 1930s.

Although local retail operations are specifically exempted from the 1935 National Labor Relations Act, interstate retail firms are subject to the act's prohibitions against interference with unions, discrimination against union members, and refusal to bargain with unions. In other words, if a majority of the employees of an interstate retail organization form a union and send representatives to talk over certain grievances, the management must negotiate concerning the complaints.[28] Whereas at an earlier time the store could decide whether to set up an agency to handle employees' complaints, today the machinery must exist in any retail establishment with organized employees. A few states have placed similar requirements upon retailers with completely intrastate operations.

Unionization has spread slowly in the retail field despite this favorable legal situation and union success in obtaining the closed shop and checkoff (automatic deduction of union dues from wages) in some department and chain stores. Probably somewhat less than 10 percent of all retail employees are unionized, although unions have made strong inroads in some cities and among some sales-supporting employee groups, such as truck drivers, warehouse workers, elevator operators, and maintenance staffs. However, membership in the major retail unions has grown substantially in recent years. The Retail Clerks International Association (AFL–CIO) had over 630,000 members at the end of 1972; the Retail, Wholesale and Department Store Union (AFL–CIO), 198,000; and the Amalgamated Meat Cutters and Butcher Workmen of North America (AFL–CIO) had about 530,000 members including a considerable number employed in wholesale and retail food firms.[29] These unions are currently trying to attract more discount house, supermarket, department store, and specialty store employee members, and have conducted some long and costly strikes in the process.

Union aims In general, retail unions have sought such goals as union recognition, the closed shop, shorter hours, higher wages, extra pay for overtime, paid vacations, health and welfare programs, grievance procedures, seniority rights, and job security.[30] In some cases, the unions have achieved formal contracts that provide substantial gains, especially in regard to hours, wages, paid vacations, and overtime pay. The efforts to achieve job security are illustrated by the provisions in some of the contracts in the supermarket industry, one of the more unionized segments of retailing. Agreements with the Amalgamated Meat Cutters in some cities forbid the retail sale of prepackaged meats.[31] The National Labor Relations Board has upheld a supermarket union contract which specified that suppliers' delivery workers could not place merchandise on store shelves (a common practice in distributing bakery products and certain other types of merchandise) since, under the contract, this work was to be reserved for store employees.[32] Supermarket plans to reduce labor costs with electronic checkout systems by using shelf price signs instead of stamping price figures on each individual can or package met with strong opposition from the unions as well as from some consumer groups.[33] To forestall union activities, retailers in some cities have formed their own voluntary agreements to establish improved wages, hours, and other benefits.

Wage and hour laws   The retail unions have supported both state and federal wage and hour laws as one step toward higher wages. A few states have had such laws for some time but it was not until 1961 that the federal Fair Labor Standards (Wage and Hour) Law was amended to cover a substantial number of retail workers. A 1974 amendment broadened the law to cover practically all retail businesses with sales at $250,000 or more per year. The minimum wage has been raised several times, reaching $2.30 per hour for all covered reatil workers (except handicapped and part-time student employees) by 1977. Workers, except executive, professional, and certain higher-paid commission sales employees, must be paid at 1½ times their regular rate for all work in excess of 40 hours per week.

Provincial laws throughout Canada provide minimum wages ranging from $1.75 per hour to $2.50 per hour, establish mandatory paid vacation periods, impose overtime pay requirements, regulate working conditions for young people, and prohibit various types of employment and wage discrimination.[34]

Certain implications of the minimum wage and hour laws for the retailers covered are quite clear. One is that retailers are compelled to maintain the differential between those whose wages are advanced by the minimum and other workers already exceeding it. Another is that the rising minimum has accelerated the move toward self-service and automation and caused many retailers to place greater emphasis on productivity.

Management reaction to unions   Although management's first reaction to the spread of unionism was to look for some method of "smashing the union," increasing numbers of enlightened retailers, like alert business leaders in all fields, soon decided to try to improve conditions and minimize grievances. The leading retailers in some cities have agreed to "codes of ethics" calling for better working conditions, shorter hours, and higher wages. A number of firms have actively encouraged a degree of employee participation in management. Other companies are distributing " 'jobholders' annual reports" and employee policy books, and making other efforts to acquaint employees with their labor policies, what management is already doing for its workers, and what it hopes to do in the future. In the past, all too often, major difficulties in personnel relations have been caused by management weaknesses. Fortunately, alert executives recognize this fact and are taking measures to correct the situation.

Since retailing is a field of relatively small establishments with close relationships between proprietor and employees, since many retail employees hope to establish their own stores at a later time, and since many employees are on a part-time basis while many others look upon retailing as a temporary means of making a living, retail unions have had difficulties in recruiting members. Yet those unions seem likely to grow and gain greater strength in the future.

Many retailers see only "bad" results from union growth, especially loss of control over personnel. In contrast, a few argue that the end result may be employees who are more appreciative of the problems of management, more willing to cooperate in making suggestions for improving operations, and—because of a greater feeling of security—are more enthusiastic about their jobs. In large measure, securing these benefits depends upon a progressive personnel program, which is believed in and adhered to by the management and made absolutely clear to all employees.

Regardless of any personal attitudes toward retail unions, retailers cannot afford to overlook their legal and moral responsibilities to their employees. Familiarity and full compliance with city, state, and federal labor regulations are essential.[35] In addition, personnel policies must anticipate and prepare for future developments. Above all, the retailer must provide an environment in which employees can work pleasantly and effectively.

■ REVIEW AND DISCUSSION QUESTIONS

1 Explain some of the major difficulties in devising a satisfactory compensation plan for retail personnel? Explain.

2 As the proprietor of a retail store, under what conditions or circumstances would you adopt each of the main methods of compensating salespeople?

3 Analyze the pros and cons for paying salespeople a straight commission in (a) a fabric store, (b) a new car agency, (c) a jewelry store.

4 Evaluate the employee discount policies of three specific retailers in your area. In each case, determine the discount percentage allowed; whether it applies to all merchandise in the store; and whether all employees are eligible.

5 As a retailer, would you consider it wise to give your employees "P.M.s" or bonuses for selling slow-moving merchandise? Why would you permit manufacturers or other vendors to offer "P.M.s" to your employees for selling selected items? Defend your answer.

6 (a) What sales-supporting personnel might be paid on a piece-rate or unit-of-work basis? Which ones might be suitably compensated under other incentive plans? Which ones should be on straight hourly, weekly, or monthly salaries? (b) What plans are generally used in actual practice? How do you explain any differences between prevailing practices and your answer to part (a)?

7 In your judgment what are the most satisfactory ways for compensating (a)

department-store buyers, (b) chain discount-house managers, (c) chain women's ready-to-wear shop managers, (d) general managers of the branches of a mail-order house, and (e) major executives in large retail firms? Explain.

8 Discuss the meaning, objectives, and methods of job evaluation.

9 Summarize the main current trends in retail working conditions. In employee service activities. How has recent legislation affected working conditions and service activities? Discuss the impact of these trends on the activities of the personnel department.

10 How do you account for the relatively slow growth of retail trade unions in this country? Comment concisely on their future growth possibilities.

■ NOTES AND REFERENCES

1 *1974 Personnel Department Research, Special Research Report #7*, Chicago: The Super Market Institute, 1974, Table 9.

2 "NMRA Survey of Incentive Programs," *Personnel News and Views*, vol. 4, no. 2 (1974), pp. 28–29.

3 "NMRA Survey of Incentive Programs."

4 U.S. Department of Labor, Bureau of Labor Statistics, *Department Stores, Occupational Earnings*, Preliminary Report S0–35, Serial No. 705, October 1974. *Average* earnings varied considerably from city to city and were generally lower than the Boston compensation cited. However, commission furniture salespeople in New York averaged $333.00 per week. Commissions earned may have been affected by the time of the year since *September* is an important month for clothing and shoe sales.

5 Gunnar Engen, "A New Direction and Growth in Profit Sharing," *Monthly Labor Review*, July 1967, pp. 6–7.

6 An additional 27 percent have profit sharing limited to certain managerial personnel. Seventy percent of the companies pay an annual bonus (21 percent to all full-timers). *The Supermarket Industry Speaks*, 1970 (Chicago: The Super Market Institute, 1970), p. 27.

7 National Retail Merchants Association, *Executive Compensation in Retailing* (New York: the Association, 1973), p. 41.

8 Forty, out of 58 stores in a midwestern city responding to a survey on the subject, said that their salespeople received some P.M.'s, but that they constituted a small portion of total compensation. Dale Varble and L. E. Bergerson, "The Use and Facets of P.M.'s—A Survey of Retailers," *Journal of Retailing*, vol. 48 (Winter 1972–73), pp. 40–47.

9 Louis Moses, *Extra Incentives for Retail Salespeople*. Washington, D.C.: Menswear Retailers of America, 1972, describes twenty-three different successful sales contests.

10 *Financial and Operating Results of Department and Specialty Stores of 1974*. New York: (Financial Executives Division) National Retail Merchants Association, 1975, pp. iv, vi. Union agreements with the Gimbel and Bloomingdale department stores in New York provide for a 25 percent discount on some merchandise categories, "Store Union, Gimbels OK New Pay Pact," *Women's Wear Daily*, June 11, 1969, p. 2.

11 Several typical bonus contracts are illustrated in National Retail Merchants Association, *Executive Compensation in Retailing*, pp. 46–62.

12 Earl Sasser and Samuel H. Pettway, "Case of Big Mac's Pay Plans," *Harvard Business Review*, vol. 52 (July-August 1974), pp. 30–46.

13 Samuel Feinberg, "Execs Favor Cash in Pocket Over Golden Handcuffs," *Women's Wear Daily*, August 14, 1973, p. 8.

14 Profit Sharing Foundation press release, reported in Bureau of National Affairs *Retail/Services Labor Report*, February 13, 1975, pp. 3–4. 1973 return on equity for the ten companies ranged

from 10.9 to 24.6 percent with the median at 13.4 percent. This compares with medians of 10.9 percent and 12.4 percent reported by *Fortune* for, respectively, the 50 largest retailers and the 500 largest industrial companies in the country.

15 Milton Moskowitz, "Profiles in Corporate Responsibility," *Business and Society Review*, no. 13 (Spring 1975), p. 33. Jewel Companies of Chicago, another chainstore company was also included in the list.

16 I. L. Sands, "Personnel Practices in Department Stores," *New York Retailer*, June 1957, p. 20. Comparable data for more recent years are not available.

17 Earl Dash: "Updated Job Policies Stressed at NRMA," *Women's Wear Daily*, January 8, 1975, p. 28.

18 Samuel Feinberg, " 'Outplacement'—Help for Person, Saving for Firm," *Women's Wear Daily*, May 27, 1975, p. 22.

19 *See* "Premium Pay Lure Drawing Sunday Help," *Women's Wear Daily*, November 3, 1969, p. 23.

20 U.S. Department of Labor, Bureau of Labor Statistics, *Occupational Injuries and Illnesses by Industry, 1972* (Bulletin 1830) (Washington, D.C.: U.S. Government Printing Office, 1974), p. 25. Only about one third of these injuries entailed any loss of working days.

21 For a good guide to Occupational Safety and Health Act requirements, *see* The Travelers Insurance Companies, Engineering Division, *OSHA Voluntary Compliance Guide for Retail Stores*. Hartford, Conn.: The Travelers, 1974. Detailed OSHA information is available from Occupational Safety and Health Administration, U.S. Department of Labor, Washington, D.C. 20210. But *see also* "Why Nobody Wants to Listen to OSHA," *Business Week*, June 14, 1976, pp. 64–72.

22 Sands, "Personnel Practices in Department Stores," pp. 20–21. More recent comparable data are not available, but these percentages have probably increased sharply.

23 Raymond B. Krieger, "Employee Benefits: Beyond the Fringe?" *Tempo* (Touche Ross & Co.), vol. 28, no. 1 (1974), pp. 20–24.

24 See p. 65, above. Also "On-Site Medical Service for Retail Employees," *Retailing Today*, August 1975, p. 1.

25 Basic hospital and medical services in Canada are provided under combined federal-provincial programs, which are primarily supported by general tax revenues, although three provinces also collect insurance premiums and one imposes a payroll tax to cover part of the program cost. Private insurance plans offer coverage for additional services. *Canada Yearbook 1974*, p. 766.

26 Canadian retirees receive incomes under the Old Age Security (OAS) and Canada Pension/Quebec Pension Plan systems in addition to any company-operated retirement programs. Private pension plans in the United States are now subject to extensive regulation under the Employee Retirement Security Act of 1974. *See* Edith M. Lynch, "Law Calls for Fast Work on Pension Plans," *Stores*, October 1974, pp. 8–10, 34.

27 P. H. Nystrom, *Economics of Retailing* (New York: Ronald Press Co., 1930) vol. 2, p. 281.

28 Actually, the union may represent the firm's employees in a given geographic area, such as greater Los Angeles, and not necessarily throughout the country. Moreover, it may represent just certain types of employees, such as restaurant workers, sales personnel, or clerical employees. *See* "Unions Will Sell Harder in Stores," *Business Week*, February 6, 1965, p. 46.

29 Bureau of National Affairs, *Daily Labor Report*, December 11, 1974, p. B-9.

30 In 1969 supermarket unions set objectives of a $4 hourly wage, "portable" or transferable pensions, and a 35-hour week. ("Clerks Want More of the Good Life," *Chain Store Age* (supermarket executives edition), February 1969, pp. 30–32. By July 1973 the average wage in unionized supermarkets was $4.24 per hour, with only baggers, wrappers, and some part-time workers averaging less than $4. *BLS Biennial Survey of Grocery Worker Wages* (Washington, D.C.: Bureau of Labor Statistics, 1975). The pension portability objective was partially fulfilled by passage of the 1974 Pension Reform Act. More recent goals, including substantially higher wages, are described in "Regional Bargaining Seen

Butchers', Clerks' Aim in '76," *Supermarket News,* January 5, 1976, pp. 1, 16, 20.

31 "Frozens Still Banned as Escape from Chicago Late Meat Sales," *Supermarket News,* October 16, 1972, p. 27.

32 *Retail Store Employees Local Union No. 876, R.C.I.A.* et al. v. *Independent Biscuit Company* et al. (70 LRRM 1213, February 12, 1969, reversal denied, CA-6, 1970, 73 LRRM 2582). The impact of such rules on retail management decision making is discussed in R. D. Michman, "Union Impact on Retail Management," *Business Horizons,* vol. 10, no. 1 (Spring 1967), pp. 79–84.

33 "Electronic Pricing Faces An Uphill Fight," *Business Week,* March 31, 1975, p. 23; "Lucky Unveils Scanner; Clerks, Shoppers Protest," *Supermarket News,* February 3, 1975, pp. 1, 30.

34 *The 1976 Corpus Almanac of Canada* (Toronto: Corpus Publishers Service Ltd., 1976), pp. 11–3, 11–4.

35 *Retailers' Manual on Union Organizing* (New York: National Retail Merchants Association, 1974) provides a guide· to the steps a retailer may take under U.S. Federal law, when faced with the possibility of employee unionization.

Merchandise management: buying, handling, control, and pricing

MERCHANDISING POLICIES
AND BUDGETS

    "Buying the right merchandise in the right quantities at the right price and at the right time" is the very heart of the retail business. Consequently, retailers must formulate sound policies about the types of merchandise they intend to offer their customers. A merchandise budget is a plan or program expressed primarily in dollars,* for buying and controlling the amount of goods purchased to meet those customers' demands.

    Not every retailer prepares a formal merchandise budget. Particularly, many small merchants simply buy goods from week-to-week or month-to-month as they seem to be needed. Supermarkets frequently place much more emphasis on watching the physical quantities of goods in the store, rather than on the dollars invested in those goods.[1] But department store, discount, furniture, clothing, and many other types of retailers can profitably use merchandise budgeting as a step toward

---

    * In the discussion that follows, we will concentrate on the dollars of retail value involved. In other words, unless the text indicates to the contrary, when we say "a merchant plans to buy $10,000 worth of goods," we will mean that the merchant plans to buy goods that will be marked to sell, at retail, for $10,000. This approach is consistent with the retail method of accounting discussed in Chapter 23 and is in accordance with the best modern practice. But our discussion, and budgeting techniques, in general, can easily be rephrased in terms of the cost of goods to the store.

developing well-balanced assortments that will successfully meet customer requirements. Some small retailers may not want or need full-scale budgeting systems for their entire assortments, but can still benefit from budgeting their two or three most important merchandise categories.[2]

"After trailing manufacturing management for almost half a century, retailers are now increasingly making use of budgets."[3] Consequently, a discussion of merchandise policies and of budgeting practices is a fitting introduction to our study of modern methods of selecting, buying, and controlling merchandise.

In this chapter, we will (1) discuss general merchandise policies. Then we will explain (2) the meaning and objectives of budgets, and (3) the requisites of a good budget. Next, in examining how budgets are prepared, we will consider (4) the preparation of sales estimates; (5) deciding on the planned turnover rate, that is, the planned size of the average inventory in relation to sales; and (6) the degree of variation desired from month-to-month in the size of the inventory. All of this will lead to (7) determination of the amount the buyer is authorized to spend in any specific period. Finally we will (8) consider the location of responsibility for budget supervision, and review the major limitations of budgeting.

■ GENERAL MERCHANDISE POLICIES

The desires and requirements of present and potential customers are the basis for formulation of effective merchandising policies. What types and qualities of merchandise do they use and what in general do they want? That is, are they attracted to luxurious goods, to the latest styles, or to the best bargains? Do they seem to want large assortments from which to choose, or will they be satisfied with more limited selections of just the most popular items? Some of the types of market information considered in Chapters 1 and 4, plus market research and personal acquaintance with the store's clientele, will help answer these and similar questions. (Also see the discussion of policy formulation in Chapter 2.)

Then the merchant must also consider what unique qualities the business and its personnel will have in appealing to those customers. Perhaps the location will dictate that the store will be primarily a convenience outlet, and must have a well-rounded assortment of only the basic staples that people want to obtain without effort or delay. Or perhaps the proprietor of a store located in a college community is particularly knowledgeable about styles that appeal to young people. In such case, the logical decision probably will be to feature clothes for the student population (and for those who want to look like students). Available funds may limit the range of items that the store will carry. The strong and weak points of competition will also indicate the possible merchandising opportunities. If none of the other food stores in a prosperous community have a gourmet food section, one merchant may gain a competitive advantage by carrying such products. The past reputation of the store will limit or encourage different types of merchandise offerings. A store that has typically sold cheap, rather sleazy products cannot suddenly successfully introduce departments with very high-quality lines. Customer preferences, influenced by the prestige and reputation of the store, will determine the opportunities for successful sale of private brands which may be more profitable and involve lower merchandise costs than national brands. The merchandise planners must keep all of these, and many other considerations, in mind as they decide on the customers they expect to serve.

☐ Scrambled or specialized merchandise lines

The most basic merchandise policy concerns the kinds of products the store will sell. Is it a shoe store, a grocery store, a sporting goods store, a clothing store, a hardware store, or perhaps a combination of some traditional types of business? As time goes on, retailers of many types often add merchandise that has traditionally been sold by other types of storekeepers. Supermarkets have added health and beauty aid products that once were sold almost entirely in drugstores and department stores. Drugstores have added stationery, hardware, household items, and toys that once were sold by specialty retailers. Many other examples could be cited. This process of adding goods from other lines has been going on for a long time and has attracted much attention. It is called "scrambled merchandising." What is not so widely recognized is that many merchants have not adopted this policy of scrambled merchandising. Some have even narrowed, rather than widened, the range of goods they offer.[4]

New retailers frequently are obliged by limited funds and space to keep their merchandise assortment within relatively narrow limits. Established stores also drop lines that become unprofitable, or that occupy space that can be better used by the remaining departments. Thus some druggists, whose stores are often called "ethical" or "professional" pharmacies or apothecaries, have found it very profitable to concentrate solely on prescriptions and health care products. They, and many other pharmacies, have also eliminated the soda fountains that once were characteristic of almost all American drugstores. Many department stores have eliminated, or sharply curtailed, their offerings in such categories as candy, books, and electrical appliances. For example, recently Goldwaters, a department store in Phoenix, Arizona, discontinued "notions, candy, gourmet shops, lamps, and rugs, to go more heavily into better china and glass and decorative housewares."[5] Some merchandise assortments prove incompatible with a store's basic nature. Supermarkets apparently can successfully sell some nonfood items that customers consider convenience goods, such as magazines, pantyhose, and baking pans. They have much more difficulty selling the apparel items that customers regard as shopping goods. As Marsteller, Inc., an advertising and marketing company reports:

Stores are also considering an "exhaustion" level—how much a woman can actually accomplish on one trip. Some supermarket experts believe they can best enhance profits and develop unique arrays of merchandise by concentrating on food—especially perishables. In other channels of merchandising— department stores, discount stores and drug stores to some extent—the trend for every type of store to carry every merchandise category is on the way out. Stores are cutting down and cutting out (major and small appliances from department stores, furniture from discount stores) to concentrate on areas they know best, and where they can best compete with each other and specialty stores.[6]

In addition to a policy decision on the range or types of products to be offered, the merchant must establish general rules about the types of vendors from whom the goods will be purchased, about the store's relations with those vendors, and about the specific items to be selected. We will consider those policies in Chapters 11, 12, and 13. At this point, we must turn to the decisions about the general quantities of goods to be purchased. These decisions will be expressed in a merchandise budget, as discussed in the next paragraphs.

■ MERCHANDISE BUDGETING: MEANING AND OBJECTIVES

A merchandise budget is a forecast and a plan for the dollar amounts that a store, a department, or a classification (a subdivision of a department[7]) expects to buy and sell during a specific forthcoming season.

Not a guide to specific items The merchandise budget does not indicate that the store should buy six pairs of misses' slacks, size 10, in blue checks, or three left-handed putters in the $17.50 price range, or one maple American Colonial dining room table with four side chairs. The budget indicates the total value of goods to be acquired in a category such as misses' slacks, golf clubs, or dining room furniture. (As noted, the planning unit may be even wider, such as all misses sportswear, all sporting goods, or all furniture.) As we shall see, information about the specific assortments desired can be useful in planning the budget (see p. 269); but the quantities of the individual items will be controlled by methods discussed in Chapter 11.

☐ Benefits of merchandise budgeting

As mentioned, a merchandise budget provides a clear-cut plan of merchandising operations for a specific period of time based upon careful study of existing needs and foreseeable conditions. Anyone who expects to spend many thousands of dollars on construction or renovation of a building would never think of going ahead without drafting definite plans, reviewing them carefully, and then abiding by them. Yet proprietors of many small stores and a few large ones make substantial investments in merchandise without similar definite plans or analysis. Such action means proceeding in the dark, not knowing what to expect or what lies ahead.

The merchandise budget provides both a definite course of future action and a yardstick for evaluating current performance. It enables retailers to obtain sales by timely buying of merchandise, to adjust inventories to meet sales requirements, and to plan promotional efforts more effectively. Moreover, it permits them to check the performance of merchandise executives and buyers and fix responsibility therefor, to coordinate all departments of the store into a profit-making entity, and assists the chief financial officer in planning the funds needed to buy merchandise.

The budget also provides a cumulative record of past results, both planned and actual, enabling the retailer to judge the accuracy of past estimates and to improve future ones. It develops a "planning consciousness" and a realization on the part of buyers of the need for facts rather than guesswork and hunches in buying and selling activities. Many retail executives believe that the planning involved in preparing the budget is even more helpful than the formal budget itself. A hardware and home center merchant in Norfolk, Virginia, has reduced inventory while substantially increasing sales through an extensive dollar budgeting and stock control system. The eight department managers receive prompt reports on purchases, sales, and stocks in 85 merchandise classifications. The system has proved very profitable even though it costs $500 per month for data processing.[8]

☐ Requisites of a good budget

To accomplish its purposes, a merchandise budget should: (1) be planned some weeks in advance of its effective date; (2) be as simple as possible and still include the elements that are considered necessary to successful merchandising operations; (3) represent the combined judgment of those whose activities influence its success; (4) cover a period no longer than that for which reliable estimates may be made; and (5) be flexible enough to permit necessary adjustments.

Most of the foregoing requisites of a good budget are self-evident and require little further explanation. It is clear, for example, that in the large organization advanced, careful planning is essential. Such planning should include a review of past years' experience, a reconsideration of the elements to be included, and the weighing of new factors influencing future results. These steps are necessary to improve the accuracy of forecasts; and the more closely the plans approximate actual results, the more valuable are the budgeted figures.

In the small store where the owner is closely associated with all operations, relatively few elements need to be included in the budget. It is perhaps enough to plan sales, beginning- and end-of-the-month stocks (merchandise inventory), reductions (markdowns, discounts to employees and others, and stock shortages and losses), purchases, and gross margin (the difference between merchandise cost and sales revenue); and this much can be done by reviewing past records, examining stock periodically, and by estimating future needs. However, plans cannot be made on such a simple basis as the store grows in size and the owner becomes further removed from the details of the business. A system must be established to provide a flow of useful information and the budget must include additional aspects of the business. Nevertheless, the budgeting system, and the entire merchandise control process, should be kept as simple and as streamlined as possible, consistent with the needs of the business.

When preparing the budget estimates, proper weight should be given to the opinions of buyers, store managers, and others whose activities influence the success of the plan. This step makes it easier to obtain each executive's cooperation in securing the desired results. And, before the plan becomes effective, the budget should be reviewed by the merchandise manager and the controller. They will usually suggest revisions to improve the reliability of the estimates; thus, the final figures will represent the composite judgment of a number of persons.

The longer the period covered by the budget the more difficult it is to make dependable estimates. Although the budget usually covers a season of six months, it is often broken down into monthly or even shorter periods. The figures should be prepared very carefully. Nevertheless, all possible contingencies cannot be foreseen; and inevitably actual results will show deviations from those planned. As soon as these occur, revisions should be made promptly to maintain the value of the budget as a planning and measurement tool.

□ Form of the budget

The form of the budget depends mainly on the kinds and amounts of information included, the way it will be used, the time periods covered, and the preferences of the people involved in the system. The forms used by retailers of similar size differ largely in the manner in which the data are presented rather than in the information itself.

Trade associations in the retail field often recommend or prepare standardized forms for use by their memberships. Figure 10–1 shows a form recommended by the National Retail Merchants Association for

FIGURE 10–1   Season merchandise budget

SIX–MONTH MERCHANDISE PLAN (BUDGET) (ALL FIGURES AT RETAIL)							
SPRING 1976	FEB.	MAR.	APR.	MAY	JUNE	JULY	TOTAL
NET SALES							
Last year							
Plan							
Revision							
Actual							
INVENTORY (Beginning of Month)							(Inventory July 31)
Last year							
Plan							
Revision							
Actual							
REDUCTIONS (Markdowns + Shortages + Discounts)							
Last year							
Plan							
Revision							
Actual							
PURCHASES							
Last year							
Plan							
Revision							
Actual							

Source: Howard L. Davidowitz, *Dollar Open-to-Buy for Smaller Stores* (New York: National Retail Merchants Association, 1975), p. 2. Reprinted with permission NRMA. Copyright 1975, NRMA.

use in smaller stores. Note that it provides space for entering last year's figures, the budgeted or planned figures for the forthcoming season, revised budget figures if conditions (and, consequently, plans) change while the budget is in effect, and a record of the actual results. At first glance the form seems to omit an essential set of figures, the end-of-the-month inventories. Those figures are provided, however, by the beginning inventories for the subsequent months. In other words, the beginning inventory at the start of business on April 1 is the same as the ending inventory at the close of business on March 31.

Although the form shown provides columns for entering monthly figures, we will first concentrate in our discussion on planning the season total. Then we will turn to the monthly breakdowns. The formulas we will use are:

(1) Total merchandise required = planned sales + planned reductions + planned closing inventory.

(2) Planned purchases = planned total merchandise required — expected opening inventory.

Let us examine each of those elements in detail.

■ BASIC ELEMENTS IN MERCHANDISE BUDGETING

□ Forecasting sales

The first step in merchandise budgeting is to forecast or plan sales volume.[9] This task is normally performed by the proprietor in a small store, perhaps with some advice from a wholesaler or other major supplier, or from the business's accountant or banker. In large firms, sales estimates may be prepared by either top management, or by the buyers and/or store managers responsible for operating units. In practice, most companies use both methods since the buyers (and the managers of chain store units) are in closest touch with the market and presumably know best how their particular merchandise lines (or communities) will be affected by changes in the economy, in popular tastes and in fashion. But these department heads are normally over-optimistic at budget time, and each foresees great opportunities for growth if assigned a greater share of the company's total resources. That is to say, the shoe buyer is likely to have a perhaps subconscious bias toward predicting substantial growth of shoe sales, since that will entitle the shoe department to more space, more advertising, and a greater portion of the company's funds for buying merchandise. The clothing buyer, the home furnishings buyer, and all the other buyers will feel the same way about their departments. So top management must prepare a realistic esti- mate of the total sales the business can obtain during the budget period.[10] Then the buyers, their supervisors and top management go through a process of discussing, revising, and reconciling the figures until agreement is obtained.

The buyers and department heads may approach the problem of estimating dollar sales by trying to judge how many units they will sell in each price line, and then multiplying the quantities by the retail price. Thus the shoe buyer may predict sales of 4,000 oxfords at $20 per pair for a sales volume of $80,000, and make similar estimates for other types of footwear and other price lines. Alternatively, the buyer may simply try to estimate total dollar sales, by reference to past experience and judgment about changing demand and supply conditions. In many cases the buyer will use both methods.

Either approach is dependent on the availability of relevant informa- tion. Forecasting sales by units and translating these into total sales fig- ures for the department or store, for instance, is impossible without records upon which to base estimates and to obtain the final results. Similarly, the direct estimation of dollar sales requires reliable data con- cerning (1) the long-term trend of sales reflecting the normal rate of growth of the business, (2) the conditions outside the business which affect its sales volume, and (3) the conditions within the business which influence future sales. Top management almost always uses this latter method and plans directly in dollars.

Long-term trend of sales A review of past experience is important in planning sales. Sales by months for several years should be listed and trends noted. Has growth been steady or have sales varied upward and downward? What are the reasons? After past results have been exam- ined, conditions affecting future sales possibilities should be investi- gated.

Outside conditions The major factors outside the business which may influence future sales include:

1. General business conditions expected during the coming period in the country as a whole and in the local community or region. This will indicate the purchasing power of the store's customers and potential customers. Although business conditions usually cannot be forecast precisely, retailers can improve their estimates with infor- mation from a variety of sources.[11]
2. The trend of population and its characteristics in the trading area in which the store is located.
3. Changes in the number, size, appearance, and promotional activity of competitive stores.

4. Broad fashion movements which affect the store's merchandise. Recent emphasis on teen-age fashions, for example, will probably help some clothing stores and harm others.

Inside conditions Analysis of present conditions within the store, and those likely to prevail in the foreseeable future are necessary in any sales forecast. Examples of such conditions are:

1. Possible revisions of promotional and credit policies such as an increase or decrease in advertising expenditures, the addition or dropping of trading stamps, and liberalization of credit policies.
2. Shifts made in the location or size of space occupied by particular departments or in the arrangement of their physical facilities.
3. Addition of new merchandise lines.
4. Possible expansion of parking facilities for customers.
5. Change in store hours, particularly night and Sunday openings.
6. Opening of new stores and branches, or the modernization of existing ones, and the effect of such actions on the "parent" store or other company stores operated in the area.

Beating last year's figures It is evident that estimating future sales requires considerable study and good judgment. Yet many retailers take the easy way and set their goal as that of "beating last year's figures." Unfortunately, the solution as to "what lies ahead" for the sales of any retailer is not this simple. For some lines of merchandise and even for entire departments, consumer demand may be on an uptrend; but for others, demand may be leveling off or actually in the declining stage. Customers constantly change and at times want higher quality goods; at other times, lower priced merchandise. Tastes and preferences also evolve; witness the way in which demand has shifted back and forth between large and small automobiles.[12] The merchant who plans to "beat last year," that is, to sell an increased amount, in every department and in every price line is likely to wind up with a heavy inventory of unwanted merchandise.*

Sales forecasts for new stores The factors we have mentioned apply chiefly to established stores. New ones have no past sales records on which to base future estimates. Therefore, retailers with new stores must rely on the sales volume of other comparable outlets or departments in similar locations and make visits to other stores to observe customer traffic and talk with their potential competitors. Other suitable means should also be employed to arrive at sound estimates of sales volume.[13]

---

* Some stores also forecast sales in terms of number of transactions, particularly during periods of changing price levels. Through studying the trend in the number of transactions, an estimate may be made of the forthcoming period. The same is true of the average sale. By multiplying the two figures, the total sales figure for the budget may be determined.

Nevertheless, the new retailer's forecasts are subject to substantial error.[14]

☐ Planning average stock

After forecasting sales, the next logical step in the budgeting process is to determine the size (in dollars) of the *average stock* that the store will have on hand during the budget period. The relationship between average stock and sales is called the *turnover* or the *stockturn rate*. It can be computed in several ways, discussed in more detail in Chapter 11, but is often calculated through the following simple equation:

$$\text{Turnover} = \frac{\text{Sales (for the period)*}}{\text{Average stock (at retail price)}}$$

In a purely mathematical sense, this equation could be transposed to read:

$$\frac{\text{Sales}}{\text{Turnover rate}} = \text{Average stock.}$$

Accordingly, it would seem that the size of the planned average stock could be set through simply dividing esimated sales by the desired turnover rate. In actuality, things are not that easy. A great deal of judgment must be used in determining the size of the average assortment. The major considerations that affect the quantities needed in the inventory at any one time are also discussd in detail in Chapter 11. They include such factors as the rate of sale of the merchandise; the speed with which replenishment inventory can be obtained from suppliers; the amount of money that can be saved through buying in large quantities rather than small ones; the danger of obsolescence and spoilage if goods remain in stock for a long period; and the need for complete assortments to satisfy customer demands.

☐ Planning monthly stocks

If customers purchased goods at a constant rate throughout the year or the season, retailers would try to have the same quantity of goods on hand at the beginning of each month. The planned average stock described above would serve as the planned B.O.M. (beginning of the month) stock for each month in the budget period. But sales normally vary considerably during a season, so that most departments and classifications will need much larger inventories some months and much smaller ones during other months. Therefore the season's sales esti-

---

* The turnover rate is often quoted on an annual basis, but may be derived for any shorter period. Four stockturns per year indicates an average of two stockturns per six-month season.

mate should be broken down into monthly figures. The estimates should give attention to the number of selling days and weekends in the month, the changing date of Easter, planned special promotions, or any other factors that might affect the distribution of monthly sales.

Then the monthly stocks can be planned to vary around the average figure so as to meet three objectives: (1) to maintain an assortment of sufficient length and breadth to satisfy customer needs; (2) to adjust the inventory to the seasonal cycle*; and (3) to control inventory investment and maintain a desired stockturn rate that will permit profitable operations.

Methods of planning monthly stocks Five methods are commonly employed to plan the needed stocks:

1. *Judgment* The planner simply makes rough estimates, based on experience and intuition, of how much the average should be manipulated up or down for each particular month or subdivision of the budget period. Alternatively, the planner may not work with the average at all, and may simply plan directly month-by-month. In such case, of course, the amounts would first be entered in the monthly columns, rather than the total column of Figure 10–1. However, it is usually best to estimate a seasonal requirement and then divide that estimate into months or shorter periods. Also, while judgment should be used to modify the figures computed under any formula, the more formal methods discussed below provide a sound basis for exercising such judgment.

2. *The basic stock method* Under this method, the beginning-of-the-month (B.O.M.) stock is computed according to the following formula:

> B.O.M. stock = Estimated sales for the month
> + (Planned average stock at retail
> − Estimated average monthly sales).

This method presumes a certain basic stock, to or from which amounts are added or subtracted as sales fluctuate. This relationship can be seen more clearly if the above formula (which was presented in the standard form used in retail accounting manuals) is transposed so as to read—without changing the results:

> B.O.M. stock = Planned average stock at retail
> + (Estimated sales for the month
> − Estimated average sales).

The basic stock method is recommended particularly for stores or departments in which turnover is relatively low (preferably six or less

---

* For example, most retailers want to have only very limited quantities of most seasonal items on hand toward the end of the season.

per year, three or less per season)* and certain minimum stock levels should be maintained throughout the season.

3. *The percentage variation (or deviation) method*   Here the beginning-of-the-month stock is increased or decreased from the planned average stock by one half of the anticipated percentage variation from the planned average of monthly sales. Or, in terms of retail prices,

B.O.M. stock = Planned average stock ×
$$\frac{1}{2}\left(1 + \frac{\text{Estimated sales for the month}}{\text{Estimated average monthly sales}}\right)$$

If stock turnover is less than six per year, this method will produce greater variations than will the basic stock method. It is useful for departments in which such fluctuation is desired. On the other hand, it provides far less fluctuation than the basic stock method if turnover is greater than six per year.

4. *The weeks' supply method*   In this method the planned stock at retail equals the estimated sales for a predetermined number of forthcoming weeks. Of course, long before that period ends, it is replenished by a sufficient amount to cover the same number of future weeks. This process continues throughout the season. The turnover rate will be high and the variation in stocks will be greater if the supply is intended to equal only a few weeks' sales; the opposite will be true if the number of weeks is larger.**

5. *The stock-sales ratio method*   In this case the planned sales volume for the month is multiplied by the planned beginning-of-the-month stock-sales ratio to ascertain the planned B.O.M. stock. The major advantage of the stock-sales ratio is that it permits comparisons with other stores and with past experience. One merchant cannot derive very much useful information if another one says: "My February B.O.M. stock in Classification X was $12,000." A comment that the February B.O.M. stock/sales ratio was 3:1 is much more meaningful.

The retailer should remember that stocks usually will not increase or decrease in direct proportion to sales. The methods discussed above tend to adjust stocks up and down less sharply than sales rise and fall. Moreover, some merchandise in which size is important, such as shoes and dresses, have minimum levels below which stock cannot go, regardless of volume. Also, planned stocks should be adjusted to the forward movement of the selling season; and to changes in the business outlook, including the availability of merchandise and price trends.

---

* As written, the formula will provide some negative results and be unworkable if turnover exceeds (and probably even if it approaches) 12 per year. A substitute formula can be used in such cases: B.O.M. stock = average stock + (estimated average weekly sales during month — estimated average weekly sales for season).

** The weeks' supply method is analogous to a moving average. Increasing the number of periods in a moving average reduces its fluctuations.

□ Planned reductions

Up to this point in the chapter, we have discussed three major steps in merchandise budgeting: (1) planning sales volume, (2) planning the size of the average stock, and (3) planning monthly variations around that average. Step three will indicate the size of the planned beginning (and ending) stocks for each month and for the period as a whole. We will now proceed to the fourth step, planning reductions. Reductions include markdowns, discounts given to employees and certain types of customers such as members of the clergy, and stock shortages. Since customer and employee discounts usually are treated as markdowns, only planned figures for markdowns and stock shortages are shown on most budget forms. These figures, like others on the form, are stated in retail prices.

Markdowns A retailer marks merchandise down so that the prices will prove more satisfactory to customers and thus stimulate sales. (As a pricing problem, markdowns are discussed in Chapter 17.) In other words, a markdown is merely recognition of a change that has occurred or will occur in the demand for an item. Markdowns are inevitable and failure to include them in the budget is a short-sighted policy. Careful planning is just as essential here as it is for sales and stocks. Actually, planning markdowns reduces their size and frequency because the buyer is made more conscious of them and tries to minimize them.

Markdowns may be placed in four main groups: (a) Preventable ones or buying errors attributable to failure to analyze customer demand adequately. These include the purchase of wrong styles, sizes, colors, and the like; (b) those caused by price adjustments outside the buyer's control, such as declining price levels, changes in price lines, and competitors' prices; (c) those attributable to store promotional policies, such as special sales events and multiple pricing, which are also outside the buyer's control; and (d) normal operational markdowns, such as price reductions on soiled and damaged goods, sample cuts and remnants, and breakage, which are practically inevitable in buying and selling merchandise. For further details on the causes of markdowns, see Chapter 17.

The markdown plans should include consideration of such factors, both within and outside the department or classification, as the sales promotional events planned for the period; the trend in business conditions and prices; the nature of the merchandise and its condition at the beginning of the period; the markdowns of comparable stores and departments; and contemplated changes in policies and in the personnel of the department.

Stock shortages Like markdowns, stock shortages are inevitable in retail stores of all kinds despite efforts to prevent them. Consequently, to be realistic they should be included in the merchandise budget.

In planning the stock-shortage figure, which is commonly done on a percentage-of-sales basis, the past experience of the store or department and that of similar stores or departments of such stores should be reviewed.[15] Wide variations exist among different stores and departments selling different merchandise. To illustrate, discount houses have larger shortages than jewelry stores and costume jewelry sections of department stores have smaller ones than those in self-service variety stores. All contemplated changes in business practices, security measures, price marking methods, store design or equipment, personnel or other factors that will affect shortages should also receive study. With this information, the retailer arrives at a budget figure for stock shortages.

☐ Planned purchases

When figures for sales, opening and closing stocks, and reductions have been planned, the planning of purchases in dollars—the fifth major step in merchandise budgeting—becomes merely a mechancial or mathematical operation through the use of certain formulas. Those in common usage, both in terms of retail prices, are as follows:

1. Planned purchases = Planned sales + Planned reductions
   + Planned increase in stock, or
   − Planned decrease in stock.

2. Planned purchases = Planned stock at end of period
   + Planned sales + Planned reductions
   − Stock at beginning of period.

These formulas may be applied, as illustrated in Figure 10–2, to an entire store, a department, a classification, or a price line for the budget period or for any part of the period. Moreover, they are applicable to control in physical units as well as in dollars. Quite obviously, they are useful only when the figures upon which they are based are accurate, timely, and tempered with the buyer's judgment. Improved equipment and EDP have speeded up the availability of the information required for sound decisions and for prompt revisions in estimates. When such adjustments are made, then the computed purchase figure adequately fulfills its function—as a guide to the buyer's judgment, not a substitute for it.*

---

* The amount and percentage of markup (the difference between cost and initial selling price) to be placed on goods purchased is an important phase of purchase planning, since the planned stock figures are at retail, whereas the store buyer is faced with cost prices in the wholesale market. Because the initial markup is discussed at some length in Chapter 16, further attention is not given to it here. However, to very briefly summarize the relationship between open-to-buy and initial markup, the initial markup percentage is deducted from the open-to-buy at retail to determine how much the

FIGURE 10–2 **Application of formulas in planning purchases**

```
Formula 1, as applied to the month of September:
    Planned sales ......................           $10,000
    Planned reductions ................             1,000
        Markdown  ..................... $900
        Shortages  ..................... 100
            Total .........................                    $11,000
    Stock on hand, September 1 ........     $20,000
    Planned stock, September 30 ........     22,000
    Planned increase in stock ...........                       2,000
    Planned purchases in dollars ........                     $13,000

Formula 2, also applied to September:
    Planned stock, September 30 ........     $22,000
    Planned sales ......................      10,000
    Planned reductions  ................       1,000
            Total .........................                    $33,000
    Stock on hand, September 1 ........                        20,000
    Planned purchases in dollars ........                     $13,000
```

The open-to-buy "Open-to-buy" is that amount, in terms of retail prices or cost, which the merchandise budget and purchasing plans permit a buyer to order for receipt during a certain period. To illustrate, and using retail prices, assume that planned purchases for October are $1,000. On October 1, therefore, the buyer is open-to-buy that amount during the month. By October 20, $700 has been spent for merchandise already received or due to arrive before the end of the month, leaving $300 for additional goods to be received during the rest of the month. In other words, open-to-buy is $300 on October 20. In practice, however, open-to-buy calculations are not so simple. Adjustments in inventories during the budget period, fluctuations in sales volume, markdowns, and goods ordered but not yet received—all complicate the determination of the amount that still may be spent. Open-to-buy figures are particularly useful to buyers when making trips to markets to examine vendors' offerings and to make needed purchases.[16]

As an example, let us review how the open-to-buy figure may be determined for a store or a department in the middle of a budget period. Assume the following figures for the month of April:

```
Actual stock, April 1 ........................ $37,000
Planned sales for the month...................   75,000
Planned markdowns and shortages for the
    month .....................................    2,500
Planned stock, April 30 .....................    35,000
```

buyer may spend at cost. For example, assume that a buyer has an open-to-buy (at retail) at $70,000 and the planned initial markup is to be 40 percent of the retail (selling) price of the goods. Then the open-to-buy at cost can only be 60 percent (100 percent minus 40 percent) of the $70,000 or $42,000.

Assume further that, during the first half of April, receipts of goods were $30,000. On April 15, goods on order for April delivery amounted to $20,000 at retail prices. The open-to-buy may be calculated in Figure 10–3.[17] However, this figure would be adjusted if sales or reductions had differed markedly from expectation during the first half of the month.

The open-to-buy form used need not be complicated or elaborate. In fact, simplicity is highly desirable. The best form is one that furnishes the needed information in the most concise manner possible. One store uses that shown in Figure 10–4.

FIGURE 10–3   Calculation of open-to-buy figures

Planned stock, April 30	$35,000	
Planned sales, April	75,000	
Planned markdowns and shortages, April	2,500	
Total goods required	112,500	
Less inventory, April 1	37,000	
Planned purchases		$75,500
Goods received, April 1–15	30,000	
Goods purchased for receipt, April 15 to April 30	20,000	
Total received or committed		50,000
Open-to-buy (at retail prices)		25,500

The open-to-buy figure is a guide rather than a set amount which cannot be exceeded. Even though the amount budgeted for purchases during a given period has been spent, further purchases are not impossible if stock is needed to meet customers' requirements. A department may be overbought but still be in urgent need of staple, fast-selling merchandise. To refuse its buyer further funds to make purchases would only serve to intensify the problem, not solve it.[18] Causes of the overbought condition should be ascertained, however, and measures taken to prevent their recurrence.

Small retailers do not collect information of the type described in as great detail or as frequently as large stores, but they should formulate definite buying plans and adhere to them rather closely. Since small operators make few trips to market, they must utilize their time and their finances while there to good advantage. Therefore, although they may not fix formal purchasing limits, they should have rather definite ideas about how much they will or may spend before going to market.

☐ Planned gross margin

Merchandise budgets, planned purchases and open-to-buy can, and in practice may be, established without attempting to set a planned gross margin figure. But decisions on merchandise selection are closely

FIGURE 10-4 A simple open-to-buy form which provides essential information

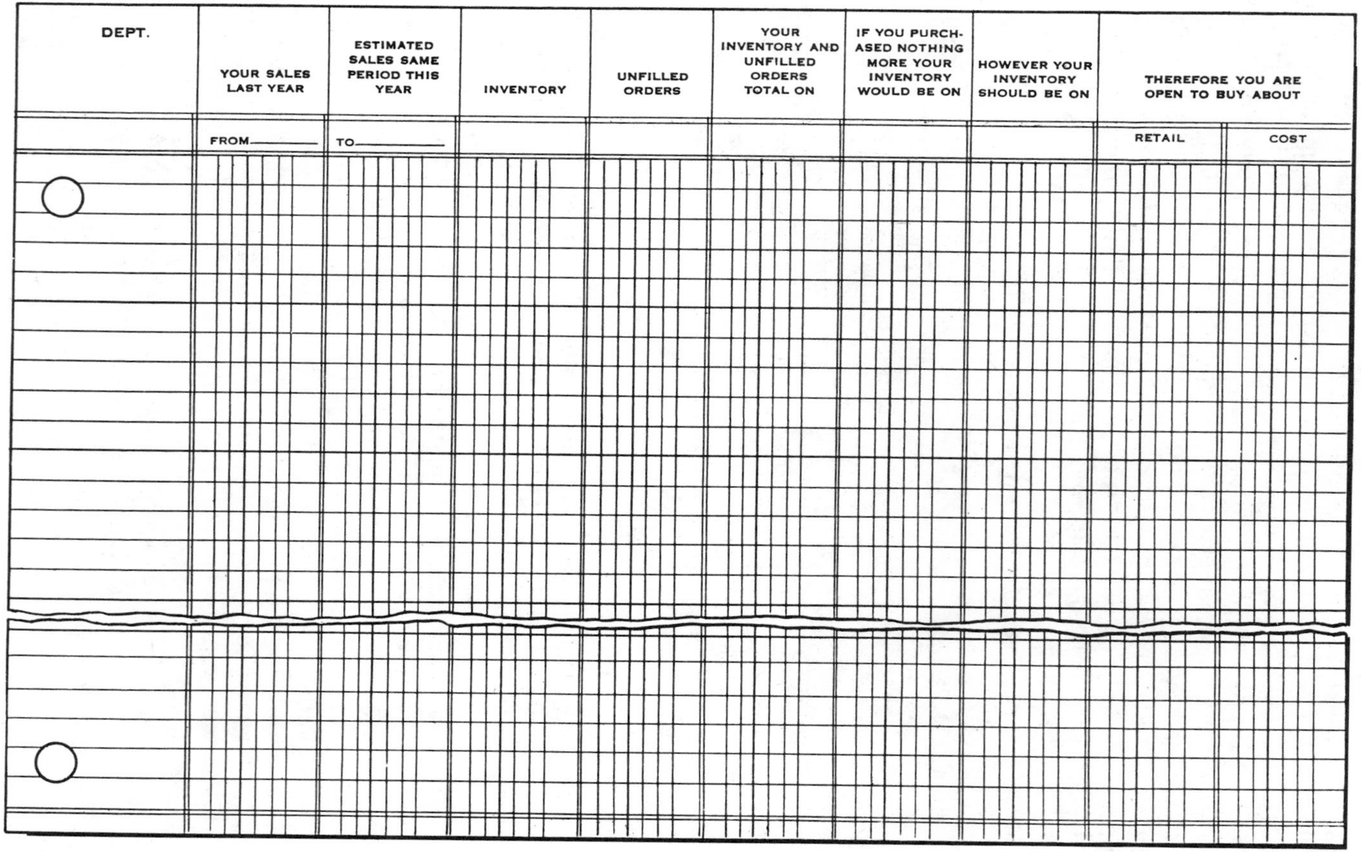

DEPT.	YOUR SALES LAST YEAR	ESTIMATED SALES SAME PERIOD THIS YEAR	INVENTORY	UNFILLED ORDERS	YOUR INVENTORY AND UNFILLED ORDERS TOTAL ON	IF YOU PURCHASED NOTHING MORE YOUR INVENTORY WOULD BE ON	HOWEVER YOUR INVENTORY SHOULD BE ON	THEREFORE YOU ARE OPEN TO BUY ABOUT	
		FROM——— TO———						RETAIL	COST

intertwined with consideration of the costs and revenue that the store will experience from its purchases. Moreover, most large and many small retailers place great emphasis upon the percentage gross margin rate (usually expressed as a percent of retail sales). This figure receives so much attention since gross margin must cover the store's expenses and any remainder will constitute the net profit before taxes.* Consequently, many retail organizations include gross margin and profit planning in their merchandise budgeting process.

The computation of gross margin is discussed in more detail in Chapter 16. Furthermore, planning gross margin involves many judgmental and policy questions. Gross margin is the difference between merchandise cost and final selling price. In other words, it is initial markup adjusted for price changes, stock shortages, and discounts to employees. Too high a gross margin may indicate noncompetitive prices that have alienated customers or failure to take necessary markdowns; too low a gross margin will indicate failure to cover expense, and possibly buying mistakes or excessive markdowns. These questions are also explored in Chapter 16. At this point we need only note that gross margin and profit are often planned.

Whether competitive factors in retailing will allow higher markups is for the future to determine. Meanwhile, the basic problem as related to budgeting remains—how best to forecast an attainable gross margin figure that will yield, after the deduction of expenses, a satisfactory and reasonable net profit.

▪ BUDGET SUPERVISION

Supervision of the budget includes more than mere checking of actual results against planned figures. It also involves follow-up to determine if information in the form desired is being promptly and accurately supplied; if purchases and markdowns are properly authorized; if the open-to-buy figure is frequently being exceeded and, if so, who has approved such action; and if the budgeted figures are being revised when necessary.[19] Furthermore, supervision involves the review of the budget at frequent and regular intervals by merchandise and control executives.

Here again responsibility for the activities described rests with the proprietor in small stores. In larger ones, it is divided between the merchandise manager and the controller, aided by those who assist in formulating the merchandise budget. Wherever responsibility lies, supervision should be thorough, consistent, and continuous.

---

* Strictly speaking, some additional profit may result from so-called "other income" such as interest on any surplus funds invested outside the store. But gross margin provides by far the greatest share of expense and profit coverage.

■ LIMITATIONS OF THE MERCHANDISE BUDGET

Despite its widespread use as a tool of management, the merchandise budget has certain limitations. First, it is an aid to the judgment of those who use it and is not designed to control their thinking. Consequently, it does not provide an automatic control over merchandise inventories; it requires review at frequent intervals, and the information it contains must be complete and current. Otherwise the budget will be a failure.

Second, the planning and the operation of the budget involve considerable time, effort, and expense. The benefits derived from its use must be greater than the cost involved in preparing and maintaining it.

Third, some buyers claim that the budget often so restricts their actions that they are unable to take advantage of exceptional buying opportunities which may arise. Since the budget is supposed to help rather than hinder the buyer, this complaint deserves further examination. In practice, the buyers ordinarily have a voice in preparing the merchandising budget, so that the planned figures reflect their judgment as well as their supervisors'. A buyer should object strenuously to any figures that seem unreasonable or unobtainable and should try to show the other budget participants why their estimates are wrong. At the same time, store officials should provide their buyers with merchandising data quickly and assist them to interpret and use it. Moreover, exceptions should be authorized and additional open-to-buy permitted whenever conditions warrant such action.

Fourth, since the planned figures are based upon analysis and interpretation of known facts and probable future conditions, they are of value only as conditions closely approximate those anticipated. When changes occur, revisions in estimates should be made in the light of these conditions.

■ REVIEW AND DISCUSSION QUESTIONS

1 (a) Briefly explain the factors a merchant should consider in deciding whether or not to add a new category of goods (line of merchandise) to the assortment offered in the store. (b) Show how these factors might affect a supermarket operator who is thinking of offering a selection of children's clothing and accessories.

2 Report on some stores in your community that seem to offer unusual combinations of goods. Visit the managers or proprietors and ask about the reasons for, and the results of, the unusual mix.

3 Define merchandise budgeting in your own words. Summarize the objectives and requisites of a good budget.

4 Concisely state the basic elements to be included in the merchandise budget. Discuss who will be responsible for preparing the budget.

5 Discuss the factors that will influence the sales forecast. Where can the merchant obtain information about those factors?

6 (a) Show by a simple example (using the desired turnover rate) how the size of the planned average stock might be calculated. (b) Describe the five main methods of planning monthly variations in the amount of stock on hand.

7 (a) What are the major components of "planned reductions"? (b) Why is it necessary or advisable to plan reductions?

8 On March 1, how much is the department manager in the following example open to buy for the month of March?

```
Stock on hand, March 1, at retail ......... $53,800
Outstanding orders for March delivery,
    at retail ............................    7,300
Planned sales, March ...................   26,500
Planned reductions, March .............    3,600
Planned stock at retail, April 1 ..........   56,200
```

9 Visit a progressive retail store in your community and determine the merchandise budgeting procedures employed. Describe the procedures in detail, using whatever forms and illustrations are necessary and available to make your description clear.

10 Explain the limitations of the merchandise budget.

■ NOTES AND REFERENCES

1 The SLIM—"Store Labor and Inventory Management"—system used in some supermarkets is a form of unit control, discussed in Chapter 14. See also T. W. Leeds and G. A. German, Food Merchandising: Principles and Practices (New York: Chain Store Age Books, 1973), pp. 71–75. A food chain, Lucky Stores, that does use merchandise dollar budgeting, is described in K. W. Cope and R. A. Watson, "Budgeting in a Large Retail Chain," Retail Control, September 1975, pp. 50–57.

2 R. Patrick Cash, "Merchandising Division," Stores, December 1974, p. 22.

3 Jerry D. Dermer, "Budgetary Motivation of Retail Store Managers and Buyers," Journal of Retailing, vol. 50 (Fall 1974), p. 23.

4 The total process of expanding and narrowing may be called "the accordion pattern" and is discussed in S. C. Hollander, "Notes on the Retail Accordion," Journal of Retailing, vol. 42 (Summer 1966), pp. 29–40.

5 "Sprawling Phoenix Feels Growing Pains," Women's Wear Daily, March 25, 1975, p. 5.

6 Checkout, November-December 1975, p. 4.

7 Sometimes called a "dis-section," but usually called a "classification." See R. Patrick Cash, "Classification Systems for Smaller Stores," Stores, April 1976, p. 19.

8 "Dollar Control by Classes," Hardware Retailing, April 1975, pp. 48–50. A more rudimentary system would be less expensive. See "Basics of Inventory Management," Stores, May 1975, pp. 15, 27, for discussion of an inexpensive manual (noncomputerized) system.

9 The Corporate Inventory Manager, Montgomery Ward & Co., says, "The development of a sound sales budget by month and by department is the first and most important basic budgeting activity of retail management." Wayne W. Gross, "Inventory Management Principles to Determine When,

What and How Much to Buy," *Retail Control,* February 1974, p. 22.

10 In one merchandise line alone, F. W. Woolworth Co. found that store managers estimated a sales volume three times as large as what central management felt could reasonably be obtained. "The Woolworth/Woolco Pattern for Growth," *The Discount Merchandiser,* August 1975, p. 22. But top management also has difficulty in predicting sales. Sears, Roebuck & Co. acknowledges its own problems in forecasting customer demand, in spite of having perhaps the most sophisticated analytical system in the retail industry. *See* John R. Lightfoot, Jr., "Forecasting: Still an Achilles' Heel?" *Chain Store Age* (general merchandise edition), March 1976, p. 9.

11 For illustrations of factors considered in making forecasts and how economic changes necessitate readjustments, *see* Howard Eilenberg, "Coping With Economic Uncertainty," *Retail Control,* October 1974, pp. 2–14; Samuel Feinberg, "Warning to Retailers: Don't Be Smug," *Women's Wear Daily,* February 24, 1976, pp. 1, 20; "Retailing: An Unexpectedly Happy Holiday," *Business Week,* January 19, 1976, p. 18.

12 "Automakers Can't Size Up the Buyers," *Detroit Free Press,* March 7, 1976, Sec. B, p. 1.

13 *See* R. F. Kelley, "Estimating Ultimate Performance Levels for New Retail Outlets," *Journal of Marketing Research,* vol. 4 (February 1967), pp. 13–19.

14 Among supermarkets opened in 1973, approximately 42 percent experienced sales above those estimated and 27 percent below. Only 31 percent obtained about the sales anticipated. See *Facts about New Super Markets Opened in 1973* (Chicago: Super Market Institute, Inc., 1974), p. 5. More recent figures are not available. How the computer may be used to estimate sales for a new retail development is suggested by D. L. Huff and Larry Blue, in *A Programmed Solution for Estimating Retail Sales Potentials* (Lawrence, Kansas: University of Kansas, 1966).

15 Department store stock shortages in 1974 were 2.01 percent of sales, down slightly from the 1969–70 peaks, but still substantially above the 1965 figure of 1.34 percent. Jay Scher, *Financial and Operating Results of Department and Specialty Stores of 1974* (New York: Financial Executives Division, National Retail Merchants Association, 1975), p. v. See also Chapter 26.

16 R. Patrick Cash, "Planning a Successful Market Trip," *Stores,* November 1974, p. 21.

For other methods of calculating the open-to-buy, see Bernard P. Corbman and Murray F. Krieger, *Mathematics of Retail Merchandising,* 2d ed. (New York: Ronald Press Co., 1972), pp. 302–36.

18 States one retailer: "To give buyers the greatest chance to do their best job . . . put the Open-to-Buy where the demand lies by recognizing that the traditional retail dollar Open-to-Buy by department often works to squelch action on the known factors of current interest. Free money for new adventures in merchandise by giving the buyers up-to-date tools for the efficient management of inventory." George Baylis, "Are the Brakes Too Tight to Let the Train Roll?" *Retail Control,* October 1965, p. 25. A similar criticism that most open-to-buy systems are too rigid and should be subject to automatic weekly or monthly revisions appears in "How to Use Your Computer As a Merchandising Tool," *Discount Merchandiser,* September 1975, pp. 44–46.

19 States W. J. Wallis, vice-president of Macy's, New York: "Top management's most important instrument of control is performance reports that are obtainable under a proper system of budgeting." "Budget Follow-Through Stressed to Controllers," *Women's Wear Daily,* May 27, 1970, p. 41.

PLANNING AND SELECTING
ITEM ASSORTMENTS

In the preceding chapter, we studied the way a well-managed retailing firm might plan the amount of money to spend each month (planned purchases) for each merchandise classification or department. Those dollar figures, however, must be translated into plans and decisions to buy specific quantities of specific items. The preparation of those plans and the item decision-making are normally the responsibility of the proprietor in the small store and of the buying executives in the large organization. The importance of this activity is illustrated by Claude Martin's comment on the differences between two stores—one successful and one failing: "The buyers for the successful store are more aggressive, more self-confident, and show a greater tendency for leadership in new merchandise trends than the buyers for the failing store."[1]

In this chapter we will (1) study two important types of assortment plans—the basic stock and the model stock; (2) consider some of the elements that enter into decisions on how much to buy; and (3) discuss the information that a buyer uses in selecting specific items. Although we have separated the topics of framing buying plans and selecting items in this chapter for convenience in study and discussion, it should be emphasized that they are closely interrelated, with each other, with merchandise budgeting (discussed in Chapter 10), and with vendor selection and vendor relations (discussed in Chapters 12 and 13). For example, even in the middle of the season, a buyer who learns from customer requests or from visits to the wholesale market that some product lines have suddenly become very popular, as Citizens Band radios did in 1974 and 1975, or that a new fad has swept the country, as pet rocks did in 1975, will immediately revise existing plans. That buyer may ask the merchandise manager to increase the departmental budget; will certainly plan to add or increase the quantity of the "hot" new item, perhaps somewhat reducing stocks of other products; and may have to add a new vendor or vendors in order to obtain the desired goods.

Similarly, a change in a vendor's prices or policies may lead the buyer to increase or decrease the quantity of that supplier's goods in the store's assortment. Consequently, all buying plans and decisions should be seen as interconnected, and should be subject to revision in accordance with changes in either the consumer market or the wholesale markets.

■ BUYING PLANS

Not all retailers prepare formal buying plans. But no merchant can operate without having at least some idea of what will be needed to serve customer demand during the forthcoming period. And the more progressive business people, including many of those who prepare dollar budgets, also draw up item plans.[2]

□ General considerations

Need for flexibility The store owner, buyer, or other executive who prepares the merchandise plan does so on the basis of past experience and current market information as to what items customers want and what products suppliers will have available. We will discuss the sources of that information later in this chapter. However, customer preferences change and new products appear on the market at various times. Therefore, all buying plans must always be considered as tentative and subject to constant review.

Breadth of selection The merchandise planner must decide not only on how many and what classifications of goods will be carried, but also on how wide a selection will be carried within each classification. For instance, should the record shop or department only sell records or should it also carry taped music; should it only sell popular and country titles, or should it also have operatic and classical albums and sets; and how extensive a variety of titles, artists and price lines should be offered within each category* A wider selection permits a closer match

---

* The question of "scrambled merchandising," discussed in Chapter 10 relates to decisions to expand into other related or unrelated lines of merchandise such as, in this

with the individual preferences of a greater number of potential customers. Moreover, many customers seem to like to shop in a store that provides a very large number of choices; witness the success of shops that offer thirty or more flavors of ice cream.[3]

Nevertheless, offering additional titles or varieties involves disadvantages and costs that must be balanced against the attractiveness of a large selection. Each new item* that is added requires some additional display and storage space. Since the available space is usually limited, and additional space, even if obtainable, is usually costly, the extra items will reduce the space that can be devoted to the core or basic items in the assortment. Even more importantly, each additional item will also use funds that could be invested in a bigger ("deeper" is the technical term) stock of the core products. Adding too many marginal items is likely to lead to carrying an inadequate supply of the basic, most-desired products, and increases the danger of being out-of-stock when customers want to purchase those products.[4] Furthermore, the marginal items normally sell more slowly than the basic ones, but still require a substantial inventory. Consequently, a wide selection usually results in a slower stock turnover rate than an assortment that is concentrated on the most popular items. That is why many discount store operators try to plan assortments that are "strong on the best [sellers] and forget the rest." Of course, each buyer must make decisions in terms of the particular items involved (for example, most customers do not particularly desire a choice of brands when buying shoelaces, although they may feel very differently about toothpaste or hairspray), store policies, price levels, and competition (a store selling at relatively high prices in a market with many competitors will generally have to provide wider selections than a store with low prices or a monopoly location), and most important of all, customer desires.[5]

A balanced assortment   The buyer will often want to include items in tne assortment to serve a variety of merchandising objectives. Some very new styles or innovative items, and some luxurious or prestigious merchandise may be added to improve the department's image. The store may expect to sell only very limited amounts of these items and will not invest in a large supply. But such merchandise will help give the whole department a reputation for leadership in introducing the best products. One Canadian merchant expresses this philosophy by saying that high style lines ". . . may only give us a small percentage of sales, but shrewd management knows they are very important because they bring customers into the store."[6] Similarly, decisions will have to be

---

case, record players, tape recorders, musical instruments, greeting cards, or school supplies.

* The technical term "stockkeeping unit" or "SKU" is often used to refer to each controllable variation in the assortment. Thus the stock of a particular style of man's shirt in blue with a size 15 collar and a 34 sleeve would be one SKU. The same style and size in tan would be another SKU, as would blue size 15½–34, and so on.

made about the ratio of private brand products to national brands, and the extent to which the buyer wants to emphasize the most profitable lines.[7]

□ Basic stock list

We will examine two types of assortment plans. The first of these is called "the basic stock list" and is used for staple goods. Staples are items that sell relatively steadily and in relatively unchanged form from year to year. Of course, demand does change and so the list must be reviewed fairly regularly. As one expert says: "Check the recent rate of sale. Last year's basic may no longer be basic. In fact, it may be this year's markdown."[8] Sometimes the most important, most-frequently-demanded, basic staples are placed on a special list called the "never-out list" or "checklist." These units will receive special attention to make certain that a supply is always on hand to satisfy customer needs.[9] Failure to have such items in stock when customers want them will result in a loss of trade to competitive, better-merchandised stores.[10]

The basic stock list will show the minimum quantity of each item that should be carried at any time—including any adjustments for seasonal requirements, and the amount that should be reordered whenever the stock sells down to the minimum point. The planned minimum stock will consist of the quantity that will normally be sold during the time required to place an order and obtain delivery from the supplier plus a safety stock to cover anticipatible fluctuations in demand or delays in delivery.*

The system just described is known as a *reorder point* system, because a new purchase is made whenever the stock drops to a specified minimum point. Many retailers find it more convenient to review their inventory and their needs periodically—weekly, biweekly, or monthly, and to place orders for desired merchandise at the time the stock is reviewed. Such systems are known as *reorder time* systems.[11] In such cases, the planned requirements will be the quantity normally sold during the interval between ordering dates plus the quantity normally sold during the delivery period plus the reserve or safety stock.

□ The model stock list

The basic stock list approach is best suited to handling staple goods that sell at fairly regular rates, that can be reordered frequently, and that consist of very distinguishable specific items or SKU's. (Lined 3" x

---

* Obviously, no retailer can afford to carry a stock that would be adequate to meet any possible (but improbable) situation. Consequently, deciding what range of possible variation in demand will be covered becomes a matter of judgment, perhaps assisted by statistical formulae.

5" index cards and unlined 3" x 5" index cards in a stationery department would be examples of items eminently suitable for a basic stock list.) That approach is not satisfactory for fashion or style goods that either change or sell at very different rates from year to year, that may be subject to reordering problems, and that may be affected by the buyer's need or desire to introduce some variation during the season. Such lines are sometimes called *maintained selection items* in that the buyer does not expect to keep reordering exactly the same chiffon evening dresses, so long as an appropriate selection of current styles of such dresses can be maintained in the popular colors and correct sizes.

The model stock lists will show the assortments that the buyer wants to have on hand on specific dates, say, at the start of the season, at the height of the selling season, and perhaps at some intermediate and end-of-season dates. The plan will be broken down by significant product characteristics such as general style (e.g., slacks, pedal pushers, culottes, and skirts); price lines; fabrics; colors and sizes in misses' sportswear; but not by specific manufacturer's style numbers. A model stock list is more "forward looking" in concept than a basic stock list since it is built around anticipated customer demand at a specified future date. However, the buyer will draw upon past sales information in several respects, as noted in the next paragraphs. The model stock list, even more than the basic list, must be subject to review and possible revision as actual sales experience develops.

Preparing the model stock list The quantities of merchandise needed in each category will be determined by the store's past experience and sales rate, as modified by the buyer's judgment about what merchandise characteristics and styles are gaining or declining in favor. Past experience also will indicate whether the customers prefer very advanced or more conservative models. A men's shoe store may find that, regardless of model changes, its sales are divided between street and sport shoes in fairly constant percentages from year to year, even though seasonal variations must be included on the buying calendar.

The size assortment of most fashion goods is also fairly constant. For example, irrespective of the year's fashion, a women's dress shop may find its sales of the various sizes divided as follows: size 12—12 percent; size 14—22 percent; size 16—30 percent; size 18—26 percent; and size 20—10 percent. However, the model stock assortment as to size and type will not necessarily be the same as the actual sales distribution. Although 10 percent of all sales in that store are in size 20 dresses, to provide an adequate assortment, this size may account for 15 percent of the model stock.

Past sales also furnish information as to the prices at which a store should offer merchandise. Past trends, by indicating how the best or the cheapest goods are moving, can show a buyer the price lines that are most popular. Finally, and as already suggested, past sales provide information on customer preferences for materials, colors, and particular styles. By keeping a running check on these factors, the buyer is better prepared in placing reorders.

■ DETERMINING QUANTITIES TO PURCHASE

We have already noted that a basic stocklist, a model stocklist or other buying plan will show the quantities of each item or group of items that the buyer wants to have on hand, either throughout the season or at specific points during the season. Thus a basic stocklist in a stationery department may set minimums of 50 units for a particular type of typewriter ribbon and 100 units for a certain type of carbon paper. Or a model stock plan for men's shirts may call for an inventory of 120 dozen striped shirts in the $12.00 price line on March 1 broken down into so much of each size, but for only 60 dozen solid color shirts in the same price line. How does the buyer decide on the relative amounts of each item and on the total quantity of goods to possess at any one time?

As already indicated, the basic determinant will be the anticipated sales of each item. Buyers naturally plan to buy more, and carry larger stocks, of those items they expect to sell in large volume. But a number of other factors, in addition to anticipated demand, will affect the quantity to be carried in the store at any one time. To cite just one example, a buyer may expect to sell 600 units of item A and 600 units of item B during a given season. Perhaps item A is imported from abroad, and the buyer knows that reorders cannot be filled during the selling season, while item B is easily obtained from a local wholesaler whenever needed. In such cases, the buyer will plan to start the season with the full requirement of 600 units of A, but with perhaps only 100 units of B. Therefore, let us review some of the factors that affect these decisions on quantity. They include anticipated sales; the nature of the items themselves; the supplier's and the retailer's policies; the store's physical and financial capacity; and the economics of purchasing in large and small quantities.

□ Anticipated sales

To repeat, the first factor that the buyer considers in planning the relative quantities needed of each item is the relative sales. But the buyer must also decide what quantity should be carried over into the next season. For example, the store may want to sell out all seasonal items such as Christmas cards by the latter part of December, but it will still want to have an inventory of birthday and "get well" cards. Therefore, the buying plan must include an allowance for the desired ending inventory.

As pointed out in discussing "breadth of selection," and "the model stock list," it is usually impossible to buy goods in exact proportion to anticipated sales. A buyer normally must purchase at least a certain minimum quantity of almost every item in the assortment, otherwise there is no point in offering the item. For example, it is difficult to imagine a shoe size in which a store would want to carry only one pair. The practicable minimum affects the slow sellers more than the popular ones and thus requires a disproportionate amount of merchandise. We have also seen how a limited amount of poor-selling prestige-items may be added to the assòrtment for their effect on total sales.

☐ The nature of the merchandise

Although all of the sales estimates mentioned above should be prepared as thoughtfully as possible, some types of merchandise require especially careful estimates. A mistake in predicting the sales of an easily resupplied staple is not as serious as an error in forecasting a novelty, fad, or fashion item. If too much of the staple is purchased, the excess will sell out in time; if not enough is planned, an emergency order can be placed with the supplier. In either case, the purchase rate can be readjusted in the future to meet actual customer demand. On the other hand, excess quantities of novelty or fashion goods may not be salable except at sharply reduced prices. Yet underordering can also be harmful, although usually safer, because supplies of the most popular items may become very limited. Sometimes an item is so new that the buyer simply cannot foretell how customers will react, and in such instances, usually must buy a very conservative small quantity as a trial order to test the market.

Merchandise characteristics may have another effect on the quantity purchased at any one time. Some items are more perishable than others. Bakery products, fresh fruits and vegetables, and many other food-store products deteriorate very quickly. Consequently, food retailers must follow a rapid turnover policy—ordering only a few day's supply of such goods at a time and constantly replenishing their inventory. Turnover must be carefully planned for fashions, fad items, and seasonal products so that the store does not have an excessive inventory when customer demand starts to decline. At the opposite extreme, a jewelry or furniture store may hold an item for a year before selling it.

☐ Vendor and store policy

A supplier may adopt policies that strongly affect the size of the orders that retailers may place at any one time and the quantity that they purchase over a season. These policies are discussed in detail in Chapter 13, but may include certain minimum-order quantities or standard packaging that does not allow a customer to buy, say, half a case-lot, and various types of quantity discounts that encourage large orders. Some manufacturers may not accept reorders once a season begins, and this will induce their customers to buy as much as they think they need on their initial order. Some retailers also set policy minima. These are illustrated by the supermarket that will only buy and handle grocery products in full-case lots or cartons that can be moved directly onto the display shelves with the least possible handling.[12] Or similarly, management may insist on large quantities to reduce the danger of being out-of-stock.

□ Financial and physical capacity

We have already seen in Chapter 10 how the amount and timing of funds available (or made available) for investment in inventory can affect the size of the stock a store or department carries. A buyer who has been allotted a very large "open-to-buy" or purchasing budget at the beginning of the season can "stock up," that is, bring in much of the season's requirements early in the period and gradually sell off the merchandise over the six-month period. In contrast, a buyer whose "open-to-buy" is more closely rationed month-by-month must place smaller initial orders and then fill in the stock requirements as funds become available during the season.

Timing of peak stocks One question in building the model stock lists concerns the dates on which the buyer wants to offer the largest selection of seasonal merchandise. The general tendency seems to be build a good selection very early, perhaps having the peak or largest assortment quite early in the season, and then "sell down." A Philadelphia merchant says: "One of our biggest problems is getting [winter] resort clothes early enough. Many of our customers are ready to go away by the middle of October."[13] The childrenswear division of the J. L. Hudson Company in Detroit begins testing fall items in May and June, and requires all displays and 50 percent of each department's stock to be in fall merchandise by July 7.[14] However, receiving goods too early will increase the amount of money tied up in inventory investment unless the vendor offers special payment terms (see the discussion of dating in Chapter 13) and increases the danger that the goods will seem "stale" when the peak selling period finally arrives.[15] Therefore, merchandisers often develop calendars, at least for their most important classifications, that show, on the basis of store experience, when their customers actually do their purchasing.[16]

Physical capacity The amount of storage space within the store* also affects the quantity of goods that can be carried. Today many chain

---

* Any separate warehouse facilities that the retailer owns or rents must be considered in addition to this in-store storage space.

store companies build stores with very limited stockroom space, so as to reduce the size of inventories and to increase the turnover rate.

☐ Turnover: The economics of small and large inventories

Definitions and measurement Turnover, also called stockturn, is the rate at which merchandise moves through the store. It is usually expressed on an annual basis, such as "four stockturns per year," although we can also compute or talk about the stockturn for a shorter period if we so desire. Four stockturns per year equal two turns per six-month season. We can talk about the turnover of a particular item, of a classification or department, or of the whole store.

The turnover rate may be calculated in any one of three different ways. In each of these methods, a figure that represents the amount of merchandise sold during a period is divided by a comparable figure representing the average inventory. In comparing these three methods, let us assume the following figures for a particular merchandise line in a store that takes inventory every three months. Assume that the items in the line cost the store $25 each and retailed for $50.

Date	Quantity on hand	Cost	Retail	Value of inventory at cost	Value of inventory at retail
January 1	300	$25.00	$50.00	$7,500	$15,000
April 1	400	25.00	50.00	10,000	20,000
July 1	100	25.00	50.00	2,500	5,000
October 1	400	25.00	50.00	10,000	20,000
December 31	300	25.00	50.00	7,500	15,000
Average	300			7,500	15,000

Sales for the year were 900 units (total cost $22, 500; retail sales $45,000).

1. *Retail method* Stores that use the retail method of accounting (see Chapter 23) would compute turnover in the above case as follows:

$$\text{Turnover} = \frac{\text{Sales (at retail)}}{\text{Average inventory at retail}} = \frac{\$45,000}{\$15,000} = 3.$$

2. *Cost method* Other merchants would normally use the following cost formula:

$$\text{Turnover} = \frac{\text{Cost of goods sold}}{\text{Average inventory at cost}} = \frac{\$22,500}{\$\ 7,500} = 3.$$

3. *Units* If we were computing turnover for a single product or collection of homogeneous items, we might also divide the number of units sold by the average inventory in units, as follows:

$$\text{Turnover} = \frac{\text{Number of units sold}}{\text{Average inventory in units}} = \frac{900}{300} = 3.$$

However, this method is not suitable for a collection of miscellaneous items and is seldom used.

Note that in each of these methods, the sales and average inventory figure must be comparable. They both must be expressed on the same base; that is, both must be figured at retail, or both must be figured at cost, or both must be in units.*

Advantages of rapid turnover The formulas cited above demonstrate that a store with a given sales volume can increase its turnover rate by reducing the size of its average inventory, and reordering goods more frequently but in smaller quantities at a time. This approach offers many advantages.

Limiting the investment in inventory at any one time reduces such expenses as interest, insurance, and property taxes (in those communities where retailers have to pay a tax on inventory). It also reduces the amount of space needed to store goods. Even more importantly, it releases funds that can be used to purchase new products or to take advantage of any especially good deals or buying opportunities that may appear while the selling season is underway. Finally, reducing the quantity on hand and, consequently, shortening the period of time that a piece of merchandise stays in stock will minimize the danger of that item becoming stale, shopworn, damaged, or obsolete. Consequently, speeding up turnover reduces markdowns.[17]

Hand-to-mouth buying The extreme version of a rapid turnover policy is called *hand-to-mouth buying*. Many retailers who want to reduce the costs and risks mentioned above follow such a policy as a regular routine. They watch their inventories very carefully and order new or additional merchandise frequently, but always in very small quantities. Other buyers use a hand-to-mouth policy only when they are uncertain about the trend in demand. Perhaps, as so often in the recent past, the leading designers and the fashion trade publications predict a major change in women's clothing styles, but the buyers doubt whether consumers will actually accept the new garments. In such cases, a hand-to-mouth policy becomes the risk-minimizing, "let's wait and see what happens" approach.

Disadvantages of a rapid turnover policy In spite of the advantages cited above, many retailers find that a rapid turnover policy can be carried too far and can harm the store. First of all, the vendor policies that we have already noted may necessitate accepting a lower turnover rate or omitting some desirable items from the assortment. Retailers who

---

* This is different from the *capital turnover* figure, sales divided by average inventory at cost, used in the manufacturing industries (where inventories are usually a much lower percentage of total assets than in retailing) and taught in most accounting courses.

will buy only small quantities may not be able to obtain the best or the newest merchandise. Moreover, such retailers often have to pay more for their purchases. They may lose quantity discounts or they may have to buy from wholesalers who charge higher prices than the original manufacturers. The freight costs for inbound shipments to the store also increase since small shipments cost more per pound and move by more costly carriers than large ones. Ordering and clerical expense rises as the number of individual orders grows.

The greatest danger of a rapid turnover policy, however, is the risk of being out of stock. The retailer who works with a small reserve (safety stock) gambles on being able to replace the items promptly when needed. Any delay in obtaining needed reorders (whether because of inefficiencies in the store's own ordering process, problems in the supplier's operations, or delays in transit) will exhaust the safety stock. Customers are naturally disappointed if a store does not have the items they desire and are likely to take their business elsewhere. Consequently, many successful retailers say that they will strive for a high (rapid) turnover only insofar as it does not interfere with having a well-stocked store that is prepared to satisfy the customers' reasonable requirements.

Speculative buying   ı extreme version of a low turnover policy consists of buying very large quantities of an item, or of merchandise in general, if the buyer thinks prices will rise sharply in the future. This is called speculative buying and is very risky. For example, due to various world conditions, sugar prices rose rapidly during the fall of 1974. A five-pound bag that had sold in supermarkets in January for 89¢ rose to about $3.99 at the end of November. But then demand fell unexpectedly in December and the average retail price dropped to about $2.79.[18] Supermarket buyers who tried to accumulate a large stock of sugar that autumn had to sell it at a loss. The typical retailer is well-advised to buy goods to satisfy the customers' normal consumption patterns, rather than to try to make a large profit through speculation in merchandise. Nevertheless, buyers often feel a need to increase purchases when prices are rising, customer demand looks good, and supplies seem limited.[19]

▪ DETERMINING WHAT MERCHANDISE CUSTOMERS WANT

The decisions about the items to be purchased and their quantities depend upon information about the types, kinds, and prices of goods present and potential customers want. We cannot here discuss all of the attributes that make products attractive to customers, since these characteristics will vary with the item, with the customer, and perhaps from time to time. The features that lead a customer to select a particular can of baked beans over another obviously can be quite different from those that lead to the choice of a particular skirt, a particular camera model, or a particular brand of spark plugs. The buyer's job includes learning what characteristics the store's customers desire in each item. This information may be gathered both inside and outside the store.

The major sources are as follows: (1) inside: past sales, returned goods and adjustment data, credit department data, customer inquiries, suggestions of salespeople, fashion coordinators' recommendations, and the judgment of buyers; (2) outside: the goods sold by other successful stores, vendors' offerings, central market representatives, trade papers, newspapers and general publications, and customer surveys.

□ Inside sources of buying information

Past sales Past sales constitute the most valuable inside source of information on customers' wants for both staple merchandise and fashion goods. We have already noted how information on past sales may be used in framing basic and model stock lists. Even if such formal buying plans are not used, the past sales experience is the best *single* guide to what customers have liked or rejected in the past. Of course, a store can only have past sales experience for items that were in stock, so the sales data only provides a hint (subject to considerable interpretation) as to how customers might react to a new item.

Returned goods and adjustment data Returned goods and customer complaints supply considerable information. Some merchandise may be of inferior material or poor workmanship and give unsatisfactory service. Women's dresses may fade, and the collars of men's shirts may fray. Knowledge of such facts is obviously of importance to buyers.

In small stores the owner-buyer usually handles merchandise complaints. In the large store, however, complaints are registered with the adjustment department and some method must be devised for passing the information on to the buyer. One method is to use the "adjustment-department notice," which contains a brief description of the complaint and the merchandise against which the complaint was registered.

Credit department data Retailers extending credit find two chief kinds of information available in the credit department useful to their buyers. One is the customers' records of purchases and the kinds and prices of merchandise they return. The second is supplied by the credit application which furnishes a variety of data about customers themselves.

Credit application analysis is relatively simple for stores that require a large amount of information from their customers. When using credit data, however, the buyer should recognize that the store's credit customers may not form a typical sample of all its customers, and that this inside-the-store information should be supplemented with customer data gathered outside the store.

Customer inquiries   A record of goods requested by customers but not in stock furnishes a helpful guide to the buyer since it reveals customer wants. Some salespeople in small stores rely on their memory in reporting such requests to the buyer-owner. More systematic procedures in which pads of "want slips" are kept near the registers, so that requests can be noted when received and assembled for the buyer, are preferable and nearly indispensable to sound purchasing.

Suggestions of salespeople   Since salespeople are customers in their own rights, with wants that frequently are similar to those of other patrons, they can afford the buyer a valuable sample of customer opinion. Urging salespeople to bring in suggestions for purchases and seeking their opinions on the merchandise offered in the market will help the buyer.

Fashion coordinators   Large retail organizations usually employ a fashion coordinator for the women's clothing division, and sometimes one is also used for home furnishings. The coordinator's job is to advise the buyers on general style trends and also to help the various departments select compatible merchandise. The coordinator develops information about what colors, materials, and "looks" are becoming important, so that, for example, the shoes and the handbags that the store features will go together.[20]

The fashion coordinator also helps the buyers and merchandisers predict style changes. Forecasting fashion changes is very difficult since one cannot be really certain about how, when, or why a particular design of color will win or lose acceptance. Various theories have been offered to explain fashion changes. One leading writer argues that fashions go through regular long-run cycles which are relatively independent of "technological inventions, social upheavals, . . . historical accidents, or the advent of a design genius."[21] Other analysts emphasize the importance of such events, or the role of various fashion "dictators" such as leading designers, elite consumers, fashion writers, or consumers who have above-average interest in style and fashion.[22] Yet numerous highly-proclaimed and widely-publicized new styles have failed to win large-scale consumer acceptance, and others have surprised both merchants and manufacturers.[23] Nevertheless, in the long run, as one veteran retailer has put it, the key to fashion merchandising is the unit control card—in careful analysis of the record of how each individual item is selling and has sold in the past.[24]

Buyer's judgment   Even a buyer who has used all or most of the inside sources discussed above and the outside information discussed in the next paragraphs must still exercise judgment. Each source must be evaluated. Is a particular salesperson—who has made a strong recommendation for a certain item—a good judge of customer tastes or simply likely to report personal preferences? Is the value of past sales data reduced because some normally popular items were out-of-stock and not available for sale during much of the last season?

In addition to appraising such information, experienced and creative buyers will use their educated intuition and even "hunches" to develop new ideas and to select new products to try in their departments. In describing a successful young buyer, the *New York Times* notes that she studies sales data from her departments, spends time on the selling floor talking to salespeople and customers, attends fashion shows in the United States and abroad, subscribes to American and foreign fashion publications, and regularly shops competitive stores. "Still, instinct is no small part of her craft."[25] Another buyer says "If you hesitate [when examining a manufacturer's line], don't buy. . . . If I don't react to a garment immediately, I forget it. I know I will not be able to sell it."[26]

□ Outside sources of buying information

Offerings of other successful stores   Turning to outside sources of information, no buyer can afford to overlook the goods offered by other successful stores in deciding what to buy. This source of information is particularly helpful to smaller retailers who cannot afford other costly ways of finding out what customers want. Considerable useful buying information may be obtained through visits to local stores and those in other cities, studies of their advertisements, and the hiring of outside "shoppers" to report on their offerings and employing one's own comparison department—if the store is large enough to maintain one. Many large stores have such departments that "shop" competitive stores in the trading area to determine merchandise offerings, prices, and customer response. Reports are prepared and submitted to the buyer for guidance in building proper assortments and establishing prices.

Despite the advantages of knowing what other successful stores are selling, some retailers owe their success to the fact that they operate unique stores—stores which offer "unusual merchandise." In the words of one highly successful, small-town retailer: " 'Tain't the money that puts your business up. It's having something that no one else has as good as."[27] In carrying out this philosophy, a small shop selling women's apparel builds its clientele on having "different" dresses or a men's clothing retailer tries to be ahead of large-scale competitors in having the latest fashions. In fact, one of the advantages of the smaller store is its buying flexibility which gives it an opportunity to "be different" from its larger competitor.

Vendor's offerings   All stores, particularly small ones, rely to some degree on the offerings of vendors* to learn what goods are "in de-

---

* "Vendor" is simply another designation for merchandise supplier or merchandise resource. The term includes manufacturers, wholesalers, rack jobbers, etc.—anyone who sells to the store.

mand." Perhaps buyers rely too much on vendors who are trying to sell what they are producing rather than first studying customer demand to find out what is wanted. Yet there is a definite trend for vendors to engage in more customer research. As they do, their offerings will reflect customers' needs to a greater degree and thus become a more dependable guide to the buyer.

Some vendors use bulletins to inform their customers what is selling. Others use sales representatives for this purpose. Still others have developed inventory control systems—some based on electronic computers—for their retail outlets to provide improved stock control, semiautomatic reordering and similar buying information. Vendors using the franchise system of servicing retailers through a voluntary chain arrangement place special emphasis on supplying "what is selling" data to their outlets.

Central market representatives Many retailers use retail central market representatives, often referred to as MR's, to furnish store buyers with information about new and popular items in the market (see the discussion of market representatives in Chapter 12). These representatives study vendors' offerings, watch fashion trends, and check promotions in large city stores. Their conclusions are transmitted to buyers by means of bulletins or verbally when the buyers visit the central markets.

Trade papers, newspapers, and general publications Retailers of all sizes depend on trade and fashion magazines and newspapers for much information as to what customers want. Retailers of women's wear find it worthwhile to study such publications as *Mademoiselle, Seventeen, Charm, Harper's Bazaar,* and *Vogue,* in which the latest fashions are pictured and discussed. *Women's Wear Daily* is another standard source of information in this field. For retailers of men's wearing apparel, *Esquire, Daily News Record,* and *Men's Wear* offer considerable data on fashion trends. Many other fields are also supplied with tradepapers, as illustrated by *Chain Store Age* with its various editions, *Discount Store News, Progressive Grocer, National Jeweler, Hardware Retailer,* and *Footwear News.*

Customer surveys Broadly, any activity designed to gather information directly from customers concerning their wants may be classified as a customer survey. Approximately 10,000 families annually report their purchases and preferences to Sears, Roebuck and Company's Home Fashion Data Bank.[28] Although most retailers do not use these surveys extensively because of the time and cost involved, they occasionally employ one or more of the following methods: questionnaires either mailed or completed through personal interviews; style counts for fashion goods; and consumer advisory groups. Since surveys may provide the store not only with data as to the goods customers want, but also with information as to the surroundings and services they want with the goods, it is essential that they be conducted and interpreted with great care; otherwise, the results may suggest courses of action not warranted by the facts.

Retailers handling fashion goods sometimes find the "style count" a useful source of customer information. The count is made by placing observers at certain points to record what people are wearing. The observation points should be selected with care, so that information will be obtained on the appropriate groups including those that act as local fashion leaders.

When consumer advisory groups or juries are used, the store attempts to organize a single small group which is representative of its customers.[29] The group may be broken down into subgroups, each representing one segment of the store's customers. One subgroup may consist of high school or college students, another of newlyweds, and another of middle-income buyers. Such groups or panels may be used not only to pass on merchandise offered by vendors but also to appraise the store's operating policies and current stock of goods.

Some agencies conduct customer surveys for retailers or on their own initiative obtain data of value in buying. Many newspapers, such as the *Milwaukee Journal*, the *Cleveland Press*, the *Chicago Tribune*, and the *New York Times*, finance research designed to provide information on consumer buying habits. The A. C. Nielsen Company and SAMI (Selling Areas-Marketing, Inc.) use consumer and dealer panels to develop valuable information. Some resident buying organizations, especially those located in New York City, also undertake investigations of various types for their members. But the storeowner or the merchandising and buying officials still have the ultimate responsibility for evaluating all of this information and reaching final decisions on what, how much, and when to buy.

Testing laboratories Both for policy and legal reasons, retailers must be concerned about the quality of the goods they offer their customers.[30] At one time many department stores and other large retailers set up their own testing laboratories to appraise the safety, durability, and quality of some of the items they sold. But operating a satisfactory laboratory today has become much more costly and is beyond the resources of all except the largest organizations. The testing machinery has become much more expensive and complex as we have learned about potential product hazards, as products have become more complicated, and as synthetic substances steadily replace natural materials. Some major organizations still maintain their own testing facilities, equipped with the necessary machines and apparatus. But most other retailers who need quality assurance rely on information from vendors, the use of outside testing bureaus, product certification from such review boards as the Underwriters Laboratory, reports in such consumer magazines as *Consumers Reports* and *Consumers Research Magazine*, and lists of unsafe products circulated by such government agencies as the Consumer Product Safety Commission.

■ REVIEW AND DISCUSSION QUESTIONS

1 Discuss the importance of preparing buying plans. Why must all such plans remain flexible or subject to adjustment?

2 Visit two stores in the same merchandise line in your hometown or college community: compare the breadth of selection in the two stores (or in the same department of the two stores). Discuss the factors that you think might help explain the differences between the two stores.

3 List and describe the differences between a basic stocklist and a model stocklist? What is the difference between a reorder point system and a reorder time one?

4 Explain why the planned assortment at any one time will contain larger quantities of some goods, and smaller quantities of others than their anticipated relative sales would suggest. (In other words, why would a buyer plan to have 10 percent of the stock in items that will produce only 5 percent of sales, and perhaps 50 percent of the inventory in another group that may produce 60 percent of the sales?)

5 How will vendors' policies and the store's policies affect the quantities that are purchased?

6 Some consumers believe that the retailers "peak" their stocks too early in the season and then sell out too early. For example, many retailers have their best assortment of bathing suits in the spring, and try to sell out their entire collection by July 1. Yet many customers take their vacations at the end of July or in August and may want new bathing suits. Discuss the merits and the disadvantages of such a seasonal selling policy from a retailer's standpoint.

7 Present the arguments for and against a rapid stockturn (turnover) rate?

8 What are the principal "inside" sources of buying information? Although such internal information is very important, it does have some limitations. What are they?

9 Describe the principal "external" sources of buying information, and indicate their weaknesses.

10 Assume that you are drawing up the merchandise plans for a particular type of store (perhaps a women's clothing store, a sporting goods store, or a record shop). You have to make many decisions about assortments, products, and price lines. What sources of information would you mainly rely on, and for what decisions would you use each such source. Explain your answer.

NOTES AND REFERENCES

1 Claude R. Martin, Jr., "The Contribution of the Professional Buyer to a Store's Success or Failure," *Journal of Retailing,* vol. 49 (Summer 1973), p. 79.

2 See "Item Control Compared to Dollar Control," *Hardware Retailing,* April 1975, p. 39.

3 John W. Wingate and J. S. Friedlander call such a selection "a dominant assortment." *The Management*

of *Retail Buying* (Englewood Cliffs, N.J.: Prentice-Hall, Inc., 1963), pp. 151–53.

4 Donald L. Belden, *The Role of the Buyer in Mass Merchandising* (New York: Chain Store Age Books, 1971), p. 51.

5 John B. Lightfoot, Jr., "On Being Important to Customers," *Chain Store Age* (general merchandise edition), April 1976, p. 9, discusses the need for a wide assortment to retain customer goodwill.

6 J.-P. Allemand, quoted in Barbara Amiel, "Trouble in Eatonia," *Mac-Lean's,* May 31, 1976, p. 30.

7 For recommendations of profitability decision models, *see* Daniel J. Sweeney, "Improving the Profitability of Retail Merchandising Decisions," *Journal of Marketing,* vol. 37 (January 1973), pp. 60–68; "Financial Measurements to Monitor Merchandising," *Stores,* April 1974, pp. 4, 31. These models recommend selecting those items that provide the highest gross margin return on inventory investment. For mixed, although somewhat favorable, results with such models, *see* John L. Schlacter, "Impact of Improved Information on Performance in the Distributive Trades," *Arizona Business,* April 1975, pp. 17–26. This approach is criticized for neglecting investment in store facilities and in accounts receivable in "Retailers Are Keeping Track of the Wrong Letters," *Retailing Today,* March 1976, pp. 2–3.

8 R. Patrick Cash, "Merchandising Division," *Stores,* September 1974, p. 22.

9 Bob Vereen, "The 'Super Sellers,' "*Hardware Retailing,* October 1975, p. 79.

10 *See* C. K. Walter and J. R. Grabner, "Stockout Cost Models: Empirical Tests in a Retail Situation," *Journal of Marketing,* vol. 39 (July 1975), pp. 56–60.

11 *Inventory: A Perspective* (Dayton, Ohio: National Cash Register Company [now NCR Corporation], 1969), p. 22.

12 Theodore R. Leeds and Gene A. German, *Food Merchandising Principles and Problems* (New York: Chain Store Age Books, 1973), p. 71.

13 "Retailing Roundtable," *Women's Wear Daily,* February 11, 1974, p. 7.

14 "Infants' and Children's Wear Departments Present Seasonal Opportunities," *Stores,* March 1976, p. 34.

15 R. Patrick Cash, "Smaller Stores Are Saying," *Stores,* March 1976, p. 25.

16 *See* R. Patrick Cash, "Peaking Fashion Stocks," *Stores,* December 1974, and Murray Krieger, quoted in "Basics of Inventory Management," *Stores,* May 1975, p. 27.

17 *See* "The Retail Push to Keep Inventories Down," *Business Week,* March 31, 1975, pp. 62–64.

18 E. H. Methvin, "Shocking Swings in Sugar Prices," *Readers' Digest,* April 1975, p. 100.

19 For an illustration of this, see " 'Hedge' Buying Pushing Fall Fur Business Up," *Women's Wear Daily,* April 20, 1976, p. 60.

20 *See* Elaine Jabenis, *The Fashion Director* (New York: John Wiley & Sons, Inc., 1972); Jil Curry, "Penney Makes Color Sense," *Home Furnishings Daily,* September 15, 1972, pp. 4–5.

21 Dwight E. Robinson, "Style Changes: Cyclical, Inexorable and Foreseeable," *Harvard Business Review,* November-December 1975, p. 121.

22 Many such theories are presented in Jeannette A. Jarnow and Beatrice Judelle, *Inside the Fashion Business,* 2d ed. (New York: John Wiley & Sons, 1974).

23 For two illustrations of difficulty in predicting fashion acceptance, *see* Fred D. Reynolds and William R. Darden, "Fashion Theory and Pragmatics: The Case of the Midi," *Journal of Retailing,* vol. 49 (Spring 1973), pp. 51–62; J. Barry Mason and Danny Bellenger, "Analyzing High Fashion Acceptance," *Journal of Retailing,* vol. 49 (Winter 1973–74), pp. 79–88.

24 Alfred H. Daniels, "Fashion Merchandising," *Harvard Business Review,* May 1951, p. 60.

25 "Shopper Par Excellence," *New York Times Magazine,* April 25, 1976, p. 93.

26 "Saks Fifth Avenue Buys High Fashion," *Tempo* (Touche Ross & Co.), vol. 20, no. 1 (1974), p. 27. Of course, this buyer has trained herself to react, not as to whether she personally would

like the garment for herself, but whether her customers will like it.

27 L. L. Bean, quoted in *Time,* December 7, 1962, p. 89.

28 "Sears Data Bank Helps Home Lines," *Home Furnishings Daily,* April 12, 1976, pp. 1, 18.

29 Wingate and Friedlander distinguish among five varieties of consumer panels: (1) The customer advisory group—which makes suggestions concerning store policies, services, and merchandise assortments; (2) the consumer jury that expresses opinion on advertising and sketches of styles; (3) the consumer experience group that reports on performance of products in use; (4) the home inventory group that reports the goods they have on hand; and (5) the continuous-purchase-record group which records and make monthly reports on their family purchasing. *Management of Retail Buying,* p. 102.

30 "Defective Product Costs Have Falling Domino Action," *Supermarket News,* April 19, 1976, pp. 1, 31. For a discussion of retailer's obligations see Elsie Fetterman and Margery K. Schiller, *Let the Buyer Be Aware* (New York: Fairchild Books, 1976).

BUYING: SELECTING
MERCHANDISE RESOURCES

In the preceding chapter we discussed the selection of specific products for the merchandise assortment. The selection of those items is closely intertwined with the selection of suppliers—called "merchandise resources" or "vendors" in the trade. Sometimes the choice of a supplier will influence the product selection as, for example, when a decision is made to carry the supplier's complete line. To illustrate, the proprietor of a hobby shop may have to choose between the model kits made by company A and company B. Both resources offer ship, automobile, and aircraft models, but B also has some stagecoach models in its product mix. The proprietor probably will not bother trying to obtain any stagecoach kits if the decision is to handle the A brand, but may carry some, for the sake of completeness or to preserve good relations with the vendor, if the B line is chosen. Even a decision to examine a particular potential resource's assortment may result in suggesting new items to be added to the store's stock. Similarly, sometimes the choice of a particular product will determine the choice of a supplier, if, for example, the product is available from only one firm.

But in many cases similar products can be obtained from competing suppliers. Moreover, the store's buyer may be able to choose between obtaining the goods from the manufacturer or from a wholesaler. The buyer must also decide how much time, money, and effort to spend in seeking vendors, or whether to let them take the initiative.

Consequently, in this chapter we will (1) investigate some general considerations in choosing vendors; (2) study the major types of merchandise resources and note their various advantages to the retailer; (3) examine the ways in which suppliers and retailers establish contact with each other; (4) pay special attention to the work of central market representatives; (5) discuss efforts to improve vendor and item selection through committee, group, and central buying; and (6) note the special problems of import buying.

■ CHOOSING VENDORS: GENERAL CONSIDERATIONS

Retailers make decisions, either consciously or implicitly, about such general matters as whether to concentrate their purchases with a few vendors or divide them among many; whether to buy from large or small suppliers; and about other essential vendor characteristics.

☐ Number of vendors: Many or few

Retailers in some merchandise fields cannot divide their orders between numerous competing vendors. Sometimes one supplier dominates the market; franchise restrictions, as in the case of automobile dealerships, may limit the merchant's choices; or each manufacturer's line may be so extensive and complicated, as again in the case of automobiles, that the retailers cannot effectively handle several brands simultaneously. But buying from numerous resources is a distinct possibility in other fields. Retailers in these fields must decide whether to concentrate their purchases with only a few, or even a single, resource, or whether to use many suppliers.

Advantages of concentrating purchases Retailers who buy all of their requirements in a particular merchandise category from one or a few vendors save time and effort in the buying process. They build goodwill with the suppliers, and the resources feel (or should feel) some special obligation to give the stores prompt deliveries, rapid handling of claims, good market advice, and generally excellent service. Concentrating purchases also leads to larger individual orders than dividing requirements, so the store receives larger quantity discounts and transportation cost savings.

Advantages of dividing purchases Spreading orders among many vendors also has advantages. It reduces the risk of supply interruption from floods, fires or strikes in a particular supplier's factory. It also provides access to a greater variety of styles or models. Contact with many resources is particularly important if the relative attractiveness of the various vendors' lines changes substantially from season to season. Merchants who buy through wholesalers are likely to concentrate their purchases; those who handle fashion goods are likely to use many suppliers.

□ Large or small suppliers

Merchants seldom set specific policies of buying only from large, or only from small, firms. The size of the suppliers chosen is more likely to be a result of other merchandising decisions. For example, a policy of featuring well-known national brands will lead to an assortment of products produced by large manufacturers. In contrast, a program of emphasizing odd and unusual merchandise will lead to a search for many small and even obscure vendors.* Sometimes, though, a store may deliberately seek different sized suppliers. Thus Joske's, a Texas department store organization, decided that the products of the leading, and best-known, junior sportswear houses were becoming too expensive, and successfully decided to aggressively promote clothes from smaller firms.[1]

□ Selecting the vendors

Primarily, retailers want resources who will supply appealing, salable merchandise at attractive prices. But they also want many other things from their suppliers: prompt delivery, quick and satisfactory adjustment of claims and disputes, perhaps the ability to return unsold merchandise, good credit and shipping terms, perhaps help in advertising and sales promotion, or perhaps exclusive rights as the product's only dealer in the retailer's community. The process of negotiating these conditions is discussed in the next chapter.

Each specific situation should be weighed carefully, but as a rule retailers should confine their purchases to those vendors having the "best buys." Hence, they should seek sources of supply which (1) have merchandise meeting their needs, (2) can be counted on as steady sources of supply, (3) are in sound financial condition, (4) have fair prices and terms of sale, (5) give good delivery service, (6) make adjustments promptly on all reasonable complaints, (7) are fair and honest in their dealings, (8) have progressive managements, and (9) deliver goods identical to their samples.[2]

Resource file Many buyers maintain a "resource file" to help in selecting the appropriate vendors. This is simply a record of each past purchase, organized and recorded under the suppliers' names. Consult-

---

* To illustrate, there are a few stores that specialize in products intended for left-handed people. The proprietors of those stores must hunt assiduously for resources that make, or can be persuaded to make, such items.

ing the record for a particular company will show the buyer whether the goods purchased from that company have sold well or poorly; whether customers returned much of the merchandise; whether deliveries were prompt and in good condition; and whether any special problems arose in the past. Obviously, a poor past record will tend to eliminate a resource from consideration for future business. Some retail trade associations and business publications now also conduct surveys and report buyers' evaluations of various suppliers.[3]

■ MAJOR TYPES OF MERCHANDISE RESOURCES

Retailers use three major sources of supply—middlemen, manufacturers, and farmers or growers. In view of the typical reader's familiarity with them from the basic marketing course, our treatment can be relatively brief. A few retailers do make some purchases from other stores. Thus the men's clothing retailer who is "out" of a shirt of a certain size may go to another retailer and secure one, rather than let a regular customer go there. Or again, so-called "discount" retailers find, on occasion, that some manufacturers and wholesalers refuse to sell them merchandise; their response may be to find other retailers to make the purchases for them. But these practices are relatively unimportant.

□ Middlemen as merchandise resources

Wholesalers Wholesalers are merchant middlemen who typically buy from manufacturers in relatively large quantities and sell to retailers in substantially smaller quantities. Most wholesalers assemble and store the merchandise that their retailer-customers need. They thus reduce the retailers' inventory costs and risks. In a sense, the wholesalers act as "purchasing agents" for their retailers in the same way that the retailers act as "purchasing agents" for the consumers. Probably almost half of all manufactured consumers' goods go through the hands of wholesalers. They handle a very high percentage of all hardware and drugstore merchandise.

1. *Service and limited-function wholesalers* Service wholesalers, also called "full function" and "regular" wholesalers, tend to carry extensive assortments. They not only assemble and store goods for retailers, but they also render other valuable services, including prompt delivery, credit extension and the provision of valuable market information.

Limited-function wholesalers extend few of the foregoing services. Cash-and-carry wholesalers in the grocery and tobacco fields, for example, only handle fast-moving items, eliminate sales representatives, and offer no credit or delivery service, thus reducing the cost of wholesaling.

Most retailers, however, still prefer to use "full function" wholesalers because of the important services they perform.

The "regular" wholesalers' services are especially valuable to small and medium-sized retailers who utilize this source of supply more than any other. In contrast, large-scale retailers such as chain stores find it more economical to take over many of the services the wholesaler performs for smaller retailers. Even large retailers, however, make some use of wholesalers, relying on them to obtain items temporarily out of stock or for which the demand is limited. Some large retailers do buy electrical appliances and other home furnishings through wholesalers who in that trade are often called distributors.[4] Some discount store chains may obtain 10 to 50 percent of their merchandise through various types of wholesalers, including the rack jobbers discussed in the next paragraph.[5]

2. *Rack jobbers* The rack jobber is a wholesaler of nonfood items who stocks and maintains an assortment of goods in special fixtures or racks in supermarkets and similar self-service stores. A specific markup percentage—usually 25 to 33 percent, depending upon the type of merchandise and competitive conditions—is guaranteed to the supermarket. The rack jobber selects the items, arranges the displays, prices the goods, provides point-of-purchase material and special promotions, removes slow-selling items and restocks the fixtures with faster-selling goods.

The rack jobber is responsible for much of the rapidity with which supermarkets added nonfoods. Without such specialized services, these retailers would have been quite reluctant to carry toys, housewares, children's books, hardware, and many other items. But since the rack jobber handles so much of the work, absorbs so much of the operating expense, and provides a guaranteed gross margin—the retailer's resistance crumbled. Independent and small-chain supermarkets particularly have used rack jobbers as sources of supply for the items mentioned above and for health and beauty aids.

Despite the widespread use of rack jobbers among supermarkets some chains have taken over their functions. Apparently the managements of these chains are convinced that they can perform the rack jobber's services effectively. This trend is in line with the chain's desire for as complete integration as is economically feasible. But it is likely that so long as rack jobbers provide needed nonfoods, give good service, and price their merchandise on a competitive basis, they will be widely used as a merchandise source.

3. *Integration of wholesale and retail functions* Among corporate chains there is often a high degree of integration of retail and wholesale activities. The voluntary chains also integrate these activities.[6] In the latter case a wholesaler and a number of independent retailers agree to coordinate their operations. In practice, the line between corporate chain and voluntary chain operations is becoming somewhat obscure. In addition to serving retailers under contract, the voluntary chain

wholesaler may have a substantial investment in, or even own, many of the so-called "independent" stores. Or a retailer may own a whole group of stores (i.e., a chain) and yet have them supplied by merchandise from a voluntary wholesaler.[7] Finally, the retailers may actually own the wholesale organization, an arrangement usually referred to as a cooperative chain. Voluntary and cooperative wholesalers have developed in hardware, drugstore, auto supply, general merchandise, and other retail fields, but probably are most significant in food distribution.

Other middlemen Other middlemen—brokers, commission houses, manufacturers' agents, selling agents, and auctions—are used as sources of needed merchandise by some retailers.

Brokers The brokers' main service is to bring buyer and seller together. They are used chiefly in buying and selling grocery specialties, dry goods, and fruits and vegetables. They are more useful to large retailers than to small-scale operators, but small retailers of men's and women's wear, household appliances, furniture, jewelry, hardware, and drugs employ their services to some degree. (See the discussion of the merchandise broker on p. 314.) Food brokers primarily act as manufacturers' representatives for food packers, processors, and manufacturers. They usually neither take title to, nor physical possession of, the goods, but sell on commission to wholesalers and large retailers, and often help the stores develop special promotional programs for their products.[8]

Commission houses These are mainly a source of supply for large retailers, especially in the food trade. They differ from brokers in that they usually handle the merchandise. They operate typically in central markets, receive merchandise that they display and sell, deduct their commission and other charges from the proceeds of the sale, and remit the balance to their principals.

Selling agents Selling agents are independent businesspeople who handle their clients' entire sales function. They are employed mostly by small manufacturers of piece goods, clothing, and food specialties who are not large enough to have their own sales organizations. Selling agents also often give their clients advice on styling, extend financial aid, and make collections. *Manufacturers' agents* sell goods similar to those sold by selling agents but they have less authority over prices and terms of sale, are restricted to a more limited area, and sell only part of their clients' output.

Auctions This type of sale is used mainly by retailers of fruits and vegetables. When produce is received at the auction, it is placed on display and sold quickly to the highest bidder, the proceeds going to the shipper after commissions and other charges have been deducted. Because they lack the skill needed to be good buyers and have little time to attend the auctions most smaller retailers buy their fruits and vegetables from wholesalers.

□ The manufacturer as a merchandise resource

Why retailers buy direct   Many retailers purchase their merchandise directly from manufacturers, even though they lose some of the services offered by the regular wholesaler. Manufacturers' sales representatives are usually better trained and better informed than those of wholesalers and can advise the retailer on advertising, display, and on the stock needed. This advice is very valuable for high-fashion merchandise. Also, manufacturers who sell direct frequently cooperate in training retail salespeople, providing demonstrators, training employees to repair and install merchandise, and providing advertising and display material.*

Direct buying also frequently enables the retailer to get fashion merchandise into the store more quickly than if a middleman is involved. For high-fashion items, time is an important consideration. Speedy supply is also essential for other goods that are somewhat perishable— crackers and cookies, for example—since customers are constantly demanding fresher merchandise.

Direct buying permits large retailers to purchase goods made to their own specification. Sears, Roebuck and Company, for example, specifies the design of 95 percent of the goods it sells. Drug and furniture chains, department stores, and discount houses also follow this practice. Nearness to the customer enables the retailer to assess customer wants; and the larger merchants have the technical expertise to prepare product specifications.

In addition to the foregoing benefits, many retailers buy direct because they are able to obtain lower net prices. In other words, the economical absorption of some of the middleman's functions by manufacturer and retailer reduces the costs of marketing and lowers prices to the retailer.

Many smaller retailers have joined together to achieve some of the advantages of direct-buying. In Cleveland, for example, direct buying by a group of hardware retailers resulted in a reported 10 to 20 percent reduction in purchase prices; and the ability to purchase directly was a major reason for the formation of Casual Corner Associates, an association of independently-owned sportswear shops.

Why manufacturers sell direct   The prevalence of direct buying is due to manufacturers' preferences as well as those of retailers. Many manufacturers prefer to sell directly to retailers because they consider it "good business." They appreciate the necessity of getting fashion and

---

* Manufacturers selling directly to large retailers cannot provide advertising and other promotional assistance unless the same assistance is offered to small retailers who buy through wholesalers. See the discussion of the Robinson-Patman Act in Chapter 13. The Combines Investigation Act imposes a similar requirement in Canada.

perishable merchandise to the retailer speedily while such goods are salable. Moreover, the growth of retailers who buy in large amounts, perform part of the storage function, and are good credit risks, encourages the manufacturer to sell direct. And relatively small retailers may concentrate their buying with a few manufacturers to make direct sale economical. Many small retailers of men's clothing, for instance, buy most of their suits and overcoats from a few sources. They also purchase substantial quantities for each season at one time, thus increasing the size of their orders.

Still other manufacturers sell directly to secure more aggressive selling, as in the grocery field where many wholesalers have developed their own private brands. The availability of public warehouses and manufacturers' branches as distributing points near their customers is also partly the cause and partly the effect of direct selling.

Manufacturer-retailer integration Just as integration has taken place between wholesaler and retailer, the manufacturer and the retailer have also been drawn together. Some retailers, having purchased for some time from certain manufacturers, have taken the initiative and "bought out"—in whole or in part—a portion of the resources. Currently, Sears, Roebuck and Company has various degrees of ownership in the manufacturers who produce about one quarter of the merchandise it sells. Bond Stores manufactures men's suits, coats, and shirts; and the Thom McAn Shoe Company produces its own shoes.

☐ The farmer as a merchandise resource

The grower is not an important source of supply for retailers, except for some foods. Small retailers may buy a large part of their fresh fruits and vegetables directly from local growers. Large chain retailers, however, may send buyers to distant farmers to procure supplies. Smaller chains cover a less extensive geographic area, but they also, frequently, by-pass central markets and go directly to growers or to cooperative marketing associations to which the growers belong. However, most food retailers still buy their agricultural products from middlemen.

■ VENDOR INITIATIVE TO FIND BUYERS

The initiative in bringing the retailer and the source of supply together may be taken by the seller or by the retailer, acting individually or in cooperation with other retailers. Sellers mainly employ two methods, (1) catalogs and price lists and (2) sales representatives.

□ Catalogs and price lists

Both manufacturers and wholesalers issue catalogs to provide information concerning their offerings. Of considerable importance at one time and still widely used by some vendors, retailers today primarily rely on catalogs for the purchase of staple merchandise needed to fill in their stocks. Catalogs can easily become quite bulky, difficult to handle, filled with out-of-date information, and generally unsatisfactory. Some vendors have substituted shorter price lists with only condensed information. But some hardware wholesalers now offer their dealers microfiche versions of the catalog in which as many as 325 large-sized printed pages are reproduced on a single, easily replaced, 4″ by 6″ card that can be inserted into a standard microfiche viewing machine (Figure 12–1).[9]

Some resident buying offices in cities such as New York prepare catalogs to assist their client stores in making purchases. One office, for example, issues a notion catalog describing all the items carried by the stores in its affiliated group. Another publishes a housewares catalog in mimeographed form containing the chief offerings of over 1,200 suppliers. (Resident buying offices are discussed later in this chapter.)

□ Sales representatives

Sending sales representatives to call on retailers is undoubtedly the most important way vendors reach their present and potential dealers. Sales visits may be made weekly, or even more often, in the distribution of fast-moving products. The sales staff in some grocery, drug, and hardware wholesaling firms telephone their customers daily. Sales visits are normally scheduled much less frequently in other fields, such as men's clothing. But the interval between visits often becomes shorter when business conditions are poor, since the sales representatives will try to exert more selling "pressure."

Store proprietors or buyers obtain advantages by waiting for the vendors' sales representatives to call. This eliminates much searching activity (which costs time and money), store salespeople can be asked to comment on the samples being shown, the actual stock can be checked to determine needs, and the vendor representatives may provide useful information or help set up displays. These, and other, benefits help the buyer do a better job of purchasing.[10]

■ RETAILER INITIATIVE TO FIND VENDORS

Increasingly, retailers are seeking sources of supply rather than depending on vendors coming to them. They prefer to compare several vendors' offerings, survey "the market," and exchange ideas with sellers

FIGURE 12–1   Wholesaler's microfiche catalog card with illustration of enlarged page

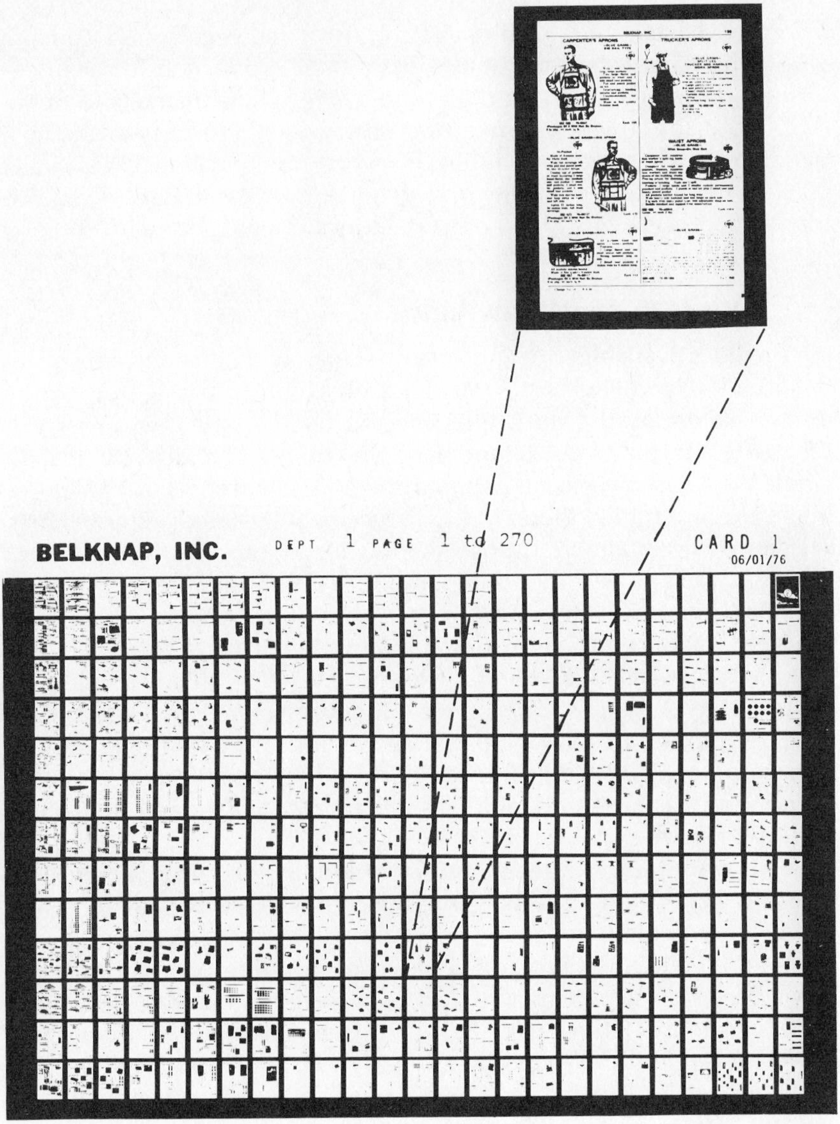

BELKNAP, INC.   DEPT 1 PAGE 1 to 270   CARD 1
06/01/76

Courtesy Belknap, Inc., Louisville, Kentucky

and retailers handling similar merchandise. Moreover, manufacturers of such high-fashion goods as women's dresses are small and geographically concentrated, thus making it economical for the retailers to take the initiative. In performing this task the retailer may visit local, central, and even foreign markets, use a buying office, and engage in group and central buying.

◻ Visits to local markets

As we have noted, small retailers of fruits and vegetables frequently visit local markets and may thus obtain their produce at lower prices. Large food retailers also send their buyers into local markets to obtain supplies at the lowest possible price. They usually deal with the local middlemen who offer the output of several farmers. Retailers may also take the initiative in dealing with cash-and-carry wholesalers in the local market and occasionally call on certain local manufacturers.

◻ Visits to central markets

Facilities available Buying in central markets is practiced mainly by medium-size and large-scale retailers and, to some degree, by all retailers of fashion goods. Most American retailers consider New York City the dominant central market for many types of merchandise, particularly women's wear, since about two thirds of all the garments manufactured in the U.S. are traded there. But, other cities are gaining as central markets, and, for certain goods, overshadow New York. San Francisco and Los Angeles have become so important for department store merchandise that even buyers from eastern stores visit these cities. For furniture, Chicago; High Point, North Carolina; and Jamestown, New York, are important markets, in addition to New York City. For many retailers, St. Louis, Dallas, and New Orleans are important central markets. In Canada, Toronto is a major central market city for furniture, home furnishings, carpeting, and hardware, while Montreal is very important in the distribution of shoes and women's apparel. Winnipeg and Vancouver are significant regional centers.

Competing vendors generally locate close together in central market cities, so that visiting buyers can easily compare the various offerings. These vendors often have permanent displays in one large, specialized exhibition building. Chicago's American Furniture Mart houses the permanent displays of many sellers of furniture and related products and its gigantic Merchandise Mart is used for display and selling purposes by vendors in practically all fields. Atlanta's Merchandise Mart likewise has displays covering many lines of merchandise, while the Apparel Mart in Dallas concentrates on all kinds of clothing.

Where central permanent displays are not used, competing vendors often sponsor temporary joint showings of their goods. Thus, New York City has its toy fair; Chicago has its home-furnishings exhibit, its semi-annual furniture markets, and its national shoe fair; and San Francisco has its home furnishings show. The Canadian National Shoe Show is held in Montreal.

Benefits and methods of central market buying Although the excitement of the large "showings" may not be conducive to careful buying, buyers find many advantages in the joint showings. In some instances catalog illustrations may be misleading. The shows permit the buyers to examine samples of the goods before they are purchased; to view all offerings in a minimum of time; to make direct comparisons; and to exchange ideas with other buyers.

One writer lists ten reasons why buyers attend central markets:*

1. To buy merchandise.
2. To seek new resources.
3. To compare a wide variety of merchandise.
4. To study market conditions.
5. To note and sense style movements.
6. To observe activities of other buyers.
7. To see showroom display ideas.
8. To obtain promotion and advertising ideas.
9. To seek special terms and purchases.
10. To consult with factory personnel.[11]

Buying in central markets is carried on mainly (1) through store buyers who make periodic trips to market, (2) through store buyers assisted by resident buying offices, and (3) directly through central buying officials. A store buyer who goes to market and buys without assistance from a resident buying office has full authority. If the resident buying office is used, it may help determine what shall be purchased. The store buyer loses much authority when central buyers assume the buying function.

Central market buying trips The frequency of visits to the central markets is determined by such factors as (1) whether or not the buyer's store has a resident buying office; (2) the type of merchandise involved, i.e., staple or fashion goods; (3) the size of the store; (4) business and supply conditions; and (5) the location of the retailer in relation to the central market. The frequency of buying trips will also be related to inventory policy. Generally buyers will go to market more often, and buy less on each trip, if the store wishes to increase its turnover rate. Globe Shopping City, a Texas subsidiary of the Walgreen Company, reduced its average inventory and raised the turnover rate by doubling the frequency with which its buyers went to markets.[12]

The brevity of the usual market trip[13] makes intensive preparation essential to insure the most productive use of the buyer's time. The buyer should carefully review merchandise plans and requirements, and available funds before leaving the store. Advance appointments may be made with major resources to be certain that the appropriate sales representatives or executives will be available when the buyer calls. If the store employs a resident buying office in that market, it should be

---

* Reprinted by permission of *Home Furnishing Daily*.

notified of the date and duration of the buyer's visit and of any assistance or services that may be desired.[14]

Many skilled buyers try to "scout" the market—that is, visit as many actual and potential vendors as possible to gather information before going back to the chosen resources to make actual purchases. Even merchants who know that they will ultimately concentrate much of their business with a few resources often try to see as many vendors as time will permit. They know that they can obtain new ideas and information this way, they may be sufficiently impressed with a previously excluded manufacturer's current offerings to add that firm to the list of resources, and such visits are also a means of remaining in touch with possible future suppliers. These buyers utilize the first visit to each vendor as a "sight-seeing" trip to note what is available. But much depends, of course, upon supply and demand conditions. When goods are in short supply, delays in making purchases may result in failure to obtain the goods desired.

On this first excursion, the buyer will keep complete notes of what seem to be the desirable prices, materials, styles, and offerings. These will be studied carefully before the second visits to the selected resources to make final choices and to place orders. This note-taking is essential to avoid confusion, since a buyer will normally review far too many lines to permit remembering the weak and the strong points of each.

Many buyers also spend some time visiting stores in the central market city to observe merchandise being displayed. Sometimes trips may be made to certain cities just to observe other stores. To illustrate, the fashion reputation of Neiman-Marcus of Dallas is so great that its fashion expositions attract store buyers from all parts of the country.

Resident buying offices Resident buying offices are institutions located in central market cities to serve out-of-town retailers. They have grown in importance in recent years and today are literally merchandising consultants for their client stores.[15] They probably serve as many as 90 percent of the country's department and specialty stores as well as many discount houses.

Resident buying offices may be classified into two groups:

A. Independent offices—profit-making businesses entirely separate from the stores they serve.
   1. *Paid or salaried offices.* Used by large stores who pay the office an agreed-upon fee, either so much per month or a certain percentage of the store's sales volume.
   2. *Merchandise brokers* Used by smaller stores, their fees are paid by the manufacturers whose merchandise they buy or recommend.

B. Store-owned offices.
  1. Those that are owned and operated by a single company, usually
     a chain store company or a department store ownership group for
     its own stores. (See Chapter 7 for a definition of ownership
     group.) The chain store company office is sometimes called a
     "private office"; the ones established by ownership groups are
     called "syndicate offices."
  2. Those that are owned cooperatively by a number of otherwise
     unaffiliated stores. For example, Associated Merchandising Cor-
     poration; Specialty Stores Association. These are often called
     "associated offices."

The various types of resident buying offices have developed most
thoroughly in the New York market but some are in such cities as Chicago, Los Angeles, and St. Louis and some have offices in London, Paris,
Hong Kong, etc. The majority of resident buyers operate in the women's
and children's apparel trades, although many purchase furs, menswear,
millinery, home furnishings, jewelry, and other lines. Some are fairly
small and serve only a limited number of stores in a few lines; others
render service in a large number of fields.

Services rendered buyers[16]   The services provided by buying offices
enable store buyers to do a much better job than they could do without
such assistance. The resident offices place orders upon request from the
buyer, check on deliveries, handle adjustments, and provide information as to goods available, fashion trends, prices, and the best sources
of supply. The store buyer gets this information from experts, and gets
it quickly. A buying office representative will accompany the store buyer
on market visits to vendors so that both can pass judgment on merchandise offers and locate the "best buys." The office also may arrange for
"showings" at which the offerings of many vendors are put on display,
thus conserving the buyer's time; and it can provide facilities such as
office space, stenographic aid, and sample rooms where vendors may
display their goods. Finally, the resident buying office often plays an
important role in making group buying arrangements. (See pp. 317–18.)

When the store buyer is not in the central market, the resident buying office may help through a constant stream of market information in
the form of letters, special reports, or regular weekly or monthly bulletins. Thus, the buyer is kept informed concerning fashion and price
trends and special buys. During recent years there has been a tendency
for resident buying offices to broaden their services to the stores they
represent. They may select and forward samples of new goods or of
exceptional values for consideration as possible purchases. A resident
office will also handle many fill-in purchases and may even consolidate
shipment on a number of small orders placed with several vendors,

thus reducing the cost of transportation. In some instances the buying office—aided by a unit-control system worked out between the store and the office—may make all the purchases of staple merchandise thus allowing the store buyers to concentrate attention on other goods. Some offices actually merchandise fashion departments in the stores they serve. Others, having foreign branches or working closely with similar groups abroad, purchase quite large amounts of foreign merchandise.

Resident buying offices sometimes offer stores two other services which are very valuable. One is to suggest goods for promotional events, prepare advertising copy, and outline the whole campaign. The second is to be a clearinghouse for information from all the stores served. Data may be gathered on expenses, markdowns, training systems, and sales promotions and distributed to all the client stores.

■ ORGANIZING THE BUYING FUNCTION

So far we have talked as though all of the decisions about items and vendors will be reached by a store buyer, that is, by a store-owner or by an employee who is part of the staff of an individual store (or of a downtown store plus its suburban branches). We have noted that this buyer may receive some help from a resident buying office, and, of course, if an employee, will be subject to supervision and control by the owner or by a senior executive. (See Chapter 7 for a discussion of the position of those buyers on the store organization chart.) But essentially we have looked at the store buyer as a solitary decision-maker. It is now time to study some other arrangements.

□ Committee buying

Most supermarket chains use buying committees that have the final power of approval or rejection over any new item that a buyer wants to add to the product assortment.[17] These committees, which normally consist of the entire buying staff (grocery buyers, meat buyer, produce buyer, and some other executives)* usually meet weekly. Each buyer decides which potential items within his or her special jurisdiction will be presented to the committee, and by simply failing to present an item, automatically rejects it. Thus the buyer does the initial screening, and moreover each specialist buyer's recommendations will naturally carry considerable weight in the committee. However, the firms that use the

---

* Since the committee usually consists entirely of headquarters personnel rather than store managers, it is also an example of *central buying,* discussed in a later paragraph.

committee system believe that the collective wisdom of the group is superior to any one buyer's judgment. Moreover, the requirement of a formal presentation to the committee (most companies have a pre-printed form that outlines the information which must be offered during the presentation) forces the buyer to assemble and analyze all relevant data about the proposed new item and its sales prospects. The weaknesses of the committee system are that: (a) it imposes delays—the buyer cannot make an immediate decision but must go to the committee; (b) it dilutes responsibility; and (c) it probably inhibits some innovation since committees in general tend to be more conservative than individuals.

Committee buying differs from group buying, discussed in the next paragraph, in two important respects. First, in committee buying, the members all come from the same company or store; and second, they have different specializations or executive positions. Group buying, on the other hand, unites similar executives, say, all of the toy buyers, from a number of stores.

☐ Group buying

Group buying involves joint purchasing by a group of buyers representing noncompeting stores. Typically, samples are gathered from various vendors and placed on display at buying offices or, in some cases, in hotel sample rooms. Sometimes vendors' labels are removed so that buying may be as objective as possible. After the samples have been examined, the committee of buyers decides, by a majority or two-thirds vote, on the items to be bought. Each buyer usually takes at least a minimum quantity of the merchandise selected.

Although done mostly by department and departmentized specialty stores, group buying is also practiced by retailers of hardware, appliances, foods, drugs, and other merchandise lines. Allied Stores Corp., a department store ownership company, created buyers' steering committees with members from 12 of its largest department store divisions (such as Jordan Marsh—Boston and Miami; Bon Marche—Seattle; Donaldson's—Minneapolis) to agree on joint purchases of such items as sweaters, refrigerators, and toys.[18]

Benefits of group buying Group buying can yield six main advantages to the participating stores. First, it permits placing large orders on certain goods and securing substantial discounts.[19] Second, it provides a pooling of knowledge as to what customers want, goods available, and fashion trends, thus enabling buyers to select items that will sell to better advantage.[20] Third, it may save the buyer's time while in the market. Fourth, it makes possible the direct comparison of samples of merchandise from several vendors in one place and results in better buying.

Fifth, in some cases, the stores will buy sufficient quantities to enable them to set their own specifications for production of the goods. Sixth, the participating stores may be able to develop a common brand name for the goods which can then be widely advertised.

Limitations of group buying In addition to the objections raised by vendors—that it results in too many price concessions, causes pressure to reduce quality, and encourages style piracy while samples are on display—group buying involves other difficulties. Many store buyers consider such buying a step toward their elimination, with their buying function taken over by central buyers. As a result, they do not cooperate in "pushing" the goods selected by the group or they place minimum orders for the selected goods. In the latter case, their action makes it difficult for the group to present a united front in asking lower prices of the vendor. The practice is also time-consuming; and not all groups have provided the expected improvement in selection.[21]

Group buying probably is best suited to stores handling medium-priced lines. Low-priced stores find that most of the goods they buy are made by manufacturers for stock, and no production savings are available when a single large order is placed. Retailers of high-priced goods realize that the individuality of customers' demands precludes their participation in extensive group-buying arrangements.

□ Central buying

Central buying implies that a large part of the authority over buying lies outside the individual retail store as is true in many chain-store organizations. Instead of the store manager or buyer choosing vendors this task is performed by headquarters executives. The central buyer is made responsible for purchasing, and the store manager for selling. Some chains follow a highly centralized policy. For example, in the 475-store House of Fabrics chain, "The home office dictates every [merchandising] detail—reorders, mark-downs, merchandise display, advertising."[22]

Growth of central buying Even department stores have adopted some central-buying practices. For example, some ownership-group department stores—Allied Stores and Associated Dry Goods—have long used central buyers for some staples and lower-priced fashion merchandise. But the loss of authority by the department store buyer should not be overemphasized. The practice has not made much headway outside of staples, and some firms have returned to individual store buying after experimenting with central buying.

Many organizations with central buyers depend to a degree on store buyers, especially in regard to shopping goods. Even such large chains as Sears, Roebuck and Company, F. W. Woolworth Company, and J. C. Penney Company let their store managers select much of their merchandise from lists supplied by headquarters. In other in-stances the managers meet and choose from the samples gathered by the central buyers, with blanket orders being placed on the items se-lected. In department store ownership-groups, store buyers may refuse goods selected by central buyers.

Yet retailing seems to go through alternating trends of centralization and decentralization. In the mid-1970s a trade magazine could com-ment: "Decentralized department stores are increasingly incorporating chain concepts [centralization] in their operations."[23] Sears, Roebuck and Company, which had always given the stores some autonomy and flexibility to offset the centralization of authority needed for its large purchases and its program of specification buying, hired a major con-sulting firm in 1975 to study the ways it might reduce "the duplication of decision-making between headquarters and stores."[24]

The "metro" concept of community-wide promotion on the part of chains that have several stores in the same city requires some trans-fer of decision-making from the individual stores to at least the metro or area manager's office (see pp. 101–2). The growth of computers and data transmission systems facilitates centralized merchandising. Never-theless experience shows that when centralization is carried too far, the limitations discussed in a subsequent paragraph take effect and the trend must be reversed. Associated Dry Goods, an 158-store ownership group, is devising more formal ways of sending advice from its central market staff to store buyers. But it says the buyers will remain auton-omous, will engage in increased travel themselves to domestic and foreign markets, and will be able to reject any central office recommen-dations.[25]

Central buyers require a constant stream of information concerning sales and customer demand. They obtain this through reports from store personnel supplemented, in some companies, by fairly frequent tele-phone conversations, and through intensive analysis of sales and in-ventory records, many of which are now computerized. Many central buyers know as much or more about the wants of customers they never see as their store counterparts. (See also the discussion of the merits and limitations of separating the buying and selling functions in depart-mentized stores on pp. 191–93.)

Advantages and disadvantages of central buying   In part, the ad-vantages of central buying are similar to those of group buying such as the lower prices secured by quantity purchases and the possibility of central planning of sales promotions. But other advantages also result. The central buyer who spends full time in buying becomes more expert in this task and often does a better job than the store buyer, for whom it usually is a part-time activity. Located in the central market, or at least closely in touch with it, the central buyer secures new merchandise immediately. Traveling expenses are reduced and inspection of goods, especially fashion items, is made easy. Finally, relieving the store buyer of considerable purchasing work frees time for sales supervision.

The benefits of central buying are greatest for staples. It may be argued that fashion goods and similar items must be purchased to meet tastes that vary from store to store. Moreover, the need for individualization reduces the quantity of any one item that the central buyer can purchase and thereby eliminates or reduces the possibility of a significant quantity discount. There is sufficient truth in these contentions, perhaps, to justify the conclusion that central buying is not really suitable for stores with upper-income clienteles. Moreover, taking too much authority away from the stores may leave the managers and other store executives ill-prepared to cope with emergencies. Yet methods of keeping central buyers informed as to what customers want are developing so rapidly that the future may well bring changes.

Ordering for specific stores in chain systems   One main problem of central buying is devising adequate systems to (1) inform store managers of the goods purchased by the central buyers and (2) to enable them to requisition such merchandise for their stores. The food chains furnish a good example of the factors involved in this problem.

These chains have usually furnished their store managers with a list of the items carried in company warehouses. Usually these lists are on a printed form that can be used for requisitioning merchandise. The store manager takes the dry grocery list, for example, and, at particular times, checks it against the quantity on hand for each item and enters the amount desired. This form is sent to the nearest company warehouse where the order is filled.

Today the food chains speed up this ordering process by the use of electronic equipment. Many Safeway stores are equipped with an ordering machine which produces a tape listing the wanted merchandise. In turn, the symbols on this tape are transmitted electronically to a warehouse from which the order is filled. The National Tea Company system has store employees place the order on cards. These cards are sent to headquarters where they are "read" by an electronic machine which automatically transmits shipping orders to the warehouse. This company, however, has experimented with a telephone-wire transmission system which reduces the time between placing an order and receiving the merchandise in the store from three days (when cards are mailed) to one day. Many chains in other fields—variety, drug, shoe, general merchandise, to mention a few—are also using electronic equipment to speed up the flow of orders to their retail units.

Not all chain systems depend on the store manager to decide on the merchandise that should be handled by the store. Some firms "merchandise" individual stores from central or regional headquarters. Through a combination of model stocks, the flow of sales tags or tickets to headquarters, and the rapid analysis of these tags, headquarters can quickly decide what merchandise is needed in the store.

■ FOREIGN MARKETS AS SOURCES OF SUPPLY

Significant fluctuations occur in the use of foreign markets as sources of supply. For example, during World War II, the inflow of goods from foreign lands dropped abruptly. During the late 1960s many large stores manifested increased interest in foreign-made goods and featured imports from Mexico, France, Italy, Japan, and other countries.[26] Rising labor and material costs in many overseas markets and changes in exchange rates for foreign currencies, particularly for some European currencies, adversely affected imports during the early 1970s.[27] Nevertheless, many stores are expanding their import programs.[28] Precise data are not available, but imports may provide 10 to 15 percent of the merchandise in U.S. general merchandise/variety chains.[29] The figure is probably higher for Canadian organizations.

Stores have three main motives in buying foreign goods, either directly or through importers. One is to obtain the merchandise more cheaply, even after paying transportation and customs tax costs, than is possible at home. This permits either a lower selling price or a greater margin between cost and selling price than can be obtained on domestic products.[30] Second, foreign markets will supply some items that are unobtainable domestically.[31] After all, U.S. and Canadian supermarkets would sell few bananas, and little coffee or tea, if they had to rely on domestic supplies. Third, some imported goods have unusual prestige and customer appeal. Laces from Belgium, furniture from Denmark, sporting goods and wood carvings from Switzerland, perfume from France, linen from Ireland, cameras from Japan, and menswear from England fall in this category.

Buying in foreign markets   Large retailers who want to have direct access to foreign sources of merchandise often send their buyers on trips to many parts of the world. Direct buying in foreign markets, however, presents many difficulties. The first is the travel expense and time involved. This is aggravated by the fact that a buyer usually needs more time to learn local business practices, to discover good sources of supply, and to cope with problems in a foreign market than is required at home. Language differences often prove frustrating. Second, the buyer must become accustomed to converting foreign price-quotations into dollars. Third, shipping arrangements, transportation costs, import (and sometimes export) duties, inspection, and international documentation are usually very complicated. Stores that send buyers overseas often use resident buying offices in the foreign markets and a variety of shipping and customs agents to help alleviate these three types of problems. Two other major problems, however, must also be solved.

Manufacturers in some foreign markets may be unskilled in producing goods for North American customers. Garments may be cut to incorrect sizes or proportions; furniture finishes or construction may prove unsatisfactory in steamheated homes; product labeling may not conform to government requirements; and the factories may have little experience in mass-production quality-control standards. Many foreign resources exhibit none of these weaknesses and, in fact, many produce highly superior goods. But when the limitations do exist, buyers do have to work very closely with their resources to obtain the necessary improvements. And regardless of the ability of the foreign resource, imported goods are susceptible to even more delivery delays than domestic lines. In one survey of apparel buyers: "The slow deliveries, especially with imported goods, were mentioned by nearly every buyer as a source of concern."[32] In view of all of these problems, some merchants—particularly the smaller retailers—prefer to buy their foreign-made goods from local importers or other wholesalers. Nevertheless, those firms that can cope with the complexities of importation do find advantages in judicious use of foreign resources.

Whether purchasing from foreign or domestic suppliers, the retailer's task is not limited to deciding how much money to invest in merchandise, determining what items customers will want and in what quantities, and locating vendors who can supply those items; those are the merchandising and buying subjects that we have examined to this point. But the retailer must also consider the prices those vendors will charge, the discounts, allowances and terms that they will grant, and the various selling helps and services that they will provide. The next chapter discusses those elements of the transaction.

■ REVIEW AND DISCUSSION QUESTIONS

1 Briefly discuss the advantages of concentrating purchases with a few resources. In spite of these advanatges, why do many retailers like to divide their business among numerous resources?

2 Describe the various types of wholesale middlemen who supply retailers. What are the distinctive characteristics and services of each type?

3 Explain the benefits retailers gain by joining voluntary and cooperative chains. Why don't all independent retailers belong to such chains?

4 (a) Why do some retailers let vendors take the initiative in establishing contact? (b) What are the two main methods that vendors use for this purpose?

5 Ask a local merchant or buyer who makes central market trips to describe a typical trip. Try to obtain answers to the following questions: (a) What planning was done before the trip? (b) Was a resident office used and what services did it provide? (c) How long did the trip take? (d) How many resources were examined? How many of those were firms that had not been previously used as suppliers? (e) How were visits to resources conducted? (f) Was there an opportunity to shop local stores?

6 Discuss the factors that have been responsible for the growth of several specific central markets.

7 Outline the principal functions performed by resident buying offices. Describe the various organizational relationships and compensation arrangements they may have with their stores.

8 As a store buyer, what would you gain and what would you lose if your store became involved in: (a) committee buying, (b) group buying, and (c) central buying?

9 Talk to a retailer who belongs to a buying group or a cooperative or voluntary chain, and report on the problems and benefits that she or he has experienced as a result of such association.

10 Explain the major problems of buying in foreign markets. Why, in spite of these problems, have large retailers increased their import volume?

■ NOTES AND REFERENCES

1 "Joske's: Big $ from Small Firms," *Women's Wear Daily,* January 4, 1974, p. 30.

2 See John S. Berens, "A Decision Matrix Approach to Supplier Selection," *Journal of Retailing,* vol. 47 (Winter 1971–72), pp. 47–50.

3 For an illustration of such a survey, see "Junior and Misses Sportswear Vendor Performance Survey," *Stores,* October 1975, pp. 2–5.

4 For example, "Macy's, Bamberger's in Switch: Buy Rival Line via Distributors," *Home Furnishings Daily,* August 22, 1974, pp. 1, 6.

5 "On Distributor Use," *Discount Merchandiser,* March 1976, p. 60.

6 For details on this form of organization see "Group Activities of Independent Retailers," in J. C. Carman and K. A. Uhl, *Phillips' and Duncan's Marketing Principles and Methods,* 7th ed. (Homewood, Ill.: Richard D. Irwin, Inc., 1973), pp. 179–87; and K. A. Adams, "Achieving Market Organization through Voluntary and Cooperative Groups," *Journal of Retailing,* vol. 42, no. 2 (Summer 1966), pp. 19–28, 60.

7 The *Progressive Grocer* reports that in 1975 wholesale grocers who sponsored voluntary chains had sales of approximately $24 billion, and those attached to cooperative chains sold about $14 billion, while unaffiliated wholesalers sold slightly less than $10 billion. "43rd Annual Report of the Grocery Industry," April 1976, p. 151. *See also* David Pinto, "Should Drug Chains Join a Co-op or Voluntary," *Chain Store Age* (drugstore edition), October 1975, p. 11.

8 "The Food Broker—Partner in Profit," *Supermarketing,* February 1972.

9 Esther Eisman, "Three Out of 4 Retailers Choose Microfiche over Paper Catalogs," *Hardware Retailing,* April 1975, pp. 72–73, 148–49.

10 For an illustration of some of the help and advice a skilled sales agent can give retailers, see Bruce Bliven, Jr., "Profile: Book Traveller," *The New Yorker,* November 12, 1973, pp. 51–113. However, not all retailers are pleased with the quality of sales presentations or the services received from sales representatives. "New Directions in the Buyer-Seller Relationship," *Chain Store Age* (supermarket edition), April 1973, pp. 64–67.

11 Ken Booth, "The Business," *Home Furnishings Daily,* January 2, 1973, p. 16.

12 Don Rhine, "We Reduced Inventory 35%," *Discount Merchandiser,* August 1975, p. 56.

13 The typical buyer attending the 1973 Housewares Show in Chicago spent only three days in the market. Advertisement, *Home Furnishings Daily,* June 19, 1973, p. 20.

14 R. Patrick Cash, "Planning a Successful Market Trip," *Stores,* November 1974, p. 21.

15 "Retailers' Ills Make Healthy Buying Offices," *Home Furnishings Daily,* March 7, 1974, p. 1.

16 For an excellent discussion of the services rendered by resident buying offices, *see* Howard Eilenberg, "Resident Buying Offices: Key Links of Marketing Channels," *New York Retailer,* Decem-

ber 1968, pp. 8–11. *See also* Herbert Koshetz, "Resident Buyers Staging Comeback," *New York Times*, November 15, 1970, p. F13.

17 See the discussion of buying committees in T. W. Leeds and G. A. German, *Food Merchandising: Principles and Practices* (New York: Chain Store Age Books, 1973), pp. 84–85.

18 "Allied Stores' Struggle with Profit Margins," *Business Week*, November 17, 1973, p. 57. Technically speaking, these steering committees differ slightly from the pure concept of group buying in that all of the members ultimately work for the same parent corporation but they would normally be considered examples of this form of buying since each member works directly for a different subsidiary.

19 For an illustration of this, see "Buying Groups Are Expected to Throw Weight Around More than Ever at Show," *Home Furnishings Daily*, January 12, 1973, p. 1.

20 "Vrontikis of NARDA Sees Buying Groups as Necessary," *Home Furnishings Daily*, July 15, 1975, p. 39.

21 For a discussion of possible legal problems in group buying, and a warning against placing too much group pressure on suppliers, see "Retailer Buy Groups May Violate Antitrust," *Home Furnishings Daily*, May 5, 1976, pp. 1, 9. *See also* the discussion of the Robinson-Patman Act on pp. 328–31.

22 "Foresight Pays Off in Profits," *Chain Store Age* (General merchandise edition), April 1976, p. 32.

23 "Futureshock/Marketing: A New Role for Buyer-Sellers," *Chain Store Age* (General merchandise edition), September 1975, p. 112. The same article also noted ilmits on centralization.

24 See "Sears' New Identity," *Business Week*, December 8, 1975, p. 52.

25 "ADG Hones Duties of Market Staff," *Women's Wear Daily*, December 3, 1975, pp. 1, 11.

26 For an excellent analysis of the advantages, disadvantages, and sources of imported merchandise see J. D. Goodnow, *The Significance of Imported Consumer Goods in Indiana Retailing* (Indianapolis: Economic Research Division, Indiana Chamber of Commerce, 1969). *Principles of Profitable Importing* by Giacomo Zanetti (New York: National Retail Merchants Association, 1971) is a very helpful text prepared from a retail point-of-view.

27 "U.S. Store Buying Offices Cut Costs," *Home Furnishings Daily*, July 25, 1974, p. 2; "Currency's Wobbles Dizzy Catalog Showrooms," *Home Furnishings Daily*, January 3, 1974, p. 16.

28 "The Rising Tide of Imports," *Chain Store Age* (General merchandise edition), March 1973, pp. 53–59; "May Company Sets Up a Program for Housewares in the Orient," *Home Furnishings Daily*, October 20, 1975, p. 2; "Hong Kong's Super Spectacular," *Stores*, May 1976, pp. 2–4.

29 "The Rising Tide of Imports." But import volume may also be affected adversely by changes in tariffs and similar legislation. *See* Eugene Farber, "The Trade Act of 1974 and Its Impact on Imports," *Stores*, April 1976, pp. 25–26.

30 "NY Dep't. Stores Keep Enlarging Import Plans Because of Markups," *Home Furnishings Daily*, October 14, 1975, p. 32; "Hong Kong RTW Festival to Stress Economy," *Women's Wear Daily*, February 23, 1976, p. 12.

31 "Trading with China," *Stores*, May 1974, p. 12; "Imports: An Antidote for Sameness," *Women's Wear Daily*, March 16, 1976.

32 "Apparel Buyers Treading Softly," *The Discount Merchandiser*, April 1976, p. 37.

BUYING: NEGOTIATIONS WITH
MERCHANDISE RESOURCES

Even after deciding that certain merchandise is suitable for their
customers' needs buyers often must negotiate a number of factors before purchasing. The prices to be paid are a major element. The amount
depends on the vendor's list price and discounts. But the retailer is also
interested in the time allowed for taking cash discounts and the date
when the bill finally becomes payable, i.e., the dating. These two elements—discounts and dating—are known as the "terms of sale." Sometimes the retailer asks the vendor to guarantee prices against decline for
a certain period; and the vendor may seek an "escalator clause," providing for upward price adjustments under certain circumstances. Finally,
transportation charges, services, and the exclusiveness of the merchandise may also be negotiated. In this chapter, we will examine these various aspects of negotiations and, more briefly, the transfer of title and
vendor relations.

■ THE INVOICE

On the pages that follow, we will frequently refer to something
called an "invoice." Although an invoice is not issued until the negotiations are completed, the purchase is made, and the goods are shipped, a
word of explanation may be helpful at this point. An invoice is simply an

■ 325

itemized statement (or bill) that the vendor sends to the purchaser by mail or along with the goods and that lists the merchandise shipped with the quantity, price, terms of sale, and other relevant data included.

■ SOME BASICS OF NEGOTIATIONS

In negotiating purchases with vendors, the buyer should recognize that the *merchandise* is the customer's first consideration rather than price. Getting the *right* merchandise is more important than getting a price concession on the *wrong* goods. Moreover, unreasonable price concessions should not be expected from the vendor. "Stiff" demands often lose the goodwill of vendors; as a result, they retaliate by being less cooperative. Prompt delivery and information about special buying opportunities are more likely to go to those with whom the vendors are on friendly terms. Consequently, a valuable asset of a buyer is the ability to obtain and keep the friendship and respect of vendors.

The buyer, however, should not be "soft" in negotiations. If the vendors are giving concessions to other comparable stores, the buyer should insist on similar terms. Also, buyers should not purchase only from their friends. But, it is to the buyer's own long-run interest to not take unreasonable advantage of a seller. Negotiations should be based on a considered mutual understanding of each other's position.

The buyer will be well advised to avoid an attitude of "knowing all the answers." An attempt to impress everyone usually ends up by incurring the vendors' ill-will. Most vendors have sufficient knowledge to pick out quickly the well-informed buyer from the uninformed one, and sometimes take pleasure in selling goods they should *not* buy to buyers who pretend to "know it all."

But before beginning price negotiations the buyer should accumulate a considerable amount of price information. The sources of these data are too numerous to mention completely but include conversations with sales representatives, newspaper items, trade journals, luncheon and telephone conversations with vendors and other retailers, past purchases, commodity market quotations, catalogs and price lists of vendors, and prices in other stores.

The buyer should also realize that the concessions granted from the asking price vary from vendor to vendor and from field to field. As a rule, when vendors are small and buyers are large, asking prices are subject to considerable haggling. To illustrate, the orders of a large department store may represent such as important outlet for a small dress manufacturer that the latter may be willing to grant a significant price concession rather than lose the account. The case for a price concession might be even stronger if the buyer represented a large chain store organization which was the sole outlet for the manufacturer. To a large food manufacturer, in contrast, the account of a small grocer is insufficient to warrant any price bargaining.

■ TERMS OF SALE: DISCOUNTS

A discount is any reduction in the list or quoted price of merchandise which is allowed the purchaser by the seller. Discounts may be grouped into six classifications: quantity, trade, seasonal, advertising or promotional, brokerage, and cash. Each of these discounts raises questions for the buyer concerning their legality under the Robinson-Patman Act.* Consequently, after explaining their nature and use, a concise review of the legal implications involved for each is presented.

☐ Quantity discounts

A quantity discount is a reduction in price granted because of the amount purchased and is usually *noncumulative,* that is, it is based on the amount** ordered at a given time. Thus, a vendor might charge $9.75 per dozen with a discount of 25 cents per dozen for purchases of 3 to 5 dozen at a time, 50 cents off for purchases of 6 to 15 dozen, and 75 cents off for orders of over 15 dozen. A *cumulative quantity discount,* on the other hand, also known as a "deferred discount" or a "patronage discount," applies to the total purchases made within a period. For example, a manufacturer of toothpaste may allow a discount of 5 percent if total purchases for the year amount to $10,000, 7 percent if purchases amount to $15,000, and 10 percent if they reach or exceed $20,000. The discount may also be based on the number of units purchased over the period.

Closely related to the quantity discount, or, in fact, a variation of it, is the "free deal" or "free goods." This practice involves including in the shipment certain goods in excess of those ordered; that is, if six dozen of an item are ordered, an extra dozen may be shipped without charge.

Why quantity discounts are granted   Quantity discounts are granted for two major reasons. One is the economies made possible for the vendor. Sales costs may be reduced when a retailer, who has formerly given a small order each week, adopts a policy of placing one large order every two months. The cost of billing and collecting may be little more on a large order than on a small one. The packaging and transportation cost per unit is less on large orders.[1] A manufacturer may find that large orders permit larger purchases of raw materials or more efficient use of plant capacity with concomitant cost savings.

However, the cumulative quantity discount does not encourage the kind of buying which results in reducing the vendor's cost so much as does the noncumulative quantity discount. Under the cumulative allowance the goods may be shipped in small lots at various times, thus in-

---

* In Canada, similar questions arise under the Combines Investigation Act.

** Sometimes the "quantity ordered" refers to the quantity of a *single* item; at other times, it refers to the quantity of *all* items included in the order.

volving higher billing, packing, transporting, and collecting costs. Although the buyer's concentration of purchases with a single vendor may give the latter a more certain market which permits (1) reducing the frequency of sales calls, (2) curtailing trade advertising somewhat, and (3) planning a production schedule to better advantage, such savings are small at best and, in the majority of cases, probably do not exist. But from the retailer's point of view, cumulative quantity discounts remove the temptation to overbuy at any one particular time, except perhaps near the end of the discount period when the merchant may be eager to qualify for a higher discount.

The second reason for granting quantity discounts is pressure from buyers. Such pressure has even been exerted in cases where higher unit costs actually have resulted from the large order. For instance, many fashion goods, such as women's dresses, are produced by relatively small manufacturers whose costs are largely direct ones. In such cases, production economies are limited. When the larger order has to be filled by overtime work and the hiring of inexperienced help, unit production cost is likely to be increased.

Trips One rather controversial type of cumulative quantity discount used primarily in the electrical appliance trade consists of inviting the dealers (and their families) on a group trip to some vacation resort or foreign site if they purchase a certain minimum quantity during a season or a year. Some manufacturers use this technique because (a) they think it motivates the dealers to buy and sell larger quantities, (b) since the manufacturers' executives and sales representatives accompany the group, it provides an excellent opportunity to cement relationships; (c) even though the program often is primarily recreational, some time will be reserved for displaying new products or conducting seminars on retailing methods, (d) the retailers naturally exchange ideas during the trip which may help each one improve selling methods, and (e) by using chartered airplanes, etc., the costs of a luxurious trip can be kept under reasonable control. The dealers, in turn, often like these trips as expense-free vacations and also appreciate the opportunity to exchange ideas. Nevertheless, some merchants feel that the trip requirements are designed to stimulate overbuying, some resent the time required away from the business, and some would prefer a reduction in merchandise cost. Others assign the trips to various employees as a reward for outstanding work.[2]

The Robinson-Patman Act Quantity discounts are subject to limits other than those resulting from the bargaining ability of buyer and seller. Under the Robinson-Patman Act, passed by Congress in 1936, a vendor selling in interstate trade may *not* give a lower price to one buyer than to another under the following circumstances:

1. If the buyers take commodities of the same grade and quality.
2. If the price difference:

a. Substantially lessens competition, or
b. Tends to create a monopoly, or
c. Injures, destroys, or prevents competition with vendor or buyer, or customers of either.

3. If the price difference is not one merely making "due allowance for differences in the cost of manufacture, sale, or delivery resulting from the differing methods or quantities in which such commodities are to such purchasers sold or delivered," or one offered "in good faith to meet the equally low price of a competitor."*

The Robinson-Patman Act does not apply directly to the prices retailers *charge*, since sales by stores to individual consumers have not been considered interstate trade for the purposes of this Act.** Also, it does not apply to the marketing of services, such as legal advice, insurance, real estate rentals, or medical assistance. It deals with the prices that retailers and other business and nonbusiness organizations are *charged* for *goods* and for certain services rendered in conjunction with their purchases of goods.

Overall appraisal of the act   The Robinson-Patman Act was promulgated during the Great Depression of the 1930s with the intention of reducing the buying advantages that large organizations enjoyed. It was part of a general wave of anti-chain store legislation† and, in fact, was sometimes called the "anti-A&P law." Even advocates of the legislation admit that it was poorly drafted, has many confusing and ill-defined provisions, and needs revision.[3] Some critics feel that the Robinson-Patman Act has failed to accomplish its purpose. It has not stopped chain store growth and may even have helped. This paradoxical effect may have occurred because the law may have encouraged chains to buy private label merchandise advantageously from small manufacturers who did not sell similar goods to other types of dealers and who thus could not be involved in chain-nonchain price discrimination.‡ Moreover, the law has been interpreted to forbid special discounts to the central headquarters of cooperative chains and thus has cut off an avenue of support that

---

* The Canadian Combines Investigation Act prohibition against anticompetitive price discrimination is more general and more recent than the Robinson-Patman Act. Consequently, considerable time will be needed for administration and judicial interpretation of the Act's implications.

** The government and the courts have avoided the question of whether interstate trade is involved and whether the Act can be invoked if the retail seller is located in one state and some of the customers who are charged different prices are located in other states, as sometimes happens in mail order selling.

† Other legislation adopted at the same time with an actual or ostensible anti-chain objective included various state tax and license laws that imposed higher fees upon chain than upon independent units, and resale price maintenance (often called "fair trade," see Chapter 17).

‡ Oversimplifying the law somewhat, a seller can be accused of price discrimination when selling to two or more customers, say, A and B, at different net prices. There can be no discrimination, as defined by the law, if the supplier only sells to A and not to B.

many independent retailers hoped to use to finance cooperative organization.*

Other critics believe that the whole purpose of the law is anticompetitive, that it favors "soft" rather than "hard" competition, and that it is bad for the company. In 1966, revision of the Act was recommended by the National Commission on Food Marketing.[4] In 1975, many high administrative officials in the federal government also recommended repeal or revision of the law, accompanied perhaps by a reinforced provision in the antitrust statutes concerning predatory pricing.[5] The law has only been sporadically enforced; while some violations have been vigorously prosecuted, others have undoubtedly continued undisturbed. Yet buyers must be aware of its existence and remember that obtaining or "knowingly receiving" an improper discount can be as illegal as granting one.[6] We will note some of the other provisions of the act when we examine advertising allowances, brokerage discounts, and promotional services.

Legality of quantity discounts Many of the firms that have been called upon to defend their quantity discounts under the Robinson-Patman Act have used the "cost defense" (item 3). That is, they have claimed a cost differential as the basis of their discount schedule. The Federal Trade Commission, which instituted most of the cases under the act, has frequently decided that evidence of a sufficient cost differential has been lacking and that the discount schedule was illegal.

Firms that want to be able to use a cost defense must have a highly accurate and well-designed cost accounting system. They must be able to demonstrate that the operating and overhead costs charged against each order (or each size of order) are allocated fairly and appropriately. For example, a seller cannot charge all manufacturing overhead costs against the first 100,000 units of production (which perhaps might be sold through wholesalers to small retailers) and then treat the next 100,000 units that go to a chain store as "extra" business on which there is no need to recoup overhead. However, establishing and defending an appropriate cost accounting system can be both difficult and expensive. The cost defense has proven to be much less effective than business people anticipated when the Act was passed.

Sometimes the facts in the case permit the defense of meeting competitive prices in good faith. The court rulings are somewhat confusing and contradictory (a typical state of affairs under the Robinson-Patman Act) on the question of whether a manufacturer can charge retailers less for merchandise to be placed under a private brand than for the identical goods when offered under the manufacturer's own national brand.

---

* Of course, a cooperative chain warehouse that buys, receives, and redistributes large quantities of goods may obtain the appropriate quantity discounts without violating the law.

Apparently, however, some "reasonable" or "customary" price differential will be permitted on the grounds of not being harmful to competition.[7]

Since the buyer who "knowingly" benefits from price discrimination is equally guilty with the vendor, the retailer must resist the temptation to bargain for a larger quantity discount than can be justified by the cost differential. To many authorities this section of the law, literally interpreted—which it probably would not be—makes the unrealistic assumption that the buyer knows the vendor's cost. The buyer must exercise restraint and should be especially wary in urging vendors to give cumulative quantity discounts, since such discounts are especially difficult to justify on a cost basis.[8]

☐ Trade discounts

The trade discount is a price reduction granted to various types of customers because of the kind of business in which they are engaged. This discount is often also called a "functional discount" since it supposedly is intended to offset the cost of the functions performed by the various types of businesses. A manufacturer selling both to service wholesalers and independent retailers, for example, may offer a 50 percent trade discount to all service wholesalers and a 35 percent discount to the retailers. This discount bears no relationship to the quantity purchased and may be given in addition to a quantity discount.

Sometimes vendors who deal with several trade groups use a string or chain of discounts. Thus, a particular vendor might offer wholesale buyers a trade discount of 30, 20, 10 or, as it might be stated, "less 30, less 20, and less 10." When such a chain of discounts is used, the discounts are deducted from the list price in sequence; that is, 30 percent off the list price, 20 percent off the balance, and 10 percent off the second balance. As a result the wholesaler would pay 50.4 percent of the list price. Such a percentage, known as the "on" percentage, may be applied to the list price to determine the actual charge.*

The manufacturer's list price is often the suggested resale price at the consumer level. If the wholesalers and retailers conform to the manufacturer's suggested prices, the trade discounts provide the margins that those dealers use to cover their expenses and, hopefully, to provide a profit. To illustrate: A drug manufacturer, selling through wholesalers for distribution to retailers, lists a product at $12 per dozen. Trade discounts are "less 33⅓ and less 15." Under these circumstances, the

---

* Based on the figures given, this percentage is calculated as follows: Assume 100 percent represents the list price shown on the invoice. Thirty percent of 100 is 30, and this amount deducted from 100 is 70. Twenty percent of 70 is 14, leaving 56 as the balance. Ten percent of 56 is 5.6, leaving 50.4 percent as the "on" percentage.

wholesaler would pay $6.80 per dozen. ($12.00 — $4.00 (33⅓ percent) = $8.00 — $1.20 (15 percent) = $6.80.) The wholesaler would resell to the retailer at $8 a dozen, realizing a 15 percent markup on selling price and allowing the retailer a 33⅓ percent markup on the retail selling price of $1 each, or $12 per dozen.

The manufacturer is willing to offer these trade discounts in part because of the cost savings resulting from selling to wholesalers instead of directly to retailers (or to retailers instead of directly to consumers) and in part because such discounts are necessary to keep these outlets in the channel of distribution.

Legality of trade discounts Trade discounts are not mentioned in the Robinson-Patman Act. To the layman, however, it would seem that vendors would have to justify those discounts on the basis of "cost of manufacture, sale, or delivery." But the Federal Trade Commission and the courts have not taken this position; instead, they have ruled that wholesale trade discounts result in no injury to competition and therefore constitute no violation of the act. But it should be emphasized that the discounts must be offered uniformly within each group and the trade groupings recognized by a seller must have a factual base.[9] In other words, a manufacturer could not arbitrarily classify one variety store as a "retailer" and give a "wholesale" rating to two other variety stores which have joined together for group buying.

□ Seasonal discounts

Seasonal discounts are percentage reductions in the billed price given to encourage ordering, and sometimes accepting delivery, in the so-called off seasons of the year. Vendors of toys may grant seasonal discounts to encourage buyers to place orders and to accept delivery in June, rather than to wait until August; and paint manufacturers may give such discounts to secure orders for spring stock in October, November, and December.

From the retailer's point of view, the seasonal discount should be large enough to compensate for the costs of (a) increased storage time, (b) risk of deterioration or loss during that period, and (c) extra interest on investment if early payment is required. The vendor's cost savings, which justify this discount, include (1) obtaining business during normal "slack" periods, thus keeping the factory in operation and permitting a more even distribution of overhead costs; (2) reducing storage costs; and (3) minimizing risks due to price changes.

Under the Robinson-Patman Act a vendor may use seasonal discounts as long as the same proportionate reduction is given to all competing comparable buyers who purchase at approximately the same time. The discount may also be altered from time to time as the seasons change.

☐ Advertising discounts or allowances

Sometimes retailers may obtain allowances for various forms of sales promotional effort. Manufacturers, for instance, may want their products advertised over the names of local department stores. They do this for several reasons: (1) The store name on an advertisement may provide prestige; (2) the stores usually obtain local advertising space and time at lower rates than the manufacturer would have to pay; (3) in addition, the store will usually pay part of the cost, so the manufacturer obtains exposure at a very low net cost; and (4) many retailers like such arrangements and favor manufacturers who use this advertising method.[10] Other manufacturers want their goods to be adequately displayed and called to the customer's attention by salespeople. A promotional allowance may be given to the retailer for these services.

Retailers obviously like advertising and promotional allowances since they represent an extra source of income or, more precisely, a reduction in costs. Sometimes, though, they resent the conditions imposed by the manufacturers (see Chapter 18). *For internal accounting purposes,* many retailers treat these allowances as reductions in the cost of the merchandise rather than as reductions in the store's advertising expense.

Impact of the Robinson-Patman Act   The Robinson-Patman Act says that advertising and promotional allowances must be made available to competing buyers on "proportionately equal terms," but "proportional *to what*" is not stated. Various cases, however, clearly indicate that a vendor should not offer, nor should a buyer accept, a promotional allowance unless (1) it is a reasonable payment for the service; (2) it is a payment for a service that all of the competing dealers could reasonably provide if they so desired; (3) it is offered on a basis that is proportionate to the dollar amount or the number of units that the retailers buy. To illustrate, a manufacturing company may offer to pay 50 percent of the newspaper, radio, or television space or time costs of dealer advertisements devoted to its product up to a limit of 5 percent of the dollar amount of the dealer's purchases; (4) if the vendor sells both to large retailers directly and to small retailers through wholesalers, the small dealers must be notified of the availability of the allowance and it must be offered under conditions that are reasonably practical for them to use if they so desire; and (5) the commission and the courts have also placed certain restrictions on a vendor's purchases of advertising space in a publication owned by a retail dealer.

As a practical matter, the "proportionally equal terms" rule may not allow the selling firm to adjust the assistance or allowance to meet its own marketing needs. "For example, a high-class store buying no more than a discount store performs a more valuable service in advertising the manufacturer's product, in that the high-class store's sponsorship carries more weight with the public and with other stores that are considering the purchase of the manufacturer's line. But the lack of objectivity in such a concept of proportionality will in all probability make it unacceptable to the Federal Trade Commission."[11]

Services The same rule, that customers must be offered "proportionately equal" treatment also applies to the promotional services that the vendor furnishes to the dealers, as well as to advertising allowances and payments. These services are discussed in a later portion of this chapter.

□ Brokerage discounts or allowances

The brokerage discount is an allowance given to a retailer who buys directly from the manufacturer and who therefore saves that manufacturer the cost of using a broker or agent. At one time many food chains that had established their own buying offices in food marketing centers and that purchased directly from food processing and packing companies received this discount, often amounting to 5 percent of purchases. But the Robinson-Patman Act contains an outright prohibition against giving a brokerage allowance (or any equivalent benefit) to anyone other than a *bona fide* independent agent or broker. This means that even those defenses that can be used to answer a charge of price discrimination* will not offset a charge of giving a brokerage allowance to anyone else.

Consequently, vendors who *use brokers for part of their sales* may not grant lower prices to reflect the nonpayment of brokerage on any direct sales.[12] And this statement is true even when the vendor can show that cost savings resulted from the performance of a brokerage service by the buyer. Only those vendors who sell *all* their output directly to retailers may grant lower prices than they might ask if using brokers.

This provision in the law produces one of the paradoxical elements of the Robinson-Patman Act. The brokerage provision keeps manufacturers and processors from turning over to voluntary and cooperative chain headquarters the selling commissions that they save on the large-scale direct orders they receive from these organizations. Thus an act that was intended to aid small merchants, particularly independent grocers, has served to eliminate a major potential support for the type of organization that seems necessary to the survival of many of these small merchants.

□ Cash discounts

A cash discount is a reduction in price given by a vendor in return for prompt payment. It is typically computed as a percentage of the

---

* The defenses are: lack of harm to competition, goods involved not of like grade or quality, meeting competition in good faith, and cost justification.

amount that remains after other discounts have been deducted from the billed amount. Thus, the discount may be 2 percent for payment within 10 days of the date of the invoice. If such terms appear on an invoice dated April 1, the buyer may take this deduction when paying by April 10. If payment is not made by that date, the buyer customarily waits 20 days longer and then pays the total price. The terms for such a transaction would be stated on the invoice as 2/10, net/30. When the net payment day is not stated, it is assumed to be 30 days from the date of the invoice, unless some other period is customary in the particular trade. If payment is not made within 30 days the vendor has the legal right to add an interest charge, usually 6 percent, although this has increased in recent years. Other cash discount terms and payment periods are discussed later in this chapter under the heading "Dating."

Significance and legality Retailers should take advantage of cash discounts even if they have to borrow the money to do so. Such action is a means of gaining the goodwill of vendors, and is immediately profitable from the retailer's point of view—so much so that one successful retailer refers to the cash discount as "a profit cushion."[13] Under the terms 2/10, net/30, the retailer who does not pay within 10 days is paying 2 percent for the use of the money for the remaining 20 days. Since there are approximately 18 20-day periods in a year, this is equivalent to about 36 percent interest. For terms of 3/10, net/60, the equivalent interest rate would be 21.6 percent;* and it would be even higher in those fields, like women's coats and suits, where the cash discount is as much as 8 percent.

As long as uniform cash discounts are granted to all competing comparable buyers, there is no danger that they will result in price discrimination and thus run afoul of the Robinson-Patman Act. In general, cash discounts have been used in a nondiscriminatory manner. But this has not always been true. One buyer may be given terms of 2/10, net/30, whereas a comparable buyer, after exerting sufficient pressure, may obtain 4/20, net/90. In such case the second buyer either pays a lower net cost than the first buyer or has the advantage of a longer credit period. In either case, the differential is illegal. As a practical matter, however, "the difficulties in the way of apprehension and prosecution are so great that the Act tends to penalize the 'gentleman' or 'ethical' buyer in his competition with the 'tough' buyer."[14]

☐ Price negotiation still legal and essential in buying

Despite the limitations placed on price bargaining by the Robinson-Patman Act, the buyer still has ample opportunity to negotiate for lower

---

* In figuring interest, the year is assumed to contain 360 days.

prices and to obtain the lowest *lawful* prices that sellers are willing to offer or accept.[15] *The act neither requires nor prevents the use of discounts of any kind; it simply places limits on them when they are used.** Hence, a vendor may decide not to grant discounts. In such a case, the buyer may need to bargain with the vendor to get even the discount that the law makes legal. In fact, some large buyers often do not receive discounts as large as the actual difference in cost, that is, as large as are legal. Moreover, in all cases in which discrimination does not exist, the buyer can negotiate for larger discounts. To illustrate, if the buyer takes the entire output of a vendor, there is no discrimination, so that any price or any discount obtained is legal. Also, buyers who prepare their own specifications and obtain products that are not of "like grade and quality" with the vendor's other goods open the way for price concessions. The buyer must frequently bargain to achieve the prices made permissible by the vendor's ability to cut prices to meet competition.

Many states have not adopted provisions similar to those of the Robinson-Patman Act; consequently, for buyers and vendors within those states, price differentials are not bound by cost differentials.** In any case, as already suggested, the buyer "has the right and obligation to seek the lowest prices given to competitors of his class . . . to assume routinely that quoted prices are standard and fixed merely because the vendor claims a one-price policy, is to be naive."[16]

■ TERMS OF SALE: DATINGS

The dating of an invoice refers to the time during which specified discounts may be taken and also to the time when payment of the invoice becomes due. As noted earlier, terms of 2/10, net/30 mean that a 2 percent discount may be taken within a 10-day period and that payment of the billed amount is due in 30 days from the date of the invoice. Of course, when no discounts are granted, the dating simply refers to the length of the period before full payment is expected. Since the retailer wants as long a period as possible during which discounts may be taken and/or final payment may be made and sellers usually want payment as soon as possible, datings are a subject of negotiation.

Datings are of two broad types, immediate and future. COD (cash on delivery) is the only form of immediate dating. There are several kinds of delayed or future datings.

---

* In a sense, the brokerage allowance is an exception to this generalization, but even here the law (a) does not require such an allowance in any case, but (b) restricts it to bona fide agents.

** This exemption, however, applies only when the seller and both the buyers who pay the higher prices and the ones who pay the lower prices are all located in the same state. "Legal Developments in Marketing," *Journal of Marketing*, vol. 40 (January 1976), p. 86.

☐ Immediate dating: COD

When merchandise is sold COD, payment must be made on receipt of goods. COD datings are relatively rare. They are so disliked by buyers that sellers use them only when they doubt the buyer's ability and willingness to pay. For instance, a buyer may be in the central market and decide to place an order with a vendor not previously dealt with. The buyer may want the goods at once, but the vendor may refuse to extend credit until an investigation has been made. In such circumstances the buyer may agree to COD terms. Some buyers are in such poor financial position that they can buy only on a COD basis. In practically all other cases, however, future datings can be arranged.

☐ Future datings

Some illustrations of future datings already have been given. The *ordinary dating* of "net 30 days" is a good example. In *extra datings* the vendor allows added time before the ordinary dating period begins. Thus, if the terms are "2/10, 60 days extra," the buyer has 60 days before the ordinary dating of 2/10, net/30 begins. *EOM dating* means that the ordinary dating period begins at the end of the month in which shipment is made. Consequently, on an invoice dated March 4, with terms 3/10 EOM, the 3 percent cash discount may be taken through April 10.*

Three kinds of future datings are used in which the invoice date is not the point from which either the discount or the due date is calculated. *Advance dating* simply sets some date following the invoice date when the ordinary dating period begins. Thus, an invoice made out on May 15 may be dated "as of September 1," so that the buyer does not have to make payment in full until 30 days following the advance date, or October 1. *Seasonal dating* is similar except that the date from which the ordinary dating begins is related to the seasons. To illustrate, many retailers want to place orders for Christmas merchandise during the summer months but do not wish to make payment until the goods have been sold. To accommodate these retailers, vendors may use a seasonal dating of December 1. *ROG (receipt of goods) dating* means that the ordinary dating period begins on the date the goods are received by the retailer. Goods with a 2/10, net/30, ROG dating which are received on April 11 must be paid for on or before April 21 to obtain the cash discount; and the invoice becomes payable on May 11.

Reason for future datings Future datings are used because most retailers, especially the smaller ones whose finances are decidedly limited, need credit for a period long enough to allow them to turn at least

---

* In practice, under EOM terms, purchases made on and after the 25th of the month usually go into the following month. Thus, on a purchase made on April 26 with terms of 2/10 EOM, the cash discount could be taken through June 10.

a part of their purchases into cash. Since the turnover of groceries is fairly rapid, terms of 2/10, net/30 are satisfactory to the buyer. Many hardware items turn over very slowly, however, and 60- or 90-day periods are desirable. ROG datings are preferred by retailers located at some distance from vendors, since part or all of the credit period under ordinary dating would be gone before the goods arrived. These datings merely put these operators in a position comparable to that of retailers who get ordinary datings and are located nearer to sources of supply. EOM datings are granted by sellers chiefly as a convenience to their customers.

Anticipation Most large retailers are financially able to pay their bills before the due dates, and if they can process the paperwork fast enough, are even able to pay before the end of the discount period. When they pay bills before the discount date, they often deduct an interest charge for the number of days of extra early payment. This interest charge is called *anticipation*.

Anticipation is practiced, particularly by department stores, far more commonly than most students of retailing realize. The stores normally have no legal right to deduct the interest from their payments, unless the contract with the vendor provides for anticipation or an implicit contract has grown up from the store's and the vendor's past dealings. But most vendors are anxious to obtain payment and actually favor stores that anticipate their bills. Moreover, when business is poor, merchants are able to impose an anticipation allowance requirement on their suppliers.

Anticipation was usually figured on the basis of a 6 percent annual rate, but since the "tight" money situation in the early 1970s, most stores have computed it on a 7.5 percent, 9.0 percent, or even higher basis.

The general rule for anticipation taken before the end of the cash discount period is as follows*: The retailer may take the cash discount plus anticipation on the balance for the number of days remaining until the end of the cash discount period. For example, an invoice for $1,000 with terms of 2/10, net/30 is paid 5 days before the end of the discount period. The 2 percent cash discount is equal to $20, leaving $980 to be paid. But this $980 balance is subject to a reduction equal to 7.5 percent interest for 5 days, that is, $1.02.** Hence, the actual payment made by the retailer is $978.98. Or again, an invoice with terms of 2/10, 30-extra, paid in 10 days, is anticipated 30 days prior to the expiration of the cash discount period. In this case, both the 2 percent cash discount and the 7.5 percent interest for 30 days are deductible.

---

* In rare instances, anticipation may be allowed after the expiration of the discount period for the number of days by which the date of payment precedes the time the invoice falls due.

** Seven and one-half percent interest on $980 for a year is $73.54. Five days is 1/72 of a year of 360 days, the number of days used for computing interest on anticipation. One seventy-second of $73.54 is $1.02.

Discount loading   A few stores that follow the practice of applying their percentage markups to the gross billed cost of goods (see the discussion of this practice in Chapter 16) will also manipulate or adjust the statement of those costs on the store and departmental records if the buyer fails to obtain a sufficient cash discount from the vendor. For example, a store may set 6 percent as the cash discount which all buyers must receive from resources. If a buyer obtains some goods on Net Terms (no discount) or at a discount of less than 6 percent, appropriate amounts will be added or "loaded" on to the price at which those goods are charged into the department on the store record. Specifically, assume that the buyer purchased some item at $96 net. Since the store wants the buyer to secure cash discounts of at least 6 percent, it treats a net cost as being only 94 percent (100 percent — 6 percent) or less of the gross cost. Consequently, dividing the actual cost of the item $96 by 94 and then multiplying by 100 provides a computed or "loaded" cost of $102.13.

Loading is practiced mainly for three reasons: (1) The large cash discount required induces the buyer to drive harder bargains; (2) all inventory and purchase figures are placed on a comparable basis; and (3) the store will probably charge higher retail prices if those prices are computed on an inflated cost basis, particularly if the store buyers usually apply fixed percentage markups to cost. Note that loading is purely an internal bookkeeping computation designed to affect the buyer's purchasing and pricing psychology. The supplier does not receive any additional compensation because of loading.

■ OTHER NEGOTIATIONS FOR MERCHANDSE

Other items that may be negotiated with merchandise resources include price guaranties, transportation terms, promotional services, and exclusiveness of goods.

☐ Price guaranties

Sometimes buyers seek guaranties against possible future price declines. For example, a buyer who places an order early to please a vendor may ask for both a seasonal discount and the vendor's agreement to rebate the difference if the wholesale price is lowered before the goods are shipped. Sometimes the guaranty applies even to goods that have already been shipped but are in the retailer's inventory awaiting the start of the retail selling season. The merchant who has placed a binding order subject to price guaranty is protected against all possible price changes, since, if wholesale prices rise, the vendor is committed to filling the order at the booked price, and if they fall, the vendor has agreed to reduce or refund the appropriate amount. Sometimes, particularly when merchandise is in short supply, when inflation is rampant or when government has imposed price controls, resources insist upon "escalator clauses" which under certain circumstances permit them to raise prices for goods not yet delivered.

The price guaranty is fairly common for seasonal items for which the vendor is especially eager to encourage early orders. It is also used to encourage buyers to place extra-large orders on staples during periods when the price structure is uncertain.

□ Transportation terms

Transportation terms offered by vendors may take any one of several forms. When prices are quoted f.o.b. (free on board) factory, the buyer pays all transportation charges from the vendor's delivery platform; when quoted f.o.b. shipping point, the vendor assumes the cost of transportation to a local shipping point but the buyer pays all further transportation charges, and when goods are sold f.o.b. store, the buyer has no transportation charges to pay. Sometimes, vendors quote prices f.o.b. certain cities, for example, f.o.b. Chicago or f.o.b. Detroit.* More complicated transportation terms are used in international trade. The buyer who wishes to purchase from foreign sources must be particularly careful in obtaining a precise agreement as to who, buyer or seller, will pay the various insurance, freight, and documentation charges (see pp. 321–22).

□ Promotional services

We have already discussed how a manufacturer may help pay for the cost of some of the retailer's promotional activities, through an advertising allowance. But retailers are often also very much interested in the promotional activities and services that the manufacturer will provide. This interest is manifested in two ways, only one of which may involve negotiation.

First, buyers of branded goods usually want to know about the manufacturers' general consumer advertising plans, since they can have such a strong impact on sales rates. Manufacturers often take space in retail trade magazines or use their own sales representatives to tell merchants how the products will be advertised to consumers.

Second, the manufacturer may supply promotional help right in the store, by offering signs, display fixtures, or even personnel who will demonstrate the product. The exact nature of these services is often subject to negotiation. Many stores have staged successful gourmet

---

* Transportation costs are rising steadily, so buyers should exert all possible efforts to reduce freight charges. Some of the steps that may be taken, in addition to inducing vendors to absorb the charges, are discussed in Chapter 15.

cooking and household appliance fairs, at which manufacturers' representatives displayed and sold new products.[17] Cosmetic manufacturers often pay the salaries of department store salespeople who concentrate on selling their brands. Other manufacturers may offer store salespeople "P.M.s," that is, monetary payments, for selling particular items. (See the discussion of "P.M.s" in Chapter 9.)

Legality   The Robinson-Patman Act applies to these services as well as to advertising allowances. A retailer should not accept a merchandising service, such as store demonstrators, from a vendor unless the service is similarly and proportionally furnished to competing dealers. In some cases, however, the Federal Trade Commission has suggested that a "substitue service" rather than the "same service" might satisfy this requirement. For example, although the store demonstrators offered by some cosmetic manufacturers might be economical in large retail stores with a heavy traffic of customers, they would be impractical in small stores. In such a situation, therefore, the manufacturer could continue to use demonstrators in the large store but offer the smaller retailers a substitute service. The practice of allowing salespeople to receive P.M.s has been subject to some question on ethical grounds, on the argument that it influences the salesperson's recommendations to customers. However, it apparently is legal even though from time to time the Federal Trade Commission has announced intentions to investigate or curb the practice.

☐ Other services

Some resources offer their dealers complete merchandising services. One of the supplier's employees, often called a "detailer," will check inventories and set up displays. Other manufacturers, such as some greeting card firms, may operate remote control merchandising systems for their retailers. A machine-readable computer card is enclosed with each shipment of each item or style. These cards are returned to the vendor as the store sells the merchandise and serve as the basis for the manufacturer's decisions on shipping new stock.

Some merchants reject these services because they prefer to make their own decisions, because they feel detailers will rearrange displays to feature their own products, and because they do not want "outsiders" going behind the counters and into the stockrooms in their stores. But there is a growing tendency to request and use this sort of help from suppliers.[18]

☐ Exclusiveness of goods

Often the exclusive right to handle certain goods is as important to the retailer as it is to buy them at low prices. In fact, many retailers of specialty goods are willing to pay higher prices for goods for which they act as exclusive distributors than for other merchandise of comparable quality. The retailer who desires an exclusive agency expects that it will yield the benefits of the goodwill the manufacturer has acquired and also eliminate all direct price competition, since no other retailers in the immediate area will be selling the same products. But the arrangement involves certain risks. The retailer may lose the agency through no personal fault because the manufacturer may change policies, or decide to use some other nearby retailer. And, in order to get the exclusive agency, the retailer may have to agree not to carry competing products of other manufacturers,[19] thereby losing the opportunity to sell to customers who prefer those products.

The retailer may also negotiate over the temporary exclusive distribution of certain goods, especially new fashion items, because it places the store ahead of competitors with "the last word" in merchandise and permits a higher markup on the new goods than would be possible otherwise.

Restricted distribution Sometimes a full-price retailer will not expect exclusivity, but will want to be certain that the manufacturer will not sell the same item to discount or bargain stores. In general, an individual merchant has the right to do business with, or refuse to buy from, any supplier one chooses. Consequently, a store is exercising a perfectly legal privilege if it decides it will not handle a product that is also being sold to lower-priced competitors. However, the exercise of this right may easily lead to buyers' attempts to place pressure on vendors.[20] At some point such pressure, although very common and not normally questioned or controlled by government, may overstep the limits set by the antitrust laws. In any event, it is clearly illegal for merchants to get together and impose joint demands upon resources who also sell to lower margin outlets.[21] In 1974, several leading New York specialty stores settled, by accepting a consent decree and and civil fines, an antitrust case that seems to have alleged improper coercion of suppliers, joint use of a shopping service to report price cutters, and some agreement on pricing practices.[22] This in turn led to customer class-action suits against the stores in 1976, and to an expanded Federal Trade Commission investigation of buying and pricing practices in fashion apparel manufacturing and retailing.

■ THE PURCHASE ORDER

When negotiations have been completed, the buyer prepares a purchase order form. In the small store, however, the vendor's order form is usually used. Actually, many such stores depend upon the vendor's representative to make out the order, after which it is examined and signed.

Large retailers provide their buyers with order forms, as illustrated in Figure 13–1. This practice is advantageous to the store since it (1) permits

FIGURE 13-1 Purchase order form

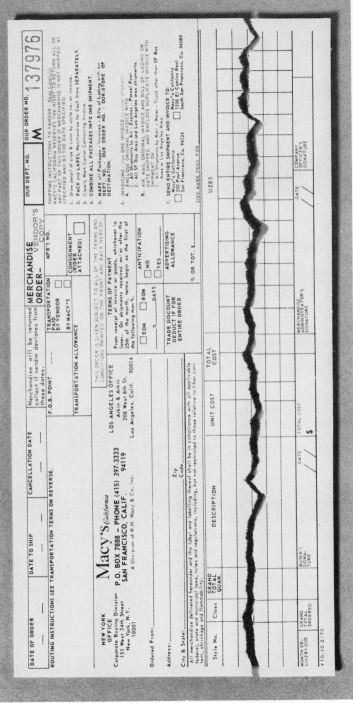

Courtesy Macy's, California

developing a form with space for whatever information the store desires and with sufficient copies for distribution to interested departments, (2) provides protection against those vendors who enter on their own forms (usually in small type) certain undesirable conditions, and (3) furnishes an ideal medium for giving vendors shipping instructions and stating the conditions under which the merchandise will be accepted.

□ Preretailing

Preretailing, practiced mainly by large firms, is the practice of placing the retail price of the items being bought on the store's copies of the purchase order (1) at the time the order is placed or (2) at least before the actual receipt of the merchandise. When the shipment arrives, price tickets may be attached without delay.

■ TRANSFER OF TITLE

Transfer of title, which means the transfer of ownership, usually takes place when the vendor releases the merchandise to a common carrier for delivery. Thereafter, responsibility for the merchandise lies with the buyer; if goods are damaged in transport, the buyer's recourse is against the common carrier, not the vendor. In dealing with certain vendors, however, buyers sometimes obtain physical possession of goods without taking title as explained in the following paragraphs.

□ Consignment buying

When goods are bought on consignment, title to the merchandise remains with the vendor. The vendor, who must accept the return of any unsold merchandise, bears the risks of price decline and obsolescence. Unless otherwise arranged by specific contract or trade custom, the retailer need not pay for the goods until sold to the final customers, and need only exercise reasonable care against loss by fire, theft, or physical damage.

We can best understand retailers' attitudes toward consigned merchandise if we first examine the two main reasons why vendors engage in this practice. First, some suppliers use it because they can't persuade the retailers to take the goods on any other basis. Second, some sell on consignment to control resale prices. As a practical matter, however, this right is being increasingly restricted by court decisions.*

The retailer's attitude toward consignment merchandise Despite the fact that consignment frees the retailer from certain risks which go

---

* For example, the courts have held that consignment selling cannot involve (1) coercion on the seller's part and (2) an agreement among buyers to fix prices. See *Simpson* v. *Union Oil Company of California* (U.S. Supreme Court, 377 U.S. 13).

with outright ownership and reduces funds tied up in inventory, most retailers hesitate to accept consigned goods. They fear that such goods may be inferior and that vendors are offering them on consignment because they cannot be sold by other methods. And prices may be higher since the vendor accepts the risks of ownership. Other retailers object to having vendors set their resale prices. The supplier may claim that returned goods have been damaged or that they could have been sold with more aggressive merchandising. This attitude, which may be justified in many cases, may cause ill-will between resource and retailer. Still other retailers may accept too many consigned items and use display space which might have been employed to better advantage for other merchandise.

In view of these disadvantages, retailers should carefully scrutinize the merchandise offered them on consignment. Even though it may be wise to place the first order for a new item on this basis, outright purchase is probably better if future sales potentialities warrant such action.

☐ Memorandum buying

The exact meaning of memorandum buying varies with the wording of the agreement between seller and buyer, but, in general, it is a method of obtaining merchandise involving features of both outright purchase and consignment buying. The major difference from consignment buying is that the retailer becomes the owner of the goods (takes title), and consequently has the right to set the retail price. In other respects memorandum buying is quite similar to consignment buying, since the retailer has the same return privileges and thus the supplier bears most of the risk.

☐ Returns of merchandise to vendors

Returns of merchandise to vendors is quite common among retailers and the reasons for such action should be understood. Some returns, of course, are fully justified while others constitute a questionable practice. Among the former are the following: The goods received may not be as described in the vendor's catalog, may fail to conform to specifications or samples, or even prove defective when used by customers; merchandise may not have arrived on time, necessitating markdowns if the peak of demand has already passed; wrong quantities may have been shipped; or the terms of sale are different from those originally agreed upon.

Some attempted merchandise returns are quite unjustified. Prices may have declined since the goods were ordered or placed in stock, and the retailer may wish to pass the loss back onto the vendor. Or an unexpected fashion change may reduce sales. Unless other factors exist, however, a vendor should not be expected to accept returns merely because the retailer did a poor job of buying. Having accepted title, the retailer should bear the risks of price and fashion changes as a normal part of the business.

Returns should be made promptly and vendors given a full explanation of the reasons.[23] This is particularly true for fashion goods; otherwise the vendor may suffer unnecessary loss. Harmonious relations with resources require mutual respect and understanding of each other's problems.

□ Joint retailer-manufacturer agreements

To minimize disagreements between retailers and vendors on cancellations and merchandise returns, these subjects are sometimes dealt with in "basic trade provisions" prepared jointly by retailer and manufacturer trade groups. A good example is the one established in the apparel trade some years ago which specified the appropriate conditions for returns and for cancellation of orders. It also set rigid time limits upon the periods in which retailers could exercise these privileges, and provided that all disputes were to be settled by arbitration under the rules of the American Arbitration Association.[24]

■ REVIEW AND DISCUSSION QUESTIONS

1 What do the guidelines outlined under the heading "Some basics of negotiation" indicate about: (a) the attributes needed by a successful buyer, and (b) how the buyer should behave in the market?

2 Describe the two major types of quantity discounts? For each type, indicate the reasons why suppliers grant it.

3 Explain the other major types of discounts and their legal status under the Robinson-Patman Act.

4 Summarize the advantages and disadvantages of advertising allowances from the point of view of (a) the retailer and (b) the supplier.

5 Has all bargaining and negotiation been prohibited by law? Explain.

6 Define each of the following terms in sufficient detail to make clear their application to a store's buying, vendor payment, or merchandise practices: (a) EOM, (b) ROG, (c) anticipation, (d) discount loading, (e) preretailing, (f) consignment buying, (g) memorandum buying.

7 Assume that merchandise shipped on April 15 was billed at $3,000 with terms of 2/10, 30 extra, f.o.b. store. Freight amounted to $150. The store paid the bill on the last permissible day for taking the cash discount. When did it pay and how much did it pay?

8 Assuming the same terms and figures as in the preceding question, what

amount should have been remitted to the vendor if anticipation was allowed, and the bill was paid on March 25?

9 Select two of the following, and for each, describe the conditions under which a buyer would be likely to seek that particular arrangement: (a) price guaranty, (b) exclusive distribution, (c) consignment or memorandum sales.

10 Discuss the conditions under which a retailer should have the right to return merchandise to the vendor.

■ NOTES AND REFERENCES

1 See "The Effect of Retailer Ordering Patterns on Wholesale Distribution Costs," *Special Research Report #2* (Chicago: Super Market Institute, 1973).

2 "How Dealers View Trips vs. Margins," *Home Furnishings Daily*, February 7, 1973, pp. 4, 5.

2A "Update—Inside Washington," *Progressive Grocer*, November 1975, p. 33.

3 *Food from Farmer to Consumer* (Washington, D.C.: U.S. Government Printing Office, 1966), p. 107.

4 B. Streeter, "White House Eyes Robinson-Patman Act; Repeal Is Possible," *Industrial Distribution*, November 1975, pp. 41–42; C. Burke Tower, "Legal News and Views," *Marketing News*, October 24, 1975, p. 3.

5 L. X. Tarpey, Sr., "Buyer Liability Under the Robinson-Patman Act," *Journal of Marketing*, vol. 36 (January 1972), pp. 38–42. For a warning against attempts by retail buying groups to obtain excessive quantity discounts, *see* "Retail Buy Groups May Violate Antitrust," *Home Furnishings Daily*, May 5, 1976, pp. 1, 9.

6 See M. L. Mayer, J. B. Mason and E. A. Orbeck, "The Borden Case— A Legal Basis for Price Discrimination," *MSU Business Topics*, vol. 18 (Winter 1970), pp. 56–63.

7 For an excellent study of the Commission's position and a summary of the court cases dealing with the cost defense, *see* R. A. Lynn, "Is the Cost Defense Workable?" *Journal of Marketing*, vol. 29 (January 1965), pp. 37–42.

8 The situation becomes quite complicated if a manufacturer sells to, say, wholesalers, chain store central warehouses that perform many of the wholesaling functions, and independent retailers. A strict interpretation of the law holds that the chain store organization cannot qualify for the same discount as the wholesaler, but only for the retailer discount plus a cost-justified allowance for any provable savings it gives the manufacturer as a result of the way or the quantity in which it buys. *See* Clair Wilcox and W. G. Shepherd, *Public Policies toward Business*, 5th ed. (Homewood, Ill.: Richard D. Irwin, Inc., 1975), p. 182.

9 *See* C. H. Sandage and Vernon Fryburger, *Advertising Theory and Practice*, 9th ed. (Homewood, Ill.: Richard D. Irwin, Inc., 1975), pp. 666–67.

10 J. W. Wingate and J. S. Friedlander, *The Management of Retail Buying* (Englweood Cliffs, N.J.: Prentice-Hall, Inc., 1963), p. 326.

11 See *Southgate Brokerage Company, Inc. v. Federal Trade Commission*, 150 F. (2d) 607 (4th Cir., 1945).

12 J. M. Ney, writing in *The Buyer's Manual*, 4th ed. (New York: National Retail Merchants Association, 1965), p. 88.

13 Wingate and Friedlander, *Management of Retail Buying*, p. 293.

14 Two of the best analyses of what can be done under the Act are R. O. Werner, "Marketing and the United States Supreme Court, 1965–1968," *Journal of Marketing*, vol. 33 (January 1969), pp. 16–23; and J. R. Grabner, "Legal Limits of Competition," *Harvard Business Review*, vol. 47 (November-December 1969), pp. 4–24 ff.

15 Wingate and Friedlander, *Management of Retail Buying*, p. 298.

16 See "Demos Come to Majors," *Home Furnishings Daily*, November 15, 1972, pp. 4–5.

17   James Snyder, "In Store Servicing Catches Fire," *Sales Management,* April 17, 1972, pp. 27–28; "More Services ... Or Else," *Chain Store Age* (general merchandise/variety edition), August 1974, pp. 34–35; "Puritan Helps Stores Keep Eye on Inventory," *Women's Wear Daily,* October 21, 1975, p. 40; Louis Carroll, "The Vendor Must Have a Plan," *Stores,* February 1974, pp. 8–9.

18   Carman and Uhl believe that such reciprocal agreements are "probably always illegal" as conspiracies in restraint of trade. *See* J. M. Carman and K. P. Uhl, *Phillips and Duncan's Marketing Principles and Methods,* 7th ed. (Homewood, Ill.: Richard D. Irwin, Inc., 1973), pp. 470–72, 636.

19   "Small Stores Hit Hard by Apparel Pressure Game," *Women's Wear Daily,* April 29, 1976, p. 11.

20   "FTC Probers: 'No Punitive Intent,' " *Women's Wear Daily,* January 11, 1976, pp. 1, 42.

21   "Another Inside Look at Retailing Case," *Women's Wear Daily,* April 14, 1976, p. 14.

22   For a more extensive discussion of cancellations and returns see D. E. Moeser, "Sound Buying Practices," in *The Buyer's Manual,* pp. 81–84.

23   Statement of the Apparel Industries Interassociation Committee, *Women's Wear Daily,* December 16, 1965, p. 35.

MERCHANDISE CONTROL

We have already noted that some merchants, particularly the more progressive ones, plan the assortment of goods that they intend to buy and carry in stock. Their planning methods may include merchandise budgets, basic stock lists and/or model lists. But all retailers, regardless of whether they use those planning techniques or not, must keep track of the rate at which items are selling. They need to know when goods must be reordered; which items are selling rapidly and perhaps should be ordered in larger quantities; and which items are selling poorly and perhaps should be reduced in price for clearance.

The various techniques for determining product sales and repurchasing needs are called merchandise control, and will be described in this chapter. The methods used range from very simple techniques, such as the merchant's casual visual inspection of the amount of each item on the store shelves or counters, to very elaborate computerized systems. Each system should be adapted to the size and needs of the particular store. The system's complexity will vary with the size of the store (and the number of stores in a multi-unit retail firm), with the number of products handled, and with the severity of the risks that result from having too much or not enough stock. Some control methods, closely related to budgeting techniques, concentrate on the dollar amount of sales and the value of the remaining inventory. These methods are called "dollar controls." Other techniques watch the sales and stocks, in individual units, of specific items. These are called "unit controls." We will study both types.

■ GOALS OF MERCHANDISE MANAGEMENT

In achieving the basic objective of a merchandise control system—a well-balanced stock—the retailer fulfills the following goals:

To meet customer demands satisfactorily As the "purchasing agent" for customers, the retailer should provide the merchandise they want, at prices they are willing and able to pay. Since customer demand varies from day-to-day and from season-to-season, this task is not easy. But proper merchandise control procedures will help the retailer attain this objective.

To improve profits Well-controlled stocks commonly result in greater sales and fewer markdowns, thereby increasing the dollar gross margin. And, if expenses remain the same or do not increase proportionately, profits will be increased. Methods and devices employed to control merchandise also contribute to improved profit by revealing trends and conditions that require executive action, by focusing attention on fast- and slow-moving items, by helping to keep stocks "clean" and "fresh," by assisting in the planning of advertising and sales-promotion events, and by enabling the buyer to reorder more frequently.

To provide buying information A good buyer needs a continuous stream of information in order to know what, when, and how much to buy. These data should include department or store sales by types and prices of merchandise, customer returns, markdowns taken to sell goods, and other similar information.

To optimize investment in inventory The store must maintain an inventory and an assortment of goods that is adequate to serve customer desires.[1] But retailers also want to, and must, limit the amount invested in inventory.[2] The merchandise control system should help the merchandiser reach the best possible balance between these two goals.

To minimize the amount of slow-selling stock The control system should help indicate the items that are selling poorly, so that price reductions or other remedial actions can be taken promptly.

To make selling easier Improved assortments and fresher stocks, the result of a good control system, permit more effective selling.

□ Some guidelines for effective merchandise control

The retailer should recognize certain guidelines that are essential to a successful control system. These are:

1. Control methods are not an adequate substitute for knowledge, experience, and wisdom on the part of the buyer. They are aids to judgment and not substitutes. This statement is equally true for staple items and fashion goods. Regardless of how "automatic" the procedures may be, the information they provide must be analyzed and interpreted.

2. Frequent appraisal of the systems adopted is necessary. Routines or procedures are set up to provide specific types of information under a given set of circumstances and need to be reviewed frequently to determine their suitability to new situations.

3. Merchandise information systems are costly to install and to maintain. The constant stream of improvements in computer design and information systems encourages increased use of technically advanced control methods. (See "Merchandise Management and EDP," pp. 362–63.) Many retailers fail to recognize the technical knowledge of design, programming, and operation required for conversion to computers as well as the necessary retraining of their staff members. In any case, the advantages of the system must be measured against the cost involved. And the system adopted should provide the desired data quickly and accurately.

4. The word "control" is probably a misnomer. Control exists only when information is interpreted and translated into action. Despite improvements in recent years, effective control of merchandise inventories still is a major problem for retail executives. Consequently, every suitable method and device should be employed to develop the information essential for sound decision making in balancing stocks and sales. Buyers cannot abdicate their responsibility for determining what, when, and how much to buy.

☐ Responsibility for merchandise management

Responsibility for merchandise management varies among retail stores. The small retailer personally assumes this function, but larger stores divide their more complicated task among a number of people. In department stores, the merchandise managers share it with their buyers. In fact, the job may be so great that a merchandise controller, under the direction of the merchandise manager or the president, may supervise these activities and work closely with the various buyers. Sometimes the controller governs stock control activities as part of the responsibility for all systems and records.

In chain stores, responsibility for merchandise control is usually centered at headquarters under the controller or a special control executive who reports to the head buyer or merchandise manager. Warehouse and store managers supply frequent detailed reports on sales of important items and on inventory conditions. Automation is of considerable assistance here.

■ BASIC TYPES OF MERCHANDISE INFORMATION SYSTEMS

Two basic types of information systems—commonly referred to as dollar control and unit control—have been developed. The distinction between them is similar to the difference between dollar and unit planning. *Dollar control* is exercised in terms of the amount of money at retail prices invested in merchandise. Dollar control usually watches the sales results and inventory position for the store as a whole, for a department, or for a departmental subdivision such as a classification (explained below) or a price line. Control by physical units—*unit control*—monitors the sale of individual items or pieces of merchandise. Dollar control answers the question "how much merchandise—in total dollar value—is on hand in the store or department"; unit control goes further and attempts to tell "what is the actual assortment."

Either dollar or unit control may be very simple, as illustrated by the case of unit control exercised through personal inspection of the items in stock at various intervals in many small stores. Sometimes the retailer may rely upon the vendor's representation to suggest what is needed to complete the stock, a common practice in the grocery, drug, and variety goods fields.

In somewhat larger stores, salespeople are often assigned definite sections of the stock to watch. They report to the proprietor or buyer when the stock of an item is low or when sales of specific products are unusually heavy. In some stores handling staple items—such as drug, grocery, and hardware stores—this reporting task is assigned to stockroom workers. Larger stores usually require more complex and carefully designed procedures because of the size and value of the merchandise inventory, the need for detailed information for buying purposes, and the element of fashion. The specific methods used will depend upon the size of the establishment, the kind and amount of data desired, and executive preferences. Let us now consider in some detail the two more formal merchandise information systems—dollar control and unit control.

□ Dollar control

Dollar control data is usually expressed in terms of the retail value. That is, if the records indicate sales they normally report them at the retail prices the customers have paid rather than at the store's purchase cost for the goods sold. Similarly, inventory information, for dollar control purposes, is usually reported at the retail selling price value marked on the collection of goods in the department or subdivision being studied. Dollar control system may be based on either perpetual or periodic inventories.

Perpetual inventory system   Under the perpetual inventory system the accounting records "perpetually" show the amount of goods that ought to be on hand in the store, department, or classification. The system works by taking the value of the opening inventory at retail prices; adding to it (at retail) any merchandise that is received in stock as well as any additional markups; and deducting both sales and markdowns as they occur. The result is the inventory that would be on hand if no shortages had occurred. Of course, a physical count must be taken at least once or twice a year to check the "book" or computed figure and to indicate the amount of error and shortage in the records. A very simplified example would be:

Retail stock on hand, August 1		$ 50,000
Retail purchases, August 1–		
January 31	100,000	
Total stock handled at retail		$150,000
Sales, August 1–January 31	84,000	
Markdowns, August 1–January 31	4,000	
Total retail deductions		88,000
Closing book inventory at retail,		
January 31		$ 62,000

If the actual physical inventory on January 31 was only $60,000, the $2,000 difference would be the shortage figure. If the store has the appropriate reporting system, the book inventory can be computed daily or as frequently as management desires, even though the shortage check can only be made when a physical inventory is taken. Since detailed records are required, the major problem of the perpetual inventory system is to obtain complete and accurate information, a task made less difficult through the use of EDP equipment. But whether handled by electronic equipment or by people, for merchandise to which it is applicable, the perpetual inventory method provides current, useful information which permits buyers and merchandisers to make prompt adjustments in their purchases and inventories.

Periodic inventory system   Periodic dollar control inventory systems provide slower and less useful information than perpetual ones, but they require less complex reporting systems. Essentially, they use fairly frequent physical inventories to ascertain the approximate dollar amount of sales. At first thought this approach seems to be a very roundabout way of gathering sales information, which supposedly could come from cash

register tapes or from customer charge account records, but as we shall
see, there are situations in which it is helpful. Using the same data as in
the discussion of the perpetual inventory system above, the periodic
system would look like this:

Retail stock on hand, August 1.......... $ 50,000
Retail purchases, August 1–
    January 31 100,000
    Total stock handled at retail.......... $150,000
Physical inventory, January 31
    at retail 60,000
Total "disappearance" of merchandise,
    August 1–January 31 .... $ 90,000

The "disappearance" of retail value from the stock of goods handled
results from sales, markdowns, and shortages, in other words, the retail
deductions shown in the earlier example. If the store has kept a record
of markdowns, it would know in this case that $4,000 of the disappear-
ance is due to that cause, and the balance, $86,000, is attributable to
sales and shortages. Unfortunately, shoplifters do not provide reports
of the items they take, so under this method the merchant can only estimate the ratio of shortages to sales.

As indicated earlier, this is a complex and relatively unsatisfactory
method of ascertaining total sales for the store. Such data can be secured more directly and more rapidly from the sales or cash registers
or from the employees' salesbooks. Moreover, the increasing sophistication of sales registers and terminals providing information at the point
of sale has reduced the instances in which the periodic inventory dollar
control system is needed. But some stores still do not have any method
for breaking sales figures down into departmental, classification, or
price-line figures. Since such an analysis is extremely helpful for merchandising decision making, periodic inventory dollar control analysis,
by department or subdivision, is a useful substitute for stores that do not
prepare detailed sales figures. We will now review some of the benefits
of controlling dollar investments by department, classification or price
line, whether done under a perpetual or a periodic inventory system.

Departmental control When control is exercised on a departmental
basis, sales, returns by customers, purchases, returns to vendors,
markup, gross margin, markdowns, rate of stockturn, and physical inventories are recorded for each department. This permits judging the profitability of each department and the performance of each buyer. Strong
and weak departments may thus be determined and improvement can
be attempted. This method, however, does not indicate strength and
weaknesses within each department. Since effective merchandise management requires more than overall figures for each department, and

since many departments have grown so large with such a variety of items that controlling them in total is meaningless, controls by classification and price-line have been developed.

Classification control Classification control, increasingly referred to as "classification merchandising," is that form of dollar control based upon classifications of related types of merchandise within departments.[3] All the information recorded departmentally under departmental control is also subdivided into classifications under classification control. Thus, in a men's furnishings department, data may be recorded separately for such classifications as shirts, neckties, hosiery, pajamas, underwear, and sweaters.

Many retailers have adopted classification merchandising and instituted programs placing emphasis on "the discovery of opportunities for increased sales" and a better "balancing of stocks in relation to sales."[4] As part of these programs, there has been a tendency not only to subdivide broad classifications into smaller groups but also to reclassify them into categories of items considered by the customer as essentially interchangeable from the standpoint of end use.

The fundamental idea of classification is to watch how sales are going, and what is happening to inventories within a meaningful category of goods.[5] Since many customers consider sport shirts and dress shirts as very different items that are intended for different occasions and are not substitutes for each other, many stores treat these two types as separate classifications. A buyer might have a very large stock of sport shirts, but still be unable to meet customer demands with an inadequate supply of dress shirts. Some stores maintain an even closer watch by subdividing dress shirts into long- and short-sleeve classifications.

In 1969, after considerable study, the National Retail Merchants Association proposed a Standard Merchandise Classification, suitable for a wide range of stores and products. However, most stores were unwilling to convert their individually developed systems to the NRMA's. The lack of response, plus the subsequent need to develop more comprehensive product characterization and coding systems for automated sales recording devices (see Chapter 25) have vitiated attempts to promote the NRMA system. Its "Standard Classification Manual" was allowed to go out of print in the mid-1970s. Nevertheless, the NRMA's Financial Executives Division annually publishes a helpful summary of merchandising statistics for U.S. department stores in which data are presented for "merchandise groupings," really classifications.[6]

Price-line control This form of dollar control is based on price lines, i.e., the particular prices at which assortments of merchandise are offered to the public. Just as departments may be divided into classifications to effect better control, so departments or classifications may be broken down into price lines to obtain more detailed information. But price-line control does not naturally follow classification control; rather, it is often used as a substitute for classification control. Price lines may also be broken down into classifications, such as material, size, and style.[7]

□ Unit control

Unit control,[8] the second basic type of merchandise information system, involves maintaining records in terms of physical units, rather than in terms of dollars. Such control commonly supplements dollar control. Both types are essential to keep stocks adjusted to customer demand.

Unit-control systems Unit-control systems vary widely among stores and departments, but they have a common attribute—provision of information quickly for any desired period. Such information may include, for instance, data on sales and stocks by style number, color, size, material, or any other characteristics of the merchandise. It may also include data on markups, markdowns, gross margin, and rate of stockturn, by price, merchandise classification, and vendor, depending on the store's needs. A major reason for the rapid growth of EDP is that it provides the required data quickly and accurately. Like dollar control, unit control may be effectuated through either a perpetual inventory or a periodic physical inventory system.

Perpetual inventory system Under this system each item is recorded when it arrives and when it is sold, permitting prompt adjustments in stock to meet sales requirements. This system provides a "book" inventory figure which may be checked for shortages by comparison with a physical inventory. It is used frequently for merchandise such as men's clothing, women's apparel, and shoes, where sales are easily recorded by units and reorders are common. Stores that use traditional sales and data recording equipment have not been able to make practicable use of perpetual inventory unit-control systems for small, rapid-selling items such as drugs, cosmetics or groceries. The work of recording each item sold has been simply too slow and costly to have been worthwhile. New electronic checkout equipment, in which optical scanners at the cash register read preprinted code markings on grocery packages and adjust computerized records promise to make perpetual inventory systems feasible for even rapid turnover staples. (See the discussion of such systems in Chapter 25.)

Physical or periodic inventory system This system is based upon periodic physical inventories. In other words, the only way to determine the quantity of an item on hand is to make an actual count. No attempt is made to record sales by units as they occur. A figure for sales—which also includes stock shortages—is obtained, however, by adding the beginning inventory of each unit to the purchases and then subtracting the ending inventory. Information for control purposes is obtained at the time of the physical inventory by analyzing the rate at which items are being sold and by comparing the goods in the previous inventory with those in the current inventory. Purchases, of course, must be analyzed in a similar manner. As we have already noted, this is a "reorder time" system, in that repeat purchases are made after the periodic stock counts are taken.

Many chain stores and wholesaler-supplied independent stores now equip the people who take these periodic stockcounts with very light, easily portable electronic devices (see Figure 14–1). These speed up the inventory-taking process and the forwarding of the resulting information

FIGURE 14–1   **Inventory-taking with electronic data entry system**

Courtesy © *MSI DATA Corporation, photograph* **reproduced** *by special permission, MSI Data Corporation*

to central buyers or merchandise controllers. Usually the device has an optical scanning wand or similar mechanism that will read and record the stock number of the item (stock-keeping unit) to be counted from a shelf tag or marker, from code markings on the package, or from a preprinted list. After the stock number is entered, the inventory taker punches in the number of units on hand, using a simple keyboard for this purpose. The process produces a tape that will transmit the data over regular telephone lines to a central office computer.

Other systems of unit control   Some other systems are designed to supplement perpetual and periodic unit controls, while another group, known as "reorder point" systems, replaces the periodic stock count methods of control.*

1. Requisition or reserve stock control   Under this system, the unit control is kept over the quantity held in the reserve stock or in the stockroom, rather than over the merchandise displayed on the sales shelves or counters. The system is best suited for small, fast-selling inexpensive items since (a) it is usually too difficult and expensive to record the numerous individual small sales, and (b) the fast-selling nature of the goods provides assurance that the display quantities will quickly move out of the store. In such cases, watching and controlling the reserve stock will closely approximate the store's actual sales experience, and is much more convenient. The information can usually be obtained and recorded on a perpetual basis. These systems are called requisition systems if the transfers of merchandise from the stockroom to the salesfloor are initiated by requisitions from the selling departments. The requisitions are then treated as the equivalent of sales for inventory control purposes. In a variation of this method, as used by a few chain store companies, the major control is applied to the warehouse stock and requisitions for merchandise transfers from the warehouse to stores are treated as "sales" data. The underlying assumption of this approach is that store managers will not request additional supplies of slow-selling merchandise, so the warehouse requisition will provide a good idea of how the items are selling.

2. Warehouse control system   This system is completely different from the warehouse requisition one just discussed, and is used for such items as furniture, stoves, refrigerators, and television sets. To save valuable space many stores only display a single "floor sample" of each item and carry most of their inventory in a separate warehouse. The customers' orders are shipped from the warehouse, but the salespeople need to know the quantities on hand there, so that they avoid selling more units for immediate delivery than the store possesses. Consequently, as soon as a unit is sold, the warehouse copy of the salescheck

---

* Of course, inventories are still taken as needed for accounting or other purposes even if a store uses a reorder point system.

goes to a control clerk who immediately revises the inventory record in the selling department. Corresponding changes are also made in the warehouse records. This system provides a perpetual inventory.

3. Reminder systems Under periodic inventory systems two methods are often used to remind the buying or merchandising staff of the need for very frequent inventories of important items. One is a "tickler system" in which a file folder is prepared for each date on which a stock count may be taken. The list of items to be counted on that day is placed in the file, which then automatically comes to the buyer's attention at the appropriate time. The other technique involves the preparation of a "checklist" of items that must be counted at certain intervals and checked against a basic stock plan or model stock plan. The success of the checklist and tickler approaches depends upon the frequency of the checks (or the diligence of the salespeople in alerting the buyer if the stock seems to be selling down faster than anticipated) and the care with which the counts are taken. (See the discussion of checklists and "never-out" lists, p. 286.)

4. Reorder point systems Sometimes, instead of relying on a periodic inventory for unit control, the buyer will want to reorder each item when its stock level reaches some predetermined level, called the reorder point. Various simple devices may be used to indicate when the stock has declined to that point. A piece of string may be tied around the predetermined quantity, say, the last two dozen packages, and the buyer or store owner notified when the string must be broken. Or, perhaps, a reorder card will be inserted in the stock at the critical point, to be mailed to the vendor when the surplus inventory has been sold.

Benefits of unit control Unit control developed to meet needs that dollar control did not fill. Specifically, its information about the physical characteristics of the merchandise is useful in buying and selling. As a buying tool, unit control yields the following benefits:

1. It reveals what merchandise is selling best and should be considered for additional purchases.
2. It indicates the merchandise that is selling slowly and that should not be reordered. It furnishes a valuable guide, therefore, in reducing the number of price lines, styles, and colors which are carried.
3. It shows the proper time to buy merchandise, thus insuring a stock of goods to meet customers' requirements. In like manner, by showing goods on order, it tends to prevent unnecessary duplicate reorders.
4. It aids in establishing model stock plans, thus insuring complete, well-balanced stocks.
5. It reveals, where the perpetual inventory system is used, the quantity of stock on hand at any time without taking a physical inventory. Moreover, by comparing this book figure with that obtained when

the physical inventory is taken, the stock shortage may be found. This comparison focuses attention on stock shortages and assists in controlling them.

As a *selling* tool, unit control provides assistance as follows:

1. It shows the age condition of the stock, thereby indicating the items requiring markdowns or special promotion. Losses are reduced when markdowns and other necessary actions are taken promptly.
2. It reveals the best-selling items and permits "playing the winners" and improving profits.
3. It minimizes "out-of-stock" situations.
4. It serves as a guide in planning special sales events by providing information on the goods available for promotion.
5. It often saves time for the customer by giving precise information on particular items in stock.

Reasons for limited use of unit control It would seem that all stores able to afford unit control would have adopted it, in view of all the benefits just summarized. But many have failed to do so for the following reasons:

1. Many executives believe that the cost of maintaining the necessary records exceeds the benefits derived from the information supplied. Frequently this is not a disadvantage of unit control itself, but rather a symptom of either poor design or poor utilization of the system.
2. The publicity given to the elaborate systems used in large stores with their expensive forms, numerous recapitulations, and involved handling of records has made proprietors of small stores skeptical of the usefulness of similar, though less elaborate, systems in their stores.
3. The failure of some retailers to define the specific purposes and uses to which the information will be put prior to its collection often results in gathering superfluous data or in generating useless reports. To quote the Director of Corporate Information Systems of the May Company: "If you really give them [the buyers] the information that they want in the way that they need it and can use it, you will have little problem with their disregarding the reports. . . ."[9]
4. The opposition of some inexperienced buyers who believe that unit-control systems are established to furnish information to merchandise managers and the controller regarding the buyers' incompetence, rather than as a means of helping them to become better buyers.
5. The fear of many buyers that a unit-control system, by supplying detailed merchandise information, would supplant part of their function. Most buyers dislike the term "automatic buying."
6. The strong conviction of some buying executives that effective control over merchandise can be maintained only through study of the merchandise itself and not by placing dependence upon records.

7. The unhappy experience of some buyers with unit-control systems has caused them to look with disfavor upon such systems. This experience may have been caused by poorly planned systems, by expecting too much of the system installed, by attempting to make the records tie in completely with dollar control, or by failure to build an adequate organization to do the unit-control job. Frequently, the "unhappy experience" is exaggerated by the buyer because of a temperamental opposition to the systematic records required for unit control. Buyers' major interests lie in buying and selling, not in accounting. However, buyer resistance to unit control, as discussed in the last four points, is becoming less and less of a problem as more buyers become experienced in unit-control techniques.

Instituting a unit-control system   If a careful review of the advantages and disadvantages of unit control, supplemented by an investigation of the conditions under which such a system of control would operate, leads to a decision to set up this type of control, the executive responsible should:

1. List all the information that it would be advisable to obtain from the system. In doing so, secure the opinion of other merchants and of employees . . . who understand the purposes of such control.
2. Examine the methods by which the desired information may be obtained to determine their suitability. . . . Review such factors as the type of merchandise, including size, color, and variety handled; the unit price; the manner in which goods are purchased and stored, that is, the frequency of orders, their size, and whether regular use is made of the reserve stock room; and the rate of stockturn.
3. Devise the forms necessary to provide information of the kind and in the form wanted. The guides in this connection should be brevity, simplicity, and clarity. Detailed explanation of the use of the forms should accompany their distribution.
4. Take a physical inventory to determine what items are in stock and the quantities of each. This step furnishes a basis upon which records may be built and also permits the desired segregation to be accomplished without difficulty. When the goods are properly segregated, they are ready to be remarked.
5. Mark the goods to permit the recording of the necessary information. This step involves (a) preparing suitable price tickets with symbols, letters, or numbers to designate style, color, size, vendor, and the like; and (b) attaching the tickets to the merchandise.
6. Provide for the accurate recording of sales. Although there are numerous ways of doing this, the most common methods consist of price ticket stubs, copies of sales checks, sales register receipt stubs, salespeople's tallies, and reserve stock requisitions. In recent years, however, technological improvements in methods of recording sales

have enabled the more progressive firms to speed up transactions, obtain more complete information, and reduce the number of errors. New-type sales registers, for example, permit sales transactions to be recorded quickly as one of the first steps in a complete system of merchandise management.[10]

7. Maintain complete and accurate control records in such a manner that the unit-control information can be summarized, tabulated, and recorded promptly and fully, and checked frequently.

When a unit-control system has been set up in the manner outlined, control has been only partially accomplished. The data recorded must be analyzed, interpreted, and used. It is in this connection that the value of the system is tested. If the information provided is not translated into improved buying practices and better-balanced stocks in relationship to sales, the system is a failure.

■ MERCHANDISE MANAGEMENT AND ELECTRONIC DATA PROCESSING

Although not absolutely essential, electronic data processing greatly facilitates the operation of both dollar and unit controls in large retail organizations and, to an increasing extent, in smaller firms. Some of the relevant types of information that can be compiled by complete systems are discussed in Chapter 15, "Handling incoming merchandise," and Chapter 25, "Control of sales transactions," and elsewhere. At this point therefore we will only sketch some of the main applications of computer technology to merchandise management.[11]

1. Copies of the buyers' purchase orders may be entered into the system to generate control data for the receiving and marking operations, to provide instructions for the distribution of goods to the branch stores, to check the invoices for proper calculation of the price extensions, etc., and to reduce the record of the amount the buyers are still open to buy.

2. When the merchandise arrives, the receiving and checking departments may check the goods against a computerized version of the purchase order; and will then insert the appropriate information into the system, thereby altering the department and store inventory records. This will initiate the process of authorizing payment to the vendor. The latter process, however, requires further check, which also may be machine-assisted, in the accounts-payable section to make certain that the store has been offered all of the discounts to which it is entitled, that the goods were not shipped by an excessively costly method, and that the supplier's bill is correct.

3. After the goods are checked in and recorded, the electronic data

processing system may print the appropriate number of price tickets or hang tags, using selling price and style number information shown on the purchase order copy.

4. Some store systems use coded price tickets, tags or other machine-readable markings that automatically record the sale of each item when it occurs at the register. These systems then correct the store inventory to show the reduction in the stock of the item or items involved. The number of such systems will undoubtedly increase substantially during the next ten years.[12]

5. The buyers then receive frequent reports (daily or weekly) that show sales and stocks broken down by style, color, size, price line, classification, branch store, or whatever data categories are considered relevant. The system can be designed to provide especially frequent "exception reports" that direct the buyer's attention to particularly rapid-selling and particularly slow-selling items, so that the appropriate action may be taken. The computer can also be programmed to print orders for additional quantities of staples, as needed, although such orders should be checked by a human buyer.

The above major steps do not exhaust all of the possibilities, and each system must be designed to meet the individual retailer's own particular situation. For example, large organizations will probably want additional information, such as each buyer's gross margin and markdown record, or analyses of the store's experiences with each vendor. Small stores will place less emphasis on immediate, or almost immediate, processing of the data and will send bundles of original records to outside data service bureaus, or in some cases, to their wholesalers, for "batch processing."[13]

■ THE PHYSICAL INVENTORY

The physical inventory—an actual counting and listing of the goods in stock at a given time, together with, the cost or retail price of each item—is considered a "necessary evil" by most retailers. Occurring once or twice a year, it is necessary to determine whether a profit has been made during the past fiscal period.[14] But in addition to this financial purpose, the physical inventory is an important aspect of merchandise control.

As of a specific date, the physical inventory shows the kinds, quantities, and values of the items in stock for the store as a whole and by departments. Moreover—depending on the store, the merchandise handled, and the information placed on the price ticket—the physical inventory makes possible the classification of items by sections or divisions of departments, by age groups, by price lines, by physical units, or by other desired groupings. It helps the retailer to improve buying and selling methods, permits checking unit control and other stock records, and furnishes the figures to compare with book inventories to determine the amount of stock shortage or overage.

□ Taking the physical inventory

Accuracy and completeness are essential in taking the physical inventory. Consequently, it should be carefully planned, the required information listed by qualified personnel, the calculations and summaries checked, and the inventory reports issued promptly. A review of the methods employed in different types of stores is helpful in understanding the activities involved.

In chain stores selling standardized goods There is no standard procedure for taking the physical inventory in all chain stores. At one extreme, for example, is the monthly inventory of the grocery chain for which there is little advance preparation. The inventory crew, usually consisting of at least two persons, comes into a store quite unexpectedly. As one checker goes through the stock, calling off the number of units at each price, the other records; or perhaps a tape or wire recorder is used, so that both can count. Although headquarters may want to know the quantities on hand for a few specific items, in general all it desires is the total value of the goods in the store; consequently, only the price-quantity relationships are required. When the count has been completed, the sheet is sent to headquarters, where the value of the stock is computed.

In department stores At the other extreme in taking the physical inventory is the department store where advance preparation for the inventory is essential.[15] Commonly, the process covers the four stages referred to previously—planning, counting and recording of the goods on hand, calculation of the value of the stock, and issuance of inventory reports.

In the planning stage, the department buyer, working under the direction of the controller or an inventory supervisor, usually takes the following steps:

1. Classifies and groups merchandise by type, price, and style.
2. Adjusts prices so that they are market prices, and makes certain that all necessary information is on the price tickets.
3. If time is available before the inventory date, sometimes plans a sale to reduce stock to a minimum and to clear out any undesirable merchandise disclosed in step 1.
4. Prepares a layout chart of the department, showing the location of each fixture with merchandise. This chart enables the controller to issue inventory sheets or tags marked for specific sections in each department.

5. Obtains the necessary inventory sheets or tags from the controller.
6. Checks the salespeople's knowledge of inventory instructions.

After plans have been completed and the designated inventory date arrives, the actual counting and recording begin. The recording may take place on inventory sheets or inventory tags but the former are used by the vast majority of firms. When sheets are used, a number of items (including description, quantity, price, and other desired characteristics) are recorded on each sheet (Figure 14–2); with tags or tickets

FIGURE 14–2   Example of a form for taking inventory

J. W. KNAPP COMPANY

RETAIL INVENTORY Date _____, 197__

Store No._____ Dept. No._____

Only One Department per Inventory Sheet

Listed By_____
Counted By_____
Checked By_____

Fixture No._____
Shelf No._____

PAGE

☐ Forward Stock
☐ Stock Room
☐ Warehouse
☐ _____

N° 220877

	DESCRIPTION	CLASS	TALLY COUNT	SALES AFTER COUNT	QUANTITY	SEASON A, B OR C	UNIT EA., BOX, PAIR . . .	PRICE $ ¢
1								⌊⌊
2								⌊⌊
3								⌊⌊
4								⌊⌊
5								⌊⌊
1								⌊⌊
2								⌊⌊
3								⌊⌊
4								⌊⌊
5								⌊⌊
1								⌊⌊
2								⌊⌊
3								⌊⌊
4								⌊⌊
5								⌊⌊
1								⌊⌊
2								⌊⌊
3								⌊⌊
4								⌊⌊
5								⌊⌊

1. Be sure price and quantity are correct for the unit (Ea., Box, Pr.)
2. Do not erase. Draw line through error and rewrite.
3. Mark a 1 in the "Sales After Count" column for any item sold after count was made.

Courtesy J. W. Knapp Company

only one item of a particular size or type appears on each ticket (see Figure 14–3). Since selling may be going on while the inventory taking is in progress, all sales are recorded either on the tags or on special deduction sheets, thus allowing computation of the stock on hand when the inventory taking has been completed. Since most large department stores use the retail inventory method, they maintain perpetual or book inventories and are thus able further to check the accuracy of their book figures against the physical inventory. In fact, a major purpose of the physical inventory is to check the accuracy of the book figures.

Once the counting and recording are completed, all sheets and tags are sent to the controller's office for calculating and summarizing. The final step is the preparation of the necessary reports, including, for in-

FIGURE 14–3 An example of an
inventory ticket in general use

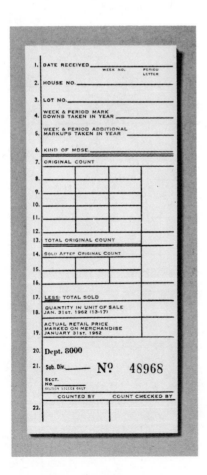

stance, those relating to the age of goods as compared with the previous inventory, the stock shortages or departments, and the warehouse stocks.

In small stores In between the simplicity of the physical inventory of the standardized chain-store unit and the rather complex procedure in the department store stands the system suitable for small independent stores. Since a physical inventory is taken only once (or twice) a year, the retailer usually inspects the stock carefully prior to making the actual count to determine the items on hand. This inspection enables sorting out slow-moving items, or "sleepers," which should be sold before the inventory is taken. It also permits adjusting costs and retail prices to market levels. The employees who help in this work should be instructed in inventory taking and the need for care and accuracy stressed. Standardized forms suitable for recording the desired information are available from a number of salesbook companies and trade associations, and their use is advisable.

■ STOCK SHORTAGES

A growing and continuous problem of merchandise management, already mentioned in Chapter 1, is the control of stock shortages—the unaccounted-for disappearance of merchandise assets. Such shortages may develop at many points in the operation of a retail store. To illustrate, merchandise may be sold for less than the price tag indicates, some breakage is inevitable, and mismeasuring plays a role. But the two chief causes of stock shortages are dishonesty and errors in records.

☐ Dishonesty as a cause of shortages

Stock shortages caused by thefts of merchandise by employees, customers, amateur and professional shoplifters, and even armed robbers have plagued retail stores for many years. And the problem has been magnified in recent years with the growth of self-service and the increase in the number of supermarkets and discount houses. The stock shortages figure was 2.16 percent of sales in 1974 in department stores with sales from $20 to $50 million, and 2.33 percent of sales in departmentized specialty stores with sales over $5 million.[16] It is not possible to determine the exact proportions of these shortages caused by thefts.

Retailers take many steps discussed in Chapter 26 to minimize stock shortages resulting from dishonesty. Burglar alarm systems and regular police protection supplementing security guards are important against professional thieves. The careful selection, training, and supervision of employees is another essential aspect of an antishortage program. Shoplifting is fought by the use of human "spotters" and television "eyes" throughout the store, and instructing employees to recognize the characteristics of the typical shoplifter—the customer who (1) hangs around without buying, (2) carries a shopping bag, (3) has a large purse, and (4) wears a topcoat in mild weather. Retailer groups have also fostered the development of local laws that protect merchants who apprehend shoplifters against claims for false arrest and false imprisonment. Under such laws a storekeeper who has "probable cause" for so doing may take a suspect into custody for a "reasonable length of time" in an attempt to recover the goods.

□ Errors as a cause of shortages

Honest mistakes made by employees which cause stock shortages are almost legion: errors in marking, in inventory taking, in handling returns, in delivering the wrong merchandise, in billing credit customers, in making change for cash customers, and in recording markdowns. While care in the selection and training of employees plus closer supervision of paper work and merchandise handling will minimize these errors, they will not eliminate them—any more than stock shortages caused by dishonesty can be eliminated. All the retailer can do, therefore, is to utilize all available techniques to minimize these shortages and maintain constant vigilance to protect earnings from further erosion.

■ REVIEW AND DISCUSSION QUESTIONS

1 (a) Distinguish between "merchandise planning" and "merchandise control." (b) What are the differences between "dollar control" and "unit control"?

2 Explain the major goals of a merchandise control system.

3 Outline some important guidelines for a successful merchandise control system.

4 Prepare a simple example that shows the figures used in a perpetual inventory dollar control system. Indicate clearly how the retailer would obtain each of those figures.

5 What are the major limitations or defects of a periodic inventory dollar control system? In view of those drawbacks, why do some stores use such a system?

6 Explain what is meant by classification control? Why is it more meaningful than departmental control?

7 Describe briefly the general nature of each of the following types of unit control and explain the type of retailing situation in which it is likely to be used: (a) perpetual inventory system, (b) periodic inventory system, (c) requisition stock control system, (d) warehouse control system.

8 Differentiate between a reorder time and a reorder point system.

9 What are the principal advantages of unit control? Why don't all stores that can afford unit control use it?

10 Discuss concisely the types of merchandise management and merchandise control information that can be processed through a computer system.

11 Describe the main steps in taking physical inventories in a department store.

12 Visit a local store and prepare a report on the system it uses to control merchandise. In your report discuss the types of stores that could profitably use the same or a similar system and the types of stores for which it would be unsuitable.

▪ NOTES AND REFERENCES

1 The importance of adequate stocks is well illustrated by two contrasting trade publication reports: "L. A. Stores That Bought Aggressively Lead Sales," Women's Wear Daily, June 24, 1975, pp. 1, 21; "We Let Ourselves Get Out of Stock and That Affected Our Sales," Discount Merchandiser, February 1976, p. 56.

2 "Inventory Turns Have High Priority," Home Furnishings Daily, March 15, 1976, p. 15.

3 See R. Patrick Cash, "Classification Systems for Smaller Stores," Stores, April 1976, p. 19.

4 Hugo Frank, "Problems in Introducing Classification Programs Successfully," Retail Control, February 1966, p. 12.

5 The characteristics of a good classification system are discussed by Jack Vivian, "Merchandise and Inventory Management in Today's Economy," Retail Control, June-July 1975, pp. 23–32.

6 Department and Specialty Store Merchandising and Operating Results (M.O.R.) (New York: National Retail Merchants Association, annual).

7 See Frank Burnside, "The Application of Taxonomy [the science of precise classification] to Retail Merchandise Data," in Readings in Modern Retailing (New York: National Retail Merchants Association, 1969), pp. 333–46.

8 On this system of control in small stores see "Unit Stock Control," Hardware Retailer, June 1970, pp. 48–49.

9 William W. Martin, "Technology and New Merchandise Information Systems," Retail Control, April-May 1975, p. 40.

10 See The Values of Total System Reports for Retailers (Dayton, Ohio: National Cash Register Company [now NCR Corporation], n.d.).

11 See also Joseph A. Lev, "Merchandise Management: How Much Can Be Mechanized?" Retail Control, October 1974, pp. 48–62.

12 See "P.O.S.: The Store Nervous System," Retail Directions, January-February 1975, p. 23.

13 "Writing the Book on Automation," Chain Store Age (Drug edition), November 1975, pp. 28–30; "Helping Retailers Use Computer Output," Hardware Retailing, October 1974, pp. 79–80.

14 See "Inventory: Asset or Liability?" Hardware Retailer, June 1970, pp. 45–47. For its significance in determining operating results of the business, see Chapter 23.

15 See National Retail Merchants Association, Inventory Taking Manual (New York: The Association, 1965).

16 Jay Scher, Financial and Operating Results of Department and Specialty Stores in 1974 (New York: Financial Executives Division, National Retail Merchants Association, 1975), p. ix.

HANDLING INCOMING
MERCHANDISE

Merchandise that is purchased must be delivered to the store and made available for sale. This process involves receiving, checking, marking, distributing, and traffic, all of which should be closely controlled and coordinated.

◼ ACTIVITIES RELATED TO INCOMING MERCHANDISE

"Receiving" means taking physical possession of merchandise (and supplies and equipment) at the store and moving it to an area for unpacking and checking. "Checking" includes matching the purchase order against the invoice, opening containers, removal and sorting of merchandise, and comparing the quantity and quality of the goods with the specifications of the order. "Marking" is placing information on or near the merchandise, to aid customers and salespeople in making selections, and to provide data for control systems. "Distributing" has to do with moving merchandise from the marking room to the stockroom or to the sales floor and from a central point to branch stores. In chain store companies, planning merchandise flow to the branches becomes very important. This function is often combined with traffic management under a vice-president for physical distribution. "Traffic" is concerned with the choice of routes for shipments, the filing and collection of damage claims, the auditing of transportation bills, and similar matters.

Efficiency in these activities is helpful to the customer, who gains from the resulting better service, and to the retailer, who benefits from greater profits. Exclusive of inward transportation, they may cost as much as 1 percent of sales. Consequently, they afford many opportunities to reduce costs and improve results through mechanization and automation. Yet merchandise handling continues to receive insufficient attention from top management in many stores.

☐ Guidelines for effective performance

Although different stores use different techniques to handle their incoming goods, they all generally try to observe the following guidelines: (1) use of specialized employees when the work is sufficient to justify the cost; (2) development (through work simplification programs) of standardized routines to increase speed and accuracy; (3) centralization of all receiving operations and provision of adequate space for this purpose; (4) the use of mechanical equipment to reduce cost wherever feasible; and (5) maintenance of adequate control records.*

Today, many retailers, forced to handle merchandise in unprecedented volume, are turning to the mechanization of receiving, marking, and related functions. Space shortages, higher labor and material costs, and keener competition are accelerating this trend.

☐ Centralization

Receiving, checking, and marking are often done on the sales floor or in a back storage space in small stores. But they are centralized in a separate room in larger stores in order to (1) afford better control over incoming merchandise by lessening the danger of lost invoices and discounts, (2) permit use of specialized employees, insuring more uniform and better quality of work at lower cost, (3) overcome the objections of salespeople who dislike doing such work, and (4) avoid the confusion and congestion that result when goods are opened and marked on the sales floor.

Frequently, ready-to-wear merchandise is opened and checked in a separate room to facilitate its removal from containers, thus avoiding wrinkling, and to speed up its movement to the selling floors. This has become less important in recent years, however, because much apparel

---

* To this list, some retailers would add a sixth, that is, the use of special bonuses or incentive payments to encourage speed and accuracy on the part of personnel performing these activities.

is now shipped by truck (or plane) on hangers. As a precaution against theft, jewelry and other high-value items are usually checked in a separate room or in a special enclosed section of the receiving area. Furniture and heavy household items are customarily received and stored in warehouses or at subsidiary receiving points located near elevators leading to the furniture department. A separate receiving room is sometimes used for merchandise going to the basement store, if one is operated and if it is large enough to warrant the facility. With these main exceptions, however, a centralized receiving room is superior to decentralized or sales floor receiving.

When department store companies first opened suburban branches, they typically received, checked, and marked the merchandise at a central facility (usually the downtown store) before sending it to the branches. Now, however, many of these firms have vendors ship directly to the branches in order to speed the movement of goods to the selling floor. In contrast, chain store companies, particularly in fields such as groceries, usually receive and distribute much of their inventory through central warehouses to obtain the economies of large shipments.[1] Many fashion and discount department store chains also price-mark some or all of their items at central warehouses.[2]

□ Location of receiving and marking facilities

Value and adequacy of the space As a rule, receiving and related activities should be concentrated in space that is relatively useless for selling purposes. Small grocery, drug, hardware, and ready-to-wear stores often handle these activities in the back room. In the large multifloor store, receiving, checking, and marking activities are usually placed on an upper floor reached by a freight elevator from a receiving point located on the ground level. The space must be adequate for the everyday needs of the store and also provide room for handling merchandise at peak periods, such as Christmas and Easter.

Location in relation to stockrooms The checking and marking room should be located as close as possible to the stockrooms to reduce the handling of merchandise. In quite a few new stores reserve stocks for various departments are now held in fixtures on the selling floor or in convenient special stockrooms near the departmental selling areas. This is possible because many of these retailers now carry much less reserve stock than they once did. (See the discussion of hand-to-mouth buying on pp. 292–93.) In such stores, goods may be opened, checked, and marked in areas adjacent to the specialized stockrooms, contrary to the general tendency toward centralized checking and marking.

Location in relation to the selling floor Since most merchants still place incoming merchandise on the selling floor as needed, it is desirable that the receiving room and the stockroom be readily accessible to the selling areas. Such an arrangement brings savings in personnel, better customer service, and greater sales. Yet, as we have noted, as long as convenient mechanisms for transferring merchandise are available, the receiving room and the sales floor may be widely separated.

Large stores operate warehouses in relatively low-rent districts, often at some distance from the stores, for merchandise sold by sample, such as furniture, radios, stoves, and refrigerators. Receiving, checking, marking (if any), and storage are performed in the warehouse, with delivery made directly to the customer's home.

■ RECEIVING ROOM LAYOUT AND EQUIPMENT

Efficiency in handling incoming merchandise depends in part upon adequate, properly utilized space, upon suitable equipment, and upon appropriate working methods. These will vary among stores of various types and size.

☐ Small stores

Small stores usually do not require any special facilities or particular layouts in the receiving area since merchandise is commonly unloaded onto a sidewalk or is carried into the back room. It is unpacked and marked at the convenience of an employee or the manager. Some stores have stationary or portable tables in the receiving area. As merchandise is unpacked, it is sorted, placed on these tables, checked, and marked.

☐ Larger stores

In larger stores the layout of the receiving area depends upon the system used in handling the merchandise received. Three methods are widely employed, while a fourth—which involves the use of mechanized conveyors—is increasing in use. Perhaps the most common one is the use of *stationary tables* or *check-marking tables,* as illustrated in Figure 15–1. These tables are frequently placed in a room large enough to allow cases to be brought in and unpacked. Merchandise is then sorted, and placed on tables. After being checked and marked, it is moved to the stockroom or to the sales floor.

The second method used is the *portable table.* Goods are placed on tables with wheels where they are sorted and checked for quantity. Tables are then moved to another section for marking. This method has an advantage over the system just described. Goods remain in the checking area for a shorter time, since they are not held there for marking. Buyers and selling department heads who are often eager to take

FIGURE 15–1 Flow chart showing checking and marking operation with stationary tables

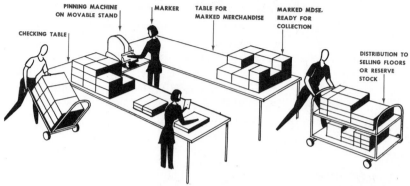

Courtesy Dennison Manufacturing Company

This method of operation is based on parallel stationary tables, with attaching machine on movable stand between them. Tables and machine stand are exactly the same height (about 36 inches) and space between tables is just wide enough for marker and machine. Overhead electric connection permits machine to move the length of the table. The operating method is as follows:

1. Receiver or stockworker brings packages containing merchandise to be machine-marked to checking table.
2. Checker matches invoice to package, opens, piles merchandise on table, checks invoice, leaving retailed invoice with merchandise.
3. Marker moves pinning machine opposite merchandise, and machine-marks, piling marked merchandise on the table at her *right*. As piles of boxes are marked, she moves machine so that merchandise to be marked, and space to pile it after marking, always are right at hand.
4. Stockworker collects marked merchandise from table, takes to forward or reserve stock.

This operating plan shows a single unit for one attaching machine. It is capable of indefinite expansion by increasing the length of the tables and adding more pinning machines. It is adaptable to portable table operation by using lines of portable tables in place of the stationary tables; or to a combination of the two systems by having the checking table stationary and the tables for marked merchandise portable.

the merchandise and put it on sale can be more easily excluded from the quantity checking area and thus cannot remove it prior to the quantity check.

A third method is known as the *bin method*. This involves dividing the receiving room into two sections, one for checking and one for marking, with a series of bins or openings dividing the sections. As merchandise is checked on tables in one section, it is shoved through the bins onto tables in the other section, where marking takes place. As with the portable-table system, this method tends to keep buyers from removing merchandise that has not been checked, since they are not allowed in the checking sections of the receiving room. But it necessitates an extra handling of all goods and may cause some confusion in marking if unlike goods are mixed in a bin.

Most large retailers use a fourth method—*mechanical conveyor belts or roller conveyors*—to move merchandise from the receiving point through the checking and marking operations. Overhead trolley systems transport clothing and any other hanging merchandise.[3] A few stores employ the overhead rail for all merchandise, placing flat-packed goods in hanging baskets.[4] At the appropriate checking point, the merchandise may be moved off the central conveyor for examination and later moved on to the marking area. Or a conveyor spur may detour it while marking is performed (Figure 15–2). Even the movement to the selling area or to the stockroom may be by mechanical equipment.

FIGURE 15–2   **Use of conveyor in marking**   The picture shows the central conveyor and several spurs.

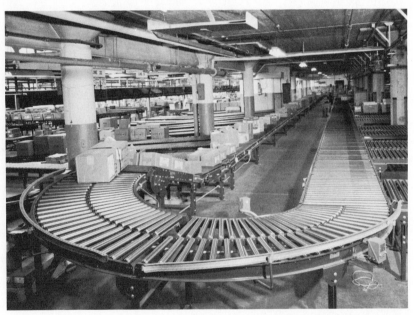

Courtesy Rapids-Standard Company, Inc.

■ RECEIVING PROCEDURES

We now turn to the actual receiving of merchandise and note the steps necessary to prepare the goods for sale.

☐ Receiving shipments

At the receiving point—station, dock, or sidewalk—all boxes, cartons, and other containers should be inspected at time of delivery for any indication of damage. If there is no such indication, the receiving clerk signs the carrier's receipt; but, if damage is detected, the receipt should be marked "damaged" before being signed. Such action facilitates the filing of damage claims later. This receiving point inspection does not involve any examination of the merchandise itself. Goods are then moved into the receiving room by means of trucks, elevators, chutes, and roller conveyors as soon as possible. If any damage, loss, or shortage is revealed when containers are opened and the goods are checked, a claim should be filed promptly against the transportation agency, the vendor, or others responsible.

□ Receiving records

Recording of incoming shipments is essential. The information commonly includes the date and hour of arrival; apparent condition of the shipment (e.g., any damage); weight; delivery charges (if paid by the retailer); shipper's name and location; form of transportation—such as railroad, express, or parcel post; person making the delivery (e.g., name of truck driver); number of pieces; amount and number of invoice;* and the department for which the merchandise is intended. Figure 15–3 shows a typical receiving record.

FIGURE 15–3 **A receiving record which permits attachment of the invoice**

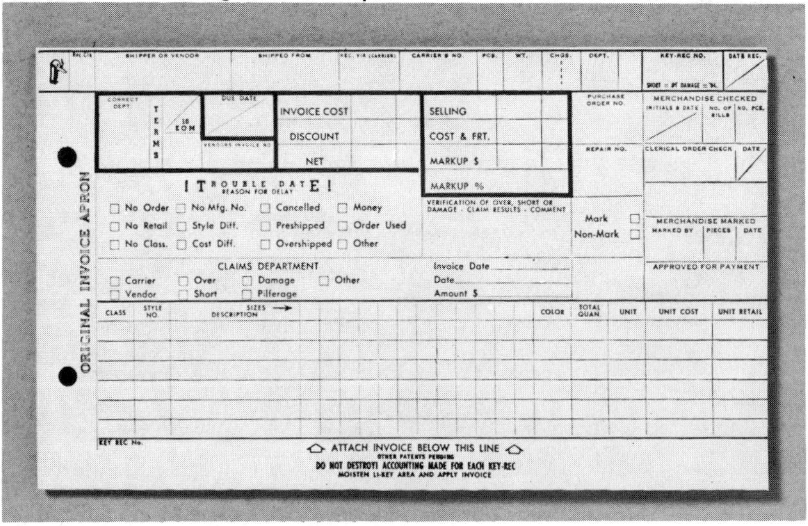
SHIPPER OR VENDOR | SHIPPED FROM | CARRIER'S NO. | PCS. | WT. | CHGS. | DEPT. | KEY-REC NO. | DATE REC.
CORRECT DEPT. | TERMS | 10 EOM | DUE DATE | VENDOR'S INVOICE NO.
INVOICE COST
DISCOUNT
NET
SELLING
COST & FRT.
MARKUP $
MARKUP %
PURCHASE ORDER NO.
MERCHANDISE CHECKED | INITIALS & DATE | NO. OF BILLS | NO. PCS.
REPAIR NO.
CLERICAL ORDER CHECK | DATE
! TROUBLE DATE !
REASON FOR DELAY
□ No Order □ No Mfg. No. □ Cancelled □ Money
□ No Retail □ Style Diff. □ Preshipped □ Order Used
□ No Class. □ Cost Diff. □ Overshipped □ Other
VERIFICATION OF OVER, SHORT OR DAMAGE - CLAIM RESULTS - COMMENT
Mark □
Non-Mark □
MERCHANDISE MARKED | MARKED BY | PIECES | DATE
CLAIMS DEPARTMENT
□ Carrier □ Over □ Damage □ Other
□ Vendor □ Short □ Pilferage
Invoice Date
Date
Amount $
APPROVED FOR PAYMENT
ORIGINAL INVOICE APRON
CLASS | STYLE NO. | DESCRIPTION | SIZES → | COLOR | TOTAL QUAN. | UNIT | UNIT COST | UNIT RETAIL
KEY REC No.
ATTACH INVOICE BELOW THIS LINE
OTHER PATENTS PENDING
DO NOT DESTROY! ACCOUNTING MADE FOR EACH KEY-REC
MOISTEN LI-KEY AREA AND APPLY INVOICE

* Invoices from local vendors and, to an increasing extent, from those located at a distance when shipments are made by truck, usually arrive with the merchandise, so that they are available to the receiving clerk when preparing the receiving record. On other out-of-town shipments, invoices come by mail and usually arrive before the merchandise. If so, they sometimes go to the receiving point, where they are held until the arrival of the merchandise. The receiving record number is placed on the invoice and on the receiving sheet or slip, if the latter is used.

The use of a receiving record offers several benefits: (1) It provides helpful information if the vendor and the store disagree about the receipt of a particular shipment. Placing the invoice number on the receiving record associates each invoice with the proper merchandise. This action is especially important for partial shipments and when many shipments are received from one vendor. (2) The receiving record allows management to check on the length of time invoices and merchandise are held in the receiving room. (3) Finally, by requiring that invoices be checked against receiving records before they are paid, the store avoids paying for merchandise not yet received.*

When the receiving records are completed and containers are properly marked, the merchandise is moved to the checking and marking room.

Electronic record systems   Large firms, and an increasing number of medium-sized ones, use computerized P.O.M. ("purchase order management") systems for receiving, checking, marking and other purposes. The data for each purchase is entered into the computer. Then each shipment received and its invoice are compared with the purchase data, often through preparation of another computerized document called "the receiver." The system can be programed to print the appropriate number of price tickets if the shipment is acceptable to the store, and will also authorize payment of the vendor's invoice. Such systems accelerate the handling of incoming merchandise; facilitate invoice payment before discounts expire; and generate valuable information, such as buyer's total commitments and remaining open-to-buy, inventory additions, and number and cause of "problem" shipments.[5]

■ CHECKING PROCEDURES

Checking consists of four quite distinct steps. First, the invoice is checked against the purchase order. Second, the merchandise is removed from the shipping containers and sorted. Third, the merchandise is checked for quantity. And finally, the goods are checked for quality. Two or more of the steps may be performed by the same employee.

☐ Checking invoice against purchase order

Comparing the invoice with the purchase order indicates (1) if the description and quantity of the goods billed are the same as those

---

* This requirement is not always fulfilled, especially in cases in which buyers are located at some distance from vendors. If past relationships have been satisfactory, goods are sometimes paid for before their receipt in order to take advantage of the cash discount. If discrepancies arise, adjustments are made without difficulty.

ordered and (2) if the terms of sale (dating and discounts) on the two forms are the same.

□ Unpacking and sorting merchandise

Despite the trend to ship wearing apparel in garment bags,* most merchandise still arrives at retail stores in containers and cannot be checked until unpacked and sorted. In some firms these tasks are not performed until invoices are available. This policy prevents removal of goods before they are checked in, thus causing a stock shortage. Or if the store makes a record of the merchandise removed from the container, places the goods in stock, and later finds a discrepancy when the invoice arrives, there is no way of rechecking the shipment. Although it generally seems wise to avoid opening containers until invoices are available, it is probably best—if the goods are needed on the sales floor —to take the chances involved and unpack the merchandise at once.

□ Checking for quantity

The two main methods of checking incoming merchandise for quantity are the direct check and the blind check. Variations of these methods—the semiblind check and the combination check—are also used by some retailers. The choice of a method depends upon how tight a control management wants and upon whom it places responsibility for careful checking.

The direct check Under this system incoming shipments are usually checked directly against the invoice. The goods are held unopened until arrival of the invoice in case of delay in receiving that document. However, some stores permit use of the combination method, described below, if the merchandise is needed immediately. In some firms the direct check is against the purchase order rather than the invoice.

The main advantages of the direct check are its speed and simplicity, its economy, and the ease of rechecking discrepancies between the checker's count and the invoice quantity. Its chief disadvantages are the possibility of careless checking and the piling up of goods in the receiving room to wait for invoices, thus delaying the movement of merchandise to the selling floor. This delay has been minimized in recent years, however, by the increased number of vendors enclosing duplicate invoices with their shipments. The direct check continues to be the most common method of checking for quantity in small stores, and probably in large ones.

---

* Dresses, blouses, coats, and similar items are frequently placed in garment bags and hung in trucks for shipment. Upon arrival at destination, the garments are easily removed, marked, and transferred to the selling floor. Problems of unpacking, eliminating wrinkles, and marking are simplified.

The blind check In this method the checker uses blank forms or blank pieces of paper on which to list the kinds and description of the merchandise, the quantities, the shipper, and other pertinent information about the merchandise received in each shipment. This procedure results in much more careful checking, allows the task to be performed immediately and the merchandise placed on sale, cost figures are not divulged to checkers, and invoices are moved promptly to the accounts payable office.

But the blind check is more expensive than the direct check since extra time is required to prepare the list and check it against the original invoice. In addition, a recheck is impossible if merchandise is removed from the receiving room before the list is checked against the invoice.

Other checking methods The *semiblind method* of checking saves time and cost as compared with the blind check. A checker is given a list of the items in a shipment but with the quantities omitted. The checker simply counts the merchandise and enters the quantities. The time saving is partially offset, however, by that required in the invoice office to prepare the lists for the checkers.

The *combination check* is a combination of the direct and blind checks. Its object is to obtain an accurate count of the goods received and speed up their removal from the receiving room. If invoices are available when the merchandise is received, the direct check is used; but if goods arrive and an invoice is not at hand, the blind check is used.

Regardless of the methods employed to check merchandise, most stores check quantities merely on the basis of the amounts listed on the outside of the packages included in the shipment. Thus a shipment of nylon hosiery, packed three pairs to the box, would be checked for quantity simply by counting the boxes and multiplying by three. Checking each package is left to the marker who attaches the price tickets. This process is facilitated by marking machines which can print any specific number of price tickets. The use of such equipment is explained on pages 383–85.

Checking *bulk merchandise* presents a different problem from that of other goods. When this merchandise is received both the number of bulk containers and the weight of the contents of each container must be checked. Care is needed in examining containers for substandard weights. Fruits and vegetables, for example, are often repacked by shippers and, in the process, loss of weight sometimes occurs; or the time element alone may be responsible for shrinkage.

Handling quantity discrepancies When the quantity check reveals a discrepancy with the invoice, and the merchandise is still in the receiving room—as it will be if the direct check is used—the checker calls a supervisor to make a recheck. In the small store, of course, the proprietor makes the recheck. If the merchandise has already been placed in stock and a recheck is not possible, the original count serves as the basis for a claim against the shipper, or against the carrier if it is at fault. When shipments contain less than the quantity shown on the invoice, it is customary for the retailer to deduct a compensating amount from the payment made to the vendor. If an overage is revealed, however, the buyer usually decides whether to accept and pay for the overshipment or to return it to the vendor.

□ Checking for quality

All too frequently the emphasis placed on the quantity check results in partial neglect of the quality factor. The usual basis of quality checking is the buyer's experience, knowledge of quality and values, and memory of the merchandise purchased. Increasingly, however, larger firms are providing their buyers with more objective standards for judging quality. Some buyers purchase samples in showrooms and check merchandise received against these samples. Others are aided by standards and specifications established by the government, the trade, the vendor, or the retailer. The National Bureau of Standards, for instance, has established standards for some items and allows manufacturers to certify that their products conform to these standards. A few of the large department stores, mail-order firms, and chain stores have testing laboratories in which samples of incoming merchandise are tested for quality. (See the discussion of testing bureaus on p. 298.) The facilities of outside testing organizations are also available.

■ MARKING MERCHANDISE

Merchandise is often price-marked by means of price tickets, gummed stickers, automatic imprinting systems, or even by hand before being placed on sale. In very recent years significant developments in electronic and other equipment for recording sales, controlling inventory, authorizing credit and other purposes has revolutionized marking systems and sharply increased the types and varieties of tickets and tags used.[6] Yet some retailers handling highly standardized goods or merchandise marked by the manufacturer, or which is sold at a single price, dispense with price marking. Even in these cases, however, some marking may be necessary to provide better stock control and to facilitate the taking of inventory.

□ UPC marking

The supermarket industry has become interested in a system called the Universal Product Code (UPC). The code markings placed on each package are machine-readable thick and thin vertical lines that indicate manufacturer or brand, item, and package size. When these markings are passed under an optical scanner at the checkout, the sales register devices automatically obtain the correct price from a computer record, add the amount to the customer's bill, and also revise the store's computerized inventory record. Other types of retailers, such as stationery and liquor dealers, have also become interested, while fashion merchants favor an alternative system. Many firms that have experimented with the UPC system want to eliminate the costly process of marking prices on each item, but this has led to controversies with labor and consumer groups. Although the UPC markings can be applied in the store, marking by the supplier (while labeling the packages) is much more accurate and far less costly. Since the UPC method is designed in part, to speed up and improve checkout operations, we will discuss it in more detail in Chapter 25. Our discussion in the following paragraphs deals with other marking methods.

☐ Some guidelines for marking

Certain basic principles guide the retailer in marking merchandise regardless of the methods or devices used in the process.

1. Merchandise should be marked legibly, neatly, and as permanently as possible without damage to the goods. The use of rubber stamps and marking machines has helped to solve this problem. But computerized point-of-sale systems that absorb information electronically from the price marks require very carefully prepared tickets and labels.

2. If possible, all necessary information should be placed on the ticket or label, at the time the goods are marked. The data should be limited to necessary information for those handling the goods, including customers, and to facts the buyers need for merchandise control and for guidance in future purchasing. Small stores usually mark the cost of the item, in code, and the retail price. In department and specialty stores, the information ordinarily includes the season letter and week in the season, department number, the size and color of the goods, the retail price, and sometimes the manufacturer and style number.

3. The marking methods should minimize manipulation of prices by employees and customers. This is usually accomplished (a) by the use of marking machines and specially prepared ink and (b) by attaching tickets to merchandise so securely that their removal is difficult. Unused price tickets should not be allowed in selling departments.

4. When a record of articles sold daily is desired for control purposes, price tickets with perforated stubs may be used. The stubs can be used in a perpetual inventory system. Tabulating the stubs indicates which items are selling best as well as the most popular colors, styles and sizes.

5. Certain items should be marked in some manner, usually in addition to the price ticket, which will prevent their wear or use by the customer before they are returned. For instance, some retail stores attach a

tag to millinery reading: "If this tag is removed, this merchandise may not be returned for credit." Other stores use specially printed price tickets indicating that certain goods cannot be returned for sanitary reasons.

6. Merchandise should be marked as quickly and economically as possible consistent with accuracy and the type of merchandise handled. The actual application of this principle is, of course, a matter of good management.

Other reasons for marking merchandise besides those mentioned above include (1) listing the price, size, color, and other data aids salespeople in serving customers, (2) marking creates customer goodwill since customers prefer to deal with retailers who treat all patrons the same, and marking is an indication (but not a guaranty) that the store does so, (3) the markings, especially, the price, encourages self-service, thus reducing sales effort, (4) marking simplifies taking the physical inventory, and (5) marking the date the goods were received aids management in deciding when markdowns are needed, thus keeping fresh merchandise in stock.*

□ Marking procedures

At least three in-store procedures are followed in marking merchandise. (For discussions of vendor marking and particularly UPC code marking for electronic checkout, see pp. 386–87 and 629–31.) *Immediate marking,* the one most widely used, involves marking each item in the desired manner as promptly as possible after its receipt. In a second method, *delayed marking,* the retail price and other necessary information is only inscribed on the outside containers or cartons. When the merchandise is needed on the sales floor, the containers are opened and the individual items marked. This procedure is practicable for canned goods and other fast-selling staples and also advisable for merchandise on which prices change frequently since it saves the expense of re-marking.** The chief disadvantage is that the marking may give insufficient information to provide adequate control of merchandise.

In the third procedure, *group marking,* containers are marked on the outside when received, as in delayed marking, and the goods moved to

---

* The adoption of "open dating" by a number of food chains is a significant development. Under this system a date that is important to the customer for determining the freshness of an item—either the date when the store obtained the item, the last date for sale (the "pull date"), or the last date on which the consumer should use the item—is stamped on the package in plain language. Previously this information was marked in a code that most customers could not decipher.

** This procedure is sometimes called "bulk marking." However, the term is used by some retailers to denote other practices. A grocer, for example, who places a large box of soap chips on the sales floor and writes "80¢ per pound" on the box considers such action to be bulk marking.

the reserve stockroom. Later, they are moved to the selling floor *without* marking the individual items; instead, the merchandise is grouped in set locations and the price indicated by a nearby price tag. This reduces the cost of marking and re-marking goods and speeds up their delivery to the selling floor. It is widely used by food stores and those selling low-priced variety goods, drug accessories, and inexpensive automotive supplies. Supermarkets and other stores which operate on a self-service basis, however, usually find it necessary to mark the retail price on most individual items; otherwise, the check-out is slow and often inaccurate.

☐ How and where merchandise is marked

The desired information may be placed on the merchandise or its container in several ways—by writing, using a rubber stamp, or by attaching labels or tickets or tags of various kinds to the merchandise by hand or by using a machine designed for this purpose. Some stores attach a print-punch tag to each item, part of which may be detached at the point of sale and fed into an electronic data processing system for automated information feedback. Whatever kind of ticket or tag is used, it must be adapted to the store's system of merchandise control and to its sales registering equipment. This is particularly true for the newer electronic devices discussed in Chapter 25, "Control of sales transactions."

Hand and rubber-stamp marking Hand marking, of course, is most common in small retail stores. In a hardware store, for example, the salesperson may write "$3.98" on each quart can of paint while placing it on the shelf; or may attach a gummed label with the price to the merchandise. Rubber stamping has largely replaced gummed labels, pin tickets, and string tickets for marking a wide variety of fast-selling packaged items such as dry groceries.

Price tickets Since marking by hand and rubber stamps is time consuming, often results in errors, and the markings may be blotted out before the merchandise is sold, many small retailers and practically all large ones attach price tickets to merchandise. A single store may use several different types, some of which are shown in Figure 15–4.

Electric or hand-operated equipment prints the designated information on the price tickets and often attaches the tickets to the merchandise. Recent improvements in equipment permit the use of all kinds of paper—gummed, ungummed, heat-seal, and pressure-sensitive, as well as heavy tag or board stocks. Hand-operated machines, such as the Monarch Model 1120—Econo-Ply® (Figure 15–5), both print and apply the label as the operator squeezes the handle. For the retailer who wants a more automatic operation, the Kimball PM75 (Figure 15–6) both prints and punches 175 to 275 tags per minute with detailed information in both human and machine readable language which is automatically

FIGURE 15–4 Some forms of price tags and tickets in common use

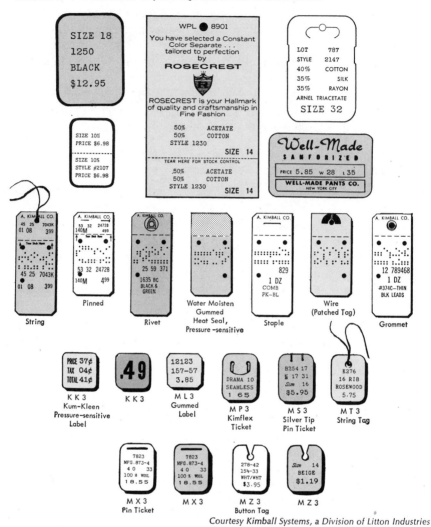

Courtesy Kimball Systems, a Division of Litton Industries

converted for processing in any conventional or computer system. Most of these machines turn out such complete price and inventory tickets that the stubs can be fed into mechanical or electronic tabulators for stock control purposes.

Where merchandise is marked As noted, small retailers frequently have salespeople do the marking on the selling floor in their spare time. But this is inadvisable because any cost saving is usually more than offset by frequent errors, slower marking, and less legible price entries or tickets. Marking should be concentrated in the receiving room or check-

FIGURE 15–5 The Monarch Model 1120 Econo-Ply®—for printing and applying labels

© Monarch Marking Systems, Inc. Courtesy of Monarch Marking Systems, Inc.

ing and marking room. Such a location also facilitates the use of marking machines.

Authorizing marking Regardless of who does the actual work, proper authorization is necessary to ensure that the marking is done correctly and promptly. A small store proprietor may do this by entering the proposed price on the invoice. In large stores the buyer usually notes the prices and other data to be marked on the invoice (or a copy) after checking the quality of the goods, and after the invoice has been com-

FIGURE 15–6 **A highly automatic machine that prints and punches up to 29 columns of information into tags, the Kimball PM75**

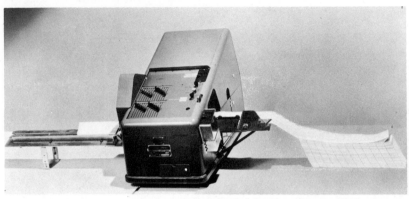

Courtesy Kimball Systems, a Division of Litton Industries

pared with the purchase order and entered for payment. In some stores the buyer gives the markers a priced-marked sample of the merchandise after making the quality check.

Numerous other stores now authorize marking through a process known as *preretailing*. This requires the buyer to place the retail prices of the items being bought upon the store's copy of the purchase order at the time the order is placed. It has two main advantages. First, it forces the buyer to consider the retail price at the time of purchase, thereby discouraging purchases which do not seem to provide the desired mark up. Second, marking is expedited because it can begin as soon as the goods arrive. In addition, preretailing fits into the modern accounting system known as the "retail method of inventory" described in Chapter 23.

Source marking Some large retailers reduce marking expenses and move goods more quickly to the selling floor by having their vendors mark merchandise prior to shipment,[7] a practice known as source marking. In some cases the stores prepare price tickets and send them to vendors for attaching to the goods; in other cases, vendors furnish the price tickets, enter the information supplied by the retailer, and affix them to the merchandise. Staple products, men's clothing, women's hosiery, and greeting cards are frequently source-marked. Source marking helps retailers utilize EDP more effectively, thus improving the feedback of information to the manufacturer and allowing prompt adjustments in production as the popularity of specific items changes. For some goods a standard tag code and format has been developed. (See Figure 15–7.)

It should be noted, however, that manufacturers marking merchandise for their retailer customers must let all competing customers know that the service is available; otherwise they will run afoul of the Robinson-Patman Act (see the discussion on pp. 332–41). Section 2(e) of the

FIGURE 15–7   Source marking standard tag code and format

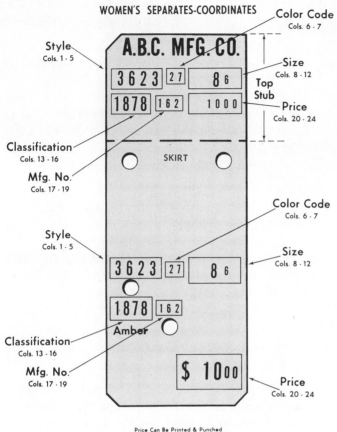

Price Can Be Printed & Punched
or Punched Only If Not Standard Priced.
Courtesy National Retail Merchants Association

Robinson-Patman Act outlaws discriminatory furnishing of "services or facilities connected with the processing, handling, sale, or offering for sale" of commodities. Practically all retailers agree that a further extension of source marking should be encouraged to reduce retail costs.[8]

Outside marking of fashion merchandise   A growing trend is the hiring of outside carrier firms to mark fashion goods. Many retailers who have lacked sufficient central facilities to mark all the merchandise for their rapidly growing branch store systems have engaged these outside services. In addition, some of these retailers believe that the carriers can process the items more rapidly than the store's own marking room, thus providing three or four days of additional selling time for fashions that may only have a short potential selling period.

Re-marking   Merchandise that has been marked and placed on the sales floor often needs remarking. Price reductions (markdowns) or price increases may be advisable; some merchandise returned by customers must be re-marked; price tickets may have become soiled, torn, or lost; and departmental transfers of merchandise may call for re-marking. Since *all* marking (at least in large stores) should be controlled by the marking-room manager, all re-markings should be done under the same supervision even if performed on the selling floor or adjacent thereto. Specialized marking machines are available for this purpose. As previously suggested, centralizing responsibility for marking assigns this activity to specialists who are faster and more accurate; maintains control over price tickets; and therefore helps ensure that all price changes will be properly recorded.

In re-marking merchandise to lower levels (markdowns), retailers follow two quite different policies. Some believe that the original (former) price should remain on the merchandise, perhaps just crossed out and the new price added, so that the customer understands a "bargain" is available. Other retailers prefer to replace the entire price tag and show just the new price. They reason that the re-marking cost is not increased by this procedure, the resulting price tag is clearer and more attractive to the customer, and the pricing psychology is better—they want to avoid the implication of "We tried to get you to pay $19.95 for it; you didn't fall for that high price, so we'll now try a lower one."

■ DISTRIBUTION OF MERCHANDISE WITHIN THE STORE

Incoming merchandise that has been marked is ready for distribution to the reserve stockroom or to the selling floor. Information as to where it shall go is supplied by the proprietor in the small store, by the manager in the chain store unit, and by the buyer or department head in the large store. In smaller stores employees marking the merchandise know what is to be done with the goods. And all employees of these stores are usually allowed in the stockroom to obtain merchandise needed on the sales floor. In larger stores, usually the receiving-room manager knows from past experience and the type of merchandise where to move the goods. In some large stores, however, the buyer may give distribution instructions when "retailing" the merchandise. Merchandise placed in the stockroom is released only on requisition from the buyer.

■ TRAFFIC MANAGEMENT

Our discussion thus far has focused on the movement of merchandise *after* it reaches the store. But retailers are also vitally interested in reducing transportation time and costs for incoming merchandise. As Dorothy E. Geiss, traffic manager of the Strauss Stores in Youngstown, Ohio points out:

The transportation factor is one of the few *cost* items that will vary sharply in direct ratio to the amount of control exercised by the retailer. In other words, the choice between *premium* services such as express (in some instances), air transportation, etc., or the normal routings of common carrier, consolidator, UPS [United Parcel Service], or Parcel Post will be reflected in substantial differences in markup and profit.[9]

Consequently, large retail firms establish traffic departments to study the complicated subject of freight rates and to develop information on the relative speed and costs of various shipping methods between vendors' supply points and the store.

Traffic department functions include selection of the best routes for shipments, tracing lost shipments, checking freight classifications and rates, including auditing transportation bills,[10] payment of transportation charges, placement and collection of loss and/or damage claims, and other activities associated with the physical movement of the merchandise. Savings and benefits realized usually far exceed the cost of performing these functions.

Since the routing of merchandise affects transportation cost, speed of delivery, and the care with which the merchandise is handled, the traffic manager should work with buyers in preparing instructions for vendors on how merchandise should be shipped. Some traffic departments hold classes for buyers to make them "transportation conscious." Vendors should be billed for any extra costs that result from failure to follow instructions. It is also advisable to audit all freight bills at regular intervals, to make certain that merchandise has been shipped in the correct classification, at the proper rate, and that computations on the bills are correct.

The tracing of delayed shipments is also important. Usually, this means maintaining contact with the carrier until the shipment is located. Filing of claims for loss or damage against the vendor or the carrier should be done promptly and full information supplied to support them.[11]

■ HANDLING INCOMING MERCHANDISE IN CHAIN STORES

Chain-store firms that operate their own warehouses often use different procedures from those so far discussed. Receiving and checking are performed at two points—in the warehouse and again in the store. In the former, special facilities are employed to handle the large volume of goods, such as pallets moved by highlift trucks, overhead track towveyor systems, towline arrangements, roller conveyors, and electronic controls.[12] The location, size, and layout of distribution centers or warehouses are also very important in the control of merchandise handling costs. Consequently, much time, effort, and expense are devoted to these problems. The Vice President of Ben Franklin Stores says: "Today we are constantly reviewing the efficiency of our distribution system."[13] The size of the facilities used by one chain is illustrated in Figure 15–8, while a system for the flow of merchandise and information from a central distribution point to the stores, with feedback to central buyers, is sketched in Figure 15–9.

But not all chain organizations find distribution centers desirable. States the former chief executive officer of Montgomery Ward:

Ward had been structured for small stores supplied by *distribution centers.* We had to eliminate the distribution centers and go to big stores. We also had to reorganize to get away from some department store concepts . . . being practiced. . . . The big thing here was a new procurement policy, which would be a part of a complete mass merchandising system extending from the suppliers at one end to the customers at the other. . . .[14]

At individual chain stores the goods are typically moved indoors from the delivery truck by conveyor or by hand. Before or during un-

FIGURE 15–8 **J. C. Penney's distribution center complex in Buena Park, California** In addition to warehousing and shipping selected lines of merchandise to Penney stores nationwide, it serves as a common stockroom permitting economic distribution of merchandise in Southern California. An automated fashion distribution facility is also provided for fast dispatch of such items to 348 stores throughout the West. Supplementing these services, among several others, is a West Coast Data Center in which computers process tickets for computer-written reordering of merchandise in 800 stores, process data for central merchandise and fashion distribution and handle all charge account records and billing as well as complete payoff records for area stores and field offices.

Courtesy J. C. Penney Company

FIGURE 15–9 **Chain store merchandise distribution system and information flow, using centralized receiving and marking**

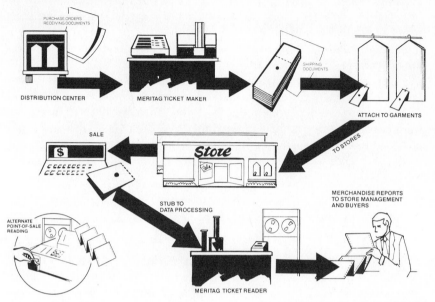

DISTRIBUTION CENTER

PURCHASE ORDERS
RECEIVING DOCUMENTS

MERITAG TICKET MAKER

SHIPPING
DOCUMENTS

ATTACH TO GARMENTS

TO STORES

SALE

Store

STUB TO
DATA PROCESSING

MERCHANDISE REPORTS
TO STORE MANAGEMENT
AND BUYERS

ALTERNATE
POINT-OF-SALE
READING

MERITAG TICKET READER

Courtesy Dennison Manufacturing Company

loading, the manager or a receiving clerk checks the number of packages against an invoice received from the driver. The driver is usually required to sign for shortages. Checking for quality is performed at the warehouse.

In some large chain units the handling of merchandise within the store is substantially mechanized. One firm, for instance, uses 1,200 feet of overhead conveyor track which electrically moves aluminum carriers from loading dock to eight different stock areas. The merchandise which has already been received, checked, and marked at a warehouse is ready for sale within 30 minutes after reaching the store.

Organizations with relatively small units set prices at headquarters; and each store manager is notified of those to be used. Actual marking is usually done in the store, although there are many exceptions to this practice. Chain supermarkets employ a wide variety of methods. Prices may be marked on cases at the warehouse or after reaching the store. Individual items may be marked when received at the store, in the back room as needed, or when placed on the shelves.

Women's apparel chains quite typically place price tickets on garments before shipment from their warehouses. Many of the drug, variety, and hard-lines chains have installed the latest type of pricing devices at their warehouses, where they pre-mark some merchandise, thus decreasing cost and increasing accuracy. Drug, hardware, and variety chains with clerk service depend largely on group marking—writing prices on large containers and bins for floor displays and using shelf tickets—while self-service stores commonly write or stamp the price on the individual item. Store employees usually perform whatever re-marking is necessary.

Merchandise shipped directly to the individual chain stores by vendors is received, checked, and marked by methods somewhat comparable to those used in independent stores. But checking for quality is frequently under the control of headquarters employees, who make spot checks. Prices are usually set at headquarters, with actual marking done in the store. Vendors generally send invoices directly to headquarters for payment.

■ ORGANIZATION FOR INCOMING MERCHANDISE

Although the proprietor of a small store, perhaps assisted by a salesperson, handles incoming merchandise, in larger ones responsibility for receiving, checking, marking, distributing, and traffic is commonly centralized in the operations manager or superintendent, with a receiving or a traffic manager exercising day-by-day control. Some large and medium-size organizations, however, place these activities under the controller or the merchandise manager. Either arrangement may be entirely logical. Yet many firms are now appointing distribution managers (sometimes with vice presidential rank) with broad responsibility over traffic, warehousing, and inventory control. The complexity of the distribution task in a particular company, the executive personalities involved, and the company's past experience will influence the decision on where to locate responsibility for distribution.

■ REVIEW AND DISCUSSION QUESTIONS

1 What are the major activities involved in handling incoming merchandise? Discuss the importance and complexity of these activities in small and in large stores. Why are they often neglected by top management?

2 Present arguments for and against centralization of receiving and marking in a large store that has no branches. Would your answer be the same if the store had several branches? Explain.

3 Where should receiving and marking facilities be located in the store, and what space should they be assigned?

4 Report on the location and arrangement of the receiving space and the types of receiving records used in two stores in your community. The stores should differ in size, type of merchandise, or ownership (chain and independent).

5 Distinguish between the direct check and the blind check methods and explain under what conditions each should be used.

6 State the procedures used in checking for quality and the person(s) who perform the quality check in (a) small stores, (b) large ones, and (c) chain stores.

7 Summarize the major requirements or essentials of an effective marking program.

8 Explain the following terms: (a) "group marking" (b) "preretailing" (c) "source marking" (d) "outside marking" (e) "re-marking."

9 Describe the major functions of a traffic department.

10 (a) What are the major differences between the receiving, checking, marking and distributing activities of single-unit and chain-store retailing companies? (b) Are there any significant trends in the way chain-store companies handle incoming merchandise functions? Explain.

■ NOTES AND REFERENCES

1 "How to Boost Profits without Boosting Prices," *Business Week,* March 31, 1973, pp. 100–101. But some food chains are shifting warehousing and distribution functions to suppliers. See Murray S. Abott, "Who Will Own the Warehouse?" *Supermarket News,* July 21, 1975, pp. 2, 11.

2 "Effective Distribution Center Keeps Liberty House First," *Stores,* August 1975, p. 11; A. Donald Bird, *Merchandise Distribution Systems for Mass Retailers* (New York: Mass Retailing Institute, 1975), p. 23.

3 "They're Highballing Hangware," *Chain Store Age* (Executives edition), March 1972, pp. E54–E61.

4 Robert E. Veale, "Systems Approach Solves Garment-Handling Problem," *Material Handling Engineering,* April 1974.

5 Jack Brill, "The Use of EDP in Receiving and Marking," *Retail Control,* March 1974, pp. 10–19; Robert M. Zimmerman, "Automated Purchase Order Management," *Retail Control,* January 1976, pp. 54–59.

6 "Tag Is a Profit Game for Ticketing Companies," *Women's Wear Daily,* June 18, 1973, p. 15.

7 Approximately 95 percent of Montgomery Ward's clothing is vendor-marked, as well as a growing share of other lines. T. J. Hills, "Vendor Marking Today," *Stores,* January 1976, pp. 6, 31–32.

8 For a cost comparison, *see* Norman Weiser, "Universal Vendor Marking: Costs and Benefits," *Retail Control,* February 1975, pp. 54–64.

9 "Traffic Management," *Stores,* February 1976, p. 27. Of course, differences in shipping costs between slow and fast services must be balanced against the benefits of speed in transport.

10 Considerable money can sometimes be saved by checking freight bills for overcharges. *See* "Cut Needless Freight Costs by Checking Bills for Errors," *Hardware Retailing,* October 1975, p. 134.

11 *See* "Freight Damage," *Home Furnishings Daily,* December 16, 1971, pp. 4–5, 18; "Stores, Makers Blame Carriers for Damage," *Home Furnishings Daily,* June 20, 1972, p. 13.

12 For examples, *see* "A Mechanized Giant," *Supermarket News,* February 26, 1973, pp. 1, 28–29; "Mechanization," *Supermarket News,* August 25, 1975, pp. 1, 20–23; "What's New in Warehousing," *Hardware Retailing,* July 1975, pp. 56–62.

13 "Distribution: Filling the Pipeline," *Chain Store Age* (General merchandise/variety edition), December 1973, p. 120.

14 Robert Booker with John McDonald, "The Strategy That Saved Montgomery Ward," *Fortune,* May 1970, p. 169.

PRICING

Sound pricing decisions are essential in retail businesses since: (1) Merchants depend upon the prices they charge to (a) cover the cost of their merchandise, (b) pay most of their expenses, and (c) provide most of their profit. They often receive some funds from other sources, such as service charges to customers, rental of space for leased departments, and income from outside investments. But normally merchandise sales provide most of the revenue. (2) The customers' opinions concerning a store's prices—whether they consider it to be expensive or inexpensive —will help determine whether they patronize it or someplace else. Thus prices must appeal to customers, cover expenses, and maximize profits.*

This calls for sound judgment in making two types of pricing decisions discussed in this chapter. (1) The first type concerns general price policy. The retailer has to decide on a general price level in relationship to competition; whether to follow a "one-price" policy; and whether to organize prices into price-lines. Then (2) the retailer (or store employees) must price the individual items in conformance with these general policies. Sometimes the supplier establishes the retail price for a product, and in such cases the retailer can only decide whether or not to handle the item at the specified price. (See the discussion of suggested prices

---

* Of course, a retailer (like every other business person) also has other goals in mind, such as company growth and the firm's prestige in the community.

and resale price maintenance, Chapter 17.) In most instances however, the retailer is the one who sets the final resale price, and consequently must consider the factors discussed on the following pages.

■ GENERAL PRICE POLICIES

The general price policies that merchants adopt will be influenced by (a) the customers (the market) to whom they hope to appeal, (b) the character of the stores they plan to operate (which also should be related to the market), and (c) competition. Moreover, making the right decisions involves as much judgment and artistry as science, but the aim should always be to further the long-run objectives of the business. We will briefly examine all of these elements of pricing.

☐ The market

Some consumers are much more price conscious than others. One might expect low-income consumers to be more sensitive to price than high-income ones, but this is not always the case. Sometimes lower-income buyers may necessarily be more interested in the availability of credit or other services rather than price. Customer awareness of, and interest in, price may also vary with education, occupation, age, type of goods involved and other factors.[1] Therefore, retailers should watch how potential and/or present customers seem to respond to various pricing and service practices in their stores and in competitive outlets.

☐ Consistency in the marketing mix

Price policies should be consistent with the other parts of the store's marketing mix—its merchandise, decor, advertising, and services. For example, shoppers will doubt that a supermarket is following a low-price policy, even though it actually charges less than competition, if it also differs from those stores by providing more services, having more modern fixtures and giving trading stamps.[2] A retailer who plans to charge relativley high prices will have to offer the atmosphere, merchandise, convenience and/or services that will make those prices acceptable to potential customers. This requires deciding which services will be subject to extra charge and which ones will be included in the price of the merchandise. (See the discussion of "free" and "fee" services in Chapter 21.)

☐ Long-run point of view

The retailer should also always maintain a long-run point of view in pricing. Upon opening a business, a merchant may plan to sell at very low prices for the first few months in order to build up trade. Short-run earnings will suffer as a result of this policy, but it may attract enough customers and build sufficient repeat business to maximize profits in the long run.

Price level and maximum profits Even in the long run the retailer may want to keep prices at a fairly low level. Selling at high prices does not necessarily produce maximum profits. Profits result from the relationships among sales, prices, costs of merchandise, and expenses of operation. Sometimes these factors will indicate that raising prices will improve profits, but other times they will show that lowering prices will improve earnings.

To illustrate, a retailing company follows a high-price policy and consequently only attracts those customers who find its location or merchandise especially appealing. Its total annual volume is $200,000, merchandise cost $140,000, operating expenses $52,000, leaving $8,000 as net profit. But the company decides to experiment with lower prices which attract trade and gradually increase sales to $300,000 a year. Since the store receives greater discounts on its larger purchases, merchandise cost expands at a somewhat lower rate than sales, becoming $204,000 and leaving a gross margin of $96,000. Although some expenses also increase as a result of the added sales, others such as rent, heat, light, and power, remain relatively unchanged. The present employees handle part of the additional work, so payroll increases at a lower rate than sales. Consequently, operating expenses only rise to $58,000. Thus in spite of selling at lower prices, the company's profit increases from $8,000 to $28,000.

□ One-price policy

The typical North American retailer claims to follow a *one-price policy*, that is, to charge the same price to everyone who buys the same item in comparable quantities under similar conditions. If the price for a particular tennis racket is $15.00, every purchaser, regardless of who that may be, will be charged $15.00 for that racket. Of course, a one-price policy does not stop a store from having clearance sales, or special promotions. It simply means that if the store reduces its price for any item, the lower price becomes available to all customers.

This policy builds up customer confidence since no one has to worry about being charged more than someone else. It also saves a great deal of time and skill that might otherwise have to be spent in bargaining with customers. The one-price policy helps routinize sales transactions, and thus facilitates large-scale retail operations.

Actually, even though one-price policies are the general rule in the United States and Canada today, we do have more deviations from those policies than we sometimes realize. Store employees are often allowed discounts on the merchandise they buy, as noted in Chapter 9. Some druggists give physicians and nurses a special "professional" discount.[3] Occasionally, a merchant may set up a special discount arrangement for a particular group, such as the members of a sport club or the workers in a nearby factory, in hopes of obtaining a large share of their purchases.[4]

But such systematic discounts affect only a very small portion of all retail sales. Individual bargaining over "trade-in allowances," a very common practice in the sale of automobiles, electric refrigerators, radios, television sets, fine cameras, and other consumer durables, is a more important deviation from the one-price system. Bargaining and haggling often occur in the sale of durables, particularly in the automobile trade, and sometimes in furniture even when no trade-in is involved.[5] Some small and medium-sized merchants dealing in other nonconvenience goods will also occasionally "shade the price" or give the customer a discount in order to close a difficult sale.

Some merchants feel that such reductions are all right if they can be disguised. Perhaps the customer can be talked into buying two items for less than the sum of their usual prices, thus making the reduction appear to be a quantity discount. Or the retailer may claim to be planning a price reduction in the very near future and thus is merely taking the markdown a few days sooner than planned. Perhaps the customer may be told that this is an exceptional case, not to be repeated. However, the risks of becoming known as a retailer who is willing to bargain argue against the use of such practices. A one-price policy builds confidence and successful retailing is built on confidence.

☐ Range of prices

Another policy decision, closely related to merchandising decisions, concerns the range of prices in the store. Will there be "something for everyone," ranging from relatively inexpensive merchandise to deluxe high-priced goods. A very large store can do this relatively easily in some merchandise lines, by grouping different price levels in different departments. It may sell budget dresses in one department, medium-priced and better models in another, and expensive designer clothes in a third section. Most merchandise categories do not generate sufficient sales volume to warrant creating several price-based departments, and even large establishments find that an attempt to cover too extensive a range can give customers a confusing store image. As a result, most merchants will tend to concentrate on a limited price/quality range.*

---

* Note that a decision on the price-quality range does not necessarily determine where the store stands in relation to its competitors. For example, some stores, particularly in large cities, specialize in offering high-style clothing at a saving. These stores normally provide very little service and have an unattractive atmosphere. Their prices

Single-price policy   The narrowest possible price range is called a single-price policy. Under this policy a store sells all of its merchandise of a given type at the same price. Generally stores that follow this practice emphasize that price in their advertising and sales promotion. Thus a specialized men's necktie store might advertise that its entire stock of ties are priced at $1.50. This approach is usually only suitable to stores with inexpensive merchandise, since it focuses attention upon price, and is a difficult policy to maintain whenever general price levels are changing substantially. The single-price policy, which is concerned with uniformity of prices among items, should not be confused with the one-price policy, which involves uniformity of prices among customers. A single-price policy is the extreme form of price living, described immediately below.

☐ Price lines

Price lining consists of selecting certain prices and carrying assortments of merchandise only at those prices, except when markdowns are taken. For example, men's ties may be carried at $2.50, $3.50, and $5.00; and women's dresses at $22.98, $29.98, and $39.98.

Reasons for price lining   Customers desire a wide assortment when buying shopping goods (to which price lining is especially applicable) but become confused by small price differences among the various items. Confining the assortments to certain specific points reduces the confusion.

Having only a few price points helps salespeople become well acquainted with their prices and reduces mistakes. This facilitates selling and improves customer goodwill. Price lining may reduce the size of the store's inventory, increase turnover, decrease markdowns, simplify stock control, and reduce interest and storage costs. It also enables the department buyer to concentrate on items that can be sold profitably at the pre-set price levels.

Establishing price lines   Price lines[6] are usually established through a careful analysis of past sales, picking out those prices at which the bulk of the sales were made. In some cases, however, past sales are disregarded; the retailer simply selects new price lines which the salespeople are then expected to "push." Although the number of price lines needed will vary in different situations, a merchant will usually

---

are *low* compared to *other, more luxurious high-style shops,* even though the garments sell for a great deal more than the average dress or suit in a popular-priced chain store. ("High Fashion at Low Discount Prices," *Consumers Digest,* September/October 1973, pp. 21–22.) Or to cite another example, one Chevrolet dealer may charge more, less, or about the same as the other Chevrolet dealers in town, although all of them will sell new Chevrolets for less than the Cadillac dealers charge for their cars.

want at least one below and one above the basic medium-price line. One popular-priced women's sportswear chain, however, has used four price lines;[7] and a large store may find that it needs six or more price lines for such merchandise as hosiery to satisfy its customers' requirements.

Some of the advantages of price lining are lost if the price lines are not far enough apart to indicate definite differences in quality. Otherwise, the customer will still be confused with several goods selling at fairly comparable prices. The retailer should have full assortments at each price line to serve the customers attracted by that line.

Good merchants also frequently check competitors' price lines to make sure that they have not found ones with greater customer appeal. One retailer expressed the need for constant reappraisal of price lines in these words: "The price line picture can seldom be considered static; testing and checking are always helpful—above and below and in between the established price lines."[8] Similarly, faced with changed customer demands for aluminum cooking utensils, a buyer at the Denver [Colorado] Dry Goods said: "By plugging in lines at price points not previously carried, we're hoping to stay ahead of the game. . . ."[9]

Effects of general price level changes Retail merchandisers face difficult problems in maintaining traditional price lines when prices in general are changing markedly. These problems became especially troublesome in the combined inflation and recession of the mid-1970s. Normally prices rise during periods of prosperity, when most customers are willing to accept new and higher price lines if the merchant cannot secure satisfactory merchandise to sell at the old price levels. Similarly, during depressed periods when customers want to "trade down" to lower price points, most suppliers usually recognize the necessity of reducing their own wholesale charges to obtain business. In either case, some merchants will be tempted to lower the quality of each regular price line. When wholesale costs rise they will want to substitute inferior merchandise to avoid changing a traditional price point; during depressed business they will reduce quality so as to lower the retail price even more than wholesale cost has fallen. But this is generally unwise. If possible, it is better to maintain the character of the goods in a price line to preserve customer confidence in the store's offerings. This may require some upward or downward adjustment in the prices of the lines during severe inflation or deflation and it may also call for adding additional higher or lower price lines to meet changed demand. To quote a well-known commentator: "Basically, an inflationary era compels a fluid approach to price-lining and price-points."[10]

Sometimes skilled buying will permit maintenance of traditional price and quality. Faced with merchandise-cost increases in 1974, the executive vice-president of Jordan-Marsh, with stores in Boston and

Florida, said: ". . . we know the price lines we have to have [to serve our customers]. We're shifting some resources to make sure we cover those price lines."[11]

Limitations of price lining Price lining does reduce the buyer's range of alternatives in selecting goods for the store. The buyer must secure merchandise that will provide a profit when sold at the store's established price lines. This requirement can increase the difficulty of obtaining adequate assortments and more than offset whatever advantages result from only having to consider those items that fit the store's price lines. Price lining also limits the store's ability to meet competitive prices.

Still other disadvantages include (1) the danger that the price lines selected will not be suited to the preferences of customers and prospective customers, (2) the difficulty, already noted, of maintaining price lines and uniform quality during periods of changes in price levels, (3) the likelihood that price lines will multiply over a period of time, and (4) the tendency to focus attention on price rather than on the merchandise.[12] Nevertheless, price lining's advantages have resulted in widespread use of the practice in selling apparel and other shopping goods. It is not as useful, however, in selling staples such as foods and toiletries, where customers generally do not want to compare an assortment of styles, colors, or sizes at one price.[13]

□ Competitive position

The most basic pricing decisions retailers make concern the relationship between their prices and those of competitors. As one might expect, most retailers tend to set their prices close to those of their major competitors. But this statement needs two qualifications: (1) Most retailers tend to think of merchants of the *same type* as their major competitors. Thus a small independent grocer will usually consider other nearby independent grocers, rather than large supermarket chains, as the competitors whose prices must be met. (2) Retailers, such as supermarket operators, who sell wide assortments of convenience and nonshopping goods, usually will not try to match their competitors' prices item for item. They expect to be higher on some items, lower on others, and are more concerned with the general price image or impression their store reflects.

Many shopping goods retailers, on the other hand, pay strict attention to item-by-item price comparisons. Practically every department store and most large specialty store organizations employ comparison shopping staffs that check their store's prices, merchandise, and service against its competitors'. Some department store firms have decided that they will run such competitive departments as drugs and toiletries and small electric appliances at a loss, if need be, in order to compete with discount stores. Some of these department stores have even offered to give a refund to any customer who finds the same item at a lower price in any other store in town.

Pricing below competitors' level Some merchants go one step beyond simply meeting competition and actually try to undersell their competitors. Many chain store, mail order, supermarket, and discount house organizations, among others, believe in seeking their profits through the use of relatively low prices to attract a large volume of sales. The net result, of course, has been a rise in their customers' standard of living, as well as an advance in the firm's profits.

Underselling retailers usually have certain definite characteristics. They are "hard" buyers, since they must acquire their merchandise at low cost to permit the profitable use of low prices. They often operate with relatively low-cost physical facilities and they may dispense with many services that other stores offer. They frequently limit their stocks to the fast-moving items; they often use self-service or semi-self-service techniques; and credit and delivery services may be either curtailed or eliminated. These retailers are often strong advocates of private brands whose prices cannot be directly compared with competitors' offerings. And these underselling stores generally devote their advertising to announcing price "specials." Some of these characteristics are illustrated by Dollar General Stores, a successful chain headquartered in Scottsville, Kentucky. The typical small country town Dollar General store has only two employees plus an extra clerk on weekends, pays a low rent ($1.25 per square foot, or less, compared to $1.50 to $3.00 plus a percentage of sales for department and discount stores in shopping centers), uses simple fixtures made by the chain itself, and features manufacturers' closeouts and irregular merchandise.[14]

In other words, retailers who adopt a low-price policy must use consistent policies in the other aspects of their business. Those who do not will soon find themselves characterized by the sign in the window of a vacant store: "We undersold everybody."

1. *Discount house pricing* Discount stores exhibit many of the low-price retailing characteristics cited above. (See the discussion of discount stores in Chapter 1.) Some of these firms are now "trading up" and offering more elaborate facilities and services, but others have been able to keep their operating costs at relatively low levels. One study of 47 discount store firms reported a weighted average expense rate of about 25 percent of total sales in 1973–74, considerably below the 32 percent typical of similarly sized department stores.[15]

Consequently, discount stores can cover their total operating expenses and earn satisfactory profits with prices below those of many competitors. Although few careful price studies are available, the concensus is that discount store nonfood prices range from 5 to 15 percent lower than those of competing stores.[16] However, not every store that calls itself a discount outlet actually has discount prices.[17]

2. *Price wars* A price war may develop when a number of competitors try to undersell each other. The warring retailers keep reducing their prices drastically in efforts to attract each others' customers. The war will often be confined to a few fast-moving items, such as milk, cigarettes, gasoline, or bread, but those items may be reduced to one half or one third their normal price before the battle is over. For example, a milk price war developed in Sacramento, California in May 1975 when local agricultural price controls were removed.[18]

These wars end in various ways. All of the competitors may simply withdraw from the struggle when they find that their rivals quickly match their price reductions. In other cases, the retailers or their suppliers may have to take some form of joint action before prices move upward. Sometimes the retailers hold a meeting and, in effect, agree upon a truce. In other cases the suppliers have used various methods to stop the retail price cutting. Major oil companies have terminated some local gasoline price wars by supplying their gasoline to the service stations on consignment and thus retaining the right to fix final selling prices.*

Legislation has often been suggested to eliminate price wars. But one careful student of the subject—with whom the present authors concur—concludes that such a program would cause further reductions in "competitive activity in an era in which competition is, if anything, too soft."[19]

Pricing above competitors' level Other retailers regularly sell some or all of their merchandise at prices above their competitors. Retailers who follow this policy recognize that many nonprice considerations, such as those outlined below, may attract customers to their stores. These merchants often can operate their businesses successfully, in spite of charging higher prices, if they offer some of the following features.

1. *Satisfactory services* Many customers will pay somewhat higher prices in order to receive desired services. They will trade with the store that provides more helpful personal attention or that has more generous delivery, credit, and returned goods policies, even if its prices are slightly above those of its competitors. By way of illustration, many traditional department stores offer such services more liberally than do, say, Sears, Roebuck or Montgomery Ward department stores. Consequently, the operators of the conventional stores can charge somewhat higher prices

---

* Some courts have cast doubt on the legality of this technique, especially when there is any evidence (1) that dealers were coerced into accepting the new program or (2) that dealers were brought together in groups, thus implying horizontal price-fixing. *Sun Oil Co.* v. *Federal Trade Commission*, CA-7 (August 1965); *Simpson* v. *Union Oil Co. of Calif.*, 377 U.S. 21 (1964).

without losing too many of their customers to the lower-priced outlets. Similarly, one study suggests that small retail stores are more likely to build profitable trade with such service elements as "speed of service," "satisfaction of customer complaints," "management and employees' knowledge about their merchandise," and "helpful and friendly attitude of employees," than by offering low prices.[20] Similarly a luxurious display of fine furniture may also permit a premium price.[21]

2. *Prestige* A store that has historically set the standard for quality in its community may have acquired considerable prestige in the eyes of its customers. This prestige helps remove the store from direct price competition with other retailers and sometimes enables it to charge a higher price than other stores. Thus a woman's coat carrying a label from Saks Fifth Avenue, Neiman-Marcus, I. Magnin, or Marshall Field seems "different" to some customers, and might command a higher price than a similar coat sold by a less prestigious firm.

3. *Convenient location* Some people will pay a premium for the convenience of being able to shop at a handy location. Neighborhood grocery, drug, and hardware stores, for example, tend to have higher prices than the big shopping center supermarkets and discount stores, but some customers will pay a little extra rather than travel to the lower-priced outlets. A drugstore or giftshop in an airport terminal, a hamburger stand in a football stadium, or a store in an isolated community may have a virtually "captive" market because of its location, and thus be able to command unusually high prices.

4. *Extended store hours* A store that is open when the other shops are closed may be able to charge more than its early-closing competitors. Many small neighborhood shops do a large share of their business in the evening and on Sunday. Chains of "convenience stores" and "bantam superettes," that sell a limited assortment of the most popular items but that stay open very long hours, have become an important part of the grocery trade. The price advantage that comes from long hours tends to disappear, however, as more and more supermarkets, discount houses, and shopping centers stay open evenings and Sundays. (See Chapter 21.)

5. *Exclusive merchandise* An assortment of items or brands that are not available in competitive stores will also give a merchant some freedom from direct price competition. Sometimes a retailer will obtain an excusive agency for a certain manufacturer's products so as to make certain that no immediate competitors can get the same goods. A letter from a cosmetic manufacturer to a dealer in Passaic, New Jersey illustrate this type of arrangement: ". . . yours is the only outlet for [our] XYZ products in the entire city. In the entire state of New Jersey, we have no city in which more than three stores handle XYZ products, and we sell to no store known as a price cutter or with a history of price cutting. We therefore believe that you will have no problem maintaining the

full retail markup in XYZ products." Similarly, a fashion goods retailer will often try to get vendors to agree that no other store within a certain radius will be allowed to purchase the same styles.

The difficulty of escaping price competition Business people generally prefer nonprice competition to price competition because (1) they believe that customers who are attracted by nonprice factors will be more loyal than those who shop around for low prices, and (2) competitors will have more difficulty in matching nonprice factors than in meeting price changes.[22]

But a merchant can seldom completely escape price competition in spite of a preference for nonprice rivalry. A store may be able to charge somewhat higher prices because of prestige, services, location, or hours, but too broad a difference will drive customers away. In fact, any price difference causes a store to lose some customers, since there are some who have little regard for a store's services or prestige. The wider the price differences become, the more customers leave and go over to the lower-priced store. Of course, customers sometimes become suspicious of quality if prices seem too low. This is one reason why pricing calls for skill and judgment.

Moreover, it is particularly difficult to escape price competition on staple clothing, household and recreational items, and well-known brand merchandise. The thriftier buyers of these items can go from store to store and learn the prices that various retailers are asking for comparable goods. Retailers who sell style items are somewhat less likely to be affected by competitive prices since customers cannot always make direct price comparisons on these items. Paradoxically, retailers, such as supermarket firms, that sell very wide assortments of low-priced staples will also escape direct price competition on many items, since most consumers seem to select only certain key products for price shopping.

Finally, most stores find that they have some competitors who have about as much prestige and offer as many services as they do. Hence, even a relatively minor price differential between such stores may cause a fairly rapid shift of trade to the lower-priced establishment. A retailer must keep such comparable stores in mind when setting prices since there may be no opportunity to charge more than others do.

Private brands Some retailers gain a certain amount of freedom from direct competition by offering some "private" brand or label merchandise instead of manufacturers' "national" brand items.* A consumer cannot compare the values of two different private brands sold by two different retailers with anywhere near the precision that is possible in

---

* A&P's Red Circle coffee and Anne Page jellies, Sears' Allstate tires, and J. C. Penney's Towncraft shirts are examples of retailers' private brands; Maxwell House coffee, Michelin tires and Arrow shirts are examples of manufacturers' brands. Also see the discussion of retailers' and manufacturers' brands on pp. 30–31.

comparing the same two merchants' prices for a specific national brand product. Some prestige stores are able to command fairly high prices for private brands that have won consumer acceptance. For example, S. S. Pierce and Company, a famous grocery firm in Boston, has successfully sold a premium-priced line of packaged, gourmet foods under its own label for many years. The products have become so popular with consumers throughout the country that Pierce now sells the line to other stores. Similarly, Eddie Bauer, a Seattle retailer with his own prestige brand of down-filled outdoor clothing and camping equipment, now has outlets in many cities.

But most private label grocery, toiletry, electric appliance, staple clothing, and similar lines normally sell at lower retail prices than comparable national brands.[23] Chain store firms and other leading users of private brands follow this policy for several reasons. (1) Consumers usually will not pay as much for a store-brand product as for a well-known, well-advertised national brand. In fact, many customers will select a national brand in preference to a private one in spite of a price differential. Private brands, for example, probably account for only about 15 percent of all chain store grocery sales.[24] (2) Low prices for the store's own brands, not available in competitive outlets, help build strong ties with the store's customers. One chain store merchant who features low-priced private brands says: "I think our private label mix has helped to reinforce our fair price-quality image. It strengthens our overall identity with the public."[25] (3) Private label merchandise usually costs retailers substantially less than comparable nationally branded goods. Consequently, they often receive much greater margins from the private brand items in spite of their lower selling prices. One chain was able to sell its own brand of paper towels for about five cents less per roll than comparable national brands and still obtains a 30 percent markup (difference between cost and selling price) as compared to 10 or 12 percent on the national brands.[26]

☐ Pricing as an art

Successful retail price setting is an art as well as a science. Formulas and general price policies provide a basis for price making, but any experienced merchant will then use judgment, intuition, and trial and error to adjust the resultant prices. Even so, one cannot be absolutely certain as to how customers will react to any specific price. Sometimes raising the price will make the item more appealing to the customers, in other instances a reduction may be needed to move the goods.[27] But over time successful merchants develop a "feel" or judgmental sense for the prices that are appropriate to their cost, market and competitive situations. In the pages that follow, we will look first at markup, which is an arithmetical way of expressing the relationship between merchandise cost (to the store) and retail price. Then we will turn to the judgmental factors that make setting individual prices an art rather than an exact science.

■ MARKUP

The concept of markup plays an important role in the retailer's thinking, both in deciding on general price policies and in setting prices for specific items. Markup formulas are often used to compute prices, and to help determine whether prices will cover operating costs. But we must remember that the marketplace provides the final test for any pricing decision. The decision is wrong, regardless of what the formula indicates, if customers won't pay the requested amount for the item.

□ Calculating markup

"Retail markup" means the amount that is added to the cost price to arrive at the retail price, a relationship which is frequently stated in the phrase "cost plus markup equals retail." The term "markup" is used to refer to the difference between merchandise costs and prices for an entire store, a department, or an individual product. This amount may be expressed in dollars. For instance, an item costing $.80 and sold for $1.20 carried a markup of $.40. More commonly, markup is discussed as a percentage, either of the merchandise cost or of the retail selling price. Therefore, in this case, the 40-cent markup can be calculated as either 50 percent of cost ($.40/$.80) or 33⅓ percent of selling price ($.40/$1.20). Expressing markup as a *percentage of selling price* is the modern approach which permits direct comparison with store expenses such as rent or wages that are also usually reported as percentages of sales. (Other arguments for the use of this base result from the retail method of accounting, described in Chapter 23.) This method is used in this book unless a cost base is specifically indicated.

However, it should be clear from the above example that any particular markup percentage expressed on one base (selling price or cost) can be easily converted to a percentage expressed on the other base (cost or selling price). This does not change the dollar markup involved but simply the way it is described. Table 16–1 shows many of these equivalent relationships.

Initial markup We must also distinguish between initial markup and maintained markup or gross margin. The initial markup, also known as the "original markup" or the "markon," is the difference between the cost and the first retail price placed on the goods. Using figures cited earlier, an item costing $.80 and originally priced at $1.20 carried an initial markup of $.40, or 33⅓ percent. But, perhaps customers refused to buy this item at $1.20, and it was finally cut to $.98 before it was sold.

TABLE 16–1

Markup table*

Markup percent of selling price	Markup percent of cost	Markup percent of selling price	Markup percent of cost	Markup percent of selling price	Markup percent of cost
5.0	5.3	18.5	22.7	33.3	50.0
6.0	6.4	19.0	23.5	34.0	51.5
7.0	7.5	20.0	25.0	35.0	53.9
8.0	8.7	21.0	26.6	35.5	55.0
9.0	10.0	22.0	28.2	36.0	56.3
10.0	11.1	22.5	29.0	37.0	58.8
10.7	12.0	23.0	29.9	37.5	60.0
11.0	12.4	23.1	30.0	38.0	61.3
11.1	12.5	24.0	31.6	39.0	64.0
12.0	13.6	25.0	33.3	39.5	65.5
12.5	14.3	26.0	35.0	40.0	66.7
13.0	15.0	27.0	37.0	41.0	70.0
14.0	16.3	27.3	37.5	42.0	72.4
15.0	17.7	28.0	39.0	42.8	75.0
16.0	19.1	28.5	40.0	44.4	80.0
16.7	20.0	29.0	40.9	46.1	85.0
17.0	20.5	30.0	42.9	47.5	90.0
17.5	21.2	31.0	45.0	48.7	95.0
18.0	22.0	32.0	47.1	50.0	100.0

* To find the desired retail markup percentage in the left-hand column multiply the cost of the article by the corresponding percentage in the right-hand or cost-markup column. The result added to the cost gives the correct price.

Note: Any markup percentage can be converted from one base to the other by using one of the following formulas:

$$\text{Markup on cost} = \frac{\text{Markup on retail}}{100 - \text{Markup on retail}} \times 100$$

$$\text{Markup on retail} = \frac{\text{Markup on cost}}{100 + \text{Markup on cost}} \times 100$$

Source: National Cash Register Company, *Expenses in Retail Businesses* (Dayton, Ohio: The Company, 1961), p. 49.

The difference between the cost and the *actual* selling price, $.18, or 18.4 percent in this case, is called the "maintained markup" or "gross margin." Note that the *final* maintained markup, $.18 is expressed as a percentage of the final price, $.98.* The gross margin or maintained markup is more important than the initial markup in determining profits. In the

---

* We will use the terms "maintained markup" and "gross margin" interchangeably. Modern department store accounting, however, draws a distinction between the two. Maintained markup, under this approach, is the difference between final selling price and cost of goods *without* adjusting that cost for any cash discounts received and/or workroom or alteration costs incurred in selling those goods. Gross margin is the difference between selling price and a cost figure that has been reduced by the cash discounts taken and increased by the workroom and alteration costs the store has borne. For a discussion of which cost figure is generally more meaningful, see pp. 408–9.

preceding case, the store lost money on that particular item if its selling and handling expenses were more than 18 cents.

A buyer will normally estimate how many markdowns or reductions of this sort will have to be made during a season. The buyer will also estimate the discounts to employees and other special customers and the probable losses through pilferage and damage. Given the total of these retail reductions, a simple formula tells what initial markup is needed to obtain a desired gross margin. Using a store as an example, suppose that the proprietor determines that operating costs will be about 29 percent of sales and a 3 percent profit is desired. So a 32 percent gross margin is needed. But the total reductions (markdowns, shortages, and discounts to employees) are estimated as 6 percent of sales. Using the formula

$$\text{Initial markup percentage} = \frac{\text{Gross margin} + \text{Retail reductions}}{100 \text{ percent} + \text{Retail reductions}}$$

the proprietor arrives at the following initial markup percentage:

$$\frac{32 \text{ percent} + 6 \text{ percent}}{100 \text{ percent} + 6 \text{ percent}} = \frac{38 \text{ percent}}{106 \text{ percent}} = 35.85 \text{ percent}$$

Thus to get a gross margin of 32 percent, an initial markup of approximately 36 percent is required in this case.

Buyers frequently have to calculate retail prices from two pieces of information: (a) the *cost* of the goods, and (b) the desired markup, expressed as a percentage of the *retail* price. A typical problem might be: What retail price will give us an initial markup of 36 percent (of retail) on an item that costs us $.96? The formula that answers this is.

$$\text{Retail price} = \frac{\text{Cost}}{100 - \text{Desired markup percentage}} \times 100$$

$$= \frac{.96}{.64} \times 100 = \$1.50^*$$

Cost of merchandise Finally we have to decide exactly what do we mean by "cost," when we say that markup is the difference between the cost of merchandise and its selling price. To clarify, a supplier charges $100 for an item. However, this $100 is subject to a quantity discount of 7 percent, a cash discount of 3 percent, and a freight charge of $5. Is the

---

* Instead of using this formula, some retailers prefer to convert the markup on retail (36 percent in this case) to a markup on cost either by using a prepared conversion table, such as Table 16–1 or the formula shown on page 407. They then go through the following two additional steps: (a) the cost is multiplied by the cost-percentage markup to obtain the dollar markup, and then (b) the cost and the dollar markup are added together to determine the retail price. Although all of these methods theoretically will produce the same result, variations in rounding fractional percentages and amounts can result in slight differences.

cost of merchandise $100 (face of invoice), $105 (invoice plus transportation), $90.21 (all discounts deducted),* or some other figure? Since we want to know the exact cost of the item delivered to the store we proceed as follows: $100 minus $7 (quantity discount), minus $2.79 (cash discount), plus $5 (freight), or $95.21. In other words, "cost of merchandise" means the invoice cost of the goods minus discounts plus inward transportation paid by the retailer. A merchant who wants an initial retail markup of 40 percent on this item that had a net cost of $95.21, would price it at $158.68** (In practice, of course, that figure would normally be rounded to $159.00, $159.50, or $160.00.)

Some retailers, however, prefer to overstate the cost of their merchandise when making this sort of calculation. Then, if they use the same initial markup percentage as other retailers, they will wind up with a higher initial selling price. The merchants who want to do this determine their cost of merchandise without regard to cash discounts. Using this method in the preceding case, the cost of goods would be stated as $98.00 and the 40 percent markup would produce a price of $163.33 (which probably would be rounded to some more customary figure from $162.50 to $165.00).

Anyone who uses this method is, in a sense, "fooling himself," much like someone who sets the alarm clock ahead at night so as to make certain of getting up at the right hour in the morning.† The modern approach treats the item's true cost as being $95.21, and considers the higher price ($163.33) as providing a markup of approximately 41.7 percent. Nevertheless, a few storekeepers feel that they set more profitable prices through this device of thinking of the cost of goods as being higher than it actually is.

■ SETTING PRICES FOR INDIVIDUAL ITEMS

Retailers have only begun to solve their pricing problems when they have determined the *average* markup needed or desired for the entire store. They will seldom want to apply a uniform markup percentage throughout the store as a whole. Markups considerably below average

---

* Seven percent from $100 leaves $93. Three percent from $93 leaves $90.21.

** The difference, or dollar markup, between $95.21 and $158.68 is $63.47, which is 40 percent of the $158.68 retail price. Note that the markup is calculated as a percentage of the *retail* price.

† A more dignified way of putting it is that some store executives prefer to treat the cash discount as a financial earning, and enter it as part of "other income" on the operating statement. This is a fairly widespread practice in manufacturing industry, where cash discounts received tend to be small and cost of goods is usually only a small part of selling price. But most modern retailers consider the cash discount to be a reduction in the cost of merchandise, as shown in the first method.

may be advantageous or necessary for some departments and some items; correspondingly, other departments and items may support sub-stantially-above-average markups.

□ Impracticality of a single markup

The same markup percentage usually cannot be used for every item in the store. Goods having the same cost may differ greatly in customer appeal and consequently will permit or require very different markups. Competitors' prices and markups, which will normally vary from item to item, will influence the markup a store may take on any particular product. Some high style and perishable products may require large initial markups to offset severe markdown rates. Higher-than-average markups may be needed for some items that involve extra handling or selling costs. Even though a single average markup percentage is often a useful starting point in price calculations, determination of the actual prices for the individual items will normally require many upward and downward deviations from that average.

Using several markups Some retailers divide their stocks into several groups and apply different markup percentages to each group. This practice is one step beyond the use of a single markup for the whole store. A food retailer will realize that markdown and spoilage costs are much greater for perishable fresh fruit and vegetables than for canned goods. Competitors, who have the same problem, normally take a higher markup on fresh produce than on canned goods, and, consequently, customers expect and are willing to pay prices that include higher markups for the perishable items. Thus the food retailer may decide that a 30 percent initial markup is necessary in the produce section, whereas 20 percent will be satisfactory for canned goods. Similarly, a shopkeeper may use different markups for different women's apparel product groups. Perhaps an initial markup of 50 percent is needed for dresses and other products most subject to markdowns; more staple goods, such as nurses' and beauticians' uniforms, might be carried profitably on a 30 to 40 percent markup.

Individual item pricing But many retailers recognize that even this practice of dividing the products into different markup groups is not flexible enough to produce maximum profits. The more skillful merchants try to mark each item with the price that will have the most beneficial effect on the store's total profits, even though some individual markups that result from this process may be above or below the desired storewide average percentage.

Some large-scale retailers have undertaken careful (and costly) studies of the turnover of various items when sold at different markups. Voluntary chain wholesalers prepare price guides which suggest to their retailers the "most profitable" markups for each item they carry.[28] Some retail trade associations offer a similar service to their members.[29] These guides help the retailer develop more flexible and more effective pricing practices.

☐ Some factors influencing markup

A number of the more significant factors that influence item price and markup decisions are outlined in the following paragraphs.

Customer appeal of the goods   Anyone who is realistic will recognize that the cost of an item sometimes has little relationship to how much it appeals to customers. A merchant may purchase two dress styles at $8.75, and find that one moves readily at the regular $16.75 price; the other may hang on the rack even after being marked down to $9.75. One of the most difficult aspects of pricing is recognizing what products and prices will or will not appeal to the customers.

One successful retailer strongly urges that: "Buyers should spend enough time in the receiving room properly appraising goods in terms of *what prices they will bring.* They should also examine the merchandise in their departments rather than rely on stock figures or unit control records exclusively. They must develop a 'feel for merchandise' that tells them almost instinctively what items and styles will sell at a profit."[30]

Customer response to lower price   Different items vary in their basic appeal to customers, and they also vary in the extent to which their sales can be increased through price and markup reductions. For example, a retailer may handle two electric appliance items, both of which cost the store $70 per unit and which might normally be priced at a 30 percent markup or $100. One is a rather new specialty item that will sell in small but satisfactory quantities to a limited market of upper income customers. Reducing markup and offering the item at a lower price will not increase sales substantially. The other product has a wider market and is subject to some price cutting in competitive stores. Perhaps this item should be priced at less than the department's customary markup.* The increased sales may provide enough total dollar margin to offset both the reduction in margin per unit and the extra operating costs of increased sales.

To illustrate, the merchant might be able to sell only two units of the second item per week at the $100 price. The gross dollar margin on that product would then be $60 per week ($100 − $70 = 30 × 2 = $60). If weekly sales increase to five units when the price drops to $89, *total* dollar margin will increase to $95 ($19 × 5 units) even though the per-

---

* Economists call the first item "relatively price inelastic,". and the second one, "relatively price elastic."

centage margin falls to approximately 21.3 percent ($19 on a selling price of $89). The net profit will increase unless the extra costs of selling the three additional units are more than $35 (the increase in dollar margin).

The profitability of this approach depends upon the rate at which sales grow in response to lower prices, and the extent to which the increase in operating costs lags behind the growth in sales. Retailers sometimes underestimate the sizable addition to sales that is needed to offset a reduction in margin. In the example above, a 150 percent addition to sales produced only a 58 percent increase in total dollar margin ($35 is 58 percent of $60). And some, perhaps all or more, of that additional dollar margin would be absorbed by the extra costs of selling the increased volume. Similarly, a 66⅔ percent increase in sales is needed simply to maintain dollar margin in the case of a 10 percent price reduction on an item that normally carries a 25 percent markup. Sales may have to double or more before the reduction becomes profitable in view of the extra expense involved in increased sales.

Leader merchandising The primary motivation for the markup reductions we have just discussed is the hope of increasing sales and profits *on the items offered at low margins.* But many retailers also price some items at very low markups for the primary purpose of attracting customers who will also buy *other products* that carry higher markups. Items intentionally sold at low prices for the purpose of drawing trade to the store are often called "leaders" or "specials." Some people apply the term "loss leader" to any such item priced at less than the store's acquisition cost; other people use the same term for all trade-attracting specials offered for less than the sum of acquisition cost and the cost of handling the items. (Legal limitations on loss leaders will be discussed in the next chapter.)

Some merchants who use leaders select a few items from various departments for this purpose; others operate an entire department, such as the food section in a discount store or the restaurant in a department store, as a leader.

But in either case the theory is that the leaders will attract a large number of customers who then purchase enough other items carrying sufficiently large markups to increase the retailer's total profit. Although many stores have used leader pricing successfully, it does require considerable skill. Customers may concentrate their purchases on the price leaders rather than buying a mix of items that yield a satisfactory average markup.[31]

If a leader policy is used, the prices of other products must also be set carefully. The specials will attract price-conscious consumers. Therefore, the prices of items cannot be raised to the point where those customers become disenchanted with the nonleader merchandise. Moreover, a very large price reduction for some kinds of merchandise may repel, rather than attract, customers. As we have already noted, customers sometimes consider the price of an item to be an indication of its quality. Consequently, too large a reduction may suggest damaged or inferior goods.

Advertising value of an item or department As the last section suggests, some items are better suited than others for use as leaders. From the retailer's point of view, the most effective leader products (1) appeal to most of the store's customers and potential customers; (2) are purchased frequently, so that at any given time most of the customers will need or want the items; (3) are not so costly that they will use up most of the customer's current purchasing ability, even when sold at a reduced price, and thus discourage sales of other merchandise; and (4) have easily recognizable values. Easily identified, well-known branded products are thus often very effective leaders. Similarly, frequently visited departments that sell relatively low-unit cost items are often most suitable for leader use.

New departments and items Relatively low markups are often used to attract customers when a store expands its merchandise offerings by adding groups of items or departments that it has not handled previously. Thus a supermarket that adds a health and beauty aids department to its merchandise mix may feature some very striking "introductory specials" and may also take a relatively low markup for the entire department.

On the other hand, rather high markups may be taken on expensive items that are truly new, in the sense of their first appearance on the market; that involve a great deal of risk of nonacceptance; and that will appeal, if at all, only to non-price-conscious buyers. High fashion items and major technical innovations such as digital watches, color television and the Polaroid camera tend, when they first appear, to fall into this category.

Seasonal and fashion goods Although some pre-season "specials" (such as an August fur sale) may be used to stimulate early business, high initial markups are often placed on seasonal fashion goods at the beginning of the regular season. The eager customers who shop then may be more interested in full selection than in price reductions, while the retailer needs some extra markup to offset the risk of heavy markdowns on fashion goods. Subsequently, average markup may be lowered as the season advances.

Merchandise cost Perhaps, somewhat surprisingly, the cost of merchandise can influence the percentage markup that a product might carry. As a result of a special "buy," the retailer may be able to place a high markup on certain goods and still meet or "beat" the prices of competitors. In contrast, a high cost of merchandise may force a store to operate on a smaller markup than it deems advisable. One drug manufacturing firm has even urged retailers of its products to place smaller percentage markups on high-cost items than on those having a lower wholesale cost—its theory being that customers for expensive drugs would otherwise pay a disproportionate share of the retailer's total operating expenses.[32]

Customary prices We noted earlier that a retailer who calculated a price of $158.68 for an item through the use of a traditional markup percentage would be extremely unlikely to offer the item at that figure. Most retailers will adjust their markups to fit the prices that have become customary in their trades. $158.68 is simply not a customary price and few retailers would use it.

The extreme form of customary price is found among those products that are usually sold at only one or two specific price points. Thus, many stores sell candy bars at the conventional points of 10 and 15¢ per bar, and the candy manufacturers themselves set wholesale prices that will facilitate this sort of retail pricing. Standard price lines, such as $7, $9, and $12 in the case of men's shirts, also shape many pricing and markup decisions. However, customary prices naturally tend to lose some of their influence on both consumer and retailer decisions during periods, such as the 1970s, when price levels and costs are changing rapidly.

Odd prices Prices that end in the digits 5, 7, 8, and especially 9, such as 29¢, $6.89, $12.97, and $29.95 are often used in the retail trade instead of round number or "even" figures such as 30¢, $7, $13, and $30. Many explanations have been advanced for these odd prices. Some people claim that they force the customer to wait for change, during which time she or he may decide on additional purchases. Also, the fact that the salesperson has to make change encourages the use of the sales register to record the sale and thus reduce the risk of employee theft. However valid these arguments may have been at one time, they have much less significance today when many stores use checkout lines separate from the sales counters; when sales taxes in many states convert practically all transactions into odd amounts; and when more and more customers regularly charge most of their purchases.

The argument most frequently voiced for odd prices concerns their supposed psychological effect. It is often claimed that a price of 49¢ will move many more units of an item than a 50¢ price, either because people subconsciously consider 49¢ much smaller than 50¢ or because they believe that any item sold at 49¢ has been subject to a deep price cut while 50¢ seems to be a "regular," full price. Modern research, however, suggests that these odd prices have very little effect upon sales rates.[33] Many department stores and many manufacturers who preticket their products are now shifting toward the use of even prices.[34]

Multiple pricing The practice of quoting a special price for a number of units, for example: 25¢ each, six for $1.39, is called "multiple pricing." Many retailers find that this technique, when used either as a regular practice or during special sales, builds up the quantity sold and increases dollar margin per transaction. Nevertheless, considerable caution should be exercised in utilizing multiple pricing. It is only appropriate, as a general rule, for items that the customer will use in considerable quantities. And some customers resent the technique because they feel forced into buying more than they really want at any one time.[35]

Operating cost   As has been suggested several times in this chapter, a retailer's freedom to vary markup is determined, in part, by operating costs. That chain food stores, in general, have long undersold independent food retailers is a well-established fact.[36] While several factors are responsible for the chains' price advantage, it is quite clear that relatively low operating cost plays a major role. Departments with low expense rates can be operated profitably at a low markup; similarly, departments and items that require substantial handling, service, or selling costs need larger markups.

Competition   As has also been indicated at several points, competitive prices will often determine the markup that a store may place on some items or classifications of merchandise.

Adjusting to changing price levels   Retailers must often adjust their markups because of changes in price levels. Let us consider three simplified examples of static, falling, and rising prices. During a stable period, a retailer buys a dozen pairs of men's socks for $8 per dozen, sells them at $1 per pair, yielding $12 total sales revenue and a gross margin of $4, composed of $3 for operating cost and $1 profit. If prices remain level the socks can be replaced at $8 per dozen and the process continued. If, however, replacement cost drops to $7, an extra $1 will be available which might be used to reduce markup. Competitors who are lowering their prices and markups might well force such action. But, if instead, wholesale prices rose to $9.50 per dozen, the retailer who had stayed at the $1 per pair price on the old inventory would be without sufficient working capital to buy a replacement dozen. (Remember sales revenue $12 minus expenses $3 left only $9).

In periods of rising prices, retailers need higher than average markups to preserve their working capital, but their ability to take the extra markup depends on competitive conditions. Figure 1–3* summarizes two interesting 1975 surveys. One asked consumers how they thought their shopping habits had changed as a result of rising food prices; the other asked store managers what they thought consumers had really done. Both groups reported more coupon redemptions (really a form of leader pricing discussed in Chapter 17), and more shopping for specials (also leaders). Consumers also purchased store (private label) brands somewhat more frequently but, according to the managers, this shift was not as extensive as the shoppers claimed.

■ MARKUP SUMMARY

We can formulate the following conclusions concerning retailers' markup policies:

* See p. 8.

First, a retailer may aim at prices which are at, below, or above those of competitors.

Second, some retailers handle most of their pricing problems by using an average markup which they apply to practically everything they sell. This is most likely to be true of small specialty shops.

Third, a larger number of retailers solve their pricing problem by dividing their goods into a number of classes and applying a set markup to each particular class. These classes may be based on differences in the cost of handling the goods, variations in markdowns, differences in cost of merchandise, or some other factor. As the number of classes increases, the retailer approaches a policy of individual-item pricing.

Fourth, the great majority of retailers find it necessary to deviate widely from any rule of a set markup, even for a limited class of goods. Factors of customer appeal, competition, price lining, time of season, customary prices, odd prices, cost of merchandise, considerations of turnover, the advertising value of an item, operating cost, price maintenance by manufacturers, and government price laws, play a part in the determination of actual markups. (Price maintenance and price legislation are discussed in Chapter 17.) Retailers must remember that they are interested in *total profits,* not in profits on any particular item. Markups on specific items should be in a process of constant adjustment in an effort to reach this goal.

This constant process of adjusting markups involves constant attempts to forecast results and such predictions are often rather inaccurate. Among other things, the retailer must estimate the effect on turnover of a certain price reduction, the effect on cost if sales increase, and how markdowns will be affected by a higher or lower initial markup. All of these forecasts are subject to correction when the change is actually implemented. In other words trial-and-error adjustments are necessary. If a certain reduction in markup does not bring the expected increase in sales, the retailer should try some other markup. Correct retail pricing involves a willingness to experiment. The retailer who tries to simplify pricing by the mechanistic use of a single markup will usually lose out to more aggressive merchants.

■ REVIEW AND DISCUSSION QUESTIONS

1 If you opened a sporting goods store in your college community, what questions would you have to decide concerning your general price policy and what specific factors in your community would influence those decisions?

2 Distinguish between the short-run and the long-run points of view in pricing at retail. Provide several illustrations of situations in which short-run and long-run points of view might lead to different price decisions.

3 Why do some retailers deviate from a one-price policy? Are these reasons

sound, from a purely commercial point-of-view? Are discounts or special prices for employees, children, students, senior citizens, or other groups ethically justifiable?

4 Describe the problems that a retailer faces in trying to price above competition. What are some of the operating practices and policies that may be used to help solve those problems? (Try to provide specific examples to illustrate those solutions.)

5 Discuss considerations that affect the width of the range of prices in a store or department. What are the advantages and disadvantages of using price-lining in (a) a menswear shop? (b) in a furniture store?

6 Visit some local stores, or watch their advertising, and compare their prices for private and national brands. What factors seem to cause the price relationships that you have discovered?

7 a. How much can a buyer afford to pay for an item to retail at $75, and yet obtain a markup of at least 45 percent of retail?
   b. Eighteen coats are purchased at $66 each. If a 40 percent markup on retail is desired, what is the retail price per coat? What is the total retail of the purchase?
   c. What markup on cost equals a markup of 25 percent on retail?
   d. What initial markup is needed to yield a gross margin of 42 percent if retail reductions equal 8 percent?

8 Select one specific type of store, such as supermarkets or department stores, and try to judge which items in those stores would usually be priced at less than the stores' average markup, and which would usually be priced above. What factors explain the difference?

9 How will changing price levels, such as those experienced during periods of inflation and deflation, affect retail markups and prices?

10 State the various arguments for the use of leaders; appraise each from the point of view of (a) the exclusive women's apparel shop, (b) the service food store, (c) the neighborhood drugstore, and (d) the discount house.

11 List the prices quoted for (a) canned vegetables, (b) men's slacks, (c) women's blouses, (d) automobile batteries, or (e) deodorants, in various retailers' advertisements in several issues of your local newspaper. Which of these are "odd" and which are "even" prices? Can you find any "customary" prices?

12 Why is pricing "as much of an art as a science?"

■ NOTES AND REFERENCES

1 K. B. Monroe, "Buyers' Subjective Perceptions of Price," *Journal of Marketing Research,* vol. 10 (February 1973), p. 71, cites conflicting research studies on price-consciousness.

2 F. E. Brown and A. Oxenfeldt, *Misperceptions of Economic Phenomena* (New York: Sperr & Douth, Inc., 1972), pp. 61–65.

3 Thomas E. Coleman, *Profitable*

Drugstore Management (Englewood Cliffs, New Jersey: Prentice-Hall, Inc., 1970) pp. 84, 86, 98.

4 "D. C. Stores Standing Firm Against Discount Pressure," *Home Furnishings Daily,* February 29, 1972, p. 2.

5 Warren Boroson, "What New Cars Really Sell For," *Money,* May 1975, pp. 30–33; Joy Browne, *The Used Car Game* (Lexington, Mass.: Lexington

Books, 1973); "Appliance Trade-Ins Increasing," *Home Furnishings Daily,* April 20, 1976, p. 1.

6   On this subject, *see also* the discussion of "Planning Price Lines," in J. W. Wingate, E. O. Schaller and F. L. Miller, *Retail Merchandise Management* (Englewood Cliffs, N.J.: Prentice-Hall, Inc. 1972), pp. 96–111.

7   *Women's Wear Daily,* October 13, 1965, p. 52.

8   F. S. Hirschler, "Price Lines and Price Lining," *The Buyer's Manual,* 4th ed. (New York: National Retail Merchants Association, 1965), p. 125.

9   J. Sebastian Sinial, "Denver Hunts a Magic Price Point," *Home Furnishings Daily,* January 13, 1975, p. 38.

10   E. B. Weiss, "Pricing Lining under Inflation," *Stores,* October 1974, p. 40. Also, "Coping with Traditional Price Points," *Stores,* May 1976, p. 40.

11   "How to Keep Quality and Markup as Well," *Women's Wear Daily,* April 4, 1974, p. 12.

12   Wingate, Schaller and Miller, *Retail Merchandise Management,* pp. 98–100.

13   Benson P. Shapiro, "The Psychology of Pricing," *Harvard Business Review,* vol. 46, no. 4 (July-August 1968), pp. 14–25 ff.

14   "How Dollar General Sells Cheaper than Anyone," *Business Week,* July 21, 1975, pp. 72–73.

15   Wendell Earle and Willard Hunt, *Operating Results of Self-Service Discount Department Stores, 1973–74* (Ithaca, New York: Cornell University, 1974), p. 51. The discount and department store figures are not directly comparable, however, since the two types of stores handle somewhat different merchandise assortments with the discount stores receiving a greater portion of their sales in relatively low expense lines. Also leased departments (whose expenses are only partially included in the store expense report) play a much more important role in discount than in department stores.

16   *See* Rachel Dardis and Louise Skow, "Price Variations for Soft Goods in Discount and Department Stores," *Journal of Marketing,* vol. 33, no. 2 (April 1969), pp. 45–50; "As Inflation Slows, Some Prices Fall," *New York Times,* March 23, 1975, section 3, p. 1.

17   *See* W. A. Smallbrook and U. C. Toensmeyer, "Analysis of Prices among Discount Food Stores," *Journal of Food Distribution Research,* September, 1973, pp. 43–46.

18   "Decontrolled-Milk Test Seen Starting Sacramento Price War," *Supermarket News,* May 5, 1975, p. 81. *See also* "Supermarket Pricing, The Gloves Come Off," *Business Week,* April 5, 1976, pp. 26–27.

19   Ralph Cassady, Jr., "Price Warfare—A Form of Business Rivalry," in *Theory in Marketing,* 2d ed., Reavis Cox, Wroe Alderson, and S. J. Shapiro, eds. (Homewood, Ill.: Richard D. Irwin, Inc., 1964), p. 379. *See also* Cassady, "The Price Skirmish—A Distinctive Pattern of Competitive Behavior," *California Management Review,* vol. 7 (Winter 1964), pp. 11–16.

20   Hal Pickle, Royce Abrahamson, and Alan Porter, "Customer Satisfaction and Profit in Small Business," *Journal of Retailing,* vol. 46, no. 4 (Winter 1970–71), pp. 38–49.

21   "Number Plus Pricing Growing: Stores Split," *Home Furnishings Daily,* April 1, 1974, p. 7.

22   *See* Jules Backman, *Advertising and Competition* (New York: New York University Press, 1970), p. 3.

23   John E. Swan, "Price-Product Performance Competition Between Retailer and Manufacturer Brands," *Journal of Marketing,* vol. 38, no. 3 (July 1974), pp. 52–59.

24   "Finds Private Label Tapering Despite Favorable Conditions," *Supermarket News,* August 5, 1974, p. 6. In contrast, Sears, Roebuck & Co. and Montgomery Ward & Co. report that private brands produce more than 90 percent of their total sales of branded merchandise.

25   "Behind the Private Label," *Chain Store Age* (supermarket executive edition), August 1968, p. 57. *See also* "Who Will Buy My Beautiful Label?" *Supermarketing* (August 1970), pp. 7–8.

26   "Trends in Share of Private Label," *Progressive Grocer,* July 1968, pp. 56–57. Many private brands, of course, are manufactured by firms selling na-

tionally advertised brands. For example, see the packaging of physically identical evaporated milk under private labels and its own label by the Borden Company. "Legal Developments in Marketing," *Journal of Marketing,* vol. 29, no. 3 (July 1965), pp. 67–68. While sometimes the merchandise sold under the two kinds of brands is quite comparable, in other instances there are significant quality differences.

27 Numerous studies of the effects of prices on consumers' evaluation of quality are summarized and criticized in Kent B. Monroe, "Buyers' Subjective Perceptions of Price," *Journal of Marketing Research,* vol. 10, no. 1 (February 1973) pp. 72–74.

28 An illustration of such a guide for food retailers is given in "A Pricing Program for Profit Makers," *Voluntary and Cooperative Groups Magazine,* April 1969, p. 28.

29 *See* The National Retail Hardware Association's *Stock Selection Guide,* as described in R. R. Mueller, "Shortest Route to Increased Profits," *Hardware Retailer,* December 1965, p. 15.

30 Morey Sostrin, "Merchandising to a Profit," *The Buyer's Manual,* 4th ed. (New York: National Retail Merchants Association, 1965), p. 282.

31 "Shopper Habits, Product Mix Shifts May Bring Higher Margins on Staples," *Supermarket News,* November 18, 1974, p. 1.

32 A prescription price study that found pharmacists using a high percentage markup on low wholesale cost items is reported in J. F. Cady and A. R. Andreasen, "Price Levels, Price Practices and Price Discrimination in a Retail Market for Prescription Drugs," *Journal of Consumer Affairs,* vol. 9, no. 1 (Summer, 1975), pp. 33–48.

33 Andre Gabor and C. W. J. Granger, "Price Sensitivity of the Consumer," *Journal of Advertising Research,* vol. 4, no. 4 (December 1964), pp. 40–44; Robert J. Holloway, "Experimental Work in Marketing," in F. M. Bass, C. W. King and E. A. Pressemeir, eds., *Applications of the Sciences in Marketing Management* (New York: John Wiley & Sons, Inc., 1968), pp. 393–94; David M. Georgoff, *Odd-Even Retail Price Endings* (East Lansing: Bureau of Business and Economic Research, Michigan State University, 1972).

34 For a contrary trend, the use of odd prices such as $4.27 in hopes of reducing attention to price increases, *see* "Odd Pricing is Expected to Cushion Mattress Pad Hike," *Home Furnishings Daily,* February 26, 1973, p. 1.

35 *See* "Multi Methods for Dual Pricing," *Supermarket News,* March 23, 1970, p. 14.

36 J. M. Carman and K. P. Uhl, *Phillips and Duncan's Marketing Principles and Methods,* 7th ed. (Homewood, Ill.: Richard D. Irwin, Inc., 1973), p. 208.

PRICING (continued)

In this chapter, we continue our discussion of retail pricing with emphasis on (1) price adjustments and reductions, and (2) legislation affecting pricing policies and practices.

■ PRICE CHANGES

Prices are constantly on trial, and often must be adjusted to meet changing conditions. Most price changes are decreases, referred to as "markdowns," but there may also be some advances or "additional markups." The pronounced effect that such price changes can have on retail earnings is illustrated by the fact that 1974 markdowns in department stores (not counting discounts to employees or stock shortages) averaged 8.93 percent of sales, compared to pretax profits of 4.97 percent.[1] Of course, markdowns in fashion departments and stores were considerably above the 8.38 percent overall average figure.

□ Markdowns

Retail accounting usually expresses total markdowns as percentages of net sales. Consequently, for purposes of *internal control and analysis,* a price reduction on an individual item is usually also stated as a percentage of the new and lower (actual selling) price. To illustrate, reducing a $50 dress to $40 is considered to be a 25 percent markdown.* Mark-down percentages are thus computed through use of the following formula:

$$\text{Markdown percentage} = \frac{\text{Dollar markdown}}{\text{New (or actual) selling price}} \times 100$$

Causes of markdowns Some markdowns result from buying and pricing mistakes. Buying mistakes are illustrated by the men's clothing merchant who added a line of male cosmetics that did not appeal to customers, and by the womenswear dealer who reordered many items too close to Easter—an error often described as "going to the well once too often." Pricing mistakes also occur because it is impossible to set exactly the right price on every item flowing through the store. The original prices are really only estimates of what the customers will pay for the merchandise. If experience proves that the original estimate is too high, markdowns are necessary.

However, a markdown does not necessarily indicate that the original asking price was wrong, or that the store buyer was at fault. Perhaps wholesale prices have declined, so competitors who bought later have lower costs for the merchandise and are charging lower prices. Newer, more stylish, or more acceptable products may have come on the market since the goods being marked down were purchased. Other markdowns must be taken because the goods have become shopworn. Even more importantly—in fact, it is one of the major reasons for markdowns—products may be reduced in price to provide attractive promotional or "sale" merchandise.

Some markdowns result from a policy of deliberately purchasing more items than the store expects to sell at full price in order to have a good assortment on hand throughout the selling season. Often the retailer is not sure which particular items in a shipment of fashion goods will sell well. Consequently the merchant may decide to place a fairly high initial markup on all the dresses, for example, and later use a mark-down to clear out those that remain.

Likewise, retailers of seasonal goods often find that they must mark down the stocks of those goods remaining at or near the end of the season. Perhaps a large number of summer suits have been purchased, but because the weather has been cold and rainy, most are still in stock at the end of July. A drastic markdown may be the only way to move them.

---

* Of course, from the customer's viewpoint, this is only a 20 percent reduction and it should not be advertised or announced to customers as more than a 20 percent price cut. This figure, which expresses the relationship of the reduction to the *former* retail price, is called "the off-retail percentage," and represents the way in which the consumer looks at the price change. The markdown percentage, which expresses the relationship of the reduction to the *new* price, is only used for the retailer's own analytical and record-keeping purposes.

Salespeople sometimes cause markdowns when they take the line of least resistance and merely show customers what they ask to see. As a result, other goods may lie in stock until the regular selling season is past. Other salespeople may be too aggressive and get customers to take several items home "on approval." Markdowns may be necessary when some of these goods are returned to the store, especially if the merchandise has been damaged or if sales were lost while the goods were out of stock.

Every store gradually accumulates "odds and ends." If it carries men's shirts, the blue ones may sell well while some of the grays remain in stock; or by chance, most of the customers may need 14½ and 15½ collar sizes and not 15 and 16. A fabric store will accumulate a large number of small pieces of cloth that remain on each bolt. Substantial markdowns are usually required in order to sell these odds and ends.

Finally, poor stock control also causes markdowns. A retailer who does not keep proper records and use them conscientiously will not have adequate warning of items that have become "slow sellers" or of seasonal stocks that are not selling according to plan. Some large retailers now use electronic equipment to provide such information quickly and economically and thus reduce the markdowns that are attributable to inadequate recordkeeping. (See the discussion of electronic data processing in Chapters 14 and 25.)

Markdowns are necessary and useful   The factors discussed above make markdowns inevitable and even useful. The successful retailer regards them as tools for keeping merchandise inventory attractive and saleable, for meeting competition and for promoting sales. Markdowns should be planned as part of the store's budget. (See "Planned reductions," pp. 274–75.) In fact the non-foods merchandiser for a successful West Coast grocery chain criticizes many supermarket firms for failing to include a sufficient allowance for markdowns in their initial markup on textile products. Consequently they retain too much out-of-style and out-of-season merchandise at full price and damage their store image.[2] Similarly, a senior executive in an East Coast discount chain says:

A buyer with minimal or no markdowns is a *poor* performing buyer. A buyer must be a risk-taker. . . . A man who experiments, looks for new items and ideas—with no markdowns, he's not performing that function.[3]

"Promotional markdowns" are undertaken to draw trade, and are a normal competitive device, particularly for stores that follow a policy of trying to undersell the market (as discussed in the preceding chapter) or during periods when business has been disappointing.[4]

Of course merchants must also avoid taking more markdowns than needed to accomplish their merchandising and competitive objectives. A survey of men's clothing stores found that the most profitable establishments had only an average initial markup, but suffered less than average markdowns.[5]

Timing of markdowns Merchants disagree as to the best time to take markdowns. Some retailers delay markdowns in the hope of additional sales at the original prices. This policy can be more suitable to a downtown store that attracts a transient (and hence, less frequent) trade than for a suburban store that relies on frequent visits from its regular customers. Other retailers only take markdowns during two or three large sale events each year; these yearly clearance sales become established in the minds of economy-conscious customers and serve to unload the shelves of the least desirable merchandise. Exclusive shops may delay taking markdowns to discourage bargain hunters and to preserve the store "image." Alternatively, they may take markdowns early and still avoid large numbers of bargain hunters by placing the garments in the next lower price line without indicating that reductions have been made.

But the great majority of successful retailers believe that markdowns should be taken early. This policy makes room for a steady flow of new goods to the store and thus keeps stocks fresh. It reduces the size of the markdowns needed to move the merchandise, since the goods will lose more of their appeal or become more shopworn as time goes on. It also avoids the cost of special sales.[6] Thrifty buyers are encouraged to visit the store regularly if some marked-down goods are always available.

1. Some general rules on timing Some retailers have set general rules to insure that markdowns are taken early enough to obtain their full advantages. They insist that a markdown should be taken as soon as sales of a fashion item begin to fall off; that is, as soon as the peak of the fashion cycle has been reached, if the store has any appreciable quantity of the item on hand. Staples are marked down before they have been in stock long enough to become shopworn. Seasonal fashion goods must be sold before the end of the season. This rule requires that the retailer take inventory as soon as the season's first rush of business ends and judge whether the stock will sell out at the original prices; if not, markdowns are in order. For instance, although many men's winter suits are sold in the months after Christmas, the majority of clothing stores reduce prices on such goods immediately after the first of the year. Figure 17–1 shows the customary dates for seasonal clearances.

But even aggressive retailers disagree about markdown policy for seasonal goods of a staple nature. Toys not sold this Christmas may be sold next year. Marbles not moving this spring may find buyers next spring. Is it better to clear these goods out at markdown prices and begin with a new stock next season, or is it better to carry the merchandise until next year? There is no one "correct" answer to this question. Holding the goods may be profitable if the retailer has available space. However,

FIGURE 17–1   A shopping calendar: When to look for sales

	J	F	M	A	M	J	J	A	S	O	N	D
Accessories	●							●				
Major appliances										●	●	
Baby needs	●				●			●		●		●
Bedding	●	●				●	●	●				
China and glassware			●									
Drugs and cosmetics	●											
Fabrics and notions	●	●		●			●					
Floor coverings	●	●				●						
Furniture	●	●				●	●	●				
Furs	●	●						●			●	
Garden supplies			●									
Home furnishings	●	●			●							
Hosiery		●				●						
Housewares			●		●							
Jewelry, diamonds	●			●								
Lingerie and sleepware	●			●		●						
Luggage	●				●							
Men's and boys' wear	●	●			●	●						
Outdoor furniture				●								
Outerwear										●		
Resort and cruise wear	●											●
Silverware											●	
Sports goods									●			
Stationery	●						●					
TV and radios	●											
White goods	●				●		●	●				
Women's apparel	●				●							

this practice ties up some funds; it involves storage costs; employees must spend time packing the goods away; and the merchandise may suffer some breakage or other damage. In view of these disadvantages, it is often better to sell the goods out if this can be accomplished by means of a moderate reduction.

2. *Automatic markdowns*   There is a tendency today toward taking markdowns earlier than ever before. Fashion merchandise retailers, who must keep their goods moving out of their stores, may follow a policy of lowering the price of any garment in stock for four weeks. A few of them have even adopted an automatic markdown plan which controls both the amount of the markdowns and the time when they take place. This policy is epitomized in the basement store of William Filene's Sons Company of Boston, where all merchandise that remains unsold after 12 selling days is repriced at 75 percent of its original price; after six more days, at 50 percent; after another six days, at 25 percent; and after a final six days, is given to charity.[7] This program has given the Filene basement a large, loyal following among bargain-minded customers. Most other stores that have tried similar methods have not pursued them as conscientiously as Filene's and have not been as successful. Generally retailers want more flexibility than the automatic plan provides.

Size of the markdowns   Table 17–1 makes it evident that markdowns vary widely from one merchandise line to another. For individual items the range would naturally be much more than that indicated by the table.

To be effective, a markdown must be large enough to induce customers to buy the product. Marking a skirt down from $16.75 to $15.75

TABLE 17–1

Typical markdown percentages for selected departments of department stores with total sales in excess of $1 million, 1974 (net sales = 100 percent)			
NRMA departmental classification number	*Department*	*Upstairs store*	*Downstairs store*
1100	Women's, misses and juniors coats	17.2	15.9
1500	Dresses	19.6	19.0
2900	Women's footwear	16.4	11.6
3200	Men's clothing	14.3	10.8
3500	Men's furnishings	8.0	9.3
5910	Cosmetics, perfume and toiletries	1.8	n.a.
7100	Furniture and bedding	8.4	n.a.
8200	Major appliances	4.9	n.a.
9610	Apparel fabric	15.7	n.a.

n.a., not reported due to the small number of stores with basement departments in these classifications. Figures include employee discounts.
Source: Jay Scher, *Merchandising and Operating Results of Department and Specialty Stores 1974*, New York: Financial Executives Division, National Retail Merchants Association, 1975.

is probably not adequate, since most people who are willing to pay $15.75 will usually also pay $16.75. Perhaps a reduction to $12.75 is needed to reach the desired number of people. The old retail adage that "the first markdown is the least costly" is still true. Put another way, any merchant who wants to clear stock, should not nibble away at the price by small successive reductions; the major correction should generally be made in one step.

Of course, the ideal markdown is the one that is just enough to sell the goods under consideration. But defining the "ideal" is quite different from deciding what is ideal in a specific case. The retailer must take into account not only tangible factors such as quantity of merchandise on hand and rate of movement but also such intangibles as how competitors will respond to a price cut and how customers who bought at the higher price will react.

The size of the markdown necessary to sell the merchandise involved is also related directly to the promotional effort put forth by the retailer and the selling effort made by sales personnel. A "P.M." with a moderate markdown may move more merchandise than a larger markdown without an incentive to the sales staff. A "P.M." is a small cash payment or bonus given to salespeople for selling specific items. See p. 237.

Price lining and markdowns   Markdowns on price-lined merchandise are handled in two ways. The usual policy is to reduce the item to at least the next-lower-price line. Some retailers state this general rule as "the next lower *active* price range." What they mean is that the merchandise must go into a price line where goods are selling in considerable volume. This policy keeps the price structure simple, so that the customer is not confused; and it also automatically determines the extent of the markdown.

The second policy uses special price lines, for marked-down goods only, located between the regular price points. It is argued that this policy minimizes the size of the reductions that the store has to take. The marked-down merchandise is also more clearly distinguishable from the regular-priced goods, and consequently may sell out rapidly. Furthermore, segregating the price-reduced merchandise from the regular lines helps build up the idea that each price line stands for a certain quality. Adding marked-down items to an established, regular price line reduces that line's homogeneity.

Publicizing markdowns   The promotional attention that will be given to a markdown will depend upon (a) the quantity of goods involved, (b) the reason for the markdown, and (c) the image the store wishes to have its advertising reflect. (See the discussion of promotional advertising in Chapter 18.) Normally advertising and window display space will not be used to announce markdowns that have been taken on isolated odds and ends of merchandise that have become soiled, shopworn, or somewhat out-of-date. The space is too expensive to use for this purpose and customers might be misled into expecting the store to have more reduced-price merchandise than is actually available. However a catalog-type listing of these items may be used, particularly in the clothing and furniture trades, if a considerable quantity of miscellaneous reduced-price merchandise is being offered during a clearance sale. In contrast, mark-downs taken for leader purposes will be vigorously publicized to attract the largest possible customer traffic. Also, some advertising may be necessary if the store has a considerable inventory of any marked-down items. Beyond this, merchants vary in the extent to which they want to feature price in their advertising, since this will strongly influence the way in which customers think of the store. Some retailers want to develop reputations for low prices and aggressive price cutting, others feel that emphasis upon marked-down items will detract from their image of quality and style leadership.

1. Coupons Some retailers and many manufacturers, particularly in the grocery trades, stimulate sales through the use of coupons that entitle the holder to a special price reduction when presented in the store. Manufacturers distributed about 16.8 billion coupons in 1970 and 29.8 billion in 1974, while the use of coupons by retailers probably increased at an even greater rate.[8] About 65 million coupons were circulated in Canada in 1974, an increase of 20 million over the preceding year.[9] Chicago supermarkets used manufacturers' coupons as weapons during a 1975 price war by offering to give customers extra or "bonus" discounts for each coupon redeemed in addition to the manufacturer's planned allowance.[10]

These coupons are sometimes included in newspaper or magazine advertising or they may be distributed by direct mail. Usually they are valid only on purchases of specific items, and in most such instances the manufacturers of those items reimburse the stores for the coupons they have redeemed. Although the work of handling any one coupon may seem trivial, the task of collecting, redeeming, assorting, and returning the enormous volume of coupons to the manufacturers is quite burdensome to retailers. The grocery industry and allied firms have taken some steps to reduce or reimburse the retailers' expenses. The A. C. Nielson Company, a marketing research firm, maintains a coupon clearing house that receives the coupons in bulk from stores and then sorts and presents them to participating manufacturers for repayment. The manufacturers also pay the stores a handling fee which covers at least part of their clerical costs in processing coupons. In 1974, Proctor and Gamble, a major issuer of coupons, raised the handling fee to five cents per coupon. The previous rate had been three cents.[11] Finally, grocery manufacturers are printing Universal Product Code (UPC) symbols on many of their coupons to make them compatible with the new electronic checkout equipment discussed in Chapter 14.

The U.S. Federal Trade Commission has issued guidelines for manufacturers using "cents-off" coupons, but the FTC rules may have discouraged honest use of the coupon promotions without detering any dishonest use.[12]

2. *Sale prices on price tickets* As noted, one technique for demonstrating markdowns to the customers is to draw a heavy line through the original price on the price ticket and enter the new one above it in different colored ink. Some merchants oppose this practice and, for three reasons, insist that new tickets be made out for each price change because (1) they feel that the altered tickets detract from the store atmosphere and create a cheap image, particularly when goods have been through two or three successive reductions; (2) requiring new tickets insures that unauthorized employees or customers will not alter the marked price to benefit themselves or friends; (3) some markdowns will go unrecorded if price changes can be made right on the selling floor. Insisting that new tickets be attached by marking room personnel insures that a record will be made. The markdown price tickets can be printed on different colored paper if the store wants to draw attention to its sale items.

Recording markdowns　There are several reasons for maintaining a record of all markdowns. Perhaps most important, a knowledge of past markdowns is essential for intelligent decisions about initial markup. The formula for initial markup, as noted in Chapter 16, is:

$$\text{Initial markup percentage} = \frac{\text{Percent gross margin} + \text{Percent retail reductions}}{100 \text{ Percent} + \text{Percent retail reductions}}$$

A retailer may estimate that a 30 percent gross margin is needed to cover estimated operating expenses of 26 percent and a desired 4 percent net profit. But the initial markup needed to provide this gross margin cannot be established until a figure for retail reductions is calculated. And the markdown rate is a major component of the retail reduction figure.

Information on markdowns is also important as a check on pilferage. Assume that, in the case mentioned in the preceding paragraph, 7 percent is allowed to cover these retail reductions (markdowns, stock shortages, discounts to employees, and others) making the initial markup 34.58 percent. Of this 7 percent figure, 2 percent is intended to cover stock shortages. However, gross margin at the end of the period is only 28 percent rather than the desired 30 percent. With records of markdowns and discounts available, the cause of the lower gross margins can be determined. If the markup was 34.58 percent, markdowns were 3 percent and discounts were 2 percent, then the reduced margin must result from a larger-than-expected stock shortage. Without records of markdowns and discounts, the retailer could locate the problem only in a very general way; that is, it would be clear that retail reductions were

too large, but there would be no indication of whether this was a markdown, a discount, or a stock shortage problem. (The importance of
markdown information for use in controlling inventory and analyzing
retail reductions is discussed more fully in Chapter 23.) Finally, a knowledge of markdowns on various types of goods and on goods of specific
manufacturers, is an important managerial and buying aid. The retailer
may discover that certain types of goods require unprofitably large
markdowns. Or, perhaps goods purchased from some suppliers have
led to larger markdowns than merchandise from other sources.

☐ Reducing undesirable markdowns

As we have noted, some markdowns are desirable for promotional
and merchandising purposes, while others, such as clearing out the last
few odds and ends of an assortment, are an almost inevitable consequence of normal retail operations. A substantial portion of all markdowns, however, can be averted through careful attention to all aspects
of the business. Skillful buying will eliminate some markdown problems.
A buyer must take some risks, but often can experiment with small quantities of new items to gauge customer reaction before making large commitments. A high turnover/low average stock policy will reduce markdowns, although it will increase purchasing costs. Proper inventory
controls will promptly identify slow sellers and thus will permit immediate corrective action, such as changed display, early markdowns, or
P.M.s, before the passage of time aggravates the problem. A record of
markdowns classified according to manufacturer or resource can also be
helpful. An apparel manufacturer, for example, may regularly produce
garments that look attractive on the rack, but are poorly cut and are
rejected when the customers try them on. The markdown record will provide warning that the buyer has experienced difficulties with that manufacturer's products. Good stockkeeping practices will help prevent damage to the goods. And salespeople should be trained to avoid suggesting
that customers send several garments home "for approval," and probable return, since this practice increases store operating expenses and
markdowns.

☐ Markdown cancellations and additional markups

As noted, some markdowns are offered for only a short period, such
as during a special sales event, after which the goods are restored to full
price. The increase from the marked-down price to regular retail is
known as a *markdown cancellation*. But sometimes, particularly during
periods of rapidly advancing prices, retailers must take *additional markups*; that is, they must raise the regular prices for some items in stock.
Generally speaking, a merchant who has to pay higher wholesale prices

to replace present stock should advance prices on the current inventory. This inventory gain will be needed to offset the inventory losses that will come when prices fall.

Moreover, considerable confusion can ensue if the merchant mingles the latest shipment of an item, at a new higher price, with somewhat older but otherwise identical merchandise at a lower price. This will be particularly true when a supermarket operator or other retailer uses an electronic check out system, such as one described on page 630, in which a scanning device reads a code mark that the manufacturer has placed on the package to indicate the product description and package size. The checkout system then queries the retailer's computer to discover the price of that size package of that product. If the store has two prices, one for old stock and one for new, special labels with a distinctive code mark must be attached to either the old or new inventory, which is a costly, cumbersome process, and the two different prices must be placed in the computer's memory bank.[13]

However, several conditions may prevent repricing the old inventory and thus taking an additional markup. (1) During emergency periods, government price controls may prohibit such repricing. (2) Competitive conditions may force the retailer to postpone desired price increases. (3) Repricing and remarking old inventory a few cents higher may not be worth the cost and effort. An experiment in First National Stores, an eastern supermarket chain, found that a policy of not repricing old inventory upwards saved $202 per week in a $3 million a year store at a time when there were about 400 wholesale price changes per week. But a competitive chain, Pathmark Stores, found that it lost about that amount of revenue from its "no repricing" policy.[14] (4) Most importantly, many consumers resent seeing an old, lower price crossed out on a package and replaced by a new higher one.[15] Consequently, a merchant must consider how customers will react to any additional markups before repricing the goods.

■ RETAIL PRICE LEGISLATION

Various special laws influence retail pricing practices or, in some cases, allow the manufacturer to set the prices the retailer must charge. This legislation has included resale price maintenance, unfair sales acts, price posting, and price advertising rules. In addition, retailers are subject to general business legislation, such as the antitrust laws which forbid price agreements in restraint of trade.[16]

□ Resale price maintenance (fair trade)

Resale price maintenance (also called "fair trade" by its advocates) has been an important and controversial issue in retailing in the past.

However, it gradually lost support in recent years and, by federal action in December 1975 was virtually eliminated as a legal mechanism for the control of retail prices in the United States.[17] In this the United States followed earlier enactments in Canada[18] and many Western European countries. Although the national resale price maintenance legislation has now been repealed, some explanation of that legislation is still advisable, since students will encounter many references to the subject. Further examination is also warranted since so many people believed so strongly that the legislation would have very beneficial or very harmful effects upon retailers, suppliers, and consumers. To understand r.p.m. we must answer two questions: (1) What was it? and (2) Who favored it?

What was resale price maintenance? Resale price maintenance was a legal arrangement that allowed a manufacturing company to set either the minimum or the exact price that retailers (and wholesalers) must charge for its product. In the United States this arrangement—where permitted—had been authorized by state laws passed under a federal enabling act.* This permission normally only applied to goods that bore the manufacturer's brand or label. The prices set in this manner were not established by any government agency, but were determined by the manufacturer in the light of its own marketing strategy. Except for special rules affecting the liquor trade in some states, the privilege of using resale price maintenance, where permitted by law, was optional for the supplier rather than mandatory; that is, the supplier could set the resale prices but was not required to do so. Most manufacturers did not use r.p.m. Probably no more than 10 percent of all goods sold at retail in the United States were ever subject to resale price maintenance, even at its height in the late 1930s and late 1940s, and the rate was down to about 4 percent in the early 1970s. But the figure was considerably higher in some other countries, reaching about 33½ percent in Great Britain.[19] A manufacturer who used r.p.m. usually had primary responsibility for stopping any dealer from selling below the minimum figures, first through persuasion and then by bringing a private lawsuit for an injunction against the dealer.

Some resale price maintenance legislation included a "non-signers clause" which also requires a word of explanation. Resale price maintenance, where permitted, is relatively easy to administer for those manufacturers who sell directly to a limited number of retail outlets while booking the annual or seasonal orders. The supplier's sales representatives can obtain signed agreements from the retailers to observe the set prices. But the situation is quite different if the product moves

---

* A manufacturer's attempt to control a retailer's price for goods that moved in interstate commerce would have generally violated the antitrust laws except for the existence of the enabling act and the allied state legislation. As indicated, the permission granted by the enabling act has now been revoked.

through indirect channels (such as large numbers of diverse whole-salers) to thousands of heterogeneous retailers. It becomes impractical for the manufacturer to obtain signed agreements from this large anonymous group. A nonsigners clause in the law required the manufacturer to conclude a price agreement with only one retailer. This then became binding upon all other dealers in the state or other area covered by the law, provided the manufacturer notified those retailers of the set prices through trade magazine advertising, notices in shipping cartons, etc.

Who favored resale price maintenance? The discussion so far might lead one to think that resale price maintenance was a privilege that manufacturers greatly desired, and the laws were written that way. Some, relatively few, manufacturers did want to control retail prices for their products because (1) they thought price-cutting damaged the product's image, (2) they feared that the price cutting dealers would try to switch customers to some other brand or would reduce services, or (3) they believed price maintenance was necessary to obtain wide distribution. Most manufacturers, however, preferred more flexible pricing at retail to encourage sales and to compete more effectively with private brands. They also disliked the legal and administrative problems of r.p.m. since an effective enforcement program in a highly competitive line sometimes cost literally millions of dollars. Small retailers and the wholesalers who served them, particularly in the pharmacy, cosmetic, hardware, and liquor trades, were the staunchest advocates of resale price maintenance and in many instances induced reluctant manufacturers to adopt a price maintenance program. These dealers believed that limitations on price cutting would stop chain store growth and would make business easier for small merchants. In actuality the price maintenance laws seem to have provided very little help for small business. The business failure rate, chain store growth and similar indicators showed no significant difference between states with, and without price maintenance laws.[20] During the 1970s consumerists attacked the laws as being inflationary, but they too, like the small retailers, probably exaggerated the effectiveness of the legislation. Throughout the late 1960s and the early 1970s an increasing number of resale price maintenance laws were either invalidated by state courts or repealed by state legislatures. Many manufacturers abandoned r.p.m. because of a desire to do business with price-cutting discount chains; and this trend was further accelerated by both the criticisms and the weakening legal position of resale price maintenance.

Finally, the federal enabling acts that permitted interstate resale price maintenance were repealed in December 1975, thus ending the legal basis for most supplier attempts to control retail prices. Both contemporary research and the immediate postrepeal experience reinforce the belief that neither the repeal, nor the legislation it removed, had much effect upon either retail operations or consumer prices in an inflationary era.[21]

☐ Suggested prices and preticketing

Manufacturers may try to influence their dealers' prices, aside from resale price maintenance, by suggesting retail prices for their products. They may even mark the goods with the prices they expect the dealers to charge. Thus a shirt manufacturer might have a $9 price printed on the plastic envelopes in which a particular style or quality of shirt is packed. This practice of pre-marking is called "preticketing."

But manufacturers cannot legally make the dealers observe those recommendations except through the device of consignment selling, which is usually impractical. Moreover, the preticketing may actually tempt some dealers into price cutting, since the pre-marked price provides dramatic evidence of the reduction the store is offering. To further complicate matters, the Federal Trade Commission holds that a preticketed price is "deceptive" if any substantial number of retailers sell the item for less than the pre-marked price, even though the manufacturer may not be able to stop their price cutting. Consequently a manufacturer should be reasonably certain that the dealers will follow any such recommendations before preticketing the products.

☐ Unfair-sales and unfair-trade
practices acts

About 26 states have unfair-sales acts, unfair-trade practices acts or sales-below-cost laws that seek to protect retailers from competitors who might sell leader items at less than cost. Whereas fair trade laws were permissive* and applied only to brand merchandise, these laws are mandatory, and apply to all goods. Eighteen of those states and fourteen additional states also have special unfair practices or sales-below-cost laws that apply to specified commodities, mainly cigarettes and milk.

Maine's Unfair Sales Act, which is fairly typical of the general statutes, requires retailers to charge a margin of at least 5.75 percent above invoice cost for all goods except damaged or deteriorated items. Lower prices may be charged, however, on clear proof that the cost of doing business is less than 5.75 percent. A law such as this does forbid deep price cutting, but the minimum required price is low enough to enable a retailer to give customers all of the benefits of low cost operation. Since the cost of retailing practically any item will usually be more than 5.75 percent, this law does not force retailers to charge more than what their own costs would normally require.

Some of the other state laws may have less desirable effects. The Arizona statute requires a markup of at least 12 percent.** Since this is in

---

* As noted above, the liquor laws of some states provide for compulsory price maintenance.

** This markup is required unless the retailer can affirmatively prove a lower cost of doing business.

excess of the markup required in retailing some goods it may result in higher prices to the consumer.[22] In California, the law forbids sales below cost except to meet competition, but then defines cost as invoice or replacement cost, whichever is lower, *plus the dealer's cost of doing business.*[23]

The California type of statute has at least two serious faults: an administrative difficulty and an economic fallacy. The administrative problem involves the difficulty of determining operating costs when a retailer is accused of violating the law. The economic fallacy is that the law seems to require the markup on each item to be at least equal to the merchant's average cost of doing business. Many items can be profitably sold at margins considerably below the store-wide average cost of doing business, and there is no sound reason for raising the prices of such merchandise.

In practice, although violations are statutory offenses and subject to action by the attorneys general of the various states, very few of these laws have been aggressively enforced. Consequently in some states wholesalers and retailers have formed associations partly for the purpose of bringing alleged violations to the attention of the attorneys general and of encouraging the enforcement of the laws. Some of these associations have themselves been prosecuted on the grounds that they were being used to encourage horizontal price fixing contrary to both state and federal laws.[24]

■ OTHER PRICE REGULATIONS

Several other forms of federal, state, or local regulation affect retailers.

□ Price ticketing and price posting

Clear, legible price tickets, signs, or other markings that enable the customer to note the price of an article at a glance are usually highly desirable for many sound business reasons and are a feature of most modern retail operations. (See the discussion of price marking pp. 380–88.) Price signs are now required by law for a few commodities. State and local laws generally specify the way gasoline prices must be shown or posted at the service station pumps. Federal law requires a label or "window sticker" showing the list price, cost of accessories, and freight and preparation costs on every new automobile sold at retail. The Federal Consumer Credit Protection Act, discussed in Chapter 22, stipulates the information that must be communicated to the customer concerning the charges for (price of) credit service.

Considerable controversy has arisen concerning the price-marking of packaged grocery products sold in supermarkets that use the new electronic checkout and automatic scanning equipment described on pages 629–31. As mentioned earlier, the packages are marked with code symbols (Universal Product Code) that indicate the brand, product, and package size. The electronic equipment reads this information, and then obtains the price, for checkout purposes, from a computer. Some retailers have felt that this eliminates the need for the costly process of marking the price on each container; that simply putting price signs on the store shelves would provide adequate information. But some consumer groups have objected, and they have received considerable support from supermarket employee unions. This had lead to many proposals for mandatory price-marking in large supermarkets.[25]

In contrast, price advertising is sometimes forbidden, usually when the dealers in the regulated commodity or service have convinced the local legislature that such advertising will lead to price wars or to "unprofessional conduct." Prohibitions on price advertising have been applied in some communities and states, to the sale of such products and services as gasoline, alcoholic beverages, prescription pharmaceuticals, haircuts, and optometric, dental and medical services. A few cities ban large price signs, visible from the highways, in gasoline service stations. One researcher found greater variation in prices among dealers in such cities than among stations in cities that allowed the large signs.[26] Until the 1970s many states prevented any advertising or display of prices for prescription drugs.* Subsequently, however, in response to consumer pressure and renewed litigation on the part of chain drug stores, some states eliminated the prohibition and others began to require that druggists display signs inside their stores showing their prices for the most frequently dispensed medicines. One careful investigator concluded that prescription prices were about 3 percent higher in states that prohibited price advertising than in comparable states that permitted such advertising.[27] In May 1976, the U.S. Supreme Court ruled that a Virginia statute that prohibited prescription advertising violated the Constitutional guarantee of free speech. This ruling will probably eliminate most state and local restraints on truthful price advertising.[28]

☐ Unit pricing

Unit pricing is a type of information that is now required in some states and that consumer advocates urge for general adoption. Under this system, the price per standard unit of weight or measure (ounce, pound, pint, quart, gallon), as well as the per-package price, is displayed or marked on goods sold in odd-sized packages. The unit pricing proponents contend that only an expert in mental arithmetic can make a

---

* Similar restrictions exist in Canada under the Federal Food and Drug Act prohibitions on pharmaceutical advertising.

meaningful comparison of prices and values between two packages of a grocery product if, for example, one contains 2–4/11 ounces and sells for $.78, while the other contains 3–7/15 ounces and sells for $1.04. Consequently, the advocates of unit pricing legislation want mandatory price marking that would show that the cost of the first package equals 33¢ per ounce, and the second one equals 30¢ per ounce. (This system is sometimes called "dual pricing," since two prices—the actual package price and the per ounce equivalent—are displayed for each item.)* This information usually appears as tags or stickers on the display shelves, although unit price information is often placed on the individual plastic wrapping in the case of store-packaged meats and fresh produce.

Unit pricing requirements, when imposed by law, have generally been limited to food, health, beauty aid, and related products, and generally apply only to large stores and supermarkets. Small retailers have usually been exempted, even though they often serve the poorest consumers who have the greatest need for such information, because of the cost and difficulty of preparing the unit price signs. However, one large chain that uses computer-printed signs estimates its cost at only $750 per store for installation of the system and $100 per-year per-store for maintenance. Other chains report maintenance expenses closer to $1,000 or $2,000 per-store per-year.[29] Consumers naturally say that they like unit price information, but researchers disagree as to whether the data have any substantial influence on actual shopping behavior. Some studies report no modification of buying behavior, perhaps due to the way the information is displayed or the fact that consumers have not been trained to use the data; however, a number of other studies indicate some rather moderate changes in buyer decisions, particularly among younger, higher-income and better educated consumers.[30]

◻ Price advertising

Truth-in-advertising standards and controls, discussed more fully in Chapter 18, are being applied increasingly to the price information offered in retail advertising. The Federal Trade Commission, for instance, has issued a helpful set of "guidelines" as to what it considers deceptive statements about retail prices. Essentially, a merchant cannot claim or imply that a price has been reduced from some former level unless the former price quoted was an actual *bona fide* one at which the product

---

* Readers who may be confused by the similarity of the terms, "one price," "single price," and "unit pricing" will find that business people and writers often use these words interchangeably. Consequently, one is forced to look at the context to determine how these words are being used. Strictly speaking, however, "one price" refers to the practice of charging *all* customers the same amount for the same item purchased under the same conditions; "single price" refers to the practice of selling *all of the items* in a store at the same price; and "unit pricing" refers to the provision of information about price per standard unit of weight and measure.

was offered to the public on a regular basis for a reasonably substantial recent period of time. For example, the retailer cannot take an item regularly selling for $7.50, mark it up to $10.00 for a day, then reduce it back to $7.50 and advertise it as "a big bargain—marked down from $10.00." A retailer who claims the price is lower than either the manufacturer's list or suggested price—or the price prevailing in other stores —must make certain that the quoted prices are those at which substantial sales are being made in the principal stores in the area. The storekeeper must clearly state all the terms and conditions in any special offer, such as "buy one—get one free," or a "half-off sale."[31] The Better Business Bureaus, voluntary business organizations, have also issued guides and suggestions on price claims. Such standards for price advertising help protect responsible merchants from unscrupulous competition and, at the same time, help provide consumers with meaningful information. In addition to national standards, many local governments have adopted ordinances governing price advertising and price marking.[32]

■ RESTRAINTS ON PRICING FREEDOM

Fair trade laws and unfair-sales acts are examples of laws which restrict the pricing freedom of retailers. Yet competitive pricing, which requires pricing freedom, is the very heart of the free-enterprise system. How far we can limit that freedom and still retain our type of economy is an important question. At some point—if we want the advantages of freedom and the high standard of living which it offers—we must be willing to accept the rigors of price competition and not try to protect everyone from its impact. There is a very encouraging aspect of these restrictive laws. As the experience of the 1960s and 1970s indicates, over long periods of time the restraints on price competition gradually tend to lose much of their force. Apparently (and fortunately) it is difficult to remove the impact of competitive factors in the retail field.

□ Emergency controls

During periods of national emergency, the government sometimes finds it necessary to suspend the normal operations of the marketplace. During the depths of the Great Depression of the 1930s, the NRA (National Recovery Administration) program was instituted to reduce price-cutting and to place floors under prices and wages. During World War II and the Korean crisis, the government imposed an elaborate system of price ceilings and other economic controls designed to curb price inflation. Similarly, in August 1971 President Nixon announced a temporary price and wage "freeze" as an antiinflationary measure. Although this freeze underwent several modifications, it was relatively short-lived and probably had little impact on the retail trade. Canada instituted wage and price controls in October 1975 under which retailers were not allowed to raise their gross margin percentages.[33]

Such measures represent the extreme degree of government control over pricing. But even in more "normal" times, as our foregoing discussion has indicated, a variety of laws and regulations affect retail pricing. Both as a merchant and as a citizen, the retailer should become thoroughly familiar with these laws and understand their effects and the obligations they impose.

■ REVIEW AND DISCUSSION QUESTIONS

1 Using a simple example, say a $7.50 item reduced to $5.00, explain the difference between the markdown percentage and the off-retail percentage. Which one should be quoted in the store's advertising and in sales presentations to customers?

2 Concisely state some of the major causes of markdowns. Which of those causes indicate poor performance or mistakes on the part of store personnel, which ones are more or less unavoidable, and which ones represent desirable uses of markdowns as a merchandising and promotional tactic? Discuss.

3 Suggest rules for timing markdowns on (a) seasonal fashion goods, (b) non-seasonal staple goods, (c) seasonal staple goods. How do merchants differ in policy on markdowns for seasonal staple goods?

4 Analyze the advantages and disadvantages of an automatic markdown policy for (a) a hardware store, (b) a phonograph record shop, (c) an exclusive women's apparel shop, and (d) the basement operation of a department store.

5 Talk to some local merchants and/or examine their advertising to determine (a) their policy in publicizing markdowns, (b) the size or amount of markdown they usually take, and (c) whether they use regular or special price lines for markdown merchandise.

6 Explain how undesirable markdowns may be reduced.

7 As a retailer, would you follow a policy for repricing merchandise upward (taking additional markups on old inventory) when replacement cost increases?

8 Briefly describe the major forms of retail price legislation in this country. How effective has each been? Discuss some of the major problems in applying and enforcing these laws.

9 Visit several stores and try to evaluate how clearly each communicates price information to its customers. Are the prices clearly and legibly marked on each item, on signs near the goods, or in some other way? Could any of the stores improve their methods of price marking without undue expense? Does the method of price marking influence you or members of your family in your choice of stores? Do you use unit price information where available?

10 A chain of automotive supply stores advertises: "Special Sale—30 percent off—X brand batteries only $28.00." What facts must be true if the advertisement conforms to the FTC rules on price advertising?

■ NOTES AND REFERENCES

1 *Financial and Operating Results of Department and Specialty Stores of 1974* (New York: Financial Executives Division, National Retail Merchants Association, 1975), page iv.

2 Robert Hearn, Nonfood Merchandiser, Von's Grocery Company, quoted in "Soft Goods Savvy," *Chain Store Age* (supermarket edition), January, 1975, p. 54.

3 Arlie Lazarus, Executive Vice President, Jamesway Corp., "Evaluating the Buyer," *The Discount Merchandiser,* August 1975, p. 64.

4 For example, see "Big Store Promotion Programs Revive Old-Time Price Pushes," *Home Furnishings Daily,* March 17, 1975, pp. 1, 11. See also Y. Kinberg and others, "Mathematical Model for Price Promotion," *Management Science,* vol. 20 (February 1974), pp. 948–59; Y. Kinberg and A. C. Rao, "Stochastic Model of a Price Promotion," *Management Science,* vol. 21 (April 1975), pp. 897–907.

5 "Menswear Retailers of America Lead the Way—In Comparison Statistics," *Retailing Today,* July 1975, p. 2.

6 R. Patrick Cash, "Smaller Stores Are Saying," *Stores,* March 1976, p. 25.

7 See "The Boston Supershoppers," *Time,* December 26, 1969, p. 27; "Filene's Basement, The 9th Wonder," *Women's Wear Daily,* June 14, 1973, pp. 1, 11.

8 "A New Look at Coupons," *The Nielson Researcher,* no. 1 (1976), pp. 2–13; "Coupons Big with Teen Age Shoppers; COED Survey Finds," *Advertising Age,* February 7, 1975, p. 32; "The Cents-Off Deluge," *Media Decisions,* August 1975, pp. 68–74; "Coupon Use by Marketers Climbed 20%," *Advertising Age,* March 1, 1976, p. 48.

9 "Coupons Gaining Ground, Says Nielson," *Marketing,* August 4, 1975, p. 5.

10 "Chicago Food Chain Price War May Spread into Other Markets," *Advertising Age,* April 21, 1975, p. 102.

11 "P&G Will Pay Stores 5¢ for Handling Coupons," *Supermarket News,* November 25, 1974, p. 6.

12 F. R. Shoat and E. L. Melnick, "Fair Packaging and Labeling Act," *Journal of Retailing,* vol. 50 (Summer 1974), pp. 3–10.

13 "Can No Repricing Work in Stores with Scanning?", *Supermarketing,* February, 1975, p. 54; "Stop, Shop Starts Testing Scanning at Mass. Stores," *Supermarket News,* April 7, 1975, pp. 36–38.

14 "No Repricing Policy Reduces First National's Labor Costs," *Supermarketing,* January 1975, p. 32. See also "Repricing: How One Retailer Improves Cash Flow," *Hardware Retailing,* December 1974, pp. 47–48.

15 Consumer preference for a policy of not repricing old stock was strongly demonstrated in a New Jersey study. F. E. Jensen, F. A. Perkins, and A. A. Meredith, *Consumer Attitudes of No Repricing Policies in New Jersey Supermarkets* (New Brunswick, N.J.: Cook College, Rutgers University 1975).

16 "Justice Explains the Do's and Don'ts of Retail Pricing," *Women's Wear Daily,* October 9, 1974, p. 9.

17 "Repealing Fair Trade Is an Anticlimax," *Business Week,* December 29, 1975, p. 25.

18 Combines Investigation Act, Section 38.

19 See W. G. McClelland, "The United Kingdom" in J. J. Boddewyn and S. C. Hollander, eds., *Public Policy toward Retailing,* Lexington, Mass.: Lexington Books, 1972, pp. 359–60, for a discussion of changes in British price maintenance legislation.

20 "Will Congress End Fair Trade?", *Business Week,* February 17, 1975, p. 82; "Much Ado . . . Fair Trade Laws Fall in State after State, but Impact is Small," *Wall Street Journal,* June 11, 1975, p. 1.

21 Bruce J. Walker, "Arizona Retailers on Fair Trade Repeal," *Arizona Business,* February 1976, pp. 20–28; James C. Johnson and Louis E. Boone, "Farewell to Fair Trade," *MSU Business Topics,* vol. 24 (Spring 1976), pp. 22–30.

22 For criticism of the Arizona law, see Robert L. Knox, "Competition and the Concept of Sales below Cost," *Arizona Business Bulletin,* vol. 16 no. 9 (November 1969), pp. 227–32.

23 *California Business and Professional Code,* division 1, part 2, chap. 4, sec. 17026.

24 See S. C. Hollander, *Restraints upon Retail Competition* (East Lansing, Michigan: Bureau of Business and Economic Research, Michigan State University, 1965), p. 39.

25 "Electronic Pricing Faces an Uphill Fight," *Business Week,* March 31, 1975, p. 23. But "Brave New Checkout," *Newsweek,* February 17, 1975, p. 79, claims most consumers do not object to the absence of individual item marking.

26 Alex R. Maurizi, "The Effect of Laws against Price Advertising: The Case of Retail Gasoline," *Western Economic Journal* vol. 10, no. 3 (September 1972), pp. 321–29.

27 John F. Cady, "Advertising Regulation and the Price of Drugs at Retail: The Cost of Information Restriction," in Edward M. Mazze, ed., *1975 Combined Proceedings* (Chicago: American Marketing Association, 1976), pp. 498–503.

28 44 *U.S. Law Week* 4686 (May 24, 1976).

29 Esther Peterson, "Consumerism as a Retailer's Asset," *Harvard Business Review,* vol. 52 (May-June 1974), p. 97; James Carman, "A Summary of Empirical Research on Unit Pricing in Supermarkets," *Journal of Retailing,* vol. 48 (Winter 1972–73), pp. 67–68.

30 Carman, "A Summary of Empirical Research," pp. 63–67; H. R. Isakson and A. R. Maurizi, "The Consumer Economics of Unit Pricing," *Journal of Marketing Research,* vol. 10 (August 1973), pp. 277–85; W. E. Kilbourne, "A Factorial Experiment on the Impact of Unit Pricing on Low Income Consumers," *Journal of Marketing Research,* vol. 11 (November 1974), pp. 453–55; J. E. Russo, G. Kreiser and S. Miyashita, "An Effective Display of Unit Price Information," *Journal of Marketing,* vol. 39 (April 1975), pp. 11–19.

31 Bureau of Industry Guidance, Federal Trade Commission, "Guides to Deceptive Pricing," January 8, 1964.

32 "In Chicago Retail Coupons Now Must Give More Price Info.," *Advertising Age,* February 17, 1975, p. 42; "Ohio Retailers Fight Discount Selling Edict," *Home Furnishings Daily,* January 27, 1975, p. 2.

33 *1976 Corpus Almanac of Canada* (Toronto: Corpus Publishers Service, Ltd., 1976), pp. 10–36. Further information about the Canadian program is available from Public Relations Director, The Anti-Inflation Board, 219 Laurier Ave. W., Ottawa, Ont. K1P 6B1.

Sales promotion and customer services

RETAIL ADVERTISING
AND DISPLAY

Once a store has been properly equipped and well-balanced assortments of merchandise have been assembled to meet the needs of prospective customers, measures must be adopted to attract those customers into the store and to induce them to make purchases. Such measures—to be really effective—should build good will for the store to insure continuous patronage from satisfied customers. When this is done, sales volume will be maintained on a profitable level. The function of sales promotion is to accomplish these purposes.

Sales promotion efforts are of two major types: (1) Those of a nonpersonal nature, such as advertising, display and mail order catalogs; and (2) those of a personal nature, such as personal salesmanship that require an individual conversation between a customer and a store employee.* The nonpersonal forms of sales promotion are considered

---

* Sales promotion provides another illustration of the fact that different business people and different writers often use the same or similar terms in different ways. Some merchants and writers, like the present authors, use the words "sales promotion" as an inclusive term covering all sales-stimulating messages directed at potential customers. Others, however, use the word "promotion" for this purpose and apply the label "sales promotion" only to miscellaneous activities (such as fashion shows or coupon distribution) that do not clearly fall under the headings of "advertising" or "personal selling." See the definitions in C. J. Dirksen and Arthur Kroeger, *Advertising Principles and Problems,* 4th ed. (Homewood, Ill.: Richard D. Irwin, Inc., 1973), p. 4.

in this and the next chapter. Personal salesmanship is discussed in Chapter 20.

■ FUNCTIONS AND GOALS OF RETAIL ADVERTISING

Advertising is "any paid form of nonpersonal presentation and promotion of ideas, goods, or services by an identified sponsor."[1] Retailers may use it to tell people what goods and services they have available, to stimulate desire for those items, to keep people interested in their stores between visits, and to develop goodwill. In other words, its main job from the retailer's standpoint is to create a desirable image in the customer's mind.

Advertising has become a very important part of many retail businesses. In 1975, for example, 50 large U.S. retailing companies spent a total of about $2.6 billion on advertising, not counting the costs of window or interior display.[2] Total retail advertising expenditures were, of course, substantially greater than those figures. One of the top 25, The F. W. Woolworth Company, alone invested about $110,000,000 in newspaper, radio, television, and magazine advertising; quite a change for a company that until 1958 relied almost entirely on window displays and location in the mainstreams of pedestrian traffic to attract trade. But retailers know that customers shop differently today from the way they did several decades ago. Now consumers usually have a choice of several shopping centers rather than automatically drifting downtown or to a few subsidiary locations; they often ride rather than walk and are less likely to be exposed to window displays; and they may be unwilling or unable to visit all possible stores in the time available for shopping. Consequently, merchants frequently need advertising to attract and to "presell" potential consumers. Well-planned advertising and display can also help partially offset deficiencies in personal selling, although this does not eliminate the need to strive for the best possible standards of salesmanship.

Advertising will not accomplish its goals unless it is carefully planned, prepared, tested, placed in appropriate media at the right times, and reviewed frequently. Moreover, it must be coordinated with other activities of the store to obtain maximum benefits.

Advertising is not a panacea for all the retailer's management problems. One expert recommends that some small retailers avoid advertising (other than window display) because of the difficulty of making a strong impression with a limited budget, but others believe this can be successfully accomplished.[3] Actually, those retailers who recognize the limitations of advertising programs and plan their programs accordingly will derive the greatest benefit from such efforts. They should keep in mind the warning voiced by two students of advertising almost two decades ago that:

1. Advertising cannot sell merchandise that people do not want to buy;
2. Advertising cannot sell merchandise in profitable quantities without the backing of every other division of the store; and
3. Advertising cannot succeed to the fullest extent unless it is used continuously.[4]

This clear warning emphasizes the fact that for long-run effectiveness, advertising must be believable, must be truthful, and must provide the customer with helpful information.

☐ Two main types of retail advertising

Retail advertising may be divided into two main types: (1) promotional or direct action, and (2) institutional or indirect action. Most advertisements represent a blending of both types.

Promotional or direct-action advertising   The main purpose of this type of advertising is to bring customers into the store to purchase specific items of merchandise. Advertising with this emphasis constitutes the greater proportion of total retail advertising. It may take one of three forms: (1) regular-price advertising, where the appeal is based on the desirability of the goods (Figure 18–1); (2) "bargain" advertising, which features price appeal in relation to value (Figure 18–2); and (3) clearance-sale advertising, whose main purpose is to close out slow-moving items, broken assortments, and remnants at reduced prices (Figure 18–3).

Institutional or indirect-action advertising   Institutional advertising seeks to develop goodwill for the store—to create confidence in its merchandise and services (Figure 18–4) and thus to build permanent patronage. There are two main kinds: prestige advertising and service advertising. The former emphasizes the store's, or the department's character and leadership in style, merchandise quality, or in community responsibility. Often these characteristics are suggested by use of appropriate type faces and illustrations rather than by flat statements in the ad. Service advertising seeks to attract patronage by stressing the various services and facilities offered by the store which make it a desirable place in which to shop. In the institutional advertisement reproduced in Figure 18–5, a men's clothing store calls attention to a local museum exhibition of clothing history (public service advertising) and then stresses the variety and stylishness of the goods it offers for sale (prestige advertising).

Promotional advertising can also be institutional advertising   Every retail advertisement helps create some impression in the reader's or

FIGURE 18–1 A regular-price advertisement promoting specific items

Courtesy Famous-Barr, St. Louis

FIGURE 18–2   Promotional advertisement with emphasis on bargain prices

FIGURE 18–3 A clearance-sale promotional advertisement Note brevity of copy.

viewer's mind about the store. So all retail advertising has some institutional effect, although the resultant image may be accurate or inaccurate, consistent or confusing, and helpful or harmful to the store. Wise merchants recognize the institutional impact of their promotional advertising and select both items and messages that will contribute to a favorable image. Thus, among three leading New York specialty shops, one stresses "elegance" in its copy and illustrations, another "avante-garde" or very original fashions, while a third emphasizes appeal to a broad-spectrum of fashion conscious customers.[5] Other merchants go beyond this and skillfully blend institutional themes and item information in the ad.[6]

Food-store advertising, often cited (incorrectly) as strictly promotional in nature, well illustrates a combination of the two main types of

FIGURE 18-4   Institutional advertisement featuring a new department in a specialty store

"The Potting Shed" is here! It's a delightful new department filled
with "every bloomin' thing" in house plants and trees. . .ivy, ferns,
philodendron and many more, from common strains to exotic
variations. . .plus an exciting array of decorative cachepots and hanging
planters, filled or just waiting for that special plant. You'll enjoy the
miniature gardening tools and "how to" books. . .and for the novice,
we offer a special planting service and lots of knowledgeable advice
to help you earn that "green thumb" status. Come in and see us soon.

LOWER LEVEL

Jacobson's

Courtesy Jacobson's, Inc., East Lansing, Michigan

retail advertising. A study of the advertisements of four competing food
chains in Philadelphia some years ago concluded that they were used
to create a favorable image to attract customers—not necessarily for the
items mentioned but for the stores' general assortment. The typical advertisement contained three categories of items, with the first two classes

greatly predominating: (a) those used to differentiate the advertiser from competitors, i.e., items not stocked or not featured by other chains; (b) those serving as a reminder list—to inform customers of the breadth of stock; and (c) a few priced to neutralize the previous advertisements of competitors, i.e., items on which competitors' advertised prices were met.[7]

■ COOPERATIVE ADVERTISING

Typically, the retailer assumes complete responsibility for the preparation and cost of the store's advertising. At times, however, merchants engage in cooperative advertising, in which they share responsibility and cost with manufacturers or wholesalers. To illustrate, the product is advertised over the retailer's name with the resource paying part—perhaps, 50 percent—of the media cost up to a maximum amount, such as 5 percent of the retailer's purchases. Perhaps as much as $2 billion is spent each year by manufacturers on cooperative advertising. The resource gains from the added interest shown by the retailer in its product, from the retailer's prestige, from the extra space or time purchased by the retailer's contribution to the media cost, and from the fact that retailers usually buy newspaper space at lower "local" rates than national advertisers are charged. Despite these advantages, many manufacturers dislike cooperative advertising. They are not satisfied with the return they obtain from the advertising allowance, and often prefer to deal directly with the media. Consequently, the trade press sometimes publishes stories of manufacturer dissatisfaction with the arrangement.*

To the retailer, cooperative advertising yields benefits such as assistance in preparing advertisements (see Figure 18–6), the tie-in posters and displays supplied for use in the store, and in the increase in the total space that can be afforded. The retailer should, however, be fully aware of the obligations involved and should be sure that the product has a suitable reputation. Moreover, retailers may be held responsible for the truthfulness of the claims made in cooperative advertisements that the vendors have prepared. On balance, the retailer should probably engage in some cooperative advertising, but be careful to select the best deals available.[8]

---

* Both American and Canadian law stipulate that firms that offer advertising allowances must make them available to all dealers on "proportionately equal" terms—that is, roughly in ratio to volume of purchases. The U.S Federal Trade Commission has issued elaborate guidelines that among things oblige manufacturers to make certain their allowance arrangements are well publicized even among small dealers who buy through wholesalers, and that prohibit requests for payment of false or fictitious charges. "Can Co-op Rid Itself of Rip-offs," *Media Decisions* (October 1975), pp. 58–59, 98–102.

FIGURE 18-6 Film for 30 second TV commercial supplied to dealers by manufacturer Five-second film tag that shows specific models can be substituted for the final frame to replace the Whirlpool logo or signature and the dealer's name and price can be superimposed on the tag.

Voice-over: Hi there! Bet you've been waiting for the right deal on a really good air conditioner. Right?

Well, look at this Whirlpool air conditioner . . . with Comfort Guard control

that automatically helps maintain a temperature range

for your comfort. Keeps you cool, cool, cool without making you cold.

Yes it's a Whirlpool air conditioner. Let's all say it—

Whirlpool. And this is the deal you've been waiting for. So hurry on down . . . .

Hey! Don't you want to hear the prices?

(Whirlpool Logo)
Courtesy Whirlpool Corporation

■ EXPENDITURES FOR RETAIL ADVERTISING

The total amount of money spent for advertising in the United States is large and continues to grow even larger. Total advertising expenditures in 1974 were over $26 billion. Twelve billion of this was local advertising, a category that includes theater and amusement, political and classified announcements, but that is very largely filled with retail advertising.[9] Retail expenditures may be about $9 or $10 billion a year. This includes the limited amounts spent by small retailers who prepare their own advertisements—often with the advice and assistance of a local printer or newspaper publisher—as well as the large expenditures of discount houses, department, and chain stores, which operate extensive advertising departments often working in cooperation with advertising agencies. In the course of a year, a small neighborhood food store may spend less than a hundred dollars for the printing and distribution of a few hand bills, while Sears, Roebuck and Company spent $487 million in 1974. Sears 1975 advertising budget included over $6 million in magazines and $73 million in network and spot television.[10]

The best available figures showing the percentage of net sales spent for advertising by various types of retailers are presented in Table 18–1. We know, moreover, that the proportion spent varies widely among both large and small stores because of such factors as the type of store, its size and location, and the competitive situation. Among department stores, for example, which are large and consistent advertisers, advertising expenditures in 1974 varied from 3.22 percent of net sales for stores with sales over $50 million to 4.38 percent for those with sales of $1–$2 million. Specialty stores averaged 3.49 percent during the same year.[11] For self-service discount department stores the 1973–74 combined dollar average was 2.63 percent of sales.[12] Among food chains the amount spent for promotional activity is 7/10 of 1 percent of sales.[13]

■ RETAIL ADVERTISING STRATEGY

Once objectives are established, conducting effective advertising involves: (1) determining the advertising appropriation; (2) planning the advertising; (3) selecting appropriate media; (4) preparing the actual advertisements; and (5) testing them. These steps should be coordinated into a complete advertising program, perhaps with the aid of an advertising agency. Some retail trade associations, such as the National Retail Furniture Association and the National Retail Hardware Association also prepare helpful materials for their members and some assistance (although not always unbiased) is often offered by suppliers and media representatives.

TABLE 18–1

Percentage of sales invested in advertising by various retail trades 1972–1973

Building materials, hardware and farm equipment stores	0.83
General merchandise stores	2.84
Food stores	0.97
Automotive dealers and service stations	0.89
Automobile and truck dealers 0.88	
Gasoline service stations 0.42	
Other automotive dealers 1.23	
Apparel and accessory stores	2.05
Furniture, home furnishings, and equipment stores	3.25
Eating and drinking places	1.63
Miscellaneous retail stores*	1.24
Drug stores and proprietary (nonprescription) stores	1.17
Liquor stores	0.50
Other retail stores*	1.39

*The miscellaneous group includes sporting goods, book and stationery, jewelry, gift, camera, luggage, toy, hobby, and sewing supply stores. Other retail stores include newsdealers, pet shops, typewriter and optical goods stores, and stores not listed in other classifications.

Data collected by *Advertising Age* from special tabulations of Internal Revenue Service statistics. Groups shown include both stores that advertise and those that don't and percentages, while most accurate available, are only approximate because of problems in classifying firms according to line of business.

Source: "Percentage of Sales Invested in Advertising," *Advertising Age* (October 20, 1975), p. 74. Reprinted with permission from the October 20, 1975 issue of *Advertising Age.* Copyright 1975 by Crain Communications, Inc.

□ The advertising appropriation

The amount a store *needs* to spend for advertising will depend primarily upon its objectives. Does it want to dominate the media and have the most prominent advertising in its community, increase sales by a certain percentage, build up certain departments or lines of merchandise, attract a certain number of new customers, perhaps from some age or income segment of the market, or remind old customers of its existence? The expense of achieving one of these objectives will be influenced by such factors as the store's age, policies, size, location, competition, trading area, and the image it has already created. Other influential factors include media costs and circulation, business conditions, and competitors' marketing strategies.

What a retailer *needs* to spend may be more than what can be *afforded*. Perhaps some of the objectives will be impossible to attain or will cost more than will be available or profitable in view of the store's present market position. In such cases, the merchant must reconsider goals and settle for ones that are more practical. The merchant must also remember that advertising results will depend, not only on how much is spent and how much time and space is bought, but also on the planning and timing of the program and the wise selection of items and prices to be featured. Nevertheless, one should not expect miracles from small advertising expenditures. Store policies and practices will also control results, since advertising can only build potential goodwill which is easily lost if the store does not live up to customer expectations.

☐ Effective planning

The care with which advertising plans are made will determine the results they produce. Careful planning has many benefits: (1) It provides a definite concrete plan based on facts rather than indefinite, last-minute decisions based on opinions and guesswork; (2) it forces a review of past experience, thus focusing attention on past mistakes and successes; (3) it requires looking ahead—adopting a long-range perspective; (4) it considers and insures attention to all phases of the advertising program including seasonal promotions, need for clearance sales, etc.; (5) it provides balanced attention to the needs of each department and each branch in departmentalized and chain stores; (6) it schedules appropriate promotional activity to accompany planned developments such as the addition of a major new merchandise line or a change in store service policy; (7) it considers probable changes in competitors' policies and programs; and (8) it facilitates coordination between various types of advertising and between advertising and merchandising, store management, and control activities.[14]

Advertising should be planned in stores of all sizes, even in the small shop where the proprietor exercises direct supervision over all promotion. As in the merchandise plan or budget, the advertising plan should cover a period of several months and be subdivided into months, weeks, or shorter special promotions. It should set forth programs for various types of promotions, including selection of merchandise to be advertised and choice of advertising media. It should also provide for the coordination of advertising and special forms of sales promotion, as well as for adjustments to meet unforeseen conditions.

Proper timing   Proper timing is vital in the planning of advertising efforts. Food retailers in some cities concentrate their advertising in Wednesday afternoon and Thursday morning papers since Thursday, Friday, and Saturday are the days when customers usually make large purchases. Department and specialty stores in the United States often advertise heavily on Sunday on the assumption that Sunday newspapers are read more thoroughly than those published on weekdays. But the growing number of discount and suburban stores open five or six nights a week and on Sunday includes many who invest heavily in midweek advertising. See Chapter 21 on this development.

For retailers of high-fashion goods, timing in terms of weather is particularly important. A large amount spent on advertising fall fashions during a warm spell may produce few sales. Likewise the promotion of lightweight summer dresses during a summer cold spell may result in a large outlay with little customer response. Some retailers study the monthly weather forecasts of the United States Environmental Services and adjust their promotions accordingly. Others go far beyond this and subscribe to weather forecasting services.[15]

Here, again, many leading trade associations, such as the National Association of Retail Druggists and the National Retail Merchants Association, furnish their members with promotional calendars and guides for various months and events throughout the year.[16] Trade publications offer a similar service.

Suitable merchandise Perhaps the greatest waste of retail advertising dollars is promoting the wrong merchandise. The best advertisements cannot sell goods the customer does not want. In contrast, relatively poor advertising is often effective in moving *wanted* merchandise.

In selecting goods to advertise, the retailer should be guided by past experience regarding proven best sellers; by the merchandise that is selling well in other stores; by pretesting goods to determine their probable rate of sale; by the desire to promote private brands; by the advice of salespeople (and by department heads in larger stores); and by considerations of timeliness, buying habits of the community, variety, frequency of purchase, and contribution to store image. New fashion items and prestige brands are often used for the latter purpose. As noted in Chapter 17, leader advertising should feature items and values that are attractive to many customers, that are purchased frequently, and that will not absorb the customer's total purchasing power.

Finally, a word of caution is in order. Too often retailers advertise certain items without first making certain that adequate quantities are on hand to meet reasonable sales expectations.* When quantities are exhausted, customers unable to buy the goods advertised are annoyed and encouraged to make their purchases elsewhere. Many alert retailers specify limited quantities or broken sizes and colors in their advertising copy if their stocks may be inadequate to meet customer demands.

□ Selecting appropriate advertising media

The retailer should carefully evaluate the suitability of available advertising media.[17] Each potential medium should be considered in terms

---

* The prevalence of this practice among food retailers has led the Federal Trade Commission to require stores to stock ample supplies on all advertised items unless stock limits are clearly indicated in the advertisement.

of (1) its coverage—whether it matches the location and reading or listening habits of present and prospective customers; (2) its suitability to the advertising message—whether general or specialized, institutional or promotional, requiring pictures or coupons, etc.; (3) its use by competitors, since a store that can make a strong presentation will often want to meet competitors "head-on" in the same medium; and (4) its cost in relation to both potential benefits and the size of the advertising appropriation. No one medium is "correct" for all retailers under all conditions.

The more important general categories of retail media are:

1. Newspapers
2. Magazines
3. Direct mail
4. Radio
5. Television
6. Outdoor
7. Public vehicles
8. Personal distribution
9. In-store

Newspaper Media choices are changing today as retailers use increasing amounts of television and radio time.[18] But newspaper advertising is still the main vehicle for large retailers and for many small stores whose trading area matches the circulation pattern of the local newspapers. Sears, Roebuck and Company invested about 73 percent of its 1974 noncatalog advertising budget in newspapers, about 16 percent in network and spot (local) TV, 7 percent in spot (local) radio, and 4 percent in magazines.[19] One trade source estimates that newspapers received about 48 percent of retailers' media expenditures in 1973, radio about 14 percent, television 12 percent and all others 26 percent.[20] Discount department stores used newspapers even more intensively, spending about three-fourths of their advertising budget in that medium.[21] These stores, and some other major chains often use *inserts* (preprinted special sections), in addition to advertising on the regular newspages, to show large selections of price specials. Supermarkets also invest heavily in newspaper advertising to show their price lists. In contrast, newspaper advertising is usually too costly for small retailers—the corner grocer, for example—whose market is very limited. However, the growth of suburban and neighborhood weekly and semi-seekly papers provides a useful medium for some small retailers who serve those markets. Appliance and used car dealers sometimes find classified advertising is worthwhile.

Many high fashion retailers seek publicity on the women's pages of newspapers. Since the editors of those pages want to provide their readers with news of fashion developments, buyers who furnish such information have little difficulty in obtaining recognition for their stores.

Retailers like newspapers because of their low cost per reader, market coverage, readership, quick response, quick check on results, availability for regular and frequent advertising, flexibility and speed, fewer size limits, and public acceptance.[22] (See Figure 18–7.) Despite these advantages, however, they possess obvious limitations such as waste circulation in certain areas and among people who are not potential customers; their numerous editions with "home coverage" not proportionately large; their short life; often an hour or less; the large number of advertisements they contain, with keen competition for the reader's attention; and the difficulty of producing good illustrations on newsprint.

Magazines   General circulation national magazines, such as *Readers' Digest, Time* and *Newsweek* do not generally fit into retailers' advertising plans, except for some firms that solicit direct mail orders, and a little institutional advertising or private brand promotion by a few big chains. But magazines that are specialized, either as to location or subject matter draw more retail advertising. *The New Yorker, New York, Chicago,* and *Toronto Life* are examples of the growing number of metropolitan magazines that, to a greater or lesser degree, appeal to residents and visitors in one particular city and thus are suitable promotional media for the stores in that city. Many firms that want mail orders advertise in specialized publications, such as *Mechanix Illustrated, Popular Photography,* and *Hobbies.* Some prestigious specialty stores, such as Bonwit Teller, I. Magnin, and Saks Fifth Avenue purchase occasional space in fashion magazines, notably *Vogue, Harpers Bazaar,* and *Town and Country* to promote a high-style dress or coat, perhaps with some of the cost being borne by the manufacturer.

The major advantages of magazines are (1) the ability to produce fine illustrations; (2) specialized readership; (3) long life; and (4) prestige among customers and employees. These are usually offset, for retailers, by (1) lack of flexibility because of long lead-time for preparation and publication; (2) waste circulation; and (3) most importantly, high cost per reader.

Direct mail   Direct mail is the major form of advertising in some small stores. A Pennsylvania shop specializing in women's sportswear, for instance, found that five direct-mail pieces each year were sufficient for its purposes, so that no newspaper advertising of any kind was used. And a small fur store on Long Island (New York), while inserting some advertisements in a local paper, relies heavily on three or four direct mailings each year to a list of 5,000 names, plus more frequent mailings to 500 to 1,000 persons. Department stores and specialty stores use direct mail extensively.

Properly used, direct-mail advertising enables the retailer to select an audience and to make the message personal in nature; it obtains concentrated attention without distraction from competing advertisements; it permits a close check on results; and it provides choice among several methods of conveying a message. But it also has definite limitations. Its effectiveness depends on a mailing list that may be costly to

FIGURE 18–7   Advertisement placed in trade publication by newsprint manufacturer urging retailers to use newspaper advertising

NEWSPAPERS, THE DAILY BARGAIN

If you're going to spend money advertising, advertise where you get the most for your money.

Everyday millions of women look into a closet full of clothes and say, "I haven't a thing to wear." There's nothing wrong with that, particularly if you're in the women's wear business. But how do you get them from the closet into your store?

Surveys show that most of these same women are also looking into the newspapers for the latest information on fashions and styles before they buy. In fact, 9 out of 10 women readers follow newspaper fashion ads every single day. That's a lot of advertising exposure, when you consider that newspapers reach more women than any other medium. 73% in one day. And 91% in five days.

"Looking" is one thing. Buying is another.

When shoppers were asked where they find the facts when they're ready to put down their money and buy, 3 out of 4 said, "Ads in newspapers." And 80% of the women respondents in a survey of 18,000 said they explore daily newspaper ads for sale items they may want to buy.

The point is women shop twice for the clothing they buy. First in the newspapers and then in the stores. So if you're in the retail women's wear business, your best buy in advertising is through your local paper. It's the most effective way to reach the most women. And the most inexpensive. Department stores know it works. Most spend 77% of their advertising budgets in newspapers.

Let's face it. Everybody in the women's wear business has to advertise. But not everybody in the women's wear business has to spend a lot of money doing it.

Newspapers, "The Daily Bargain." Use it. And you'll spend your money where it does the most good.

CrownZellerbach
Newsprint Division

WOMEN'S WEAR DAILY, TUESDAY, SEPTEMBER 9, 1975

Courtesy Crown Zellerbach Corporation

compile and maintain, specialized skill is required to prepare the material, and the cost per unit is rather large for materials, production, postage, and preparation for mailing. Direct mail often gives very good results per dollar of expenditure when sent to present customers; it is often less efficient in reaching and selling prospective patrons.[23]

Broadcast media Broadcast media (radio and television) have steadily gained popularity with retailers because of the number of people who primarily listen to or watch those sources rather than read print media. The rising cost of newspaper space, the development of relatively inexpensive television production techniques such as videotape, and the growing amount of experience retailers have in using TV also contribute to the trend.[24]

The retailer using radio or television may choose from a wide variety of programs and vary appeals so as to reach all members of the family. The broadcast advertiser may reach customers at times when they are receptive to suggestions of merchandise suited to their needs, and may also make last-minute changes which appear advisable. Merchandise can be shown in a convincing and effective way on television. Finally, radio and television advertising lend prestige to some types of retailers and create confidence and enthusiasm among employees.

Broadcast commercials are ephemeral; customers cannot save the ads for reading when convenient or for comparison shopping. Also cost tends to restrict usage to large and medium-sized stores or to combinations of small stores although relatively small retailers can afford spot announcements in some communities.[25]

Other media The shopping-news type of publication, one form of personal distribution, is typically owned cooperatively by its advertisers, but some are nonretailer controlled. Usually published once or twice a week, each issue consists of retail advertisements plus some brief articles of interest to prospective customers. These papers are distributed free to households in the paper's area.

Some stores, especially those in small cities, often use hand bills or flyers, which may be distributed in the store or from house to house. Because of increased postal costs, many retailers now run their circulars as newspaper inserts or distribute them through house-to-house carriers.[26] Even some large stores such as Sears and Penney's make extensive use of circulars. Properly prepared, they are quite effective in stimulating the sale of general merchandise, household items, foods, and other goods. They are especially useful for special sales events discussed later in this chapter. We will also discuss some forms of in-store advertising under the heading of "display" in this chapter.

Billboards (outdoor posters), signs on or in buses and taxicabs, and other miscellaneous media are primarily forms of reminder advertising. They are quite useful in specific instances, but involve only a small portion of total retail advertising expenditures.

☐ Preparing advertisements

Television commercials are almost always prepared by specialists, either by outside advertising agencies, by a merchandise supplier under a cooperative program, or in some large retail firms, by the company's own TV expert. The most important rules a retailer should remember in working with the TV specialist, in providing merchandise and in approving commercials apply to all advertising. They are: (1) each advertisement should contain a "unique selling proposition," that is, it shows why an item, an idea, or a store image, should appeal to the customer;[27] (2) the more specific the advertisement the better; and (3) only a limited amount of information can be transmitted in any one advertisement.[28] Print advertising is more likely to be prepared in the store and involves three steps: writing copy, selecting illustrations, and designing the layout.

The copy The term "copy" refers to the reading matter of an advertisement, including both the text and the headline. Copy may be said to be the heart of a retail advertisement, although color, illustrations, and typography must be coordinated with it to obtain the desired results.

Since human wants and needs are the basic influences motivating behavior, the retailer's advertising copy should reflect a close familiarity with them. That is, copy should interpret the want-satisfying qualities of the retailer's offerings in terms of the consumer's needs and desires. The retailer should also bear in mind that "efficiency in advertising seems to depend on the use of simple language—simple direct presentation of sales arguments—and the avoidance of tricky attention-getting devices unrelated to the product itself."[29] Unless these guiding principles are followed results are certain to be disappointing.

When the copy has been written, it should be subjected to certain tests to determine its value. Kleppner mentions the following qualities that should be examined:

Does it present the benefits that the product offers to the reader? Is it clear? Is anything in it liable to be misunderstood? Is the most important benefit given the most prominence? Does it give adequate information? Is it accurate? Is it plausible? Can it be made more specific? Can the story be told in fewer words, in shorter words, or in fewer sentences? Does it make the reader want the product advertised? As to the headline, does it attract attention and create interest in the rest of the copy?[30]

The illustration There is an old saying that one picture is worth a thousand words. Although illustrations are not invariably required—effective food advertising, for example, often contains no picture—retailers use illustrations frequently to attract attention, to show the merchandise and/or its use, to lend "atmosphere," and to confine the reader's attention within the advertisement. Small retailers find the advice and assistance of the local printer and the manufacturers whose products they handle of much value in choosing illustrations. Large retailers have their own specialists who, singly or in cooperation with advertising agencies or newspaper artists, devise appropriate illustrations to suggest the effect desired. These specialists sharply disagree in preferences for using drawings or photographs as illustrations.[31] Often the choice seems to be to use whichever one will differentiate the store from its competitors.

The illustration should be simple, clear, and appropriate; focus attention on the points desired; help sell the product or the ideas being advertised; and "face" into the advertisement and toward the copy if possible. Otherwise the reader's eyes may be directed toward a competitive advertisement in the next column.

The layout   The layout is a sketch showing the location of the text, headline, and illustration in the advertisement. It enables the advertiser to visualize the complete advertisement and to provide instructions to the printer for setting up the advertisement.

There are certain guidelines concerning layout just as there are for other phases of retail advertising. Specifically, the layout should (1) have attention value, presenting a complete and balanced picture pleasing to the reader; (2) provide the desired emphasis through focusing attention on the more important parts of the advertisement; (3) reflect the character or image of the store; and (4) make effective use of type faces and sizes, white space, and illustration in conformity with the best standards of advertising practice.

□ Testing retail advertising essential

Retailers naturally need to check or test the effectiveness of their advertising. These tests involve (1) checking the advertisement before it is used—the precheck;* and (2) check of the results produced—the aftercheck.

Checklists have been developed to insure proper coverage of all essential points in the precheck. The advertising department of the *Chicago Tribune* has long used the following and variations of it:

1. Has the advertisement maximum attention value?
2. Is it "in character" for the store it represents?
3. Does it dramatize the offer? This point includes the appeal to the reader's emotions.
4. Does it satisfy the sense of value of the prospective purchaser? This point could be elaborated to ask: Does it give conviction that price

---

* In the words of one advertising specialist, "An ounce of copy pretesting is worth a pound of presumptions."

is right, that quality is good, that the merchandise will be beneficial and useful?

5. Does it inspire confidence in the advertiser?
6. Have necessary details been included as to size, color, style, price, address, phone, store hours, time of sale, free parking?
7. Has it a selling "hook" or unusual inducement for direct action?

Other pretesting methods, such as showing the advertisement to a selected sample of consumers, are often used in national (manufacturers') campaigns, but these techniques are generally too time-consuming, too expensive, and insufficiently informative for most retail advertising purposes. The aftercheck presents similar problems. As one well-known expert says: "To measure the effectiveness of advertising is probably analogous to finding a needle in a haystack."[32] Survey research can discover how many people report seeing or remembering the advertisement, but this method is imprecise, time-consuming, and doesn't answer the central question: Did the advertisement help sell the item? Most retailers rely on records of how well the merchandise sold before and after the advertisement appeared. Of course, sales will be influenced by many factors: the quality of the item, in-store display, the weather, and competitors' activity.[33] Nevertheless, sales results probably provide the best practical measure of advertising effectiveness for most retailers, if the results are interpreted carefully and if decisions are reached by observing many advertisements over time rather than on the basis of a single ad.

■ TRUTH IN ADVERTISING

The effectiveness of retail advertising is dependent upon the confidence of readers in the honesty of the advertiser. As two students have written: "If advertising does not have the confidence of most consumers, it will lose its influence and surely die. If people grow to disbelieve a substantial percentage of the advertising messages that come to them, they will soon tend to reject most or all advertising."[34] Consumers, for example, have become skeptical of price-reduction claims in sale advertising.[35] Yet, some retailers continue to be guilty of misleading and exaggerated claims in their advertising, thus bringing discredit to themselves and undermining faith in all advertising statements. Consequently, leading retailers, manufacturers, advertising people, the government, and others have long tried to curb the unfair advertising practices of these unrepresentative merchants. These efforts have been conducted by Better Business Bureaus (voluntary organizations of local business people), by some industry trade associations, by advertising media that are concerned with the honesty of the messages they convey, and by local, state, provincial, and federal government action. The major federal bodies concerned with retail advertising are The Federal Trade Commission in the United States (Wheeler-Lea Act, 1938), and the Department of Consumer and Corporate Affairs in Canada; but, in addition, many other agencies have jurisdiction over the advertising of particular items.[36] Yet, much remains to be done. As a well-known business scholar says: "Much of the political and social concern about advertising in its varied manifestations would be relaxed, perhaps even resolved, by self-enforced or governmentally enforced standards reflecting simple honesty."[37]

Each merchant owes the trade full support for activities that will eliminate untruthful advertising.

■ SPECIAL SALES EVENTS

An important part of the retailers' advertising program is the planning and execution of special sales events—that is, the heavy promotion of merchandise at reduced prices for a limited period of time. Most retailers believe these events contribute significantly to sales and profits, and that they maintain the customers' interest in the store. As one successful retailer has said, "store business is show business."

We may note three kinds of special sales events: (1) Distress sales —those designed to raise money quickly regardless of their effect on future business; (2) turnover sales—those conducted to sell slow-moving merchandise or to close out a line, brand, or department; and (3) promotion sales—those used to attract new customers, introduce new goods, or secure favorable publicity. These events may include: a clearance sale, anniversary sale, white-goods sale, back-to-school sale, Mother's Day sale, one-cent sale, or fire sale. In addition to special *sales* events, which feature reduced prices, many large retailers conduct special events which may attract considerable publicity and arouse customer interest. These are discussed in the next chapter.

The types of special sales events used by a retailer, and their frequency will depend upon past experience, the competitive situation, group efforts undertaken with other retailers as in a shopping center, aid obtained from manufacturers, the seasonableness of the weather, the accumulation of slow-moving merchandise, and similar factors. Many large stores use special sales extensively to obtain a satisfactory sales volume,* but when used too frequently, they undermine customer confidence in "regular" prices. In addition, customers become indifferent to such events, employees lose their enthusiasm, accounting and control problems are complicated, and merchandise returns are in-

---

* Sears, Roebuck and Company, for example, commonly features such events during the last four days of each week and often supplements them with extra specials on Saturdays, Sundays, and Mondays.

creased. Special sales events often require extra sales personnel and great diligence in controlling shoplifting while satisfactorily handling large numbers of customers.[38]

☐ Joint promotions

Special sales events are often organized by groups of retailers. This practice is not new. But the growth of shopping centers has brought group promotional activities to a new peak. Retailers in these centers have long engaged in joint promotions, often organized around the visit of a celebrity, a circus, an outdoor party on the parking lot, an art exhibit, a concert, or a beauty contest. As shopping centers grew in size and number, and as they became competitive with one another, special sales events became even more desirable as a means of drawing customers to a particular center; and this trend was furthered as free-standing discount houses became more numerous and gave the centers formidable competition for customers. In turn, the special events of shopping centers and discount houses have forced downtown merchants to undertake joint events of their own.[39]

☐ Planning special sales events

Special sales events must be planned with care so that all activities are effectively coordinated. Store-wide sales, for instance, are often planned three to six months in advance. Buyers should approach resources in ample time to obtain the best price concessions, which are frequently made possible through production in dull periods or because of vendors' overstocks. When these arrangements are completed, time is required for production, delivery to the store, receiving, and marking. Time is necessary, also, for preparation and release of advertising—a task superimposed on the regular daily activities of the advertising staff—and for securing additional selling and nonselling employees to handle the customer traffic. Otherwise, the value of the advertising in bringing customers into the store is diminished, since sales are lost and customers become disgruntled because of poor service.

■ DISPLAY

The growth of self-service has brought increased emphasis on display in stores of all types and sizes. However, window display has been neglected, deemphasized, or even completely eliminated in many retail outlets. As one Sears, Roebuck and Company executive stated in 1960: "Show windows to display merchandise were justified when people rode buses and streetcars. Now most of our customers come by automobile. They enter the stores through the rear parking lot. Advertising, not display, brings them in." But downtown merchants know, or should know, that window displays—which occupy the most valuable footage along the front and sides of the building—can be used effectively to stop passersby from passing by. Similarly, windows that face on to the pedestrian concourse in a shopping center can be of major help in inducing customers to enter the store. Good interior display contributes to the atmosphere of the store, breaks up the monotony of a rectangular layout (see pp. 152–53), enhances the featured merchandise, and stimulates impulse buying. Consequently, display warrants very close attention from all merchants.

□ Window displays

Item promotion and image building Stores normally use their display windows to feature merchandise items, although some may occasionally be donated to civic or charitable causes or devoted to nonmerchandise purposes such as fascinating scenes for children at Christmas. The careful selection of merchandise that is distinctive, timely, stylish, or specially good value for the displays contributes to the successful sales of those items. At the same time, the use of appropriate merchandise, careful choice of the right fixtures and mannequins, and taste and imagination in designing and executing the displays contributes greatly to the total store image.

Some chains have headquarter experts set up the forthcoming displays, and then send photographs and complete instructions for their reproduction to their store managers. In department stores, however, window display experts usually are part of the regular staff, sometimes supplemented with outside professionals who provide ideas and materials for such special occasions as the Christmas season. These large stores, as a rule, plan their window displays several weeks in advance, carefully select merchandise to be displayed, arrange definite time schedules for each window, and assign display space to various departments upon the basis of need, prevailing conditions, and other similar factors.

Unfortunately, many other retailers neglect to plan their window displays properly, to "dress" them effectively, and to change them frequently. Too many merchants still consider window dressing as a necessary evil, delegate the responsibility to employees uninterested in such work, and refuse to spend money on fixtures and supplies necessary to do the job properly. The inevitable result is that sales are lost because the store appears unprogressive.

Productive window display Actually a small merchant does not have to spend a fortune on display paraphernalia to have effective windows. Generally, such retailers should follow the advice of Virginia Paxton, window display manager at Marshall Field and Company: "The best display is one in which the background doesn't fight the merchandise."[40] In other words, the emphasis usually should be on the merchandise rather than on background or fixtures. We hardly need mention that the window and the display area should be kept scrupulously clean and well dusted. Any faded or discolored merchandise should be removed immediately. The window should be checked frequently (something that is often neglected) so that any items that have fallen out of place or backing material that has come loose can be quickly restored to proper condition. Vendor-supplied display materials can be very helpful in trimming windows in the small store, but they should be reviewed carefully to be certain that they fit in with the store's own selling program rather than simply being suppliers' billboards used to fill up space.

A good window display can usually convey effectively only one message. This message, of course, may relate to any one of a number of ideas—the variety of values offered; the fashion leadership of the store; or the tie-in with holidays such as Easter, Independence Day, Thanksgiving, and Christmas, or with special occasions such as Mother's Day.[41]

The value of window displays is influenced by the frequency with which they are changed. Although much depends on the location of the store, both as to the site occupied and the size of the city or shopping center, probably stores in small cities *should* change their displays more frequently than stores in the central shopping areas of the large cities or those in regional shopping centers. In practice, however, the reverse is likely to be true, but small city retailers now change displays more often than in the past. Finally, management should make certain that the salespeople are thoroughly familiar with the merchandise in the windows so they can properly respond to customer inquiries.

☐ Interior displays

Interior displays constitute practically the only method of inside sales promotion other than window displays in some stores—particularly supermarkets, variety stores, and many small grocery, drug, and hardware stores. Other retailers coordinate such displays with newspaper advertising featuring the same kinds of merchandise. Or they use them to induce their customers to purchase additional items. Perhaps one-half or more of the purchases made in some types of stores are the result of decisions made by the customer *after* entering the store. And with impulse buying so prevalent in many stores, the correct use of interior displays requires continuous attention. Among food chains, for example, where self service is so common, the number and use of special displays continues to increase. Research suggests that tie-ins between media advertising and point-of-purchase displays to promote identical messages or items may prove especially effective.[42]

Types of interior displays Interior displays may be conveniently classified into three groups: (1) merchandise displays, (2) vendor displays, and (3) store signs and decorations. These classifications are rather arbitrary and overlappings among them are inevitable.

1. Merchandise displays Merchandise displays constitute the main type of interior displays. Three forms may be distinguished: open, closed, and architectural displays.

Open displays are those that make merchandise accessible to customers for examination without the aid of a salesperson. Their variety is legion—shelf displays, as in self-service food stores; counter-top displays, as in drugstores; island displays and mass displays, as in supermarkets; and table-top displays and rack displays, as in department stores. Open displays permit customers to handle merchandise, are readily adjustable to meet variations in customers' demands, are simple and inexpensive to set up, and utilize space that otherwise might be wasted. Interestingly enough, some experiments have concluded that "jumble" (rather than neatly stacked) displays encourage the customer to handle, and to buy more merchandise.

Closed displays consist of merchandise shown inside a wall case or showcase and inaccessible to customers without the aid of a salesperson. Their chief advantages are protection against theft and maintenance of merchandise in saleable condition. For example, jewelry, fur coats, silverware, and expensive cosmetics are so valuable that close control must be exercised. Men's and women's clothing needs protection from excessive handling to prevent soiling and wrinkling. Coats may be chained to an open rack, and the cords of electric appliances may be fastened down to provide a measure of theft protection along with some advantages of open display.

Architectural displays provide an appropriate setting showing various articles of merchandise in use, such as model homes or complete kitchens or complete bathrooms.[43] Their main advantage is that they dramatize the merchandise by showing it in a realistic setting.

2. Vendor displays Vendor displays, also known as point-of-sale (or point-of-purchase) advertising, consist of signs, banners, display racks, and other selling aids provided by the manufacturer, including those used in windows. The Stanley Company, a manufacturer of hand-tools, for example, offers its dealers hexagonal pegboard units that display 198 different kinds of tools, show pictures of tools in use, and hold a 1,000-item reserve stock.[44] Some manufacturers, such as General Electric Company, and Burlington (hosiery) Mills, even supply audio-visual units that show taped commercials for their products.[45] Vendor displays encourage sales in two ways—by reminding salespeople of the product and its merits, thus encouraging suggestion selling, and, more significantly, by informing the shopper of a product at the very moment he or she is in a buying mood. From the manufacturer's point of view, such displays can present the advantages of the product pictorially and dramatically. And this presentation is made to the very people most interested in the product since they are in a store where such merchandise is sold.

Although many valuable displays are furnished retailers by manufacturers either as a gift or at a moderate charge, the increasing volume of point-of-sale display material, coupled with the much slower expansion of available space in the store where this material may be placed, has created problems both for the retailer and the supplier. The manufacturer encounters greater difficulty in getting the displays used and retailers find that many of the displays are too large, poorly designed, and ineffective as sales tools. (See Figure 18–8). It is evident, therefore, that the retailer must consider each display piece on its own merits and find satisfactory answers to such questions as: Is the display suitable to my type of operation? Does the merchandise concerned justify the area occupied by the display? Does the attached sign, taken in conjunction with the merchandise, tell the customer the full sales story, or is a salesperson still needed? What is the cost of the display rack or case?[46]

3. *Store signs and decorations*   The term "store signs" includes counter signs, price cards, window signs, hanging signs, posters, elevator cards, flags, banners, and similar devices. These selling aids are used by all retailers but mostly by stores making frequent use of special promotions and sales events. They are helpful in directing customers to items being featured and in calling attention to particular merchandise values.[47]

Decorations refer to distinctive displays and other related preparations for such occasions as Christmas, Halloween, and for anniversary and birthday sales. Seeking to generate a spirit that will be conducive to buying, retailers probably devote more attention to their Christmas decorations than to those of any other time.

■ RESPONSIBILITY FOR ADVERTISING AND DISPLAY

Regardless of store size, responsibility for advertising and display activities carries with it the obligation to originate and to appraise such activities and to combine them effectively to attain the desired results. In small stores the responsibility rests with the proprietor. In larger ones this responsibility is delegated to qualified individuals, so that the proprietor may devote full attention to coordinating all activities of the business.

In department stores responsibility for sales promotion is centered in the publicity director or the sales promotion manager, who may have the assistance of an advertising agency in planning and carrying out this assignment. This executive may supervise a display manager who is responsible for window and interior displays; an advertising manager who directs the work of the advertising department—including copy, art

FIGURE 18–8 Cartoon suggested in somewhat exaggerated fashion the effects of accepting too many inappropriate display pieces from manufacturers

Oh – for more manufacturer displays!

▶ This cartoon first appeared in HARDWARE RETAILING several years ago to dramatize the problem involved in some of the merchandising displays being developed and offered to the industry, and what happens to retailers who do not exercise proper controls.

Since that time, tremendous improvements have been made, but unfortunately there still are displays being produced that are too large, sometimes hazardous, ill-conceived, etc.

Manufacturers and the people working with and for them responsible for the development of merchandising display units must remember that the *best* dealers — the ones who will sell the *most* merchandise — are the ones who will be most discriminating in selecting units.

Those are the ones to remember when designing time comes. ◀

Reprinted courtesy of Hardware Retailing Magazine, *Indianapolis*

work, and production for various media; and an individual in charge of miscellaneous methods of promoting sales including special events (see Chapter 19). Sometimes this person may be called the "fashion coordinator." And growth in use of television and market research has led some stores to create new positions such as "broadcast coordinator" and research director.

Chain stores have problems that are not encountered in single-store operation. For example, traveling window-display crews may be employed, and advertisements in the form of matrices or proofs, television films or slides, and radio tapes may be sent to individual stores for use. The J. C. Penney Company, for instance, takes the latter step some 30 days before a particular program goes into operation. Items that are "newsworthy and will create a response" are selected jointly by buyers and by sales promotion specialists—who are located in New York City—about four or five months in advance of the use of the advertisements. The central office of Ben Franklin Stores, a national voluntary chain of about 2,000 independent variety stores works out a 52-week promotional program that the store owners can tailor to their individual needs. The program includes quarterly shipments of posters, monthly and weekly newspaper advertising "mat" series sent to the stores about six weeks prior to publication, fourteen monthly and bi-monthly circulars that can be ordered in 4 to 16 page editions and many other promotion services.[48]

A Canadian study, conducted by Urwick, Currie Partners, shows that chain store companies are (1) hiring new marketing experts, (2) using advertising agencies more extensively, particularly for special campaigns and media; (3) using more TV, (4) increasing the ratio of "theme" or institutional advertising to "item" or direct action advertising; (5) using a longer planning period; and (6) centralizing more advertising decisions at headquarters.[49] Except for the increase in relative share of institutional advertising, much the same trends seem to be occurring in the United States. These tendencies are interrelated. The use of a marketing approach with careful planning, and more complex media (TV) require longer planning periods, more centralization and help from agencies, while both centralization and the use of agencies increase the time needed to plan and execute the campaign. But whether an agency is used or not, the final responsibility for the honest and skillful use of advertising rests with the sales promotion executives and ultimately, in both small and large businesses, with top management.

■ REVIEW AND DISCUSSION QUESTIONS

1 Explain the reasons for the growing importance of advertising in the retail store sales promotion program.

2 What are the two main types of retail advertising? Which would you empha-size, and why, if you operated (a) a phonograph record shop, (b) a fine jewelry store, (c) an interior decorator and home furnishings studio, or (d) a chain of automobile tire, battery, and spare-parts stores?

3 What are the advantages and disadvantages of cooperative advertising to the retailer? To the vendor? Why then do some vendors and some retailers reject or discontinue cooperative advertising?

4 Describe in some detail the five major steps that follow determination of the objectives in conducting an effective retail advertising strategy.

5 Why have retailers traditionally used newspapers for most of their advertis-ing? Why are they now shifting some of their advertising budgets into broad-cast media, and why are they still keeping a large portion in the newspapers? What are the merits and drawbacks of other media?

6 Bring a number of retail advertisements to class and discuss how well each seems to meet the guidelines for copy, illustration and layout presented in the text.

7 Suggest special sales events that might be appropriate for a toy store that wants to increase its business during the winter, spring and summer seasons. Would you recommend a similar schedule of special sales events for a store that sells expensive and rather conservatively styled men's clothing?

8 An association of small retailers who do not have display directors have asked you to talk to them on the subject of "planning, timing and preparing good window displays." Write your speech.

9 In a conversation with a wholesaler, J. R. Doe, who operates a super-market, says: "Customers are interested in merchandise and merchandise makes the only good display. Printed materials, cardboard stands, etc., are just a waste of valuable space. Moreover, I won't use manufacturers' mer-chandise displays because they try to steal more space than the items are worth." Discuss Doe's statement.

10 Why are some chains centralizing responsibility for advertising at head-quarters?

■ NOTES AND REFERENCES

1 This definition was formulated by the Definitions Committee of the American Marketing Association. See the report of this Committee in the *Jour-nal of Marketing,* vol. 13, no. 2 (October 1948), p. 205. It continues to be widely accepted.

2 Louis J. Haugh, "Top 50 Retail-ers Spend $2.55 Billion for Advertising," *Advertising Age,* November 29, 1976, pp. 19–20.

3 Laurence W. Jacobs, *Advertis-ing and Promotion for Retailing: Text and Cases* (Glenview, Ill.: Scott, Fores-man and Co., 1972), p. 60.

4 C. M. Edwards, Jr., and R. A. Brown, *Retail Advertising and Sales Pro-motion,* 3d ed. (Englewood Cliffs, N.J.: Prentice-Hall, Inc., 1959), p. 14.

5 "Lifestyle—That Special Ingre-dient," *Women's Wear Daily,* January 10, 1972, p. 24.

6 J. R. Rowen, "Meaningful Themes Give Continuity," *Stores,* June 1974, p. 24.

7 Wroe Alderson et al., *The Structure of Retail Competition in the Philadelphia Market* (Philadelphia: Wharton School of Finance and Com-merce, 1960), p. 32.

8 "Retailers Seek More Co-op TV Freedom," *Home Furnishings Daily,* October 14, 1975, pp. 1, 36; Nancy L. Buc, "Retailers Liable for Ads Prepared by Resources," *Stores,* December 1975, p. 26.

9 R. J. Coen, "Advertising Volume in the U.S. in 1973 and 1974," *Advertising Age,* December 16, 1974, p. 23. These figures are based primarily on space and time costs and only include the planning, production and preparation costs that are covered by media commissions to advertising agencies.

10 Haugh, "Top 50 Retailers Spend . . . ;" "Top 100 National Advertisers in 1975," *Advertising Age,* May 24, 1976, p. 32.

11 Jay Scher, *Financial and Operating Results of Department and Specialty Stores of 1974* (New York: National Retail Merchants Association, Financial Executives Division, 1974), p. xvii. Of these totals from .75 to 1.5 percent were the costs of advertising and publicity management, display and special exhibits.

12 Wendell Earle & Willard Hunt, *Operating Results of Self-Service Discount Department Stores,* 1973–74 (Ithaca, New York: Cornell University, 1975), p. 32. This figure is expressed as a percent of total store sales. It was 2.85 percent of owned-department sales, which excludes volume done by leased-department concessionaires.

13 "42nd Annual Report of the Grocery Industry," *Progressive Grocer,* April 1975, p. 94.

14 One study, for example, showed that extra sales increases resulted when in-store display material contained the same pictures as were used in the store's TV commercials. John P. Dickson, "Retail Media Coordination Strategy," *Journal of Retailing,* vol. 50 (Summer 1974), pp. 61–69.

15 The *American Investor,* the magazine of the American Stock Exchange, reports a study that revealed a loss of retail sales of 1 percent for every degree of temperature below normal any day in the spring or above normal any day in the fall. It was found, also, that "every one-tenth inch of rain that falls between 7:00 and 11:30 a.m. on any day inevitably depresses sales by 1 percent."

"Economic Theory," *Time,* March 19, 1965, p. 98. *See also* "Can You Plan for Rain?" *Chain Store Age* (general merchandise edition), March 1975, p. 24.

16 These aids are illustrated in *Attracting and Holding Customers* (Dayton, Ohio: National Cash Register Company, n.d.), pp. 13–16.

17 For a concise explanation of the main factors governing the choice of media by small retailers and other businesses, *see* H. R. Cook, *Selecting Advertising Media: A Guide for Small Business* (Washington, D.C.: U.S. Government Printing Office, 1969).

18 H. W. McMahan, "Retail Advertising Grows Up" *Advertising Age,* November 12, 1973, pp. 63–67.

19 "How Sears Plans Media," *Media Decisions,* September 1975, p. 53.

20 Larry Goodman, "National Retailers Grow, Lean on Newspaper Ads," *Advertising Age,* September 30, 1974, p. 56. The figures were prepared by the Newspaper Advertising Bureau.

21 Mass Retailing Institute, *Advertising Practices, Budgets, and Costs of Self-Service General Merchandise Retailers* (New York: the Institute, 1974), p. 11. More recent figures are not available.

22 See C. H. Sandage and Vernon Fryburger, *Advertising Theory and Practice,* 9th ed. (Homewood, Ill.: Richard D. Irwin, Inc., 1975), p. 450.

23 That Marketing Man, "Memo on Direct Mail," *Home Furnishings Daily,* September 8, 1972, p. 8; "NRMA Panel Urges a Media Mix for the Big Sell," *Women's Wear Daily,* January 8, 1974, p. 30.

24 For example, "Woodies [Woodward & Lothrop, Washington, D.C.] Shifts Advertising Emphasis to Television on a Large Scale," *Women's Wear Daily,* October 1, 1975, p. 36; "TV Ads Costly, But Win Chains," *Supermarket News,* September 8, 1975, pp. 1, 4; "Multi-Store Retailers Reduce Newspaper Ads to Go on TV," *Home Furnishings Daily,* February 23, 1976, p. 2.

25 *See* Gregory Lincoln, "What TV Can Do (and at What Cost) for Retailers," *Advertising Age,* September 30, 1974, p. 54. *See also* "TV Advertising . . . New Horizon for Hardware Retailers," *Hardware Retailing,* June 1975, pp. 88–89.

26 Ellen Hackney, "If Not the Postal Service, What?" *Hardware Retailing,* February 1976, pp. 88–92.

27 That Marketing Man, "Admen and U.S.P.," *Home Furnishings Daily,* December 17, 1973, p. 18.

28 M. A. Rosenbloom and Judy Y. Ocko, *The Secret of Good Retail Ads: A Handbook for Buyers and Their Bosses.* New York: National Retail Merchants Association, 1974, is a very helpful guide for merchandisers who will work with the advertising staff.

29 Alfred Politz, "The Dilemma of Creative Advertising," *Journal of Marketing,* vol. 25, no. 2 (October 1960), pp. 1–2.

30 Otto Kleppner, *Advertising Procedure,* 5th ed. (Englewood Cliffs, N.J.: Prentice-Hall, Inc., 1966), pp. 108–9.

31 Annalee Gold, "Draw and/or Shoot," *Stores,* May 1976, pp. 13–15, 35–36.

32 Jagdish N. Sheth, "Measurement of Advertising Effectiveness: Some Theoretical Considerations," *Journal of Advertising* vol. 3, no. 1 (1974), p. 11.

33 Alfred Politz, "The Function of Advertising and Its Measurement," *Journal of Advertising,* vol. 4 (Spring 1975), p. 11.

34 Sandage and Fryburger, *Advertising Theory and Practice,* p. 29.

35 J. N. Fry and G. H. McDougal, "Consumer Appraisal of Retail Price Advertisements," *Journal of Marketing,* vol. 38 (July 1974), pp. 64–67.

36 For more details, see James M. Carman and Kenneth P. Uhl, *Phillips' and Duncan's Marketing: Principles and Methods,* 7th ed. (Homewood, Ill.: Richard D. Irwin, Inc., 1973), pp. 137–45; E. J. McCarthy and S. J. Shapiro, *Basic Marketing,* 1st Canadian ed. (Georgetown, Ont.: Irwin-Dorsey Ltd., 1975), pp. 456–58.

37 E. T. Grether, "Marketing and Public Policy: A Contemporary View," *Journal of Marketing,* vol. 38 (July 1974), p. 5.

38 *Selling for Special Occasions* (personnel checklist series) New York: National Retail Merchants Association, 1975.

39 *See* A. K. Kleimenhagen, D. G. Leesberg and B. A. Eilers, "Consumer Response to Special Promotions of Regional Shopping Centers," *Journal of Retailing,* vol. 48 (Spring 1972), pp. 22–29; John H. Fulweiler, *How To Promote Your Shopping Center.* (New York: Chain Store Age Books, 1973).

40 "Prop Stoppers," *Women's Wear Daily,* September 22, 1975, p 20.

41 "F. W. Woolworth Building Displays to Stress One Item," *Chain Store Age* (general merchandise/variety edition), November 1973, p. 70. This constitutes a major change in display policy, since firms such as Woolworth previously tried to show a wide assortment in each window.

42 J. P. Dickson, "Retail Media Coordination Strategy," *Journal of Retailing,* vol. 50 (Summer 1974), pp. 61–69. However, another supermarket study reported that special displays were effective in increasing sales, particularly for items in the mature stage of the product life cycle, but that amount of outside advertising did not affect the percentage sales gain resulting from the displays. Michael Chevalier, "Increase in Sales Due to In-Store Display," *Journal of Marketing Research,* vol. 12 (November 1975), pp. 426–31.

43 A comparable concept is "shop merchandising" in which related groups of merchandise are displayed together in the proper setting. See Chapter 7.

44 "New Stanley Concepts," *Home Furnishings Daily,* November 14, 1973, p. 3.

45 "New Ways to Make a Sale," *Chain Store Age* (general merchandise/variety store edition) June 1974, p. 18; "Audio-Visual Pitch Prods Hosiery Sales," *Women's Wear Daily,* May 23, 1975, p. 1, 16. *See also* "L & T [Lord & Taylor] Communicates With Videotape," *Women's Wear Daily,* September 8, 1975, p. 30.

46 "What to Consider When Selecting a Manufacturer's Display Unit," *Hardware Retailing,* September 1975, p. 66.

47 "Good Signs Point Way to

Easier Shopping," *Supermarket News,* December 24, 1973, p. 11.

48 "Budgeting for a 52-Week Sell," *Chain Store Age* (general merchandise/variety store edition), December 1973, pp. 108–10.

49 "The Multi Market Retailer," *Stimulus,* May/June 1975, pp. 12–17.

OTHER NONPERSONAL METHODS OF RETAIL SALES PROMOTION

Retailers use other nonpersonal methods of retail sales promo-tion in addition to advertising and display as discussed in the previous chapter. Telephone and mail-order selling, packaging, labeling, con-sumer premiums, including trading stamps, special events, and pub-licity, can be very helpful and will be considered in this chapter.

■ TELEPHONE AND MAIL-ORDER SELLING

Soliciting purchases or accepting orders by telephone or mail on the part of retail stores is not a new development.[1] As long ago as 1905, Strawbridge and Clothier of Philadelphia used a full-page advertisement to tell potential customers that it was "The telephone store."[2] But a substantial growth in telephone selling did not take place until the de-pression of the 1930s. In contrast, mail-order selling by retailers has long been accepted as an easy and convenient method for customers who wanted merchandise sent to their homes.

□ Extent and importance

Today both large and small stores actively encourage telephone or mail orders in their advertising.[3] The extent of this practice is evident from the advertisements in the Sunday or, in Canada, Saturday issues of metropolitan newspapers many of which contain the statement "Mail and phone orders filled." Large downtown stores that may be closed to the public on Sundays often keep their switchboards open to receive telephone responses to the newspaper advertisements. Sometimes reply coupons are also included in the copy, to facilitate ordering by mail (see Figure 19–1). In fact, ordering by telephone and by mail has become so prevalent that on occasion customers must be reminded that no mail or telephone orders will be accepted for special merchandise offerings.

Retailers have many other ways of soliciting mail and telephone orders in addition to using newspaper advertisements. Those that use radio or TV may emphasize their telephone number as part of the commercial; some include "stuffers"—small circulars and order blanks— with the monthly statements sent to charge customers; others send direct mail advertisements to old customers or selected lists of prospective customers; and a number issue small catalogs or booklets, particularly during the Christmas selling season.[4] In fact, the tremendous growth of mail-order selling is one of the most striking retailing developments in recent years. Many illustrations of telephone and mail-order selling by retailers are readily available. In 1966 the J. C. Penney Company purchased a small mail-order firm and placed order desks in many of its stores in order to ultimately provide a nationwide mail-order service. About 80 percent of Penney's catalog business is handled at those order desks and in specialized catalog stores and agencies. Only about 20 percent is direct mail order.[5] Sears, Roebuck and Company also receives about 4 percent of its catalog volume by mail; about 50 percent of that volume is received by telephone, and the remainder is obtained over the counter at catalog order desks and catalog stores. The catalog business amounted to about 21 or 22 percent of Sears total sales in 1975.[6] Since 1973 Simpson-Sears, a chain jointly owned by Sears, Roebuck and Simpsons, Ltd. of Toronto, has been experimenting with a system that permits customers in that city who have touch-tone (push

FIGURE 19–1 Coupon used by department store to facilitate ordering by mail

```
ALEXANDER'S MAIL ORDER DEPT.                                    ST-6-28-70
P.O. Box 107, Fordham Station, Bronx, New York 10458
Enclosed please find check or money order for $_____.
Please send the following knit dresses:

| STYLE | QUANTITY | SIZE | COLOR          |     Name_____
|       |          |      | 1st choice 2nd choice |
|       |          |      |                |     Address_____
|       |          |      |                |
|       |          |      |                |     City_____
|       |          |      |                |
|       |          |      |                |     State_____ Zip Code____

Add 60c for delivery of each knit. Add 6% sales tax within N.Y.C. No phone orders. No C.O.D.'s.
```

button) telephones to use those telephone buttons to transmit orders directly to the Simpson-Sears computer.[7] The Robert Simpson Company, another Simpson's department store division, reports great success with telephone order service in selling well-known basic clothing and household items, when the advertisement gives the customer sufficient information for ordering purposes, and when the store maintains adequate stocks to cover the telephone orders.[8] Favorable results from telephone selling are also being shown by such other firms as Montgomery Ward and Company, Spiegel, and Aldens—each providing telephone service through telephone offices, catalog offices, and retail stores.

In the department store field, many firms now sell 5 to 13 percent of their volume by telephone.[9] Carson Pirie Scott and Company of Chicago; T. Eaton Company, of Toronto,* the J. L. Hudson Company of Detroit; and numerous others have long promoted sales by this medium. The same is true for many small and large retailers of other types in all parts of the country; many neighborhood and downtown drug and food stores, for instance, have long depended on the telephone to bring in many of their orders. Telephone selling is also an effective sales tool for specialty stores.

□ Reason for growth of telephone and mail-order selling

Both customers and retailers like telephone and mail-order shopping for many reasons.

Customer's viewpoint Telephone service is convenient. Approximately 94 percent of all households have telephones.[10] Customers can call and place orders, without having to walk or drive to the store, thus avoiding travel, parking, and gasoline costs. Telephone shopping is especially helpful when the customer has to take care of small children, is ill, or wants to avoid bad weather. As noted, some firms accept telephone orders at night or on Sundays when the store is closed, and some arrange for toll-free long distance calls (800, Enterprise, and Zenith numbers). Ordering by mail can also be easy, particularly if the store provides preprinted order forms and postage-paid envelopes. A catalog or mailing piece may show the item more effectively than a crowded display on the store shelves. During inflationary periods, the catalog's prices, which were printed in advance, may offer a saving in comparison to in-store prices that have risen with market changes.[11]

Retailer's viewpoint Telephone and mail-order sales are "plus" sales. Surveys indicate that many such orders come from customers who do not engage in in-store shopping in the same store. The average tele-

---

* But contrary to the general trend, Eaton's discontinued its mail order and catalog division, which had very substantial dimensions, in Spring 1976.

phone sales check is perhaps 40 percent higher than the average floor check.

Retailers can also take the initiative and use the telephone as a business-builder, rather than merely waiting for customers to phone in. To illustrate, one department store encourages its cosmetic saleswomen to call their regular customers bimonthly. Telephone calls can be used in the following ways:

1. Customers can be notified of the receipt of merchandise which was not in stock at the time of their visit to the store or which has been ordered especially for them. Such service prevents lost sales and builds customer goodwill.
2. As the business grows and each of the employees builds up a personal following, there is an increasing opportunity to make use of the telephone to get business by personal calls to customers who are pleased to be notified when some new merchandise arrives.
3. New residents can be tactfully solicited on the telephone, although this practice should be followed carefully. Some shop owners do not approve of it, as they claim that a blind solicitation by telephone often annoys a customer; if she is a busy housewife any interruption of her duties may be considered a nuisance. Therefore, it is often better to build customers' confidence by securing their permission to telephone them.
4. The telephone can be used in an effort to revive inactive credit accounts. With friendliness and a desire to obtain facts, one can: (a) express regret over the decreasing volume of business from such credit customers; (b) ascertain any cause for dissatisfaction; (c) make what commitments are deserved by the circumstance; and (d) solicit an increase of future business.[12]

Improved telephone equipment that is closely adapted to retail selling needs is now available. One new device enables a salesperson to handle four computer based telephone conversations simultaneously with consequent cost savings.[13]

Many large stores also feature a "shopping service" designed to assist telephone or mail-order customers in finding suitable merchandise for all types of occasions. Some of them use special names to identify this service. In San Francisco, for example, the Emporium has its "Barbara Lee" and I. Magnin and Company its "Kitty Steele."

☐ Limitations of telephone and mail-order selling

Despite the growth of telephone and mail-order selling, and despite some evidence to the contrary, many retailers are still reluctant to employ these forms of sales promotion because they fear customers will be kept from visiting their stores. Consequently, some of them still run the line "no mail, no phone, no COD" in their advertisements, hoping this will induce store visits and result in other purchases being made. Retailers also know that telephone solicitation may irritate some customers who resent being disturbed at home. Overly aggressive "high pressure" sales tactics and the poor ethical standards of some firms have fostered suspicion of telephone approaches when the consumer does not know and respect the store that is calling. Other retailers object to this type of selling because the merchandise sold is more likely to be returned than that bought in the store, resulting in increased costs and reduced profits.[14] Of course, if a retailer trains the telephone staff to say, "Let us send you several dresses from which you can select one or two," high returns on telephone sales are to be expected. A similar result follows the sending out of merchandise—for instance, fruits and vegetables—which over-the-counter customers refuse to purchase. If the store makes an honest effort to treat telephone and mail-order customers as well as it treats those who come to the store, there is no reason for excessive returns on such sales.

Some practical operating disadvantages must also be overcome. Sufficient stock should be maintained to permit fulfillment of all orders, thus avoiding customer disappointment when goods are unavailable; delivery service must be provided; and arrangements made to collect on COD transactions and/or to extend credit to telephone customers who desire to purchase on this basis. The telephone salesperson also has the disadvantage of not being able to see the customer and thus note facial reactions to suggestions made. Moreover, some expense and trouble is involved in training and maintaining a telephone and mail-order staff.

□ The future of telephone and mail-order selling

Disagreement exists among retailers concerning the future importance of this business. Those who have obtained satisfactory results from these sales promotion methods are convinced they have a bright future, but those who have not obtained the benefits expected often reach an opposite conclusion. On balance, it seems to the authors that the current sales increases from these methods of selling are in line with fundamental trends, and that further gains may be expected. But each retailer must determine the extent of utilization of these sales promotional devices based on a judgment of their effect on sales volume, the costs involved, and their relationship to the store's other forms of selling effort.

In conclusion, it should be emphasized that sales by telephone and mail-order do not just happen; they are the result of proper planning and the continuous, effective execution of these plans. Successful telephone selling, for example, depends in no small degree upon (1) proper selection and training of personnel; (2) a satisfactory wage scale, which will attract the desired type of employee; (3) proper working conditions, including the provision of adequate facilities; and (4) competent supervision.

■ PACKAGING FOR MODERN SELLING CONDITIONS

The past three decades have witnessed a sharp increase in the attention given to packaging by manufacturers and by retailers. Today, well-conceived packages are essential both in self-service stores where displays perform most of the sales task, and in retail outlets which rely mainly on salespeople. Packaging influences both store layout and display, since the maximum effectiveness of packages cannot be obtained without good display techniques and appropriate fixtures. Business people and consumers, however, must also be concerned with the monetary and ecological costs and benefits of various packaging techniques.

☐ Current attention to packaging

Four main factors have led to the growing interest in packaging by manufacturers and retailers: (1) their desire to meet their customers' wishes, (2) the realization that the package is an effective tool of sales promotion, (3) the growth of the self-service and self-selection store, and (4) various technological and environmental changes. All of these factors are interrelated; each factor is partly cause and partly effect of the others.

Customers have favored the "packaging revolution" since it aids them in buying convenient amounts, keeps products more sanitary, protects fragile items, provides convenient containers for the storing of items while being used in the home, and offers a way to communicate product differences and information. Good packaging reduces product deterioration and thus helps reduce waste.

In addition to pleasing the customer, the manufacturer or the private-branding retailer who packages products gains a valuable sales promotion tool.[15] In fact, some marketing experts rate package appeal as the main reason why a consumer buys one product rather than another. Although the authors do not agree with this statement, because in the long run it is the customer's satisfaction with the contents of the package which results in repeat purchases, there is little doubt but that the appeal of the package—including its style, color, utility, and attractiveness—plays a role in the product's salability. Consequently, the manufacturer who devises an attractive package often has an important advantage over competitors. This competitive factor has been especially significant in self-service stores, where there are no salespeople to extol the merits of the less distinguished package or the unpackaged merchandise.

Technological changes have made possible the greater emphasis on packaging. To illustrate, when the packaging of fresh meat was first attempted the available materials led to discoloration. Gradually the research laboratory turned out today's plastics, including transparent trays, which allow the meat to "breathe" and retain its natural color, thus increasing its salability. Similar technological changes in the wood, paper, metal, and glass industries have produced an almost unbelievable variety of containers.[16]

Societal attention to packaging and its effects has, however, begun to influence seriously the amount and types of packages used in marketing consumer goods. Packagers today are being asked to incorporate five new elements in their package designs: (1) conservation of natural resources, (2) reduction in litter, (3) reduction in pollution potential, (4) increased informative labeling, and (5) package safety.[17] Improved packaging and the disposal of used containers are matters of growing concern. Used package material is now increasingly being recycled.

□ Packaging to meet the customer's needs

Retailers want packages that attract customer attention, protect the product, make the product available in proper amounts or sizes, reflect the nature and use of the product, offer convenience in handling and placing on the shelves and in customer use, make effective displays,[18] are moisture-proof, provide space often called a "white spot," for easy price-marking, and are easily identified so that the customer is aided both in the selection process and in the rejection of substitutes. Many leading retailers feel that their customers will resist excessive or "overly romanced" packages that increase prices unnecessarily. The director of packaging for F. W. Woolworth says that packaging is important for almost every product category, but "We try to use as little packaging as required."[19]

In order to deter shoplifting, merchants often prefer having small, easily-concealed items, such as lipsticks and pens, securely packaged on large, less easily-hidden cards. Storekeepers want packages that conform to all local and national laws concerning reusable containers, size requirements, childproof caps and closures for medicines, and other substances that may be hazardous if used improperly, etc. They also want packages which are not deceptive to the customer, such as results from slack filling. Manufacturers and private-branding retailers who engaged in this practice had only themselves to blame when the late President Kennedy urged a government program for "improving packaging standards and achieving more specific disclosure of the quantity and ingredients of the product inside the package. . . ."[20]

■ LABELING TO MEET CUSTOMERS' NEEDS

Labeling is the placing of text or pictorial material upon a product or attaching such information to its container. It is illustrated by the gummed paper sheet on the package, the printed material placed inside the container, and the tag attached to the product itself. Some label designs have become so popular, at least for a little while, that people collect them, decorate their clothes with label replicas, and buy souvenir products that display familiar labels. In 1975, for example, the Coca Cola Company distributed 8 million sets of glasses bearing the Coke label, as a premium promotion.[21]

Labeling has long been used to identify the manufacturer or distributor of a product, disclose the amounts and ingredients of the contents, and inform the customer as to how the product should be used. In recent years—with the expansion of self-service stores and federal legislation requiring certain product information on various consumer goods—labeling has become an important tool of sales promotion. A tag attached to a television set contains a brief listing of the set's special features. Directions on a tag attached to a woman's Orlon sweater emphasizes the ease with which the sweater can be washed. The gummed label on a package of cake mix employs both text and picture to convey the message that in a few minutes the customer can produce a cake superior to that which "mother made."

Product labeling, in the sense of providing product information and brand identification, is usually the manufacturers' responsibility.* Some merchants have their suppliers go beyond this and attach labels that show various amounts of "store information," such as season code (for example S77 for Spring 1977), style number and price, before shipping the goods to the store. Decisions on whether to mark goods in the store or to have suppliers "preticket" them depend on the size and efficiency at the store's marking facilities; whether, in the case of chains, the goods go first to a central warehouse or directly to the stores; the willingness of suppliers to cooperate; and the amount of information the retailer wants to give the supplier. Some retailers like packages that are automatically labelled with the manufacturer's suggested selling price. Paradoxically they may desire this either because they intend to

---

* Even in the case of private brands, this information is generally placed on the merchandise or package, under the retailer's direction, during the manufacturing process.

charge the suggested price, or because they intend to sell the item for less than the suggested amount and feel that the higher preprinted price will convince consumers that they are being offered a bargain. (Also see the discussion of "preticketing" in Chapter 13 and of suggested prices in Chapter 17.)

□ Retailers' interest in labeling

Retailers can gain from the awakened interest in labeling. Labels build additional sales and reduce selling costs by requiring less aid from salespeople. The added information helps customers select merchandise better suited to their needs, thereby increasing goodwill and reducing returns. As with packaging, however, the retailer suffers if the labeling is misleading. Consequently, regardless of whether the manufacturer or the retailer does the labeling, accuracy is essential.

□ More informative packaging and labeling

Under certain circumstances, food processors and retailers are now required to show the nutritional content (for example, protein, mineral and vitamin levels) of packaged foods, and some private brand retailers have also adopted voluntary nutritional labeling programs.[22] "Open dating" or programs in which food packages are clearly and legibly marked with the date of processing, the last appropriate date for retail sale ("the pull date"), or the last date for consumer use, are also becoming prevalent. Such programs reduce spoilage and increase shopper satisfaction.[23]

Governmental efforts are also being directed toward more accurate practices: witness the 1966 enactment of the "Fair Packaging and Labeling Act" commonly referred to as the "Truth-in-Packaging-Act." The Act became effective July 1, 1967, and gave the Federal Trade Commission and the Food and Drug Administration expanded responsibility in areas covered by the Act's title. It authorized the Commission and the FDA to move against such misrepresentations as: (1) misleading pictorial matter on labels; (2) packages or labels not listing the ingredients, the net quantity, and the size of serving when the number of servings is specified; (3) the use of such words as "jumbo" or "giant" quart; and (4) the employment of "cents off" deals other than on a short-term basis. However, numerous problems have been encountered in enforcing the Act.[24]

Despite the need to eliminate deception in packages and labels, some retailers and manufacturers are concerned that government regulations in this area may result in unnecessary restraints. Specifically, they "fear that negative rules against misrepresentation and deception may lead into detailed, positive regulative requirements and standards" which will weaken the competitive positions of honest companies. Consequently, they feel that Congress should "strike a proper balance so that only packaging and labeling that in fact do confuse and deceive consumers are proscribed."[25]

▪ CONSUMER PREMIUMS TO PROMOTE SALES

The use of consumer premiums* as traffic builders and sales stimulators tends to vary with economic conditions, changes in consumer attitudes, retailers' marketing needs, and competitive conditions. Consumers avidly collected trading stamps and sought other premiums as well during the economic boom of the 1950s and 1960s. By the 1970s, however, the twin forces of inflation and recession (plus possibly some boredom and over-use of those devices) tended to shift customer interest toward price-reduction offers rather than traditional premiums.[26] Nevertheless, many retailers profitably use premiums to attract new patrons, to introduce a new store, to induce customers to pay bills on time, to obtain an audience for merchandise demonstrations, to sell specific items under either their own or a manufacturers' brand, and to promote continuous customer patronage.[27]

☐ Types of consumer premiums

A premium offer is a tie-in arrangement in which one product, (the premium), usually not a part of a seller's regular sales assortment, is sold at a discount or given away in return for the purchase of something else in the regular sales assortment, or in return for visiting the store. There are two major types of premium arrangements, (1) the single transaction offer in which the customer may obtain the premium with a single purchase from the regular assortment; and (2) the continuity offer involving a series of purchases to accumulate coupons, cash register tapes, trading stamps or the like to obtain a premium.[28] Illustrations of the first type are: (a) a backpack for $1.25 with a purchase of a McDonald's hamburger, and (b) the gift of the Encyclopedia of Sports with a Gillette razor. Continuity premiums are exemplified by offers of sets of dishes that can be obtained one item at a time with weekly purchases of some minimum amount in a supermarket. The purpose of a continuity offer is to build up regular habits of visiting the store which, hopefully, will continue after the offer is completed.

---

* Although many manufacturers use premiums to promote the sale of their merchandise, the present discussion is restricted primarily to activities of retailers. See, however, "Coupons" in Chapter 17, for a discussion of manufacturers' "cents off" coupons.

Careful planning and proper execution of a premium program is essential, including establishing guides for selecting products to use as premiums, providing adequate publicity, arranging operating details, and maintaining close cooperation with the manufacturer.

□ Trading stamps and games

Trading stamps are a form of continuity premium that retailers have used in varying amounts since the beginning of the century to satisfy customer desires, to attract and hold trade away from competitors, and to build sales. However, many stamp issuing retailers have done so only in response to competitor's actions and customer tastes. These storekeepers have tended to resent the necessity of buying and distributing the stamps. Similarly, some gasoline station operators have claimed that the major refiners pressured them into using stamps.[29] Supermarkets, which for a long time were the leading users of stamps, began to discontinue them when food prices started to rise in the mid-1960s and some consumers blamed the price increases on the cost of stamps. Only 17 percent of all U.S. supermarkets issued stamps in 1974, as compared with 78 percent in the 1961–63 period.[30] Similarly, the 1973–74 gasoline shortage sharply reduced stamp distribution through gasoline stations.

Stamps appeal to many customers. Despite the decline in the use of trading stamps among supermarkets and the negative reaction of some customers to this promotional device, quite a few retailers continue to offer them to satisfy the preference of their other customers.[31] A 1974 study revealed that trading stamps were saved by 54 percent of all the respondents and that 67 percent regarded stamps as desirable.[32] Many factors probably contributed to this favorable response.

To some customers, stamps are a relatively painless way of saving. To others, they offer certain psychological satisfactions: a reputation for being thrifty, a response to the collecting instinct, and a sense of accomplishment in filling one's stamp books and redeeming them for merchandise. But the basic answer is economic in nature; the belief that the store offering trading stamps gives them more per dollar spent (when both the merchandise purchased and that obtained through the stamps are considered) than does the nonstamp store.

Requirements for successful use of trading stamps   Trading stamps are best suited to certain retailing situations. Competitive conditions will not usually allow a retailer to raise prices to compensate for the cost of stamps, and the discontinuance of stamps involves many serious problems. Before adopting them the retailer should be reasonably sure that they will increase sales or reduce other operating costs. These goals can be achieved only if some or all of these characteristics are present: (a) sufficient excess capacity to permit absorbing a 10 to 20 percent increase in sales without an appreciable change in total overhead costs; (b) a location in reasonably close proximity to a group of stores in various fields who do not provide harmful competition but who do use the same brand of stamp and thus facilitates stamp accumulation by consumers; (c) a willingness to promote the stamps, i.e., a willingness to encourage customers to take them, save them, and redeem them; and (d) the ability to meet competitors in terms of convenience of location, prices, selection and quality of merchandise, courteous and friendly service, cleanliness of housekeeping, and type and quality of services. In the words of one supermarket executive: "Whether stamp or discount, the best operated store is the one which succeeds."

Since not all retailers have these four characteristics, or do not have them in the same degree, the success they have achieved with stamps varies widely. Some have so increased their sales that their profits have advanced, despite the cost of the stamps, others have suffered lower profits.

Games of chance The customer is assured of receiving a designated item or selection of goods from a premium or accumulation of trading stamps. Games, lotteries, drawings, and similar devices differ in that they distribute the rewards to only a few customers, usually chosen by luck or chance. They may be simple in design, and offer a relatively small prize, such as "your purchase free if a lucky star appears on the cash register tape." Or they may involve complicated continuity requirements, such as to assemble a set of cards, issued with purchases over a period of weeks, in which hidden letters spell out the name of the sponsoring store. Games of this sort became very popular as replacements when the stamp boom began to decline. But they involved complex legal problems for the retailer, including the danger of violating anti-lottery postal laws; there were serious accusations that some firms "rigged" or designed the administration of their contests so that a disproportionate number of prizes went to stores that faced strong competition; there were also accusations that some firms misrepresented the chances of winning; and many consumerists objected to games of chance as unduly expensive and unrewarding. Consequently, they soon lost popularity.

The future of trading stamps and games Current trends in consumer behavior are not very favorable to trading stamps and games. Although trading stamps carry a connotation of thriftiness and saving, they actually are most popular when consumers feel most prosperous. Consequently, stamp usage goes through long cycles of expansion and decline, seemingly related to the business cycle and the general price level. Games of chance are more of a fad that bursts into sudden, widespread use at sporadic intervals and then rapidly disappears again. In the minds of many people, they involve more questions of morality or ethics than do stamps, and they also involve the danger of stimulating resentment among non-winning customers. Therefore, retailers should weigh their decisions very carefully when considering the use of such games. But if past history is any guide, both stamps and games may enjoy a renaissance.[33]

In these days of constant change in retailing it is more difficult to forecast developments, perhaps, than ever before. Each retailer, therefore, must analyze the particular situation with great care, and review customers' preferences and competitors' policies thoroughly before deciding whether to use trading stamps or games.

■ SPECIAL EVENTS

We have already noted the importance of special sales events in which goods are offered at reduced prices to attract trade (see pp. 464–65). Other special events that offer customer entertainment or information, rather than price bargains, also draw people to the store, contribute to the store atmosphere and add excitement to a department or to the store as a whole.[34] Merchandise stunts, such as inviting a star baseball or football player to a sporting goods store or department to meet customers and assist them in their purchases or to autograph goods purchased, affords a type of showmanship which often stimulates sales. Abercrombie and Fitch, a deluxe New York City sporting goods store, has a rooftop pool in which a diver has demonstrated aqualung techniques.[35]

Authors of best selling books may be invited to the book department to autograph their volumes or to speak at an "author luncheon." Fashion shows, in which the newest designs in women's ready-to-wear are featured on live models, are widely used by department stores and by some specialty and limited line stores. Bridal fairs, which may be sponsored by an individual store or a group of merchants, provide an opportunity to display fashions, bridal bouquets, wedding invitations, jewelry, furniture, and honeymoon travel.[36] Flower shows, such as those held by Macy's of San Francisco and the May Company in its Denver store, attract numerous "observers" and undoubtedly many buyers. Contests of various sorts—related to cooking, photography, and craftsmanship—are sometimes used by retailers.

The current interest in gourmet cooking, and profitable sales, can be fostered through demonstrations of new cooking utensils and appliances, sampling of unusual foods, and cooking schools.[37] Rich's, a department store in Atlanta, attracts 200 students at a time at a $60 tuition fee for each offering of its five week gourmet cooking course.[38] The Dayton Company in Minneapolis conducts ten-week seminars on homemaking and household decor.[39] Fashion magazines, such as *Seventeen* and *Mademoiselle* will join with stores in staging events that help sell advertisers' products.

In many communities, retailers cooperate in the planning and execution of an annual sidewalk arts and crafts fair to attract customers to the shopping district and thus to increase sales. Some stores sponsor parades to advertise the store and promote business. R. H. Macy and Company's parade inaugurating the Christmas season and using mammoth balloon animals and comic strip characters is probably one of the best known.

The variety of such events that a store can conduct is limited only by the imagination and energy of its personnel, and also by its budget. As suggested by the preceding comments, manufacturers and other suppliers will sometimes cooperate and absorb much of the cost if their items are featured. As a practical matter, large stores are more likely to receive such assistance than small stores.* Even the large stores must scrutinize offers of cooperation carefully and make certain that the items and promotional techniques involved meet store standards and are acceptable to their customers. Special events can also consume an inordinate amount of staff time and divert attention from the day-to-day work of running the store. Nevertheless, such events do help give a store a distinctive personality. Wisely used, they contribute to immediate sales results and also help build a loyal store clientele.

■ PUBLICITY

Publicity consists of unpaid news stories and editorial features about the store, its products, events and people, placed in broadcast or published media. Outsiders often have exaggerated ideas about the ease with which publicity can be secured and the effect it will have on sales. One editor talks about "the tremendous crush of 'Gimme's'"—the army of individuals, firms, and other organizations that keep saying in effect, "please give me a lot of free newspaper space."[40] Consequently, editors must be very selective in choosing the publicity stories they will print. They only want newsworthy ones, and they ordinarily will not feature any one store in the continuous, repetitive manner that is essential to a sound promotional program. An individual whose name or picture appears even once in the newspaper is likely to be very conscious of it, but the general public is not that easily impressed.

However, publicity can be a useful adjunct when something newsworthy happens at the store. It helps create "visibility and identity" or in other words, it helps build a desirable store image in the consumer's mind.[41] The topics that may provide suitable material for publicity releases include interesting special events, such as were described in the preceding section of this chapter, fashion shows and news of styles for the forthcoming season; significant community or public service activ-

---

* Even under the "proportionately equal" doctrine, the subsidy or allowance available to a small customer may be inadequate for conducting a significant event.

ities of the store; and announcement of a new store, branch, or department. Particularly in small towns, where people are very much interested in local institutions, publicity can be obtained for any major change or remodeling of a local business.

The publicity release should be written in news style. It should be factually accurate, and should not contain any "puffery" or adjectives praising the store. The essence of the publicity release should be concentrated in the first paragraph and then amplified with successively less important details in each of the following paragraphs so that the editor may easily cut it to any desired length. The release itself should be typed, double-spaced on one side of the page only, and clearly marked with the name and address of the issuing organization, name and telephone number of the individual who prepared it and who can provide further details if desired, date of issuance, and date (either immediately or some specified point in the future) when the material may be printed.[42]

■ SOME GENERAL OBSERVATIONS

We should note several further aspects of sales promotion.

□ Variety

The types of nonpersonal promotion described above do not exhaust the list of techniques that retailers can, and possibly will use to increase sales. Some stores sell gift certificates, often mounted in attractive presentation folders, that are redeemable in merchandise, so as to serve customers who want to send presents but who do not know the recipients' sizes or exact preferences.[43] Stores that sell merchandise for children sometimes offer a special little treat or send a greeting card on the customer's birthday. Many stores offer samples of new foods or candies. One retailer may provide merchandise to be used, with proper credit, in another dealer's window displays. Thus a dress shop may lend clothes and a clothing dummy to fit into a luggage store's display, and the luggage merchant may lend some suitcases for a travel agent's window. Fashion shows, exhibits and demonstrations may be conducted off the store premises as well as in the store building. The manager of the stationery department in a Texas store increased his sales of pocket electronic calculators substantially by lecturing to high school classes on how to use the machines. This list of promotional methods could be extended almost indefinitely.

Moreover, technology may provide new avenues of sales promotion. Many merchants and writers expect widespread use of cable television that would permit customers to view merchandise displays at home and ultimately to transmit orders from their household consoles.[44] While such systems are technically feasible today, they are still far too costly and inadequately matched to customer shopping habits to be practical. Nevertheless, alert merchants will watch for possible developments in this area.

☐ Limitations

A retailer must consider the cost, possible disadvantages, and appropriateness of any technique before deciding to use it. Rising costs for postage, newspaper space, premiums, and other components of promotional programs have made many retailers reevaluate their choice of sales-stimulation techniques. Some of these techniques have other disadvantages besides cost. As noted, contests and games may evoke resentment among disappointed nonwinners, while special events may require an inordinate amount of effort. Such events may also attract numerous people who come to watch rather than buy. The resulting congestion can interfere with regular business and also increase the danger of shoplifting. Finally the techniques must be suited to the store and its merchandise. Issuing trading stamps would harm rather than help an expensive, high-fashion dress shop, since the stamps would not be appropriate to the store image. A record shop would hardly want to take national brand or national label records out of albums to repackage and relabel on its own.

☐ Governmental control

As has been emphasized at several points, both government and voluntary groups now monitor promotional practices and exercise increasing control to insure truthfulness in promotional statements. For example, according to one knowledgeable attorney, the Federal Trade Commission is likely to consider a promotional claim as false, misleading, deceptive, or unfair if it is false, is partially true and partially false, is unsubstantiated, contains insufficient information, creates a false impression, is based on false proof, motivates some relatively helpless group such as children to take harmful action, or offers promises that are unlikely to be fulfilled.[45] Packaging, labeling, and prize contest programs are also subject to strict controls. Retailers should seek advice from their trade association or from competent lawyers before undertaking any such program. Other promotional media, such as publicity and special events, normally involve fewer regulatory problems except to insure that such events are conducted without violating safety and fire rules. Nevertheless, all promotional activities should conform to high ethical standards that will maintain long-run customer goodwill.

■ REVIEW AND DISCUSSION QUESTIONS

1 Describe the factors that are likely to lead to an increase in the percentage of business that stores receive by telephone and mail order. Will anything tend to reduce that percentage?

2 Assume that you are a member of the buying committee in a large supermarket company and that you are going to speak at a grocery manufacturers' convention on the topic. "Our desires in grocery packaging and labeling." What will you say? Would your remarks differ if you were a department store merchandise manager talking to group of men's furnishings manufacturers?

3 Based on observations in local stores, give four examples of labeling used to promote sales. In at least two of these examples suggest how the labeling might be improved.

4 Based on observations in local stores, give four examples of packages or labels that contain information presented to conform to government regulations. Explain the regulations involved and discuss how helpful the information might be to you or to other consumers in making purchasing decisions. What additional information, if any, would you like?

5 Distinguish between single transaction and continuity premiums and give examples of both types. What are the reasons why a retailer who wants to give premiums might decide to use a single transaction offer? What are the reasons for using a continuity premium?

6 How do you account for the decline in the use of trading stamps since 1961–63, and how do you explain their previous growth?

7 What is the difference between a special event and a special sales event? Suggest some special events that might be appropriate for two of the following: (a) a pet shop; (b) a ski shop; (c) a lumberyard and building supply store that sells to consumers, and (d) a record shop.

8 Examine several issues of a local newspaper and see if you can find any examples of retailers' publicity efforts.

9 What are some of the rules for preparing publicity releases? Prepare a press release for an imaginary fashion show in accordance with these rules.

10 Review the types of sales promotion discussed in this chapter, and indicate the major drawbacks or limitations to the use of each type.

■ NOTES AND REFERENCES

1 As used throughout this section, "mail orders" refers to such sales made by retailers who predominantly sell over the counter. Of course specialized mail order firms also do a substantial volume of business. The 1972 U.S. Retail Census reports sales of approximately $4½ billion for mail order establishments, but this figure may include some mail order warehouses operated by general merchandise chains. Bureau of the Census, *1972 Census of Retail Trade, Area Statistics, United States* (RC72–A–52) (Washington: U.S. Government Printing Office, 1975), p. 8.

2 *Philadelphia Bulletin,* June 3, 1905.

3 A Michigan State University study reveals that mail and telephone shopping has doubled in recent years despite the expansion of suburban shopping centers. See P. L. Gillett, "An Analysis of Demographic, Socioeconomic and Attitudinal Characteristics of the Urban In-Home Shopper" (Unpublished Ph.D. dissertation, Michigan State University, 1969), p. 5.

4 Retailers disagree about the profitability of such seasonal catalogs. Some department stores have discontinued or deemphasized housewares catalogs in favor of newspaper and broadcast promotion. Earl Lifshey, "Fading Glory," Home Furnishings Daily, January 23, 1975, p. 10. Yet Lowe's Companies, Inc., a very successful regional chain of home supply and hardware stores was pleased enough with 1973 results to increase its 1974 catalog from 128 to 160 pages. "Lowe's Guide Has 80 'How To' Pages," Home Furnishings Daily, July 24, 1974, p. 22. See also "Costs Up but Catalogs Help the Bottom Line," Women's Wear Daily, November 19, 1975, p. 16.

5 "Mail Order or Catalog Sales?", Retailing Today, October 1974, p. 4.

6 "Cost Control, Better Markup Hike Big Chain Catalog Net," Home Furnishings Daily, November 11, 1975, p. 2.

7 "Shopping by EDP: The Magic Touch," Women's Wear Daily, October 8, 1973, pp. 1, 12.

8 "Phone-Orders: Profitable Sales Potential," Stores, July 1975, p. 49; W. D. Hill, "Profitable Mail and Phone Business," Stores, February 1976, p. 34.

9 National Cash Register Company, "Attracting and Holding Customers" (Dayton, Ohio: n.d.), p. 27.

10 Statistical Abstract of the United States, 1974. Washington: U.S. Government Printing Office, 1974, p. 500.

11 "Mail Order or Catalog Sales?"

12 "Attracting and Holding Customers," p. 27.

13 "Marketing Observer," Business Week, September 23, 1975, p. 84.

14 See "Chicago's Boiler Room Business," Home Furnishings Daily, December 19, 1972, pp. 4–5; "Catalog: Merchants Battle Returns," Chain Store Age (general merchandise edition), May 1976, p. 36.

15 For illustrations of this point, see Walter Landor, "What's Wrong (and Right) with Today's Packages," Advertising Age, April 29, 1974, pp. 29, 44.

16 W. P. Margulies, "Materials, Shapes, Marketing Segmenting Are Packaging Keys," Advertising Age, April 29, 1974, p. 53; "Package Design Faces Up to the Recession," Packaging Design, Summer 1975, pp. 18–19.

17 "The Billion Dollar Packaging Snarl," Modern Packaging, April 1973, p. 30.

18 See "Says Packaging Should Reflect Retail Surroundings," Supermarket News, August 4, 1975, p. 5.

19 "Chains Eagle-Eye Packaging," Chain Store Age (general merchandise edition) April 1975, p. 30.

20 Message to Congress of March 15, 1961, as reported in full in the New York Times, March 16, 1961.

21 "Logo Lovers," Forbes, November 15, 1975, p. 39.

22 "Grand Union Labels List Nutrients," Supermarket News, October 15, 1973, p. 4; "Nutritional Labeling," Chain Store Age (supermarket edition), October, 1974, pp. 43–50.

23 U.S. Department of Agriculture Food Dating (Marketing Research Report No. 984). Washington: the Department, 1973. But also see P. Nayak and L. J. Rosenberg, "Does Open Dating of Food Products Benefit the Consumer?", Journal of Retailing, vol. 51 (Summer 1975), pp. 10–20.

24 For a discussion of problems leading to passage of the Act and difficulties in enforcing it, see William T. Kelley and Etienne Gorse, "The Fair Packaging and Labeling Act of 1966: Does it Protect the Consumer?" in W. T. Kelley, ed., New Consumerism (Columbus, Ohio: GRID, Inc., 1973), pp. 425–50.

25 E. T. Grether, Marketing and Public Policy (Englewood Cliffs, N. J : Prentice-Hall, Inc., 1966), p. 47.

26 "Dealer, Salesmen Incentives Lead Premium Growth," Advertising Age, September 22, 1975, pp. 1, 30.

27 "Premium Suppliers Report

Gain in Supermarket Use," *Supermarket News,* October 6, 1975, p. 10.

28 Another classification of consumer premiums used by grocery manufacturers is as follows: (1) self-liquidators (the price charged the consumer reimburses the firm for the cost of the premiums), (2) in-pack premiums, (3) coupon plans, (4) on-pack premiums, (5) free mail-in premiums, and (6) container premiums, with the container itself a useful object. "How the Industry Uses Premiums," *Grocery Manufacturer,* September 1969.

29 "S&H Fights a Slump in Trading Stamps," *Business Week,* August 25, 1973, pp. 72–74; "Sharp Drop in Gas-Station Business Brings Trading Stamp Industry More Woes," *Wall Street Journal,* March 1, 1974, p. 26.

30 *The Supermarket Industry Speaks, 1971; The Supermarket Industry Speaks, 1975* (Chicago: The Super Market Institute, 1971, 1975), p. 12; p. 15.

31 "Surprise!! Shoppers Still Like Trading Stamps," *Incentive Marketing,* March 1974, pp. 93–94; Herbert Kosehtz, "The Trading Stamp Tries for a Comeback," *New York Times,* June 20, 1976, sec. 3, p. 3.

32 "Marketing Briefs," *Marketing News,* July 18, 1975, p. 3. The study was one of a continuing series commissioned by a major stamp company. Although it reported a persistance of favorable attitudes toward stamps, it also showed a decline in the prevalence of those attitudes.

33 Supermarket chains experimented with bingo and other game promotions in about twelve states in 1974–75. See "Bingo Promo's Back in Three Supermarket [Chains]," *Advertising Age,* September 29, 1975, p. 52; "Around the Circle Again—With Games," *Retailing Today,* January, 1975, p. 3. Also some retailers have adopted stamps. *See,* for example, "Zayre Held Near Trading Stamps," *Home Furnishings Daily,* October 2, 1975, p. 4; "In Birmingham, Battle of Stamps Continues," *Supermarket News,* September 8, 1975, p. 10.

34 A prominent Japanese merchant comments that American department stores are outstanding in technical merchandising and marketing skills, but that they lack "excitement" in com-

parison to stores in his country. He believes that there should be many more of these special events, and that department stores should also sponsor athletic contests, show movies and plays, and have pet shops, exhibit halls, roof gardens and customer clubs, as is customary in Japan. *See* Samuel Feinberg, "Japanese Retail Exec: 'U.S. Stores Need More Excitement,'" *Women's Wear Daily,* July 1, 1975, p. 11, quoting Hideo Yamanaka.

35 "A and F Sporting Its Old Look," *Women's Wear Daily,* July 9, 1973, p. 8.

36 For example, see "The Bridal Fair at Valley Forge," *Stores,* June 1974, pp. 2, 26.

37 Earl Lifshey, "Cooking Up Gourmet Sales," *Home Furnishings Daily,* August 21, 1975, p. 5.

38 "Rich's Cooking School Stirs Gourmet Sales," *Home Furnishings Daily,* September 18, 1975, p. 12.

39 "Dayton's Launches Seminars on Home Making, Decor," *Home Furnishings Daily,* September 16, 1975, p. 2.

40 Oxie Reichler, editor, Yonkers (N.Y.) *Herald-Statesman,* quoted in Raymond Simon, *Casebook in Publicity and Public Relations,* 3d ed. (Columbus, Ohio: GRID, Inc., 1972), p. 43.

41 Terry Mayer, "Public Relations for Retailers," in Philip Lesly, ed., *Lesly's Public Relations Handbook.* (Englewood Cliffs, N.J.: Prentice-Hall, Inc., 1971), p. 212.

42 Most of the points in this paragraph are drawn from J. C. Cumming, *Making Fashion and Textile Publicity Work* (New York: Fairchild Books, 1971), pp. 41–51.

43 "Gift Certificates Spur Store Sales 15%," *Home Furnishings Daily,* December 9, 1974, p. 6.

44 "N-M Tests Cable TV as a Sales Vehicle," *Women's Wear Daily,* January 16, 1974, p. 66. However, this Nieman Marcus experiment did not succeed. "The New Way to Exploit Profits," *Chain Store Age* (general merchandise edition), September 1975, p. 132.

45 Dorothy Cohen, "The Concept of Unfairness as It Relates to Advertising Legislation," *Journal of Marketing,* vol. 38 (July 1974), p. 8–13.

PERSONAL SELLING

Except for self-service stores and purchases from vending machines or by mail, a customer-salesperson relationship is essential to complete a sale. The impression customers receive from salespeople often determines their opinions of stores.[1] The actions and attitude of the salesperson can nullify the sales promotion efforts that brought the customer to the store. Stated positively, the customer should be treated pleasantly and courteously, should be made to feel welcome in the store, should be given honest and useful assistance in purchasing suitable merchandise, and should obtain a feeling of confidence in the store and its offerings. These are the goals of retail salesmanship; it should be the goal of every salesperson to aid in their accomplishment.[2]

■ CURRENT IMPORTANCE OF
RETAIL SALESMANSHIP

Salesmanship is "selling goods that won't come back to customers who will." Customers will remain loyal to a store if the merchandise that is sold to them meets their needs adequately, if the prices charged represent good values, and if they are satisfied with the services rendered by the store. Stores need this regular patronage which is based upon goodwill—the disposition of a pleased customer to return to the store where she or he has been well treated. The importance one retail organization attaches to customer goodwill is indicated by these lines which are constantly reiterated to all store personnel: "Let no man and no woman leave this store at night without being able to say, 'I have done something today to preserve and increase the goodwill of Rich's.' "[3] The commercial effect of building goodwill is demonstrated by the experience of an employee in a department store's interior design studio. She sold a $10,000 Oriental rug to a repeat customer who had originally dropped into the studio to find some fabric for reupholstering kitchen chairs and had become impressed with that employee's friendly, helpful assistance.[4]

This customer-is-king concept of salesmanship—to look at everything from the customer's point of view—is relatively new. For many years the doctrine of *caveat emptor* (let the buyer beware) prevailed. Under this doctrine the forces of persuasion and cunning were brought to bear upon the prospective customer, so that one would buy regardless of one's intentions or the suitability of the goods for perceived requirements. Today, however, in contrast to that concept of salesmanship, the idea is to help people to buy. The preference of satisfied customers for particular stores and particular salespeople is built upon the faith they have in the honesty and the sincere desire of management and salespeople to serve the customers' interests.[5]

☐ Personal salesmanship still needed

Some observers contend that the era of informed, creative personal selling in stores has passed and that we are now in an age of impersonal trade. One discount house operator has said: "We don't want salesmen in our organization. Our people are educated order-takers. . . . Our clerks are trained to be courteous, to answer his (customer) questions, and give him what he wants, but not to waste time trying to sell him anything. I believe this is the coming pattern of retailing—for every kind of merchandise—cars, motor-boats, everything. Selling has become an unnecessary vocation."

Those who take this "personal salesmanship is unnecessary" point of view are influenced by a number of developments, such as the preselling of customers by national advertising; the growing part of the selling task assigned to merchandise displays, packaging, and labeling; the rise of self-service and self-selection stores as illustrated by the supermarket and the discount house; and by the thought that the automated store lies just ahead. A few of them even forecast the end of the retail store as we know it, with the customer "shopping" at home over a television set or ordering by telephone from a "warehouse with no floor traffic" establishment.[6]

Even though those factors have lessened the importance of personal selling in some establishments, selling is, and is likely to continue to be, essential in many stores. Customers still need help in selecting items and in coordinating personal assortments,[7] they require information about complex products, and they want advice and reassurance. In fact, some supermarkets are now expanding service operations in delicatessen and other departments.[8] Consequently, the great need is to improve, rather than eliminate, personal selling. Management must also increase the productivity of the sales staff in order to offset rising wage and fringe benefit costs.

☐ Need for improvement of retail salesmanship

In spite of the critical importance of retail salesmanship, the actual caliber of performance in many stores leaves much to be desired. Customers complain that salespeople are often rude, disinterested, uninformed, and unhelpful.[9] Frequently, customers have to wait an excessive length of time, even when the store is not busy, before anyone will help them.* In a few instances, stores that sell very luxurious, expensive merchandise to impressionable customers seem to have encouraged their salespeople to be disdainful and arrogant, so that the patrons come to feel privileged in being allowed to buy the products. A writer describes one such store: "[Its] staff has mastered the art of the drop-dead put-down and the icy stare, flashing signs that the customer is unworthy. . . ."[10] But this crude approach will not work for the great majority of stores, or with most sensible customers. Consequently, it is apparent that retail salesmanship should be improved. Management has a pressing obligation to adopt whatever measures are necessary to accomplish this objective.

In stores where retail salespeople are necessary, management may take measures to obtain better productivity by salespeople. Probably the most important is the selection, training, and supervision of the sales staff. (Also see the discussion of these topics in Chapters 8 and 9.) Qualified personnel cannot be hired without carefully prepared job descriptions and tests to determine if applicants possess the required characteristics. And they cannot perform adequately without proper training in their duties, including emphasis on proven sales techniques.

Supervising and evaluating salespeople is essential to the attainment of sales goals. (See "Management's responsibility for personal salesman-

---

* The problem of providing timely service is complicated, however, because some customers like to browse and examine the merchandise before entering into a conversation with a salesperson. Acknowledging their presence and saying, "Please let me know when you want some help and I'll be glad to assist you" is often the best way to handle such customers. The size of the sales staff relative to the number of customers also affects the speed with which service can be provided.

ship," p. 509.) The basics of sound sales supervision have been summarized by one authority as follows:

1. Know what you expect the salesman to do.
2. See that he knows what you expect him to do.
3. Know that he does what you expect of him.
4. Let him know you know that he has done it.
5. Let him know you appreciate what he has done.[11]

Although these points apply to the sales staff in general, they have equal
relevance to retail salespeople. Numbers (1) and (2) have been covered
in the previous paragraph. Concerning numbers (3), (4), and (5), it is
evident that everyone deserves recognition of his or her accomplishments, encouragement in seeking continued improvement, and adequate rewards when the desired results are achieved.

Engineering approach   Many firms have adopted an "engineering
approach" to improve sales efficiency. Essentially, this approach involves
the use of mechanical equipment, store layout improvements, scientific grouping of merchandise, and the better planning of the flow of
work so that the salesperson has more time to devote to selling. Various
forms of automation have substantially reduced the time needed for
nonselling activities. Mechanical devices have speeded the movement of
merchandise from receiving areas and stock rooms to the selling floor;
electronic equipment has decreased the time that sales personnel must
give to recording sales transactions; and inventory-taking has been facilitated through the use of various sophisticated devices. But such measures are only a good beginning; future years are certain to bring many
more significant developments as competition increases the need to
reduce selling costs and to increase sales productivity.

Some manufacturers and trade associations provide retailers with
the means of evaluating the productiveness of their salespeople in relation to selling cost. For example, the National Cash Register Company
has prepared the chart shown in Figure 20–1.* To understand its use, let
us assume that a salesperson receives $90 per week in a store whose
salary cost percentage is 15.0. To determine how much that person
should sell to earn the salary we proceed as follows:

Under the column headed $90 (1), find the figure 15.0 (2). To the side in the
"amount of weekly sales" column, you will find that the salesperson should
sell $600 (3) worth of merchandise to justify the salary received.

But suppose at the end of the week the individual has sold only $500
worth of merchandise. Obviously, this is below quota. Now locate this figure
(4) in the weekly sales column and then follow along the line to the left until
you reach 15.0 (5). At the top of this column . . . a weekly salary of $75 (6) is

---

* Current dollar figures would be higher than those used in the example, but the
principle remains the same.

FIGURE 20–1 Form for evaluation of salespeople in retail stores

SALARY COST

$72.50	$75.00	$77.50	$80.00	$82.50	$85.00	$87.50	$90.00	$92.50	$95.00	$97.50	$100.00
48.3	50.0	51.7	53.3	55.0	56.7	58.3	60.0	61.7	63.3	65.0	66.7
45.3	46.9	48.4	50.0	51.6	53.1	54.7	56.3	57.8	59.4	60.9	62.5
42.6	44.1	45.6	47.1	48.5	50.0	51.5	52.9	54.4	55.9	57.4	58.8
40.3	43.0	44.4	45.8	47.2	48.6	51.0	51.4	52.8	54.2	55.6	
38.1	39.5	40.8	42.1	43.4	44.7	46.1	47.4	48.7	50.0	51.3	52.6
36.2	37.5	38.7	40.0	41.3	42.5	43.8	45.0	46.3	47.5	48.8	50.0
34.5	35.7	36.9	38.1	39.3	40.5	41.7	42.9	44.0	45.2	46.4	47.6
32.9	34.1	35.2	36.4	37.5	38.6	39.8	40.9	42.0	43.2	44.3	45.5
31.5	32.6	33.7	34.8	35.9	37.0	38.0	39.1	40.2	41.3	42.4	43.5
30.2	31.2	32.3	33.3	34.4	35.4	36.5	37.5	38.5	39.6	40.6	41.7
29.0	30.0	31.0	32.0	33.0	34.0	35.0	36.0	37.0	38.0	39.0	40.0
27.9	28.8	29.8	30.8	31.7	32.7	33.7	34.6	35.6	36.5	37.5	38.5
26.8	27.8	28.7	29.6	30.6	31.5	32.4	33.3	34.3	35.2	36.1	37.0
25.9	26.8	27.7	28.6	29.5	30.4	31.3	32.1	33.0	33.9	34.8	35.7
25.0	25.9	26.7	27.6	28.4	29.3	30.2	31.0	31.9	32.8	33.6	34.5
24.2	25.0	25.8	26.7	27.5	28.3	29.2	30.0	30.8	31.7	32.5	33.4
23.3	24.1	23.8	24.6	25.4	26.2	27.1	28.5	29.2	30.0	30.8	
20.7	21.4	22.1	22.9	23.6	24.3	25.0	25.7	26.4	27.1	27.9	28.6
19.3	20.0	20.7	21.3	22.0	22.7	23.3	24.0	24.7	25.3	26.0	26.1
18.1	18.8	19.4	20.0	20.6	21.3	21.9	22.5	23.1	23.8	24.4	25.1
17.0	17.6	18.2	18.8	19.4	20.0	20.6	21.2	21.8	22.4	22.9	23.5
16.1	16.7	17.2	17.8	18.3	18.9	19.4	20.0	20.6	21.1	21.7	22.2
15.3	15.8	16.3	16.8	17.4	17.9	18.4	18.9	19.5	20.0	20.5	21.1
14.8	15.0										
13.8		14.8	15.2	15.7	16.2	16.7	17.1	17.6	18.1	18.6	19.0
13.2		14.1	14.5	15.0	15.5	15.9	16.4	16.8	17.3	17.7	18.2
12.6	13.0	13.5	13.9	14.3	14.8	15.2	16.7	16.1	16.5	17.0	17.4
12.1	12.5	12.9	13.3	13.8	14.2	14.6	15.0				
11.6	12.0	12.4	12.8	13.2	13.6	14.0		14.8	15.2	15.6	16.0
11.1	11.5	11.9	12.3	12.7	13.1	13.5		14.2	14.6	15.0	15.4
10.7	11.1	11.5	11.8	12.2	12.6	13.0	13.3	13.7	14.1	14.4	14.4
10.4	10.7	11.1	11.4	11.8	12.1	12.5	12.9	13.2	13.6	13.9	14.3
10.0	10.3	10.7	11.0	11.4	11.7	12.1	12.4	12.8	13.1	13.4	13.7
9.7	10.0	10.3	10.7	11.0	11.3	11.7	12.0	12.3	12.7	13.0	13.3
9.3	9.7	10.0	10.3	10.6	11.0	11.3	11.6	11.9	12.3	12.6	12.9
9.1	9.4	9.7	10.0	10.3	10.6	10.9	11.3	11.6	11.9	12.2	12.5
8.8	9.1					10.6	10.9	11.2	11.5		

PERCENTAGES | **WEEKLY SALARIES / AMOUNT OF WEEKLY SALES**

$160.00	$165.00	$170.00	$175.00	$180.00	$185.00	$190.00	$195.00	$200.00	$205.00	$210.00	$215.00	$220.00	$225.00	$230.00	$
106.7	110.0	113.3	116.7	120.0	123.3	126.6	130.0	133.3	136.6	140.0	143.3	146.6	150.0	153.3	150
100.0	103.1	106.3	109.4	112.5	115.6	118.8	121.8	125.5	128.1	131.2	134.3	137.5	140.6	143.7	160
94.1	97.1	100.0	102.9	105.9	108.9	111.7	114.7	117.6	120.5	123.5	126.4	129.4	132.3	135.2	170
88.9	91.7	94.4	97.2	100.0	102.7	105.5	108.3	111.1	113.8	116.6	119.4	122.2	125.0	127.7	180
84.2	86.8	89.5	92.1	94.7	97.4	100.0	102.6	105.2	107.8	110.5	113.1	115.7	118.4	121.0	190
80.0	82.5	85.0	87.5	90.0	92.5	95.0	97.5	100.0	102.5	105.0	107.5	110.0	112.5	115.0	200
76.2	78.6	81.0	83.3	85.7	88.1	90.4	92.8	95.2	97.6	100.0	102.3	104.7	107.1	109.5	210
72.7	75.0	77.3	79.5	81.8	84.1	86.3	88.6	90.9	93.1	95.4	97.7	100.0	102.2	104.5	220
69.6	71.7	73.9	76.1	78.3	80.4	82.6	84.7	86.9	89.1	91.3	93.4	95.6	97.8	100.0	230
66.7	68.8	70.8	72.9	75.0	77.1	79.1	81.2	83.3	85.4	87.5	89.5	91.6	93.7	95.8	240
64.0	66.0	68.0	70.0	72.0	74.0	76.0	78.0	80.0	82.0	84.0	86.0	88.0	90.0	92.0	250
61.5	63.5	65.4	67.3	69.2	71.1	73.1	75.0	76.9	78.8	80.7	82.7	84.6	86.5	88.4	260
59.3	61.1	63.0	64.8	66.7	68.5	70.3	72.2	74.0	75.7	77.7	79.6	81.4	83.3	85.1	270
57.1	58.9	60.7	62.5	64.3	66.0	67.8	69.6	71.4	73.2	75.0	76.7	78.5	80.3	82.1	280
55.2	56.9	58.6	60.3	62.1	63.8	65.5	67.2	68.9	70.6	72.4	74.1	75.8	77.5	79.3	290
53.3	55.0	56.7	58.3	60.0	61.6	63.3	65.0	66.6	68.3	70.0	71.6	73.3	75.0	76.6	300
49.2	50.8	52.3	53.8	55.4	56.9	58.4	60.0	61.5	63.0	64.6	66.1	67.6	69.2	70.7	325
45.7	47.1	48.6	50.0	51.4	52.9	54.2	55.7	57.1	58.5	60.0	61.4	62.8	64.2	65.7	350
42.7	44.0	45.3	46.7	48.0	49.3	50.6	52.0	53.3	54.6	56.0	57.3	58.6	60.0	61.3	375
40.0	41.3	43.0	43.8	45.0	46.2	47.5	48.7	50.0	51.2	52.5	53.7	55.0	56.2	57.5	400
37.6	38.8	40.0	41.2	42.4	43.5	44.7	45.8	47.0	48.2	49.4	50.5	51.7	52.9	54.1	425
35.6	36.7	37.8	38.9	40.0	41.1	42.2	43.3	44.4	45.5	46.6	47.7	48.8	49.9	51.0	450
33.7	34.7	35.8	36.8	37.9	38.9	40.0	41.0	42.1	43.1	44.2	45.2	46.3	47.3	48.4	475
32.0	33.0	34.0	35.0	36.0	37.0	38.0	39.0	40.0	41.0	42.0	43.0	44.0	45.0	46.0	500
30.5	31.4	32.4	33.3	34.3	35.2	36.1	37.1	38.1	39.0	40.0	40.9	41.9	42.8	43.8	525
29.1	30.0	30.9	31.8	32.7	33.6	34.5	35.4	36.3	37.2	38.1	39.0	40.0	40.9	41.8	550
27.8	28.7	29.0	30.4	31.3	32.1	33.0	33.9	34.7	35.6	36.5	37.3	38.2	39.1	40.0	575
26.7	27.5	28.3	29.2	30.0	30.8	31.6	32.5	33.3	34.1	35.0	35.8	36.6	37.5	38.3	600
25.6	26.4	27.2	28.0	28.8	29.6	30.4	31.2	32.0	32.8	33.6	34.4	35.2	36.0	36.8	625
24.6	25.4	26.2	26.9	27.7	28.4	29.2	30.0	30.7	31.5	32.3	33.0	33.8	34.6	35.3	650
23.7	24.4	25.2	25.9	26.7	27.4	28.1	28.8	29.6	30.3	31.1	31.8	32.5	33.3	34.0	675
22.9	23.6	24.3	25.0	25.7	26.4	27.1	27.8	28.5	29.2	30.0	30.7	31.4	32.1	32.8	700
22.1	22.8	23.4	24.1	24.8	25.5	26.2	26.8	27.5	28.2	28.9	29.6	30.3	31.0	31.7	725
21.3	22.0	22.7	23.3	24.0	24.6	25.3	26.0	26.6	27.3	28.0	28.6	29.3	30.0	30.6	750
20.6	21.3	21.9	22.6	23.2	23.8	24.5	25.1	25.8	26.4	27.1	27.7	28.3	29.0	29.6	775
20.0	20.6	21.3	21.9	22.5	23.1	23.7	24.3	25.0	25.6	26.2	26.8	27.5	28.1	28.7	800
		20.6	21.2				24.8	25.4							

Source: *Expenses in Retail Businesses* (Dayton, Ohio: National Cash Register Company, n.d.), p. 45.

indicated. This means that the salesperson's efforts for the week have earned only $75 in salary—$15 less than actually paid! This difference must be advanced to the employee from the store's earnings or from those of other profitable employees. . . .[12]

Since rising prices and changing wage rates tend to distort year-to-year comparisons expressed in dollars, some retailers also measure sales employee productivity in terms of *transactions per employee/hour*.[13] But regardless of the measure used, merchants must recognize the urgent need for better performance in all phases of the retail selling function. Also, sales volume or number of transactions alone may not be an adequate measure of a salesperson's contribution. One employee in a floor covering store may sell $150,000 worth of bargain and low-margin carpet per year and thus contribute less to store profits than a colleague who sells $125,000 worth of regular-price merchandise.[14] Attention must also be given to the amount of nonselling work each salesperson performs such as stockkeeping, handling complaints, and training younger employees. Yet salary and commission payments as a percent of dollar sales is a commonly-used measure, in part because of its simplicity and in part because it indicates each salesperson's selling cost.

◻ Direct selling

Direct selling establishments primarily sell merchandise "by house-to-house canvass, by party plans, by telephone, or from a truck," and account for slightly less than one percent of all U.S. retail trade.[15] In addition, however, some small scale direct selling activities are not enumerated in the census, and more importantly for our purpose, some conventional store-based retailers also send salespeople to customers' homes and offices to sell such items as draperies, floor coverings and major appliances. Total direct-sales volume may be twice the census figure.[16] Some direct selling firms retail convenience items, such as ice cream, that require only routine handling, but many deal in specialty goods, such as encyclopedias, vacuum cleaners, cooking utensils or cosmetics, that require demonstrations or other elaborate sales presentations. Consumers often are suspicious of, or irritated by, direct selling,[17] and resentment against "high pressure" tactics has led to the passage of numerous "cooling-off" laws that give purchasers a short period (usually one to three days) in which they can rescind (cancel) any order over a stipulated amount given to a direct salesperson.[18] Yet a sizable number of consumers derive considerable information and satisfaction from visits of direct sellers whom they like and who have inspired confidence. Recreation is a significant aspect of party plans, in which small groups of friends are invited to a customer's home for entertainment and a product presentation.[19] In-home demonstration and fitting may be very helpful in selling some items such as custom-made draperies or wall-to-wall carpeting. Recruiting and training an effective sales force is, of course, especially necessary for successful direct selling.[20]

◼ FUNDAMENTAL ELEMENTS IN A RETAIL SALE

The basic elements in any retail sale are (1) the store (or direct-selling firm) and its policies (2), the customer, (3) the merchandise, and (4) the salesperson.

◻ The store and its policies

Policies of the store in which the sale takes place govern the selling methods pursued and the actions of salespeople. For example, in mass-selling stores, little individual attention is given the customer: one salesperson may serve three shoe customers at the same time. In contrast, some other stores emphasize high standards of salesmanship and outline detailed procedures to be followed during the selling process.

☐ The customer

The customer is the very heart of the sale, a fact which the famous retailer Marshall Field recognized in his phrase, "Give the lady what she wants." And Jack I. Straus of R. H. Macy and Company stated some years ago: "We are embarking on a major effort to demonstrate that we care that the customer finds what she wants, gets the help she desires, and derives satisfaction from every contact with Macy's."

The modern informed consumer ". . . chooses the store that cares about her, the store where salespeople give each shopper the consideration one human being expects from another."[21] And today, ". . . an era characterized by a continual stream of innovation, it is not surprising to find a renewed emphasis on the old adage that 'Your best salesman is a satisfied customer'."[22] Salespeople, guided by this understanding, will sell from the customer's point of view. To do so, they should recognize the customer's growing sophistication. They should know something about consumer psychology and about buying motives—what pleases or irritates customers and what considerations motivate their buying.[23]

A moment's reflection will bring an awareness of the fact that in the long run the interests of the customer, the salesperson, and the store are identical, since successful operation is impossible without continuous satisfaction of customers.

☐ The merchandise

The third important element in a retail sale is the merchandise. A thorough knowledge of the lines offered is essential to successful salesmanship. The information needed varies with the type of merchandise sold and the clientele served, but, in all stores, the salesperson should be able to give a clear picture of the sizes, styles, designs, finishes, patterns, qualities, and colors of the merchandise. The salesperson should know how to bring out points of superiority such as durability, utility, service, safety, prestige, satisfaction, and comfort, and possess the facts pertinent to the uses and care of the merchandise. One should also be aware of the offerings of competing stores.

The knowledge of merchandise required for effective selling may be obtained in many ways: experience; handling goods; asking others, including wholesalers' sales staff, the head of stock, and the buyer; learning from other salespeople and from customers; through manufacturers' representatives and printed material; trade journals, home and fashion magazines, advertisements, newspapers, and books; and also by reading information on tags and labels that come on the product.[24]

Despite all the information available to them, many retail salespeople still have insufficient knowledge of the merchandise they are attempting to sell. Responsibility for this condition is twofold: First, salespeople are to blame for failing to prepare themselves adequately for the selling task. Second, store management—either through the proprietor in the small store or the training division in the large store—sometimes fails to impress employees sufficiently with the importance of knowing merchandise, neglects to provide proper instruction concerning it, and does not offer the supervision and follow-up necessary to determine how the selling job is being done.[25]

□ The salesperson

The final essential element in a retail sale is the salesperson.[26] Customers probably prefer to deal with salespeople who seem relatively similar in tastes and lifestyle, and who exhibit some expertise about the merchandise.[27] But other attributes are also important. Good or neat appearance, a pleasant normal voice,[28] the right attitude, and courteous treatment of customers are fundamental to success in selling. Merchandise knowledge, awareness of customer traits, and even the store's other sales promotional efforts may be of no avail unless the salesperson demonstrates a sincere interest in determining and satisfactorily filling the customers' wants.[29]

In general, the qualifications of a successful salesperson are much the same as those necessary for success in any line of business: hard work; confidence in oneself, one's company, and one's merchandise; courage to meet disappointment and defeat; judgment; discrimination and good sense; creative imagination or the capacity to develop ideas; a talent for getting along with one's associates and superiors; and knowledge of the job to be done. If the salesperson also possesses or develops such qualities as a genuine interest in people, enthusiasm, the ability to instill confidence, and some flair for showmanship, the chances for success are enhanced.[30]

The salesperson must be positive, active, creative, and self-confident, so as to be able to overcome the customer's natural causes for hesitation. He or she should also be a good loser. It is not possible to close every sale attempted; but if the salesperson does the best possible and then closes with a smile, the customer probably will come back either after having shopped around or sometime in the future when desirous of the type of merchandise in question.

In summary, it is apparent that the responsibility of the salesperson is a vital one in retail selling. Much of this responsibility may be summed up in one word: *courtesy*.[31]

FIGURE 20–2 The essences of courtesy in retailing have been well expressed by O'Neil's, an Akron, Ohio department store

Hints about courtesy

Courtesy is taking a genuine interest in your customer and showing it these ways:

. . . Being considerate of your customer's time by serving each in turn and as quickly as possible.

. . . Extending a warm greeting when approaching customers and recognizing "waiting" ones.

. . . Attempting to understand your customers' needs and helping them arrive at solutions.

. . . Listening closely to your customers' requests and politely answering their questions.

. . . Being patient and pleasant with customers who are slow in making up their minds.

. . . Showing your appreciation for your customers' patronage by thanking them sincerely.

"COURTESY IS A FEELING BEST CONVEYED WITH SINCERITY AND A SMILE!"

Source: *O'Neilogram* (November 1, 1974), p. 4.

■ THE SELLING PROCESS

An appreciation and understanding of the major elements of a sale is essential to successful participation in the selling process.[32] This process may be thought of as involving seven steps, as follows: (1) approach and greeting, (2) determining the customer's needs, (3) presenting the merchandise effectively, (4) meeting objections, (5) closing the sale, (6) suggestion selling of additional items, and (7) developing goodwill after the sale.

In discussing these steps certain qualifications should be recognized at the outset. First, any classification of steps must be arbitrary and some steps may be omitted in consummating some sales. Second, the sequence of the steps performed will often vary, depending upon the customer and the skill of the salesperson in defining the customer's wants. Third, the salesperson should remember that the major task is to help the customer in a courteous, intelligent manner. If too much attention is devoted to the sequence of steps in a sale, the sale may be lost. The successful salesperson develops the ability to analyze each selling opportunity and utilizes the appropriate approach and tactics for the particular situation.

□ Approaching and greeting the customer

A proper approach to the customer is a matter of skill and judgment. It requires friendly interest and a sincere desire to be of service, balanced by proper reserve and self-confidence. The customer should be welcomed with a genuine smile and a pleasant greeting and made to realize that the salesperson and the store appreciate the opportunity to be of service.[33]

In many stores customers are greeted by name and given a hearty welcome. Most people like the recognition and appreciation of their patronage that this type of greeting indicates. The number of customers served by salespeople in large stores makes it difficult to remember names, but this practice should nevertheless be encouraged.

Alertness and promptness on the part of the salesforce are essential to an effective approach. Yet all too often salespeople gather in groups to converse and neglect customers. Occasionally, customers are deliberately avoided for fear of delayed lunch hours or postponed departure at closing time. This condition can be corrected through proper instructions and effective supervision.

□ Determining the customer's needs

After the customer has been properly greeted, his or her needs should be defined as quickly as possible. This task is easy for staple, branded items, such as toilet articles, but much more difficult for ready-to-wear or furniture. The salesperson may obtain some indication of the customer's tastes and preferences from clothes, appearance, and manner of speech, but this can be misleading. Experiments in dress shops in Canada and in automobile dealerships in the United States show that salespeople are often discourteous to poorly dressed customers.[34] These salespeople forget that customers who dress very casually when shopping may want luxurious and elegant merchandise for their other activities. The answers to a few well chosen exploratory questions and close observation of the customer's reactions to the merchandise first shown will provide a more reliable guide to what is wanted. By eliminating quickly those articles which do not meet the customer's requirements, attention can be concentrated on those that appear to be suitable.

Many salespeople mistakenly define a customer's needs and judge the desirability or suitability of merchandise by reference to their own tastes and purchasing power. This should be avoided since it serves to irritate and confuse the customer and often results in lost sales.

☐ Presenting the merchandise effectively

No sharp line of demarcation exists between determining the customer's needs and presenting merchandise, since some demonstration often is needed to ascertain requirements. Nevertheless, an effective presentation requires a knowledge of the customer's needs.

Presenting the merchandise to customers in a manner that will induce purchases involves (1) knowledge of its location in the store or department, (2) wise selection of what is shown or demonstrated, (3) proper display of the merchandise, and (4) careful selection of its chief selling points and their effective presentation.[35] The importance of these factors is obvious. The proprietor or manager of a small store carries the responsibility of seeing that salespeople receive this information. In large organizations, the merchandising, training, and sales promotion staffs may share this task.[36]

☐ Meeting objections

Meeting objections satisfactorily is probably the most difficult step in the selling process. Although objections should be anticipated and answered as much as possible in the sales presentation, all of them cannot be foreseen. They may be divided into two groups: (1) genuine objections, constituting honest and sincere reasons for failure to buy; and (2) mere excuses, used to conceal the real reason for failure to take action. Since genuine objections are definite obstacles to consummating a sale, they should be met squarely and without evasion. In contrast, excuses may often be ignored, although they may be recognized and answered by the salesperson. Sometimes excuses are more difficult to handle than genuine objections, since they do not really reflect the opinions of the customer and, consequently, furnish no solid basis for answering them.

Some general rules for meeting objections Certain "proven" general rules are helpful in meeting customer objections.

1. Never argue with a customer. An argument may be won but a sale and a customer lost.
2. Anticipate objections and incorporate answers to them in the presentation.
3. Deal with objections fairly and completely, making sure not to belittle the customer's opinions.
4. Inspire confidence on the part of the customers and contribute to their self-esteem by the tactful handling of questions.

5. Avoid, if possible, mention of competitors and their merchandise. If the customer mentions them, speak well and briefly of them.

Conformance to these rules and experience in handling specific reasons customers give for failing to buy will enable the salesperson to meet most selling problems successfully.

Handling the price question Because of the many and varied wants of *all* people and the limited incomes of *most* people, the fundamental objection to purchase for nearly all people is price. "I cannot afford it" and "I like it very much, but the price is too high," are common customer expressions with which salespeople are constantly faced.

In most cases, perhaps, price should not be mentioned until the suitability of the merchandise to the customers' needs has been demonstrated. This tends to reduce the importance of the price factor to the customer. Many customers, however, inquire about prices at the outset. In such instances, the salesperson should not hestitate in stating prices; but should immediately stress the values at these prices. It is often advisable to show higher-priced merchandise of better quality to demonstrate the difference between the various items. Some firms have their salespeople follow a practice of "trading up"—of attempting to induce customers to buy better-quality merchandise at higher prices.[37] The president of an audio systems retailing firm that follows such a policy says that his sales staff should never ask customers "How much do you want to spend?" Instead they should casually demonstrate very fine equipment to arouse the customers' interest in better merchandise.[38]

☐ Closing the sale

If the transaction has been properly handled, the sale[39] will be closed naturally and without particular notice by the customer. But many sales are not closed. The best way to avoid such occurrences is for salespeople to try to analyze each sale they lose, determine the mistakes made in their presentations, and correct these errors in subsequent contacts with customers. The more common avoidable errors include: "pushing" customers into decisions before they have evaluated all aspects of their purchases; failure to ask for the order when the customer is ready to buy; not meeting questions or objections fully and truthfully; failure to know and to emphasize important characteristics of the merchandise; evidencing irritation and making caustic comments about the customer's delay in making a selection; and failing to provide the courteous and considerate service the customer deserves as a guest of the store.

Knowledge of the reasons why sales are lost, however, is insufficient preparation on the salespersons' part. They must translate this knowledge into improved salesmanship and do all they can to minimize the mistakes that cause sales to be lost. In this connection, their own experiences should prove a valuable guide, since they will tend to use more frequently those methods they have found effective and to avoid using those they have found ineffective. In all instances, however, they should attempt to close sales in a manner pleasing to their customers.

☐ Suggestion selling

Once the sale has been closed on the merchandise desired by the customer, the salesperson has an excellent opportunity further to serve the customer and promote both personal and store interests through suggestion selling. This may take any of the following forms, among others:

1. Increasing the amount of the sale by suggesting better quality merchandise and pointing out the advantages of buying the better item, a form of the trading-up process referred to previously. However, this should not be done if it will damage the already-completed sale.
2. Increasing the sale by suggesting larger packages and explaining the saving they represent and by selling larger quantities or groups of the same item. For example, the $1.00 size of an item may contain three times the quantity of the 50-cent size, or three men's shirts may be sold at $18.50 instead of one at $6.50.
3. Suggesting related, associated, or companion items. To illustrate, the woman buying shoes may need hosiery, gloves, or a bag. Similarly, the man buying razor blades may need shaving cream or soap.
4. Suggesting seasonable, timely merchandise in demand by customers. During the winter many people require cold remedies and vitamin tablets. At Easter, millinery, spring clothing, and flowers are appropriate.
5. Suggesting any special values or bargains that the department or store offers. These values may result from reductions in the prices of regular goods for a limited period or from particularly advantageous purchases which permit lower-than-usual prices for such merchandise.
6. Suggesting new merchandise which has just arrived. Since some people like to be the first to wear or to exhibit something new, such a suggestion ordinarily arouses interest and may result in a sale if the goods appeal to the customer.

The emphasis placed on suggestion selling by Edison Brothers Stores, a large retail footwear chain, is indicated by what a company executive said some years ago: "Edison does not believe in selling one pair of shoes. . . . A sale is not complete until two or three pairs are sold. [Other stores] now advocate this but Edison was the first to develop the principle and do a really scientific training job." The shopper also is invited "to look at matching handbags, hosiery, and other accessories that account for about one fifth of [our] volume."[40] These efforts, along with others, resulted in increasing suggestion sales to about 30 percent of total sales, and stock turnover and sales per store also increased sharply.

Suggestion selling is often neglected, since most retail salespeople dislike the mental and physical effort required, and since training and supervision are frequently lax in this direction. Although some customers resent suggestions, others welcome them. The customer's attitude toward this practice depends upon the manner in which it is made, upon the merchandise offered, and upon the situation. Suggestions are useless unless they are appropriate, definite, and helpful in the light of the customer's needs. Properly used they are a valuable method of increasing sales, but if used incorrectly they may lose sales and customers.

□ Developing goodwill after the sale

When the customer makes the original purchase or even after buying additional goods as a result of suggestions made by salespeople, the selling process still has not been completed. The goods purchased must be carefully wrapped for carrying home or for delivery when promised, and correctly billed if credit has been extended. The customer should also be satisfied with the purchase, and recall favorably the store and the department as a desirable place to trade. These goals call for effective action on the salesperson's part even after the customer has said, "I'll take it."

A customer will remember, and react favorably to, a cheerful and sincere expression of gratitude for the purchase. For example: "Thank you very much. I hope you will enjoy this article and that you will come in again. It was a pleasure to serve you." The words used when customers depart are just as important as those used in greeting them.

Even if no sale is made, the customer should be thanked for having shown an interest in the store and its goods. By doing so, the salesperson builds goodwill and makes friends for the business. Failing to do so, or expressing resentment at the customer's inability to decide on a purchase at that time only creates ill-will and loses customers for the store.

In some small stores, salespeople are often responsible for placing the merchandise on a delivery cart or truck as soon as possible, for wrapping the goods for mailing or for gifts, and for checking on the performance of articles such as washing machines or carpet sweepers after they have been used for several days. The interest evidenced in performing these activities is a mark of good salesmanship and builds patronage for the store.

■ MANAGEMENT'S RESPONSIBILITY FOR PERSONAL SALESMANSHIP

Successful personal salesmanship in retail stores involves more than the development of proper attitudes, knowledge, and practices on the part of salespeople and other employees. It is management's responsibility through alert leadership and adequate supervision, to provide the storewide direction and atmosphere that is conducive to effective selling. When this is done, customers will be pleased with the surroundings in which they shop; employees will be satisfied with their working conditions and will have congenial relationships with each other and their supervisors.

Management's major responsibilities for the guidance, supervision, and stimulation of the sales force include fair distribution of work among employees, assignment of definite responsibility to each worker, even-tempered supervision, and continuous interest in and encouragement of the salespeople. Executives should recognize that the maintenance of high standards in selling efforts necessitates rather close and constant observation of the selling process. Alert merchants spend time on the selling floor to emphasize the importance of the sales task and to boost salesperson morale.[41] Allied Stores Corporation, for example, has developed a rotating schedule for constant sales supervision by department managers and other executives.[42] Sales development also requires detailed study of performance records; and demands correction of sales methods as a result of such observation and study.[43]

Management must conduct regular sales meetings to inform and stimulate salespeople. Moreover such meetings should be conducted skillfully and with judgment. An attitude of superiority should be avoided and employees should be encouraged to participate. When these responsibilities are met, personal selling efforts will be improved and profit possibilities enhanced. Fortunately, there are signs that management is increasingly aware of its obligations in attaining these goals.

■ REVIEW AND DISCUSSION QUESTIONS

1 Define retail salesmanship. Why is retail salesmanship still important in spite of the growth of self-service stores?

2 Point out some of the major faults or weaknesses of retail salespeople today. What causes these deficiencies in selling? What can management do to improve the situation?

3 Explain "the engineering approach" to sales productivity improvement.

4 How would you measure a salesperson's performance? What are the weaknesses of measures that are based on dollar amount of sales?

5 How important is direct selling in the total retail economy? What are some of its weaknesses and limitations? Some of its strengths and advantages? Why do some retail store firms also engage in direct selling?

6. Describe how the selling process will be affected by each of the following three fundamental elements in a sale: (a) the store and its policies, (b) the customer, and (c) the merchandise.

7 Discuss the characteristics and personality that tend to make a retail salesperson effective.

8 Prepare a critical evaluation of the "Courtesy Platform" of O'Neil's, reproduced on p. 503.

9 Indicate the major stages of the selling process. For three of these stages, describe some of the most common weaknesses or errors of retail salespeople. In your answer draw, if possible, upon your own experiences as a salesperson and as a customer.

10 How can (a) salespeople and (b) management remedy the specific weaknesses cited in your answer to the preceding question?

■ NOTES AND REFERENCES

1 See "Customer Is Created at Point of Purchase," *Stores*, February 1969, pp. 33–34.

2 Retail selling is discussed in detail in O. P. Robinson, W. R. Blackler and W. B. Logan, *Store Salesmanship,* 6th ed. (Englewood Cliffs, N.J.: Prentice-Hall, Inc., 1966).

3 F. H. Neely, *Rich's: A Southern Institution since 1867* (New York: The Newcomen Society in North America, 1960), p. 14.

4 *Lazarus Enthusiast,* September 19, 1975, p. 3.

5 "It is no exaggeration to appraise pleasing, cordial attention and service as being the prime factors in making people want to patronize a store." *Attracting and Holding Customers* (Dayton, Ohio: National Cash Register Company, n.d.), p. 24.

6 William G. Nickels, "Central Distribution Facilities Challenge Traditional Retailers," *Journal of Retailing,* vol. 49 (Spring 1973), pp. 45–50; F. K. Shuptrine, "The Distribution/Retailing Institute of Tomorrow," *Journal of Retailing,* vol. 50 (Spring 1974), pp. 20–32.

7 "Sales Help—Lack of It—Bugs Store Execs' Wives," *Women's Wear Daily,* June 27, 1973, p. 22.

8 "Why Supers Are Swinging to Service," *Chain Store Age* (Supermarket edition), February 1976, pp. 70–72.

9 M. M. Brown, "Women Shoppers Feel Insulted the Way Salesmen Treat Them," *Home Furnishings Daily,* November 6, 1972, p. 14; "Consumer Panel Is Unanimous, Most Salespeople Turn Them Off," *Home Furnishings Daily,* March 12, 1975, p. 16.

10 Mimi Sheraton, "The Rudest Store in New York," *New York,* November 10, 1975, p. 44.

11 J. C. Aspley, *The Sales Manager's Handbook* (Chicago: Dartnell Corp., 1968), p. 708.

12 *Expenses in Retail Businesses* (Dayton, Ohio: The National Cash Register Co., n.d.), p. 46.

13 "Motivated Sales People: Key to Independent's Productivity," *Stores,* March 1975, p. 7.

14 Jack Cox, "Selling Costs Cut the Bottom Line," *Home Furnishings Daily,* June 12, 1975, p. 15.

15 U.S. Bureau of the Census, *Census of Retail Trade 1972, Area Statistics* RC72–A–52 (Washington, D.C.: U.S. Government Printing Office, 1975), pp. 8, A10.

16 C. R. Patty, A. R. Haring and H. L. Vredenburg, *Selling Direct to the Consumer* (Fort Collins, Col.: Robinson Press, 1973), pp. 6–9.

17 M. A. Jolson, *Consumer Attitude Toward Direct-to-Home Marketing Systems* (New York: Dunellen Publishing

Co., 1970), pp. 121–22; M. Granfield and A. Nicols, "Economic and Marketing Aspects of the Direct Selling Industry," *Journal of Retailing*, vol. 51 (Spring 1975), p. 34, n. 2.

18 Patty, Haring and Vredenburg, *Selling Direct . . .* , pp. 218–27; D. H. Tootelian, "Potential Impact of 'Cooling-Off' Laws in Direct-to-Home Selling," *Journal of Retailing*, vol. 51 (Spring 1975), pp. 61–70. Direct sellers also face so-called "Green River" ordinances in some communities which make uninvited entry upon private residential property for the purpose of selling goods a misdemeanor.

19 See "Tupperware Shores Up Dart," *Business Week*, May 5, 1975, p. 63.

20 Granfield and Nicols, "Economic and Marketing Aspects . . . ," pp. 33–50.

21 Anne Saum, a retail personnel expert, quoted by Samuel Feinberg, "From Where I Sit," *Women's Wear Daily*, April 15, 1975, p. 14.

22 J. F. Engel, R. J. Kegerreis, and R. D. Blackwell, "Word-of-Mouth Communciation by the Innovator," *Journal of Marketing*, vol. 33, no. 3 (July 1969), p. 15.

23 "To sell Mrs. Smith what Mrs. Smith buys, you must see what's seen through Mrs. Smith's eyes." Ralf Shockey, "Selling Is a Science," part IX, *Department Store Economist*, December 1965, p. 88. Also see "How Housewives See the Discount House Today," *Discount Merchandiser*, March 1970, p. 77.

24 Selling guides for 21 merchandise lines are given in A. E. Zimmer, *The Strategy of Successful Retail Salesmanship* (New York: McGraw-Hill Book Co., Inc., 1966), pp. 165–209.

25 E. B. Weiss, "Great Days Ahead for Training Salespeople," *Stores*, August 1975, p. 40. See also "Management's responsibility for personal salesmanship," p. 509.

26 States one keen observer of the retail scene: "The worst thief in the store is the employee who figuratively beats up the customer, not the employee or shopper who actually steals the merchandise. The worst thief is one who, by not doing a proper job of selling goods and services, hurts volume and net profit, darkens the future of more efficient and effective fellow workers, and endangers the company's continued existence and the community's economy." Samuel Feinberg, "From Where I Sit," *Women's Wear Daily*, September 25, 1970, p. 13.

27 A. G. Woodside and J. W. Davenport, Jr., "The Effect of Salesman Similarity and Expertise on Consumer Behavior," *Journal of Marketing Research*, vol. 11 (May 1974), pp. 198–202.

28 "How to Sound Good," *Women's Wear Daily*, July 19, 1974, pp. 14–15.

29 On the part played by store personnel—and the salesperson is most important here—in attracting retail patronage, see P. R. Stephenson, "Identifying Determinants of Retail Patronage," *Journal of Marketing*, vol. 33 (July 1969), pp. 57–61.

30 The difficulties faced by retailers in securing and keeping good salespeople are discussed in "Wanted: Someone to Watch the Store," *Business Week*, September 19, 1970, pp. 52, 57.

31 See "Martin's: Courtesy Is Long-Time Policy," *Women's Wear Daily*, April 3, 1974, pp. 22–24.

32 The persuasive and perceptive aspects of the selling process are discussed in R. M. Baker, Jr., and Gregg Phifer, *Salesmanship: Communication, Persuasion, Perception* (Boston: Allyn and Bacon, Inc., 1966), pp. 240–415. See also Lawrence Leemaster, "Sales Improvement with Psychology," *New York Retailer*, May 1969, pp. 11–13. The examples given all deal with a summer tourist in a souvenir store.

33 See "First Impressions Vital to Success," *Hardware Retailer*, June 1969, p. 126. See also " 'May I Help You?' Is Not the Way a Salesperson Greets a Customer in the Newest Neiman Marcus Store," *Chicago Tribune*, March 8, 1976, sec. 3, p. 2. ("Welcome to Neiman Marcus, Northbrook" is the recommended phrase.)

34 "Girls' Test Finds It Pays to Be Rich," *New York Times*, January 9, 1973, p. 4, reporting a study at the University of New Brunswick; Gordon L. Wise, "Differential Pricing and Treatment by New Car Salesmen," *Journal of Business*, vol. 47 (April 1974), pp. 218–30.

35 One study reported inadequate determination of customers' needs by retail salespeople of television sets and refrigerators, yet the salespeople largely controlled the number of products examined and the sales points considered for each product. Richard W. Olshavsky, "Customer-Salesman Interaction in Appliance Retailing," *Journal of Marketing Research,* vol. 10 (May 1973), pp. 208–12.

36 "Coordinating Sales Training," *Stores,* May 1975, p. 12.

37 A study of the bargaining on price and other factors which takes place between customers and appliance salespeople is reported in A. L. Pennington, "Customer-Salesman Bargaining Behavior in Retail Transactions," *Journal of Marketing Research,* vol. 5 (August 1968), pp. 255–62.

38 "Salesmen Trained in Trade Up Techniques Key to Cal Hi-Fi Gains," *Home Furnishings Daily,* August 9, 1972, p. 8.

39 Factors governing the close of a sale are explained and illustrated in C. A. Pederson and M. D. Wright, *Salesmanship, Principles and Methods,* 5th ed.

(Homewood, Ill.: Richard D. Irwin, Inc., 1971), pp. 442–60.

40 "New Shine for a Master Retailer," *Business Week,* April 16, 1966, p. 112.

41 Annalee Gold, "Selling Fashion: How Management Can Show It Cares," *Stores,* April 1974, p. 12.

42 Samuel Feinberg, "Intensive Hunt Underway for Solution to Walkouts," *Women's Wear Daily,* December 26, 1973, p. 13.

43 Reports one investigator: "Two issues are at the bottom of most selling problems: (1) Failure of retail management to appreciate the real contribution that creative personal sales effort can have on the final sale; and (2), management's lack of interest in scientifically determining the causes of salesmen's behavior in situations where various forms of salesman-customer interaction, such as bargaining and negotiation, are important in the final sale." J. C. Cotham, "Case for Personal Selling: Some Retailing Myths Exploded," *Business Horizons,* vol. 6 (April 1968), p. 81.

CUSTOMER SERVICES

The retailer's most basic service consists of assembling a satis-factory assortment of desirable merchandise and offering it for sale, at reasonable prices, in an attractive, conveniently-located store. But in addition the customers may expect many traditional extra services, such as clothing alterations, gift wrapping, merchandise delivery, and assurances of complete satisfaction with their purchases. Such services are normally offered at cost, less than cost, or free of extra charge, and are intended to encourage customer purchases. Competent, prompt, cheerful, and courteous performance of the appropriate services is a significant form of nonprice competition and a necessary element in developing a favorable store image.

Many retailers now also offer an increasing number of "income producing" services, such as tool and equipment rental or insurance sales, to meet their customers' changing demands. These activities also contribute to the store image, since their availability suggests that the store is trying to satisfy all of its customers' desires. The income services may also lead to sales of related merchandise, as, for example, when golf instruction leads to the sale of clubs or other equipment. But while the traditional services represent expenses that the store incurs in order to sell its wares, the income services are undertaken to produce their own direct profits or contribution to overhead. Large retailers, who are seeking additional ways to serve their customers profitably, will probably offer even more income services in forthcoming years. One estimate is that by 1990 services will provide 50 percent of sales revenue in general merchandise stores.[1]

■ SCOPE OF THE CHAPTER

Although we will consider both traditional and income-producing services, we cannot and need not examine every possible service in detail in this chapter. The customer services that result from having an attractive and well-designed store with air conditioning, good lighting, and convenient vertical transportation have already been discussed in Chapter 5. Similarly, the services that a helpful and attentive sales force can provide have been noted in Chapter 20. Some other services, for example "piped-in" background music, present relatively few managerial problems, and only require brief mention. In contrast, credit activities are so important to so many retailers, are so complex, and have been subject to so many recent changes that a separate chapter is needed for adequate discussion, Chapter 22, "Retail credit and collections."

Consequently, we will first look at some basic service policies. We will next examine some traditional "extra" services in detail, and then consider the rising market for income-producing services.

■ SERVICE POLICIES

The number and variety of services Decisions on the number and variety of services to be provided, and on the policies, procedures, and conditions under which they will be offered require considerable judgment. Overly elaborate and inappropriate services may create a false image and make the customers *think* that the store is expensive even though its actual prices are competitive with other establishments. And inappropriate extra services that do not generate suitable extra sales volume will increase costs and absorb profits inordinately. Moreover, customers' expectations concerning service are often difficult to judge, and, in many instances, experimentation is needed to provide the answer. Yet the retailer must provide the services that the clientele needs and expects. Fortunately, some of the following guidelines will help in deciding on the services to be offered.

Guides to services offered (1) Competitors' policies and practices are important guides. Customers will expect comparable service or compensating advantages. (2) The type of merchandise handled will influence the services rendered. Heavy merchandise, such as electric refrigerators, stoves, washing machines, and furniture, usually requires delivery service. Moreover, some form of deferred payment is essential for these high unit value items. In contrast, customers can readily carry cosmetics, shoes, and hosiery, and may not desire credit when buying these products. (3) The customers' income, location, and buying habits influence the services that must be provided. Generally speaking, the higher the income group, the greater the number of services expected and offered. (4) The type of store is important. Customers may expect more personalized service in a small specialty store than in a large establishment; and more service in a traditional department store than in a mail-order company branch. (5) The store's pricing policy affects the nature and extent of its services, since customers expect less service in a "bargain" outlet. (6) Store location also plays a role since a downtown retailer may have to offer delivery service while a suburban competitor may rely on customers carrying their own purchases. Similarly, a hardware retailer in a suburban area, where "do-it-yourself" is common, is often expected to rent tools and equipment.

Realistic service standards The retailer should remember that services are intended to contribute to the store's *long-run* profitability. An attempt to satisfy every possible customer would be both costly and futile. A few people will make demands that are impossible to fulfill. The retailer should take all reasonable steps to minimize unpleasant situations. A merchant should normally avoid offending a good customer just to win a small argument, and should carefully investigate all complaints, no matter how unwarranted they may seem. But if such investigation shows that the policies and procedures are sound, the loss of an occasional unreasonable customer should not be considered to be a catastrophe. The important thing is to be certain that the store's merchandise and services will satisfy the great majority of its present and potential customers—the people who can provide the repeat business that is essential for ultimate success.

Service charges Decisions must be made, not only as to the number and variety of services to be offered, but also as to whether fees will be charged for any of them, and if so, how much. In some cases, the decision is obvious. Some traditional services must be offered without any extra charge. A merchant could hardly request a fee for listening to customer complaints, or for telling customers where to find goods in the store!

In contrast, charges will naturally be imposed for the income-producing services that are instituted to earn profits.* And some of the customer-convenience services are so costly to the store that no one expects them to be available without charge. Department stores, for example, often operate their restaurants as a service that will attract people to the store and induce them to spend more time there. In such cases, the meals may be priced so low that the restaurant inevitably loses money. But none of the patrons expect the meals to be totally

---

* A store-operated travel agency may be an exception to this generalization, since some or all of its revenue will consist of commissions paid by hotels, carriers (airlines, steamship companies), and tour operators.

free. And today many store restaurants are operated as profit-generating income centers.[2]

Policy concerning certain other services varies from store to store or from community to community. But currently an increasing number of merchants charge at least partial fees for services once included in the price of the merchandise. A number of stores now charge for delivery service, especially on small orders. Many retailers now charge extra for alterations to women's—and to an increasing extent, men's —clothing.

The tendency to reduce the number of totally "free" services results in part from rising labor and supply costs and in part from increased competitive pressure. The store that offers services without extra charge must recover the costs of those services in the prices it receives for its merchandise. Competition from self-service or self-selection stores, such as discount houses, has forced many traditional merchants to reconsider the services that they offer and the price levels they must charge to provide those services. Retailers are also increasingly aware of the fact that many customers are willing to pay directly for many of the services that they use.[3]

But competition among retailers is a competition of services as well as merchandise. Many factors must be considered in deciding to add or to reduce services. What do customers expect? What will the service cost? Can the store charge for the service, or offer it "free," and still retain its existing price policies? Are the customers of the type and income group that requires the service? What are competitors doing? Is the service well adapted to the store's merchandise? Retailers should ask these questions about each service they currently offer. Without doubt, a careful analysis will lead certain merchants to the conclusion that they are offering too many services, whereas others will decide to add still more.

Some major services are discussed on the following pages.

■ ALTERATIONS

Alterations are widely expected and required in selling clothing. Women's dresses often need to be shortened, made longer, or taken in at the hips. Men's clothing and even childrenswear often also require adjustment. Clothing stores must provide for these alterations.

Originally alteration was usually a "free" service, but this has changed considerably in the last four decades. Even now, though, the charge doesn't always cover the full cost of the work. Charges are typically made for alterations on women's clothing, but not for minor adjustments (cuffing trousers, lengthening or shortening sleeves, altering waistlines) on men's clothing. Many merchants charge for adjustments on bargain sale items and an increasing number charge for major alterations to menswear, such as recutting trousers or adjusting the degree of fullness across the back of the coat. Many small retailers oppose this policy and claim they would prefer to raise their prices rather than charge for alterations on men's and boy's clothing. In spite of these charges, net alteration costs average about 5 percent of men's clothing sales volume.[4]

■ WRAPPING MERCHANDISE

Practically all U.S. and Canadian retailers wrap or bag* their customers' purchases,** although the amount and kind of wrapping service varies widely from store to store. A high-fashion store, for example, utilizes far different wrappings than does a drugstore or supermarket. Attractive paper and plastic shopping bags have become popular with many customers. These bags, which are available in many sizes, shapes, colors, and designs, help display the store's name or insignia on the street, and in buses and suburban trains, at very low cost.[5] But the individual items still must be wrapped in many cases, even though the customer is carrying a shopping bag. This may be desirable as a security measure, to show that the merchandise has not been shoplifted, as well as a customer convenience.

□ Wrapping arrangements

Three major types of wrapping systems are in common use—clerk wrap, department or floor wrap, and central wrap.

Clerk wrap   The salesperson who waits on the customer also does the wrapping under a clerk wrap system. The customer usually prefers this since one person carries out the whole transaction. This saves the customer's time and provides a feeling of having really received service —a feeling that is lost when required to go to a wrapping station and wait in line for the package. The clerk wrap system is by far the most practical and most widely used system for small- and medium-sized service (as distinguished from self-service) stores. Large stores also use it for departments, such as handkerchiefs, hosiery, and toilet goods, that do not require special packaging facilities.

Department wrap   Under the department or floor wrap system, each department or group of departments has a conveniently located

---

*The term "wrapping" includes "bagging" (that is, placing the merchandise in bags), as generally practiced in supermarkets, discount stores, and self-service outlets.

** This statement would not always be true of other countries. In some European supermarkets (and in a few discount supermarkets here), customers bundle the purchases themselves after they have passed the check-out cashier. Of course, very large items, such as furniture, major appliances, automobiles, and boats are often delivered unwrapped.

FIGURE 21-1 An attractively-designed shopping bag

Courtesy Gimbels, Milwaukee

station where specialized employees wrap all the merchandise sold in those departments. Sometimes, especially during busy seasons, the station may employ one or several full-time wrappers; in other cases one individual may act as both cashier and wrapper. The salesperson may carry "take-with" merchandise to the wrapping desk, wait until it is wrapped, and return it to the customer; or may simply conduct the customer to the wrapping station. In some stores the customer is expected to carry "take-with" purchases to the wrapping desk. The salesperson usually takes "send" merchandise to the station.

Central wrap Central wrap localizes the store's wrapping service in one or a few places, thereby achieving the advantages of greater specialization. It also permits the use of wrapping machines which can handle as much as 70 percent of the merchandise in some stores at substantial savings in both space and wages. The wrapping department is usually placed in the basement of the store, but large stores that require two or three centers locate them on various floors adjacent to selling departments. In a sense, the check-out counter in a self-service store is a central wrap system. In such cases, the cashier or a "bagger" typically performs the wrapping—really the bagging of the items—at a point near the exit from the store.

☐ Prepackaging

Some manufacturers assist the retailer by placing their goods in packages that contain the number of units the customer usually purchases. This practice is called "prepacking" or "prepackaging." Lamps, china, glassware, and other breakable items are often prepackaged to reduce damage and handling costs.

☐ Gift wrapping

A large number of stores offer gift wrapping throughout the year, but it is most important during the pre-Christmas season. It is a fairly expensive service. Good quality gift boxes range in cost from relatively small sums to as much as $5 each. Specially expert wrappers will be assigned to this service, if the volume is sufficient, since customers want their gift packages to look especially well. Some customers will buy gifts in a low-grade store and then bring them to a higher-grade one for wrapping. Because of these factors, some stores make a charge for gift wrapping service. But most department and specialty stores that are eager for gift business continue to provide their standard grade of free gift packaging (sometimes called "the store wrap") the year round, charging only for specially elaborate wraps.[6]

■ DELIVERY SERVICE

Despite customers' increased willingness to carry goods home and the growth of self-service "cash and carry" stores, merchandise delivery remains one of the most important services rendered by many retail stores. Such service is generally provided for large or heavy items—including furniture, stoves, refrigerators, washing machines, television sets, rugs, mattresses, and mirrors. Delivery service can even be arranged in some supermarkets and chain stores where "cash and carry" is the standard practice. Moreover, many people who are unwilling to cope with the traffic problems of metropolitan shopping areas now buy increasing amounts by mail and telephone order and have the purchases delivered to their homes.

Delivery costs, already high, are increasing rapidly, largely because of rising labor and gasoline costs. Per-package cost for delivery now exceeds 75¢ in the larger cities*; and department store delivery costs now average one half of one percent of net sales, or more.[7] Nevertheless, delivery is usually performed on a "free" basis. Some retailers require a minimum purchase of $2 to $5 for free delivery and levy a small charge (such as 50¢ to 75¢) when the minimum is not reached. Likewise

---

* Information received from a major delivery company.

charges are commonly imposed for shipments to addresses outside the store's normal delivery service area.

□ Delivery systems

Retail delivery systems may be divided into five categories: (1) individual-store system, (2) mutual system, (3) consolidated system, (4) express, and (5) parcel post.

Individual-store system   Under this system the individual store uses its own personnel and equipment to provide delivery service. The proprietor of a small store may make the deliveries personally, or if volume warrants, a clerk may be employed part- or full-time to make deliveries by bicycle or truck. Regular delivery routes are not maintained; and, when necessary deliveries may be made immediately. Otherwise, the employee making deliveries waits until a few orders accumulate. No special system is used to check out goods for delivery or to check in returned goods.

Medium-sized and large stores use much more highly organized systems. The delivery department is responsible for all goods as they leave the wrapping department. It usually also collects the goods from the sales floors if clerk or department wrap systems are used. The merchandise is sorted in the delivery department and transported along carefully laid-out routes.

The individual-store delivery system is the most flexible one any store can use. The store can set routes and schedules to meet its own requirements. Famous-Barr, a St. Louis store, telephones customers before delivering furniture and other large items to make certain someone will be home, and uses a two-way radio system to reroute its drivers if the planned delivery times have to be changed.[8] Furthermore, the delivery-person is a store employee who can serve the company's interests, for example, in reporting customer complaints and messages to the proper store authorities. In addition, the store enjoys the advertising of its name on its trucks. And if the volume of work is sufficient to keep the department fully utilized, the cost of a store-owned system may be nearly as low as that of any alternative arrangement.

Mutual delivery system   In some cities the retailers have formed mutual or cooperative delivery systems. They usually set up a separate delivery corporation, with the ownership shared and expenses divided among the participants according to some agreed basis. The delivery company picks up the goods from each retailer, takes them to its own sorting station, sorts the merchandise, makes delivery, collects COD accounts, and returns goods that cannot be delivered or that customers do not want.

The mutual delivery system has two main advantages over the individual store system: (1) combining packages of all cooperating stores provides sufficient volume for more frequent, and hence better delivery service; and (2) savings in space, personnel, equipment and management supervision result in lower costs to the stores.

The major problems of mutual delivery systems include (1) building an organization and providing equipment to accomplish the objective; (2) determining an equitable basis for allocating expenses among the members of the group; and (3) maintaining effective control over the system to insure customer satisfaction. Consequently, mutual delivery systems are not spreading rapidly at present, although some have been very successful.

Consolidated delivery systems Consolidated delivery systems operate much the same way as mutual ones. But instead of being owned by the stores they serve, they are formed and operated by independent firms that hope to make a profit from the fees they charge the stores. The United Parcel Service, with facilities in 44 states, is an illustration of these systems. Its growth demonstrates the need for such services.

Consolidated systems have the same advantages as mutual ones and avoid some of the problems that can arise in joint or cooperative activities. Moreover, management often prefers having an independent outside company handle delivery activities since retail unions frequently gain their first toehold among the drivers in store-owned delivery departments. Consequently, United Parcel Service and similar organizations seem likely to continue to grow in the future.

The difficult problem of determining delivery charges arises whenever a consolidated or a mutual system is used. Each system may impose (1) a per-package charge (which may vary with either or both the size or weight of the package), (2) a flat weekly rate based roughly on the number or value of orders delivered for each merchant over a period of time, or (3) a combination of the flat weekly rate and a charge per package.

Parcel post and express delivery The delivery systems already discussed handle most retail deliveries. All large stores, however, use express companies and parcel post service to some extent, especially for mail orders and gift shipments sent to points outside the store's delivery area. A small store that has few packages to deliver may also find these services very suitable to its needs. Greyhound and other bus package services are sometimes used for intercity shipments.

The rates for parcel post and express shipments tend to become quite high if the packages are heavy or bulky. Parcel post rates, package size limitations, and other rules have been subject to several changes in recent years. The decline in total parcel post shipments during the last two decades, in spite of the economic expansion of the period, indicates that current rates, rules, and services are not competitive with alternative delivery services.[9]

■ COMPLAINTS AND ADJUSTMENTS

No retailer, no matter how skilled, can completely eliminate customer complaints. An occasional complaint is not upsetting; in fact it is a welcome source of information about things that may be wrong in the store.[10] All complaints should receive attention and be investigated. Moreover, the merchant should try to adjust them to both the customer's and the store's satisfaction and, if practical, rectify whatever causes the complaints.

Warranty responsibilities The Magnuson Moss Warranty Act, a U.S. federal law, which became effective July 4, 1975, creates additional responsibilities for retailers in handling products that sell for $5 or more and that are accompanied by warranties that promise total or partial refunds, adjustment, exchange, or repair service. Since the law applies primarily to manufacturers, the retailer's prime obligation will usually merely be to transmit information to the customer about any limitations in the producer's warranty. Manufacturers may also appoint retailers as their representatives to collect or repair unsatisfactory products. Retailers become subject to additional stipulations of the law if they add their own warranties to those of the vendors; if they sell service contracts; or if they offer merchandise under their own brand or label.[11]

□ Major causes of complaints

In general, complaints may be traced to one or more of four factors:

Improper buying The purchase of goods unsuited to customers' needs is an important cause of complaints. The store's buyers may lack experience; they may not know what the customer wants; or perhaps they are simply careless in their buying. Whatever the reason, poor buying cannot help but result in customer complaints.* Consumers generally expect the store, rather than the manufacturer, to provide redress if an item proves unsatisfactory.[12]

Inefficient store system A weak store system results in many complaints. If a delivery order fails to specify the number of packages, the driver may leave a certain address after having delivered one package instead of two. The result is a complaint that the delivery is "short."

Inadequately trained and careless personnel Salespeople who do not know the proper procedures for preparation of sales checks and credit slips, who do not dispatch "sends" to the delivery department promptly, and who fail to give all customers courteous service, con-

---

* Frequently, it is unfair to place all blame for unsatisfactory merchandise upon the buyer. For example, variations in sizes of ready-to-wear among manufacturers are an important cause of complaints and returns.

tribute to the number of complaints. Likewise, some retailers have inadequately trained repair personnel to service the appliances and television sets which they sell.

Carelessness and mistakes can produce complaints even in the store that has developed an adequate system and has given its employees detailed training. Incorrect addresses may be placed on "sends," wrong sizes may be delivered, and another account credited when goods are returned. Better supervision of employees can minimize much of this carelessness.

Habitual complainers Some customers are habitual complainers. They always seem to assume that they should have received even better merchandise or better service. If an automobile tire shows wear at the end of 25,000 miles, the customer feels that it should have gone 30,000. The $7 shirt which begins to fray on the cuffs after repeated washings is returned as being defective. In brief, every store has a few customers who will complain even though everything possible has been done to give satisfaction.

☐ Handling complaints

Maintaining goodwill A customer who feels that a complaint has not been settled satisfactorily is likely to turn to some other retailer. That customer may also voice the grievance to friends, who may be influenced to give their business to a "more responsible" merchant. This can be very damaging to the store. There is no point in spending large sums on advertising to develop goodwill and then lose it through inadequate attention to customer complaints and adjustments. The personnel who handle complaints vitally influence the customer's image of the store and should appear friendly and sympathetic to the customer's point of view. In an effort to turn complaints into goodwill many retailers have very liberal adjustment policies. Throughout the discussion that follows, an *adjustment* refers to the action taken by the retailer in an effort to satisfy the complainant. Sometimes the adjustment consists of making an *exchange*, that is, the merchandise returned by the customer is exchanged for other goods. Such exchanges may be even or uneven. See the distinction between even and uneven exchanges in Chapter 25. Typical of these policies is that of Sears, Roebuck and Company; "Liberal and prompt adjustments to our customers, *even if we may think they are wrong,* are desirable as a matter of policy. . . . The Sears motto, *Satisfaction guaranteed or your money back,* is a real policy, to be faithfully observed." Some retailers who follow such policies quite automatically make the adjustment the customer requests. Others quickly make any adjustments called for by a failure on the part of the store; but otherwise they try to distinguish between (1) customers who honestly feel they have a legitimate complaint, and (2) those who are

FIGURE 21–2 Work flow for efficient and responsive processing of customer complaints and adjustments

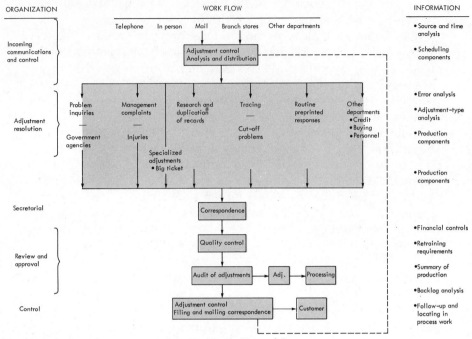

Source: Ronald Siegel, manager, retail services, Touche Ross and Company.

merely taking advantage of the store's "the customer-is-always-right" policy. While adjustments are made in the first case, they may be refused in the second instance.

Minimizing complaints In addition to building goodwill, the adjustment of complaints should provide basic data that will enable the store to reduce future complaints. A careful analysis might show, for example, that many complaints arise because of delayed deliveries, because of improper handling of charge transactions, or because of defective merchandise sold in a certain department. This information will indicate where remedial measures are needed. Too often, however, executives fail to take prompt and effective action upon the basis of such data; therefore the complaints continue.[13]

□ Systems for handling complaints

The proprietor or manager usually deals with most of the complaints in a small store, although the salespeople may handle some minor matters directly. Some other arrangement is needed for medium-sized and large stores, where the chief executive could not possibly handle all of the complaints. A store may adopt (1) a centralized system, (2) a decentralized one, or (3) a combination of certain elements of both.

Centralized system   Under this plan, every complaint, regardless of its nature, is referred to the adjustment department. The customer benefits in that (1) the grievance is handled by people who are trained to hear complaints and to make adjustments, and (2) the adjustment is more likely to be satisfactory since an impartial adjuster, rather than the salesperson involved in the transaction, hears the complaint.

The store also gains. Skilled adjusters, selected for their patience, tact, and ability to deal with all types of aggrieved customers, can handle difficult situations uniformly and build goodwill. Salespeople and buyers are relieved of the task of handling complaints and can devote more time to their other duties. Complaints are discussed in at least semi-privacy in the adjustment department, instead of being debated in front of other customers on the selling floor. Finally, centralized adjustments make it easier to keep and analyze records of all complaints, so that the data may be used as a means of reducing future complaints.

But most customers naturally expect that the salesperson, or at least the department, that sold the goods should adjust the complaint. They resent having to take the time and effort to go to a central adjustment department, possibly having to wait in line to be heard, and having to explain the whole matter to a third party. The presence of other customers, also complaining, creates a negative impression of the store. Moreover, it is difficult to arrange merchandise exchanges in the central adjustment department since the goods are not readily at hand. Instead, the customer may insist upon a full refund.

Decentralized system   In this system, the department heads, supervisors or, in some cases, head salespeople have authority to settle complaints, especially when the store is obviously at fault. Only executives, however, are allowed to refuse adjustments, and as one knowledgeable analyst urges, customers should always have a way to present their complaints to management if they so desire.[14] The decentralized system eliminates the disadvantages of a central adjustment department, but it also eliminates the advantages of using specialized, skilled, well-trained, impartial adjusters to handle complaints. Yet Rich's, an Atlanta department store that is well-known for its high level of service, handles all complaints and adjustments in the selling departments.[15]

Combination system   Many medium-sized and large stores try to gain the advantages of both systems by combining the two. The decentralized system, which the customers prefer, is used for the great majority of complaints. Only difficult complaints, that is, those that seem unreasonable to the department head or that involve fairly substantial amounts of money, are referred to the specialists in the adjustment department. This seems to be the most satisfactory arrangement for the bigger stores.

■ RETURNED GOODS

The returned goods problem is closely related to the problem of complaints and adjustments. Few customer services are as widely used, and abused, as the return privilege. To cite but one example, returns by and allowances to customers averaged over 8.5 percent of gross sales in department stores of various sizes in 1974.[16] Some departments, such as toilet articles, books, and groceries naturally have very low return rates, perhaps 1 to 3 percent of sales; but returns of women's dresses, furniture, rugs, and some electrical appliances may range from 8 to 25 percent.

□ Cost of handling returns

Customers seldom appreciate all the costs and difficulties involved in handling returns. In many cases, the store may be required to deliver the merchandise and then pick it up, incurring double expense without sales revenue. Additional recordkeeping is required. The goods have to be reinspected, re-marked, and placed in stock again. Salespeople must devote additional time to resell returned merchandise. Markdowns are often required; probably more than 50 percent of returned goods must be sold at a reduced price. Also, the store has a considerable sum invested in goods that are in the hands of customers but that will be returned to the store. The interest on this investment is another cost of handling returned goods. All of these costs substantially increase the cost of doing business.

□ Causes of returns

The great bulk of all returns are due to merchandise problems, inadequate store service, and store policies that foster returns. Still other returns result from irresponsible practices on the part of the customers. But some returns are inevitable and will always be part of the retail business.

Unsatisfactory merchandise Items may be returned because of poor workmanship and manufacturing defects, incorrect size designations, or inadequate informational labeling. Poor assortments and overpricing also lead to returns when the customer finds a better "buy" in another store.

Faulty store service Delayed deliveries, delivery of incorrect items, poor alterations, and damages during delivery also result in returns.

Store policy Store policies can cause many returns. The salespeople may be encouraged to use high-pressure methods that force sales of items the customers are unwilling to keep. Salespeople may also urge customers to take items home for further consideration, with assurance that whatever is not wanted may be returned without obligation. Such

No Questions Asked . . .

What's a bride gonna do with ten toasters?

Make a lot of toast maybe. And wish they'd been nine other things she needed. Or, if they were bought at Lazarus, she can simply pop 'em back. And get those other necessities instead. She most likely wouldn't have the problem if she'd listed her wants and needs with our Bridal Gift Registry girls. Then we could have kept a record of what was bought for the bride and passed the word to other gift-gatherers. To help avoid such duplications. And frustrations. And also because it's standard practice for us to take our things back with no questions asked.

LAZARUS

a bride's best friend

Courtesy F. and R. Lazarus Company, Columbus, Ohio

a sales policy usually results in large returns. Easy credit policies encourage credit purchases, and returns are higher from credit customers. A very liberal return policy, accepting the great majority of returns without question, also induces a high return rate. Some merchants, however, feel that such a policy is necessary to build customer confidence and encourage purchases.

Customer responsibility for returns Customers change their minds about price, color, quality, or style. Other returns result from buying gifts that do not completely please their recipients. Some customers "buy" merchandise for a special occasion, such as a wedding or a football weekend, and then return it after use. The blame for such returns is obvious.[17]

Returns cannot be totally stopped. People will change their minds; and if one store refuses to accept returns they will take their business to other retailers who extend this privilege. The customer often needs to see how furniture and other items will look at home, and expects to return whatever is unsuitable. But the stores are not without fault. For example, much customer dissatisfaction is due to delivery delays. Hence, except for bargain clearances conducted with the stipulation that "all sales are final," the retailer must expect to allow some returns. The best that can be done is to minimize unnecessary ones.

□ Minimizing returns

Retailers are not overly concerned when merchandise is returned within a three- to ten-day period, undamaged, with the price ticket intact, and accompanied by the sales check. The main problems involve merchandise that has been "out" for some time, that has to be remarked because the price ticket is gone, or for which there is no sales check. Even some of these returns are inevitable. But retailers have tried to minimize returned goods and still retain customer goodwill through (1) individual store action and (2) cooperative action by retail groups.

The individual store approach The individual store's attempt to reduce returns should start with analysis of what causes excessive returns. If merchandise defects and overpricing are responsible for disproportionate returns, the buying operations should be improved. If unsatisfactory service causes returns, then steps should be taken to improve the service—for example, to decrease damage, delays, and errors in delivery. Employees should be kept "return-conscious." The store's overselling practices and policies of urging "on approval" sales should be modified if they lead to a very high rate of returns. A policy of charging for picking up returns may replace a free pickup policy.

A store may impose a "no return" policy for some wearable and personal items. Most customers will actually welcome this rule on sanitary grounds. Return policy may vary with the type of sales transaction. Cash customers may receive less than full refunds or be required to accept merchandise certificates. Other stores use certificates when merchandise is returned without sales checks, on the theory that the certificates lead to the purchase of other items in the store while cash may be used to make purchases elsewhere. But rigid rules of this sort usually break down over time, and can easily engender serious ill-will while in operation.

The group approach   The retailers of a community, as a group, can afford to do many things that the individual store cannot undertake. By joining together, the merchants can activate educational campaigns on the costliness of returns, provide material for publicity drives, frame sanitary provisions and seek local ordinances establishing sanitary controls over returns, exchange information about customers with records of excessive returns, and exchange return-ratio data.

Merchants sometimes act as a group to set uniform time limits for returns, to refuse to pick up certain types of merchandise, or to impose standardized pickup charges for collecting returns. Such agreements, if successful, eliminate competitive pressure for increasingly liberal return policies, but may be contrary to the antitrust laws. But attempts to reach such agreements often fall apart in disputes over what the policies should be. This problem is aggravated if the group is large and includes stores of different types offering a variety of services. Moreover, suspicion may arise among the members as to whether everyone is complying with the stated policies, or whether some are seeking competitive advantages through more liberal practices. In such case the agreement is likely to lose its effectiveness very quickly.

■ REPAIR SERVICE

Various retailers regard repair service as a profitable business, a necessary step in maintaining goodwill, or as a major problem. Some retail dealers, particularly in such durable goods fields as automobiles, automotive supplies, television and major electrical appliances, maintain large repair departments that offer repair services for a fee on products that the customer has purchased elsewhere or on which the warranty has expired. As most consumers know, service, and repair charges may be substantial. One study estimates the cost of the average 1980 color TV set repair call at $50, and concludes that service expenses will be about one third of the set's total cost (including purchase price and electricity) during a ten-year life span.[18]

But even merchants who do not want to engage in extensive repair activities as a source of income know that customers usually expect some remedy or reparation from the store where they purchased the item if a defect or difficulty develops within a reasonable time after purchase. The easiest and best solution may be to give the customer a replacement if the product is inexpensive and if the complaint occurs

infrequently. But when the items involved are expensive and complicated durables on which a certain amount of warranty-period repair
work is inevitable, the store must arrange for such repairs, either by returning the product to the vendor for the customer; by subcontracting
the work to a specialized service firm; or by maintaining its own staff of
repair technicians. The first approach, sending the item back, involves
some shipping costs and packing and clerical routines, but even worse,
is slow and irksome to the customer. The use of specialist firms involves
problems of supervision and maintenance of standards; while operation
of the store's own department includes all the difficulties of recruiting,
training, and coordinating a group of skilled mechanics. Moreover, as a
result of consumer dissatisfaction, repair work is increasingly being subjected to licensure and other legal requirements.

◻ Responsible servicing practices

In view of the prevalence of consumer complaints, merchants who
provide repair services, either directly or through subcontractors, should
make certain that their operations conform to the following Code of Responsible Servicing Practices recommended by the National Business
Council for Consumer Affairs:

1. Customers should be offered an estimate of cost in advance of
   services to be rendered.
2. Customers should be promptly notified if service appointments cannot be kept.
3. Only repairs authorized in writing by the customer should be performed, except where other arrangements have been made to the
   customer's satisfaction.
4. A written itemized invoice for all parts, labor, and any other charges,
   should be given to the customer upon completion of the work.
5. All repair services should be guaranteed for a reasonable length of
   time.
6. Appropriate records of services performed and materials used
   should be maintained by the service company for at least one year.
7. Service technicians should not be paid on a basis that is contingent
   upon the size of the customer's repair bill.
8. The service dealer should maintain insurance coverage adequate
   to protect the customer's property while it is in his custody.
9. Service dealers should cooperate with consumer protection agencies at all levels of government to insure satisfactory resolution of
   customer complaints.
10. Customers should be treated courteously at all times, and all com-
    plaints should be given full and fair consideration.[19]

■ STORE HOURS

The days and hours of the week the store should be open to serve its customers is an increasingly important problem. Although customer preferences are probably the chief determinant, competitors' policies, employee attitudes, and government regulations are also basic considerations. (The impact of wage and hour regulation is covered on page 253.) Retailers' desires to serve their customers have led to long hours of business for retail stores in comparison to other firms. The present trend toward night and Sunday openings has extended current store hours substantially beyond the practices of 20 or 30 years ago.

□ Night openings

Probably beginning with supermarket operators in Southern California, the night opening movement has spread rapidly throughout the United States. Faced with the inroads of discount houses and other competitors, many stores have reluctantly added evening (and in many cases, Sunday) openings. Today almost all kinds of stores in all sections of the country are open some late hours each week. Downtown retailers have tried evening hours in order to compete with the pulling power of shopping centers, and in many cities, are open one, two, or three nights per week.[20] Shopping center merchants consider evening hours essential, and are usually open five or six nights. Many retailers make 25 to 35 percent of their sales during evening hours, and this figure rises to 60 percent in some stores.

Nevertheless, evening hours are expensive. One retailer with a chain of hosiery stores says: "It costs us $40,000 [per year] for one [extra] hour of operation of a Parklane store per week. In the last year and a half we've eliminated eight of those hours."[21] In 1975, Dayton Hudson Corporation improved profitability by a reduction of store hours in both its Detroit and Minneapolis units.[22] Before deciding on night openings, a merchant must resolve such questions as:

1. Do the potential customers prefer this time for shopping? Since the retailer exists to serve the customers this question is the key one.
2. Are night openings profitable? That is, do they result in increased sales without a proportionate increase in expenses, or do they merely shift part of the volume to the night hours with no overall sales gain?
3. Are night openings necessary to meet competition from other stores, whether downtown or in suburban centers?
4. Do night openings impair or improve customer service?
5. Do night openings raise or lower personnel standards? Does the practice aid or retard the retailer's ability to obtain qualified personnel?
6. What combination of staggered hours, part-time employment and

"shift" schedules will be needed to remain open at night and still give the employees the shorter hours they now demand?

7. Two additional questions arise if a policy of night openings is adopted: (a) How many nights will the store be open? (b) What night or nights and what hours shall be chosen?

□ Sunday openings

Some stores, such as drug and food retailers, newspaper shops, and service stations, have long operated on Sunday, but many other types of stores have now adopted this practice. The rapid expansion of shopping centers and highway stores is a major factor in this development. The roadside and shopping center retailers quickly found that night and Saturday hours were especially important because of the opportunities for family shopping. Sunday hours gave them another substantial sales gain.

State and local ordinances have often been used, at times successfully, in attempts to prevent Sunday openings. Canadian local and provincial retail hour legislation, which tends to be stricter than the U.S. laws, in some cases controls evening as well as Sunday sales.[23] Retail trade unions oppose Sunday selling, even if overtime wages are paid and a 40-hour week is maintained through "staggering" of employees' hours. Some retail groups have sponsored joint advertisements that condemn Sunday retailing and urge customers to refrain from shopping on that day. Opinions differ regarding the effectiveness of the plea. In practice, however, increasingly stores are yielding to competitive pressures and remaining open on Sundays.[24]

The widespread adoption of Sunday openings by retail stores of almost all types has raised questions for management similar to those already mentioned for night openings and need not be repeated here. These questions should be carefully considered, however, before a decision is made.

■ SOME OTHER SERVICES

Many other services are also useful in attracting and holding customers. Some of these services are briefly discussed in the following paragraphs.

□ Personal shopping

Many large department stores and departmentized specialty shops, as well as some smaller specialty shops, offer personal shopping services. These stores will select merchandise for their customers in response to mail or telephone requests. Some stores will send their shopping department representatives to other establishments if the desired items are not in the store's own stock. Sometimes the name of a fictitious individual is used to personalize this service. For example, Marshall Field and Company promotes its services under the names Pauline Shaw (P for personal, S for shopping) and Mary Owen (M for mail, O for order) even though it actually has a large staff of shoppers. Numerous retailers also employ a number of especially well-trained salespeople, either year-round or during the pre-Christmas peak, to accompany customers from department to department and to assist in making selections. Some stores call these persons "escort shoppers" to distinguish them from "personal shoppers" who shop in response to written and telephone communications. Both escort and personal shopping business is growing rapidly in many establishments and stores are seriously competing for this business.

Interior design   Interior decoration or design service is similar to much personal and escort shopping, in that knowledgeable people on the store staff help the customers select the right items. Stores that sell the more expensive furniture and home furnishings lines often feature their design service. It may be offered without extra charge, or the fee will be waived if the customer buys a certain amount.[25]

☐ Helping customers locate merchandise

Most small retailers find it unnecessary to do more than provide salespeople to help the customer find desired items. But the problem of helping customers locate what they want becomes more complicated in large stores. The merchandise may be on several floors, or the sales floor may be so large—as in the modern supermarket and discount house—that all the merchandise cannot be seen from any one spot. Under these conditions, several steps may be taken to aid customers. The salespeople may be trained to answer customer's questions about the location of goods; signs can be placed over each department or category of merchandise, as is done in most discount stores and supermarkets; store directories may be placed near the store entrances or in and near the elevators; elevator operators may be trained to direct customers to the various departments; and floor supervisors and information clerks may be provided to direct customers.

☐ Providing merchandise information

Many retailers are intensifying their efforts to give their customers more information about merchandise. Some grocery chains are providing increased information about the packaging date and freshness of grocery products. Some large firms can obtain merchandise data from their own testing bureaus while other smaller organizations may use commercial testing firms. R. H. Macy and Company has its Bureau of Standards, and Sears, Roebuck and Company has its merchandise laboratory. Both large and small retailers now ask their suppliers to furnish more details about such factors as color fastness, shrinkage, and washability. These data are passed on to the salespeople to improve their selling efforts. In an increasing number of cases, at least part of this information is placed on labels attached to the merchandise.[26]

□ COD and layaway

Many retailers sell some merchandise on a COD basis. Buying COD is especially convenient for the customer who places an order by mail or telephone and who does not have a charge account at the store. But CODs are expensive to handle and also result in a high percentage of returns—almost double that of cash and charge sales. Consequently, many stores now add an extra fee for the service and some now refuse to accept COD orders unless a down payment is made or unless the total order is in excess of a specified amount.

Layaway   Layaway or will-call is another convenience for the customer who does not have a charge account and does not want to pay cash. The store sets aside the merchandise the customer wants in return for a deposit, usually about 20 percent or more of the purchase price. Depending upon store policy, that deposit may or may not be refunded if the customer later decides not to complete the purchase, but any limitation on refunds should be clearly explained at the time of sale. Layaway service tends to tie up inventory and presents storage and clerical problems, but it does stimulate extra sales.[27]

□ Check cashing and EFT

Many workers who are paid by check prefer to cash those checks in stores, particularly in supermarkets, rather than at banks. According to one survey, about 70 percent of all checks issued in the U.S. in 1970 were cashed in stores, rather than in banks, and the average supermarket today cashes checks that amount to about 125 percent of its sales volume.[28] A Detroit supermarket chain received over 20,000 applications in a month-and-a-half for its "plus 50 courtesy check cashing card" that allowed a cardholder to cash a personal check for $50 without a purchase, or for a purchase plus $50, seven days a week.[29] Customers enjoy the convenience of such service, and merchants gain from the flow of patrons with funds for shopping. Unfortunately, the number of bad checks (fictitious or forged signature or endorsement, checks drawn on nonexistent accounts and accounts with insufficient funds) has increased alarmingly and has forced many retailers to cancel or curtail check cashing services. A few retailers have now allowed financial institutions to place experimental electronic terminals within their stores, so that customers can execute their financial transactions without leaving the retail premises. (See Chapter 25.)

☐ Still other miscellaneous services

Many other services may be offered to induce customers to patronize the store. A few stores have established playrooms, where children may be left during a shopping trip. Others provide auditoriums for use without charge by local organizations. Beauty parlors may be operated at a loss to attract customers, and "free" educational classes may be conducted in knitting and sewing. The store may provide a branch post-office to accommodate its customers. Through a personal service bureau, theater and transportation tickets may be purchased. Or a lost-and-found department may be operated.

Adequate and convenient parking facilities attract many customers. As parking has become more difficult, some retailers have provided their own facilities or made arrangements for their patrons to park in nearby garages or parking lots; others offer bus service at frequent intervals from parking lots to their stores; and still others have placed their stores in locations (1) where there is ample parking room in the streets, (2) where the store may operate its own parking lot, or (3) where several retailers may join together to offer parking facilities, as in a shopping center. Supermarkets may offer assistance in transferring packages to cars, and a slowly increasing number of stores are offering services or facilities for the physically handicapped.

■ INCOME-PRODUCING SERVICES

The services previously mentioned, and numerous others that could be mentioned, are usually primarily intended to increase the sale of the store's merchandise. But, as we have already noted, many retailers are now adding services that produce their own direct revenues.

A U.S. government report predicts that large department store chains will offer an array of financial services. "These may include insurance (automobile, property, liability, life, and unusual risk), mutual funds and the origination and servicing of mortgage loans on residential property."[30] Others expect that general merchandise chains will some day derive 50 percent of their revenue from the sale of services rather than products.[31] Meanwhile, both small and large merchants are offering an increasing number of income producing services. TV and appliance dealers provide repair work; hardware stores rent rug cleaning equipment; numerous stores collect camera film for developing; supermarket delicatessens will prepare sandwiches for parties; restaurants and snack bars are operated as profit centers in many stores; some retailers also act as car rental agencies; others will remodel kitchens or build home garages. The list of possible services is almost endless and the volume is expected to grow with the increase in working wives and the decline in time available for housekeeping.

We cannot examine this range of income producing services here, but one, rental service, is so closely related to merchandise sales as to warrant special attention.

□ Rentals

Merchandise rental has grown rapidly during the past two decades. Consumers can rent automobiles, furniture, power mowers, floor polishers, electric power tools, stapling guns, ladders, chain saws, glasses and dishes for parties, and a host of other items. Many stores have established separate rental departments to meet the needs of their customers.

At least five basic considerations have led hardware retailers and others into the rental business: (1) the high profit potential of a well-controlled rental operation; (2) the absence of strong competition, since many chain and department stores have neglected the potential of renting; (3) the additional sales created by customer decisions to buy the products they have rented; (4) the sales of related supplies used with the equipment rented; and (5) the overall store growth generated by new customers with needs for other merchandise and services.

But a rental service is not an automatic source of easy profits. Some major problems include (1) the size of the inventory investment required to provide a balanced stock of suitable merchandise;[32] (2) the difficulty of effectively displaying a variety of used and unrelated items; (3) the setting of equitable rental rates; (4) the provision of adequate insurance protection for the retailer, the customer, and the equipment or tools rented; (5) the establishment of proper controls over the insurance, care, and return of the rented items; and (6) conformity to government regulations concerning advertising of rental service.[33]

■ PUBLIC SERVICES

The retailer's social contributions have already been discussed in Chapters 2 and 3. But it is only fitting to conclude this discussion of retail services with mention of the wide and increasing variety of public service activities that socially conscious retailers are rendering. These activities range from parades, civic celebrations, and art festivals to efforts to encourage disadvantaged and minority citizen enterprises. They include, among many other endeavors, voter registration drives, community health programs, scholarships and charitable efforts in depressed areas, consumer education conferences for home economics teachers, vocational training seminars, employment of the handicapped and mentally retarded, fund raising for a working boys' home, and maintenance of a cultural center in the store for exhibitions of local talent in the arts.

■ REVIEW AND DISCUSSION QUESTIONS

1 Describe the information and guidelines that will help a retailer decide on (a) the services to be offered; (b) the standard or quality of service; and (c) whether fees will be charged, and if so, how much.

2 Should merchants offer free alterations whenever their products need some modification to be suitable to the customer's use?

3 In a large store, what are the arguments for and against having all packages wrapped at a central wrap department? What are the arguments for and against handling all complaints and adjustments in a central complaint department.

4 Distinguish the major types of delivery systems. Under what conditions might each type be used?

5 Summarize the chief causes of customer complaints in retail stores. How can complaints be reduced?

6 Discuss both sides of the question "Should stores drastically curtail the return privilege? If not, how can they successfully reduce the return percentage?"

7 What are the major rules for providing satisfactory repair service?

8 Point out the factors that a retailer should consider in deciding on night and Sunday openings.

9 Try to compile a list of all the "traditional" or "nonincome" services that local retail stores offer as part of their business of selling merchandise. Compile another list of the income services. Do you think either list will grow or shrink during the next ten years? Why?

10 What are some of the problems and benefits of a rental department in a hardware store?

■ NOTES AND REFERENCES

1 "Future Shock/Customer Services," *Chain Store Age* (general merchandise edition), September 1975, p. 124.

2 "Profit in Expanded Food Services," *Stores*, April 1974, p. 11; Robert H. Kaiser, "A Profit Center for Sage-Allen," *Stores*, September 1975, p. 26.

3 This arrangement is more equitable, since customers who do not want and do not use a particular service do not share its costs. *See* "Conclusions and Recommendations of the Committee on Distribution" in Paul W. Stewart and J. Frederic Dewhurst, *Does Distribution Cost Too Much?* (New York: The Twentieth Century Fund, 1939), pp. 351–52, for a "classic" marketing study that recommended the use of separate service charges to pay for individual services.

4 *1974 Annual Business Survey* (Washington: Menswear Retailers of America, 1975), p. 25.

5 In order to satisfy an ecological need, a British chemist has developed an inexpensive bio-degradable

plastic shopping bag that will disintegrate when buried in the ground. It is being used by a 4,000 store grocery voluntary chain. "The Vanishing Carrier-Bag," *Retail and Distribution Management*, September-October 1975, p. 40.

6 For illustrations of gift wrapping raised to the level of a highly esthetic craft see: Hideyuki Oka, *Tsutsumu: The Art of the Japanese Package* (New York: American Federation of Artists, 1975).

7 Jay Scher, *Financial and Operating Results of Department and Specialty Stores in 1974* (New York: Financial Executives Division National Retail Merchants Association, 1975), pp. 19, 27, 35, 43, 51.

8 "Famous-Barr Helps Profit Grow with More Efficient Deliveries," *Home Furnishings Daily*, May 22, 1975, p. 20.

9 *1955 Annual Reports of the Postmaster General* (Washington, D.C.: U.S. Government Printing Office, 1956), table 201, p. 51; and *Annual Report of the Postmaster General 1972–73* (ibid., 1974), p. 44. *See also* "Parcel Post: Pricing Itself out of the markets?" *Women's Wear Daily*, June 16, 1975, pp. 1, 10.

10 Arthur L. Pugh, Jr., "Using Customer Complaints to Improve Operating Efficiency," *Retail Control*, vol. 43 (June-July 1975), pp. 45–49.

11 "The Guesswork on Warranties," *Business Week*, July 14, 1975, p. 14; Nancy L. Bue, "The New Warranty Act," *Stores*, August 1975, p. 23; Ellen Hackney, "The Warranty Law," *Hardware Retailing*, April 1976, pp. 69–78.

12 John R. Thompson, "Consumers, Complaints and Cognition," paper presented at the Southwestern Social Association annual meeting, March 30, 1972.

13 *See* Thomas E. Wightman, "Quality Control: The Way to Cut Big Ticket Adjustments," *Stores*, April 1976, pp. 30–31, 40.

14 E. B. Weiss, "Recapture the Human Touch," *Stores*, October 1975, p. 40. For a more general comment on the need for responsiveness to complaints, *see* William G. Nickels and Noel B. Zabriskie, "Corporate Responsiveness

and the Market Correspondence Function," *MSU Business Topics*, Summer 1973, pp. 53–58.

15 "Rich's Southern Comforts," *Women's Wear Daily*, April 26, 1976, p. 6.

16 Jay Scher, *Financial and Operating Results of Department and Specialty Stores of 1974*, pp. x, xi.

17 Noel B. Zabriskie, "Fraud by Consumers," *Journal of Retailing*, vol. 48 (Winter 1972–73), pp. 22–27.

18 *The M.I.T. Report—Consumer Appliances: The Real Cost* (Washington, D.C.: RANN Document Center, National Science Foundation, n.d. [1975]), pp. 21, 24.

19 National Business Council for Consumer Affairs, Sub-Council on Performance and Service, *Product Performance and Servicing* (Washington, D.C.: U.S. Government Printing Office, 1973), pp. 39–40.

20 But in some cities the downtown stores have suffered from very low customer traffic and sales volume during the evening hours. *See* "Downtown Areas: Night Sales Slow," *Women's Wear Daily*, October 23, 1969, pp. 1, 14. Consequently, some stores have reduced selling hours.

21 Herbert M. Somekh quoted in "Streamlining the Corsetorium," *Women's Wear Daily*, February 8, 1973, p. 21. *See also* "Experimenting with Hours," *Retailing Today*, June 1975, p. 2.

22 "Dayton Hudson Cost Cuts Pay Off," *Women's Wear Daily*, July 30, 1975, pp. 1, 8.

23 "Ontario Bill Would Set Fines for Violation of Sunday Laws," *Women's Wear Daily*, October 27, 1975, p. 20; "Sunday Laws under Review," *Canada Weekly*, August 9, 1975, p. 3.

24 "LA Stores Mull Staying Open on Sunday, Like the Broadway," *Women's Wear Daily*, January 25, 1974, p. 2; "Retail Unions in New Try to Clean Up Sunday Laws," *Women's Wear Daily*, January 21, 1974, p. 2; Art Graham, "Protests on Sunday Selling," *Home Furnishings Daily*, October 16, 1975, p. 22.

25 *See* S. C. Hollander, "Buyer Helping Businesses . . . And Some Not So Helpful Ones," *MSU Business Topics*,

vol. 22 (Summer 1974), pp. 52–68, for a discussion of other advisory and related services.

26   Federal legislation requires distribution of care information for textile products, but compliance has been relatively poor. *See* "The Care Labeling Law: Unobserved and Unpoliced," and "Retailers Comment on Label Policy," *Women's Wear Daily*, March 13, 1974, pp. 1, 18–19. *See also* the discussion of labeling in Chap. 19.

27   "Layaway—Nuisance or Sales Builder?" (leaflet; New York: National Retail Merchants Association, 1972).

28   Bob Curtis, *Security Control: External Theft* (New York: Chain Store Age Books, 1971), p. 150; W. H. Bolen and A. J. Faria, "Bad Checks = Bad Problems," *Retail Control*, February 1975, p. 21.

29   "Allied Check Cashing Plan Thriving," *Supermarket News,* January 1, 1973, p. 16.

30   U.S. Department of Commerce, *Service Industries: Trends and Prospects* (Washington, D.C.: U.S. Government Printing Office, 1975), p. 48.

31   "Futureshock/Customer Services: The New Way to Exploit Profits," *Chain Store Age* (general merchandise edition), September 1975, p. 124.

32   "Although a hardware store might begin with a rental inventory worth only $2,000 or $3,000, normal requirements will be at least two or three times that figure"; see "Rentals," *Hardware Retailing,* June 1975, pp. 41–43.

33   "Rentals," p. 43. "Product Rental Ads, Promotion Come under FTC Scrutiny," *Chain Store Age* (drugstore edition), March 1974, pp. 3, 12.

RETAIL CREDIT
AND COLLECTIONS

As noted in the previous chapter, an ever-growing number of customers now demand credit service. Credit buying has become so well established that our society is sometimes justifiably called "a credit economy." Consequently, in this chapter we will first note (1) the importance of credit, (2) its effect on retailing, and (3) the major types of credit plans used in retail sales. Then we will study the basic steps in (4) credit management and (5) collection management. Finally, (6) we will look at the important laws governing credit practices.

■ VOLUME OF RETAIL
CREDIT SALES

Total consumer credit outstanding at the end of the year, aside from single payment cash loans which were also often used to finance purchases of goods and services, grew from approximately $4 billion in 1945 to $182 billion in 1974. Of this latter amount, $162 billion was installment credit (including $53 billion automobile debt) and $20 billion noninstallment. In addition, consumers had about $13 billion worth of single payment personal loans outstanding at the close of 1975.[1] Some 50 percent of all American households use at least one of the two leading national credit cards—Mastercharge and Bank Americard.[2]

Exact figures are not available, but we can safely estimate that credit business constitutes at least one third of total retail sales. Probably about one out of every three retail firms offers to sell on credit but the importance of credit varies widely between different types of stores. More than two thirds of all furniture, household appliance and jewelry store sales are made on credit. While 60 percent of department store and 67 percent of specialty apparel store sales involved credit in 1963, those figures had declined to 54 and 53 percent, respectively, in 1974.[3] About 34 percent of all hardware store and 52 percent of all home center sales were made on credit in 1974.[4] Some discount chains that originally operated on a cash basis now offer credit. Supermarkets, however, have resisted the trend toward widespread credit. Some have experimented with credit cards and other plans but generally have found them too expensive for implementation.[5]

Credit is now widely used by consumers in all income groups and for most kinds of merchandise and services. Even income tax payments and church donations may be charged by means of credit cards in some communities. This growth in credit outstanding has worried both economists and retailers who fear that consumers may not be able to handle their debt burden successfully. However, many consumers reacted conservatively to the 1974–75 problems of debt, recession, and inflation, and, by curtailing purchases, increased their rate of savings. Although this reduction in purchasing had adverse effects on current business, it helped preserve consumer financial liquidity. Many retailers and other credit suppliers also began to impose stricter standards for allowing credit, partially because of apprehensions about consumers' ability to repay their debts and partially because limitations on credit charges in some states (discussed on p. 566) made the riskier accounts unprofitable.[6] Furthermore, even though some writers expressed alarm over a supposed rapidly rising rate of personal bankruptcy, the 168,767 such bankruptcies in 1974 was actually only slightly higher than the 1965 figure of 163,413.[7] All credit-conscious retailers, however, believe that our highly dynamic economy requires close supervision and control over credit accounts.

■ ADVANTAGES OF CREDIT SELLING

Retailers offer credit service because it helps increase sales. Some merchants have grown very rapidly as a result of featuring and intensively advertising "easy credit terms." In fact, some firms rely so heavily on credit account earnings that they might be called "finance companies that also have merchandise for sale."[8] But many retailers who place less emphasis upon credit terms also find that their customers expect and demand credit services. Moreover, retailers who operate their own credit departments can use those departments as a point of contact with their customers, as a means of developing mailing lists, and as a sales agency.

□ Customer demand

Customers desire credit since it makes shopping more pleasant and convenient. With credit, customers do not have to carry sizable sums of money on shopping trips or limit purchases to planned items. Stores usually let credit customers take goods on approval, and items bought on credit can be returned more easily since the store merely credits the customer's account. Credit facilitates telephone and mail order sales. Children may be sent to make credit purchases without the risk of entrusting money to their care.

Individuals who receive their income periodically or irregularly, such as employees who are paid monthly and farmers who sell crops annually, often require credit for a part of their purchases during the period between paychecks or income receipts. A large portion of the customers who want to buy television sets, electric refrigerators, and expensive clothing either do not have sufficient liquid funds to pay in full or do not want to deplete their bank accounts for that purpose.

□ Competitive pressure

Retailers who do not offer credit, when faced with these customer desires and needs, will drive much of their potential business to competitors, unless they can offer strong inducements, such as sharply reduced prices, to stimulate cash sales. Some well-known firms that once were famous for their "cash-and-carry" policies, have turned to credit selling. For example, in 1958 the J. C. Penney Company introduced selling on credit in a few of its stores; today credit is available in all Penney stores and accounts for a substantial share of the firm's annual business.*

□ Continuous contact with customers

Many retailers are convinced that credit customers are likely to be steadier patrons and, hence, to buy a greater proportion of their goods from one source than the cash customers.** It has always been difficult to

---

* The Company has made a strong appeal to "young moderns" as users of its credit facilities. It says, ". . . it is more important than ever for young people to learn thrift and sound money management. A good reputation for financial responsibility, established early, will be a valuable asset all their lives. . . ." Annual Report for the year ended January 31, 1970.

** Cash customers, of course, often resent the implications of this fact and make protests against the superior treatment accorded the credit customer.

determine whether this belief was correct as a general rule applicable to all retailing, and it may be even less true today since so many customers now have credit privileges in a large number of stores. But experience has convinced many merchants of its truth. To illustrate, Montgomery Ward found a few years ago that its average credit customer purchased $329 worth of goods per year while the typical cash customer only spent $180.[9]

☐ Aids in building a mailing list

Credit also helps produce sales by providing a selected mailing list of persons who have liked the store enough to have opened a charge account there. The retailer who has this information about customers can send them advertisements and announcements of special sales at minimum expense. This can result in appreciable additional business.

☐ Credit department help in building sales

In addition to the general sales-increasing advantages of credit extension, discussed in the preceding paragraphs, the credit department itself should be a valuable sales agency. The department should adopt a marketing philosophy and constantly ask: "How can we help increase the store's sales?" It should exercise judgment, tact, wisdom, and imagination in (1) soliciting new accounts, (2) handling active accounts, and (3) revitalizing inactive accounts. Appropriate telephone calls and letters may persuade former customers, whose accounts have become inactive, to return to the store.

■ PROBLEMS OF SELLING ON CREDIT

Although selling on credit has its advantages, it does involve additional expenses and does create some significant management problems for the retailer.

☐ Credit costs

Credit selling creates three additional major costs for the store: (1) credit, billing, and collection department payroll, (2) losses from bad debts, and (3) interest on the funds tied up in accounts receivable. Credit activities also use extra space, equipment, supplies, postage, and communications service. (Stores that use outside agencies, such as bank credit card plans, to handle their credit function pay most of these costs indirectly, through their fees or commissions to those agencies.) Different types of stores, and stores with different annual sales volumes experience various credit expense rates, but the typical rate for department stores in 1974, not counting interest costs, was about 2.08 percent of *total sales*.[10] Since credit sales were only about 55 percent of *total sales*, the credit expense really amounted to 3.8 percent of *credit volume*. Automation of some credit operations may eventually reduce this cost ratio somewhat but probably not by any significant amount.

Despite care in extending credit, some bad debt losses are inevitable. In the smaller store, where the proprietor's personal relationship with customers may lead to carelessness in granting credit and reluctance to apply pressure in making collections, losses of from 0.5 to 2 percent on credit sales are common. Bad debt losses in men's clothing stores averaged 0.3 percent of total sales (0.6 percent of credit sales) in 1974.[11]

Credit card companies reported that delinquent accounts (more than 30 days past due) amounted to about 5 to 5.4 percent of total credit outstanding at the end of that year.[12] BankAmericard's bad debt and fraud loss equaled about 1 percent of customer payments.[13]

The interest cost on funds tied up in credit accounts varies with (a) the interest rate the firm pays for the capital used to finance its accounts and (b) the amount of time customers take to pay for their purchases. A very conservative estimate for large department stores, prepared in 1969 when interest rates were low, was about 2.5 percent of credit sales. A more recent study of stores in New York state produced an estimate of 5.73 percent for revolving credit accounts.[14]

Credit stimulates merchandise returns. Customers are more willing to take home several items "on approval" for selection purposes when they do not have to lay out the cash for them. Consequently, the cost of handling those extra returns should be considered as a cost of extending credit.

Installment credit is even more costly than open-account credit. Since open-account customers are likely to keep their accounts active for several months or years, one credit investigation may result in the opening of an account that produces a considerable volume of business. In contrast, installment credit customers tend to be less loyal so that more accounts must be opened and more investigation undertaken per dollar of sales. Bad debt losses on installments run even larger than for open-account credit. Moreover, the tracing of goods to be repossessed involves considerable expense, and the longer period of payment for installment sales increases interest expenses.

□ Impact on prices and profits

But the extra costs of credit selling do not *necessarily* result in higher prices, greater total expenses (as a percentage of net sales), or lower profits for a store that offers credit. Credit may generate sufficient additional business, without a proportionate increase in other expenses, to lower the total expense rate. Or it may raise the expense rate somewhat, and thus lower the profit *percentage* if there are no increases in prices; but yet stimulate a sales growth that will yield an increased *dollar* profit. In spite of the many possibilities, however, credit selling is probably generally accompanied by somewhat higher expense rates, higher prices, greater sales, smaller net profit percentages, and larger total dollar profits than would result from operating the same stores on a cash basis.

■ TYPES OF RETAIL CREDIT

Retail credit, one form of consumer credit, may be defined as present purchasing power based upon the seller's confidence in the buyer's willingness and ability to pay bills as they mature. Historically, retail credit took two forms: open account and installment. However, additional forms such as revolving credit, option terms credit, and other variations in the two basic types have become important during the past 35 years or so.

☐ Open-account credit

Under "regular charge account" or open-account credit, the customer (1) receives the goods without any down payment and without pledging either those goods or any other asset as specific collateral for the debt; (2) is billed for the full amount of the charged purchase at the end of the billing period (usually one month); and (3) is then supposed to pay that bill in full within a conventional period (usually 30 days) from the time the bill is mailed. Most of the stores that offer open-account credit consider the costs involved as an operating expense to be covered by the price of the goods they sell and do not make a separate charge for this service. Some retailers, however, now impose a "service" charge when payments are delayed beyond the due date. They do this both to encourage prompt payment and to cover part of the extra costs that result from slow payment.

Retailers receive little or no credit charge revenue from open-account credit. They also have minimum formal security, since they receive no down payment and cannot repossess the merchandise if the customer fails to pay the bill. They basically depend upon the customer's financial capacity and personal character, although expensive and complicated legal procedures can be used as a last resort in case of nonpayment. Open-account credit is the traditional form extended by department stores and at one time was offered only to well-to-do customers. Many credit managers believe that more conservative and stricter standards should be followed in approving open-account credit than for other types of accounts.

□ Installment credit

The installment credit customer's payment obligation is divided into parts, or installments, which come due at set intervals in the future.* It thus differs from open-account credit where the customer is normally expected to make a single, full payment for goods bought following receipt of the first bill. Along with this basic difference, installment credit usually, although not invariably, differs from open-account credit in the following ways: (1) A down payment is usually required when the item is purchased or delivered; (2) the seller often requires some security that may be repossessed in case of nonpayment; (3) a written contract is used; and (4) a separate "finance" or credit charge is usually imposed for the installment service. To illustrate, the Sears, Roebuck catalog "payment table" shows that customers who divide purchases of $290.01 to $310.00 (after down-payment) into 18 monthly installments have to pay a finance charge of $48.10.[15]

Secured transactions The installment seller often retains security rights in the merchandise sold, particularly if expensive or durable items are involved. In most states those rights are now specified in a standardized contract, called a Security Agreement or a Retail Installment Sales Contract. This contract has eliminated many complicated technical and legal questions that formerly arose when the security arrangements were embodied in conditional sales, chattel mortgage, and bailment lease contracts.[16] The Security Agreement allows the seller to repossess the merchandise if the purchaser fails to make the required payments as they come due.** The seller may also sue the buyer for any remaining deficiency if the full balance owed cannot be recovered by reselling the repossessed item.† Or, instead of repossessing, the seller may sue for the entire unpaid balance in case of default.

□ General credit contracts

The general credit contract, another type of installment agreement, does not give the seller the right to repossess. If the buyer defaults on payments, the seller's only recourse is to sue for the amount due.

---

* Installment contract terms are subject to a considerable amount of local regulation. Each retailer selling on installment should become familiar with the appropriate state or provincial laws.

** In practice, of course, delayed payments are usually accepted in lieu of other collection action.

† The Uniform Consumer Credit Code, adopted in some states and discussed on p. 567, modifies the right of repossession and generally prohibits suit for the remaining deficiency after repossession. Several practical business considerations, discussed on pp. 552–53, also limit the benefits the seller can gain from repossession.

☐ Revolving credit

Installment credit originally developed to allow customers to use and enjoy large items, such as furniture, major electrical appliances, and automobiles, while paying for them out of future income. But during the last 25 years or so, many major retailers have also developed plans that (1) permit the purchasers of smaller items to divide up their payments if they so desire, and (2) involve a service charge to set against the costs of extending liberal credit. The principal plans they created, "revolving credit" (discussed in this section) and "option terms" (discussed in the following section) combine many of the aspects of installment and open-account credit.

Under the revolving credit plan the customer agrees to pay a fixed amount, for example $25 per month, during any month that there is an unpaid balance outstanding at the store. The store then agrees to provide a "line of credit" or credit limit, which in this case might be $300. Whenever the debt to the store drops below the $300 limit the customer is entitled to charge additional merchandise up to that figure. A "service charge," often at the rate of 1.5 percent per month on the unpaid balance, is usually imposed and will be included in the regular monthly payment.[17]

The customer has the convenience of being able to purchase miscellaneous items (up to the limit) without having to sign a separate contract for each purchase as would normally be required with installment credit. Yet the payments can be spread out over a number of months. The fixed maximum credit line provides relatively tight control over the amount the customer is allowed to charge (although some stores will relax the limit for approved customers during peak buying periods such as Christmas and Easter) in contrast to the vague and indefinite limits usually associated with open-account credit.

☐ Option-terms

The option-terms plan allows the customer to choose between paying the bill in full during the option period (generally 25 to 30 days after the billing date) or, if preferred, only paying some minimum portion (usually one tenth or one twelfth) of the amount at that time. No service charge is imposed if the bill is completely paid during the option period, but a charge (often 1.5 percent of the unpaid balance per month) automatically goes into effect if the customer chooses the deferred payment arrangement.

This plan, sometimes called "option-terms revolving credit," is much more flexible than the basic revolving credit plan outlined above. The dollar amount of the monthly payment is fixed under the basic plan, while it varies under option-terms in proportion to the size of the customer's unpaid balance. Option-terms gives the customer a wider choice of payment alternatives than open-account does. The automatic service charge is easier to collect and induces much less customer resentment than would an equivalent penalty fee for late payment of open-account bills. Many retailers consider the option-terms plan as an "ideal" credit arrangement which will ultimately be the most widely used of all credit plans.

□ Other types of retail credit

Several other credit plans should be mentioned briefly. The "90-day" or "3-pay" plan used for men's and women's clothing typically requires a one third down payment with the balance split into three equal amounts payable over a period of three months. A service charge may or may not be added. "Ten-pay" and "twenty-pay" plans are also in use, but they are paid off in ten or twenty weeks, not months.

Under "coupon book" plans the customer receives the credit limit in the form of a book of coupons which can be spent as cash in the store. Advertised as providing "instant credit" to their users, these coupon books appeal chiefly to consumers who cannot qualify for other types of credit or who like the convenience of the coupon. Books are available in denominations of $25, $50, and $100, with individual coupons valued at 50 cents, $1, $2, and $5, and payments are made on a monthly basis.

■ BANKS, FINANCE COMPANIES, AND CREDIT CARD COMPANIES

This chapter deals primarily with the techniques and problems involved in the granting of credit by retail stores. But we should recognize that consumers finance some purchases with credit from non-store institutions and agencies. To cite a few examples: Credit unions—cooperatives organized to extend small loans to members—have become a source of funds for many persons who wish to buy on credit. Increasingly, banks are advertising their small-loan services, and many of these loans are arranged for repayment on an installment basis. The sales finance company, which provides so much of the credit for sales of automobiles and other consumer durables, is still another example of a nonstore source of credit.

□ Assistance from finance companies and banks

Although retailers *originate* most of the installment credit extended to consumers for the purchase of goods, most merchants do not hold their installment contracts to maturity. Instead, they sell some or all of them to banks and finance companies. This step provides cash at once and the finance company may also assume responsibility for collections. In return for this immediate cash, the retailer accepts something less than would be received by carrying the contract until all payments are made. In other words, the finance company takes over the retailer's "paper" at a discount.

Limitations on the "holder-in-due-course doctrine"   Until recently, a consumer who bought merchandise on credit could not refuse to pay a third party, such as a bank, credit card, or finance company, to whom the retailer had sold the account if the merchandise proved defective of unsatisfactory. The law held the third party was "a holder [of the account or the note] in due course" and was entitled to payment, while the consumer's only right was to pay and then seek a refund from the store. (In practice, of course, reputable stores would cancel the charge and, in effect, buy back the account from the third party if they thought the customer's complaint was justified.) Now Federal Trade Commission rulings and the Fair Credit Billing Law of 1975 generally allow consumer debtors, but not business debtors, to assert most of the same defenses against a third party that they could advance against the original creditor.[18]

☐ Credit card plans

Credit card organizations have become a major nonretail source for consumer purchasing credit in recent years. Banks, gasoline companies, travel and entertainment card firms, and independent credit card companies have sponsored credit card plans, but the bank plans have by far the greatest significance for general retailing.

Travel and entertainment cards, such as American Express and Diners' Club, are used primarily for hotel and restaurant bills and similar travel services and are also accepted in some stores that cater to travelers. The cardholders, who are mainly in the upper income brackets, pay an annual fee for the service. The travel card companies receive most of their revenue from commissions paid by the hotels and other

TABLE 22–1

Credit card plans, June 1975 (amounts outstanding in billions of dollars)

Bank credit cards	8.2
Oil companies (consumer accounts)	1.8
Travel and entertainment (consumer accounts)	.2

Source: Tabulation prepared by the Board of Governors, Federal Reserve System, November 1975.

suppliers who honor their cards. Airlines and hotel and motel chains also issue cards and sometimes arrange to have those cards accepted in cooperating establishments.

The gasoline company cards are mainly intended for use in stations that sell the company's brand of gasoline, and thus are of greatest significance to the petroleum, tire, battery and accessory industries. The gasoline cards are also accepted in many motels, hotels, and other establishments that serve motorists. Both the gasoline companies and the travel card firms try to sell some general merchandise to their cardholders through direct mail solicitation along with their monthly bills.[19]

Bank credit cards The bank card plans have grown meteorically in recent years. Two Federal Reserve Board studies show a 4,000 percent increase in the number of banks offering credit cards, from approximately 200 to a little more than 8,500, between September 1967 and December 1972.[20] Most such banks are members of either the Interbank (Master Charge) or the BankAmericard system, but some now issue their own cards or participate in smaller systems that emphasize the local bank's own identity. Master Charge and Chargex are the two leading systems in Canada.

The various bank plans are basically similar to each other, although they vary somewhat in details. Essentially, the sponsoring bank acts as a "collective credit department" for all the merchants who join the plan.* Customers may apply for credit either at the bank or at one of the cooperating retailers. In either case, however, it is the bank—rather than the retailer—who passes on the merits of the application. Once approved, the customer gets a credit card which serves as identification and is valid at any cooperating store. The retailer who participates in the plan can make small sales without special authorization, but may call the bank if an unfamiliar customer wants to make a large purchase. The merchant sends the salescheck to the bank, where the amount involved is credited to the store's account after deduction of a charge of 3 to 5 percent, depending upon store volume.

The bank handles collections, usually without recourse to the merchant, and the customers typically have the option of paying their bills in full monthly or paying a percentage of the bill each month with a service charge on the unpaid balance. The banks and stores that participate in interchange systems, such as Master Charge and BankAmericard, agree to accept cards issued by any member bank. Their cards thus acquire national acceptability.

Benefits and limitations The bank credit card plans are especially

---

* Some merchants belong to more than one plan and/or also maintain some individual store charge accounts along with the bank plan(s). In such cases, of course, each bank system acts as the "collective credit department" only with regard to its own accounts.

advantageous to small retailers who normally have difficulty in competing with the large retailer's credit service. The plans handle the investigation of new accounts, the subsequent maintenance of up-to-date credit information and of accounting records, the collection of accounts, and the credit risk itself. The retailer's cash is not depleted by the growth of accounts receivable. Since the same credit card is valid in several stores, each may also gain business from the customers of other participating retailers.

The major limitations of the plans are (1) the store's loss of "personal hold" on the customer; (2) the charge for credit service; and (3) the losses from fraudulent use of credit cards. The customer's loyalty to any one store is reduced since the credit relationships are largely with the organization issuing the card and since that card is usually valid at several competing stores.[21] The usual 3 to 5 percent charge may be more expensive than the rate at which some merchants are able to handle their credit costs, including losses; but many others would reduce their costs if they used an outside plan. Many department and chain store firms believe that maintenance of their own credit departments, with all of the attendant advantages, is no more costly and may be less expensive than the use of an outside credit card plan. Some large stores now accept BankAmericard, Master Charge, or American Express cards as supplements to their own systems so as to attract additional customers, but most major department stores and many national chains rely solely on their own credit services.[22] Nevertheless, an increasing number of smaller chains and independent stores are using outside credit card plans to compete with the larger firms. Some banks offer so-called "private label card plans" for large stores or chains in which the card bears only the retailer's name and is only valid at that firm's establishments.[23]

■ CREDIT MANAGEMENT

When a store sells on credit, accounts must be solicited; and someone must decide who is to get credit, what amount is to be granted, the time during which it is to be extended, and how collections shall be handled, including delinquent accounts and those involving customer bankruptcies. Specialized procedures have to be established for the activities of (a) opening accounts, (b) maintaining credit information, (c) identifying customers for whom accounts have been opened, (d) authorizing credit purchases, (e) billing customers, and (f) collecting past due accounts. Credit extension also creates problems in providing the necessary additional working capital, in deciding on the extent to which credit operations will be computerized, and in conforming to credit regulations established by the government.

□ Promoting credit accounts

Most retailers who regularly extend credit actively solicit new accounts, since the cost of obtaining each new account will normally be returned several times over in profit. Salespeople may be instructed to suggest the advantages of a charge account to their cash customers, and they may be rewarded for every new account they obtain. The retailer may use telephone or direct mail to solicit prospective credit customers chosen from club membership lists or telephone directories, lists of new arrivals in town, taxpayers' lists, and similar sources. Stores also use various forms of advertising to emphasize the benefits of credit accounts and the ease with which such accounts may be secured. Some retailers have actively solicited student accounts but the results have been mixed.[24]

□ Setting credit standards

Decisions on accepting or rejecting credit applications involve two closely related questions. First, management must set standards; that is, it must decide on the credit standing (degree of creditworthiness) needed to obtain an account at the store. Second, prospective credit customers must be evaluated as part of the account-opening procedure discussed on pp. 553–56, to determine whether they qualify under those standards.

The credit manager (or the proprietor in a small store) faces a dilemma: with low standards, the store will obtain greater sales than would result from a more conservative credit policy. But low standards also entail greater bad debt losses, heavier collection expenses, and the need for more credit department personnel. High standards reduce these cost elements but, as we have just noted, check the expansion of sales. The credit manager's task is to balance sales stimulation and expense reduction in order to maximize the store's net profits. A high-margin pricing policy also allows more latitude for handling credit risks than does a low margin policy.

Standards for installment credit As noted previously, installment sales agreements often give the seller some lien or claim on the merchandise sold, which permits repossession in case of nonpayment. Because of this, some retailers feel that they can set lower standards for installment credit transactions and that they can safely omit scrutinizing installment credit applications with the care they use in approving open-account and option-terms credit.

But changes in the laws and several practical factors have reduced the protection the retailer receives from the right of repossession. First among these factors is the extension of installment selling to soft goods and services, such as travel, which usually have little or no repossession value. Second, even for durable goods, repossession value has become less certain. Fashion is becoming more important, and even the market values of durable items are influenced by unpredictable changes in fashion. Third, some durable goods, such as automobiles and television sets, may be wrecked or damaged. Finally, competition on installment terms has tended to stretch out the payment period and thus allow increased time for deterioration to further weaken the security afforded by repossession.

Moreover, the long-term nature of the installment contract can create special collection problems since the customer's financial circumstances or willingness to pay for the item in question may change before the contract is completed. Consequently, the establishment of installment credit standards and the evaluation of installment applications call for as much skill and judgment as in any other type of credit.

☐ Account-opening procedures in the small store

The close personal contact between the proprietor of the small store and the customers facilitates decisions about who should be granted credit. The proprietor usually knows something about the customers, and hence, does not feel the need of the "red tape" which the large stores impose before extending credit. But this personal contact will prove detrimental if sympathies and emotions influence business judgment. It is difficult to refuse credit to friends, to impose a reasonable credit limit upon them, and even more difficult to pursue sound collection policies.

The large credit losses of many small stores indicate that their proprietors need to exercise better judgment in evaluating the credit qualifications of their customers. Although they do not require the formal credit-granting organization of the large store, they should use the same techniques. Data should be gathered from references and from the local credit bureau. When a credit bureau does not exist or is considered too expensive, the local banker may be a good source of information.

The small retailer will find it a good practice to adopt a credit limit even though it may be quite flexible. And, like larger competitors, the small merchant should explain to each customer the general rules governing credit extension, when bills will be rendered, and when payments are expected.

☐ Account-opening procedures in medium-sized and large stores

Among such stores, five basic steps are usually followed when a customer desires to open an account. These are the credit interview,

obtaining outside information, approving the credit application, establishing the credit limit, and informing the customer.

The interview Stores that aggressively seek credit accounts may
accept, and even promote, mail applications for new accounts but
personal interviews with the customers provide better control. During
the interview, the credit department obtains information from the customer, explains credit policies and procedures, and (hopefully) tries
to project a favorable image of the store.

Obtaining outside information Some stores extend credit solely
on the basis of the interview—especially when the customer desires
to make an immediate purchase. Most stores, however, gather additional data and check the interview information before opening the
account. In most communities, a local retail credit bureau is usually the
central source for outside information. Many of these bureaus are
cooperatively owned by the participating stores, but both cooperative
and commerically owned bureaus function similarly. Each of the participating stores furnishes detailed data on each of its credit customers,
showing amounts of credit extended and promptness of payment. The
bureau collates this information into a *credit report* on the customer,
which it will then furnish to any member that is considering opening an
account for that individual. It may also compile an *investigative credit
report,* which includes information gathered from neighbors, employers,
etc. Credit bureaus in different cities will often exchange or transfer
information if the customer moves to another community. The information that can be included in a credit report and many other aspects of
reporting are now subject to strict regulation under the Fair Credit Reporting Act, discussed on p. 568.

Approving credit applications The credit manager's decision on
whether or not to approve credit is usually not difficult, since the majority of applicants easily meet the store's requirements. The evidence may
indicate that credit extension is clearly undesirable for a small percentage of the applicants, and the manager may have difficulty in deciding about another relatively small group. Additional information
or a second interview may be required in these latter cases.

1. The "three Cs" Credit decisions are usually made on the basis
of three criteria: character, capacity, and capital, called the "three Cs."
Character, the most important of the three, means willingness to pay
obligations when due. It is primarily demonstrated by the prospective
customer's payment record with other retailers. Capacity refers to the
ability to pay out of current income, generally indicated by the applicant's and/or the applicant's spouse's job, years of employment, and
other sources of income. Capital, that is, financial resources or assets
such as bank accounts, real estate, and securities, provides another indication of ability to pay.

2. Scoring techniques Some large retailers employ a rapid, semiautomatic credit application evaluation procedure called *numerical* or *point scoring*. This technique, sometimes called statistical scoring, is based upon a rather elaborate statistical analysis of large samples of the firm's customers with good and poor payment records. The aim of the analysis is to find those objective characteristics that distinguish one group from the other, and to assign a precise weight to each such attribute.

An analysis may show that the good-risk group includes higher percentages of people who are employed in certain types of jobs, who own a home and a car, who have lived for three years at the same address, and so on. Moreover, it will indicate that professional employment adds a certain score, perhaps 10 points, and that owning an automobile adds another grade, perhaps seven points, to the evaluation of a credit application. These points are added to obtain a total score. Management can then set cut-off levels that depend upon how anxious it is to add new credit accounts. Perhaps all applications scoring below 40 points will be rejected automatically and all above this figure accepted; or an intermediate zone may be established, for instance, 40–50 points, calling for individual appraisal of the applicant. The basic statistical analysis has to be repeated periodically since the relative importance of the different characteristics varies considerably from time to time.[25]

Establishing the credit limit   Along with approving the account, the credit department commonly sets a limit on the amount of credit to be allowed. A fairly conservative rule is that the limit should be set at about twice the customer's estimated weekly income. But other factors, such as general business conditions, the existing unemployment rate, and the individual's credit reputation have an important bearing on the limit.

The credit limit is not an ironclad maximum. Usually, it is set for control purposes. If a customer reaches the credit limit, the facts of the case are reviewed. Under revolving credit, the use of partial payments and service charges permit considerable flexibility regarding the credit limit.

Informing the customer   The customer should be informed promptly of the credit department's decision. When it is unfavorable, every effort should be made to avoid antagonizing the customer. Letters are useful since they avoid involving the credit manager in a face-to-face argument. A brief paragraph stressing the advantages of trading at the store on a cash basis may help retain some goodwill.*

If the store has decided to extend credit, a letter still seems the best medium for informing the customer. This saves time for both customer

---

* According to law, the credit applicant must be informed if credit is denied or limited because of an adverse credit report, and must be given a specific explanation upon request if refusal is for any other reason. See the discussion of the Fair Credit Reporting and Equal Credit Opportunity Acts, pp. 568 and 569.

and credit manager, and enables the store to provide the customer with a written statement of its credit rules. Information concerning billing dates and when payments are expected may be included as well as a description of the system used to identify customers. (Federal law requires a written statement of much of the information if credit or service charges are imposed. See pp. 567–68.) The necessary coin, card, or "Charga-Plate" may also be enclosed in the envelope. Some stores inform the customer of the credit limit, although this is not the usual practice.

Store's initiative in opening accounts Although most credit accounts are opened at the request of the customer involved, retailers sometimes establish accounts for potentially good-credit customers who have not requested credit privileges. This is done by sending letters to them stating that an account has been opened in their names.

The accounts that the store establishes on its own initiative can be profitable and create relatively little risk if the list of names is properly screened. Many firms, however, formerly included credit cards and credit plates in the promotional letters sent to these invited customers, thus causing considerable resentment among people who feared liability for lost or stolen cards that they had never requested and did not want. The Federal Trade Commission now prohibits the mailing of unsolicited credit cards.

□ Maintaining current credit information

Unfortunately for the retailer, a person's credit standing is subject to rapid change. Financial reverses, a death in the family, and sickness with its attending expenditures are only a few of the factors that may cause change. As a result, retailers must keep their information on credit customers up to date. Maintenance of current information is seldom difficult in the small community or neighborhood store, where "everybody knows what everybody else is doing."

The large store finds this problem more serious, but periodic review of the store's own records will reveal which accounts are gradually deteriorating. "Revolving credit" and service charges may prove helpful in dealing with such accounts. Local newspapers also need to be scrutinized for information on day-to-day happenings such as accidents, deaths, and bankruptcies.

□ Customer identification

Installment customers will normally sign contracts for each purchase, and thus automatically identify themselves. But open-account, revolving-credit, and option-terms customers require some means of identification that will permit them to make frequent purchases against their accounts.

Personal identification   Identification presents no problem in the small store. Even in the medium-size store, the salespeople will know many of the customers, while others will use a driver's license or similar device for identification. But the task is more complicated in large stores.

Identification devices carried by the customer   Most large retailers give their credit customers plastic cards or metal plates that show name, address, and account number. The customer making a credit purchase hands the card to the salesperson, thereby both establishing identity and providing much of the information needed in preparing the salescheck. In highly automated systems the card may be inserted directly into the sales register.[26] Other stores use small hand-operated machines that will imprint the sales slip with the customer's name and address as recorded on the "Charga-Plate" or credit card. Stores in some cities have cooperated in establishing a group "Charga-Plate" plan under which only one plate need be carried for use in several stores.

The card suffers two serious disadvantages. First, many customers do not carry the plate or card all the time, although the habit of carrying the identification device is growing steadily. Second, it may be lost. Unless the store is promptly informed of the loss, the token may be found and used by an imposter.

Signature identification   Another identification plan compares the customer's signature with one obtained during the credit interview. Under this plan, the clerk asks the customer to sign the sales slip which is then forwarded to the credit department for comparison. This method avoids the defects of the card or metal-plate method, although it makes the customer wait—perhaps a minute or two—to establish identification. It is difficult to use in a branch store, where other identifiers, such as a driver's license, may be needed to supplement the signatures.

☐ Approving credit purchases

"Charge-take" transactions   Credit customers often desire to take their purchases with them. The manager of a small store will usually combine the two steps of identification and authorization by allowing any recognized customer to take charged merchandise away without waiting for a formal check on his or her credit standing.

Large stores that use "Charga-Plate" or credit card systems normally permit customers to take small credit purchases (perhaps less than $25) without waiting for approval from the credit department. This figure is called a "floor limit." Larger amounts, however, must be authorized by this department. This may be done by (1) sending the sales slip to the credit department through a conveyor or tube system, (2) calling the authorizer by telephone, or (3) using new electronic communications systems. (See Figure 22–1.)

The credit department usually provides its authorization within a very short period, ranging from about 30 seconds to, at the most, three

FIGURE 22–1 Credit sale authorization process using the IBM Retail Management System The Retail Credit Management System causes a credit sale to pass two checks before it can be approved. First the account number is checked against the restricted file on the store controller disk file. Second the sale is checked against the host credit data base. If the account number is on the restricted file, or if the sale exceeds the open-to-buy or transaction-count limits, then the purchase must be referred—a human intervention occurs in the authorization process, either by the salesperson or a central credit authorizer—before cedit is approved or denied.

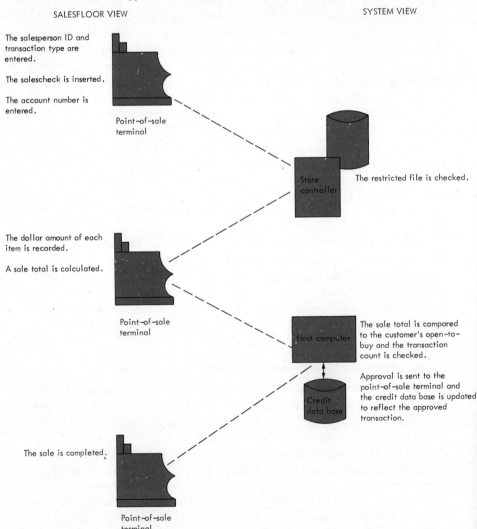

SALESFLOOR VIEW

SYSTEM VIEW

The salesperson ID and transaction type are entered.

The salescheck is inserted.

The account number is entered.

Point-of-sale terminal

Store controller

The restricted file is checked.

The dollar amount of each item is recorded.

A sale total is calculated.

Point-of-sale terminal

Host computer

The sale total is compared to the customer's open-to-buy and the transaction count is checked.

Approval is sent to the point-of-sale terminal and the credit data base is updated to reflect the approved transaction.

Credit data base

The sale is completed.

Point-of-sale terminal

Source: Reprinted by permission from *Retail Store System: Credit Management Concepts* © 1973 by International Business Machines Corporation.

minutes. Large stores employ several authorizers, each of whom handles the records of customers whose names fall in a certain part of the alphabet. The authorizer extends an immediate approval if the customer's record is clear. If the customer has exceeded the credit limit by a relatively large amount or if some other irregularity is evident, the authorizer may request that the customer be referred to the credit office; or the authorization may be granted and the irregularity taken up with the customer by letter. New mechanical and electronics systems which decrease the time required for authorization still further are now coming into greater use.[27]

"Charge-send" transaction The need for speed in authorizing these sales is not so great, since authorization can be handled at any time before the goods leave the store. Yet, although authorization may not take place immediately upon sale of the goods, the majority of stores use the same system for authorizing charge-sends as for charge-takes.

☐ Billing the customer

The final step in most credit sales is billing the customer for purchases made during the previous month.* For many years, all stores did this at the end of each calendar month, although those with a large number of accounts adhered to a "cutoff" date near the end of the month to facilitate the preparation of bills for mailing on the first of the following month.

Cycle billing Today, although most small stores probably still bill all of their customers on or near the first of the month, many large stores and some medium-size ones use cycle billing. They divide the names in their credit files alphabetically and statements are sent to a different group on a fixed billing date within the month. Thus, customers in the alphabetical group "A-B" may be billed on the second of the month; those in group "C" on the fifth day; and so on throughout the month.

"Country club" billing One method of preparing monthly bills, still used by many small stores, involves recording each sale on the customer's ledger card or record when the sales slip is received by the accounting department, and then, at the end of the month, preparing a detailed, itemized statement to mail to the customer. Many larger stores have switched to a labor-saving method called "country club" billing. Instead of making ledger entries, the sales slips are simply filed in folders or dockets prepared for each customer. Microfilm copies of these slips are made for the store's records at the end of each billing period, and the original sales slips, plus a simple statement of the total outstanding, is mailed to the customer.

---

* The billing and payment arrangements, either weekly or monthly, for installment contracts will be specified at the time the sale is made.

Descriptive billing An increasing number of large stores now use "descriptive billing," an even more efficient and economical electronic data-processing method. Sales slips are not sent to the customer but are retained in the files for future reference. The monthly bill is a machine-produced statement that shows (1) the previous balance, (2) a dollar figure for each purchase together with an indication of the department selling the item (the customer who wants to know the specific item covered by each figure must refer to the original copy of the sales slip), (3) total purchases and credits, (4) service charges, (5) amount due currently, and (6) the due date. This EDP billing system saves considerable clerical labor and eliminates many human errors.

A provision of the Fair Credit Reporting Act which became fully effective on July 1, 1976 requires more explicit indication of the item purchased and the date of the transaction than some firms and credit card companies had previously provided. However, some analysts believe that so-called descriptive bills could be made even more informative (for example show which family member had purchased the item and/or identify it fairly specifically as a "shirt" or "skirt," etc.) and thereby increase customer satisfaction.[28]

Sales promotion and the monthly statement Sales promotional material is often enclosed with the monthly statements. Inserts announce dates for special sales, colorful pamphlets promote specific items, gift certificates are suggested, and customers using revolving credit are informed as to the dollar amounts which can be added to their accounts without an increase in the monthly payments. These steps again emphasize the opportunities that credit accounts provide for sales promotion.

□ Automating the credit function

As the foregoing discussion indicates, many credit department activities are highly repetitive and involve the accumulation and use of vast amounts of standardized data. Alert credit managers, particularly in the larger organizations, are constantly seeking ways to speed service and to reduce costs through the use of computers and electronic data-transmission equipment. A shift from manual operation to EDP can be a major problem for a large store requiring detailed planning, much interdepartmental cooperation and substantial overtime work. Often two complete credit systems, one manual and the other electronic, have to be maintained side-by-side until the "bugs" or difficulties are eliminated from the electronic one. Customers' accounts become confused and considerable customer irritation seems inevitable in converting to credit EDP.[29]

In the long run, however, computer-based systems can provide faster service; improve the quality of floor authorization for credit sales; strengthen financial control; help in collection follow-up; and also provide useful sales information for soliciting credit accounts, reviewing inactive accounts, and analyzing departmental sales. In addition, they often permit substantial reductions in personnel expense through elimination of many manual operations. And the benefits of computerized credit operation need not be restricted to the large retailer. Smaller firms can obtain speedy and economical data processing through the use of commercial computer service centers.

Automation in the future We have already noted, that some supermarkets have accepted experimental installation of banking (or savings and loan association) terminals that enable customers to carry out banking transactions (make deposits, withdraw funds, and charge purchases to their bank accounts) while in the store. Quite conceivably these terminals could be used for credit purchases by permitting the customer to charge the transaction against a line of credit established at the bank, much like a credit card sale. But these electronic funds transfer systems also involve many complex legal, operating, and consumer problems (see Chapter 25). When, and if, ever fully adopted they will not lead to a completely "cash-less" society, since we will undoubtedly need some small sums for minor purchases, but most forecasters believe that we will handle far less cash and fewer checks in the future.[30]

■ COLLECTION MANAGEMENT

Retailers who sell on credit* need to understand the merits and limitations of various collection policies, as analyzed in the following pages.

□ Collection activities

The collection function includes more than just obtaining cash from the negligent credit buyer. It begins with careful preparation of sales checks by the salesperson, since they are the first record of the amount due the store; proceeds through the maintenance of records of the customer's debits and credits; includes all activities associated with trying to collect actual cash from the customer—sending statements, letters, and making telephone calls; and does not end until cash has been received and a receipt given or until the account has been deemed uncollectible.

The collection function should maximize sales and minimize losses, while retaining the highest possible level of goodwill. Sound policies and procedures are required to achieve this objective.[31]

The collection problem and credit policies A store's credit policies will directly influence its collection problems. A store that gives credit to

---

* Strictly speaking, collection management is a part of credit management, as evidenced by the fact that the credit department manager normally supervises the store's collection manager. The collection function is of sufficient importance, however, to warrant discussion as a separate section of this chapter.

practically all applicants must expect more difficulty in collecting its accounts and more credit losses than one that restricts the credit privilege more carefully. The collection problem of a given store is also somewhat influenced by the credit policies of other stores. A company that is substantially stricter than other stores will simply drive its customers to competitors. This inability to escape the impact of competitors' policies has fostered attempts to develop uniform community credit programs. These programs are usually channeled through the local credit bureaus.

Advantages of early collections Prompt follow-up on past-due accounts has many advantages. It saves interest charges on funds tied up in accounts and reduces payroll, postage, and telephone expenses for issuing collection notices. The longer an account is outstanding, the harder it becomes to collect. Some people become more and more reluctant to pay as time elapses from the receipt of the merchandise and their initial enjoyment of it steadily diminishes. Early collections also lead to increased sales. Many customers hesitate to patronize a store when their accounts are overdue; but, once the account is paid, they again become regular customers.

Granting the desirability of early collections, the retailer should handle collections with tact. In some cases, this means putting pressure on the debtor as soon as the account becomes overdue. But, in the majority of instances, accounts can be collected with less loss of customer goodwill if the store reserves its pressure until it has tried a few gentle reminders of the overdue account. Apparently, most credit customers intend to pay their obligations; but many of them sometimes find that some delay is necessary. Collection procedures should aim to reduce this delay as much as possible while retaining the customer's patronage.

Similarly, installment sellers will normally make every effort to help the customer complete the payments, even after default on a contract, rather than reclaim the goods. Merchants feel that they are better off to increase the length of the payment period, either by decreasing the size of each payment or by skipping a payment and adding it on at the end, rather than to take back the article. To minimize the number of defaulters, however, a charge is usually made when any such extension of payment is arranged.

□ Collection policies[32]

Retailers differ as to the collection policies they follow. Unfortunately, many small retailers follow no carefully worked-out collection program; and this deficiency is responsible in no small measure for their low collection ratios.* Yet some small retailers have effective collection

---

* A collection ratio expresses the amount collected during a month as a percentage of the uncollected amount at the end of the previous month.

programs. Collection policies may be either uniform (that is, applying uniformly to all customers) or nonuniform (that is, treating customers differently according to their past records and the facts of the present situation).

Uniform collection policy   Although it is difficult to generalize about the uniform collection policies of various retailers, the usual steps seem to be as follows:

1. *Past-due statements*   If a customer's regular open account or re-volving credit bill, or installment payment goes unpaid beyond the regular payment date, a second statement* (usually not itemized) is sent unless the customer has discussed the situation with the credit manager. If the retailer places an interest charge on past-due accounts, it should be shown on the second statement—which is usually accompanied by an appropriate insert as illustrated in Figure 22–2. The time that elapses be-

FIGURE 22–2   **Effective inserts for use with statements on past-due accounts**   These forms are used interchangeably.

Penneys   NOTICE OF PAYMENT DUE

ACCOUNT NUMBER

DATE

AMOUNT DUE

PERHAPS ITS HAPPENED AGAIN...

NOW AND THEN WE SEND CUSTOMERS A REMINDER ABOUT THEIR OVER-DUE ACCOUNT... ONLY TO RECEIVE A CHECK IN THE VERY NEXT MAIL. SO IF YOUR PAYMENT IS ON ITS WAY, PLEASE DISREGARD THIS FRIENDLY NOTICE. OTHERWISE, WON'T YOU SEND IT TO US... BEFORE IT SLIPS YOUR MIND.

J. C. PENNEY COMPANY, INC.

CUSTOMERS SAY THEY APPRECIATE...

BEING INFORMED WHEN THEIR ACCOUNTS BECOME PAST DUE. SO WE HOPE YOU WILL ACCEPT THIS FRIENDLY REMINDER IN THE SAME SPIRIT. IF YOU HAVE JUST SENT US YOUR CHECK, PLEASE DISREGARD THIS NOTICE AND ACCEPT OUR THANKS.

J. C. PENNEY COMPANY, INC.

DID YOU FORGET US?

WE KNOW HOW BUSY ONE CAN GET THESE DAYS AND WE FEEL PERHAPS THAT'S WHY YOU MAY HAVE FORGOTTEN THAT YOUR ACCOUNT IS NOW OVERDUE. IF YOUR PAYMENT IS ALREADY ON THE WAY, PLEASE ACCEPT OUR THANKS.

J. C. PENNEY COMPANY, INC.

Courtesy J. C. Penney Company

---

* First, if an installment account, since customers usually know when their install-ments are due and consequently do not receive a regular monthly bill. If the store continues to extend new credit to the deliquent customer, any penalty fee imposed on the account is likely to be considered as a finance charge under Section 226.401 of the Truth-in-Lending Act and will be subject to all provisions of that Act.

tween the date an account becomes past due and a second statement varies from retailer to retailer and from field to field; it also depends upon whether the account is open-account or installment credit. In general, retailers selling goods consumed rapidly (for example, food) will mail reminders within a week after the account is past due; whereas department stores and furniture stores may wait from 30 to 60 days unless, of course, revolving credit is used. On installment contracts the first notice will go out within 10 or 30 days following the due date.

2. *Letters and telephone calls* When a customer fails to respond to the reminders enclosed with the statements, the retailer may send a letter that, although mild in tone, requests prompt action by the customer. As an illustration, the text of the letter used by one retailer for accounts overdue from 60 to 90 days is as follows:

To retain your good will . . . is always of first consideration. That's why we have to be so patient . . . even though you haven't replied to any of our reminders that your account is long over due. Naturally, when customers don't get in touch with us, we can only assume that they are no longer interested in this convenient way to shop. And, obviously, that means it might be necessary to restrict future purchases. Of course, you don't want this to happen . . . and neither do we. So won't you please mail us a check at once . . . or get in touch with us within the next five days?

Sincerely,

Collection Department

AD:GW
Amount Due $_____
Account No. _____

Most credit managers believe that more pressure should be used if there is still no response. The installment seller can sometimes repossess, but the open-account seller must use other tactics. Letters may be sent pointing out that the customer's credit rating will be damaged in case of nonpayment and that the past due account will be reported to the local credit bureau. Legal action may be threatened, but only if the store sincerely intends to take such action in case of nonpayment. Sometimes a telephone call, which is more personal, will evoke a response when a letter fails.[33]

3. *Collectors* If the store has been reasonably careful in extending credit, the preceding steps will collect most of the accounts. For those that are still outstanding, the personal collector is the next step. Depending upon the size of the store, the collector may be employed on a part-time or a full-time basis. Some stores use salespeople for collecting during periods when they are not needed in the store; or in the small

store, the proprietor may make the necessary calls. Several noncompeting stores may cooperate—usually through the local credit bureau—and employ a full-time collector. If personal collection fails, legal action is about all that remains, unless the store desires to turn the account over to a collection agency.*

4. *Legal action and garnishment* Legal action may be too expensive if only a small account is involved, so the account may be closed out as a bad debt. In other cases the merchant may find it advisable to sue. Retailers sometimes may obtain a garnishment order that may be served on the defaulting debtor's employer. This court-issued order requires the employer to pay a portion of the employee's wages directly to the seller to satisfy the debt.** The federal "Truth-in-Lending" law (see pp. 567–68) limits the portion of an employee's wage that may be subject to garnishment.

Nonuniform collection policy Some retailers believe that the collection program should be varied in accordance with the delinquent customer's past payment record and present situation. They hesitate to begin collection activity immediately if a customer who has a long record of prompt payments should fall behind in meeting one bill. Some special situation or circumstance probably explains the delay, and they do not want to send overly hasty collection letters that might offend a good patron.

Some other customers may withhold payment because they feel they have a valid, unsettled grievance or claim against the store. And still others may be classified as "slow pay, but sure," in that they are frequently tardy in making payments but always eventually settle their bills in full.

Many other factors may also cause delayed payments. Consequently the store faces many different types of collection problems. Although the large store cannot treat each account individually, it can classify accounts and submit comparable accounts to similar collection methods.

This does not imply that the store should be lax in its collections.[34] Rather, it means recognizing that differences do exist and that successful collections and the holding and building of customer goodwill demand that these differences be recognized. But once customers have been grouped according to their similarities, the store should have a definite collection routine which operates quite automatically. Persistence and promptness are two great virtues in a sound collection policy.

---

* Many credit bureaus also act as collection agents. Apparently, fees for this service equal 15 to 40 percent of the amount collected. An increasing number of stores are able to employ lawyers to perform this service at fees of 10 to 15 percent of the sums collected.

** A wage assignment is a similar arrangement negotiated directly with the buyer at the time of making the installment sale and attached to or embodied in the installment contract for purposes of providing additional security. A number of states forbid, and others strictly limit the use of, wage assignment contracts.

□ Credit counseling services

Many major retailers, banks, finance companies, and chambers of commerce have joined together to set up credit counseling service bureaus, designed to improve consumers' ability to handle credit problems and to help reduce the large number of personal bankruptcies. About 270 such bureaus already operate in the United States and Canada, mostly on a nonprofit basis, as affiliates of the National Foundation for Consumer Credit or of the Family Service Association of America.[35]

The counseling bureaus do not lend money, are not collection agencies, and do not sell anything. Their major function is to provide professional guidance and budgeting advice to families who have overextended their use of credit or are having trouble managing their debts. The bureaus also help set up prorating plans, under which the debtor pays off the same percentage of outstanding debts to all creditors in cases where acute difficulties make this the most satisfactory solution to all concerned. Some bureaus also maintain educational programs dealing with the economics of credit and try to distribute sound credit advice as widely as possible.

Since both credit-grantor and credit-user have a mutual long-run interest in the maintenance of sound credit relationships, counseling bureaus fulfill a real need in our "credit economy." They are helping reduce the number of consumer bankruptcies and at the same time affording protection to creditors. Their services are either free or offered at a very nominal charge. They should not be confused with the commercial profitmaking debt-adjustment organizations that operate in some parts of the country.

■ GOVERNMENT REGULATION OF CONSUMER CREDIT

State laws As we have noted, state laws affect many phases of credit operations. Installment sales of practically all types of merchandise are subject to special laws in approximately 41 states, the District of Columbia and Puerto Rico, while eight additional states regulate installment sales of automobiles. In addition, a number of states have credit reporting, anti-credit discrimination, and other credit-related legislation. These laws cannot be easily summarized here, since they vary widely and some are likely to be changed in the near future. However, most state laws affecting installment purchases require written contracts; many specify the information that must appear on the contract (cash price, down payment, credit charges and fees, etc.) and the form in which it appears; some establish maximum rates for finance charges;[36] and some give the buyer the right, subject to some exceptions, to cancel the contract within two or three days after signing. Other provisions often control the creditor's remedies in case of default.[37]

All of the states have "bad check" laws and also establish bankruptcy procedures. Many regulate other phases of collection work, including in some cases debt adjustment and prorating services. Moreover, legislation has been enacted quite widely that parallels, supplements, or replaces the federal "Truth in Lending" law discussed later in this section.

Uniform consumer credit code   Since credit sellers who operate in more than one state often have difficulty in adjusting to the state-by-state differences in credit legislation, the National Conference of Commissioners on Uniform State Legislation (a semiofficial body appointed by the state governors) developed a standard law for adoption in all 50 states.[38] This proposed Uniform Consumer Credit Code, or "U3C" as it is often termed, establishes uniform limits on finance charges, provides that installment contracts can be cancelled within three days after signing, and recommends the regulation of many other aspects of credit. It has encountered considerable criticism, however, and so far has been adopted in relatively few states. Nevertheless, many of its provisions will probably be enacted in additional states in the reasonably near future.

Canadian regulation of credit practices   In addition to the traditional types of legislation dealing with usury, bad checks, and bankruptcy, Canadian statutes and court decisions now affect such credit matters as the information that can be collected and reported by credit bureaus,[39] truth in lending, and installment buying. However, these regulations have been adopted by the provincial governments and vary from province to province.[40]

☐ The "Truth-in-Lending" Law

Practically all retail credit sales that involve a finance charge, service charge, time-price differential or similar charges, are now subject to the federal Consumer Credit Protection Act of 1968, often called the "Truth-in-Lending" law; and also to Regulation Z of the Board of Governors of the Federal Reserve System issued under the provisions of the 1968 Act.[41] Moreover, any advertisement that offers a purchase plan of five or more payments without extra charge (such as is frequently used in selling silverware) must contain a specific statement that the "retail price includes the cost of credit."[42]

Under this legislation, the seller must give each new customer a written statement that shows, among other things, exactly how much payment time is allowed before the finance charge is imposed; to what balances (end of the month or beginning of the month) the finance charge will be applied; exactly how the charge will be calculated; the minimum payment that must be made on each statement submitted; and any additional charges or penalties that may be imposed in connection with the account. The customer's statements must also show similar information, including the specific amounts involved. Purchases made on the installment basis are subject to some additional disclosure requirements.

The most controversial element of the law is its requirement that the equivalent annual percentage rate must be shown for all finance charges. To illustrate, if the store's service charge is 1.5 percent per month on the unpaid balance, the customer's notice and bills must indicate that this charge represents an annual percentage rate of 18 percent. Many firms that use "option-terms" plans consider this requirement unfair because (a) they are not allowed to reduce the annual rate figure shown to reflect the 25 or 30 days of free credit before the service charge goes into effect, and (b) customers who settle their bills in less than a year don't actually pay such a rate. Advocates of the law claim, however, that consumers require a uniform system of describing credit charges (the annual rate method) to facilitate comparison of the costs of using different sources of credit.[43]

Credit card controls   The Truth-in-Lending Law also now stops credit grantors from sending unsolicited cards to lists of prospective customers, a method many companies formerly used to obtain new credit patrons. The cardholder's liability, in case of a lost or stolen card, is now limited to $50 and even that limited liability is waived if the card-issuer has not provided a special, postpaid form on which to report the loss or theft.[44] Both federal and state laws provide very severe penalties for fraudulent or unauthorized use of a credit card.

□ The "Fair Credit Reporting" Act

This federal law,[45] which became effective on April 25, 1971, controls credit bureau practices in compiling and distributing consumer credit ratings. The law gives consumers an opportunity to examine their files in the bureau's records, and to rebut any erroneous adverse information contained therein. Any merchant who rejects a credit application because of an adverse report from a credit rating bureau must notify the applicant of the name and address of the bureau that supplied the report. The consumer may insist upon reinvestigation of any statements in the record that seem inaccurate, and if not satisfied with the investigation, may prepare a brief rebuttal statement to be included in the file. Except in specified circumstances, the bureau may not use any adverse or derogatory information that is more than seven years old, and most adverse information that is more than three months old must be reverified before being used. The consumer must be notified in writing before interviews are conducted with friends, neighbors, or associates to collect information for an Investigative Credit Report about character, reputation, or mode of living, and must also be notified if certain types of derogatory credit reports are likely to affect the chances of securing a job for which a person has applied.[46]

☐ The Equal Credit Opportunity Act

The Equal Credit Opportunity Act prohibits discrimination in credit granting on the basis of sex or marital status. Its provisions, which became effective in steps on various dates in 1975, 1976, and 1977 prohibit credit grantors from asking about marital status or childbearing intentions when a credit applicant wants a separate individual account, or from using such information in a point-scoring formula. The point-scoring formula cannot treat income from part-time employment differently from equal amounts earned in a full-time job and it cannot pay any attention to the name (husband or wife) in which a home telephone is listed. Rejected credit applicants have the right to demand information about the reason for rejection. Questions can be asked about the spouse if (a) the spouse will be allowed to use the account, (b) the spouse will be liable for payment of the account, or (c) the credit applicant relies primarily upon the spouse's income or any separation or alimony awards for payment of the bills. Reports on a joint account made to a credit-reporting agency or to anyone else must be made in the names of both spouses if (a) the account was opened after November 1, 1976 or (b) at the request of the participants in an account opened prior to that date.[47] This last provision is intended to remedy a problem many women faced when they suddenly found, after becoming widowed or divorced, that they had not accumulated any personal credit history while their accounts were recorded in their husband's name.

☐ The Fair-Credit Billing Act

The customer's rights, in case of dispute over an error in billing, are the central element in the Fair Credit Billing Act. Creditors must give their customers a detailed statement of those rights when a new account is opened and then either (a) send them the same notice twice a year or (b) enclose a brief statement with each bill. In either case, every monthly bill must show the address to which all complaints and inquiries should be addressed. The customer has 60 days in which to complain about an alleged billing error; then the credit grantor must acknowledge receipt of the complaint in 30 days; must make reasonable efforts to investigate the matter and must reach a final decision in 90 days. The credit grantor cannot file an adverse report on the account because of an unpaid amount in dispute, and, if the firm was in error, cannot collect a finance fee or penalty because of the unpaid overcharge. Other provisions of the law specify that bills must be mailed at least 14 days before due if the account allows a free period before finance charges go into effect; payments must be credited to the account as of the day received—not as of when finally posted to the customer's account; and that a credit card company cannot *forbid* participating stores from giving discounts up to

5 percent for cash. However, stores do not have to allow such discounts unless they so desire, and most merchants probably will not provide such discounts.[48]

Other legislation regulating credit is likely to be enacted in the near future. The increase in this legislation testifies to the constantly growing importance of credit in our economy.

■ EVALUATING THE CREDIT DEPARTMENT

The prime function of the credit department is to generate profitable business. Consequently the ideal measure of a credit department's effectiveness, from a managerial point of view, would be margins or profits on incremental credit business (incremental business here meaning the sales that would not have occurred if the store had insisted on cash) minus expenses and losses that resulted from credit operations. But determining which sales are incremental ones is very difficult; moreover, much of the credit business done in any one year is the result of much earlier decisions on accepting credit applications, so that *current* credit volume does not necessarily indicate the wisdom of *current* credit policies. In view of these factors, therefore, stores that try to evaluate their credit operations generally use more easily-obtained measures, such as: (1) the number of new accounts opened in a given period; (2) the number of credit applications refused; (3) the number of delinquent accounts—usually obtained through a process of "aging" accounts; (4) the overall service rendered, as reflected in the number of complaints received and the time required for authorizing purchases on credit; (5) the percentage of delinquent accounts collected; (6) losses from bad debts; (7) the cost of credit department operations; and (8) the department's knowledge of, and full compliance with, the relevant laws and government regulations. Credit operations require the closest possible attention to trends and changes in the firm's credit volume, expenses and losses, to fluctuations in external economic conditions, and to new developments in credit regulation.

■ REVIEW AND DISCUSSION QUESTIONS

1 What evidence supports the statement that we live in a "credit economy"? What evidence exists of limits on the extent to which consumers use credit for their retail purchases?

2 How do you explain the fact that so many retailers offer, and even encourage, credit in spite of the costs and risks involved?

3 How is credit granting likely to affect retailers' expenses, prices, sales vol-

ume, net percentage profits and net dollar profits? Discuss the various possibilities and explain your answer.

4 (a) Describe, and clearly distinguish among open-account, installment, revolving, and option-terms credit. (b) Why do some credit managers think option-terms is the "ideal" form of credit?

5 (a) As a retailer, would you prefer to issue your own credit card or would you prefer to accept one or more of the national cards? State your reasons. (b) What aspects of your business might affect your answer to this question? Discuss.

6 Describe the five basic steps in opening accounts in medium-size and large stores.

7 Explain any five of the following terms and in each case indicate the advantages (and disadvantages, if any) it has for retailers: (a) statistical point scoring; (b) signature identification; (c) floor limit; (d) cycle billing; (e) descriptive billing; (f) nonuniform collection policy; (g) credit counseling.

8 Talk to the owners or credit officials in some local stores and obtain their views on the extent to which the credit function is currently automated and what are the likely developments of the next ten years.

9 Describe the principal provisions of one of the following pieces of legislation: (a) Truth-in-Lending Law; (b) Fair Credit Reporting Act; (c) Fair Credit Billing Act; (d) Equal Credit Opportunity Act; (e) the local consumer credit laws of your state or province.

10 How would you, as general manager of a large retail organization, judge whether your credit department is operating effectively?

■ NOTES AND REFERENCES

1 Statistical releases prepared by the Board of Governors of the Federal Reserve System (R & S—1960; C–19—February 6, 1976). Installment, department store, furniture store, other retail, and credit card company credit in Canada grew from about $2.7 billion in 1966 to $3.6 billion in 1974, exclusive of bank credit cards. During the same period, bank and credit union loans to individuals increased markedly. *Canadian Statistical Review,* March 1976, p. 98.

2 "The Big Charge Cards Adjust to a Different Future," *Business Week,* August 4, 1975, p. 53.

3 Jay Scher, *Financial and Operating Results of Department and Specialty Stores of 1974* (New York: National Retail Merchants Association, 1975), pp. v, vii.

4 *Management Report, Retail Hardware Stores 1974 Financial Operating Results* (Indianapolis: National Retail Hardware Association, 1975), p. 7; and

Bottom Line 1974 Home Center Financial Operating Results (Indianapolis: Home Center Institute, 1975), p. 7.

5 "Using Credit Cards to Buy the Groceries," *Business Week,* November 9, 1974, p. 50; S. Goldenberg, "Credit Cards Sidle Up to the Supermarket Queues," *Financial Post,* October 26, 1974, pp. 1, 4.

6 *See* "Will Consumers Stop Buying?" *Business Week,* October 12, 1974, pp. 94–96; "Insecure Consumers Are Socking It Away," *Business Week,* October 19, 1974, pp. 92–96; Ernest A. Dauer, "The Consumer's Financial Position," *Consumer Credit Leader,* August 1974, pp. 9, 22–23.

7 *Annual Report of the Director of the Administrative Office of the United States Courts 1974* (Washington, D.C.: U.S. Government Printing Office, 1975), p. 158.

8 Some of the major finance companies have purchased interests in

retail organizations, in part as a means of expanding their investments in consumer credit. Thus Beneficial Corporation (formerly Beneficial Finance (Co.) now controls Western Auto Supply Co. (an automotive supply, sporting goods and hardware chain) and Spiegel's, Inc. (a large mail order firm). Household Finance Company owns a large number of furniture, hardware, appliance, variety, and grocery stores.

9 Richard Cremer, "Retailer's Viewpoint for Maintaining Company Credit Cards—Only," *Retail Control,* September 1973, p. 52.

10 Jay Scher, *Financial and Operating Results,* p. xii. Handling or service charges received by the stores amounted to about 2.15 percent.

11 *1974 Annual Business Survey,* (Washington, D.C.: Menswear Retailers of America, 1975), p. 27.

12 "The Recession Catches Up With the Credit Cards," *Business Week,* February 17, 1975, p. 47.

13 National BankAmericard, Inc., *Report to Members,* 1974, p. 7.

14 See *Economic Characteristics of Department Store Credit* (New York: National Retail Merchants Association, 1969), p. 55; J. T. Presby and C. B. Duncan, "What Is the Cost of Revolving Credit?" *Tempo* (Touche Ross & Co.), vol. 20, no. 1 (1974), p. 34.

15 Winter 1975, catalog, p. 643; rate applicable in Illinois, Kentucky, and Minnesota.

16 Ernest A. Rovelstad, ed., *Credit Manual of Commercial Laws 1971* (New York: National Association of Credit Management, 1970), pp. 16–21, 131–35, 160.

17 In approximately 40 states, specific legislation establishes the maximum rate, usually 1.5 percent per month, that may be imposed as a service charge on revolving credit accounts. In some of the other states, the courts have held that, in the absence of specific legislation, credit account service charges may not exceed the state's maximum legal rate of interest for cash loans which, in some cases, is only 1 percent per month. See George Kholik, editor, *Credit Manual of Commercial Laws 1975* (New York: National Association of Credit Management, 1974), pp. 161–63, 169–73.

18 "FTC Issues New Credit Regulations," *Home Furnishings Daily,* November 18, 1975, p. 8. U.S. Federal Trade Commission, Bureau of Consumer Protection, *Staff Guidelines on Trade Regulation Rule Concerning Preservation of Consumers' Claims and Defenses* (Washington, D.C.: The Commission, May 4, 1976). *See also* the Fair Credit Billing Act discussion on pp. 569–70.

19 Jack M. Starling, "Syndication: Direct Merchandising to Credit Clientele," *Journal of Retailing,* vol. 49 (Winter 1973–74), pp. 23–36.

20 *Bank Credit-Card and Check-Credit Plans* (Washington, D.C.: Board of Governors, The Federal Reserve System, 1968), p. 1; "Credit Card and Check-Credit Plans at Commercial Banks," *Federal Reserve Bulletin,* vol. 59 (September 1973), p. 646.

21 M. J. Etzel and J. R. Donnelly, "Consumer Perceptions of Alternative Retail Credit Plans," *Journal of Retailing,* vol. 40 (Summer 1972), pp. 67–73, report that consumers perceive bank credit card plans as being more efficient and convenient, while individual merchant plans may seem more prestigious and conducive to greater service.

22 Steven Richards, "Bank Cards: Retail Management's Dilemma," *The Credit World,* March 1975. But *see also* Richard Cremer, "Retailer's Viewpoint for Maintaining Company Credit Cards Only," *Retail Control,* September 1973, pp. 42–63.

23 "Master Charge Offers Private Label Card," *Financial Post,* April 20, 1975, p. 12; "Private Label Credit Cards: Coming or Going?" *Women's Wear Daily,* August 4, 1975, p. 6.

24 Irving Penner, "The College Credit Market," *Stores,* vol. 52 (September 1970), pp. 14–16; Arlene Holyoak and Martha Plonk, "Commercial Credit Use by High School Students," *Journal of Consumer Credit Management,* Summer 1972, pp. 19–25; "Jacobson Stores Decentralize Credit Control," *Stores,* October 1974, p. 11.

25 William P. Boggess, "Screen Test Your Credit Risks," *Harvard Business Review,* vol. 45 (November-December 1967), pp. 113–22. Some credit analysts feel that point scoring is too rigid and arbitrary since it deals with average behavior and makes no allowance for the individual whose payment potential may be significantly better or worse than that of most people with the same set of objective attributes. One critic notes that military service personnel are likely to receive lower scores than their actual payment potential would warrant because they move frequently and usually don't own homes, and because a considerable portion of their total earnings are fringe benefits that do not contribute to the usual point score. R. L. Johnson, "Does Point Scoring Treat Servicemen Fairly?" *Credit World,* October 1974, pp. 25–26. E. N. Maledon, Jr., and C. T. Rucks, "Bank Card Profitability: User Characteristics," *Journal of Consumer Credit Management,* vol. 6 (Summer 1974), pp. 22–34, argue that point scoring systems should pay more attention to those characteristics that indicate likelihood of heavy usage, rather than simply concentrating on repayment probabilities.

26 "NCR Ties Retail Unit to Outside Credit Card," *Women's Wear Daily,* April 21, 1975, p. 14.

27 A chain of 25 dress shops found it could handle up to 600,000 accounts with a system in which store personnel communicated via pushbutton (touch-tone) telephones with a central computer and with human authorizers who could override the computer in borderline cases. The system cost $150,000 installed, far less than the price of more elaborate electronic display terminals. "Phone Computer Credit Check Saves Money," *Chain Store Age* (executive edition), May 1973, p. E45.

28 M. B. Tomme, Jr., "Computer Descriptive (?) Billing," *Retail Control,* vol. 43 (January 1975), pp. 13–41.

29 Robert M. Grinager, "What about Conversion," *Credit Management Yearbook, 1968–1969* (New York: National Retail Merchants Association, 1970), pp. 60–64.

30 "Future/Shock: Mechanization: Transaction Cards to Eliminate Cash," *Chain Store Age* (General merchandise edition), September 1975, p. 146.

31 *See* "Stock Control, Collections Cited as Keys to Retail Profit, Liquidity," *Home Furnishings Daily,* October 24, 1975, pp. 1, 29.

32 For a detailed survey of the use and importance of various collection methods—particularly of litigation and court orders—*see* Douglas F. Greer, *Creditors' Remedies and Contract Provisions,* National Commission on Consumer Finance, *Technical Studies, vol. 5* (Washington, D.C.: U.S. Government Printing Office, 1974).

33 J. C. Stewart, Jr., "The Business of Getting Your Money," *Credit World,* October 1975, pp. 11–12.

34 "I have found it almost impossible to ruin the business by making people pay their bills. Once in a while I stir up a hornet's nest, of course, and wonder whether the gain was worthwhile. But usually the man who is forced to pay me the bill he owes gets over it. In the long run the results are either that I get rid of a bad customer for good, or he gets over it and forgets." R. E. Gould, *Yankee Storekeeper* (New York: McGraw-Hill Book Co., Inc., 1946), p. 91.

35 "Advice to the Debt-Lorn," *Money,* January 1973.

36 The way in which a low maximum rate for finance charges may cause credit suppliers to restrict marginal customers is discussed in William C. Dunkelberg, "An Analysis of the Impact of Rate Regulation in the Consumer Credit Industry," in National Commission on Consumer Finance, *Technical Studies, vol. VI* (Washington, D.C.: U.S. Government Printing Office, 1974), pp. 7–45.

37 George Kohlik, ed., *Credit Manual of Commercial Laws, 1975* (New York: National Association of Credit Management, 1974), Chapters 8 and 9.

38 For an excellent summary of this law, *see* Robert W. Johnson, "Uniform Code for Consumer Credit." *Harvard Business Review,* vol. 46 (July-August 1968), pp. 119–25. The U3C is also summarized in Kohlik, *Credit Manual of Commercial Laws 1976* (New York: National Association of Credit Management, 1975), pp. 192–96.

39 John M. Sharp, *Credit Reporting and Privacy* (Toronto: Butterworth & Co. (Canada) Ltd., 1970).

40 E. J. McCarthy and S. J. Shapiro, *Basic Marketing,* 1st Canadian ed. (Georgetown, Ont.: Irwin-Dorsey Limited, 1975), p. 97.

41 Public Law 90–321; 82 Stat. 146; *Code of Federal Regulations,* Title

12, Chapter II, Part 226. The Federal Reserve Board may exempt credit transactions from Regulation Z in any state where the Board finds that state laws impose substantially similar requirements and are effectively enforced.

42 Public Law 93–495, 93d Cong., 2nd Sess., October 28, 1974; Alan R. Feldman, "Amendments to Truth in Lending," *Stores,* May 1975, p. 22.

43 Considerable debate exists as to whether the Truth-in-Lending Law has improved consumers' knowledge of credit terms or the wisdom of their credit utilization decisions. One set of studies suggests that knowledge about Annual Percentage Rates (APR) has increased among affluent, higher educated consumers as well as a small improvement in low income consumers' awareness of the dollar amounts of finance charges, but great gaps remain in consumer information and the law has had little effect on buying decisions. See: The National Commission on Consumer Finance, *Technical Studies,* vol. 1 (Washington, D.C.: U.S. Government Printing Office, 1973); W. K. Brandt, G. S. Day and T. Deutscher, "Information Disclosure and Consumer Credit Knowledge: A Longitudinal Analysis," *Journal of Consumer Affairs,* vol. 9 (Summer 1975), pp. 15–32; and T. A. Durkin, "Consumer Awareness of Credit Terms," *Journal of Business,* vol. 48 (April 1975), pp. 253–63.

44 *Federal Register,* vol. 36, no. 15 (January 22, 1971), pp. 1040–42.

45 Public Law 91–508, October 26, 1970.

46 Kohlik, *Credit Manual of Commercial Laws 1975,* pp. 179–86.

47 Board of Governors of the Federal Reserve System, *Regulation B* (12CFR202); "Special Report," *MRA Business Newsletter* (Menswear Retailers of America), October 27, 1975.

48 "New Credit Laws Give You a Better Break," *Changing Times,* November 1975, pp. 29–31.

Accounting controls

BASIC ACCOUNTING CONTROLS

Retailers, like all other business people, need accurate and informative accounting records in order to run their businesses properly. The basic accounting reports take two forms: (a) *the balance sheet,* also called *the statement of assets and liabilities,* which measures what the business is worth at a specific point in time, and (b) *the operating statement,* often called the *statement of profit and loss* or *the income statement,* which measures what the business has earned or lost over a specific period of time, such as a month, a quarter, or a year.[1] In effect, the income statement reports on what has happened to the business during the period from the date of one balance sheet to the next one. Since we cannot duplicate an accounting course in this one chapter, we will concentrate on some of the main aspects of the *operating statement* for two reasons: (a) a special method of calculation, which we will describe, is sometimes used in determining this statement for a retail business, while the preparation of a retailer's balance sheet does not differ substantially from what is done in any other major type of business; (b) the income statement figures tend to influence many day-to-day operating decisions about prices and margins.[2] After a brief review of the balance sheet we will look at two methods of preparing the operating statement: the traditional or cost method, and the retail method. Finally, we will examine a technique called Merchandise Management Accounting which was proposed as a remedy for some of the defects of the standard accounting methods. However, before we discuss any of these details, we will note the reasons why accounting is so important in retailing.

■ PURPOSES OF ACCOUNTING

Accounting records serve five main purposes, as follows:

To report financial results of past operations One cannot find out what has happened, and is happening, to a business, without adequate accounting records. Such records are necessary to determine if such figures as sales, operating expenses, merchandise costs and profits have been increasing or decreasing. A knowledge of financial results is also essential in deciding how much can be paid out in any one year to the owner, partners, or stockholders of the business.

Profits, of course, result from the maintenance of a satisfactory relationship among sales, the cost of the goods sold, and total operating expenses. Otherwise, losses occur. As we shall see, these three elements are important parts of the operating statement. But balance sheet accounts such as cash, accounts receivable, merchandise inventory, and accounts payable are likewise significant. All must be properly controlled to maintain the business in satisfactory condition.

To help evaluate current results and prepare future plans Knowing the results of past operations is not sufficient for wise management. The results of the last period, or periods, should be appraised by comparison with previous periods, with the results of other stores, and with planned results. (See the discussion of External Standards in Chapter 27.) Such an evaluation helps indicate whether the business is fully realizing its opportunities or whether some aspect needs improvement. Future plans, in turn, are based in good part on information from past records.

To furnish information for establishing credit lines From time to time, most retailers must borrow money from banks to finance their operations. Before making loans, bankers require complete and up-to-date financial statements from applicants. The chances of favorable action upon the application are considerably reduced if the needed information is not available in proper form. Vendors, likewise, require ample evidence of financial soundness before credit will be granted. Proper accounting records are evidence of good management, and merchandise resources are favorably inclined toward merchants who submit current and accurate statements. Likewise, a prospective purchaser of a retail business reviews accounting records in appraising the worth of the firm.

To safeguard company assets Proper accounting records help retailers safeguard their assets in three ways: (1) If correctly prepared, the frequent reports and summarized statements direct attention to the present value of the various assets: cash, merchandise inventory, accounts receivable, furniture and fixtures, equipment, buildings, etc. Changes in any of these figures may signal a need for prompt examination. Perhaps, for example, accounts receivable has been growing far more rapidly than either sales or total assets. This may be a warning that the store has been extending credit too liberally. (2) As we shall see, the retail method of determining profits and losses is especially helpful in pointing out "shrinkage," i.e., a shortage in cash and/or merchandise. The retail method doesn't usually explain what is causing the shrinkage (whether it is employee theft, carelessness, or shoplifting), but it alerts management to the need for investigation. (3) Good accounting records are necessary to obtain adequate protection and satisfactory settlement under business interruption insurance and many other types of insurance.

To meet government regulations   Today, more than ever before, retailers must make detailed reports to various local, state, provincial and federal governmental agencies. These include, among others: reports on taxable income; old-age pensions and unemployment insurance; withholdings of federal and state income taxes; and sales or retailers' occupational taxes collected. They must be filed promptly to avoid penalties.

☐ Accounting knowledge required by retailer

Proprietors of small stores certainly do not have to be experts in accounting techniques, but should have sufficient knowledge to maintain a satisfactory recordkeeping system and to interpret the reports it provides. A study of stores in four cities in a southern state showed that those that obtained and analyzed accounting data were, on the average, two to four times larger than stores that did not.[3] Small retailers can often use accounting services run by independent accountants; specialized accounting organizations such as the Mail-Me-Monday plan; wholesalers, for example, McKesson & Robbins' Economost for drugstore retailers, or trade associations. These services prepare reports, often through computerized methods, from the store's sales and expense records. As an illustration, the Pennsylvania and Atlantic Seaboard [Retail] Hardware Association provides 24 different reports for participants in its accounting system and will also prepare customer bills and tax returns for stores that have joined the system.[4] Large retail organizations, of course, have highly skilled and highly specialized accounting and financial control staffs.

■ THE BALANCE SHEET

As we have already noted, the balance sheet describes the financial position of the firm. The assets (resources of the firm) include such items as cash (both held in the store and deposited in the bank), accounts receivable (money that credit customers owe to the store), merchandise inventories, and fixtures and equipment. The firm's indebtedness—the nature and amount of claims against the assets—are the liabilities. Net worth—the amount by which total assets exceed total liabilities—is especially important, as are the changes in the nature and amount of the assets and liabilities during the period. The very simplified balance sheet of Table 23–1 shows some of these elements.

Although many students are familiar with these concepts from their accounting courses, a few words about some of the assets may be helpful. The cash account obviously is worth its face value, in that a deposit in a solvent bank can easily be converted, dollar for dollar, into an equivalent amount of money. To be conservative, however, and avoid overvaluing the business, many of the other asset accounts must be adjusted downward to reflect the loss of value over time. Thus, when it is new, a store fixture will be shown on the books at the price the store paid for it, but that value must then be reduced each year to reflect the way the unit has aged and used up some of its useful life. This reduction is called depreciation and is considered as one of the expenses of running the business. Similarly, experience has shown that some customers fail to pay their bills in full, so that the store will not receive the total amount due. Consequently, the value of accounts receivable is the total due *minus* an estimate or "reserve" for bad debts.

The most important adjustment for our purposes is in the value of the merchandise inventory. The conservative approach is to value most items at what the store paid for them since that figure supposedly represents what might be realized if the items had to be sold quickly in order to obtain cash. If the goods on hand include a dozen shirts that were purchased at $6 to retail for $10, they should normally be inventoried at $6 each or $72 for the dozen. But suppose that subsequently the manufacturer reduced the wholesale price to $5, or suppose that the

TABLE 23–1

Balance sheet, December 31, 1976 and June 30, 1977		
	June 30, 1977	December 31, 1976
Assets		
Cash	$12,000	$10,000
Customers' accounts receivable (less reserve for bad debts)	8,000	8,000
Inventory (at actual or current cost, whichever is lower)	42,000	38,500
Fixtures and equipment (after depreciation)	15,000	15,600
	$77,000	$72,100
Liabilities and net worth		
Accounts payable (to suppliers)	$28,000	$27,000
Loan from bank	7,000	6,000
Owner's Net Worth	42,000	39,100
	$77,000	$72,100

style has become a little less popular so that merchants generally would only be willing to pay $5 wholesale for them. In such cases, the proper asset valuation is $5 each or $60 per dozen. This rule is known as "valuation at actual or current cost, whichever is lower" (sometimes called "cost or market, whichever is lower").[5]

▪ THE OPERATING STATEMENT UNDER THE COST METHOD

Most retail stores, including practically all small ones, use the cost method to prepare the operating statement.* In practice, this usually means that each item that is purchased for resale must be marked with the cost price (usually in code) as well as the retail price, although in some cases separate cost records can be maintained. Physical inventories are then taken on a cost basis at appropriate intervals, with adjustment to make them conform to the axiom, "cost or market, whichever is lower." The code marking and the need for physical inventories can be quite burdensome, but the accounting is simpler than under the retail method which we will examine a little later on.

☐ Major elements in the operating statement

To repeat, the operating statement summarizes the results of operations carried on during a specific period of time, such as a month, six months, or a year. It shows the relationship that has prevailed for the period among sales, cost of goods sold, and expenses, and thus indicates the resulting profit or loss. This relationship (shown in the highly simplified operating statement of Table 23–2) is as follows: net sales minus cost of goods sold equals gross margin; gross margin minus operating expenses equals net profit before income taxes. Let us look at each of these elements.

Net sales The term "gross sales," which appears at the head of Table 23–2, refers to the total of the prices charged for goods at the time when they were sold (in the example, $110,000). But customers returned some goods for refunds (or for credits against their charge accounts). And in some instances they received financial adjustments for defects discovered *after the merchandise had been purchased*. To illustrate, a customer may have found a rough spot in the finish on a $250 table the store had delivered, and consequently may have received $25 from the store to pay for refinishing the item. The value of such allowances and of returns is deducted from gross sales to derive the *net sales* figure.

---

* Retailers who employ the cost method of accounting are more likely to use a periodic inventory system, rather than a perpetual inventory system, if they utilize any formal inventory control method at all.

TABLE 23-2

Operating statement, January 1–June 30, 1977 (cost method)		
	Dollars	Ratio to sales
Gross sales	$110,000	
Returns and allowances	10,000	
Net sales	$100,000	100.0
Cost of goods sold	65,000	65.0
Gross margin	$ 35,000	35.0
Operating expenses	30,000	30.0
Net profit before income taxes	$ 5,000	5.0

Cost of goods sold The accounting term, "cost of goods sold" really means "the cost of merchandise required to obtain the sales of the period" and includes the cost-value of all items that were sold, stolen, or destroyed during that period. Measuring the cost of goods used in this way during a given month, season, or year involves a problem in a continuing business such as the normal retail store. Some of the merchandise sold in any period, say, a six-months' season, will have been acquired by the store before the season began. Similarly, some of the products that have been shipped into the store during the season will remain on hand to become part of the goods sold during a subsequent period. Consequently, "cost of goods sold" is not the same thing as the cost of merchandise received during the period.

To determine "cost of goods sold," we must go through two basic steps. (1) The value of the goods obtained from the preceding period (the opening inventory) must be added to the cost of goods received. The resulting figure is often called "cost of goods handled" or "cost of goods available for sale." Then (2) the value of the goods remaining on hand (the closing inventory) must be subtracted to measure the cost of goods sold.

The $65,000 cost of goods sold figure shown in Table 23–2 might have resulted from the following set of circumstances:

Opening inventory (at cost or market) January 1, 1977	$24,000*
Purchases at cost	61,000
Total cost of goods handled	$85,000
Closing inventory (at cost or market) June 30, 1977	20,000
Cost of goods sold	$65,000

* This figure, of course, is the same as closing inventory, December 31, 1976.

FIGURE 23–1   **Relationship of "cost of goods sold" to "cost of goods handled,"
to purchases, and to opening and closing inventories**

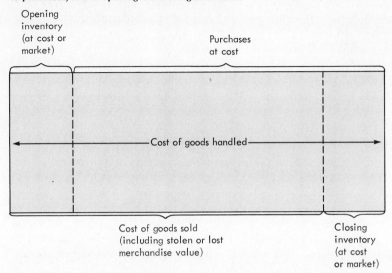

Opening inventory (at cost or market)

Purchases at cost

Cost of goods handled

Cost of goods sold (including stolen or lost merchandise value)

Closing inventory (at cost or market)

Two types of adjustments had to be made in order to produce the numbers. (1) The cost of purchases includes whatever the store paid for incoming shipments after adding the freight costs it paid and deducting any cash or trade discounts that it received. This figure is the true cost of the merchandise.* Thus the $61,000 cost for purchases may have resulted from:

Purchases at gross billed cost	$66,000
Minus discounts	6,000
	$60,000
Plus freight and express	1,000
	$61,000

(2) Earlier in this chapter we discussed the need to adjust the closing and opening inventory figures so that they represent cost or market, whichever is lower, at the time inventories are taken. Damage, age or

---

* Some retailers prefer to show the gross cost of merchandise on a *departmental* statement without deducting any discounts, thereby showing a higher purchase cost for the goods. They then treat the discounts as "other income." The theoretical rationalization for this approach is that the cash discounts do not result from any buying or merchandising skill, but from the store's financial resources. This does not change tax liabilities or reduce taxes in any way (as some students assume), but it may lead the department manager or buyer to think of the goods as being more expensive than they really are, and therefore lead to higher price decisions than would otherwise be made. But this technique is not recommended. (See p. 409.)

style changes will almost always have reduced the salability of some goods in the closing inventory. Therefore, when taking that inventory, the merchant must adjust the values assigned to those goods down to a conservative, true worth figure. The $20,000 closing inventory figure in the example may have resulted from a $25,000 inventory minus $5,000 deterioration in value. Only the final figure, the $20,000 in this case, is usually shown on the published operating statement, while the adjustment figure is included with other markdowns in the store's internal records.

Gross margin As reference to Table 23–3 will indicate, gross margin is the amount that remains after cost of goods sold is deducted from net sales. Although stores often receive some additional funds, called "other income," from various sources such as interest on outside investments, gross margin is the primary source of the funds needed to pay operating expenses and to provide a profit.

TABLE 23–3

Operating statement January 1–June 30, 1977 (cost method)			
Gross sales		$110,000	
Returns and allowances (to customers)		10,000	
Net sales			$100,000
Opening inventory (cost or market), January 1, 1977		$ 24,000	
Purchases at gross billed cost	$66,000		
Discounts	6,000		
	$60,000		
Freight and express (inbound)	1,000		
		$ 61,000	
Total cost of goods handled		$ 85,0000	
Closing inventory, June 30, 1977 ($25,000 — $5,000)		20,000	
Cost of goods sold			$ 65,000
Gross margin			35,000
Operating expenses			30,000
Net profit before income taxes			$ 5,000

Operating expenses Chapter 24 deals with the costs shown as "operating expenses" in Table 23–3. At this point we should note that "operating expenses" includes all the costs of running the store, such as payroll, rent, advertising, insurance and supplies. Deducting all these expenses from the dollar gross margin indicates net profit before income taxes.

A recapitulation of all the figures discussed above is shown in Table 23–3.

☐ Preliminary evaluation of the cost method for computing profits and losses

Although the merits and limitations of the cost method will be more evident following the discussion of the retail inventory method later in this chapter, a few words should be added here. Relative simplicity of records and ease of understanding are evident in the cost method. But profits cannot be computed without a physical inventory. (This statement is not valid for retailers who can maintain a perpetual inventory figure. See p. 353.) This is true because the daily or weekly records that most retailers typically maintain under the cost system provide information about incoming merchandise on one basis (cost) and about sales on another basis (retail price). Consequently, the merchant who relies on the cost method cannot subtract sales from total goods handled to determine closing inventory, yet that figure is necessary before cost of goods sold and profits can be measured. Since most retailers find it too time-consuming to take an accurate cost inventory more than once or twice a year, the cost method does not provide a profit figure as often as may be desired by many retailers. Moreover, it does not provide data on stock shortages. Despite these limitations, the great majority of retailers find the cost method suited to their needs and continue to rely upon it.

☐ The cost method and large retailers

The discussion in the preceding paragraphs has been deliberately over-simplified to emphasize the point of view of the small retailer. Larger retailers operating under the cost method must maintain more detailed records. These are usually prepared for each department or classification and include estimated gross margin figures. Since physical inventories are not taken at such frequent intervals, book inventory figures are determined from the estimated gross margin. This procedure becomes more difficult as the number of departments or classifications within a store increases. Consequently, practically all large stores, most chains and many medium-sized stores use the retail method which we will now examine.

■ THE OPERATING STATEMENT UNDER THE RETAIL INVENTORY METHOD

The retail method of accounting derives its name from the fact that its procedures rely heavily on records at retail prices rather than on cost. The concept is not new but its widespread adoption came following its qualified approval by the Bureau of Internal Revenue in 1920.

Most large department stores and general merchandise chains have adopted the retail method. Some, however, have subsequently modified their accounting approach to include some version of the LIFO valuation technique mentioned in footnote 5. Sixty-six percent of the independent supermarkets and 36 percent of the chains responding to a Super Market Institute survey used the retail method.[6]

□ Fundamentals of the retail inventory method

Basic approach   The retail method enables a merchant to estimate two important figures without taking an actual physical inventory. The first such figure is the estimated value at *retail prices* of the inventory on hand at any point in time. This figure is often called "the book inventory." Then that figure can be converted to an estimated closing inventory at "cost or market, whichever is lower." Of course, if the inventory has actually been counted at retail, that is, if a physical inventory has been taken, it also can and will be converted to its cost value, as we shall see later on. Even though inventorying the retail value of the goods in the store is much easier than taking a physical inventory at cost, it is still a laborious task. Even the retailers who use the retail method normally only take their retail physical count once or twice a year. Much more frequent counts may be made in some departments and classifications for merchandising purposes but they usually are not regarded as being sufficiently precise or comprehensive for accounting purposes. Book inventories and estimated profit will be calculated several times a year or even monthly.

The retail inventory method requires records of both opening inventory and purchase figures at retail and at cost. Any additional markups are included in the retail figure. Physical inventories are taken at retail prices, and it is not necessary to place cost information on the merchandise. All markdowns must be reported.

Let us now review the method for determining the book inventory figures (estimated closing inventory at retail). Then we will see how it is converted to a cost basis. For this purpose, let us assume that a store had the following experience during the first three months of 1977:

	Cost	Retail
Opening inventory (January 1, 1977)	$24,000	$28,000
Purchases (received in stock		
January 1–March 31)	56,000	72,000
Net sales (January 1–March 31)		78,000
Markdowns (January 1–March 31)		5,000
Estimated stock shortage (January 1–March 31)		2,000

All of the above figures except the shortage estimate are obtained from the store records. That estimate is based on past experience and is checked when a physical inventory is taken. For simplicity, the cost of purchases is shown here *after* adjustment for discounts and inbound freight, which are computed in exactly the same way as under the cost method.

1. *The book inventory* If we look at the prices marked on the goods at the beginning of the period (the opening inventory), or when they were subsequently received (the purchases), we can see that the store originally expected to obtain $100,000 for them:

	Cost	Retail
Opening inventory	—	$ 28,000
Purchases	—	72,000
Total goods handled		$100,000

If we then ask what happened to that $100,000 worth of valuation, we find that $78,000 was removed from the inventory by sales. In other words, sales took $78,000 worth out of the inventory. Theft and carelessness removed another $2,000, which we call stock shortage or shrinkage. Finally, style obsolescence, merchandise damage, competitive pressure and other forces eliminated another $5,000 in value from the inventory, which was recognized by markdowns in the price of the goods. It is important to note that sales, shrinkage and markdowns all have the same effect on the value of the closing inventory, even though the last two figures differ greatly from sales in their effect on store profits. These three figures are usually called retail reductions. In short, we must think of the merchandise handled as an assortment or bundle of physical assets that is reduced in value whenever any of those assets leave the store, either through sale or theft, or whenever any of the items loses some of its salability. Selling a piece of merchandise replaces the physical asset with a financial asset such as cash or an account receivable, but it reduces the value of the physical stock (see p. 588). We can now compute closing inventory at retail.

2. *Estimating closing inventory at cost* We still have the problem of converting the retail value of the closing inventory ($15,000) to a basis

	Cost	Retail
Opening inventory .... —	$28,000	
Purchases	72,000	
Total goods handled		$100,000
Sales	$78,000	
Markdowns	5,000	
Stock shortage	2,000	
Total retail reductions		$ 85,000
Closing inventory		$ 15,000

of cost or market, whichever is lower. The courts, the Internal Revenue Service and the accounting authorities who have accepted the retail method say that the appropriate cost valuation can be estimated by applying the store's own initial cost percentage (the complement of the initial markup percentage) to the retail inventory. The resulting figure is only a computed estimate, but it is regarded as being close enough for both business and tax purposes. To compute the initial cost percentage, we must return to the records of opening inventory and purchases at both cost and retail.

	Cost		Retail	Cost percentage
Opening inventory $24,000		$28,000		
Purchases 56,000		72,000		
Total goods handled	$80,000		$100,000	80%
				$\left(\dfrac{80,000}{100,000} = 80\%\right)$
Sales		$78,000		
Markdowns		5,000		
Stock shortage		2,000		
Total retail reduction			85,000	
Closing inventory	12,000		$ 15,000	
	(80% of $15,000)			

Note that the initial cost percentage resulted from dividing total goods handled at cost by total goods handled at retail. This percentage is the complement of the initial markup percentage. (In the illustration, $100,000 — $80,000 equals a dollar markup of $20,000 or 20 percent on the *retail* base of $100,000.) Then that cost percentage is applied to the closing inventory at retail to estimate closing inventory at cost or market.

Summary of steps in the retail inventory method The foregoing illustrations suggest that six basic steps are involved in the retail inventory method: (a) charging merchandise to a department or to an entire store at both cost and retail prices; (b) keeping complete and accurate records at retail prices of all additions to and deductions from this stock; (c) determining the markup percentage and through this the cost percentage on the total merchandise handled; (d) calculating from the records the closing retail book inventory, that is, the retail value of the merchandise in the closing inventory; (e) applying the cost percentage to the retail book inventory; (f) taking a physical inventory at retail prices, usually semiannually or annually, to check the accuracy of the retail book inventory. If this check reveals that the retail book inventory exceeds the physical inventory, which is the usual situation, a stock shortage exists; if the physical inventory is larger than the book inventory, there is an overage.

☐ The operating statement

The remaining steps necessary to prepare an operating statement under the retail inventory method are similar to those under the cost method. If the store we have just been discussing had operating expenses of $8,000 for the period, its operating statement would show:

Sales			$78,000
Opening inventory	$24,000		
Purchases	56,000		
Total goods handled		$80,000	
Closing inventory		12,000	
Costs of goods sold			68,000
Gross margin			$10,000
Operating expenses			8,000
Net profit (before income taxes)			$ 2,000

☐ Advantages and limitations of the retail inventory method

We can now evaluate the retail method and the reasons for its growth.

Six advantages   The six main advantages of the retail method are:

1. *Permits frequent operating statements*   An operating statement can be prepared under the retail method without taking a physical inventory. A store management that uses the retail method can easily obtain timely monthly reports on trends in profits, and can react quickly to any changes in those trends. In contrast, only semiannual or annual reports are likely under the cost method, because of the expense and difficulty of taking a physical inventory.

2. *Facilitates taking the physical inventory*   There is less chance of error because no decoding is necessary, and entries on the inventory cards or sheets are made more rapidly. Moreover, personnel unfamiliar with the stock can list and count it. Since inventory-taking is easier, it may be done more frequently; thus, slow-moving items and irregularities in the stock may be detected more quickly.

3. *Helps provide effective merchandising control*   It is not sufficient to know whether profits are increasing or decreasing; an alert manage-

ment wants to know what is causing the change. We have already noted that profits depend on the relationships between sales, margins and expenses. Gross margin, which is the result of initial markup and subsequent price changes, is a key figure in today's highly competitive environment. For example, a study of men's apparel shops showed that the highly profitable stores had approximately the same initial markup, but a much lower markdown rate (and a lower expense rate) than the industry average.[7] The retail method requires detailed records of, and provides current information about, such significant profit elements as initial markup, additional markup and markdowns. It provides a basis for merchandise control on a dollar basis. (See the discussion of dollar control on pp. 353–56.) It thus focuses the attention of department heads, buyers and top management on major merchandising variables, and warns when corrective action is needed.

4. *Aids in controlling stock shortages* Currently, shortage problems are a major concern in many retail stores. By providing a book inventory figure, the retail method permits a comparison of book and physical inventories, at retail, and consequently indicates if any serious shortages exist. If so, their causes may be studied and steps taken to reduce the losses.

5. *Furnishes basis for proper insurance coverage and claim adjustment* Accurate and reliable records that regularly show the value of goods on hand and profits help retailers secure adequate inventory and business interruption insurance. Such records are very helpful, even essential, in settling any disputed claims.

6. *Permits valuation of inventory on conservative basis* The retail inventory method permits a conservative valuation for the closing inventory. As noted, this result is achieved by applying the cost percentage to the book inventory at retail. But the question arises: Why does this procedure yield an inventory valuation on a conservative "cost or market, whichever is lower" basis? The answer lies in the fact that the cost percentage is calculated *after* additional markups but *before* markdowns. Further explanation will clarify this point.

Assume that a retailer purchases a man's suit at $60 and marks it to sell for $100, the cost percentage being 60 percent. Assume, further, that the retail price is increased to $120 by taking an additional markup of $20, so that the cost percentage drops to 50 percent. The new cost percentage, 50 percent, when applied to the new retail price, $120, will correctly indicate the actual cost of the suit, $60. If the old cost percentage, 60 percent, were applied to $120, the cost of the suit would be shown as $72, which is clearly in error.

Now let us make another assumption. Suppose that another suit costing $60 is marked to sell for $100 so that the original cost percentage is also 60 percent. But it fails to sell and is marked down $10. This leads to the question: Does $60 represent a fair valuation of a suit which had to be marked down $10 to be sold? If the accounting maxim—anticipate losses but never profits—is adhered to, the loss caused by the markdown will be taken in the current period rather than in the following one. Consequently, the original cost percentage, 60 percent, will be applied to the reduced price of $90, yielding a book value of $54. Thus, the fundamental rule is that the cost percentage should always be calculated by including the additional markups but excluding the markdowns.

Limitations of the retail method   The retail inventory method has five important limitations which the retailer should recognize.

1. *An averaging method*   This system of accounting suffers from the fact that it is an averaging method. That is, the cost percentage is based on the total cost of the merchandise handled and its total *retail* value (see page 588). The resulting closing inventory only approximates the true cost of the merchandise.*

2. *Great care needed in recording of price changes*   The book (retail) inventory figure, a key element in the retail method, can be calculated accurately only if great care has been exercised in recording all charges for merchandise delivered to the department, price changes such as markdowns and additional markups, transfers of goods to and from the department, and sales. Some unscrupulous buyers, however, may manipulate records—for example, markdowns—to their own advantage, with the result that the final figures are incorrect. This manipulation, of course, will result in higher stock shortages if the buyer is unable to alter the physical inventory figures. Only close supervision by management can overcome this danger.

3. *Unsuited to some stores and departments*   The retail inventory method is not suitable for certain kinds of merchandise—such as bakery goods and soda fountain sales—where composition or manufacturing takes place. Similarly, the accounting records for drapery and furniture workrooms, devoted to preparing merchandise for use by customers, must be kept on a cost, rather than a retail, basis. However, this is not a serious disadvantage since many retailers have little difficulty in operating the large majority of their departments on a retail basis and the remaining small number on a cost basis.

4. *Costly to operate*   The retail inventory method is costly to operate satisfactorily. The expense involved is greater than for the cost method because of the numerous records it requires. In the final analysis, of course, these costs are offset by the savings in inventory-taking

---

* Since low-markup merchandise tends to sell faster than high-markup goods, the former is represented in the total dollar purchases to a greater degree than it is at any time in the stock on hand. Consequently, when the closing book inventory at retail is reduced to cost by applying the cost percentage, the resulting valuation is higher than would be obtained by tabulating the specific costs of the items on hand. This disadvantage is particularly significant for stores and departments having (a) wide variations in markups and (b) many special sales events featuring merchandise at lower-than-usual markups.

effort, and more importantly, by the value of the information the system provides.

5. Concentrates on markup percentages The retail method places great stress on *percentage* relationships, and particularly on the initial markup percentage and on its complement, the cost percentage. Consequently, both senior executives and buyers in stores that use the retail method may concentrate on markup percentages in making or evaluating all buying and pricing decisions and may not pay sufficient attention to the dollar markup. A piece of furniture that costs the store $60 may not be profitable unless sold for $120 (a 50 percent markup when expressed as a percent of retail), but this does not mean that a $600 cost item will be unprofitable unless sold at $1,200 (also a 50 percent markup). Perhaps the store's expenses in selling the first item are $55, but handling and selling the second one only costs $400. In fact, a $1,200 retail price may leave the store vulnerable to being undersold by an aggressive competitor. Yet the use (or, really, the misuse) of plans prepared in accordance with the retail method may have caused the merchandise managers and buyers to insist on a uniform 50 percent markup. Such insistence upon uniform percentage markups put many department stores at a disadvantage when faced with competition from hard-goods discount houses during the late 1940s and 1950s and led to experiments with Merchandise Management Accounting, discussed below.

■ MERCHANDISE MANAGEMENT ACCOUNTING

Just as the limitations of the cost method stimulated the growth of the retail inventory method, so, too, the shortcomings of the latter system encouraged the search for a new approach that would improve merchandising decision-making under modern conditions. Merchandise management accounting was one result of this research. Strictly speaking, it is more a method of merchandising and pricing rather than a form of accounting. Since it relies so heavily on accounting records and demands some accounting information not required for other purposes, however, a few paragraphs concerning it are advisable here.

Merchandise management accounting (MMA) seeks, among other objectives, to improve *dollar* profit (rather than *percentage* profit) through better determination and interpretation of costs by individual items. In other words, merchandise management accounting attempts to measure the *dollar* cost of handling and selling each specific item in stock or under consideration as a potential addition to the stock. An analysis of records may show that customers request delivery service on half of all purchases of item A and on one third of all purchases of item B. If the store's delivery company charges $1 for handling an item such as A or B, the average dollar delivery cost for A is 50¢ and 33⅓¢ for B. Similar analyses are made of buying, receiving, marking, selling, wrapping and other costs. (See the discussion of expense analysis methods, especially production unit accounting, in the next chapter.) The advocates of merchandise management accounting claimed that a buyer or merchandiser could combine this cost information with a good intuitive estimate of the demand curve for each item (i.e., expert judgment as to the quantity that would be sold at each possible price) and thus make a profit-maximizing decision about the price to charge and the quantity of each item to buy. They felt that the retail inventory method placed too much emphasis on department or store-wide gross margin percentages and deplored "the fixed habit of looking at departmental expenses, both direct and allocated, as applying across the board to all the goods sold in the department."[8] They pointed out that this traditional approach discouraged retailers from purchasing merchandise which might move in great quantity if priced with a lower-than-normal markup.

Despite management's recognition of the need for more information of the type furnished by merchandise management accounting and the strong advocacy of this concept by certain accounting firms and students of retailing, only a relatively few stores have adopted the system. Adherence to traditional methods, unavailability of the required cost data and unwillingness to provide it, and lack of understanding of the techniques involved, among other reasons, are responsible.[9]

It seems certain, however, that the future will continue to bring frequent and critical evaluations of all accounting systems used by retailers as well as constant search for improved methods and devices to strengthen control. Such actions are necessary in view of the numerous current technological developments having particular application to retailing (some of these are discussed in Chapter 25, "Control of sales transactions"), the growing competition among retailers for consumer patronage, the continuous pressure of personnel for higher wages and better working conditions, and the need to control prices and costs to insure a reasonable profit.

■ REVIEW AND DISCUSSION QUESTIONS

1 Jones, who plans to open a store, says: "I'm a merchant, not a bookkeeper. I'm not going to bother with accounting records, but at the end of the year I'll see if I have more money than I started with." What may go wrong with Jones' plans?

2 (a) If Jones eventually becomes convinced of the need for accounting records and reports, what is the minimum amount of accounting knowledge

required? (b) Where can a small merchant obtain help with accounting problems?

3 Visit two local retailers and ask them to discuss the accounting records and reports they use, and what help they obtain in preparing and interpreting those documents.

4 (a) What is a balance sheet and what are the principal items it contains? (b) How does it differ from an operating statement? (c) Describe the downward adjustments that normally have to be made in some of the items on the balance sheet.

5 Explain the difference between (a) "gross sales" and "net sales," (b) between "total cost of goods handled" and "cost of goods sold," and (c) between gross margin" and "profit before income taxes."

6 (a) Two stores, A and B, have identical sales, purchases, closing inventory and expenses, but A has a higher opening inventory. Which one has the greater profit? (b) Store X has the same sales, opening inventory, purchases and expenses as Store Y, but X has a higher closing inventory. Which one, X or Y, has the greater net profit?

7 Explain the meaning of the following terms used in the retail method of accounting: (a) cost percentage, (b) retail reductions, (c) book inventory, (d) physical inventory.

8 During a six months' period, a store had the following experience: Opening inventory at cost $50,000, at retail $90,000; purchases (after adding freight and deducting discounts) at cost $550,000, at retail $910,000; sales $860,000; markdowns $45,000; estimated shortages $15,000; and operating expenses, $270,000. Compute total goods handled at cost, and at retail; the cost percentage; retail reductions; closing inventory at retail, and at cost; cost of goods sold; gross margin; and profit before income taxes.

9 Cite the advantages of the retail method over the cost method. What information does the retail method provide that is missing under the cost method?

10 Describe some of the defects of the retail method. Explain how merchandise management accounting tried to remedy some of the weaknesses of the retail method.

■ NOTES AND REFERENCES

1 A third analysis is a cash-flow statement. This differs from the income or profit and loss statement in that (a) it is concerned with changes in the amount of cash in the store's bank account or otherwise available to pay bills rather than with changes in total assets, and (b) it is generally prepared as an estimate of future developments rather than as a record of completed events. See any standard accounting or business finance text, such as J. D. Edwards, R. H. Hermanson, and R. F. Salmonson, *Accounting: A Programmed Text* (Homewood, Ill.: Richard D. Irwin, Inc., 1974).

2 Nevertheless, the balance sheet is also important, for example, by indicating whether the business has incurred excessive debts or has too much money tied up in fixed assets (such as buildings and fixtures) that will not turn into sales revenue. An old retailing maxim is: "Many retailers live by the income statement and die by the balance sheet." ("What's Behind W. T. Grant & Co.," *Retailing Today*, November 1975). This means that merchants who fail to guard against taking on excessive liabilities (debts) become very vulnerable to failure. (Again, for more information on bal-

ance sheet analysis, see any standard accounting or managerial finance text.)

3 Robert E. Stevens, "Using Accounting Data to Make Decisions," *Journal of Retailing,* vol. 51 (Fall 1975), pp. 23–28.

4 "Computerized Retail Accounting," *Hardware Retailing,* October 1974, p. 99.

5 In modern accounting practice, this basic rule has been subjected to a wide variety of interpretations, in part because of attempts to deal with the problems that inflation has introduced into the determination of inventory values, merchandise cost, profits and taxes. The general concept of so-called Lifo-Fifo adjustments in inventory valuation is discussed in all standard accounting textbooks. For retailing applications see John Hammond, "Lifo-Not Quite a Money Tree," *Hardware Retailing,* January 1976, pp. 94–102.

6 "1975 Inventory Valuation Practices: A Status Report (Special Research Report #9)" (Chicago: Super Market Institute, 1975), p. 5. Many of the other respondents used some modification of the retail method.

7 *1974 Annual Business Survey* (Washington, D.C.: Menswear Retailers of America, 1975), p. 14.

8 M. P. McNair and E. G. May, "Pricing for Profit: A Revolutionary Approach to Retail Accounting," *Harvard Business Review,* vol. 35 (May-June 1957), p. 111.

9 For an analysis of these reasons see Roger Dickinson, "Marginalism in Retailing: The Lessons of a Failure," *Journal of Business,* vol. 39 (July 1966), pp. 353–58. This source contains an excellent explanation of the fundamental concepts of merchandise management accounting.

ANALYZING AND
CONTROLLING EXPENSES

Retailers, faced with rising costs, intensified competition, and consumer resistance to price increases, have had to institute increasingly strict control over their operating expenses.[1] But merchants cannot control those expenses unless they know how much they are spending to keep their businesses operating, what activities have created those expenses, and what benefits have resulted from the expenditures. In this chapter we will look at several ways of analyzing expenses. First, we will consider expense classification schedules (including expense center analysis) that report on the major categories of expenses. Then we will examine two methods (the net profit and the contribution methods) of charging expenses against the various merchandise departments and branches of departmentized and chain store firms. After this, we will study production unit accounting, a method of measuring costs and output for standardized tasks in retail stores. Finally, we will discuss expense budgeting as an approach to expense control and reduction.

Multiple analysis A large retail organization will examine its expenses in many different ways, and even a small merchant may want to analyze some expenses on two or three different bases. But while multiple analyses increase the store's information about expenses, they do not increase the actual expenses. To illustrate, Mary Jones, a salesperson in the furniture section of Store 82 in the XYZ chain received a salary payment of $195 on December 16, 1976. That $195 was a part of the XYZ Company's wage expense, it was also a part of its selling expense, of its furniture department expense, of its expenses for Store 82, and of its December 1976 expenses. Yet the amount actually spent, $195, remained unchanged and did not increase fivefold just because the XYZ Company analyzed it in five different ways.

■ EXPENSE CLASSIFICATION

Expense classification divides all the expenses of retailing such as rent, advertising, and salaries into a number of clearly defined groups. Its purposes are to provide a detailed breakdown that can be used year after year: (1) to note expense trends for each classification and (2) to allow comparisons with other stores. These comparisons reveal expenses that are "out of line" and indicate need for remedial action.

Expenses are classified in various ways among different types and sizes of stores, both multi- and single-unit. These variations are clear when the expense classifications used in different types of stores are examined. Department stores and departmentalized specialty stores, however, have given the greatest attention to expense classification, distribution, and analysis. Consequently, our discussion of these topics emphasizes the terminology and procedures used in these institutions.

□ Natural system of classification

The first classification schemes that we will examine mainly divide or group expenses into "natural" categories. These are relatively traditional categories that are easy to use and understand. In general, the categories report on *who was paid,* rather than on what task or function within the business received the benefit of the expenditures. For example, a natural system will always have an account called "wages," but without further analysis that account will only indicate the total amount the employees received as wages. It will not show what portion of that total was spent for work in the warehouse, for work in the credit office, and for cashiering. This point will become clearer after studying expense center (also called responsibility center) classification. However, even though natural systems are not as informative as expense center ones, they are still very useful and their simplicity is conducive to use in medium-sized and smaller firms.

Hardware store expense classification   Although the majority of small independent retailers employ a simpler expense classification, the one recommended to its member stores by the National Retail Hardware Association is shown in Table 24–1.

TABLE 24–1

Classification of expenses in hardware stores
Payroll and other employee expenses
Salaries—owners, officers, managers
Salaries—other employees
Federal and state payroll taxes
Group insurance
Benefit plans
Total payroll and other employee expense
Occupancy expense
Heat, light, power, water
Repairs to building
Rent or ownership in real estate*
Total occupancy expense
Other costs of doing business
Office supplies and postage
Advertising
Donations
Telephone and telegraph
Bad debts
Delivery (Other than wages)
Insurance (Other than real estate and group)
Taxes (Other than real estate and payroll)
Interest on borrowed money
Depreciation (Other than real estate)
Store and shop supplies
Legal and accounting
Dues and subscriptions
Travel, buying and entertainment
Unclassified
Total other costs of doing business

* Ownership in real estate includes taxes, insurance and depreciation on land and buildings.
Source: *Retail Hardware Stores 1974 Financial Operating Results* (Indianapolis: National Retail Hardware Association, 1975), p. 6.

A food store expense classification Another system, developed for industry-wide comparisons among food chains, is shown in Table 24–2. It also is based on a natural system and is quite similar to the hardware store classification, in spite of some differences in terminology. In practice, the accounts may be broken into detailed subgroups for further identification of the expenses.

Expense classification for smaller department stores The National Retail Merchants Association suggests two types of expense classification—by natural divisions for smaller stores and by expense centers for larger ones. The recommended 20-point natural classification of operating costs for the smaller stores is shown in Table 24–3. Along with sixteen basic, natural divisions of expense, four additional category groups are provided for redistribution and offset purposes.[2] As noted,

TABLE 24-2

Classification of expenses in food chains

Payroll
Supplies
Utilities
Communications
Travel
Services purchased
Promotional activities
Professional services
Donations
Insurance
Taxes and licenses (except on income)
Property rentals
Equipment rentals
Depreciation and amortization
Repairs
Credits and allowances
Unclassified
Interest

Source: Wendell Earle and Willard Hunt, *Operating Results of Food Chains, 1974–75* (Ithaca, N.Y.: Cornell University, 1975).

this grouping is called a natural classification because it assigns expenses on a simple, understandable basis that most retailers have used for many years.

☐ Expense center accounting

The expense center system takes each expense item that has originally been classified according to the natural plan and regroups it according to the major business task or function involved. Each such function is called an "expense center." (Some accountants prefer the term "responsibility center.") Use of the expense center system tells management what it has spent in order to accomplish each of these significant functions.

Department stores The National Retail Merchants Association recommends that larger department stores first classify their expenses into the natural divisions and then reanalyze them in 23 expense centers, with each center designating a particular activity or service essential to the operating of the store such as management, sales promotion, and delivery. These 23 centers are shown in Table 24–4. Expenses are classified under both the appropriate natural division and the expense center. Thus, top management salaries (a part of natural division 01—payroll) and managers' traveling expenses (natural division 09) are also charged

TABLE 24-3

National Retail Merchants Association natural division of expenses

	Expense division	Illustrations of costs included
01	Payroll	Salaries, wages, commissions, bonuses, prizes for contests, etc., received by all employees.
02	Fringe benefits	Not in itself a pure natural division, but provided to permit optional redistribution of fringe benefits from expense center 630 to other expense centers.*
03	Advertising	Space costs in newspapers, radio and television time, direct mail, and other media.
04	Taxes	Federal (excluding income taxes) state, county, city, unemployment, social security, disability.
06	Supplies	All items consumed in operation of business such as stationery and wrapping, packing, and cleaning materials.
07	Services purchased	Nonprofessional services by outsiders—delivery, repairs, armoured cars, collection agencies, etc.
08	Unclassified	All expenses not included in other natural divisions—net cash shortages, policy adjustments, want ads., etc.
09	Traveling	Out-of-town travel expenses for all employees.
10	Communications	Postage, telegrams and cables, telephone service and rental of communications equipment.
11	Pensions	All payments to retired employees in nature of pensions, retirement allowances, and contributions to pension funds.
12	Insurance	All types of insurance coverages—fire, liability, and others.
13	Depreciation	Depreciation of book value of buildings, furniture, fixtures and equipment, rolling stock, etc.
14	Professional services	Services of a highly specialized and professional nature such as legal fees, public accountants' fees, and appraisal fees.
15	Donations	Contributions to welfare, charitable, and educational institutions.
16	Bad debts	Bad debts, bad checks, and fraudulent purchases less recoveries.
17	Equipment costs	Costs of all equipment rented or leased (except communications equipment)
20	Real property rentals	Expenses incurred or rent paid for real estate used in the business, less any income received from sub-rentals.
91	Expense transfers	Expenses transferred from one expense center to another to reflect actual operating costs of each center.
92	Outside revenue and other credits	Transactions involving credits related to such items as advertising and cost of merchandise in workroom departments as well as outside revenue not classified as gross or other income.
93	Multiple-store distribution	Designed to provide a vehicle for redistribution of accumulated central organization expenses to individual selling units.

* Expense center 630—Supplemental Benefits—is shown in Table 24-4.
Source: *Retail Accounting Manual* (New York: National Retail Merchants Association, Controllers' Congress, 1962), pp. III-1 to III-5.

TABLE 24–4

National Retail Merchants Association expense centers
110   Management
120   Property and equipment
210   Accounting and data processing
310   Accounts receivable
320   Credit and collections
410   Sales promotion
510   Service and operations
550   Telephone and other utilities
570   Cleaning
580   Maintenance and repairs
610   Personnel [management]
630   Supplementary benefits*
720   Maintenance of reserve stock
740   Receiving and marking
750   Shuttle service (transfer hauling)
810   Selling supervision
820   Direct selling
830   Customer services
860   Wrapping and packing
880   Delivery
910   Merchandising
920   Buying
930   Merchandise control

* See special explanation for Expense division 02 in Table 24–3.
Source: *Retail Accounting Manual*, p. IV–1.

to expense center 110 (management), while buyers' salaries (also a part of natural division 01) and buyers' traveling expenses (09) are charged to expense center 920 (buying).[3] Note that these accounts can be broken down into finer detail, if the store so desires. Thus expense center 610 (personnel) which concerns personnel management—not the wages and salaries of store employees—can be divided into such subcenters as recruiting, employment, and training. Similarly, the accounts shown can be combined to determine the total cost of even more basic groups of activities. Thus, all of the 800 series centers deal with customer service, and all 900 series centers are part of buying and merchandising.

Food chains The same report that presents the natural classification of food chain costs shown in Table 24–2 also contains an analysis of the same costs classified into eleven major responsibility (or expense) centers as shown in Table 24–5. For illustration, we have shown the natural categories from which costs are drawn for three of these centers, although the full report, of course, shows similar breakdowns for the other eight. The more meaningful nature of the information provided

TABLE 24–5

**Expense responsibility centers—
food store chains**

Accounting and office services
Advertising and sales promotion
Employee benefits
Field supervision
General administration
Merchandising and buying
Occupancy (other than store)
Store occupancy

> Utilities
> Insurance
> Taxes and licenses
> Property rentals
> Depreciation and amortization
> Repairs
> Unclassified
> Credits and allowances

Store operations

> Payroll
> Supplies
> Communications
> Travel
> Services purchased
> Unclassified
> Credits and allowances

Transportation

> Payroll
> Supplies
> Travel
> Services purchased
> Insurance
> Taxes and licenses
> Equipment rentals
> Depreciation and amortization
> Repairs
> Unclassified
> Credits and allowances

Warehouse operations

Source: Wendell Earle and Willard Hunt, *Operating Results of Food Chains, 1974–75* (Ithaca: New York State College of Agriculture and Life Science, Cornell University, 1975), pp. 51–53.

by the responsibility (expense) center approach should become evident upon comparing Tables 24–2 and 24–5.

Evaluation of the expense center system   The expense center classification provides much more useful information than the natural method because one natural account may be a substitute for another. A store that operates its own trucks will have higher wage and purchased supply expenses and lower purchased services expenses (all natural accounts) than a similar store that contracts out its delivery work to a consolidated delivery company, but the important cost question for management is: Which system has the lower total delivery (expense center) costs? Expense center analysis facilitates such comparisons.

■ DISTRIBUTION (ALLOCATION) OF EXPENSES

Once expenses have been suitably classified, they can be distributed or allocated to selling departments within a store, and/or to the stores within a chain. In other words, the accountant attempts to determine the costs of operating each department or branch store. This is the next step in expense control, but it is difficult because not all retail expenses can be clearly traced to specific departments, branches, or to individual units of a chain.*

☐ Direct and indirect expenses

Expenses are of two types—direct and indirect. Generally speaking, direct expenses are those occasioned by the existence of a particular department, and would disappear if the department were dropped. Such costs include the department's payroll and the supplies it uses. In contrast, indirect expenses result from operating the business in general rather than a particular department, and include such items as store rent,** the president's salary and office overhead. They would not disappear if a particular department were discontinued. It is generally agreed that all direct expenses should be carried by the department causing them, but opinions differ concerning the allocation of indirect expenses.

☐ Methods of allocating expenses

Three methods are employed to distribute retail expenses, as follows:

---

* The discussion which follows refers to distribution of costs among selling departments, but the reader can easily transfer the basic ideas to the units of a chain or to a branch organization.

** This statement must be modified if the store has a percentage lease.

The net profit plan Under this plan all expenses, both direct and indirect, are divided among the departments of the store. Direct expenses are charged directly to the selling departments causing them, and indirect ones are distributed to those departments on a predetermined basis. For example, general management expense may be divided up in ratio to the net sales of the various departments, accounts payable cost may be assigned in ratio to the number of invoices involved, and checking and marking expense allocated on the basis of the number of pieces marked. Net sales are used as the base for indirect cost distribution when no other logical base can be found.

When the total expenses assigned to a specific department are deducted from the departmental gross margin, the net profit is determined. In brief, each department is considered as a separate profit-making entity and is judged on its ability to produce profit.

The chief merits of the net profit plan are that it furnishes a basis for judging and rewarding the overall performance of the department heads and makes them conscious of the need to control both direct and indirect costs (although in many cases they will have little, if any, control over the indirect ones). Its major limitations are the lack of control by department heads over certain expenses (as just mentioned), the arbitrary allocation of many indirect expenses to departments which consequently distorts the reported "profit" figure and the time consumed and the costs involved in determining the expense allocation.

Widespread dissatisfaction with the net profit plan, particularly the allocation of indirect expenses, led to the development of the contribution plan.

The contribution plan This plan of expense distribution was probably first enunciated by the late Carlos B. Clark of the J. L. Hudson Company in 1933 under the title "Reservoir concept."[4] Currently, however, the "contribution plan," as it is now known, is used by many large retailers. This plan is designed to overcome the arbitrariness of allocating indirect expenses to selling departments by providing that only the direct or escapable expenses be so assigned. That is, each department is charged with the expenses directly incurred by it and which would disappear if it were discontinued;* all other expenses are placed in a general bracket with no attempt at departmental distribution. The department statement shows: sales — cost of goods sold = gross margin — direct expenses = contribution. The contributions—i.e., the portion of gross margin that all departments have remaining after direct expenses have been charged off—constitute the reservoir to cover indirect expenses and provide store profits.

Besides its simplicity, the contribution plan forces selling departments *and* people performing such services as credit, delivery, and ac-

---

* For example, selling, delivery, and newspaper and direct mail advertising expenses.

counting to concentrate on those expenses over which they have some control. Its three major disadvantages are (1) it does not provide a total expense figure for the department, so it is of little aid in pricing; (2) all departments may show positive contributions, which may make the department heads feel they have performed satisfactorily, and yet the total reservoir may be inadequate to cover all other expenses and yield a profit; and (3) selling department heads may make inordinate demands for credit, delivery, and other services for which they are not assigned a share in the cost.

Combined net profit and contribution plan Some retailers desire more complete information than the contribution plan provides. Although interested in gross margin, controllable expense and "contribution" for evaluation of department performance, they also want to study the relationship between indirect expenses and departmental results. Consequently, they prepare reports which show both a department's "contribution" and its "net profit." First, they deduct direct expenses from dollar gross margin to measure the contribution, and then indirect expenses are deducted from that figure to show the net profit. This combination plan, as illustrated below, really involves the same steps as the net profit plan discussed earlier except that two figures, contribution and net profit, are highlighted for analysis:

Net sales	$600,000
Cost of merchandise sold	400,000
Department gross margin	$200,000
Direct expense of the department	120,000
Contribution of the department	80,000
Indirect expenses charged to the department*	54,000
Department net profit	$ 26,000

* In some cases, these indirect expenses would be classified into two groups: (1) those assigned to departments in ratio to net sales and (2) those assigned on other bases.

Another approach that is quite similar to the combination plan involves the computation of rent or occupancy charges for the departments in a departmentalized store. Rent is a direct, variable cost for each department if the store has a percentage lease with its landlord. In such stores, rent fluctuates with each variation in sales. But occupancy is, in a sense, an indirect or uncontrollable cost for the departments when the store pays a fixed dollar amount in rent or in mortgage interest and amortization, taxes, and property insurance. Nevertheless, the amount of space occupied and its location in the building is so important to departmental results, and department heads usually vie so vigorously for improved space (especially if no charge is computed) that many stores do calculate a rental charge. This charge is then added to direct costs before measuring contribution. Since rent is the main item of indirect expense, this step brings the contribution plan close to the net profit measure and may leave only a relatively small amount of unallocated overhead.

■ PRODUCTION UNIT ACCOUNTING AN ADDITIONAL METHOD

Production unit accounting is quite different, in applicability and scope, from the two expense analysis methods we have just discussed. Expense classification is suitable for all stores (with smaller stores using the natural system and larger ones the expense center approach) and covers all expenses. Expense allocation applies to any multi-department or multi-store organization and covers either all expenses (net profit and combination plans) or all direct expenses (contribution plan). Production unit accounting is practicable only for fairly large firms, and is suitable only for measuring cost and efficiency in performing highly standardized tasks, such as wrapping packages or preparing checks for payment of suppliers' bills. Furthermore, it can be used meaningfully only when those tasks are handled by specialized employees who do the work on a repetitive basis.

Production unit accounting considers three chief elements in any such activity: (a) the "work load" or amount of work to be done; (b) the speed or rate at which it is done, termed "productivity"; and (c) the labor cost per hour of performing the job, called the "effective pay rate." The workload is defined in standard units, such as "number of packages wrapped" or "number of suppliers' bills processed." The cost accountants often express the relationships among these elements in a single equation: "Work load (units) ÷ Productivity = Hours used × Pay rate = Payroll expense." In practice, this will be transposed and broken down into two or three equations, such as: "Work load ÷ Hours worked = Productivity" and "Payroll expense ÷ Hours worked = Pay rate." The resulting figures permit comparisons with past periods and with other stores to see if the performance or production per employee/hour and the pay rate are satisfactory. This technique is inappropriate for tasks that are unstandardized or highly qualitative, such as decision-making or planning advertising campaigns.[5]

■ EXPENSE COMPARISONS AND ANALYSES

After expenses have been classified into groups and properly allocated to assure comparability both over time and with other firms, the important task of expense analysis may begin. A complete analysis includes three steps: (1) a review of the store's expense trends over a period of time; (2) a comparison of them with other retailers; and (3) a comparison with the expense budget.

☐ Reviewing expense trends and making comparisons with similar firms

Dollar and percentage-of-sales reports   One effective way to review the long-run cost trends is through a five- or ten-year expense table. Consisting of dollar and percentage of sales figures for each item in the expense classification, this table is a constant reminder of expense trends and calls for frequent study. Some cost ratios may be rising and others falling. What are the reasons? For example, are more customers demanding delivery service or are salespeople failing to encourage customers to carry their purchases? Has enough been spent to keep store fixtures and equipment up to date? Is more advertising being done or more expensive media being used? By answering these and other questions the retailer decides on the expense control steps that are needed.

This emphasis on long-run trends does not imply that expenses should be analyzed only once a year. Many large retailers prepare daily, weekly, and monthly reports to improve their expense control.

Comparisons of a retailer's expenses with those of similar firms are made possible through reports expressing each cost as a percentage of sales.

The corporate headquarters of an ownership group (see page 194) usually circulates comparative expense figures among the semi-autonomous stores it controls. The central organization in voluntary and cooperative chains, some resident buying offices and many national retail trade associations compile average expense figures reported by their clients or members.[6] Retailers who have access to this information (the trade association reports are widely circulated) can readily see if their expenses are "out-of-line." (See also the discussion of figure comparisons in Chapter 27.)

☐ The expense budget

Nature and purposes   An expense budget is an essential tool for controlling retailing costs. It is simply an estimate or a forecast in dollars of the various expenses a store will incur in a designated period. This period, as with the merchandise budget, normally consists of one season or six months; but it is usually broken down into months, or even weeks or days, depending on the needs of the store. The primary purpose of the budget is to make a careful forecast of expenses of all kinds, so that adequate provision can be made to meet them and the store's profits can be safeguarded. The expense budget, together with the merchandise budget, is incorporated into an overall store financial budget. The expense budget provides a definite goal and fixes responsibility on certain individuals in the store for attaining this goal. Moreover, the extent of and reasons for any variations between planned and actual expense figures can be analyzed at the end of the budget period. In other words, each expense classification can be studied both *before* and *after* the actual expenditure takes place.

Requisites An expense budget should be planned carefully, constructed with discrimination and judgment, and judiciously administered. It should be simple and still provide the necessary information to permit effective control. Each executive who has responsibility for expenditures should understand the budget and participate in its formation.

The budget should also be flexible. If business conditions change suddenly and sales fall or rise more rapidly than was expected the expense budget should be adjusted to the new level of business activity. But there must be reasonable certainty that business conditions (including competitive changes) and not poor management were responsible for the variations shown. After all, the budget is a control mechanism: it sets a goal and permits measurement of progress toward that goal. If the goal changes too frequently and if disagreement exists regarding the need for such changes, confidence in the budget is lost. Original estimates should be formulated with care and require few significant revisions.

The budget should be an effective device for localizing responsibility and authority. In most large stores, the general manager is responsible for the entire budget, with heavy reliance on the controller both for preparing it and using it. Responsibility is also delegated to the department heads to hold expenses within the limits set for their departments. But one person, or a top management team, must have the final obligation to see that the store remains within its expense budget and must have final authority to approve or reject any particular expenditure.

Some objections to expense budgets Despite the foregoing advantages some executives still object to using a budget. They claim it may make the organization so penny-conscious that outlays will be insufficient for growth and development; or that it may be based upon over-optimistic sales estimates, with resulting large totals for operating expenses, and these latter sums will be spent even if the estimated sales fail to materialize; and, finally, that it may be too inflexible to meet changing conditions.

These claims have some validity, although they are directed more at misuse of the budget than at the budget itself. If the executives understand the purpose of the budget as a tool for long-run profit maximization, they should not become too penny-conscious. Likewise, if those responsible for the budget consistently overestimate sales, the moral seems to be to let someone else do the estimating, not to throw out the budget. Moreover, if adequate controls are maintained, all budgeted funds need not be spent if sales fall below expectations. The budget is a guide, not a strait-jacket; and it is an aid, not a substitute for, management judgment.

Budgeting procedure   Three steps are involved in setting up an expense budget: (1) establishing store-wide (or company-wide in the case of chains) control figures or estimates for total expenses and for each classification; (2) establishing departmental budgets (or individual store budgets in chain store companies); and (3) breaking down the control and departmental budgets into monthly or even shorter-period budgets. These steps are discussed below.

Store-wide control figures   Retailers who prepare expense budgets usually obtain their overall control estimates by combining two methods: (1) through estimating planned sales for the budget period and (2) by using the total expense figure for the previous year adjusted for changes anticipated during the budget period. When the first method is used, the cost of merchandise must also be estimated to secure a dollar figure for gross margin. (How the retailer obtains a planned sales figure has already been discussed, see "Forecasting sales," pp. 268–71.) A permissible or planned overall expense figure is obtained by deducting desired net profit from this gross margin figure. This amount is then adjusted on the basis of previous expense experience and the retailer's judgment of conditions that will prevail in the budget period.

Many small retailers are unable to use this method because they lack the appropriate records. But it is a sound approach to expense planning if the records are available. Adequate records are required when the overall expense estimate is based on past experience. In this process, many stores start with "fixed" expenses—those that do not vary much with total sales, such as taxes, property rentals, and insurance. The "controllable" accounts can then be added to these costs.

Actually, these fixed costs are not so predetermined as one might expect. Property rentals, for example, will be increased if the size of the store should be expanded, or reduced if a part of the building is sublet. Again, this amount might be reduced by negotiating with the landlord. To quote an accounting expert, "Many retailing costs that had formerly been considered 'fixed'—taxes and energy, for instance, are now variable and rising rapidly. So we are seeing a heavily intensified effort to wring more profit out of every dollar of sales [through cost control]."[7]

Each expense item over which the retailer has even more control should also be reviewed for a possible increase or decrease over the preceding comparable period. Possibly some full-time employees may be replaced by part-time ones. Or a new method of compensating employees may result in increased productivity, thus reducing the number needed and decreasing payroll costs. On the other hand, close analysis may indicate that there are too few employees and that better service to customers with more employees will increase sales.

The estimates for each expense center should be prepared very carefully. Methods of cutting costs and the consequences of such reductions, as well as the possible advantages gained from increasing expenses in certain areas, require study. The net result of such action is a careful estimate for each kind of expense which, when totaled, furnishes the overall expense figure.

But even with great care in constructing overall and major account expense figures, adjustments are often necessary to accommodate unforeseen developments.

Departmental and chain-unit budgets In departmentized stores or in chain organizations, the control figures previously set up are commonly broken down by departments or by individual stores. (Chain store managers may subdivide their budgets by departments.) The best approach is to have department heads or individual store executives participate actively in the formulation of the budget.* These individuals may prepare preliminary estimates of their own based on their previous experience and the conditions expected during the budget period.**

To obtain realistic departmental budgets, however, the department head should be supplied with all available pertinent information. This is necessary because no budget is better than the information upon which it is based. In addition to the data needed from within the store, similar information for comparable departments in other stores is also necessary, plus the outlook for general business, price trends, competition, and contemplated changes in store policy. The total number of transactions in relation to number of employees is likewise important. And, where feasible, particularly under the net profit system, the department head should be told how much of the general store overhead will be charged against the department and the bases upon which it will be allocated. Departmental expense budgeting under the contribution plan only involves direct expenses.

With the data suggested, the department head can make estimates of the direct expenses for the section for the budgeted period. This process requires a careful review of the departmental needs in consultation with the assistant manager and other trusted employees. Since wages and salaries typically constitute one half or more of total operating costs, sound judgment is necessary in estimating the payroll figure. We will, therefore, briefly review the procedure followed in establishing such a figure. (See also the discussion of personnel scheduling on p. 214.) Other major items in the expense budget, for instance, advertising, should be estimated just as carefully.

---

* Although the practice of budgeting probably is more highly developed among industrial firms than among retailers, a lower level of management is used by retailers in making up and using the budget than in industrial firms.

** To facilitate the discussion, the following analysis is expressed in terms of department budgets. However, the same method is used for stores in a chain-store system, with the store manager building the budget rather than the department buyer.

1. Determining a department payroll budget A logical approach to this task is to (1) set a control figure; (2) consider the work to be done; (3) estimate the number of employees needed to perform that work; (4) determine the total payroll needed; and finally, (5) adjust this "total-payroll-needed" figure to the control figure.

In a selling department, the control figure may be obtained by taking the payroll-to-sales ratio of previous years, let us say, for example, 8 percent of sales. This figure should be compared with the payroll ratios for the same department in other stores, and for comparable or related departments in the same store.

The number of transactions expected during various weeks of the budget period indicates the work to be done. To illustrate: Estimated sales for the first week of the period may be $9,500 and past experience may indicate that the average sale is $5.25. Consequently, slightly over 1,800 transactions may be expected ($9,500 ÷ $5.25). (Similar estimates will be prepared for all the subsequent weeks of the budget period.) Past experience also shows that, on the average, each salesperson handles about 360 transactions per week, so that at least five people will be needed for the 1,800 sales. (Moreover, this estimate may have to be increased to insure that there are enough salespeople on the floor at all times to provide customer service, arrange merchandise, and prevent shoplifting.) But if the average salesperson's wage is $180 per week, five salespeople will cost $900. This is about 9½ percent of the estimated $9,500 sales and thus exceeds the 8 percent control figure.

The discrepancy between the control and built-up figures tells the responsible executives, the department head or buyer, the merchandise manager and the controller, that a problem exists. They will then try to see if the size of the average transaction can be raised, if the number of transactions per employee-hour can be increased, perhaps by greater reliance on part-time workers, or if the control figure is unreasonable and should be changed.

2. Adjusting department (or store) budgets to control figures Similarly, the total budgets prepared by each department (or chain store) manager will be reviewed with the merchandise manager, the controller, and the budget committee (if one exists) and checked against the control figures. The departmental budgets (or branch store budgets) will be added together and compared with the overall company budget. If the budget estimate totals built up from the departments and branches differ from the company-wide control estimates, appropriate downward or upward adjustments will be made. Usually, the burden of change will be placed on the departments or branches, but if management is thoroughly convinced that those units cannot be expected to achieve more than they have estimated, the company-wide control figures will be revised.

Breaking down the budget period into smaller divisions The final step is to divide all of the expense budgets, including those for departments and branches, into monthly or weekly portions of the six month period. This process is not difficult if records of past experience are available, since seasonal expense patterns vary little from year-to-year.* Each executive responsible for controlling expenditures can then watch those expenses from month-to-month or week-to-week and can institute the necessary remedies almost as soon as expenses deviate from the budget.

Analyzing expenses through the budget We have emphasized that the expense budget permits analysis of each expense classification *before* and *after* the expenditure of funds. A well-planned expense-budget form provides space for entering both planned and actual figures for each expense item. At the close of each budget period, these planned and actual figures should be scrutinized to determine the reasons for any variations. For example, why did actual advertising cost exceed the planned figure? Did we use too many media rather than concentrating on the more productive ones? Was the budget figure unrealistic in the light of unexpected developments? This kind of diagnosis gives the retailer the information needed for corrective action.

■ TAKING CORRECTIVE ACTION

Classifying, distributing, and analyzing expenses—although essential steps in the control of expenses—are just means to an end: the corrective action they make possible. In other words, expense control does not actually take place until someone does something about the expenses which the analyses show are out of line.

There are few instances in which sizable savings are effected through major economies in one phase of operation. More often, small savings can be realized in a variety of store activities through close and continuous scrutiny of all expense items, with the aggregate of such savings being substantial.

Expense control does not always mean expense reduction. On the contrary, by increasing certain expenses the retailer may increase sales enough to improve profit despite higher costs. Certainly this is the aim of all advertising expenditures and of customer services. Hence, expense control should be thought of as deciding upon and limiting actual expenses to those that are necessary for the maximization of profit.

A main advantage of the expense budget is that it permits early remedial action. Even in small stores where budget preparation is limited, monthly comparisons of actual expenditures with budget inform the proprietor about expense trends and problems. Larger stores, where

---

* Some variation can be estimated in advance, since it results from known differences in the calendar, such as the changing date of Easter or annual differences in the number of weekends and selling days in any calendar month.

many individuals are responsible for expenditures, must keep a tighter rein over actual expenses. Consequently, more attention is given to budget figures and to deviations from them. Some retailers, for instance, require prior approval by an expense controller for any significant expenditure, even if it is within the limits of the budget. A department manager needing additional supplies must submit a requisition to the expense controller. If the cost involved is within reasonable limits of the departmental budget, it will be authorized. Otherwise, it is referred to the controller for approval. All expenses, of course, should not require requisitions, since some are indirect costs over which the department heads have no control. But all important direct expenses should be subject to this kind of control.

Compensation plans in which the heads of revenue-producing departments are rewarded, at least in part, on the basis of their net profits or contribution help keep them interested in cost control as well as in obtaining sales and gross margin. Similar incentive plans can be developed for managers of the sales supporting departments.

In conclusion, we need to emphasize once again that records are a step to control, and not control. Some retailers, in the mistaken belief that records alone will provide the necessary control of expenses, have piled form on top of form and analysis on top of analysis. For one English retailer this situation became so absurd that it was necessary to junk 80 tons of record-keeping forms, thus saving an estimated $14 million in the cost of filling them out and substantially adding to net profits.[8] While many small retailers still need additional data as a basis for improving operations, many large ones need fewer forms and more executive action.

■ APPENDIX

The following reports, issued annually, summarize operating expenses, and other aspects of business operations in various branches of retail trade.

Chain Store Age, Drug Store Edition. *Annual Report of the Chain Drug Industry.*

This report concentrates on the sales, margins and expenses of drug store chains. Eli Lilly and Company, a pharmaceutical manufacturer in Indianapolis, Indiana, publishes *The Lilly Digest* which contains similar statistics for other drug stores.

Menswear Retailers of America. *Annual Business Survey.* Washington, D.C.: The Association.

These expense figures are classified according to the annual sales of each store.

NCR Corporation [formerly National Cash Register Company]. *Expenses in Retail Businesses.* Dayton, Ohio: The Company.

This small volume stresses the importance of expense control and provides expense data for a variety of retail stores.

National Retail Furniture Association. *Operating Results of Furniture Stores.* Chicago: The Association, annual.

These reports are of much value to all retailers of home furnishings.

National Retail Hardware Association. *Management Report.* Indianapolis: The Association.

Expenses, sales and other financial data are analyzed according to store size (both sales volume and floor space), type of ownership, location and geographic region.

National Retail Merchants Association, Financial Executives Division. *Department Store and Specialty Store Merchandising and Operating Results.* New York: The Association.

Known as MOR, data are now broken down by classification and store volume.

————. *Financial and Operating Results of Department and Specialty Stores.* New York: The Association.

Known as FOR, these reports are designed to provide "store management a tool to aid in the forecasting and formulation of future operations, plans and policies."

Operating Results of Food Chains. Ithaca, N.Y.: New York State College of Agriculture, Cornell University, published under the direction of Wendell Earle and Willard Hunt.

This summary of expenses provides valuable information on chains of various sales volumes. The same source also issues a similar annual report, *Operating Results of Self-Service Discount Department Stores.* The Mass Retailing Institute, a trade association that cooperates in the preparation of the latter report also publishes *Mass Retailers' Merchandising Report* (New York: The Institute, annual), which tabulates departmental results.

Progressive Grocer. *Annual Report of the Grocery Industry,* usually published in the April issues.

This comprehensive collection of grocery retailing and wholesaling statistics provides information about expense, sales, profit, and other trends in the supermarket, convenience store, and related industries. Another useful compilation has been published annually by the Super Market Institute under the title "The Super Market Industry Speaks." However, the Institute is now in the process of merging with the National Association of Food Chains, and the merged organizations will assume a new name, Food Marketing Institute.

The True Look of the Discount Industry.

Published annually by *The Discount Merchandiser,* this volume contains detailed data on operating and merchandising results as well as significant trends.

■ REVIEW AND DISCUSSION QUESTIONS

1 Discuss the reasons why any one store or firm would use several different methods for analyzing its expenses.

2 What are the differences between the natural and the expense center (also called functional or responsibility center) systems of expense classification? Which one would a small store use? Why would a large organization use the other?

3 (a) Differentiate between direct and indirect expenses. (b) Is rent (space occupancy) a direct or an indirect expense of a selling department within a department store? Explain. Would your answer vary depending upon whether the store had a percentage lease or a dollar lease with its landlord? Why?

4 Define or describe (a) the net profit and (b) the contribution plan of allocating expenses to departments. What are the advantages and disadvantages of each approach?

5 On what basis would you allocate each of the following expenses to departments: (a) general management, (b) institutional advertising, (c) receiving inbound merchandise, (d) credit office, (e) delivery? State your reason in each case.

6 (a) Why would production unit accounting be unsatisfactory for measuring the work done by buyers and merchandise managers? (b) Why is it useful in measuring the performance of credit office billing clerks?

7 Assume that you are a senior executive of a retailing company that has several branch stores. You are reviewing the expense figures reported for the company as a whole and for each branch for the past six months. What comparisons will you want to make and why?

8 (a) What are the major steps in preparing an expense budget? (b) Explain the difference between a control figure and a built-up figure. Which one is usually adjusted if there is a discrepancy between the two? Why?

9 Describe in detail how you would construct a six month payroll budget for a department in a department store or for a moderate-sized establishment.

10 (a) Explain the difference between expense analysis and expense control. (b) What are some of the methods retailers use to control expenses? (c) Does control always lead to a reduction in expenses? State your reasons.

■ NOTES AND REFERENCES

1 For example, "Cost Control Not Just for Giants," *Supermarket News,* May 14, 1973, p. 13; "Dayton Hudson Cost Cuts Pay Off," *Women's Wear Daily,* July 10, 1975, pp. 1, 8.

2 *Retail Accounting Manual* (New York: National Retail Merchants Association, Controllers' Congress, 1962), p. iii–1.

3 It is not practicable here to discuss all aspects of expense classification covered in the *Retail Accounting Manual*. Readers interested in a more comprehensive treatment should consult

that source, especially Chapter VI, "Elements of reports and statistics."

4 " 'Reservoir Concept' Is Keynote of Future Profits," *Retail Ledger,* December 1933, p. 13.

5 For further details concerning production unit accounting, see Chapter XII of the *Retail Accounting Manual.*

6 *See Expenses in Retail Businesses,* Dayton, Ohio: NCR Corporation, annual). *See also* the list of expense reports published by trade associations in the appendix to this chapter.

7 Arnold Becker, Vice President of Cresap, McCormick and Paget, in "A Lackluster End to Summer," *Business Week,* September 8, 1975, p. 17. To illustrate Mr. Becker's point, many retailers are now installing sophisticated devices to monitor and reduce electrical energy consumption.

8 "The English Unorthodoxy of Marks & Spencer," *Dun's Review and Modern Industry,* October 1966, p. 128.

CONTROL OF
SALES TRANSACTIONS

All retail sales to customers involve such activities as furnishing sales checks or sales register receipts, receiving and safeguarding money, and recording desired information about the transactions. Responsibility for establishing a suitable transaction-control system may be centered in the proprietor, the controller, a systems committee or department, or a research department. We will study such systems with regard to (1) the variety of transactions that can occur in a modern store; (2) the nature and goals of the systems; (3) the particular functions of two seemingly simple but important sales record documents, the sales check and the sales register receipt; (4) traditional, and (5) modern transactions systems equipment; (6) code marking for optical scanning purposes; and (7) considerations in selecting equipment.

■ TYPES OF SALES TRANSACTIONS

The types of sales to be handled is a basic consideration in planning the transaction system. Ideally, a decision about the types of transactions to be expected should be made even before the store is opened, so that the right equipment can be purchased and properly installed in a well-designed floor plan. It is easier and less expensive to install equipment as the store is being built or remodeled than at a later date.

About one half or more of all retail stores make both cash and credit sales. The other stores sell for cash only. There are many variations of these two types, however, and knowledge of them is necessary to understand the procedures they require.

□ Cash sale

In a cash sale the customer pays for the merchandise at the time of purchase. It may be either a *cash-take ("take-with"* or *"take-transaction")* in which the customer carries the purchase away or a *cash-send* (or *"send-transaction")* in which the goods are delivered.

□ COD sale

In a COD transaction, usually considered a form of cash sale, the customer pays for the merchandise upon delivery. The amount collected may be either the full amount of the sale or the balance that remains after a deposit has been made at the store. The latter type of transaction is frequently referred to as "part-pay COD." Some stores make an extra charge for COD service.

□ Charge sale

In a charge sale the amount of the purchase is charged to the customer's account with payment expected at some later date. Cycle billing has brought variations in payment dates; while the revolving credit plan permits payment over a longer period than the normal 30 days. (On cycle billing, see p. 560; on revolving credit, see p. 547.) As with cash sales, there are both charge-takes and charge-sends.

□ Budget, on contract, or installment sale

Originally limited to sales of high-value items, the budget or installment transaction now extends to many other types of merchandise. The customer signs a contract or agreement to make weekly or monthly payments of a specified amount until the total amount of the sale, plus a carrying charge, is paid. The store retains title to the merchandise and may repossess the goods in case payments are discontinued.

□ Will-call (layaway or deposit) sale

In the will-call sale the customer pays a percentage of the selling price of an item, usually 10 to 20 percent, to reserve it for an indefinite period—during which time payments are continued until the merchandise is fully paid for and released. Merchandise purchased under this plan is held in the department or moved to a "will-call" office, where it is always available on customers' calls. The will-call sale is really a form of installment selling except that the store holds the merchandise until payments are completed. Many stores have discontinued this kind of transaction in recent years.

☐ Discount sale

A discount sale takes place when a discount or reduction from the regular price is granted the purchaser. Such reductions are given store employees and certain types of customers such as members of the clergy, physicians, and dentists, depending on the type of store. Although employees may pay cash for their purchases and still receive the discount, it is common practice to charge the goods to their accounts and to deduct the amounts from their wages at monthly intervals.

☐ Budget-book sale

In a budget-book transaction, which resembles both a cash and an installment sale, merchandise certificates, purchased upon a definite contractual basis, and often bound together in a "budget book" are used as cash when goods are bought. The budget book contains certificates of various denominations aggregating $15, $25 or $50 in value. The customer ordinarily pays a small carrying charge, as in the case of budget or on-contract sales; and agrees to make payments for the certificates on specified dates.

☐ Exchange sales

Exchange sales transactions occur when customers return merchandise and purchase additional items. In an even exchange the retail price of the goods returned is the same as that of the new selection, whereas in an uneven exchange the price of the goods selected is different from the original purchase.

☐ Other types

The above list does not exhaust all of the types of transactions. The customer may present coupons from a newspaper or direct mail advertisement in partial payment, bottles or other containers may be returned for a refund, or the customer may redeem a gift certificate. Usually, the last case is treated as a cash sale, with the endorsed gift certificate being treated as money, but the sale can become more complicated if the certificate is not for the exact amount of the purchase.

■ OBJECTIVES AND REQUIREMENTS OF TRANSACTION SYSTEMS

After determining the probable or actual variety of transactions to be recorded, the retailer (or the system designers) can select and install the equipment needed to implement the system. That system should, above all, provide fast, efficient and dependable service to customers who otherwise can easily become dissatisfied and take their patronage elsewhere. It should also satisfy all of the other objectives outlined in the next paragraph.

□ Characteristics of an effective system

A satisfactory transaction system has the following characteristics:

1. Provision of prompt customer service. Regardless of how well the system meets the store's other requirements, it must permit satisfactory customer service. Customers expect their transactions to be completed promptly and courteously without delay from the system.
2. Economy in installation and maintenance. The system's cost should be reasonable in the light of the benefits to be derived from its use.
3. Simplicity. Instructing employees in new procedures is difficult at best and a relatively simple system minimizes this task. The system should also minimize errors, in part by reducing the amount of handwritten material as much as possible and in part by "fail-safe" procedures that preclude mistakes.*
4. Furnishing of desired information quickly and accurately. Up-to-date, useful information is especially necessary in today's competitive economy. Its value frequently depends on its timeliness. Management may want reports on item or department sales, coupon redemptions, sales and excise tax collections, individual salesclerk or cashier productivity, hourly variations in sales activity (useful for labor-scheduling purposes), ratio of credit to cash transactions, and the like. Of course, the system is likely to become more elaborate and more expensive as more data are desired, so the value of each additional type of information must be subjected to a careful cost-benefit analysis.

---

* For example, some modern sales registers illuminate various parts of the keyboard in succession in the order in which those parts are to be used. Other machines will lock unless the keys are operated in proper sequence. Relatively simple registers today will calculate the change due the customer in a cash sale and some issue the appropriate coins to the customer.

5. Adequate protection of assets. The system must provide adequate safeguards for the company's cash and merchandise. Such safeguards are necessary to afford protection from customers, employees and shoplifters. Some unscrupulous customers attempt to take advantage of stores in such matters as refunds, exchanges, and adjustments. Employees, also, sometimes appropriate cash and merchandise for themselves or for relatives and friends who pretend to be customers.* The system should minimize these temptations.

☐ Selecting and evaluating sales-handling equipment

Selecting equipment for an original installation that will have the above characteristics, or evaluation of a possible change of system, are difficult tasks for the retailer. These decisions require a careful definition of needs, thorough investigation of available equipment and its cost, and, where feasible, a comprehensive test of potential selections. The latter step is most common among large firms.

Defining requirements   As noted, the first element in defining the system requirements is a determination of the transactions to be handled and the conditions under which they will occur. Will there be many small transactions where the customer is in a hurry; or will there be a more leisurely atmosphere, with a comparatively small number of large sales? Will the business be mostly cash or largely charge? Will the number of salespeople be fairly constant, or will many "extras" be required at certain times? Will salespeople be closely supervised? The next task is to decide what information the system must provide. Much of it will be dictated by accounting needs, some by the type of store and clientele, and some by the desires of the owner or executives.

Investigation of equipment available   After ascertaining these requirements the retailer is ready to investigate the available equipment. Particular attention might be given to the newer electronic machines but all applicable types should be studied. Original cost and economy of operation require special study. Sometimes several types of equipment may provide the same information, the same control, and approximately the same customer service; but one will cost less than the others. Although cost alone should not be the decisive factor, it should certainly be given constant attention.

Testing equipment   Large retail firms that want to avoid the choice of inappropriate equipment generally make test installations of the machines that seem likely to meet their needs. This testing prior to purchase, and continuous evaluation thereafter, are certain to increase as the variety of equipment multiplies and decisions become more com-

---

* A common statement in the retail business is "Employees are 99 percent honest. The system must be designed to protect the store from the 1 percent."

plex. Even the decision to test cannot be made lightly. For example, a Montreal supermarket chain spent a considerable period of time redesigning and remodeling the checkout counters, bringing in additional power lines and training employees in a test store before undertaking a five months' trial of a new electronic point of sale system.[1] But even such laborious testing is more economical than a commitment to the wrong system. A small supermarket chain in Los Angeles found that two potential systems, tested over a 10-month period, failed to yield results that justified their costs.[2]

■ RECORDING SALES

The sales transaction system usually must create a record of the transaction for the benefit of both the customer and the store. Typically, this recording is achieved through (1) handwritten sales checks—also called sales slips—and (2) sales register receipts and tapes. Most small stores probably rely solely upon sales (cash) registers, although sales checks are often used for credit sales. Larger stores use sales registers in some departments and sales checks in others, but the typical supermarket, drugstore, or discount store—regardless of size—relies entirely on the sales register. Some stores, however, require both registers and sales checks in all departments; the sales check providing merchandise control information and a shipping ticket for delivery purposes.

□ Increasing use of sales register receipts

Sales register receipts are increasing in use because improved modern registers produce receipts that can now fulfill several functions formerly assigned to the sales check. These machines are now called "sales registers" rather than "cash registers" because they can handle a wide variety of non-cash transactions. Even charge-send transactions can be recorded in detail by inserting the sales slip in the slot provided on the register. (See the discussion on pp. 628–29.) Simultaneously, rising wage rates have encouraged many retailers to forgo some information which could be furnished by the more expensive sales check.

Nevertheless, even though the handwritten sales check will be less frequently used in the future, we should examine some of its purposes and functions under present conditions.

□ The sales check

Functions and uses The major purposes of the sales check are: to provide a definite record of sales transactions; to permit analysis of sales and to allocate them among departments, salespeople, and classifications of merchandise; to furnish a receipt to the customer as well as a record of monies turned in to the cashier by the salespeople; to provide a shipping ticket for merchandise deliveries; and to furnish a record upon which merchandise returns and adjustments may be adjudicated.

Depending upon the size of the store, the information placed on the salescheck may include the date; salesperson's number; department number; the kind of sale, e.g., cash, charge, or COD; name and address of the customer and/or name and address of the person to whom the goods are to be delivered; and a brief description of the merchandise sold. Transactions other than "cash" require additional data such as disposition of the merchandise, i.e., whether "taken" or "sent," and the purchaser's signature. A sales check used by one large retailer is shown in Figure 25–1.

FIGURE 25–1 "Take" sales check

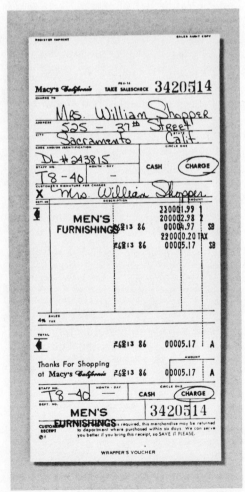

Courtesy Macy's, California

Many stores that use sales checks prepare them in triplicate. The original copy is the store's record of the sale and can be used for analyzing and classifying sales, for preparing reports, and for similar purposes. The duplicate or customer's copy accompanies the merchandise, regardless of its disposition. The triplicate (tissue) copy remains in the sales book. Sales books containing these copies are filed and are helpful in tracing and investigating inquiries and complaints. Some stores use specially designed sales checks for sales of "warehouse" merchandise and for telephone orders.

Sales checks and books of checks are usually numbered, generally serially, to permit close control by the auditing department. All sales checks should be accounted for when the original copies pass through the sales audit department.

Recent changes in sales checks The improvements in sales-registering equipment have permitted many changes in sales check format. These newer forms furnish pertinent information quickly and eliminate much handwriting. One firm has devised a punch card form for charge-take sales which account for over 80 percent of its total sales. This single check with a perforated customer receipt stub can be completed in four steps in contrast to the eleven operations needed for the tri-part sales check used previously.

Other firms employ new automatic equipment which records all basic sales data on the sales register in a single "pass" across the keyboard by the salesperson. Automation also permits the economical use of separate sales checks for major types of sales transactions. Thus, Macy's of California has different sales checks for these kinds of transactions: "take," "send," "COD," and "returned merchandise vouchers" covering cash refunds and credits to accounts. The "take" and "send" checks are used both for customers' and employees' transactions, for cash and credit sales and also, with appropriate notations, for "even" and "uneven" exchanges. A printed form made available by electronic developments is shown in Figure 25–2.

■ TRANSACTION SYSTEMS EQUIPMENT

The sales recording devices that retailers are using today range from traditional registers, through electronic equipment, to the latest UPC point-of-sale scanners.

□ Traditional equipment

The two main types of traditional equipment which are still widely used are (1) sales (or cash) registers and (2) carrier systems, such as the pneumatic tube, which transport the sales slip and the customer's money to a central "cash office" in the store for handling, approval and change

FIGURE 25–2 Newer form of printed sales check made possible by electronic equipment
Name of store and customer are fictitious.

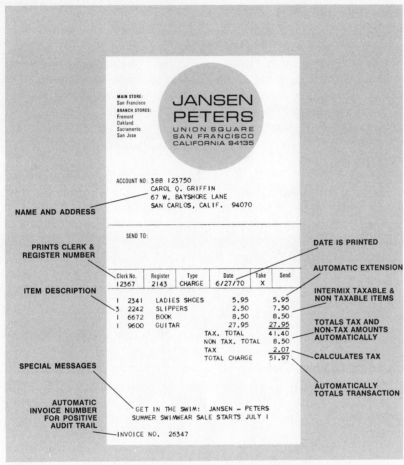

NAME AND ADDRESS

PRINTS CLERK &
REGISTER NUMBER

ITEM DESCRIPTION

SPECIAL MESSAGES

AUTOMATIC
INVOICE NUMBER
FOR POSITIVE
AUDIT TRAIL

DATE IS PRINTED

AUTOMATIC EXTENSION

INTERMIX TAXABLE &
NON TAXABLE ITEMS

TOTALS TAX AND
NON-TAX AMOUNTS
AUTOMATICALLY

CALCULATES TAX

AUTOMATICALLY
TOTALS TRANSACTION

Courtesy American Regitel Corporation

making. Manufacturers of pneumatic-tube systems have attempted to meet the challenge of improved sales registers by making improvements of their own.* Sales registers and pneumatic tubes offer retailers the following benefits:

---

* In the retail trade, the term "decentralization" is used to describe that method of handling transactions in which sales are consummated locally in departments by means of sales registers. Frequently, also, the term is applied to those instances in which floor cashiers or inspector-cashiers are used. The term "centralization," on the other hand, refers to that method under which all sales—cash, charge, and others—are handled in a central location or locations (1) by means of a conveyor or tube system or (2) when the customer brings all packages to one point as under a check-out system in self-service operations.

Advantages of sales registers The major arguments favoring the use of sales registers are as follows:

1. They permit fast, efficient and courteous service to customers. Registers make this possible by enabling salespeople to give customers receipts and change without delay. Registers have been adapted to handle "cash send" and "charge" transactions effectively as well as "cash takes." Even though "cash sends" and "charge sends" require sales checks or other shipping tickets, those documents can be receipted or authorized by insertion into a slot in the register before the amount of the sale is recorded. This eliminates the need to send the salescheck to a central cashier. Similarly, on the newer registers, credit cards can be inserted into special readers that will record the card number on the register tape.

2. They are sufficiently flexible to permit handling peak periods of activity without confusion. They can also be moved to various locations within the store, as, for example, during a special sale.

3. The cost of register tapes is economical compared to sales checks.

4. Their use tends to reduce the number of packages delivered. Exerience reveals that the customer is more likely to take the package when a salesperson handles the complete transaction, including wrapping of the merchandise.

5. The newer machines furnish a sales record for quick and economical auditing, and provide other information for improving departmental operations. Some models supply receipts and validate sales checks in the conventional manner and also record all basic sales data on tape in computer language. These sales data include the department number, the class of merchandise and unit control number shown on the price ticket, amount of the transaction, and the salesperson's number.

6. Register models intended for almost continuous usage, such as at self-service store checkout counters, are constantly being modified to provide trouble-free service under such heavy-duty conditions. They can also be equipped with numerous attachments that speed up customer service, including change-makers and trading stamp dispensing devices.

Advantages of pneumatic tubes Some retailers find carrier systems advantageous despite many improvements in sales-registering equipment and despite the growth of self-service and the use of check-outs in supermarkets and other stores. In the carrier system, a sales check is prepared at the point-of-sale, and is then sent, usually by pneumatic tube, to a central cashier along with the customer's money or credit card. The cashier receipts the salescheck and returns it with any change through the same tube mechanism. Although they require the customer to wait until the check returns from the central cashier, tube systems do have the following advantages:

1. They provide maximum control by requiring sales checks for each transaction, by using qualified cashiers to handle cash, and, when cashier-inspectors are used, by providing a check of the goods wrapped against those listed on the sales check.
2. They are particularly suited to the handling of peak sales periods since they can absorb a large number of carriers simultaneously and permit salespeople to do interdepartmental selling in rush periods.
3. They afford greater opportunity for suggestion selling during the time the tube is in transit, thus tending to increase the average sale.
4. They avoid the technical training necessary for salespeople in the use of sales registers as well as the mental strain on salespeople of "balancing out" their cash receipts each day.
5. They require sales checks, thus giving the customers an itemized receipt.
6. They facilitate authorization of charge sales, because checks for such sales can routinely be sent to the credit authorizer for approval.
7. They serve as mechanical messengers in the distribution of reports, requests, and messages among various departments of the store.

☐ Electronic sales-recording equipment

Previous reference has been made to the increase of automated devices in retailing operations, particularly merchandise control, credit authorization, and the registering of sales (see pp. 138–40, 362–63, and 560–61). Even more of tomorrow's sales-handling equipment will be electronic in nature.

Actually, the variety of computerized systems now being offered often leaves retailers confused. This confusion is confounded by the costliness and complexity of the new systems. As two experts say:

> The system behind the retail terminal is already complex and getting more so—in terms of hardware, software, communications, systems planning, training requirements, and more. The familiar cash register sat out there, stolid and self-sufficient, doing its job without causing much concern. On the other hand, the electronic terminal needs much care and feeding in terms of instructions (programming), communications (in-store wiring and external phone lines), control (a minicomputer that tells it what to do and when), and so forth. Of course, a computer is needed at the other end to run the whole system and produce usable data. This computer is now generally referred to as the "host," to distinguish it from secondary computers that may exist in the system.[3]

Some electronic terminals are built as convertible units that can be used independently until incorporated into a store-wide or company-wide computer system.[4] One might ask why so many types of computerized point-of-sale equipment are being offered to retailers at this time. The answer is not difficult; retailing is one of the least computer-ized industries and now constitutes an enormous market for computer-ized systems. A single department store system of 80 terminals and an in-store computer cost about $400,000 in 1975.[5] In spite of their costs, these systems can be of enormous benefit to the stores and their cus-tomers. In their fully-devleoped form, they will not only speed up sales transactions, but will also maintain perpetual inventory records and pro-vide valuable management information.[6] Nevertheless, the investment involved, uncertainties about possible obsolescence if superior equip-ment comes on the market in the future, and difficulties in converting to fully automatic systems have deterred many potential applications. Such major manufacturers as RCA, General Electric, and Singer have incurred severe losses and have discontinued manufacturing retail terminals.[7]

Point-of-sale recorders Two point-of-sale recorders are illustrated in Figures 25–3 and 25–4, and many other models are also available. Some, such as the illustrated models, require only a limited number of keys, which simplifies training and operation. Built-in controls also may guide the salesperson through the proper sequence of operation. Some terminals will verify entries, thereby reducing mistakes, and information may be transferred automatically from merchandise tags and credit

FIGURE 25–3 **The NCR-280 point-of-sale recorder**

Courtesy The National Cash Register Company

FIGURE 25–4   Unitote/Regitel Model 420 with only

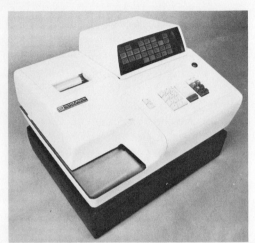

Courtesy General Instrument Corporation

cards. A hardware chain in Alabama collects considerable information about each customer, for market research purposes, through the entries into its point-of-sale registers, while simultaneously automatically preparing the sales documents and revising its perpetual inventory records.[8] As we have noted in Chapters 21 and 22 point-of-sale registers may also be redesigned to obtain approval for a credit card sale from a central credit authorization facility, or even to handle deposits, withdrawals and charges against a customer's bank account under an Electronic Fund Transfer System (see pp. 534–35, 560–61). Various terminals are designed to interact directly with a central computer (on-line systems) and/or produce a tape that can be used for computer processing at the end of the day or at other intervals. The latter alternative is helpful to medium-sized retailers who cannot afford an in-store computer and who want to use the services of an outside data processing bureau.

Optical scanner   The optical scanner or reader, like the point-of-sale recorder, is another means of activating the computer. Designed either as a wand or as a fixed device, it rapidly reviews typed, coded or handwritten letters and numbers, translating them into "machine language" or electrical impulses. The speedy and accurate "reading" of sales register slips and sales checks by the optical scanner permits prompt forwarding of data to the computer with resultant savings in both time and money. Optical scanners can be programmed to read symbols or markings in plain language, or in a company's own code system. But interest is now growing in industry-wide codes, discussed in the next paragraph.

☐ Optical scanning and industry code marking

Supermarkets As discussed in Chapter 15, food product packages are now being pre-marked by the manufacturer with a series of thick and thin vertical lines that identify each item under the Universal Product Code (UPC). These symbols replace the conventional numerical prices usually stamped or written on each item. Food retailers who use the UPC system place price and inventory information in a central computer. As the customer's purchases pass along the checkout counter, the optical scanner obtains the prices from the central computer and enters them into the sales register, for totaling and printing on the customer's sales slip. Simultaneously, the central perpetual inventory records are revised to show that the purchases have been removed from the inventory. Although this system has many advantages, in speeding transactions, reducing errors, eliminating costly handwork, and generating practical management and inventory control data,[9] it also involves at least five problems: (1) accurate, precise code marking has proven to be difficult but quite manageable when applied to standardized prepackaged groceries; correctly marking variable-sized store-packed items such as fresh meat and produce is more complex:[10] (2) the systems are costly to purchase and install: (3) difficulties arise if a new shipment is placed on the shelves at a higher price while older units of the same item are still displayed at the old, lower price (see p. 430): (4) The department store and textile products industries seem to prefer a different code system which is difficult to reconcile with the grocery industry's UPC.[11] Yet many textile products, such as hosiery, are sold in both types of stores. Hardware items present similar problems. Conceivably, manufacturers will have to mark such items with both codes or maintain separate supplies for different types of retailers.

Most important of all the problems, (5) comsumerists and retail labor unions object to the elimination of conventional (human readable) price marking on the individual containers. They claim that the little shelf signs that would replace the individual price markings in a pure UPC system are often inaccurate or illegible. Yet the elimination of handstamping and marking has often been advocated as one of the major cost savings in using UPC machine-readable code markings.[12]

A study conducted in the Spring of 1976 under grocery industry sponsorship showed that consumers were less aware of prices and less able to make price comparisons in test stores that eliminated conventional item price marking and substituted only the UPC and shelf signs. Consequently the industry committee that sponsored the study recommended retention of item price marking.[13] Some supermarket companies have felt that the information received from scanning systems justifies their cost even if item marking must be retained, while some other firms say they intend to test customer reactions in their own stores.[14] But most experts believe that the rate of new scanning installation will be considerably slowed by the price marking recommendation and other problems.[15]

Department and specialty stores The typical department store item is much more expensive than the typical grocery store product; department stores carry much larger assortments (perhaps 20 to 25 times as many items as supermarkets); and a large portion of department store merchandise is identified by hang tags rather than being prepacked by manufacturers. But department stores also have fewer transactions per employee/hour and sell fewer items per transaction. Because of these factors department and other textile and fashion stores have very different transaction-handling and information needs than grocery stores. The fashion-oriented retailers want much more complete item identification, including color and size, than the UPC can provide; at the same time they do not require the high-speed productivity of the supermarket industry. Consequently, the department store industry has adopted code symbols that both humans and machines can read called OCR-A (Optical Character Recognition). In contrast to the ten digit code numbers established by the UPC, these OCR characters are used in a much more informative but more difficult to handle 31 digit code called the Voluntary Retail Identification Standard developed by the National Retail Merchants Association. The adoption rate of OCR-A/VRIS (also known as UVM—Universal Vendor Marking) has been slower than for UPC.

Other types of retailing Codes that are compatible with the UPC seem likely to develop in many other consumer goods fields, including drugstore, stationery store, and liquor store merchandise. However, many hardware retailers and wholesalers believe that a system similar to the NRMA's OCR-A would be more practical for their purposes.[16]

☐ Electronic funds transfer systems

EFTs (Electronic Funds Transfer) systems, which received test installation in several supermarkets in the mid-1970s, provide a direct link between in-store terminals and a bank or savings association. Customers can withdraw funds from their bank accounts or charge purchases directly to those accounts, as shown in Figure 25–5. The systems appeal to merchants since they reduce the costs and risks of cashing checks for customers and, when used for customer purchases, immediately credit the amounts involved to the store's bank account. But EFTs also involve many problems: Are the terminals branch banks for banking regulation purposes, and thus subject to a number of state limitations

FIGURE 25–5 **Point-of-sale EFT system**

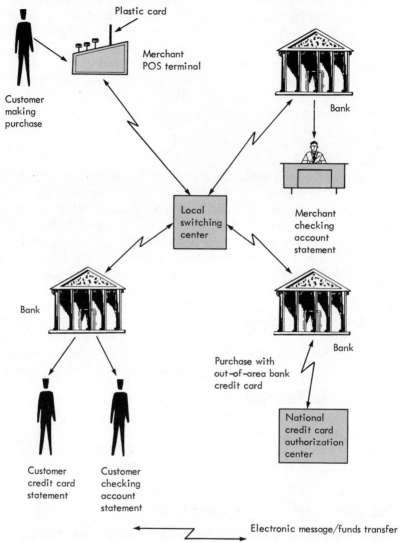

Source: *Point of Sale Systems—The Ultimate EFTS?* (Washington, D.C.: Funds Transfer Research Department, U.S. League of Savings Associations, 1973), p. 2.

and prohibitions? Can consumers be certain of the accuracy and privacy of the banking services offered under EFTs? Who will be liable in case of error? How should the system costs and benefits be shared? Are the systems worth the costs? Widespread adoption of the EFTs will depend upon satisfactory resolution of these, and other, questions.[17]

☐ Final comment on choice of equipment

Many different types of sales transaction equipment provide satisfactory service to different kinds of stores. Sometimes complaints and arguments for or against a particular type of equipment are based on prejudice, on personal preference and belief, and on experience with poorly operated equipment rather than on solid facts. Frequently, the equipment is blamed for poor service when the particular model or type does not meet the store's needs, or when the system or layout is at fault.

Poor service blamed on equipment often is caused by a management attitude of cost-consciousness rather than an attitude of customer-consciousness. No equipment, whether conventional or electronic, can provide satisfactory service unless it is properly selected, operated by knowledgeable personnel, and is adapted to the particular needs of the store or department.

Finally, it should be kept in mind that the equipment comprises but one part of the sales transactions system designed to provide fast and courteous customer service at the lowest cost to the store, to protect cash receipts, to furnish the data required to control merchandise, to permit auditing of all kinds of sales, and to prepare the necessary statistical and managerial reports. It is imperative, of course, that the sales transactions system should be related to other systems of the store to provide overall operating efficiency.

■ REVIEW AND DISCUSSION QUESTIONS

1 Describe the major types of sales transactions. What special information might a store want to obtain for each type of sale?

2 What types of transactions would be likely to occur in a jewelry store; a gift shop; a department store; a discount store?

3 Summarize the major objectives and characteristics of a satisfactory sales transaction system.

4 Select a fairly large store in your college (or home) community and very briefly describe the types of merchandise that store sells, and its customer characteristics. Drawing on that information, and anything else you know about the store, describe its requirements for transaction-handling equipment.

5 Why are large retail firms more likely than smaller firms to test new systems before final adoption?

6 What information can the handwritten sales check provide? Why is it increasingly being replaced by the use of register receipts?

7 Considering only traditional systems, briefly explain the arguments for and against using sales registers (decentralization) rather than pneumatic tube carrier systems (centralization)?

8 Describe the benefits that retailers can gain, in return for the costs involved, if they install electronic point-of-sale registers or recorders.

9 Discuss the merits and disadvantages of the UPC from the viewpoint of (a) consumers, (b) supermarkets, and (c) department stores.

10 A retail consultant says: "As in the early days of the computer, some installations of electronic point-of-sale systems will be enormously successful and some will be dismal failures." What can management do to obtain a successful system?

■ NOTES AND REFERENCES

1 "Steinberg's Market, Patrons Prepared for Montreal Trial of Scanner System: Scanner Test Culminates Months of Preparation," *Supermarket News*, July 22, 1974, pp. 1, 22.

2 "Hughes Drops ECR Checkout," *Supermarket News*, May 5, 1975, p. 1.

3 W. D. Power and D. R. Huisien, "What's Next at the Point-of-Sale," *Tempo* (Touche Ross & Co.), vol. 20, no. 1 (1974), p. 38.

4 *Summary of Super Market Point of Sale Systems* (Chicago: Super Market Institute, 1975).

5 "The Coming Battle at the Supermarket Counter," *Fortune*, September 1975, p. 105.

6 Irving Geller, "The Master Machines of Retailing," *Dun's Review*, October, 1969, p. 107. More recent data may be obtained from major equipment manufacturers such as NCR Corporation and American Regitel Corporation. *Women's Wear Daily* also frequently publishes a page on "The New Technology" which describes new equipment and systems.

7 "Singer to End Computer Sales," *Detroit Free Press*, December 30, 1975, p. A8.

8 "How P-O-S Works in a 42 Store Chain [Moore-Handley, Inc., Pelham, Ala.]," *Hardware Retailing*, October 1974, pp. 82–83, 100.

9 M. S. Moyer and B. L. Seitz, "The Marketing Implications of Automated Store Checkouts," *The Business Quarterly* (University of Western Ontario), vol. 40 (Spring 1975), pp. 68–77.

10 Techniques for in-store code labeling are discussed in *Approaches to UPC Implementation* (Chicago: Super Market Institute, 1974), pp. 33–36. In contrast, David L. Fleisher, "The Case for the Readable Code," *Tempo* (Touche Ross & Co.), vol. 20, no. 1 (1974), p. 43, argues that the cost of in-store code labeling is prohibitive—about 14 times as great as the cost at point of manufacture.

11 "Optical Scan and Grocery Code: What's the Crossover?" *Chain Store Age* (executive edition), March 1974, p. E75; "When Food and Soft Goods Use Different Codes," *Business Week*, March 30, 1974, pp. 64–66.

12 Nancy Verser, "POS: Automation without Representation?" *Computer/Decisions*, November 1975, pp. 27–31.

13 "Scanning Stalls, Item Prices Stay Put," *Progressive Grocer*, May 1976, pp. 75–80.

14 "Industry Group Recommends Item Price Marking; Some Scanner Users Say They Will Not Go Along," *Supermarket News*, March 29, 1976, p. 1.

15 "Mandatory Pricing Will Slow, Not Kill, Scanners," *Progressive Grocer*, December 1975, p. 52; "See Full UPC Use in Canada Distant," *Supermarket News*, May 17, 1976, pp. 2, 12.

16 Bob Vereen, "Automated Checkouts—A Dream or Reality," *Hardware Retailing*, May 1975, p. 13.

17   "Those Buck-Passing Bank Machines," *Money*, February 1976, pp. 46–48; "Disagree on EFT Potential, Agree on Working Together," *Supermarket News*, May 10, 1976, p. 19; "Legal Muddle Slows EFTS," *Chain Store Age* (Supermarket edition), May 1976, p. 81. *See also* "Symposium: Electronic Funds Transfer," *Maryland Law Review*, vol. 33, no. 1 (1975), pp. 3–114.

RETAIL SECURITY AND
LOSS PREVENTION

The term "security" refers to protection of the store, customers, employees, executives, and property against loss from crime, carelessness, accidents, or natural hazards, such as fire, tornadoes, and floods. Sometimes the word "security" is used to indicate only the work of uniformed guards and plainclothes store detectives, and the terms "loss prevention" or "loss control" are then used for the total group of protection activities. However, in the discussion that follows we will regard security as synonymous with loss control—the responsibility of all employees and executives, and especially of top management. "Loss prevention is an attitude which must start at the top of the company and permeate to the lowest level. . . ."[1]

In this chapter we will emphasize protection of merchandise and cash against criminals—currently a very serious problem in retailing. After a few general comments, we will study protection against external thieves, such as shoplifters and burglars. Then we will turn to internal security or the control of employee misconduct. Finally we will look briefly at other types of security such as accident and fire protection.

■ SHRINKAGE: AN INDICATION OF THE PROBLEM

You will recall from your study of the retail method of accounting, in Chapter 23, that shrinkage is the amount by which the actual physical inventory in the store and the warehouse falls short of what the books indicate should be there. In other words, it is the amount of merchandise value that has mysteriously disappeared.

Some of the loss is a natural unavoidable consequence of normal selling practices. A salesperson cutting lengths of fabric in a piece-goods department cannot measure the cloth with the precision of a laboratory scientist, and it is always better to give the customer just a little extra fabric rather than short measure. Similarly, if chocolates are weighed out and boxed at the candy counter, the clerk will have to give slight overweight rather than cut pieces of candy into fractions to achieve the exact weight. Some discrepancies between book and physical inventory result from bookkeeping errors, such as failures to record all markdowns properly. But these "legitimate" causes of shrinkage probably explain only a small portion of the total loss.* Moreover, a poor, sloppy accounting system or an ill-enforced one that permits many bookkeeping errors will also permit many deliberate attempts to steal merchandise and cash from the store. Most shrinkage results from deliberate dishonesty.

The National Retail Merchants Association reports that inventory shrinkage (stock shortages) amounted to 2.04 percent of sales in department stores and 2.30 percent in large specialty stores in 1974.[2] These figures may be compared with average after-tax profit rates of 3.14 percent for department stores and 1.18 percent for the specialty stores. The Small Business Administration estimates the impact of crime falls much more heavily on small firms than on large ones. Because of crime, businesses with sales under $100,000 per year lose three times as high a percentage of total receipts as businesses with sales between $1,000,000 and $5,000,000. American retailers were estimated to suffer $6.5 billion crime losses in 1975.[3] One authority estimates that five cents out of every dollar spent in retail stores goes to pay for the cost of crimes against retailing and for the necessary security measures.[4]

□ A controllable problem

Although some loss and shrinkage is inevitable, the amount can be kept under control through diligence and sound management. A Washington, D.C., department store used a number of control programs over

---

* Supermarkets often treat the losses resulting from produce spoilage and withering and from weight loss in soft cheeses over time as part of shrinkage, rather than as something to be reported as formal markdowns. Consequently, a higher portion of supermarket shrinkage than of department store shrinkage is due to legitimate causes.

a three-year period to reduce shrinkage due to shoplifting and internal theft from 5 percent of sales to 2 percent.[5] Theoretically, a store could reduce its loss rate to zero, by keeping all merchandise under lock and key, by requiring two or more cashiers to check and verify every sales transaction, and so forth. But such restrictive measures would seriously reduce sales volume. So the management task is to find control measures that are not oppressive to customers or employees, that will not inhibit business, and yet will provide the necessary protection.

■ EXTERNAL CRIME

People who are not store employees may obtain merchandise or money illegally through shoplifting; price-ticket switching; currency, check, charge account, and credit card frauds; and burglary and robbery.

□ Shoplifting

Shoplifting is stealing goods from a store's displays or shelves while posing as a customer or other legitimate visitor to the store. Contrary to popular impression, a person may be apprehended for shoplifting before removing the goods from the store. Under the law in most jurisdictions, anyone who conceals goods with an apparent intent to steal may be held for shoplifting.

There are many types of amateur and professional shoplifters. A study of over 18,000 shoplifters apprehended in supermarkets and drugstores showed that about 31 percent were in the 12- to 17-year-old group and about 26 percent were 18 to 29. About 55 percent were male and 45 percent female.[6] Although most shoplifters, or at least the most frequently caught shoplifters, are amateurs, professionals steal more expensive merchandise and probably cause greater losses.[7] The professional steals to resell the merchandise at a profit, or occasionally, to return it for a cash refund, while the amateur is likely to keep the item or even give it away. Some professionals use clothing with numerous inner pockets, trick boxes or attache cases with hinged bottoms that can be placed over a merchandise display and surreptitiously filled, and other intricate devices. But more skillful professionals shun such equipment, which can be used against them as evidence of intent to steal in case of detection and prosecution.

Danger signals Security staffs and store personnel in general should be especially alert to shoppers who:

1. Carry open shopping bags, loose parcels, umbrellas, newspapers or other objects in which merchandise may be concealed.
2. Wear bulky or loose-fitting coats (especially if unsuitable to the weather, worn half-open, or carried over the arm), boots with wide tops, or other clothes that may conceal goods.

3. Who appear nervous, who seem to constantly look about the store, or who actually look past the merchandise while pretending to examine displays. One security expert recommends that store detectives first be trained to learn how normal customers behave, so that they can then recognize deviant behavior.[8]
4. Who spend considerable time browsing in the store, who carry merchandise from one counter to another, or who want to see every item in stock.
5. Who cause a disturbance, perhaps by pretending to faint or have an accident or by starting an argument, or who engage a salesclerk in a long conversation, often while maneuvering to block the clerk's view of the rest of the store. This may permit an accomplice to shoplift at leisure.[9]

Obviously, many people who exhibit some of the above characteristics will never steal, and some shoplifters will not manifest any of those warning signs. Nevertheless the actions listed above indicate a greater-than-average possibility of shoplifting. Truck drivers, rack jobbers, route workers, and other vendor representatives or repair people who wander into stockrooms or browse in portions of the store that are unconnected with their duties are also suspect.

Control measures   Anti-shoplifting measures include proper store design and fixturing, detection devices, adequate floor coverage, joint campaigns and many other approaches.[10] Some important steps are:

1. Store design and layout   Anti-shoplifting security is increased when store managers, employees, and security people can easily watch large areas of the store. Straight aisles, bright lighting and low fixtures may or may not be suitable for the shopping atmosphere management wishes to create, but they facilitate selling surveillance. Self-service departments should alternate with staffed ones in combination stores, so that sales personnel can also help watch the self-service sections. The Walgreen Company has designed an L-shaped self-service drugstore with unimpaired visibility from the prescription booth located at the intersection of the two arms of the L.[11] Opening up the entire storefront, for a shop in an enclosed mall, or having a large number of wide entrances and exits will encourage customers to enter the store, but may also encourage shoplifters to leave without paying. Subject to fire safety needs, all exits in a self-service store should require passing through a checkout counter.

Fitting rooms present special problems, since customers may misappropriate garments, exchange their old clothes for new ones, or use the privacy of the booth to rearrange and to more securely hide stolen merchandise. Many stores now use only half-doors or partial screens on the booths and arrange for frequent patrols by store detectives of the appropriate sex.[12]

Opinion differs as to the value of convex mirrors, closed circuit television, visible observation booths, and signs warning of prosecution for shoplifting.[13] The National Institute of Law Enforcement and Criminal Justice notes that closed circuit TV can very effectively catch shoplifters in the act of concealing merchandise, and may deter other potential shoplifters. But it also observes that the systems are very expensive and require considerable staff-time for monitoring.[14] A Brooklyn shopping center reports very good results from closed circuit TV.[15] The other visible anti-shoplifting devices, such as convex mirrors and prosecution warnings, may deter some potential thieves, but according to Bob Curtis, a well-known security specialist, will actually stimulate and challenge others. Moreover, the optical limits of convex mirrors may help shoplifters more than security people by reflecting a clear picture of employees approaching the point of the theft.[16]

2. *Displays and fixtures* Very valuable products, such as fine jewelry, should be kept in locked display cases. The glass top of the sales counter should be surrounded by a raised molding, so that a shoplifter who is examining several items cannot surreptitiously slide one off into a bag or pocket. Expensive garments, such as fur or leather coats, may be chained to the display fixtures if the loss rate is becoming excessive, although this practice may also reduce sales volume. Garments or other items may also be protected by securely-attached metal discs that customers cannot easily remove. Unless a salesperson or cashier removes or desensitizes the tag, as an indication of a legitimate purchase, the metal will activate an alarm system located near the store or department exits. This method, which is called "article surveillance," has proven effective in many shops; it reduced shrinkage in the Paul Harris stores of Indianapolis by as much as 80 percent.[17] But salespeople must be certain to remove or cancel the tags on all properly sold items, to avoid embarrassing legitimate customers.[18] Appliance cords may be securely fastened to the display racks. Only one unit of items normally sold in pairs, for example shoes, should be placed on open display. Small, easily purloined products, such as lipsticks, are often mounted on large cards in impenetrable "blister packs" that reduce casual theft. From a security standpoint, items on open display should be arranged neatly, in even rows that will direct the salesperson's attention to any missing units.

3. *Floor coverage* Sufficient personnel should be on the selling floor at all times, so that shoplifters, and customers, do not feel unobserved. A department should never be left unattended (see the discussion of sales floor coverage in Chapter 8. Salespeople and other employees should greet customers, or offer a pleasant remark. This builds goodwill with all customers, and is a psychological deterrent to shoplifters. Salespeople should be trained to watch for the warning signals mentioned earlier, to keep stocks and displays in a neat and orderly manner, and to safeguard their supply of saleschecks, refund slips and similar

FIGURE 26–1   Sensitized tag used to alert electronic article surveillance system

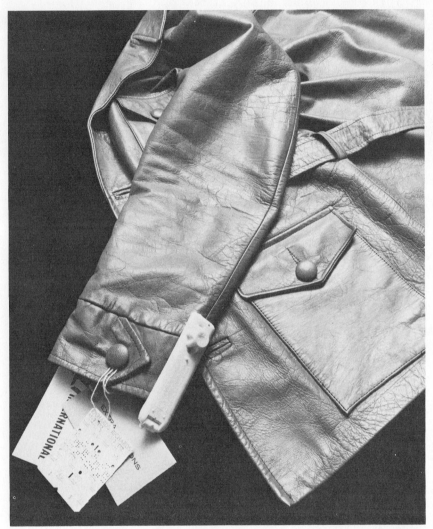

Courtesy Sensorimatic Electronics, Inc.

documents. Salesclerks should control the number of garments customers take into fitting rooms, even if a checker is employed, and should
give the customer fairly frequent attention. Checkout cashiers and
package bundlers should be especially alert for hidden items, for instance, products slipped inside the cardboard core of a role of paper
toweling. They should also check the lower tray on the customers' carts
as they pass the checkout. Awards to salespeople who report shoplifters
stimulate vigilance.[19] Salespeople who lack special training, however,

generally should not apprehend shoplifters because of the danger of violence and of liability for false arrest.[20]

Uniformed guards can implement security measures and may help direct customer flow and provide other services. They also create a "police state" atmosphere that may clash with the store's desired impression, and some hired contract guard services are poorly trained and supervised.[21] They may be unarmed, probably the best arrangement, or because of lack of weapons training and for other reasons, they may wear imitation guns which makes them vulnerable during armed robberies. The guard service's insurance policy may not protect the store against all possible claims arising out of improper or inefficient guard service.[22] However, some companies have found agency services very satisfactory.[23] Plainclothes detectives, if well selected and well trained are best prepared to cope with professional shoplifters.

4. *Community campaigns* Intensive publicity campaigns tell young people that shoplifting is not a game, but a serious crime; and that being convicted will have very adverse consequences. At the very least, conviction of shoplifting will create a criminal record and other, more severe penalties may also be imposed. Major educational campaigns that have seemed to reduce juvenile shoplifting include the S.T.E.M. ("Shoplifting Takes Everybody's Money") program in Philadelphia; the "Shoplifting in Nevada Is a Handful of Trouble—Don't Risk It" campaign (see Figure 26–6); and an anti-shoplifting drive in Washington, D.C.[24]

Apprehension and prosecution Legislation in some states allows merchants to detain persons if the merchants have (a) probable cause for believing that the persons have concealed unpurchased merchandise, and (b) that such detention will permit recovery of the merchandise. Detention of this sort, if effected in a reasonable manner and limited to a reasonable period of time, does not constitute arrest in the states with such laws, and will not render the merchants liable to possible claims for false arrest.[25]

Nevertheless, the terms "probable cause," "reasonable manner" and "reasonable time" are vague and require judgment in application.[26] In addition, shoplifter apprehension may occasionally produce dangerous or emotional incidents. Consequently, most experts agree that only security people, and storeowners and supervisors with training should detain shoplifters. Anyone who has this responsibility should obtain full information about applicable legislation from the store's attorney or retail trade association secretary. Many security people prefer to wait until the shoplifter has left the store, then approach the suspect very calmly and lead a return to the store with some remark such as "Let's see if we can straighten this out."[27] Some merchants prefer to stop apparent amateur shoplifters within the store and ask some "face-saving" question, such as "Would you like to have that wrapped?"[28] The interview with the apprehended suspect should be conducted very carefully,

FIGURE 26–2 One of a series of advertisements used in Nevada antishoplifting campaign

Courtesy Nevada Antishoplifting Committee

preferably with a second store officer or employee as a witness,* also preferably taped, and with due regard for the suspect's legal rights.

Eventually, a decision must be made as to whether to call the police and to prosecute. Some experts recommend prosecuting only 15 to 20 percent of all apprehended shoplifters, to avoid investing too much security personnel time in court appearances. The current tendency though is toward higher prosecution rates. Almost 40 percent of all shoplifters apprehended in self-service discount stores in 1973 were prosecuted[29] and many stores are moving closer to 100 percent.[30] At a minimum, stores will almost always prosecute at least those shoplifters who (a) refuse to sign a release form, (b) have no identification, (c) resist or attack store personnel, (d) have professional equipment, (e) appear to be intoxicated or under the influence of drugs, or (f) have a prior record.

□ Ticket switching

Some unscrupulous customers will remove the regular price tag or price-marked container top from an expensive item and substitute a tag or lid from a less costly one. This is tantamount to shoplifting the difference between the true price and the one actually paid. Some food processors protect their retailers by placing luxury products in bottles or jars that will not accept caps from cheaper items. Tag switching can also be controlled by securely fastening all price marks or hang tags and by placing two price marks on each item. One fashion accessories store puts a code mark, consisting of the first three digits of the price, on the label of each garment. Similarly, some stores require new price tags for markdowns, rather than just crossing out the old price and writing in the new one. This stops any customer from picking up a crayon and writing in his or her own markdown. The number of price tickets should be carefully controlled. Above all, checkout cashiers and salespeople should be alert for any price that seems inordinately low.

□ Currency, bad check, charge account and credit card frauds

Counterfeit money Retailers, cashiers, and other employees who handle large amounts of money should learn to recognize counterfeit bills and coins.[31] The U.S. Secret Service issues two booklets, *Counterfeiting and Forgery* and *Know Your Money,* that point out the distinctive characteristics of most counterfeits. (Figure 26–3) The Commercial Crimes Branch of the Royal Canadian Mounted Police provides similar guides to Canadian currency called *Counterfeit Detection Bulletins.*

---

* If the suspect is a female, at least one of the interviewers should also be a female.

FIGURE 26–3   Detecting counterfeit currency

POSITIONS OF IMPORTANT FEATURES ON PAPER CURRENCY

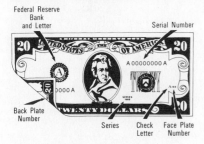

Federal Reserve Bank and Letter

Serial Number

Back Plate Number

Series

Check Letter

Face Plate Number

RECOGNIZING THE COUNTERFEIT NOTE

The best method of detecting a counterfeit note is to compare the suspect note with a genuine note of the same denomination and series. Look for the red and blue fibers in the paper. Often counterfeiters attempt to copy these fibers by printing colored lines on the paper.

If the note that you question does contain these fibers, then compare its other features with the genuine note. LOOK FOR DIFFERENCES—NOT SIMILARITIES.

The counterfeiter does not have access to equipment as sophisticated as the Government's. Nor does he possess the skill of the Government's master craftsmen. Therefore, his notes are inferior. Most counterfeits are made by a photo-mechanical process. The printing appears flat and lacks the three-dimensional quality of genuine notes.

Further, the lines in the portrait background, if you look closely, form squares. On counterfeits, some of these squares may be filled in, and many of the delicate lines in the portrait may be broken or missing.

Source: U.S. Secret Service.

COUNTERFEIT	GENUINE
PORTRAIT	
Portrait is lifeless and the background is usually too dark. Portrait merges into the background. The hairlines are not distinct.	Portrait appears lifelike and stands out distinctly from the fine screen-like background. The hairlines are distinct.
COLORED SEAL	
Saw-toothed points on the circumference are usually uneven, blunt and broken off.	Saw-toothed points are even, clear and sharp.
BORDER	
The fine lines that crisscross are not clear or distinct.	The fine lines are clear, distinct and unbroken.
SERIAL NUMBERS	
The serial numbers may be in the wrong color. They may not be properly spaced or aligned.	Serial numbers are evenly spaced and aligned. They have a distinctive style.

Banks, retail trade associations and local police may also advise when unusual amounts of bogus money have been distributed in a community.

Check frauds   Stolen checks (falsely endorsed), checks drawn on nonexistent bank accounts, checks drawn on accounts with insufficient funds and checks with forged signatures create additional problems for retailers, and particularly for those that normally offer check-cashing services. One percent of all checks accepted by retailers in the Atlanta Federal Reserve district proved to be defective.[32]

The major controls against bad check losses are: (1) have definite policies on accepting and cashing checks, (2) limit authority to accept checks to as few employees as practical; (3) require positive identification and (4) examine the check carefully. The Springfield, Ohio, police recommend obtaining at least two pieces of identification, one or more with photograph. The picture, physical description, and signature on the identification should be compared with the individual cashing the check. The customer's address and telephone number should be noted on the check, along with all ID numbers. Checks should be refused if they appear strange or unusual, show any sign of alteration, are written in pencil, are dated ahead or more than 30 days old. Any check already endorsed should be reendorsed in front of the cashier.[33] Many stores either refuse or exercise additional care when either the check or the customer is from out-of-town. Some stores also now photograph the customer and/or require a thumbprint. The photo machines, which cost about $600 to $700, plus about one cent for each picture, help deter bad-check passers and also assist in collecting.[34] Merchants in small and medium-sized communities have also cooperated in setting up volunteer telephone warning networks to alert each other when a stranger attempts to offer fraudulent checks or credit cards.[35]

Credit card and charge account frauds   Similar precautions to those used against bad checks will also provide protection against customers who offer stolen, fictitious, cancelled, or expired credit cards. Positive identification should be required; credit card numbers should be checked against lists of stolen or cancelled cards; and all take-with purchases above the appropriate floor limit should be verified by phone or through a point-of-sale terminal authorization system.[36] Procedures for controlling the misuse of charge accounts were discussed in Chapter 22, but again involve obtaining proper identification and upon verifying the current status of the customer's account.

□ Burglary and robbery

While burglary (illegal entry for purposes of theft) and robbery (theft in the presence of the victim, usually through the use or threat of force) are much less frequent than shoplifting or bad check incidents, they are potentially much more dangerous to employees and to the business.

The best protection is built in to the store building. Strong, solid core doors; unbreakable and uncuttable plastic door and window panes instead of glass, especially near locks; protective "dead locks" instead of more easily-opened spring locks; adequate and well-maintained metal grids over windows, cellar entrances, ventilator shafts, etc.; and sturdy walls and ceilings that cannot be easily breached help make the store more secure.[37] Good perimeter (outside) lighting, and burglar alarm systems that can alert private or municipal police or that scare burglars away are also helpful. They are not, however, infallible.[38] If burglars do enter they are likely to attack sales registers and safes, or attempt to steal lightweight, high-value, easily-sold merchandise. Little cash should be left in the building overnight, and register-drawers should be left empty and open to avoid damage. The safe should be securely locked, visible from outside and unless of very heavy weight, securely fastened to the building structure. If possible, serial numbers of high value electrical appliances, cameras, watches, etc., should be recorded to help recapture stolen items. In general, good housekeeping will reduce burglary risks.[39]

Many of the measures intended for protection against burglary will also reduce the likelihood of armed robbery. A group of ex-convicts who acted as consultants to a grocery store franchising company successfully reduced the frequency of robbery attempts by recommending: (a) improve outside visibility into the stores; (b) locate cash registers near windows; (c) improve parking lot lighting; (d) block escape routes; and (e) reduce amount of cash kept on hand.[40] Although only limited amounts of cash should be retained in the store, bank deposits (unless sent by armored car) should be made at different times from day-to-day and the person(s) making the deposit should vary their route to the bank. Police and other authorities agree that storekeepers and employees should never try to resist armed robbers, but should try to retain as clear a mental picture as possible of the robbers and their mannerisms for subsequent identification.

■ INTERNAL THEFT

The internal theft problems that can arise in a retail business include pilferage of merchandise and supplies by employees at various levels, retention of store money by employees who handle cash, collusion between employees and outsiders, and major forms of embezzlement. Internal theft losses are probably far greater than those due to external theft.[41]

Internal theft can best be controlled by maintaining an atmosphere of scrupulous honesty and by following good business and administrative policy. The employees will always be influenced by the ethical standards the store itself sets. A retailer who uses, encourages, or permits trickery or misrepresentation toward customers should not be surprised by employee dishonesty toward the store. The employees should also feel that they are being treated fairly. The business cannot operate successfully if the personnel are treated as a group of dangerous criminals. Nevertheless, employees will usually accept fairly rigorous security rules —in fact, they may welcome them as a shield against temptation and as a control on the more crime-susceptible members of the staff—provided those rules appear reasonable and are enforced uniformly without exception or favoritism.

□ Employee screening

Careful selection of applicants and careful review of employees provides useful protection against internal theft. (See also Chapter 8.) Application blanks should be examined very carefully for omissions and inconsistencies. An unexplained gap in the reported years of educational and work history should be questioned. References and previous employers should be checked, preferably by telephone.[42] Psychological and personality tests may be administered: one company reports developing a personality test that measures honesty.[43] Polygraph (lie-detector) tests and audio-machines that analyze voice tremors for signs of nervousness are sometimes used at the preemployment stage but are often reserved (if used at all) for specially sensitive jobs or for investigations of suspected dishonesty.

However, retailers must be careful to avoid violating applicants' and employees' legal and civil rights. Some states prohibit use of polygraph tests. Application questions and psychological tests must not have any discriminatory implications. Checks on police records may be illegal. An applicant must be notified before an investigative credit report is ordered from a credit agency.[44]

Problem and high risk employees and applicants include those who live substantially beyond their means; those who are heavily involved in gambling, narcotics, or other expensive habits (unless on an acknowledged control program); and those who are consistently maladjusted, complaining, and violative of store rules. Long-term, apparently devoted employees, especially bookkeepers and executives, who never take a vacation or a day off and never allow anyone to have access to their records are also suspect.[45] Temporary employees may feel less moral obligation to the store than do regular workers.[46]

□ Pilferage control

Pilferage is attacked by controlling the ways in which employees can remove merchandise from the store, warehouse, and trucks. Large stores usually require employees to enter and exit through special doors that security guards can monitor. Employee packages and purchases are checked, often on a random basis. Duplicate copies of sales slips for employee purchases, especially charge or lay-away transactions, should be controlled and audited to make certain that records of amounts due the store have not been destroyed. Some stores require that sales personnel leave handbags and packages in a secure locker room. This not only protects the store, but gives the employee protection against purse-snatching.

Goods being loaded onto delivery trucks (as well as goods coming into the store) should be carefully counted and compared with invoices and manifests. (See the discussion of receiving control in Chapter 15.) The activities of repair and delivery people and others who regularly come to the store for business purposes should be controlled. Trash and waste removed from the store should be inspected frequently since it is a favorite hiding place for stolen objects that will be picked up after the store closes. Such inspection will also reveal carelessness in the use of store supplies, or thoughtless discards of valuable merchandise.[47]

☐ Cash theft and embezzlement

Precise accounting and cash-handling methods and periodic tests of the system provide the greatest control over monetary losses. Cashiers and salespeople who handle money should be required to give customers a complete and accurate register receipt or sales slip for each transaction. Register error corrections and use of the "no-sale" key (for example, to open the register for someone who wants to change paper money to coins) may require a supervisor's approval. If not, register tapes should be checked for excessive use of the "no sale" key. Periodic test shoppings by trained investigators will often disclose improper practices.

Refund slips and incidental, on-the-spot cash payments to suppliers should be verified. Insofar as practical, the individual who makes a cash (or other) payment to a customer, supplier, or employee should not be the same individual who authorizes that payment. This double-checking should prevail, to the extent practicable, throughout the entire system. In addition, periodic cash counts, checks, and audits are needed.[48] All saleslips, refund vouchers, petty cash vouchers, and similar forms should be numbered and should be accounted for at all times. Large retail firms often must establish even more elaborate auditing systems to prevent or detect major forms of embezzlement.[49] Some symptoms of possible embezzlement, however, are unusual and unexplainable decreases in sales revenue, profit or debt collections, or equally disturbing increases in expenses, bad debt writeoffs or merchandise returns in a department or store. All warrant investigation, for business as well as security reasons.[50]

☐ Collusion

Collusion between an employee and an outsider is not so much a *type* of crime as a *way* of committing one of the crimes discussed elsewhere in this chapter.* It may take many forms and covers a wide range in dollar amount. A salesperson or cashier many undercharge a friend or relative; a receiving clerk may sign for more merchandise than the store actually obtains and divide the proceeds with the delivery truck driver, or a buyer may accept bribes from vendors.[51]

While careful employee selection and the maintenance of high standards and morale are the major weapons against collusive offenses as well as individual ones, other steps are also helpful. Proper selling-

---

* In the legal sense, of course, conspiracy (or collusion) to commit a felony is itself a crime in addition to the actual felony.

floor and checkout-counter surveillance will decrease the number of free and reduced-price "gifts" to friends.[52] Double checking merchandise receipts and keeping accurate inventory records and spot checking will reduce receiving room problems.[53] Buyer and purchasing agent bribery can be countered by selecting honest, capable executives; by requiring countersignature (approval) of all purchases by knowledgeable senior officers of the company; by making it known that the store will never do business with any vendor who bribes one of its buyers; and by watching for any pattern of questionable or unwise purchasing.

■ CARELESSNESS AND ERROR

The sources of loss that we have discussed to this point involve deliberate wrong-doing. Some losses, however, arise from honest mistakes and from carelessness. While such losses do not involve moral culpability, they can amount to a considerable sum and should be minimized.

Illustrations of this type of loss include the item that is sold for less than full price because the price-marking is illegible or missing;* the invoice that is paid in full because no one noticed the availability of a discount; and the merchandise that is tossed away with the store's refuse because the shipping carton was not completely emptied. An apparent shortage will appear in the store's books under the retail method of accounts unless all markdowns, discounts, and allowances to customers are properly recorded (see Chapter 23). Vigilance, training, and leadership are needed to offset the human tendency toward carelessness.[54]

■ FIRE AND ACCIDENT PROTECTION

The creation of a secure environment requires more than efforts to control crime and reduce paperwork mistakes. The customers, the employees, the merchandise and the buildings should be protected against fire, accidents, and other hazards.

□ Fire protection

No building is absolutely fireproof, although some types of construction are much less susceptible than others. (See the discussion of building design in Chapter 5.) But even retail stores with so-called fire-resistant or noncombustible buildings usually contain inflammable merchandise, packing and wrapping supplies, and display materials. Store restaurants, cafeterias, and other cooking facilities, trash chutes,

---

* Salesclerks and cashiers who guess at prices will often underestimate the amounts, perhaps to avoid any possible customer resistance or objection.

electrical wiring, and heating and air-conditioning systems pose special problems. Oddly enough, fires can originate in the water-filled wooden cooling towers that are part of normal air-conditioning facilities, and those towers must be equipped with sprinkler systems.[55]

Measures to reduce fire risks include (a) proper building design and construction, (b) fire detection and alarm equipment, perhaps connected to a fire patrol company outside the store as well as to an internal security center or switchboard,[56] (c) an adequate, well-maintained sprinkler system, (d) a supply of hand-operated fire extinguishers in good working condition as well as automatic systems at vulnerable points, (e) adequate fire exits and a set of battery-powered emergency lights in case of power failure, (f) good housekeeping practices that prevent accumulation of rubbish and that will not permit merchandise inventories to be piled so high they will block the water flow from the sprinklers,[57] and (g) rigorous enforcement of smoking rules. Employees, especially full-time supervisors, should be trained to respond to fire situations and to evacuate customers, if necessary, without creating panic. Duplicate safety copies of important records and computer files, such as accounts receivable, should be kept at some location away from the main store building.[58]

☐ Accident prevention

We have already noted that retail store employees incur a large number of accidents, although fortunately most are relatively minor in nature (see Chapter 9). Customers also may stumble or trip over steps, display platforms or merchandise left in the aisles, may cut themselves on broken pieces of counter glass, or may be hit by merchandise falling from high shelves. Good lighting; safe construction with nonslip floor surfaces; decals or other prominant markings on glass doors; elimination of sharp edges and protruding rods from counters, display racks and other fixtures; and control of housekeeping standards will reduce customer and employee accidents. Care should also be exercised to insure that employees know *and use* the proper methods for lifting heavy parcels, for handling electrical equipment, for working with hand tools, ladders, meat-cutting equipment and other hazardous items, and for performing other tasks.[59]

☐ Other problems

Store safety and security personnel, as well as top management if needed, should be prepared to cope with many other types of problems. These include individual difficulties, such as sudden illness of a customer or employee (which may require first aid facilities in the large store and a knowledge of how to obtain help in a small store) or a noisy argument between two customers or between an employee and a customer (they should be separated and guided to a quiet spot).* More general problems include natural calamities such as (depending on the store location) tornadoes, floods and hurricanes, or human disturbances, such as riots. Management should have plans for handling all such situations.[60]

■ CONCLUSION

As noted in the preceding paragraphs, retail businesses are susceptible to a surprisingly large number of criminal, negligent, and natural hazards. Management should, however, be more concerned with prevention than with apprehension.[61] It is far better to remove temptation than to catch someone who has succumbed to temptation. Similarly, it is better to prevent a fire than to have to extinguish one. Some aspects of financial loss can be covered by insurance, although insurance merely spreads the financial burden over the whole group of policy holders—it doesn't eliminate the loss. Moreover, some financial risks cannot be insured, including shoplifting losses or any deterioration in store reputation and goodwill if the store has to close because of fire or other calamity.** But no insurance can cover the human costs of calamities or of becoming involved in criminal acts.

Consequently, management should strive to avert trouble. Proper building design, sensible precautions in merchandise display, insistence upon compliance with well-planned control and bookkeeping systems,[62] and above all, maintenance of an atmosphere of fairness and honesty will do much to prevent difficulties. At the same time, management simply cannot act as if it is engaged in a war against either employees or customers. One experienced merchandiser says that some security people would like to "close the store" to prevent loss.[63] That is, of course, totally impractical. Security measures must be reasonable. They should allow sales transactions to be handled efficiently and courteously; they should give the customers convenient opportunities to see and inspect the merchandise; and they should help develop harmonious labor relations.

■ REVIEW AND DISCUSSION QUESTIONS

1 Visit a local merchants' association, a police department juvenile officer, or some merchants to discover (a) how serious they consider retail crime

---

* Note that shoplifters, working in teams, sometimes create an "emergency" or a disturbance to distract attention while an accomplice removes the merchandise. Employees not needed to handle the apparent problem should not become curious onlookers but should remain alert to the store's other needs.

** Business interruption insurance only protects against direct loss of sales while closed.

problems to be, and (b) what suggestions they have for reducing crime. Also try to ascertain the law in your community on shoplifting, citizen's arrest, and the merchant's right of detention.

2 Define "shrinkage." What are the major causes of shrinkage? Present some figures on its relationship to total retail sales.

3 Distinguish between "professional" and "amateur" shoplifters. Do they take different types of merchandise and do they present different problems to the security force? Summarize some of the symptoms of suspicious conduct.

4 What are some of the principal measures for combating shoplifting? Which ones are generally regarded as effective by all or most experts, and which ones are subject to debate? Briefly describe the arguments for and against the debated measures.

5 Outline a training session for salesclerks in proper methods of handling cash and checks.

6 Suggest measures retailers can adopt to reduce the risks of burglary and armed robbery.

7 (a) Outline the techniques you would use as a retailer employing, say, 100 people, to reduce losses through employee pilferage. (b) What techniques would you use to curb internal cash thefts and fraud?

8 Describe the fire prevention methods that you would recommend for a discount department store.

9 Explain some of the likely causes of accidents in supermarkets. In hardware and electrical appliance stores. How may customers and employees be protected against these accidents?

10 Discuss the statement: "Everything that the security people want to do will interfere with sales and the merchandising people must fight them at every step."

■ NOTES AND REFERENCES

1 David Steeno, "Loss Prevention in Retail Stores," *Security World*, December, 1973, p. 50.

2 Financial Executives Division, National Retail Merchant Association, *Financial and Operating Results of Department and Specialty Stores of 1974* (New York: The Association, 1975), pp. iv–vii.

3 U.S. Department of Commerce, *The Cost of Crimes against Business* (Washington, D.C.: U.S. Government Printing Office, 1974), pp. 7–8.

4 "Expert Says Consumer Pays 7 to 8 Cents on Every Dollar as Toll to Dishonesty," *Women's Wear Daily*, March 21, 1975, p. 2. The estimate, 7 to 8¢, includes costs of crimes against nonretail as well as retail businesses.

5 "Woodies Slashes Shrinkage to 2%," *Women's Wear Daily*, January 11, 1973, p. 26.

6 Roger K. Griffin, "Shoplifting," *Security World*, September 1973, pp. 16–19. See also Amin El-Dirghami, "Shoplifting among Students," *Journal of Retailing*, vol. 50 (Fall 1974), pp. 33–42, and M. D. Geuris, R. R. Andrus and J. Reinmuth, "Researching Shoplifting and Other Deviant Behavior," *Journal of Retailing*, vol. 51 (Winter 1975–76), pp. 43–48.

7 Bob Curtis, *Security Control: External Theft* (New York: Chain Store Publishing Co., 1971), pp. 24–26.

8 Curtis, *Security Control: External Theft*, pp. 71–73.

9 For an extensive, similar list, see "Spotting the Shoplifter," *Chain Store Age* (general merchandise/variety edition), February 1974, pp. 46–48.

10 For another review of anti-shoplifting measures see Anthony J. Faria, "Shoplifting Methods, Detection, Prevention and Apprehension," *Retail Control*, March 1975, pp. 44–57.

11 "Plain Naked-Eye Coverage," *Chain Store Age* (Executive edition), October 1974, pp. 33–34.

12 "May Co. Boosts Fitting Room Security," *Chain Store Age* (Executive edition), March 1974, pp. E70–71.

13 Alfred Alexander and Val Moolman, *Stealing*, New Revised ed. (Hollywood, Florida: Distribution Advisors International, 1973), p. 124; Addison H. Verrill, "Reducing Shoplifting Losses" in Richard S. Post, ed., *Combating Crime Against Small Business* (Springfield, Ill.: Charles C. Thomas, 1972), p. 121; and U.S. Department of Commerce, *Crime in Retailing* (Washington, D.C.: U.S. Government Printing Office, 1975), p. 15, all recommend signs and mirrors.

14 U.S. Department of Justice, *Fixed Surveillance Cameras* (NILECJ-Guide 0301.00) (Washington, D.C.: The Department, 1974).

15 "TV Gives Guards Visibility," *Chain Store Age* (Executive edition), October 1974, p. 37.

16 Curtis, *Security Control: External Theft*, pp. 49–52.

17 Colin N. Jones, "New Electronic System Aids Industry Environment," *Security World*, October 1973, p. 25; Arthur Ratz, "New Accounting Approach Includes Security," *Security World*, January 1976, pp. 32–33; "Bugged Tags Help Finger Shoplifters," *Chain Store Age* (Executive edition), June 1973, p. E–20.

18 In one New York store two-thirds of the alarms resulted because cashiers forgot to remove the tags. "Alexander's Gets Its Man—Often the Wrong One," *Women's Wear Daily*, October 1, 1973, pp. 1, 11.

19 Curtis, *Security Control: External Theft*, pp. 59–61; Edith M. Lynch, "Personnel Division," *Stores*, December 1975, p. 22.

20 The Colorado Retail Security Association and the Colorado Retail Council have developed two successful videotape training programs. The one for salespeople emphasizes the seriousness of the shrinkage problem and the indications of shoplifting; the one for supervisors includes apprehension methods. Melvin L. Baumgartner, "Imposing Security Awareness," *Security Management*, May 1973, pp. 33–34.

21 *The Cost of Crimes Against Business*, p. 14; James S. Kakalik and Sorel Wildhorn, *Private Police in the United States: Findings and Recommendations*, vol. I (R869/DOJ), Rand Corporation for National Institute of Law Enforcement and Criminal Justice (Washington: U.S. Government Printing Office, 1971), pp. 32–37, 86–92; James Parry, "Make Sure You Hire the Right Security Guards," *Canadian Business*, March 1976, pp. 73–75.

22 Bruce Brownyard, "Are You Buying Security—or Trouble?" *Security Management*, November 1974, pp. 18–20.

23 "Security Guards: Earning Their Keep," *Chain Store Age* (drug edition), July 1975, p. 45.

24 Carol Messenger, "State Campaigns Fight Shoplifting," *Stores*, October 1975, pp. 25–26; "The Philadelphia Method Helps to STEM Shoplifting," *Women's Wear Daily*, October 10, 1973, p. 66; *Crime in Retailing*, p. 23.

25 John J. Sullivan, "Legal Authority of Security Personnel," *Security World*, February 1973, pp. 20–26.

26 See Daniel T. Clancy, "Authority of Private Police," in *Business and Industrial Security: Practical Legal Problems 2d* (New York: Practicing Law Institute, 1972), pp. 61–146.

27 For a detailed and very specific approach, see Curtis, *Retail Security: External Theft*, pp. 85–86. *See also* Robert Griffin, "Shoplifting Policy Guide for Retailers," *Security World*, December 1973, pp. 34–36.

28 See Curtis, p. 53.

29 *Store Thieves and Their Impact* (New York: Mass Retailing Institute, 1973), p. 9.

30 "Those Who Help Themselves," *Money*, September 1975, p. 84.

31 "You Can Spot Bogus Money," *Chain Store Age* (general merchandise-variety edition), April 1974, pp. 74–76.

32 "How BIG Is the Bad Check Problem?" *Security World,* July/August 1974, p. 35. However, a 1973 study showed that about one out of every 139 checks cashed in the typical chain supermarket was returned as "NSF" ("not sufficient funds"), amounting to about $300 per store per week, but that 80 percent of the amount involved was eventually recovered. *Bad Check Losses: A Report on Current Trends* (Chicago: Super Market Institute, 1973), pp. 2, 4.

33 Quoted in Mass Retailing Institute, *MRI Security Bulletin,* August 1975, p. 5. Similar suggestions appear in *Crime against Retailing,* p. 20; Verne A. Bunne, "Business Management for Crime Prevention," in Richard S. Post, ed., *Combating Crime against Small Business* (Springfield, Ill.: Charles C. Thomas, 1972), pp. 60–66; and Curtis, *Retail Security: External Theft,* pp. 153–64.

34 *MRI Security Bulletin,* August 1975, p. 2; "Reduces Bad Check Losses," *Stores,* June 1975, p. 10; Marian Rothman, "Bad Checks," same source, June 1976, pp. 18–25; William H. Bolen and Anthony J. Faria, "Bad Checks = Bad Profits," *Retail Control,* February 1975, pp. 23–26.

35 Carroll W. Boze, "Retail Red Alert," *Security World,* April 1973, pp. 21–23.

36 *Crime in Retailing,* p. 21; Timothy J. Keane, "Credit Card Fraud," *Security Management,* January 1974, pp. 17–21.

37 "Security Begins with the Blueprint," *Chain Store Age* (Executive edition), July 1973, pp. E40–E42.

38 "Alarm Systems: Which Is Best for You?" *Chain Store Age* (Supermarket edition), April 1974, pp. M7–M8.

39 Bunne, "Business Management for Crime Prevention," pp. 42–48.

40 "Southland Cuts Stickups 30% in Calif. Using Former Convicts as Consultants," *Supermarket News,* January 5, 1976, sec. 1, p. 21.

41 See John Osbon, "Ward's: 5,000 to 'Resign' in Theft Probe," *Women's Wear Daily,* October 27, 1975, pp.

1, 25. "U.S. Report: Retail Theft Is Mostly an Inside Job," same source, March 18, 1976, p. 11; "Ripoff," *Progressive Grocer,* February 1976, pp. 45–50.

42 See Carol Messenger, "Shortage Control: Store Managers Hear Remedies," *Stores,* December 1974, pp. 28–29; D. L. Wood, "Pre-Employment Background Investigations" and J. S. Alden, "Background Investigation: Well Worth the Cost," both in Sheryl Leininger, ed., *Internal Theft: Investigation and Control* (Los Angeles: Security World Publishing Co., 1975), pp. 197–214.·

43 George W. Lindberg, "A Test for Honesty," in Leininger, *Internal Security,* pp. 215–22.

44 See Timothy J. Walsh and Harvey I. Saferstein, "Screening of Employees" in Clancy, ed., *Business and Industrial Security: Practical Legal Problems 2d,* pp. 31–60; *Private Police in the United States,* pp. 59, 66, 96–97; *see also* Chapter 8.

45 See Bob Curtis, *Security Control: Internal Theft* (New York: Chain Store Age Books, 1973), pp. 34–46 for a more extensive list.

46 Charles F. Hemphill, Jr., "If Christmas Means 'Temporary,'" *Security World,* December 1974, pp. 27, 62.

47 Charles F. Hemphill, Jr., "Trash Tests Your Security," *Security World,* August 1973, pp. 42–45. Curtis, *Security Control: Internal Theft,* pp. 241–90, analyzes a number of methods of curbing pilferage.

48 Peter A. Gergay, "The Detection of 'Lapping' in Retail and Service Organization," *Retail Control,* April-May 1974, pp. 22–28.

49 Such systems are beyond the scope of this chapter, but are discussed in standard textbooks on auditing such as Arthur W. Holmes and Wayne E. Overmyer, *Auditing: Standards and Procedures,* 8th ed. (Homewood, Ill.: Richard D. Irwin, Inc., 1975).

50 U.S. Small Business Administration, *Preventing Embezzlement,* quoted in "FYI: Ideas for Independents," *Stores,* June 1974, p. 22.

51 Samuel Feinberg, "The High Cost of Dishonesty by Purchasing

Agents," *Women's Wear Daily*, October 24, 1975, p. 6.

52 Curtis, *Security Control: Internal Theft*, pp. 292–313, discusses cashier controls.

53 Joseph E. Bernstein, "The Prevention and Detection of Internal Theft," *Retail Control*, December 1974, pp. 58–61; A. Alexander and others, *Stealing*, new, revised ed. (Hollywood, Florida: Distribution Advisers International, 1973), pp. 62–63.

54 See Richard L. Silva, "The Buyer's Role in a Stock Shortage Control Program," *Retail Control*, November 1974, pp. 34–52; James A. Brogan, "The Control of Paperwork Problems That Can Cause Inventory Shortage," *Retail Control*, March 1975, pp. 18–27.

55 Elliot R. Berrin, "Property Loss Prevention for the Retailer," *Retail Control*, April–May 1974, pp. 2–11; also, Gordon L. Williams, "Fire Prevention," *Stores*, October 1975, p. 23.

56 W. J. Christian and P. M. Dubiusky, "Basic Information on Fire Detection Devices," *Security World*, March 1974, p. 71.

57 J. S. Barrett, "Fire-Fighting Tactics for Racked Storage," *Security World*, March 1974, p. 16.

58 Many of these suggestions are listed in Berrin, "Property Loss Prevention."

59 See George J. and Helen Matwes, *Loss Control: A Safety Guidebook for Trades and Services* (New York: Van Nostrand Reinhold Company, 1973), especially "Department Stores," pp. 198–232; "Small Stores and Shops," pp. 302–03; and "Supermarkets," pp. 309–17.

60 John H. Fulweiler, "Resolve Now to Prepare for Emergencies," *Chain Store Age* (executive edition), December 1973, p. E8. Also, National Retail Merchants Association, "Riot Precautions" (New York: The Association, n.d.).

61 R. D. Furash, "Shortage Control," *Retail Control*, January 1974, pp. 16–25.

62 Studies of a number of stores suffering increasing shrinkage losses revealed that they generally had well-designed control systems, but had failed to enforce those systems and had permitted careless record keeping. F. P. Rieser and J. A. Polan, "Inventory Shortage Control," *Retail Control*, January 1976, pp. 17–25.

63 Richard L. Silva, "The Buyer's Role in a Stock Shortage Control Program," *Retail Control*, November 1974, p. 37.

Coordination and management

MANAGEMENT COORDINATION
AND LEADERSHIP

Management's prime responsibility is to operate profitably. Without a profitable business the retailer cannot serve the public, provide jobs at competitive wages, or support community projects.

■ COORDINATION ESSENTIAL TO PROFITABLE OPERATIONS

A profitable operation requires coordination of all store activities. Every retail firm needs some individual, or a very small group of individuals, to keep the various departments or divisions functioning as well-integrated units. Moreover, the management must make certain that the organization is well adjusted to present conditions, and ready to meet future requirements. In this chapter we will discuss (1) some of the major factors involved in coordination, including (a) certain questions that the leadership must ask and (b) the responsibility for answering them: i.e. the necessary coordination for effective performance. Then we will examine (2) standards, (3) figure comparisons, (4) budgeting, and (5) retail research, all of which are important management tools that facilitate coordination. Finally, we will briefly consider (6) some aspects of leadership style in retailing and (7) management's social responsibilities.

□ Adjustment to present and changing conditions

To discover the adjustments called for by current conditions the retailer should possess an inquiring, critical mind. Associates should be consulted continuously to find answers to such questions as the following: Are our merchandising and sales promotional activities adequate to hold our place in the community in which we operate? Would it be better, considering the competition of a nearby discount house, to "trade up" in services and merchandise or to reduce prices? Do we have enough salespeople to give the degree of service expected by our clientele? Is it desirable to appoint a fashion coordinator for wearing apparel and one for home furnishings to insure greater uniformity of quality and prices in the offerings of the various selling departments? What innovations have been adopted recently by our chief competitors? Which, if any, of these should we adopt to preserve or strengthen our "image" in the minds of our customers?

The coordinator must also be responsible for the adjustment of the organization to changing conditions, a difficult task because the rate of change today is constantly accelerating.

Changing technology   We have already discussed many of the ways in which automation and electronic data processing are changing merchandise control, sales transaction methods, and credit procedures. These automated techniques will become increasingly important in the future, and retailers may also expect the development of many other new technologies. The basic retailing problem of presenting the right merchandise at the right time at the right price in the right way will remain unchanged, but new equipment will undoubtedly appear to help solve that problem.

Changing labor conditions   The number and qualifications of the people interested in working in retailing, and their attitudes toward the work vary with such factors as population changes, economic fluctuations, unionization, and the changing nature of retailing positions. Reductions in labor supply or increases in wages and salaries may induce more automation; that automation in turn will affect the attractiveness of some retailing positions.

Changing supplies   The quantity, variety and quality of goods available for resale; the ease or difficulty of importation; and the number and selling practices of suppliers will necessarily change. Fifteen years ago few retailers would have even thought of creating electronic departments to sell digital wristwatches and pocket calculators. New retailing opportunities will continue to appear and some established lines will lose their place.

Market changes   Retailers particularly must be prepared to cope with market changes. The consumer market constantly evolves, both in objective characteristics such as numbers, age distribution, residence location, and income; and in subjective elements, such as tastes and attitudes. Successful retailers are increasingly adopting a marketing approach to discovering what services and products present and potential customers want.[1]

Social changes Closely allied to market changes are changes in public attitudes and beliefs, as illustrated by the upsurge of consumerism in the 1960s and 1970s. These attitudes affect retailers both directly and indirectly through the process of government regulation. Again, a marketing attitude is required.[2]

In brief, only by a continuous adaptation to changing conditions can retail organizations render satisfactory customer service and achieve optimum profits. Indeed, the retailer must look ahead, note the trends, plan adjustments carefully, utilize the newer management tools, and coordinate the entire organization to effect necessary changes, otherwise the business may end. Retailing history is filled with examples of retailers, both large and small, who have failed at this task.

☐ Responsibility for coordination

Who in the retail organization should be responsible for coordination? The answer is clear: Coordination is a function of the general manager of the organization or of a small executive committee of two or three people. In practice, one-person responsibility for coordination seems desirable; and in the majority of retail organizations the general manager or chief executive has this assignment.

In the large retail organization the general manager finds that day-to-day contact even with the more important activities of the business is impractical; this necessitates reliance upon numerous individuals to whom authority is given and responsibility is delegated. The personnel manager, for example, must coordinate all activities relating to the employment, training, compensation, and welfare of employees. The merchandise manager, likewise, must assume responsibility for the maintenance of well-balanced stocks of goods in all selling departments. These individuals and others should report to the general manager either orally or in writing as frequently as warranted by the importance of the particular function or tasks over which they exercise control. After all the facts are assembled, however, it makes for speed of action and centralizes responsibility if one person "has the final word."

Nevertheless, the management of the highly successful Federated Department Stores ownership group believes that each major division should have "two top bosses, one to look after the merchandise, the other to run the store. 'Somebody . . . with enough authority and responsibility to disagree with you.' "[3] In the Federated organization, one such individual is usually designated as chairperson, the other as president.

▢ Major tools of coordination

Some retailers rely heavily on what they term "instinct." One chain-store executive said: "I believe I run my business by feel. I instinctively know when a thing is wrong and realize its value when it is good, but to sit down and enumerate these things is rather difficult to do." By no means are all those who follow this procedure failures in business; in fact, the executive just quoted built a food chain which was a financial success. Many years of daily contact with the organization had created an ability to sense trends and make adjustments without being conscious of the thought processes involved.

Typically, however, the retailer needs more than "instinct"; and, fortunately, there are a number of tools available for carrying out the coordination function. Four of these tools are especially important—internal standards, comparisons of operating and merchandising results with those of other retailers, the budget, and research.

■ STANDARDS

Standards are quantified yardsticks for measuring business performance. They can, and should, be used to set objectives in addition to evaluating and diagnosing results. Retailers use many different types of standards, and they obtain the figures for those standards in many different ways. The most common source is the store or firm's own past performance. However, any standards set on the basis of what happened in the past must be adjusted (a) for current changes in business conditions and (b) for improvement of any weak spots in past operations. Retailers also often use figure comparisons with other stores as a source of standards, and some aspects of this approach are discussed on pp. 665–70. Finally, a few standards may come from miscellaneous sources; time and motion study may be used to develop a physical production standard for a routine job, while gross margin and expense standards serve as a check on each other.

▢ Types of standards

While standards may be classified in many ways such as the method of setting the standard or the method of measurement, we will discuss them below in terms of the aspects of the business to which they apply.

Sales standards The store's total sales may be compared with past volume to measure the trend in business, but more precise figures are often desirable for comparison with other stores, for comparison between departments, or for more thorough analysis. Retailers often measure sales per square foot of the floor space (that is, dollar sales divided by square footage) to permit comparison between stores or departments of different size. Other sales standards include dollar sales per employee, number of transactions, amount of the average sales-check, and relationship of net sales to gross sales (to measure the return rate).

Some organizations devise standards for the division of dollar sales among various departments. Thus, a food chain may decide that 55 percent of its business should be in dry groceries and dairy products, 12 percent in fruits and vegetables, 28 percent in meats, and 5 percent in nonfoods. If the meat department sales drop below 28 percent, management is warned that the department may not be operating as it should. Such a warning is useful, but should be placed in the proper perspective. In this type of analysis, the total figure for all departments is always 100 percent. If one department has exceptionally good sales, the other figures will be reduced proportionately even if those other departments are performing satisfactorily. In the example, if the grocery department increases its share to 58 percent, the other departments will automatically lose 3 percent.[4]

Still another type of sales standard measures the store's sales results against its competitors'. Information may be gathered by shopping competitors' stores (and trying to estimate their business volume), by using published statistics on retail sales in the community, or by asking customers and potential customers where they buy certain kinds of goods. (A market research study of this type is discussed on p. 672.) The resulting figures help show the retailer's "share of the market."

Merchandising standards   These standards concern the effectiveness of store buying and pricing practices. Some of the major measures are average initial markup, markdown rate, gross margin, and merchandise turnover. Turnover rate, like the division of sales mentioned above, is called a physical standard, since it really expresses a physical activity —in this case the average speed at which a quantity of goods moves through the store's stock. This is true even though the turnover rate is usually calculated by dividing one dollar figure by another dollar figure, for example, dollar sales divided by average inventory at retail price.

Operating expense standards   These standards take three forms (see also the discussion of expense analysis and control in Chapter 24):

1. *Percentages*   Operating expenses are usually expressed as a percentage of net sales. A department store management may decide that buying (buyers' salaries, travel, etc.) should not cost more than 1.8 percent of net sales and selling and sales supervision should not exceed nine percent.

2. *Unit cost standards*   Some expense guides are established as unit cost standards, that is, they set forth the cost of performing a specific act. Frequently the standard for wrapping is of this variety, the

store calculating that its cost of gift wrapping during the Christmas season should be 50¢ per package; its wage cost per average sale should be 80¢; and its delivery cost per package, $1.35.

3. *Production per employee-hour* These measures, which can also be considered physical standards, describe the amount of work that an employee is expected to accomplish in an hour, or a day or some other finite period. Such standards may describe the number of cases of groceries an employee is expected to price mark in an hour or the number of sales registers that an auditing employee should check per day.

Service standards These standards normally relate to the service customers receive, and include such criteria as: the number or percentage of packages misdelivered, the number of customer complaints, the average amount of time customers have to wait for sales service or in a checkout line, and the number or percent of cashier errors. Similar standards may be set for the services facilitating departments render to the rest of the store, for example, how long on the average selling departments have to wait for merchandise to go through receiving and marking operations.

Financial standards Much of the financial and accounting data discussed in Chapter 23 can be converted to ratios that serve as standards for the solvency and profitability of the business.[5] One such ratio, current assets divided by current liabilities, helps indicate the ability to pay bills as they come due. Current assets are those assets that can be quickly converted to cash without great difficulty, and include cash, notes, accounts receivable (less estimated loss from bad debts), merchandise inventory (at true market value or less) and securities (also not in excess of market value). Current liabilities are all debts falling due within one year.

Profitability measures One important set of financial measures concerns the important question of profits. Profits are usually expressed as a percentage of net sales and, for financial analysis, as a percentage of net worth. Net worth represents the owner's or stockholders' equity in the business and is obtained by subtracting total liabilities from total assets. Large companies may use somewhat different and more complex measures of return on investment, but the aim is still the same—to judge how well the business is rewarding its investors. Large retailers who use the contribution method of accounting for departmental analysis (see pp. 604–6) must of course set departmental standards in terms of contribution rather than net profit.

Social indicators Some people believe that businesses should set standards for their societal performance as well as for their commercial results. Forty-four percent of the executives responding to one survey expected that a social audit would be required in the fuutre.[6] Developing precise measures of good business citizenship has proven very difficult and will require resolution of many deep philosophical, conceptual, theoretical and technical questions. But at least one major retailer publishes an annual report of its community contributions.[7]

☐ Using standards

Establishing standards   Setting standards is beneficial, and most retail businesses probably have too few, rather than too many, such yardsticks. Nevertheless great care should be exercised in setting standards to make certain (1) that they are reasonable and attainable, and (2) that they will have the desired effect. For example, low expense rates may be set as standards and may be achieved. However, reducing expenses may involve reducing services or advertising to a point where sales are adversely affected with harmful results on final profits. Similarly, management may set a high initial markup or a low markdown standard that damages the store's competitive position.[8]

Standards not applicable in all areas   It is not possible, of course, to set up objective standards for all areas in which the retailer is interested. Standards cannot be set for the courtesy with which salespeople treat customers, the quality of wrapping done by the personnel performing this task, or for the wisdom of long-run management decisions. Yet standards can be devised for so many important matters that they become an essential device in the successful coordination of retail activities.

Written standards advisable   Too many merchants (especially small ones), decide to set standards, and then fail to put them in writing. As a result, they are seldom used. If standards are to fulfill the purposes for which they are intended, they should be in written form, compared with actual results, and prompt action initiated when significant differences are revealed.

■ COMPARATIVE FIGURES

The second major tool of coordination for the retailer is the comparison of operating, merchandising and financial results with those of comparable retailers. Perhaps the employees are poorly trained, a fact that would be reflected in comparatively low sales per salesperson, a high returned goods ratio, and a low ratio of actual buyers to the number of people entering the store. Direct comparisons indicate weaknesses and enable management to adopt measures to correct them. A few of the detailed statistics published by the Financial Executives Division of the National Retail Merchants Association for department stores and departmentized specialty stores are illustrated in Table 27–1, while some of the ratios for many lines of retailing published in *Dun's Review* are shown in Table 27–2, p. 668.

FIGURE 27–1 **Fourteen key business ratios (financial standards)**

Current Assets to Current Debt Current Assets are divided by total Current Debt. Current Assets are the sum of cash, notes and accounts receivable (less reserves for bad debt), advances on merchandise, merchandise inventories, and Listed, Federal, State and Municipal securities not in excess of market value. Current Debt is the total of all liabilities falling due within one year. This is one test of solvency.

Net Profits on Net Sales Obtained by dividing net earnings of the business, after taxes, by net sales (the dollar volume less returns, allowances, and cash discounts). This important yardstick in measuring profitability should be related to the ratio which follows.

Net Profits on Tangible Net Worth Tangible Net Worth is the equity of stockholders in the business, as obtained by subtracting total liabilities from total assets, and then deducting intangibles. The ratio is obtained by dividing Net Profits after taxes by Tangible Net Worth. Tendency is to look increasingly to this ratio as a final criterion of profitability. Generally, a relationship of at least 10 percent is regarded as a desirable objective for providing dividends plus funds for future growth.

Net Profits on Net Working Capital Net Working Capital represents the excess of Current Assets over Current Debt. This margin represents the cushion available to the business for carrying inventories and receivables, and for financing day-to-day operations. The ratio is obtained by dividing Net Profits, after taxes, by Net Working Capital.

Net Sales to Tangible Net Worth Net Sales are divided by Tangible Net Worth. This gives a measure of relative turnover of invested capital.

Net Sales to Net Working Capital Net Sales are divided by Net Working Capital. This provides a guide as to the extent the company is turning its working capital and the margin of operating funds.

Collection Period Annual net sales are divided by 365 days to obtain average daily credit sales and then the average daily credit sales are divided into notes and accounts receivable, including any discounted. This ratio is helpful in analyzing the collectibilty of receivables. Many feel the collection period should not exceed the net maturity indicated by selling terms by more than 10 to 15 days. When comparing the collection period of one concern with that of another, allowances should be made for possible variations in selling terms.

To cite one further example, among hardware retailers the average net profit before taxes in 1974 was but 4.98 percent of sales; yet the most profitable one-third of those reporting averaged 10.40 percent.[9] Hardware retailers who compare their own experience with that of stores in both groups obtain valuable information concerning points of strength and weakness in their operations.

□ Sources of comparative data

The meaningfulness of comparative figures increases with the degree of similarity among the stores being compared. Consequently, department stores that belong to an ownership group, such as Federated Department Stores, Allied Stores Corporation or Associated Dry Goods

FIGURE 27-1   (continued)

Net Sales to Inventory   Obtained by dividing annual Net Sales by Merchandise Inventory as carried on the   balance sheet. This quotient does not yield an actual physical turnover. It provides a yardstick for comparing stock-to-sales ratios of one concern with another or with those for the industry.

Fixed Assets to Tangible Net Worth   Fixed Assets are divided by Tangible Net Worth. Fixed Assets represent depreciated book values of building, leasehold improvements, machinery, furniture, fixtures, tools, and other physical equipment, plus land, if any, and valued at cost or appraised market value, Ordinarily, this relationship should not exceed 100 percent for a manufacturer, and 75 percent for a wholesaler or retailer.

Current Debt to Tangible Net Worth   Derived by dividing Current Debt by Tangible Net Worth. Ordinarily, a business begins to pile up trouble when this relationship exceeds 80 percent.

Total Debt to Tangible Net Worth   Obtained by dividing total current plus long term debts by Tangible Net Worth. When this relationship exceeds 100 percent, the equity of creditors in the assets of the business exceeds that of owners.

Inventory to Net Working Capital   Merchandise Inventory is divided by Net Working Capital. This is an additional measure of inventory balance. Ordinarily, the relationship should not exceed 80 percent.

Current Debt to Inventory   Dividing the Current Debt by Inventory yields yet another indication of the extent to which the business relies on funds from disposal of unsold inventories to meet its debts.

Funded Debts to Net Working Capital   Funded Debt are all long term obligations, as represented by mortgages, bonds, debentures, term loans, serial notes, and other types of liabilities maturing more than one year from statement date. This ratio is obtained by dividing Funded Debt by Net Working Capital. Analysts tend to compare Funded Debts with Net Working Capital in determining whether or not long term debts are in proper proportion. Ordinarily, this relationship should not exceed 100 percent.

Corporation, have an advantage in that the subsidiary stores tend to be very similar in merchandising philosophy. Also, the stores within such a group normally exchange figure reports with each other quite freely, usually with each store's results being identified as to source. This permits the user to make allowance for any unusual market or operating conditions when studying the figures from one of the other stores. Most chain organizations also prepare comparative reports for their stores, in some cases showing the results of individual units and in other instances showing the averages for districts, regions or the company as a whole. The amount of individual store detail shown will depend on (a) the number of stores involved, (b) the items being reported, and (c) the executive receiving the report. Some resident buying offices also

TABLE 27–1

Selected operating results for department stores with annual sales of $20–50 million in 1972, 1973, and 1974			
Item	1972	1973	1974
Net company sales—percent change			
this year/last year	10.55	12.51	6.93
Average gross sale ($)	8.46	9.03	9.66
Gross margin*	36.69	36.93	36.81
Net operating expenses*	32.77	32.61	33.13
Pre-tax earnings*	3.67	3.28	3.07

* Percent of sales. Pre-tax earnings represent income from merchandising operations adjusted for net other income or deductions but before federal income taxes.

Source: Jay Scher, *Financial and Operating Results of Department and Specialty Stores of 1974* (New York: National Retail Merchants Association, Financial Executives Division, 1975), p. 39.

collect, summarize, and report merchandising and operating figures for their clients, who also will generally be relatively similar in size and merchandising approach.

Merchants who are not part of a chain or ownership group, or of a buying office clientele, can still obtain comparative figures from many other sources. Although these sources usually publish national averages

TABLE 27–2

	Current assets to current debt (times)	Current debt to tangible net worth (percent)	Inventory to net working capital (percent)	Net profit on net sales (percent)	Net profit on net working capital (percent)
Lines of retail trade					
Clothing and furnishings,					
men's and boys'	2.83	50.5	96.4	1.79	7.69
Department stores	2.78	45.2	81.5	1.72	7.01
Discount stores	2.06	81.3	146.4	1.47	11.06
Furniture	2.68	60.0	67.3	2.16	6.73
Groceries	1.58	73.4	167.9	1.00	25.60
Hardware	3.11	39.8	87.5	1.93	10.07
Jewelers	3.22	38.0	82.8	3.50	8.15
Lumber and other					
building materials	2.80	42.6	82.6	2.93	12.87
Shoe stores	3.22	41.8	108.9	1.60	5.77
Women's ready-to-wear					
stores	2.52	52.4	80.9	1.77	7.48

Median financial ratios in selected lines of retail trade, 1974

Source: "The Ratios of Retailing," *Dun's Review* (October 1975), p. 83.

and do not identify individual company results,* many provide analyses of the data divided according to region of the country, store size, city size, or other significant grouping. Only a few such sources can be mentioned here.

The United States Department of Commerce releases information from time to time on such matters as credit, collections, and monthly sales for several types of stores. The Small Business Administration of the federal government also prepares helpful booklets containing comparative data. The NCR Corporation publishes several compilations of expenses and other operating results based on various sources. The annual *Fairchild's Financial Manual of Retail Stores* reports, among other things, capital, surplus, assets, liabilities, and 10-year comparisons of sales and profits for over 450 publicly owned retail organizations. Even more detailed data on a limited number of fields will be found in the reports released by some university bureaus of business research such as the one at Cornell University. The Cornell data, for example, cover the operating and merchandising aspects of food chains and discount department stores.

For certain purposes—such as determining whether a store is holding a desired percentage of business in a community—the releases of the U.S. Bureau of the Census are of interest. Statistics Canada provides monthly reports on retail sales by type of business (merchandise line) and province, and on department store sales and inventories,[10] as well as other periodic information of interest to merchants.

In addition to the National Retail Merchants Association, valuable data are available from many other trade associations such as the National Retail Furniture Association, the National Association of Retail Druggists, and the Retail Council of Canada. *Discount Store News, Chain Store Age, Women's Wear Daily, Supermarket News* and other trade papers are still other sources of information.

Comparative statistics are very helpful aids in evaluating a store or department's performance, but they should not be used as a substitute for careful judgment. The following points should be kept in mind: (1) The store being compared with the group average may have used different recordkeeping classifications or faced different market conditions, so that the data or the situation are not truly comparable. (2) Many published reports only show average (mean or median) numbers, and most merchants should strive to do better than average.** (3) To overcome the objection just mentioned, some associations also publish "goal" figures, usually those of the 25th or 33d percentile. In other words, figures are presented for the best one-quarter or one-third of the

---

* Financial manuals that reprint statistics from the annual reports of publicly-held corporations are an exception to this rule.

** By definition, not all can succeed at being better than average.

stores reporting that item. Unfortunately, however, these figures are often calculated item by item, which means, for example, that the "goal" figure for initial markup may have been produced by one set of stores within the survey, while the "goal" for markdowns may have come from different stores. Thus these figures will not really fit together to produce a practicable "ideal" operating statement. The National Retail Hardware Association and the Menswear Retailers of America, to mention two organizations, use a better technique in that they publish an average of the figures of the most profitable stores as well as a general average.

■ THE BUDGET

The budget is a third major tool used by retailers for effective co-ordination of activities. Setting up budgets forces the various executives of the store to plan, coordinate and integrate their activities, even before effort is expended in the actual buying and selling of merchandise. Each official in the organization is given a goal in very specific terms—some in terms of goods to be handled, others in terms of sales to be achieved, and still others in terms of advertisements to be prepared and media to be used—and a definite amount of money is allocated for the attainment of these goals. Week by week, and month by month, actual operations should be checked against the planned goals. This checking demands a constant stream of reports covering all aspects of the organization's operations: monthly profit and loss statements; weekly and monthly sales; gross margin data; expense figures; reports on purchases, stocks on hand, and goods in transit; original markups and markdowns by various departments and classifications; turnover data; and others. Deviations from the firm's desired goals are noted by the general manager, and prompt explanations are expected. Only through such action can the full benefits of the checking process be realized.

Because of detailed discussions of the budget in previous chapters, it is unnecessary to devote more attention to it here. (See Chapter 10, "Merchandise policies and budgets," and Chapter 24, "Analyzing and controlling expenses.") Its importance as a coordinating device, however, cannot be overemphasized and it is advisable for the reader to restudy these sections from this point of view.

■ RETAIL RESEARCH

Research, the fourth important tool used to coordinate activities, may be defined as the organized search for, and the analysis of, facts related to problems in the field of retailing to derive useful recommendations for improvement.

Many retailers fail to recognize the benefits that research can yield and consequently use it very little. This situation is especially acute among small and medium-sized independent stores.[11] One of the dominant reasons for the slow progress of many small stores and some larger ones is that their proprietors have been unable or unwilling to undertake research.* Clearly, one of the large retail organization's main advantages (not always fully utilized) is that it can employ qualified personnel to carry on necessary research activities.

☐ Main steps in retail research

After the problem upon which information is desired has been recognized and defined, four steps are involved in retail research; (1) gathering and summarizing the data; (2) analyzing and interpreting them; (3) preparing recommendations for improvement; and (4) following up to see that the recommendations, when endorsed by management, are actually put into effect and noting the results of their adoption.

Research departments in some large firms perform all four of these steps; in other stores, only the first two or three steps are handled there, with the general manager taking care of the fourth one. Among smaller firms the proprietor or general manager is usually closely associated with all four steps.

Retail research cannot be carried on effectively unless management is research-minded. Specifically, management must recognize the importance of developing information to aid in making decisions; it should not be so impatient for results that studies are hurried and conclusions lack full support; and it should recognize and appreciate the costs involved. Moreover, research should be conducted by qualified personnel under the direction of one whose experience and knowledge justify management's confidence in the recommendations. (See pp. 676–78 for a discussion of the research director's qualifications.) Just as essential is the raising of provocative questions for consideration by top management.

☐ The nature and scope of retail research

An understanding of retail research can best be provided by a brief examination of some of the areas to which it is currently being applied.[12]

Customer research   In recent years no subject in the field of marketing, perhaps, has received more attention from social scientists and

---

* Of course, all research does not have to be of the formal type, nor does it even have to be thought of as research by the executive. A good manager can recognize many problems and sense their solutions through day-by-day contact with the business.

practitioners than consumer motivation and behavior. Retailers need information regarding consumers as a means of improving their decisions on the goods and services to provide. And they continue to seek ways to create favorable images of their stores and merchandise as inducements to continuous patronage.

Broadly speaking, customer research refers to studies of customer demographics (age, stage in life cycle, income, location), attitudes, beliefs, buying habits, and motives. Telephone surveys, mail questionnaires, and personal interviews are often used for this purpose. Thus Federated Department Stores was able to find new growth opportunities and identify weak spots for one of its subsidiary stores by asking a 1,200 customer sample where they purchased various products—in the Federated store or in competitors'. The resulting information was worth far more than the $4,500 the telephone interviews cost.[13]

Valuable information can also be obtained from customers' credit account records and from observation of customers' shopping behavior. Commercial agencies in practically every state can supply the names and addresses of the car-owners if given the license numbers of customers' cars in the store lot or parking ramp. Retailers can analyze such data to find out whether, and why, their stores appeal to high or low income consumers, whether to young or old, to women or men, etc.[14]

Image research Image research is an important type of consumer research that asks: What do consumers think about the store? Do they consider it friendly or cold, honest or deceitful, fashionable or stodgy, expensive or moderately priced, etc.? This research almost always uses a questionnaire, although some other psychological testing techniques may also be applied. Alert storekeepers are becoming interested in image research and its acceptance is increasing. Sometimes the customers' evaluation of a store turns out to be very different from what the storeowner believes it to be.[15]

Sales projections In our discussion of the merchandise budget in Chapter 10 we noted that "the first step . . . is to plan sales." While some retailers do their sales planning "by guess and by gosh," others recognize that considerable research is necessary to establish reliable estimates. Sears, Roebuck and Company projects its sales five years in advance, correcting those forecasts from time to time as conditions warrant. About six to nine months prior to a specific selling season (for example, in January for the following fall season), this forecast is "firmed up" for that season.

Product and assortment research Research concerning the products and assortments to handle in the light of expected sales and available floor space may involve sales tests, customer studies and other information.[16] The increasing variety of products available today makes such research even more essential for profitable operation.

Commercial organizations such as SAMI (Sales Area Marketing, Inc.)

and the A.C. Nielsen Company provide "monitoring" or "store audit" services that watch the relative sales of major brands and product categories in national samples of the wholesale and retail outlets in the food, drug and hardware trades. Some of the resultant information is restricted to the manufacturers who pay for the services, but retailers can also obtain many useful analyses from these organizations.

Merchandising research   This research includes gathering, summarizing, and interpreting merchandising statistics such as markup, markdown, sales, turnover, and profit figures.

Retailers can now obtain these figures much more easily and promptly than in the past, since modern data processing methods provide internal statistics rapidly and external statistics (comparative results of other stores) are available through figure exchanges. At the same time, merchandising decisions have become more complex, so that such research is more vital than ever before. To cite one illustration, a study done for a retailer of children's clothing and toys showed that the company was using generally satisfactory pricing tactics, but was carrying too broad an inventory that included too many low turnover items.[17]

Management research   Research on the overall management of a retail organization is illustrated by a study of the responsibility and authority of all key management positions. Such a project may involve comparing the firm's organization structure with its competitors. Another example is a study of the various reports flowing to top management. One study of this type recommended that some reports be dropped or consolidated, that others be added, and that the timing and methods of preparation for others be changed.

Advertising and display research   A few illustrations will indicate the nature of this form of research. In one store the jewelry department was showing unsatisfactory sales results. Investigation revealed that unimpressive unit displays were used with most of the stock in drawers behind the counter; while a competitor, whose volume was rising, had extensive counter displays of jewelry with spotlights focused on them. Displays were improved; volume gained 15–20 percent immediately and remained at a satisfactory level. Another retailer made a specific study of direct-mail pieces to be sure the recipients were not already being reached by the firm's newspaper advertisements. And a food chain has used advertising and display research to test the effectiveness of special displays in the sale of specific food products, to determine how best to group products on the shelves of a self-service operation, to analyze a number of special promotions, and to measure the sales effectiveness of various product labels.

Sales tests are often used in advertising research—How many of the advertised items were sold? Although most retail advertising is intended to produce immediate sales of specific items, these tests are not always valid measures of advertising effectiveness. Other variables, such as product desirability, price, competition and weather can affect sales results; also some advertising effects such as store image do not show up in immediate sales results. Customer surveys, to discover who saw and who remembers the advertising, may supplement sales tests.[18]

Personnel research Personnel research studies selection, training, compensation, motivation, appraisal, and human relations problems concerning employees and executives at all levels. Research is now underway in many stores on such questions as: Are aptitude tests desirable in the selection of employees? What is the correlation between results of aptitude tests and the way employees perform under actual working conditions? Are we competitive with other stores in the city in training methods, salaries, and promotional schedules? How effective is our follow-up on transfers and training assignments?

Operating research This type of research examines the store's operating activities.* It includes such matters as store layout; building maintenance; all forms of customer service; and receiving, marking, and warehouse operations. For example, one establishment, concerned over high marking room costs found that checkers were opening each box of hosiery and similar packaged items to determine the total quantity in the shipment. The store changed to only counting the number of boxes, since any short-filled boxes would become apparent later on when the markers attached price tickets to the merchandise. This reduced costs. Supermarket operators and other retailers who handle large volumes of merchandise on low margins have been the leaders in applying operating research to storekeeping.

Systems research The increasing complexity of business, accompanied by the growing demand for prompt and accurate data upon which to base decisions, has generated the need for improved information systems based on such technological advances as the vastly improved sales registers and EDP. And the role of systems in store management is certain to expand still more in the future as advances in equipment technology continue. Systems research studies the types of information that should be collected on a regular basis for management decision-making, the way it should be tabulated and how it should be reported.[19] It also includes studies of the flow of paperwork and data in routine matters such as credit authorization and payment of vendors' bills.[20]

Communications research This research examines the store's correspondence and telephone and telegraphic communication with customers, employees and vendors for clarity, effectiveness, impact on store image, and cost. Studies may be made to see whether letters seem friendly and helpful; whether form letters or paragraphs may be sub-

---

* The term "operations research" is often applied to all forms of scientific research in retailing, particularly operational problems and customer studies. We shall use the term here in its more limited sense. Studies of warehousing, inventory control and product handling are often called "physical distribution" or "logistics" research.

stituted for individually composed messages; how often telephone callers receive busy signals; or whether long distance telephone costs are excessive.

Location research   A new store location decision or an appraisal of an existing location should be based on facts elicited by location research, as well as upon sound judgment. The techniques used in such research were discussed in Chapter 4, "Store location."

Other research   The foregoing list does not exhaust all of the subjects that are being studied by farsighted retailers, retail trade associations and others interested in the trade. Another field is public relations research (very closely akin to image research). A food store association is studying whom consumers blame for high food prices.[21] Some research directors are studying store expenses, really a form of operating research. Store security and theft control are also being studied, and a few retailers are even using, or considering, long-range weather forecasting services. Sears, Roebuck and Company employs two meteorologists for the latter purpose.[22]

Basic retail research   As indicated by the foregoing paragraphs, most of current retail research deals with day-by-day operating problems. Such research draws "upon a reservoir of existing ideas and techniques —psychological, managerial, and technological. It is directed at meeting current competition, but not through innovation; it strives to increase sales, but only through customary inducements; it looks to more efficient customer services, but only within the framework of traditional procedures."[23]

Certainly research on day-to-day operating problems is necessary and should be expanded, but even more basic research is needed. That research might study such problems as the following:

1. What are the predictable changes in consumer tastes, wants, and satisfactions deriving from the single fact that twice as many youngsters are going to college now as did a decade ago?

2. Are our stores properly organized to capture more and more consumer dollars? Do traditional department and classification breakdowns we have lived with for years parallel what the consumer thinks of when she comes in to buy? How can these classifications be flexible?

3. How much do we really know about the potentials of after-hours, Saturday night, and Sunday selling, or merchandising geared to convenience?

4. Have we really thought through the automobile revolution that General Wood (retired head, Sears, Roebuck) foresaw? Are we even now meeting more than a fraction of the customer's needs centering around the auto?

5. Have we given adequate thought to the tremendous field of services of all kinds—insurance, travel, gift shopping, perhaps using our mailing lists effectively to sell the services of other businesses?

6. Have we really learned the full lesson that the discount house taught us about how appliances can be sold more cheaply if one sells them according to clearly defined services or the lack of them?

7. Are we right in assuming that the millions of dollars we spend year after year in taking markdowns is really the only way to move slow merchandise? Would premiums, such as the soap people use, perhaps move them faster?

8. Are we keeping close watch on the fact that children are getting bigger in planning our stocks to predictably "popular" sizes? Or are we losing a lot of sales because we do not have big enough sizes—or big enough shoes, for example? Who really knows?

9. What sort of systems and equipment, designed especially for our needs, are we developing to reduce the delays, errors and monumental foul-ups in our so-called customer services, merchandise handling methods, and office procedures?

10. What are we doing to develop simpler, more effective, less costly information and communications systems, to replace the frightful ones we have to live with simply because we have failed to demonstrate how unproductive, misleading and expensive they really are?

11. Who has started an experimental store simply to try out and pilot new ideas? If not, why not?[24]

The above list was prepared more than a decade ago, yet the readers can judge how many of the questions remain unanswered, or even unstudied today. They can undoubtedly add a list of new questions that retailing should be trying to solve, such as those that arise from changes in population trends, fluctuations in economic climate, product and energy shortages, the new status of women and other groups, the impact of consumerism, variations in life-style, and technological innovations.

□ Conducting retail research

Productive research requires proper management attitudes and qualified personnel. Where can a "research-minded" management find the needed knowledgeable personnel? Shall an independent research agency be employed or shall a company build its own department? The answers largely depend on the size of the organization, the nature of the problems currently demanding executive attention, the availability of relevant information, and the research interests and capabilities of present staff members.

An independent agency or a salaried research department? It is easy to conclude that an independent agency should be employed to conduct research in small firms and a full-time, salaried research department established in larger ones. In practice, however, some large retail organizations find that the use of independent researchers reduces their costs, since their research needs are not continuous. Such a policy allows the firm to employ a research counselor who is especially well equipped to handle the particular problem to be investigated, and who has a completely objective point of view. An outsider can be thorough and make the most advisable recommendations without fear of harming close associates in the company.*

At the same time, it can be argued that a large retail organization should be conducting research at all times, and doing so through independent agencies is too expensive. Also, a full-time department can acquire a vast amount of information about the firm for which it is working—information on policies, clientele, and competitors—which enables it to do its work more rapidly and with less bother to the executives of the firm.

The advantages of continuous research are so great that many large retailers employ full-time salaried research directors. Special research jobs requiring skills that the director or the staff do not possess, or investigations that directly concern the job security of the director's close friends, however, are usually assigned to an independent agency.**

Qualifications of the research director   The research director, whether independent or a full-time employee, needs to be well trained in the principles and methods of research and to have had experience both in research and (preferably) in retailing. The recommendations of someone who lacks retail experience are likely to be considered "theoretical"; and they probably will be less sound than those a more experienced person would make. The director should be able to win the confidence and cooperation of the firm's executives, be objective and thorough in analyzing and interpreting data, understand the current subjects requiring practical research in the company, and have the capacity to raise pertinent questions regarding future plans. Finally, the abilities to write and to present orally short, convincing reports are essential.

The research report   The report made to management should be concise and yet provide all the data needed for proper interpretation of the findings. Unfamiliar terminology should be avoided. Effective organization and presentation are necessary to spotlight the important conclusions. Many executives are not "figure-minded," and dislike detailed statistics. They are primarily interested in the study's results, their relationship to the problem at hand, and the reasons for and the recommendations concerning future action. These facts should guide the report writer.

---

* One very successful retail organization reports to the authors that a shift from a company-owned to an independent research organization resulted in uncovering many facts not previously known. Of course, much depends on the quality of the outside researcher; some companies have discovered to their sorrow that the methods of some market researchers leave much to be desired.

** Some firms assign particular problems demanding study to young college trainees in their organizations. Such a plan enables the employee to acquire a vast amount of information about the company in a short time, gives the company an objective analysis of the problem, and provides an opportunity for the employee to demonstrate ability to organize and present findings effectively.

Research assignments The research director in the large store should both report to and be considered an "arm" of the chief executive, by assisting the latter in coordinating store activities. Thus, a large number of the projects handled by the research department will originate with the general manager. But a research director who wins the confidence of the various department heads will receive many requests for help from those executives. The merchandise manager needs assistance in evaluating sales-recording equipment to control inventories in various departments. The operating manager is concerned with the causes of an increase in customers' returns of merchandise. The sales manager of the automotive accessory chain wants to know how to get better cooperation from store managers in carrying out suggestions from headquarters.

Some firms also allow or encourage the research director to originate many projects subject to the general manager's approval. This is now being done to an increasing degree. But if this practice is followed, the research director must be a person of broad background in retailing and familiar with current developments in the field.

■ KEEPING "CURRENT"

As suggested early in this chapter, all retailers, regardless of size, should keep abreast of changing conditions and adapt their policies and practices to these changes. This two-fold obligation is difficult to fulfill. How, then, does the retailer learn about current developments and plan appropriate adjustments?

Small retailers secure this knowledge through the efforts of the proprietor or chief assistant. A vast amount of information can be acquired by watching competitive developments in the immediate vicinity; reading trade papers; traveling; attending conventions; and talking with sales representatives, manufacturers, and competitors. Trade associations can provide invaluable help.

Even among large organizations, executives rely heavily upon these same sources, although in a minority of firms they are supplemented in various ways. The director of research may be expected to watch and report on all significant developments. The firm may subscribe to advisory services that forecast manufacturers' inventories, the business situation, or wholesale and retail prices. Or it may employ an economist to keep executives informed regarding external changes and to suggest what might be done in the light of these conditions. This sort of staff specialist, who is free of day-to-day operations, can have a broad perspective and is not "too close to the trees to see the forest."

Forecasting, whether so recognized or not, is an implicit or explicit element of budgeting and of all retailing decision-making. A decision to leave policies unchanged is really a forecast that the external situation will not change; policy revisions always rest on some view of the future. Retailers should, and often do, use many types of information in making those forecasts.

■ EXECUTIVE LEADERSHIP IN RETAILING

A supply of current information and the coordination tools we have discussed (standards, comparative figures, budgets and research) alone will not produce a successful retail business. As we have noted before, some one individual, or a small group of chief executives, must serve as leaders, to be "sparkplugs" or energizers as well as coordinators of the organization.

There is no magic formula, no "one sure-fire trick," for successful leadership in retailing. Much depends on the personality of the leader and the personalities of the other people in the organization. Some people respond best to very tight control, others will do their best work when given considerable freedom to exercise initiative without close supervision. Similarly, some executives are quite informal by nature, and can easily establish relationships with subordinates in a casual but effective manner. Others are more formal by nature, and only seem silly or awkward if they pretend to be "one of the gang." Yet all capable business leaders, and particularly those in retailing, seem to have some characteristics in common.

☐ Leadership characteristics

Willingness to assume responsibility The chief executive(s) must accept the responsibility for making decisions and seeing that they are implemented. This does not imply an unwillingness to hear all points of view and to consider all sides of a question. Moreover, a wise senior executive will not unnecessarily interfere with a subordinate's decision, even while perhaps silently disagreeing, if the decision is not a critical one for the department or the firm, and if such interference will sap the subordinate's initiative. But a leader is prepared to act when necessary or advisable.

Checks up It has been said that Queen Victoria of England never looked back when sitting down; she simply expected that someone would place a chair underneath her. This apparently worked for the Queen, but retail executives learn to be less confident. Things can go wrong, unforeseen developments occur, and instructions are not always implemented. The successful leader follows up on all plans and activities to see how well things are going. The president of a very prosperous retail business, with annual volume over $250 million, receives and reads sales reports from the store's EDP system three times a day, even interrupting important meetings for that purpose. These extremely frequent reports satisfy a genuine desire for information; they also let the entire organization know that the president is interested in what is happening.

Plans ahead The competent executive does not merely observe current conditions and react to changes. It is essential to anticipate changes (hence the importance of research and forecasting), to plan ahead, and wherever possible to initiate change. This requires a receptivity to change and willingness to accept new methods when a critical evaluation indicates their desirability. Truly outstanding merchants tend to have developed an ability to watch current details (perhaps in a selective manner) without losing sight of "the big picture." Stanley J. Goodman, chairman of May Department Stores, calls this "bifocal management, focused on both the near and the far view."[25]

Fairness Regardless of personal style or method of working, the leader who wants to build an effective organization must be fair and equitable in dealing with the members of that organization, and must be perceived as being fair.

Communicates People have varying desires for information and news about their organization. The chief executive must keep many things confidential, in part because some information is received in confidence, and because some premature statements might stir up needless worries or rumors. Senior officials of large firms must be very careful in circulating information, even internally, that might affect the price of the company's stock or that might have certain antiunion implications. But on the whole, most people cannot feel that they are part of an organization if they are not informed of the developments that affect their business lives. Similarly, the chief executive(s) need a constant flow of data, information and opinions from the entire organization. Consequently, management must constantly strive to establish good channels of communication throughout the entire firm.

□ Management by objectives

A management style that holds much promise for success is management by objectives (MBO). It is a participative process in which executives and specialists at all levels prepare their own detailed job descriptions, *in cooperation and consultation with their supervisors,* agree on standards and set objectives. Then their performance is subject to quarterly review and annual appraisal.[26]

Standards, which have already been discussed, are continuous measures that often can provide daily, weekly or monthly indications of performance. Objectives are annual or semi-annual targets. Usually the two are set at different levels of accomplishment, one representing satisfactory work while the other constitutes very superior to excellent achievement. Lipmans, a department store in Portland, Oregon, sets the standard at good performance, while accomplishing the objective is much more challenging.[27] O'Neills, an Akron, Ohio, store calls the standard "the base line of excellence" to be achieved over time and then sets objectives as steps toward reaching that level.[28]

Sound objectives meet the following tests:

1. The people responsible for carrying out the objectives have had a role in setting them.
2. Senior management has participated in setting the objectives.
3. The objectives have some 'reach' [since] many people work better when there is a reasonable challenge.
4. The objectives are realistic in light of internal and external environmental constraints and trends.
5. The objectives in different parts of the company have been examined to see if they are mutually consistent.
6. The objectives are contemporary [based on recognition of the fact] that they must be updated and revised [from time to time].
7. The key objectives are stated simply [to insure their] being borne in mind constantly by people responsible for carrying them out.
8. The objectives are innovative [especially in periods of rapid change] such as we are experiencing today.[29]

Some experts feel that MBO has been widely discussed, but seldom actually implemented.[30] Yet the experience of the two stores mentioned and others illustrates successful use. But an author who has looked at the application of MBO to the retail trade says: "There must be a total company commitment to the new way of life which is planning, organizing, directing, controlling and appraising results."[31]

☐ Social responsibility of retailing management

The responsibilities of modern retailing management go far beyond the emphasis placed on "management by objectives." They should (and to an increasing extent do) also encompass a strong sense of social responsibility and community involvement. As one leading retailer points out, merchants must not merely serve as figureheads on committees but must be both leaders and active in "serving in the middle ranks of important community programs."[32] All retailers, both large and small, face the task a well-known management scholar has outlined for corporation in our society.

... there exists a powerful move to seek continued improvement in the quality of life for the entire population. All institutions, including business firms are expected to participate in achieving this end. . . . The great challenge ahead for managers of corporations is to establish policies and programs which will pursue both economic and social goals which will be mutually supportive.[33]

Abundant opportunities exist for retailing manifestations of social responsibility. To mention a few: employment and training of minority groups to alleviate unemployment and reduce the number of welfare recipients; providing management assistance to minority businesses, particularly in their initial operations; furnishing advice and counsel on consumer credit uses and abuses; and serving on community boards that seek solutions for urban and suburban problems.

Steps that some retailers have taken in this direction include (1) the development and implementation of affirmative action training and employment programs for women, minority, handicapped and disadvantaged workers over and beyond minimum legal requirements;[34] (2) service, either before or after retirement, as a voluntary consultant to local or overseas small business groups, minority enterprises, and public agencies;[35] (3) deep involvement in local charitable, educational, cultural, and community improvement organizations; and (4) the creation of product testing, supplier control, advertising review, complaint handling, and other procedures that meet consumeristic objectives.[36] Such programs may in the long run, be quite compatible with financial objectives. "The social action of a corporation *can* improve image and contribute to favorable economic results."[37]

In closing our discussion of the social responsibilities of business, the following editorial comments by *Business Week* appear appropriate:

While the effectiveness of [businessmen's] efforts cannot yet be measured, it is clear that the contribution of business to such critical areas as employment of minorities, air and water pollution, and urban rehabilitation has been enormous. . . .

At the same time, it is now clear that far too much was expected—far to fast—by many of those who rallied business to take on new responsibilities in the critical areas. These are not simple problems and they do not yield to simple, cheap solutions. . . . Involvement with the great social problems of our times is not an ordinary business proposition . . . race relations, urban decay, and environmental deterioration are threats to the whole structure of U.S. society, including the U.S. business community. To deal with these problems, the nation must draw on the resources and skills of business. And business has no choice but to make its resources and skills available. . . .[38]

■ REVIEW AND DISCUSSION QUESTIONS

1 Why is the coordination function so important? If a retailing company, even a large one, has competent middle-level executives and supervisors, couldn't they handle all problems satisfactorily, either individually or as a group? Explain.

2 Discuss the major predicted changes in the economic, social, legal, and technical environment that may affect retailing in the next 20 years, and their likely effects upon retailing.

3 (a) How would you set standards in a retail business? Suggest the sources that could be used to provide the standards (or the information needed to set those standards. (b) What are some of the limitations of those sources and consequently what adjustments might they require for use in a particular store?

4 (a) Describe several sales standards. Why should a merchant bother with any other sales standard than total sales? (b) Explain three other types of standards.

5 (a) Examine and report upon the comparative information contained in a trade association or similar report on retail operating, merchandising and financial results in a major line of retail trade. (The annual *M.O.R.* and *F.O.R.* reports issued by the Financial Executives Division of the National Retail Merchants Association are examples of such publications. They and others may be available in your library or from a cooperative local retailer.) (b) How, as a merchant, might you use such information? What are its limitations? Discuss.

6 Explain precisely how management may use the budget as a coordinating tool.

7 (a) Select one retailing function or activity, such as site selection, advertising, store operations or personnel, and give several illustrations of how research might be used to help solve problems in that aspect of the business. (b) Drawing on the examples cited in the text, and other retail research applications with which you may be familiar, discuss the statement: "Research is simply a matter of going out and asking consumers what, where, and why they buy the products they do."

8 What are the relative advantages and disadvantages of using an internal research department versus using an outside research agency?

9 How can the proprietor of a small or medium-sized retail business "keep current" about present and future developments in the trade?

10 Explain concisely what you consider to be some of the major characteristics of a good leader.

11 Describe "management by objectives" as practiced in retailing. Be sure to include its principal elements.

12 Do retailers have any social responsibilities beyond observing the law, paying their bills and keeping their businesses profitable enough to continue in operation? If so, what are the other responsibilities? Discuss.

■ NOTES AND REFERENCES

1 Samuel Feinberg, "Widened Marketing Services Vital to Profitable Future," *Women's Wear Daily*, May 23, 1972, p. 16; E. B. Weiss, "The Coming Marketing Era in Department Store Retailing," *Stores*, January 1975, p. 40.

2 Samuel Feinberg, "Marketing Has to Fill Research, Advertising Gaps," *Women's Wear Daily*, January 11, 1973, p. 14; "Retail Management: Red Owl Listens to the Consumer," *Supermarket News*, July 16, 1974, pp. 6, 8.

3 "This Peacock Won't Be Tomorrow's Feather Duster," *Forbes*, June 15, 1975, p. 26.

4 "The Dangers of 100%," *Retailing Today*, November 1974, p. 2.

5 *Dun's Review* annually publishes fourteen key financial averages

for various types of retail business, usually in its September or October issue. These ratios are described in Figure 27–1 and are illustrated in Table 27–2. *See also* Richard Sanzo, *Ratio Analysis for Small Business* (Washington, D.C.: U.S. Government Printing Office, 1970).

6 J. J. Corson and G. A. Steiner, *Measuring Business's Social Performance: The Corporate Social Audit* (New York: Committee for Economic Development, 1974), p. 37.

7 Dayton-Hudson Corporation, *Contributions for Community Improvements for the Year of —*, annual.

8 See: "What Does 'M.O.R.' Mean?" *Retailing Today*, January 1973, pp. 1–2.

9 *Management Report—Retail Hardware Store 1974 Financial Operating Results* (Indianapolis: National Retail Hardware Association, 1975), p. 6.

10 Published in the *Canadian Statistical Review*.

11 For suggestions on the conduct of research in small firms, see H. M. Anderson, "Managing Applied Research in a Small Company," *Management Review*, January 1970, pp. 31–35.

12 Some of the illustrations were prepared by Robert Arkell and are used here with his permission. For other classifications of research which are important, see Frank Mayans, "Research in Retailing," *Retail Control*, May 1966, pp. 33–44; and "Retailers Only Recently Began to Research Market," *Marketing News*, June 15, 1973, p. 12.

13 Barry Miller, "How Federated Measures Performance against Competition," *Stores*, June 1976, p. 27.

14 For an example, *see* "Computer Gives Carson's the Complete Customer," *Women's Wear Daily*, March 11, 1974, p. 21.

15 See "Store Image Special Issue," *Journal of Retailing*, vol. 50 (Winter 1974–75).

16 Ronald C. Curhan, *On the Conduct of In-Store Field Experiments*, Preliminary Research Report (Cambridge, Mass.: Marketing Science Institute, 1975).

17 J. L. Schlacter and J. E. Withers, "Analysis of a Retail Firm's Marketing Strategy Through the Use of a 'Return on Investment Model,'" *Retail Control*, December 1973, pp. 2–32.

18 Laurence W. Jacobs, *Advertising and Promotion for Modern Retailing* (Glenview, Ill.: Scott, Foresman & Co., 1972), Chapter 8; Shirley F. Milton, *Advertising for Modern Retailers* (New York: Fairchild Publications, Inc., 1974), pp. 214–21.

19 *See* M. S. Moyer, "Market Intelligence for Modern Retailers," *California Management Review*, vol. 14 (Summer 1972) for a discussion of one important type of information system.

20 *See* "The Computer: A Helpful Partner in Achieving Efficiency," *Hardware Retailing*, October 1974, pp. 53–78, for a discussion of how systems research and data processing systems are being used within voluntary organizations to help small and medium-sized merchants handle both routine and major decisions.

21 Speech of William R. Bishop, Jr., Vice President, Super Market Institute, to the Retail Research Society, New York, May 29, 1975.

22 "Everybody Talks About the Weather," *Retailing Today*, November 1972, p. 1; "Can You Plan for Rain?" *Chain Store Age* (general merchandise edition), March 1975, p. 24.

23 H. F. Clark and H. S. Sloan, quoted by Samuel Feinberg, "From Where I Sit," *Women's Wear Daily*, February 14, 1962, p. 4.

24 H. S. Landsman, quoted in Samuel Feinberg, "From Where I Sit," *Women's Wear Daily*, February 9, 1966, p. 12.

25 "Raising the Image of Business," *Stores*, March 1974, p. 11.

26 The MBO concept was developed by G. S. Odiorne. See his *Management by Objectives* (New York: Pitman Publishing Co., 1965) and *Management Decisions by Objectives* (Englewood Cliffs, N.J.: Prentice-Hall, Inc., 1969).

27 C. R. Rogers, "Management by Objectives and Participative Management," *Retail Control*, December 1975, p. 23.

28 Company manual.

29 C. H. Granger, "How to Set Company Objectives," *Management Review*, July 1970, pp. 3–5.

30 Stephen Singular, "Has MBO Failed?" *MBA*, October 1975, pp. 47–50.

31 Claire Maluso, *Management By Objectives Tailored for the Men's Wear Retailing Industry* (Washington, D.C.: Menswear Retailers of America, 1975), p. 82.

32 "NRMA Convention: Lazarus to Retailers: Serve Community," *Women's Wear Daily*, January 10, 1974, p. 13.

33 George A. Steiner, "Institutionalizing Corporate Social Decisions," *Business Horizons*, vol. 19 (December 1975), p. 18.

34 For a discussion of the status of minority recruitment and training programs in food retailing see: "Minority Hiring: Quiet Progress or Benign Neglect?" *Supermarket News*, September 9, 1974, pp. 1, 32–33.

35 Some examples are cited in Isidore Barmash, "Executives Retire to Work," *New York Times*, October 18, 1970, pp. F1–F2; and Samuel Feinberg, "Retired Executives SCORE as Small Business Counselors," *Women's Wear Daily*, May 15, 1973, p. 38.

36 Larry J. Rosenberg, "Retailers' Response to Consumerism," *Business Horizons*, vol. 19 (October 1975), pp. 37–44. Also see Marcus Alexis and Clyde M. Smith, "Marketing and the Inner City Consumer," *Journal of Contemporary Business*, vol. 2 (Autumn 1973), pp. 45–80; and "Special Issue on Consumerism," *Journal of Retailing*, vol. 48 (Winter 1972–73).

37 M. C. Burke and L. L. Berry, "Do Social Actions of a Corporation Influence Store Image and Profits?" *Journal of Retailing*, vol. 50 (Winter 1974–75), p. 70.

38 November 1, 1969, p. 136. *See also* the special report, "The War That Business Must Win," pp. 63–74.

INDEXES

NAME INDEX

A

Abercrombie and Fitch, 488
Abott, Murray S., 232, 393
Abraham and Straus, 194 n
Abrahamson, Royce, 418
Adams, K. A., 323
Aiken, Eric, 35
Alden, J. S., 655
Aldens, Inc., 478
Alderson, Wroe, 56, 418, 472
Alexander, Alfred, 654, 656
Alexis, Marcus, 685
Allemand, J.-P., 300
Allied Stores Corporation, 20, 109, 194, 317–18, 509, 666
Allied Supermarkets, Inc., 227
Amalgamated Meat Cutters and Butcher Workers of North America, 252
American Arbitration Association, 346
American Express, 549, 551
American Marketing Association, 472
American Stores, 20
Anderson, H. M., 684
Andreasen, A. R., 419
Andrus, R. R., 653
Applebaum, William, 96, 119
Arkell, Robert, 684
Arlen Realty and Development Corporation, 13, 63
Aspley, J. C., 510

Associated Dry Goods Corporation, 12–13, 318–19, 666–67
Avis, 27
Avon Products, Inc., 30
Ayr-Way discount stores, 13

B

Backman, Jules, 418
Baker, R. M., Jr., 511
Bamberger's, 130
Bank of America, 66
BankAmericard System, 540, 550–51
Barmash, Isidore, 685
Barrett, J. S., 656
Basco, Inc., 25
Bass, F. M., 419
Bata, Ltd., 30
Bauer, Eddie, 405
Baumgartner, Melvin L., 654
Baylis, George, 282
Bean, L. L., 301
Beasley, Norman, 56
Becker, Arnold, 616
Belden, Donald L., 300
Bell, James E., 33
Bellenger, Danny, 300
Ben Franklin Stores, 390, 471
Beneficial Corporation, 572
Berens, John S., 323
Bergdorf-Goodman, 52, 194 n

Bergerson, L. E., 255
Berkovin, Beth, 33
Berkwitt, G. J., 56
Berlew, D. E., 56
Bernstein, Joseph E., 656
Bernstein, Louis M., 88
Berrin, Elliot R., 656
Berry, L. L., 685
Best Products Company, 25
Bird, A. Donald, 393
Bishop, William R., Jr., 684
Blackler, W. R., 510
Blackwell, R. D., 511
Bliven, Bruce, Jr., 323
Bloomingdale's, 124, 130, 194 n, 255
Blue, Larry, 282
Boddewyn, J. J., 35, 439
Bogart, Leo, 35
Boggess, William P., 572
Bolen, W. H., 539
Bon Marche, 194 n, 317
Bond, R. C., 205
Bond Stores, Inc., 309
Bonino, J. A., 34
Bonwit Teller, 117, 458
Booker, Robert, 393
Boone, Louis E., 34, 440
Booth, Ken, 323
Boroson, Warren, 417
Boston Store, 194 n
Bouton, Donald, 232
Boze, Carroll W., 655
Brandt, W. K., 574
Braun, Harvey, 88
Braun, Richard J., 87
Brenninkmeyer, C. & A., 30
Bride's Showcase International, Inc., 27
Brill, Jack, 393
British American Tobacco Company, 30
Broadway Department Store, 109
Brogan, James A., 656
Brown, E. J., 206
Brown, F. E., 417
Brown, M. M., 510
Brown, R. A., 472
Browne, Joy, 417
Brownell, B. A., 121
Brownyard, Bruce, 654
Brunner, J. A., 98 n
Bue, Nancy L., 473, 538
Bullock's, Inc., 126, 128, 145
Bullocks-Magnin Co., 194 n
Bunne, Verne A., 655
Burch, David L., 34
Burchfield, D. V., 145
Burke, M. C., 685
Burlington Mills, 468
Burnick, Stanley I., 88
Burnside, Frank, 369
Business Week, 682
Buzzell, R. D., 36

C

Cady, John F., 419, 440
Canadian Anti-Inflation Board, 14
Canadian Department of Consumer and
    Corporate Affairs, 464
Canadian Food Price Review Board, 13
Canadian Safeway, 21
Carey, Marlene A., 87–88
Carlson, David, 121
Carlson, Mary R. S., 121
Carman, James, 440
Carman, J. C., 323
Carman, James M., 34, 348, 419, 474
Carrefour Company, 26
Carroll, Louis, 348
Carruth, Eleanore, 206
Carson Pirie Scott & Co., 230, 478
Carter-Hawley-Hale Stores, Inc., 30, 194
Carusone, P. S., 120
Cash, R. Patrick, 281–82, 300, 323, 369, 439
Cassady, Ralph, Jr., 418
Casual Corner Associates, 308
Cavenham, Ltd., 30
Chain Store Age, 29, 669
Chain Store Age, Drug Store Edition, 613
Chargex, 550
Chevalier, Michael, 474
Chicago, 458
Chisholm, Robert F., 206
Christian, W. J., 656
Cities Stores Company, 194
City Products, 20
Clancy, Daniel T., 654–55
Clark, Carlos B., 604
Clark, H. F., 684
Coca Cola Company, 483
Coen, R. J., 473
Cohen, Dorothy, 494
Coleman, Thomas E., 417
Collins, Dorothy, 34
Colonial Stores, Inc., 159, 197–98
Commercial Crimes Branch of Royal Cana-
    dian Mounted Police, 644
Consumer Distributing Company of To-
    ronto, 25
Consumer Product Safety Commission, 298
Cook, H. R., 473
Cope, K. W., 281
Corbman, Bernard P., 282
Corkley, Carrell B., 231
Cornell University, 669
Corson, J. J., 684
Cort, S. G., 36
Cotham, James C., III, 231, 512
Cox, Eli P., 120
Cox, Jack, 510
Cox, K. K., 170
Cox, Reavis, 418
Crawford, L. C., 231
Cremer, Richard, 572

Cumming, J. C., 494
Curhan, Ronald C., 170, 684
Curry, Jil, 300
Curtis, Bob, 539, 640, 653–56

D

Daggett, R. V., 230
B. Dalton, bookshop chain, 29
Dana, Margaret, 56
Daniels, Alfred H., 300
Darden, William R., 300
Dardis, Rachel, 418
Dash, Earl, 256
Dauer, Ernest A., 571
Davenport, J. W., Jr., 511
Davidowitz, Howard L., 267
Day, G. S., 574
Dayton Hudson Corp., 20, 29, 194, 531
Dayton's, 74, 76, 78, 109, 488
Dennison Manufacturing Company, 374, 391
Dermer, Jerry D., 281
de Somogyi, Jan, 230
Deutscher, T., 574
Dewhurst, Frederic J., 537
Dias, Robert M., 88
Dickinson, Roger, 35, 595
Dickson, J. P., 474
Diners' Club, 549
Discount Merchandiser, 23, 614
Discount Store News, 669
Doktor's Pet Centers, 27
Dollar General Stores, 401
Dominion Stores Ltd., 21
Donaldson's, 194 n, 317
Donnelly, J. R., 572
Drew-Bear, Robert, 36, 88, 206
Dubiusky, P. M., 656
Duncan, C. B., 572
Dunkelberg, William C., 573
Dun's Review, 665
Durkin, T. A., 574

E

Earle, Wendell, 36, 418, 473, 599, 602
T. Eaton Company, Ltd., 21, 116, 478
Jack Eckard Corp., 63
Edison Brothers Stores, Inc., 507
Edwards, C. M., Jr., 472
Edwards, J. D., 594
Eilenberg, Howard, 282, 323
Eilers, B. A., 474
Eisman, Esther, 323
El-Dirghami, Amin, 653
Elliott, Burton, 36
Emporium, The, 245, 479
Emporium-Capwell Company, 141, 154, 194 n
Engel, J. F., 511
Engen, Gunnar, 255
England, Wilbur B., 205

Etzel, M. J., 572
Evanson, R. V., 170

F

Fairchild's Financial Manual of Retail Stores reports, 669
Fairlane development, 110–11
Family Service Association of America, 566
Famous-Barr Co., 74–76, 157, 169, 446, 520
Faria, Anthony J., 539, 654–55
Federated Department Stores, 20, 54, 63, 125, 194, 661, 666, 672
Feinberg, Samuel, 56, 87–88, 120, 145, 205, 230, 232, 255–56, 282, 494, 511–12, 655, 683–85
Fetterman, Elsie, 301
William Filene's Sons Company, 205, 425
Fingerhut Corp., 63
First National Stores, 430
Fisher, W. A., 56
Fleisher, David L., 634
Food Fair Properties, Inc., 109
Food Fair Stores, 20, 109
Forecast Shop, 134
Fox, Harland, 87
Fram, E. H., 56
Frank, Hugo, 369
Frank, R. F., 170
Friedlander, J. S., 299, 301, 347
Fry, J. N., 474
Fryburger, Vernon, 347, 473–74
Fulmer, Robert M., 88
Fulweiler, John H., 144, 474, 656
Furash, Richard D., 230, 656

G

Gable, Myron, 231
Gabor, Andre, 419
Gaines, L. A., 120
Gamble Development Co., 109
Gamble-Skogmo, Inc., 104, 109, 124
Gayfer's, 194 n
Geiss, Dorothy E., 388
Geller, Irving, 634
Gemco Discount Store, 133, 154
General Electric Company, 468, 628
General Instrument Corporation, 629
Georgoff, David M., 419
Gergay, Peter A., 655
German, Gene A., 281, 300, 324
Geuris, M. D., 653
Giant Food, 203
Giddings-Jenny, Inc., 107
Gillett, P. L., 493
Gimbel Brothers, Inc., 119
Gimbels, 30, 255
Ginther, Steve, 88
Globe Shopping City, 313
Gold, Annalee, 474, 512
Goldblatt, Inc., 148 n
Golden, L. S., 145

Goldenberg, S., 571
Goldstucker, J. L., 87
Goldwaters, 263
Goodman, Larry, 473
Goodman, Stanley J., 680
Goodnow, J. D., 324
Gordon, Ben, 37, 170, 206
Gorgano, Ronald, 145
Gorman, Walter P., 35
Gorse, Etienne, 493
Gottman, Jean, 120
Goudchaux's branch store, 124
Gould, R. E., 573
Grabner, J. R., 300, 347
Graham, Art, 538
Grand Union, 30
Granfield, Michael, 37, 511
Granger, C. H., 684
Granger, C. W. J., 419
W. T. Grant Company, 18
Great Atlantic & Pacific Tea Company
   (A&P), 18, 20, 404 n
Green, P. E., 56
Greer, Douglas F., 573
Grether, E. T., 474, 493
Griffin, Robert, 654
Griffin, Roger K., 653
Grinager, Robert M., 573
Groeneveld, Leonard, 56
Gross, Wayne W., 281

H

Hackney, Ellen, 474, 538
Hadden, Jeffrey K., 120
Hammond, John, 595
Haring, A. R., 510–11
Harpers Bazaar, 458
Paul Harris Stores, 640
Hartley, Robert F., 231
Harvey, Michael, 119
Harwell, E. M., 171
Haugh, Louis J., 472–73
Hauser, P. M., 120
Hayghe, Howard, 34
Hearn, Robert, 439
Hedges, Janice N., 34
Hemphill, Charles F., Jr., 655
Hermanson, R. H., 594
Hertz, 27
Hirschler, F. S., 418
Hobbies, 458
Holiday Inns of America, Inc., 27
Hollander, S. C:, 35, 37, 439–40, 538
Holloway, Robert J., 419
Holmes, Arthur W., 655
Holt, Renfrew and Co., 194 n
Holyoak, Arlene, 572
Homart Development Co., 109
Hopke, William E., 88
House of Fraser, 30

House of Nine, 27
Household Finance Company, 572
Howe, E. D., 230
Hudson, J. L., 145, 290, 478, 604
Hudson's Bay Co., 21
Huff, D. L., 282
Huisien, D. R., 634
Hunt, Shelby, 87
Hunt, Willard, 36, 418, 473, 599, 602
Hypermarché Laval, 26

I

IBM Data Processing Division, 145
IBM Retail Credit Management System,
   558
Interbank (Master Charge) System, 550
International Executive Service Corps, 48
International House of Pancakes, 27
Isakson, H. R., 440
ISR Newsletter, 34
Israel, Lawrence J., 36

J

Jabenis, Elaine, 206, 300
Jackson, Terence, 88
Jacobs, Laurence W., 472, 684
Jacobson's, Inc., 449
Jancer, Allen R., 231
Jarnow, Jeannette A., 300
Jensen, F. E., 439
Jewel, 200
Jewel Companies, 20, 79, 256
Jewel Supermarkets, 60
Jewelco, Inc., 25
Johnson, James C., 34, 440
Johnson, R. L., 573
Johnson, Robert W., 88, 573
Jolson, Marvin A., 34, 510
Jones, 194 n
Jones, Colin N., 654
Jordan-Marsh Co., 126, 142, 194 n, 317, 399
Joske's, 194 n, 304
Jucius, Michael J., 230
Judelle, Beatrice, 300
Jupiter discount houses, 80

K

Kahn, Robert, 87
Kaiser, Robert H., 537
Kakalik, James S., 654
Katz, R. L., 56
Kaufmann's, 134, 153
Keane, Thomas J., 655
Kegerreis, R. J., 511
Kelley, R. F., 282
Kelley, William T., 493
Kennedy, John F., 483
Kentucky Fried Chicken Corp., 27
Kerin, R. A., 119
Kilbourne, W. E., 440

Killian, Ray A., 230
Kimball Systems, Inc., 384, 386
Kinberg, Y., 439
King, C. W., 419
King's Supermarket, 161
Kleimenhagen, A. K., 474
S. Klein department store, 165
Kleppner, Otto, 461, 474
K-Marts discount stores, 7, 22, 30, 80, 113,
    120
Knox, Robert L., 440
Kohl Corporation, 30
Kohlik, George, 231, 572–74
Koontz, Harold, 88
E. J. Korvette, Inc., 113–14
Koshetz, Herbert, 324, 494
Kotzman, J. A., 170
Kozoll, Charles E., 231
Kreiser, Russo G., 440
Krieger, Murray F., 282, 300
Krieger, Raymond B., 256
Kroger Company, 20, 79, 197, 200
Krone, Paul R., 87
Kurtz, D. L., 34

L

Landor, Walter, 493
Landsman, H. S., 684
Langeard, Eric, 36
Laws, Dwayne, 119
Lazarus, Arlie, 439
Lazarus, Ralph, 54
F. R. Lazarus and Company, 130 n
Leathan, J. T., 146
Lechmere discount chain, 29
Leeds, Theodore R., 300
Leeds, T. W., 281, 324
Leemaster, Lawrence, 511
Leesberg, D. G., 474
Leininger, Sheryl, 655
Lev, Joseph A., 369
Levitz Furniture Corporation, 25
Lewis, Arthur M., 87
Lifshey, Earl, 493–94
Lightfoot, John B., Jr., 300
Lightfoot, John R., 282
Lincoln, Gregory, 473
Lindberg, George W., 655
Lion, 194 n
Lipmans, 680
Lit Brothers, 127, 132
Liu, Ben-chieh, 119
Loblaw, Inc., 30
Logan, W. B., 510
Long's Drugstores, 63, 129–30, 155
Lord & Taylor, 117, 128
Lowe's Companies, Inc., 241, 493
Lucky Stores, Inc., 20, 133, 154, 211, 281

Lynch, Edith M., 231, 256, 654
Lynn, R. A., 347

M

McAlpin's, 194 n
Thom McAn Shoe Company, 309
McCabe, R. W., 94 n
McCarthy, E. J., 33, 120, 474, 573
McClelland, W. G., 439
McCord, Bird, 231
McCreery, James, 56
McCrory Corporation, 13
McDonald, John, 393
MacDonald's, 27
McDonald's Corporation, 240
McDougal, G. H., 474
McFarland, Dalton E., 205
McKesson & Robbins'Economost, 579
McMahan, H. W., 473
McNair, M. P., 595
R. H. Macy and Company, 129–30, 136,
    166, 489, 501, 534
Macy's (California), 343, 623
Macy's of San Francisco, 488
Mademoiselle, 488
I. Magnin and Co., 403, 458, 479
Maledon, E. N., Jr., 573
Mallen, Bruce, 35
Maluso, Claire, 685
Marcor, Inc., 20
Margulies, W. P., 493
Marks & Spencer, Ltd., 30
Marshall Field & Co., 117, 127–28, 228, 403,
    466, 501, 533
Marsteller, Inc., 264
Martin, Claude, 283
Martin, Claude R., Jr., 299
Martin, William W., 369
Mason, J., 98 n
Mason, J. Barry, 35, 119, 300, 347
Masotti, Louis H., 120
Massy, W. F., 170
Master Charge, 540, 550–51
Mattheiss, T. H., 231
Matwes, George J., 656
Matwes, Helen, 656
Mauger, E. M., 170
Maurizi, Alex R., 440
May, E. G., 595
May Company, 360, 488
May Department Stores, Inc., 20, 109, 680
May Realty and Investment Company, 109
Mayans, Frank, 684
Mayer, Morris L., 35, 347
Mayer, Terry, 494
Mazur, Paul M., 184–85, 205
Mazze, Edward M., 440
MBA, 87
Mechanix Illustrated, 458
Meijer, Inc., 26

Melnick, E. L., 439
Menswear Retailers of America, 613, 670
Mercantile Stores Company, 194
Meredith, A. A., 439
Messenger, Carol, 654–55
Methvin, E. H., 300
Meyer, W. G., 231
Midas Muffler, 27
Miller, Barry, 684
Miller, F. L., 418
Milton, Shirley F., 684
Mitchell, W. N., 56, 146
Miyashita, S., 440
Moeser, D. E., 348
Monarch Marking Systems, Inc., 385
Monroe, Kent B., 417, 419
Moolman, Val, 654
Morano, R. A., 230
Moses, Louis, 255
Moskowitz, Milton, 256
Moyer, M. S., 634, 684
MSI Data Corporation, 357
Muczyk, J. P., 231
Mueller, R. R., 419
Murphy, G. C., 80

N

National Association of Retail Druggists, 456, 669
National Bureau of Standards, 380
National Business Council for Consumer Affairs, 530
National Cash Register Company, 407, 498–99, 628
National Commission on Food Marketing, 330
National Conference of Commissioners on Uniform State Legislation, 567
National Foundation for Consumer Credit, 566
National Institute of Law Enforcement and Criminal Justice, 640
National Retail Dry Goods Association, 184
National Retail Furniture Association, 231, 453, 614, 669
National Retail Hardware Association, 25, 68, 87, 143, 150, 231, 453, 597–98, 614, 670
National Retail Merchants Association, 150, 217, 237, 243, 267, 355, 456, 598, 600–601, 614, 631, 637, 665, 669
National Tea Company, 30, 320
Nayak, P., 493
NCR Corporation, 613, 669
Neely, F. H., 510
Neiman-Marcus, 194 n, 314, 403, 494
New York, 458
New Yorker, 458
Newspaper Advertising Bureau, 9, 473

Newsweek, 458
Ney, J. M., 347
Nickels, William G., 510, 538
Nicols, Alfred, 37, 511
A. C. Nielsen Company, 298, 427, 673
Nixon, Richard, 437
Nystrom, P. H., 257

O

Ocko, Judy Y., 474
Odiorne, G. S., 684
Oka, Hideyuki, 538
Olshavsky, Richard W., 512
O'Neills, 681
Operating Results of Food Chains, 614
Orbach's, 30
Orbeck, E. A., 347
Osbon, John, 655
Oshawa Group of Toronto, 26
Overmeyer, Wayne E., 655
Oxenfeldt, A., 417

P

Padberg, Daniel I., 206
Palamountain, James M., 35
Parry, James, 654
Patty, C. R., 510–11
Paule, M. A., 120
Paxton, Virginia, 466
Pay-Less Drug Stores, 165
Pederson, C. A., 512
Penner, Irving, 572
J. C. Penney Company, 7, 11, 20, 29–30, 43, 80, 84, 88, 141, 145, 158, 166, 211, 232, 318, 390, 404 n, 460, 471, 477, 542
Pennington, A. L., 512
Pennsylvania and Atlantic Seaboard Hardware Association, 579
Perkins, Donald S., 87
Perkins, F. A., 439
Peterson, C. C., 121
Peterson, Esther, 203, 440
Peterson, Robert A., 36
Petrie Stores Corp., 63
Pettway, Samuel H., 255
Phifer, Gregg, 511
Pickle, Hal, 418
S. S. Pierce and Company, 405
Piggly-Wiggly grocery stores, 165
Pinto, David, 323
Plonk, Martha, 572
Polan, J. A., 656
Politz, Alfred, 474
Popular Photography, 458
Porter, Alan, 418
Post, Richard S., 654–55
Power, W. D., 634
Presby, J. T., 572
Pressemeir, E. A., 419

Proctor and Gamble, 427
Progressive Grocer, 323, 614
Pugh, Arthur L., Jr., 538

Q–R

Quaker Oats Company, 223–24
Ralph's, 170, 194 n
Rao, A. C., 439
Rapid-American, 20
Ratz, Arthur, 654
RCA, 628
Readers' Digest, 458
Reichler, Oxie, 494
Reinmuth, J., 653
Retail, Wholesale, and Department Store Union, 252
Retail Clerks International Association, 252
Retail Council of Canada, 669
Reynolds, Fred D., 300
Rhine, Don, 323
Richards, Steven, 572
Rich's, 488, 525
Rieser, F. P., 656
Robinson, Dwight E., 300
Robinson, O. P., 510
Rogers, C. R., 684
Romans, D. B., 146
Rosenberg, Larry J., 493, 685
Rosenbloom, M. A., 474
Rothman, Marian, 655
Rouse Co., 119
Roush, Ann, 56
Rovelstad, Ernest A., 572
Rowen, J. R., 472
Rucks, C. T., 573

S

Saferstein, Harvey I., 655
Safeway Stores, Inc., 20, 30, 63, 200, 320
St. Marie, Satenig S., 35
Saks Fifth Avenue, 30, 124, 403, 458
Salmon, Walter J., 36, 63
Salmonson, R. F., 594
SAMI (Selling Areas-Marketing, Inc.), 298, 672
Sandage, C. H., 347, 473–74
Sands, I. L., 256
Sanger-Harris, 125–26
Sanzo, Richard, 684
Sasser, Earl, 255
Saum, Anne, 511
Schabacker, Joseph C., 56
Schaller, E. O., 418
Scher, Jay, 35–36, 282, 369, 425, 473, 538, 571–72, 668
Schiller, Margery K., 301
Schinkel, Thomas, 37
Schlacter, John L., 300, 684
Schneider, J. B., 120
Scott, Peter, 94 n

Sears, Roebuck and Company, Inc., 20, 22, 29–31, 63, 80, 84, 109, 114, 124 n, 163, 194, 197, 201, 211, 218, 282, 308–9, 318–19, 402, 404 n, 418, 453, 457, 460, 464 n, 465, 477, 523, 534, 672, 675
Home Fashion Data Bank, 297
Seitz, B. L., 634
Selfridge's, 127
Seventeen, 488
Shapiro, Benson P., 418
Shapiro, S. J., 33, 120, 418, 474, 573
Sharp, John M., 573
Shepherd, W. G., 347
Sher, Herbert, 88
Sheraton, Mimi, 510
Sheth, Jagdish N., 474
Shillito's, 194 n
Shoat, F. R., 439
Shockey, Ralf, 511
Silva, Richard L., 656
Simon, Raymond, 494
Robert Simpson Company, 478
Simpson-Sears, Ltd., 21, 477–78
Simpsons, Ltd., 477
Singer Company, 30, 628
Singular, Stephen, 685
Sinial, J. Sebastian, 418
Sirota, David, 230
Sizemore, R. C., 119
Sklar, June, 33
Skow, Louise, 418
Sloan, H. S., 684
Smallbrook, W. A., 418
Smith, Clyde M., 685
Larry Smith Associates, 115
Snyder, James, 348
Somekh, Herbert M., 538
Sorenson, Ralph Z., 36
Sostrin, Morey, 419
Southdale Shopping Center, 109
Southland Corporation, The, 20
Spath, Walter F., 34
Spiegel, Inc., 478, 572
Stanley Company, 468
Starling, Jack M., 572
Steeno, David, 653
Steichen, Everett, 121
Steinberg's, Ltd., 21
Steiner, George A., 684–85
Stephenson, P. R., 511
Stevens, Robert E., 595
Stewart, J. C., Jr., 573
Stewart, Paul W., 537
Stone, Gregory, 34
Stop and Shop Companies, The, 79, 227
Straus, Jack I., 501
Strauss Stores, 388
Strawbridge and Clother of Philadelphia, 476
Streeter, B., 347

Sullivan, John J., 654
Sunset House, 194 n
Super Market Institute, 150, 165, 586
Supermarket News, 669
Supermarkets General Corp., 87
Swan, John E., 418
Sweeney, Daniel J., 300
Szalai, Alexander, 34

T

Target discount chain, 29
Tarpey, L. X., Sr., 347
Tauber, Edward M., 10, 34
Team Central high-fidelity stores, 29
Tempo-Buckeye stores, 124
Thompson, Bryan, 120
Thompson, John R., 538
Thrift Drug Company, 29
Time, 61, 458
Toensmeyer, U. C., 418
Tomme, M. B., Jr., 573
Tootelian, D. H., 511
Toronto Life, 458
Tower, C. Burke, 347
Town and Country, 458
Trunzo, Candace E., 37
Tupperware Co., 30
Turner, Alan, 121
Tysons Corner Regional Center, 119

U

Uhl, Kenneth P., 323, 348, 419, 474
Underwriters Laboratories, 298
United Parcel Service, 521
U.S. Civil Service Commission, 215–16
U.S. Department of Commerce, 27, 34–35, 71, 87–88, 104, 119, 155, 669
U.S. Department of Justice, 12, 104
U.S. Department of Labor, 86–87, 236, 255–56
United States Environmental Services, 456
U.S. Federal Reserve Board, 550, 567, 571, 574
U.S. Federal Trade Commission, 12–13, 103, 330, 332, 334, 341, 428, 433, 436, 440, 464, 484, 491, 549, 556
U.S. Food and Drug Administration, 484
U.S. National Labor Relations Board, 252
U.S. Secret Service, 644–45
U.S. Small Business Administration (SBA), 14, 70, 72, 155, 637, 669
Currie Urwick Partners, 471

V

Val-U-Mart Stores, 63
Varble, Dale, 255
Varro, Paul, 230

Veale, Robert E., 393
Vereen, Bob, 35, 300, 634
Verrill, Addision H., 654
Verser, Nancy, 634
Vivian, Jack, 369
Vogue, 458
VonRiesen, R. Dale, 230
Vredenburg, H. L., 510–11

W

Walgreen Company, 79, 166, 313, 639
Walker, Bruce J., 440
Wallis, W. J., 282
Walsh, Timothy J., 655
Walter, C. K., 300
Montgomery Ward and Company, 22, 31, 80, 82, 84, 144, 176, 194, 197, 199–200, 205, 237, 393, 402, 418, 478
Water Tower Place, 117, 128, 130
Watson, R. A., 281
Weaver, Charles N., 231
Weiser, Norman, 393
Weiss, E. B., 34, 119, 171, 231, 418, 511, 538, 683
Werner, R. O., 347
Western Auto Supply Co., 572
George Weston Ltd., 21, 30
Whirlpool Corporation, 224, 452
Wickes Hardware, 30
Wiggs, Garland D., 87
Wightman, Thomas E., 538
Wilcox, Clair, 347
Wildhorn, Sorel, 654
Williams, Gordon L., 656
Wilson's, 135
Wingate, John W., 299, 301, 347, 418
Winn-Dixie Stores, Inc., 20
Wise, Gordon L., 511
Withers, J. E., 684
Woll, Milton, 192
Women's Wear Daily, 669
Wood, D. L., 655
Woodside, A. G., 511
Woolco units, 120, 170
F. W. Woolworth Co., 20, 30, 80, 120, 158, 160, 164, 282, 318, 444, 482
Wright, M. D., 512

Y–Z

Yamanaka, Hideo, 494
Zabriskie, Noel B., 538
Zanetti, Giacomo, 324
Zayre Company, 88
Zimmer, A. E., 511
Zimmerman, Robert M., 393
Zion's Cooperative Mercantile Institution (ZCMI), 142

SUBJECT INDEX

A

Accessibility of store, 100–101
Accident prevention, **651**
Accordion pattern, 281
Accounting, retail, 575–656
  balance sheet, 577, 579–81, 594
  basic controls, 577–95
  cost method, 581–85
  financial standards, 664, 666–67
  knowledge required, 579
  operating statement; see Operating
    statement
  purposes of, 578–79
  reports, 577, 579–92
  retail inventory method, 486–92
Accounting and control division, opportunities in, 78–79
Acquisitions, 12, 194
Additional markup, 420, 429–30
Adjustments, 523–24; see also Complaints
  of customers
  present and changing conditions, 660–61
  systems of marking, 525
Administrative ability of executive, 47
Advance dating, 337
Advanced management programs, 227
Advertising, price, 435–37
  prescription drugs, 13, 435
Advertising, retail, 443–75; see also specific
  types and media
  appropriation for, 454–55

Advertising, retail—Cont.
  copy, 461
  defined, 444
  expenditures, 444, 453
  functions, 444–51
  goals, 444–51
  illustration, 461–62
  layout, 462
  media, selection of, 456–60
  opportunities in, 77
  planning, 455–56
  preparation, 461–62
  prechecking, 462–63
  proportionately equal terms, 451 n
  responsibility for, 469, 471
  special sales events, 464–65
  strategy, 453–63
  suitability of merchandise, 456
  testing, necessity for, 462–63
  timing, 455–56
  truth in, 463–64
  types, 445–51
Advertising discounts and allowances,
  333–34
  proportionately equal terms rule, 333–
    34
  reasons for, 333
  Robinson-Patman Act, 333–34
  services, 334
Advertising manager, duties and responsibilities of, 187–88
Advertising research, 673–74

Advertising value, 413
Age Discrimination in Employment Act of 1967, 230
Age distribution, 56
Air conditioning, 137–38
Aisle tables, 163–64
Alterations, 516–17
  charges for, 516–17
Amalgamations, 13
Anchor stores, 102–3
Anchorless malls, 31, 112–13
Annual Percentage Rates (APR), 574
Anti-A&P law, 329
Anticipation, 338
Anti-inflationary controls, 13–14
Antique row, 108
Anti-shoplifting measures, 639–42; see also Shoplifting
Antitrust regulation, 12–13
Antitrust statutes, 330
Apartment dwellers, 10
Apathetic shoppers, 10
Apparel chain stores, organization of, 195–96
Applicants for jobs; see Employment procedures and Personnel
Application forms
  credit, 554–55
  personnel, 217
Aptitude tests, 218
Architectural displays, 468
Area supervisors, 83–84
Article surveillance, 640–41
Arts and crafts fair, 489
Assets and liabilities, statement of, 577
Assortment research, 672–73
Athletic contests, 64
Auctions, 307
Auditoriums for community use, 535
Author luncheons, 488
Automatic vending machines, 15
Automation; see also Electronic data processing equipment and Electronic equipment
  credit operations, 544
  impact of, 12
  merchandise control systems, 11
Automobile; see also Parking facilities
  significance to retailer, 105
Average initial markup, 663
Average stocks, planning of, 271

B

Bad check laws, 567
Bad check losses, 655
  controls against, 645–46
Bad debt losses, 544
Bagging; see Wrapping merchandise
Balance sheet, 577, 579–81, 594

Banks
  credit assistance from, 548–49
  credit card plans, 550, 572
Banners, 469
Bantam stores, 28, 60
Bantam superettes, 403
Bargain advertising, 445, 447
Bargain squares, 164
Basic stock list, 286, 288
Basic stock method, 272–73
Beauty parlors, 535
Better Business Bureaus, 437, 463
Billboards, 460
Bin method of receiving, 374
Bingo, 494
Bio-degradable plastic shopping bag, 537–38
Blind check, 379
Blister packs, 640
Blue Cross and Blue Shield plans, 249
Bonus discounts, 427
Book inventory, 586–87
Boutiques, 60, 148
Branch post office, 535
Branch stores, 53, 190–91
  benefits and problems of, 114
  site selection factors, 101
Brands; see National brands and Private brands
Bridal fairs, 488
Broadcast coordinator, 471
Broadcast media advertising, 460
Brokers, 307
Brood hen and chick organization, 190
Bubble-gum junior population, 5
Budget-book sale, 619
Budget sale, 618
Budget stores, 186 n
Budgets; see Expense budget and Merchandise budget
Building, store; see Store building
Bulk marking, 382 n
Bulk merchandise check, 379
Burglary, 646–47
Bus service, 535
Buyers
  bonus compensation to, 238–39
  functions and responsibilities of, 186–87
Buying, 302–48
  anticipated sales, 288–89
  balanced assortment, 285–86
  basic stock list, 286
  breadth of selection, 284–85
  central, 318–20
  changing plans for, 284
  committee, 316–17
  concentration of, 303
  determining quantities for, 288–93
  determining what customers want, 293–98

Buying—*Cont.*
  dividing of, 303–4
  financial capacity, 290–91
  general considerations, 284–86
  group, 317–18
  information sources, 294–98; *see also*
    Information sources for buying
  inside sources of information for,
    294–96
  mistakes, 421
  model stock list, 286–88
  nature of merchandise, 289
  negotiations with merchandise re-
    sources, 325–48
  organization of function of, 316–20
  outside sources of information for, 296–
    98
  physical capacity, 290–91
  plans for, 284–88
  responsibility for, 283
  selecting merchandise resources, 302–
    24
  store policy, 289–90
  timing of peak stocks, 290
  turnover; *see* Turnover of stock
  vendor policy, 289–90
Buying habits, 95, 99–100
Buying and selling activities, separation of,
  191–93
Buying trips to central markets; *see* Central market buying trips

C

Cable television, 490
Calamities, handling of, 652
Capital requirements; *see* Financing
  methods
Capital turnover, 292 n
Captive market, 403
Careers in retailing, 58–88
  pros and cons of, 84–85
Carelessness and error, 368, 650
Carriage trade, 100
Cash awards, 237–38
Cash-and-carry policies, 542
Cash-and-carry stores, 519
Cash-and-carry variety stores, 100
Cash-and-carry wholesalers, 305
Cash customers, 542
Cash discounts, 334–35
  defined, 334
  legality, 335
  significance, 335
Cash-flow statement, 594
Cash registers; *see* Sales registers
Cash sale, 618
Cash theft, 649
Cashless society, 561
Catalog order desks, 477

Catalog showrooms, 23, 25
Catalog stores, 477
Catalogs, 310–11, 477, 493
Caveat emptor doctrine, 496
Ceiling finishes, 132
Central buying, 316 n, 318–20
  advantages and disadvantages of, 319–
    20
  growth of, 318–19
  ordering for specific stores in chain sys-
    tem, 320
Central management positions, 83–84
Central market buying trips, 312–16
  benefits, 312–13
  brevity of, 313–14
  facilities available, 312
  frequency of, 313
  methods of buying, 312–13
  reasons for, 313
  resident buying offices, 314–15
  scouting, 314
Central market representatives, 297
Central shopping districts, 106–7
  future trend, 115–17
Central wrap, 518
Centralization, 319
  chain stores, 197, 200–201
  customer complaint handling system,
    525
  receiving merchandise, 371–72
  training employees, 221–22
Cents-off coupons, 428
Chain stores, 17–18
  advertising problems, 471
  area supervisors' positions, 83–84
  central management positions, 83–84
  centralization, 197, 200–201
  common characteristics of, 195
  decentralization, 197–201
  incoming merchandise, handling of,
    389–92
  integration of wholesale and retail func-
    tions, 306–7
  managers' compensation, 239–40
  merchandising of individual stores, 320
  opportunities in, 79–84
  ordering for specific stores in system,
    320
  organization of, 195–201
  physical inventory, 364
  prototype layouts, 156
  prototype stores, 123
  recruiting personnel, 84
  recruiting programs of, 79
  regional training centers, 231
  retail inventory method, 586
  site selection factors, 101
  store management and supervision, op-
    portunities in, 80–83
  training programs, 80–83

Changing conditions, adjustment to, 660–61
Charga-Plate, 556–57
Charge account frauds, 646
Charge sale, 618
Check cashing services, 534–35
Check frauds, 645–46
Checking merchandise
  defined, 370
  invoice against purchase order, 377–78
  procedures, 377–80
  quantity discrepancies, handling of, 379–80
  unpacking and sorting, 378
Checklist system, 286, 359
Checkmarking tables, 373
Circular advertising, 477
City store location, selection of, 93–97; see also Trading area selection
Civil Rights Act of 1964, Title VII, 230
Claim adjustment; see Complaints of customers
Classification control, 355
Classification merchandising, 355
Clearance-sale advertising, 445, 448
Closed displays, 468
Clusters of stores, 108, 114
COD dating, 337
COD transactions, 480, 534, 618
Code of Responsible Servicing Practices, 530
Collection of credit accounts, 561–66; see also Credit and Credit management
  activities involved in, 561–62
  advantages of early collection, 562
  collectors, 564–65
  credit counseling services, 566
  credit policies influencing, 561–62
  garnishment, 565
  legal action, 565
  letters, 564
  nonuniform policy, 565
  past due statements, 563–64
  policy on, 562–65
  problem of, 561–62
  steps in, 563–65
  telephone calls, 564
  uniform policy, 563–65
Collection agents, 564–65
Collection letters, 564
Collection management; see Collection of credit accounts
Collection period ratio, 666
Collection ratio, 562 n
Collective credit department, 550
Collusion, 649–50
Color combinations and zoning, 132–33
Combination check, 378–79
Combination drug stores, 23
Combination supermarkets, 23

Combines Investigation Act (Canada), 308 n, 329 n, 439
Commission houses, 307
Committee buying, 316–17
  group buying distinguished, 317
  weaknesses of, 317
Communications research, 674–75
Community activities
  contributions to, 48–49
  participation in, 53
Community responsibility, 681–82
Community services, 536–37
Comparative data, 665–70
  sources of, 666–70
Comparison shopping, 203
Compensation, 233–42; see also Salaries
  average earnings, 255
  bonuses, 238–40
  buyer's bonus, 238–39
  chain store managers, 239–40
  drawing account, 236, 239
  job evaluation for, 242–43
  managerial, 238–42
  objectives of plan of, 233–34
  quota bonus, 235–36
  salary plus commission on all net sales, 235
  salary supplements, 237–38
  sales-supporting employees, 238
  salespeople, 234–38
  senior executives, 240–42
  straight commission, 236–37
  straight salary, 234–35, 238
  tax aspects, 241
Competition
  markup factor, 415
  pricing policy factor, 400–405
  regulation of, 12–13
  services offered by retailers, 516
  site selection factor, 98, 100
  trading area selection factor, 96–97
Competitive developments, 18–33
Competitive pricing, 437
Complaints of customers, 294, 522–25
  adjustments, 523–25, 590
  causes, 522–23
  centralized system of handling, 525
  combination system of handling, 525
  decentralized system of handling, 525
  goodwill, maintaining of, 523–24
  habitual complainers, 523
  handling of, 523–24
    systems for, 524–25
  improper buying, 522
  inadequately trained and careless personnel, 522–23
  inefficient store system, 522
  minimizing, 524
  systems for handling of, 524–25
  warranty responsibilities, 522

Complaints of employees, 250–51
Computer revolution, participation in, 11
Computers; see Electronic data processing
    equipment and Electronic equipment
Concessions, 23
Conglomerates, 194
Consignment buying, 344–45
Consumer advistory groups, 298, 301
Consumer credit; see Credit
Consumer Credit Protection Act of 1968,
    434, 567–68
Consumer economics, 7–9
Consumer experience group, 301
Consumer juries, 298, 301
Consumer location, changes in, 6–7
Consumer panels, types of, 301
Consumer premiums; see Premiums
Consumer psychographics, 9–11
Consumer representation, 203
Consumerism, 8, 11, 661
Consumeristic controls, 13
Consumers
    appeal of goods to, 411
    classification of, 10
    complaints of; see Complaints of cus-
        tomers
    evaluation of stores, factors influencing,
        11
    help in locating merchandise, 533
    importance of, 43
    price negotiation with, 397
    response to lower price, 411–12
    retail sale factor, 501
Container premiums, 494
Contingent force of employees, 220
Continuous-purchase-record group, 301
Control division, organization of, 189
Controller, responsibilities of, 189–90
Convenience foods, 9
Convenience-type stores, 27–28, 60, 403
Cooperative advertising, 451–52
Cooperative chains, 29, 307
Coordination; see Management coordina-
    tion
Corporate form of business, 72
Cost of goods sold, 582–84
Cost of merchandise, 408–9
    markup factor, 413–14
Cost departments, 189
Cost method of accounting, 581–85
    cost of goods sold, 582–84
    gross margin, 584
    gross sales, 581–82
    large retailers and, 585
    major elements in, 581–85
    net sales, 581–82
    operating expenses, 584–85
    periodic or physical inventories, 581
    perpetual inventory, 585
    preliminary evaluation of, 585

Costs, 123
    credit selling, 543–44
    crimes, 653
    delivery service, 519–20
    electronic data processing equipment,
        139
    returned goods, handling of, 526
    store modernization, 141
Counseling bureaus, 566
Counter signs, 469
Counter-top displays, 468
Counterfeit money, 644–45
Country club billing, 559
Coupon book credit plans, 548
Coupon sales, 427–28, 619
Courtesy, essence of, 502–3
Credit, 9, 540–74; see also Collection of
        credit accounts and Credit manage-
        ment
    advantages of, 541–43
    aids in building a mailing list, 543
    aids in building sales, 543
    automation of operations, 544
    banks, assistance from, 548–49
    competitive pressure, 542
    continuous contact with customers,
        542–43
    costs of, 543–44
    coupon book plan, 548
    credit card plans, 549–51
    customer demand, 542
    defined, 545
    delinquencies, 544
    extension of, 551
    finance companies, assistance from,
        548–49
    general credit contracts, 546
    government regulation of, 566–70
    growth in, 541
    holder in due course doctrine, limita-
        tions on, 549
    ideal credit arrangement, 548
    impact on prices and profits, 544–45
    installment, 544–47
    instant, 548
    interest cost of, 544
    military service personnel, 573
    90-day plan, 548
    open-account, 544–46
    option-terms, 547–48
    phone-computer system, 573
    problems of selling on, 543–45
    regular charge account, 545
    repossession for default in, 546
    revolving, 547
    secured transactions, 546
    service charges, 572
    state laws governing, 566–67
    ten-pay plan, 548
    3-pay plan, 548

Credit—*Cont.*
twenty-pay plan, 548
types, 545–48
volume of, 540–41
Credit bureaus, 554, 565, 568
Credit card frauds, 646
Credit card plans, 549–51
banks, 550, 572
benefits of, 550–51
government controls of, 568
individual merchants, 572
limitations of, 550–51
private label card plans, 551
types, 549–50
unsolicited, 556
Credit counseling services, 566
Credit department, evaluation of, 570
Credit economy, 566
Credit management, 551–61; *see also* Collection of credit accounts *and* Credit
account-opening procedures, 553–56
approving applications for credit, 554–55
approving credit purchases, 557–59
authorization process, 558
automating the credit function, 560–61
billing the customer, 559–60
charge-send transactions, 559
charge-take transactions, 557–59
customer identification, 556–57
establishing the credit limit, 555
floor limit to credit, 557–58
identification devices carried by customers, 557
informing customer of decision, 555–56
interview of account applicant, 554
maintaining current credit information, 556
personal identification of customer, 557
procedures for, 551
promoting credit accounts, 552
sales promotion material in monthly statement, 560
setting credit standards, 552–53
signature identification, 557
standards for, 552–53
store's initiative in opening accounts, 556
Credit reports, 554, 568
Credit unions, 548
Crime, 11, 637; *see also specific types*
cost of, 653
external, 638–47
internal, 647–50
Current assets, defined, 664
Current assets to current debt ratio, 666
Current debt to inventory ratio, 667
Current debt to tangible net worth ratio, 667
Current liabilities, defined, 664

Customary prices, 414
Customer entrances, 130
curtains of air, 130
Customer inquiries, 295
Customer-is-always-right policy, 524
Customer-is-king concept, 496
Customer research, 671–72
Customer services, 188, 513–39; *see also specific types*
policies regarding, 514–16
Customer surveys, 297–98
Customer traffic, equipment for handling, 136–37
Customers; *see* Consumers
Cycle billing, 559

D

Dating, 325, 336–39
defined, 336
kinds, 336
Decentralization, 59, 115
chain stores, 197–201
customer complaint handling system, 525
training employees, 221–22
Decorations, 469
Deferred discount, 327
Delayed marking, 382
Delivery service, 519–21
consolidated delivery systems, 521
costs of and charges for, 519–20
express delivery, 521
individual-store system, 520
mutual delivery system, 520–21
parcel post delivery, 521
systems of, 520–21
Demographics, 4–7
Demotions, 246
Department managers, responsibilities and functions of, 186–87
Department stores, 10, 18
accounting and control division opportunities, 78–79
branch organization, 190–91
branches of, 22
control division organization, 189
discount; *see* Discount houses
divisions, changes in number of, 193–94
expense classification, 598–601
four-function organization chart, 184–90
free-standing, 114
junior executive training programs, 73–74
leased departments, 23–25
Mazur plan, 184–90
deviations from, 190–94
merchandising division opportunities, 74–77

Department stores—*Cont.*
  merchandising division organization, 186–87
  operating division opportunities, 77–78
  operating division organization, 188–89
  opportunities in, 72–79
  optical scanning and industry code marking, 631
  organization of, 183–94; *see also subtopics hereunder*
    changes in, 190–94
  ownership groups, 194
  personnel division opportunities, 79
  physical inventory, 364–67
  publicity division opportunities, 77
  publicity division organization, 187–88
  salaries, 73
  separation of buying and selling responsibilities, 191–93
  service division opportunities, 77–78
  small, 183–84
  store management division organization, 188–89
  two-function organization chart, 183–84
Departmental control, 354–55
Departmentalization, 179–82
  advantages of, 180
  borderline merchandise, 181
  problems of, 181–82
  regrouping of merchandise, 181–82
  steps in, 180–81
Deposit sale, 618–19
Descriptive billing, 560
Direct-action advertising, 445
Direct buying, 308–9
  foreign markets, 321
Direct check, 378
Direct mail advertising, 458, 460, 477
Direct mail sales, 619
Direct selling, 117, 500, 511
Discount arrangements, 397
Discount department stores; *see* Discount houses
Discount houses, 13, 18, 22–23, 111–12, 148
  characteristics of, 22–23
  displays in, 162
  free-standing, 113–14
  leased departments, 23–25
  opportunities in, 80–83
  pricing, 401–2
Discount loading, 339
Discount retailers, 305
Discount sale, 619
Discount stores; *see* Discount houses
Discounts, 325, 327–36
  advertising, 333–34
  brokerage, 334
  cash, 334–35
  customers, 274, 397, 619

Discounts—*Cont.*
  employees, 212–13, 237, 274, 619
  price negotiations, 335–36
  quantity, 327–31
  seasonal, 332
  trade, 331–32
Discretionary spending power, 4
Dishonesty, 367–68
Display, 159–64, 465–69
  aisle tables, 163–64
  bargain squares, 164
  cabinets or cases, 162–63
  considerations in, 163
  customer inducement, 161
  defined, 160
  exterior, 163
  interior, 162–63
  layout factor, 159–64
  mass, 163
  merchandise islands, 162–63
  outside, 163
  responsibility for, 469, 471
  shelves and racks, 162
  silent salesclerks, 163
  talking signs, 163
  variations among types of, 162–63
  Y arrangement, 164
Display research, 673–74
Distress sales, 464
Distributing merchandise, 388
  defined, 370
Distributors, 306
Diversification, 29
Divisional group managers, 205–6
Dollar controls, 349, 352–56
  defined, 352
Dominant assortment, 299
Door-to-door salespeople, 9
Doors, types of, 137
Downtown malls, 115–16
Drawing account, 236, 239
Drawings, 487–88
Drug chains, opportunities in, 83–84
Dual pricing, 436

E

Ecological controls, 13
Ecological records, 11
Economical shoppers, 10–11
Educational activities, 249
Educational classes, 535
Electronic data processing equipment (EDP), 138–40
  costs, 139
  credit function uses of, 560–61
  current uses of, 139
  descriptive billing of customers, 560
  future of, 139–40
  inventory taking with, 357–58
  leasing of, 140

Electronic data processing—*Cont.*
  limitations, 139–40
  merchandise management and, 362–63
  sales checks, 624–25
  sales transactions systems, 627–29
  time sharing, 140
  uses of, 11
Electronic equipment, 11, 138–40
  ordering for specific stores in chain system, 320
  research, use for, 11–12
Electronic fund transfer systems (EFTs), 629, 631–32
Electronic record systems, 377
Elevator cards, 469
Elevators, 136–37
Embezzlement, 649
Emergency controls, 437–38
Emergency situations, 651–52
Employee benefit plans, 249–50
  group insurance, 249
  mutual-aid associations, 249–50
  retirement pensions, 250, 256
  savings and loan plans, 250
Employees; *see also* Personnel
  clubs, 64
  discounts; *see* Discounts
  induction of, 219–20
  large number of, 59–60
  pilferage by, 647–49
  requirements of, 212
  return-consciousness of, 528
  salaries, 62–63
  screening of, 647–48
  service activities for, 248–50
  skills required of, 212
  stability of employment of, 60
  theft by, 11
  turnover rate, 210–11
Employment aspects of retailing, 59–65
  changing opportunities, 60
  decentralization, 59
  different occupations available, 60
  kinds of stores, 59
  large number of employees, 59–60
  salaries, 62–64
  stable employment for full-time employees, 60
  training for key positions, 61–62
  women, opportunities for, 60–61
  working conditions, 64–65
Employment procedures, 215–21
  contingent force of employees, 220
  job orientation, 219–20
  job studies, 215–16
  prospect file, 220
  review of, 221
  selecting personnel, 217–19
  sources of personnel, 215–17

Employment tests, 218–19
  aptitude, 218
  intelligence, 218
  personality, 218
  skill, 218
Energy problem, 124–27
Environment of work, 64
Environmental changes, 209
Environmental controls, 13
EOM dating, 337
Equal Credit Opportunity Act, 569
Equal store structure, 190–91, 201
Equipment; *see* Fixtures and equipment
Errors; *see* Carelessness and error
Escalator clause, 325, 340
Escalators, 136–37
Escort shoppers, 533
Esprit de corps, 64
Ethical shoppers, 10
Exception reports, 363
Exchange sales, 619
Exclusiveness of goods, 341–42
Executives, retail
  administrative ability, 47
  character, 47
  community services, 48–49
  compensation plans for, 240–42
  conceptual skill, 47
  decisiveness, 46
  drive, 44–45
  effective expression, 47
  experience, 43–44
  friendliness, 45
  functions, 42
  human skill, 47
  judgment, 46
  knowledge of, 43
  leadership of; *see* Leadership
  market orientation, 43
  personal qualities, 42–48
  personal requirements, 41–49
  rewards other than dollars, 63–64
  salaries, 63, 73
  short-term changes, sensitivity to, 42 n
  social contribution, 48–49
  technical skill, 47
  vision of future, 46–47
Exhaustion level, 264
Expansions, 211
Expense budget, 607–12
  advantage of, 612–13
  analysis of expenses through, 612
  breaking budget period into smaller division, 611–12
  chain unit, 610–11
  departmental, 610–11
  nature of, 607–8
  objections to, 608–9
  payroll budget, 611

Expense budget—*Cont.*
  procedure for setting up, 609–12
  purposes of, 607–8
  requisites for, 608
  store-wide control figures, 609–10
Expense center, defined, 599
Expense center accounting, 599–603
  evaluation of, 603
Expense workrooms, 189
Expenses, 596–616
  allocation of, 603–6
  analyses of, 596, 606–12
  budget, 607–12; *see also* Expense budget
  classification, 597–603
  combined net profit and contribution plan of allocation, 605–6
  comparisons, 606–12
  contribution plan of allocation, 604–5
  control, 607, 612–13
  corrective action, 612–13
  direct, 603
  distribution of, 603–6
  dollar and percentage-of-sales reports, 607
  expense center accounting, 599–603
  fixed, 609
  food chain classification, 598–99, 601–3
  hardware store classification, 597–98
  indirect, 603
  larger department store classification, 599–601
  multiple analysis of, 596–97
  natural system of classification, 597–98
  net profit plan of allocation, 604
  percentages, 663
  production per employee-hour standards, 664
  production unit accounting method, 606
  rent, 605, 609
  review of trends in, 607
  smaller department store classification, 598–99
  standards, 663–64
  unit cost standards, 663–64
Experimental stores, 7
Extra dating, 337
Extra workers, training of, 227–28

F

Failures in retailing, 67–68
Fair Credit Billing Law of 1975, 549, 569–70
Fair Credit Reporting Act, 554, 560, 568
Fair Labor Standards Law, 253
Fair Packaging and Labeling Act, 484
Fair trade, 329 n, 430–32, 437
Farmers, 309

Fashion coordinators, 203, 295, 471
Fashion goods, 413
  marking of, 387
Fashion shows, 488, 490
Feedback, 63, 232, 386
Finance companies, credit assistance from, 548–49
Financial standards, 664, 666–67
Financial structure, 49
Financing methods, 69–72
  capital needed, 69–70
  franchise operations, 71–72
  requirements, 70
  sources of funds, 70, 72
Fire protection, 650–51
Fixed assets to tangible net worth ratio, 667
Fixtures and equipment, 50, 122–46
  electronic equipment, 138–40
  equipment defined, 133
  expenditures for, 123
  fixtures defined, 133
  leasing of, 140
  receiving room, 373–75
  sales-supporting activities, 138
  selection of, 133–34
  selling activities, 138
Floor finishes, 132
Floor plans, 158–61
Flyers, 460
Flying squad of employees, 220
F.o.b. transportation terms, 340
Food chain expense classification, 598–99, 601–3
Food chain mergers and acquisitions, 12
Forecasting sales, 268–71
  beating last year's figures, 270
  inside conditions affecting, 270
  long-term trend of sales, 269
  new stores, 270–71
  outside conditions influencing, 269–70
Foreign markets as sources of supply, 321–22
  direct buying, 321
  manufacturers in, 321–22
Franchising, 27–28, 60, 67, 201
  defined, 27
  financing of, 71–72
  kinds of businesses, 71
  profitability, 67
  training of franchisees, 62
  types, 27
  vendor's offerings for, 297
Free deal, 327
Free goods, 327
Free mail-in premiums, 494
Free-standing stores, 113–14
Full function wholesalers, 306
Functional discount, 331

Funded debts to net working capital ratio, 667
Furniture warehouses, 25
Future dating, 337–39
Future prospects, 65

G

Games of chance, 487–88, 494
Garment bags, shipping in, 378
Garnishments, 565
General management, primary obligations of, 182–83
General merchandise stores, opportunities in, 80–83
Gift certificates, 490, 619–20
Gift wrapping, 519
Goodwill
  building of, 496
  development after sale, 508
  maintaining, 523–24
  repair service to maintain, 529
  value of, 69
Gourmet cooking courses and demonstrations, 488
Government assistance, 14
Government regulation, 11–14
  credit, 566–70
  pricing, 430–37
  restrictive shopping center leases, 103–4
  sales promotion, 491
  trading area selection factor, 97
Green River ordinances, 511
Gross margin, 407–8, 428, 584, 590, 663
  defined, 279
Gross sales, 581–82
Group buying, 317–18, 324
  benefits of, 317–18
  committee buying distinguished, 317
  limitations of, 318
Group insurance, 249
Group marking, 382–83

H

Hand bills, 460
Hand marking, 383
Hand-to-mouth buying, 292
Handicapped persons, consideration of needs of, 123–24, 535
Hanging signs, 469
Hard goods, 22, 25
Hardware store expense classification, 597–98
Headquarters buyers, 206
Health and beauty aids, 306
Health services, 248–49, 256
High-price policy, 402–4
Home centers, 25–26
  defined, 25–26
Home furnishings stores, 25–26
Home inventory group, 301

Hours of work; see Store hours
House-to-house selling, 15, 117
House organs, 64
Household management, 9
Human relations, 209–10; see also Personnel management
Hypermarkets, 26

I

Identification of credit customers, 556–57
Image research, 672
Immediate dating, 337
Immediate marking, 382
In-home purchasing systems, 117
In-pack premiums, 494
In-store code labeling, 634
In-store display, 473
In-store task forces, 54
Income, as trading area selection factor, 95–96
Income distribution, 8–9
Income-producing services, 513, 535–36
  charges imposed for, 515–16
Income statement, 577
Incoming merchandise, handling of, 370–93; see also Receiving merchandise
Independent stores, 17–18, 307
Indirect-action advertising, 445
Indirect expenses, 603
Industrial engineering staffs, 203
Inflation, 7, 399, 478, 485, 541
Information sources for buying, 294–98
  adjustment data, 294
  central market representatives, 297
  credit department data, 294
  customer inquiries, 295
  customer surveys, 297–98
  fashion coordinators, 295
  general publications, 297
  hunches, 296
  inside, 294–96
  judgment of buyer, 295–96
  newspapers, 297
  offerings of other successful stores, 296
  outside, 296–98
  past sales, 294
  returned goods, 294
  style count, 298
  suggestions of salespeople, 295
  testing laboratories, 298
  trade papers, 297
  vendor's offerings, 296–97
Initial markup, 406–7
  formula, 428
Installment credit, 544–47
  standards for, 552–53
Installment sale, 618
Instant credit, 548
Institutional advertising, 445–51
Insurance coverage, 590

Integration of retail and wholesale functions, 306–7
Integration of retailer and manufacturer, 309
Intelligence tests, 218
Interior design services, 533
Interior displays, 467–69
Internal expansion, 12
Internalization, 30
Interviews; see Personnel
Inventory control systems, 297; see also Merchandise control
Inventory to net working capital ratio, 667
Inventory turnover; see Turnover of stock
Inventory valuation, 590–91
Investigative credit reports, 554, 568
Invisible windows, 131
Invoice, 325–26, 376
  checking against purchase order, 377–78
  datings of, 336–39; see also Dating
Island displays, 468
Item assortments, planning and selection of, 283–301

J

Job analysis, 215–16
Job classifications, 60
Job evaluation, 242–43, 244 n
  committee for, 243
  defined, 242
  methods, 242–43
  objectives, 242
Job orientation, 219–20
Job performance form, 245
Job security, 65
Job specification, 215
Job studies, 215–16
Job tests, 218
Job training, 225–26; see also Training employees
Joint promotions, 465
Joint retailer-manufacturer agreements, 346
Junior executive training programs, 73–74

L

Labeling, 483–85
  defined, 483
  function of, 483
  information required on, 484–85
  misrepresentations, 484–85
  responsibility for, 483
  retailers' interest in, 484
Labor conditions changes, 660
Labor-saving devices, 138
Labor unions; see Unions
Land expenditures, 123
Large stores, 18
  competitive developments, 22–26
  cost method of accounting and, 585

Large stores—Cont.
  credit account-opening procedures, 553–56; see also Credit management
  delivery system, 520
  departmentalization, 179–82
  forecasting sales, 268
  free-standing, 113–14
  general management of, 182–83
  merchandise budget supervision, 279
  merchandise complaints, 294
  organization of, 178–83
  personnel evaluation, 244–46
  policies of operation, 50
  promotion from within policies, 61
  receiving merchandise, organization for, 392
  receiving room layout and equipment, 373–75
  retail inventory method, 586
  stock assortment plan, responsibility for, 283
Layaway sales, 534, 618–19
Layout, 147–71
  advertising, 462
  characteristics, 151–55
  checklist of space needs, 150–51
  customer point of view, 151–52
  definition, 147
  display factor in, 159–64
  emphasis on, 148–49
  end-cap fixtures, 170
  factors influencing, 147–48
  flexibility, 158
  floor plans of various stores, 158–61
  functions of design for, 148
  gondola ends, 170
  hardware stores, 159
  magic core, 156–57
  mall-type aisle, 152–53
  procedure, 149–59
  receiving room, 373–75
  recommendations from outside sources, 155–56
  relation to profit, 153
  retailer point of view, 152–55
  sales forecast to estimate space requirements, 149–50
  sales-supporting departments, location of, 156–58
  self-selection and self-service, 164–69
  selling departments, location of, 156–58
  sources of information on, 155
  survey of space requirements, 149–51
  variations in space value within store, 156, 158
  visit new stores of same type, 155
  wandering aisle, 152
  wide central aisle, 152–53
Leader merchandising, 412–13

Leadership, 45–46, 679–82
  characteristics, 679–80
  management by objectives, 680–81
  social responsibility of retailing manage-
      ment, 681–82
Leased departments, 23–25, 418
Leasing arrangements, 102–4
  electronic data processing equipment,
      140
  fixtures and equipment, 140
Legal form of organization, 72
Licensed departments, 23
Life style changes, 9–10
LIFO valuation technique, 586, 595
Lighting, 134–36
  diversity in, 133
Limited-function wholesalers, 305–6
Loading, 339
Local market buying trips, 312
Location, store; see Store location
Location research, 675
Long-range planning staffs, 202
Loss control; see Loss prevention
Loss leaders; see Leader merchandising
Loss prevention, 636–56
  defined, 636
Lost-and-found departments, 535
Lotteries, 487–88
Low-price policy, 401–2
Luxury purchases, 8

M

Magazine advertising, 458
Magnuson Moss Warranty Act, 522
Mail-Me-Monday plan, 579
Mail order, defined, 492
Mail-order business, 15
Mail-order houses, 22
Mail-order selling, 117, 476–81; see also
      Telephone selling
Mail-order shopping, 9
Maintained markup, 407
Maintained selection items, 287
Management
  prime responsibility of, 659
  social responsibility of, 681–82
Management by objectives (MBO), 680–81
Management consultants, 66
Management coordination, 659–85
  adjustment to present and changing
      conditions, 660–61
  budget as tool, 670
  comparative figures, 665–70
  keeping current, 678–79
  major tools of, 662
  profitable operations, necessary for,
      659–62
  research, 670–78
  responsibility for, 661–62
  standards, 662–65

Management information services, 202–3
Management research, 673
Managerial compensation, 238–42
Manufacturers, 308–9
  direct buying from, 308
  direct selling by, 308–9
  foreign markets, 321–22
  retailer integration with, 309
Manufacturers' agents, 307
Manufacturers' brands, 404
Manufacturers' representatives, 307
Manufacturing departments, 189
Markdown rate, 663
Markdowns, 274, 420–30
  automatic, 425
  cancellation of, 429–30
  causes of, 421–22
  ideal, 426
  necessity for, 422–23
  off-retail percentage, 421 n
  percentage expression of, 420–21
  planning for, 422
  price lining and, 426
  publicizing, 426–28
  recording on, 428–29
  remarking for, 387–88
  size of, 425–26
  timing of, 423–25
  undesirable, reduction of, 429
  usefulness of, 422–23
Market changes, 660–61
Market factors, 4–11
Marketing concept, 43
Markets, 3–37
  retail, changes in, 104–6
Marking merchandise, 380–88
  authorization for, 385–86
  defined, 370
  guidelines for, 381–82
  manner of, 383–88
  outside marking of fashion merchandise,
      387
  places for, 383–88
  procedures, 382–83
  reasons for, 381–82
  types, 380
Markon, 406
Markup, 275 n, 276 n, 406–9
  adjustment to changing price levels, 415
  calculation of, 406–9
  defined, 406
  factors influencing, 411–15
  percentage of retail price, 409 n
  percentage of selling price, 406
  several, 410
  summaries of policies concerning, 415–
      16
  table of, 407
Markup percentages, 592
Mass displays, 468

Mazur Plan, 184–90
deviations from, 190–94
Mechanical equipment, 138
Mechanization, 60
Mechanized conveyors, 373, 375
Medical services, 248–49, 256
Medium-sized stores; see also Small
stores
credit account-opening procedures,
553–56; see also Credit management
delivery system, 520
opportunities in, 65–72
receiving merchandise, organization for,
392
Megalopolis, trend toward, 106
Memorandum buying, 345
Merchandise
effective presentation of, 505
incoming, handling of, 370–93; see also
Receiving merchandise
providing information concerning, 533–
34
retail sale factor, 501–2
Merchandise budget, 261–82
basic elements in, 268–79
benefits of, 265
coordination tool, 670
defined, 261, 264
forecasting sales, 268–71
form, 266–68
formal versus informal, 261–62
limitations of, 280
objectives of, 265
planned gross margin, 277, 279
planned purchases, 275–77
planned reductions in stock, 274–75
planning average stock, 271
planning monthly stocks, 271–74
requisites of, 265–66
supervision of, 279
Merchandise complaints; see Complaints
of customers
Merchandise control, 349–69
basic types of, 352–62
defined, 349
dollar controls; see Dollar controls
guidelines for, 350–51
methods used, 349–50
objectives of, 350
physical inventory, 363–67
stock shortages, 367–68
unit controls; see Unit controls
Merchandise displays, 468
Merchandise groupings, 355
Merchandise information systems; see
Merchandise control
Merchandise management, 259–440; see
also specific topics
budgets, 261–82

Merchandise management—Cont.
buying, 302–48
electronic data processing and, 362–63
goals, 350–52
incoming merchandise, handling of,
370–93
merchandise control, 349–69
planning and selecting item assortments,
283–301
policies of merchandising, 261–82
pricing, 394–440
responsibility for, 351–52
Merchandise Management Accounting
(MMA), 577, 592–93
Merchandise managers, 186
functions and responsibilities of, 186
Merchandise planning, 349
Merchandise resources; see also Vendors
auctions, 307
brokers, 307
commission houses, 307
farmer as, 309
foreign markets, 321–22
major types of, 305–9
manufacturer as, 308–9
middlemen as, 305–7
negotiations with, 325–48
selection of, 302–24
selling agents, 307
wholesalers, 305–7
Merchandise stunts, 488
Merchandise testing departments, 203
Merchandising, policies of; see Policies of
merchandising
Merchandising control, 589–90
Merchandising division
opportunities in, 74–77
organization, 186–87
Merchandising research, 673
Merchandising services, 341
Merchandising standards, 663
Merchants' associations, 112
Mergers, 12, 194
Method of analogies, 98
Metro concept, 101–2, 319
Metropolitan area
clusters of stores, 108, 114
defined, 104–5
large free-standing stores, 113–14
neighborhood business streets, 107–8
newer shopping centers, 108–13; see
also Shopping centers
older central shopping district, 106–7
older secondary shopping districts, 107
retail structure of, 106–14
shopping plaza, 108
scattered stores, 108
Middlemen, 305–7
Mini-computers, 139
Mini-malls, 113

Minimarkets, 104
Model stock list, 286–88, 290
    preparation of, 287–88
Modernization, store; *see* Store modernization
Monitoring services, 673
Monthly stocks
    basic stock method of planning, 272–73
    judgment method of planning, 272
    methods of planning, 272–73
    percentage variation or deviation method of planning, 273
    planning of, 271–73
    stock-sales ratio method of planning, 273
    weeks' supply method of planning, 273
Monument store, 145
Morale surveys, 211
Motives, 10–11
MR's, 297
Multiple pricing, 414–15
Multiunit stores, 18
Multi-use buildings, 116–17
Mutual-aid associations, 249–50
Mutual delivery services, 520–21

N

National brands, 30–31, 37, 404–5
National Labor Relations Act of 1935, 252
National Recovery Administration (NRA), 437
Negotiations with merchandise resources, 325–48
    basics of, 326
    miscellaneous, 339–42
    purchase order, 342–44
    transfer of title, 344–46
Neighborhood business streets, 107–8
Net profits on net sales ratio, 666
Net profits on net working capital ratio, 666
Net profits on tangible net worth ratio, 666
Net sales, 581–82
Net sales to inventory ratio, 667
Net sales to net working capital ratio, 666
Net sales to tangible net worth ratio, 666
Net terms, 339
Never-out lists, 286, 359
New departments and items, 413
New, experienced employees, training of, 225
New, inexperienced employees, training of, 223–25
New towns, 117
Newspaper advertising, 457–58
    mail and telephone orders, 477
Newspaper as information source, 297
Night openings, 152, 403, 531–32, 538

No return policy, 528–29
Noisy arguments, 651–52
Nonpersonal methods of retail sales promotion; *see* Telephone selling *and other specific topics*
Nonprice competition, 404

O

Occupations in retailing, 60
Odd prices, 414, 419
Omnistructures, 116–17
On contract sale, 618
On-pack premiums, 494
One price, defined, 436 n
One-price policy, 394, 396–97
One-stop self-service outlets, 10
One stop shopping, 26
Open-account credit, 544–46
Open-to-buy, 276–78, 282, 290
Open dating, 382 n, 484
Open displays, 468
Operating activities, 188
Operating cost, 415
Operating division
    opportunities in, 77–78
    organization of, 188–89
Operating expenses, 584–85
    standards, 663–64
Operating research, 674
Operating statement, 577
    cost method, 581–85
    retail inventory method, 586–92
Operations research, 674 n
Opportunities in retailing, 58–88
    chain stores, 79–84
    department stores, 72–79
    medium-sized stores, 65–72
    small stores, 65–72
    specialty stores, 72–79
Optical Character Recognition (OCR), 631
Optical scanner, 629
Optical scanning and industry code marking, 630–31
Option-terms, 547–48
    revolving credit, 547
Ordinary dating, 337
Organization, 173 ff.; *see also specific topics*
    buying function, 316–20
    chain stores, 195–201
    charts, 176–77, 183–85, 203
    defined, 176
    department stores, 183–94
    departmentalization, 179–82
    flexibility of plans of, 177
    general management, 182–83
    informal, 177
    large store, 178–83
    management information services, 202–3

Organization—*Cont.*
  personnel management, 207–57
  receiving merchandise, 392
  small store, 178–79
  staff services, 202–3
  structure of retail firm, 175–206
  summary of changes and trends in, 203–4
Original markup, 406
Outdoor posters, 460
Outshopping, 104
Ownership groups, 194

P

Packaging, 481–83
  current attention to, 481–82
  customer's needs, 482–83
  elements in design of, 482
  factors leading to growing interest in, 481
  information required on, 484–85
  misrepresentations, 484–85
  sales promotion tool, 481
Paid holidays, 238
Parades, 489
Parking facilities, 535
Part-time employees, 210
  training of, 227–28
Partnership form of business, 72
Patronage discount, 327
Patronage motives, 10–11
Pedestrian malls, 115–16
Pedestrian trade, 99–100
Pensions, retirement, 250, 256
Percentage lease, 102–3
Percentage variation method, 273
Periodic inventory system, 353–54, 356–58
  cost method of accounting, 581
Perpetual inventory system, 353, 356
  cost method of accounting, 585
Personal income, 7–8
Personal requirements of management, 41–49
Personal selling, 495–512
  basics of, 498
  defined, 495
  direct selling, 500
  engineering approach to improvement in, 498–500
  goodwill, building of, 496
  importance of, 495–500
  management's responsibility for, 509
  need for, 496–97
  need for improvement in, 497–500
  timely service in, 497
Personal shoppers, 533
Personal shopping services, 532–33
Personality tests, 218
Personalizing shoppers, 10

Personnel: *see also* Employees
  application forms, 217
  competency of, 55
  demotions, 246
  final interviews, 219
  loyalty of, 55
  physical examinations, 219
  preliminary interviews, 217–18
  promotions, 246
  references, 217
  selection of, 217–19
  sources of, 215–17
  store manager's responsibilities, 189
  terminations, 246–47
  tests, 218–19
  transfers, 246
Personnel division, opportunities in, 79
Personnel evaluation, 244–46
Personnel management, 207–57; *see also* Employees *and* Personnel
  causal factors within retailing, 209–12
  compensation, 233–42; *see also* Compensation *and* Salaries
  complaints of employees, handling of, 250–51
  conducting personnel activities, 213–14
  employment procedures, 215–21; *see also* Employment procedures
  environmental changes, 209
  evaluating personnel, 244–46
  external factors, 209
  factors causing increased emphasis on, 208–12
  functions, 207–8
  importance of, 208
  objectives, 207–8
  persons involved in, 213–14
  policies essential for, 212–13
  relocating personnel, 246
  service activities for employees, 248–50
  stimulating satisfactory personnel performance, 243–54
  terminations, 246–47
  training of employees, 221–29; *see also* Training employees
  unions, 251–54
  working conditions, 247–48
Personnel performance, stimulation of, 243–54
Personnel planning, 214–15
Personnel policies, 212–13
Personnel relocation, 246
Personnel research, 674
Personnel review committee, 244–46
Phased construction techniques, 124
Physical facilities of stores; *see* Fixtures and equipment
Physical inventory systems, 363–67; 589; *see also* Periodic inventory system
  cost method of accounting, 581

Physical inventory systems—*Cont.*
  defined, 363
  form of taking, 365
  taking of, 364–67
  ticket, 366
Pilferage of merchandise, 11, 647–49
  check on, 428
Piped-in background music, 514
Planned gross margin, 277, 279
Planned purchases, 275–77
Planned reductions, 274–75
Planned sales, 609
Planned shopping centers; *see* Shopping
  centers
Planning committee, 202–3
Planning retail advertising, 455–56
Planning special sales events, 465
Planograms, 201
Playrooms for children, 535
Pneumatic tubes, 624–27
Point-of-purchase displays, 467–68
Point-of-purchase material, 306
Point-of-sale displays, 468–69
Point-of-sale recorders, 628–29, 632
Point scoring techniques, 554–55, 572–
  73
Policies of collection of credit accounts,
  562–65
Policies on customer service; *see* Service
  policies
Policies of merchandising, 261–82; *see also*
  specific topics
  buying, 302–48
  general, 262–64
  item assortments, planning and selection
    of, 283–301
  scrambled or specialized merchandise
    lines, 263–64
Policies of pricing; *see* Pricing
Policies of retailing, 50–55
  areas of decisions, 52–53
  changing conditions, adjustment to, 54–
    55
  changing conditions, effect of, 50–51
  considerations influencing choice of,
    51–52
  coordination, 54
  defined, 50
  enforcement, 53–55
  large stores, 50
  membership in trade associations, 53
  need for effective policies, 50–51
  operating procedures and, 53
  participation in community action, 53
  personnel management, 212–13
  promotions from within, 61
  responsibility for formulation of, 52
  review, 53–55
  small stores, 50
  steps in formulation of, 51–52

Policy committee, 202–3
Population growth, 4–5
  trading area selection, 94
Population mobility, 6–7
Population shifts in trading area selection,
  94
Portable tables, 373
Posters, 469
Predatory pricing, 330
Premiums, 485–88
  classification of, 494
  continuity offer, 485
  single transaction offer, 485
  types, 485–86
Preretailing, 344, 386
Prescription drugs, price advertising of, 13,
  435
Prestige advertising, 445
Prestige and pricing, 403
Preticketing, 433
Price advertising; *see* Advertising, price
Price cards, 469
Price changes, 420–30, 591
Price differential, 331
Price discrimination, 329–31, 334
Price guaranties, 339–40
Price level adjustments, 415
Price-line control, 355–56
Price lines, 394, 398–400
  effects of general price level changes,
    399–400
  establishment of, 398–99
  limitations of, 400
  markdowns and, 426
  reasons for, 398
Price lists, 310
Price negotiations, 335–36
  with customer, 397
Price posting, 434–35
Price/quality range, 397
Price signs, 434
Price tickets, 383–86, 434–35
  sales prices on, 428
Price/wage controls, 437–38
Price/wage freeze, 437–38
Price wars, 402
Pricing, 394–440
  art of, 405–6
  changes in, 420–30, 591
  competitive position, 400–405
  consistency in marketing mix, 395
  convenient location, 403
  difficulty of escaping price competition,
    404
  emergency controls, 437–38
  exclusive merchandise, 403–4
  extended store hours, 403
  general policies, 394–406
  importance of sound decisions in, 394–
    95

Pricing—*Cont*
  individual items, 409–11
  legislation, 430–34
  long-run point of view, 395–96
  markdowns, 420–30
  market considerations, 395
  markup, 406–9
  mistakes, 421
  one-price policy, 394, 396–97
  overselling competitors, 402–4
  prestige, 403
  price level and maximum profits, 396
  price lines, 394, 398–400
  private brands, 404–5
  range of prices, 397–98
  regulation of, 434–37
  restraints on freedom of, 437–38
  satisfactory services, 402–3
  single-price policy, 398
  underselling competitors, 401–2
Private brands, 30–31, 37, 309, 418–19
  pricing, 404–5
Prize money (P.M.'s), 237, 255, 341
  markdown, 426
Product research, 672–73
Production unit accounting, 606
  effective pay rate, 606
  elements in, 606
  productivity, 606
  suitability of, 606
  work load, 606
Professional discounts, 397
Profit cushion, 335
Profit and loss statement, 577
Profit sharing, 241
Profitability measures, 664
Profitable operations, coordination essential to, 659–62
Program Evaluation and Review Technique (PERT), 123
Promotion sales, 464
Promotional advertising, 445–51
Promotional allowances, 333–34
  proportionately equal doctrine, 489 n
Promotional department stores, 22
Promotional markdowns, 422
Promotional services, 340–41
Promotional training, 226
Promotions, 246
Proprietorship form of business, 72
Prospect file, 220
Protection of store and merchandise, 188
Public services, 536–37
Publicity, 489–90
Publicity division
  opportunities in, 77
  organization of, 187–88
Publicity manager, duties and responsibilities of, 187–88
Pull date, 484

Purchase order, 342–44
  checking invoices against, 377–78
  form, 342–43
Purchase order management (P.O.M.), 377
Purchases of merchandise; *see* Buying
Purchases of supplies and equipment, 188
Purchasing agents, 305
Purchasing arrangements, 102–4
Purchasing power, 7, 95

Q

Quality check, 380
Quantity check, 378–80
Quantity discounts, 327–31
  cumulative, 327–28
  defined, 327
  legality of, 330–31
  noncumulative, 327
  reasons for, 327–28
  Robinson-Patman Act, 328–30
  trips, 328
  why granted, 327–28
Quota bonus, 235–36
Q.S.C. standards, 240

R

Rack displays, 468
Rack jobbers, 306
Radio advertising, 457, 460
Ratios, 664, 666–67
Real per-capita disposable income, 7
Receiving manager, 392
Receiving merchandise, 370–93
  activities related to, 370–73
  centralization, 371–72
  chain stores, 389–92
  defined, 370
  guidelines for effective performance, 371
  location of facilities for, 372–73
  organization for, 392
  procedures for, 375–77
  space for, 372–73
Receiving records, 376–77
Receiving room
  equipment, 373–75
  layout, 373–75
  location, 372–73
  manager, 388
Receiving shipments, 375–76
Recording sales, 622–24
Recreational activities, 249
Recruiting personnel in chain stores, 84
Recruiting programs, 217
  chain stores, 79
Reductions, retail; *see* Discounts; Markdowns; *and* Stock shortages
Regrouping of merchandise, 152, 181–82
Regular charge accounts, 545
Regular employees, training of, 225–27

Regular-price advertising, 445–46
Regulation Z, 567–68
exemptions from, 574
Relatively price elastic, 411 n
Relatively price inelastic, 411 n
Re-marking, 387–88
Reminder systems, 359
Rental services, 536
Reorder point system, 286, 358–59
Reorder time systems, 286
Repair service, 529–30
responsible servicing practices, 530
Repossession, 546
Requisition stock control, 358
Resale price maintenance, 430–32
defined, 431
non-signers clause, 431
Research, 670–78
basic, 675–76
conducting, 676–78
defined, 670
independent agency to conduct, 676–77
nature of, 671–76
qualifications of director of, 677
salaried research department to conduct, 676–77
scope of, 671–76
steps in, 671
Research assignments, 678
Research department, 676–77
Research director, qualifications of, 677
Research report, 677
Research units, 202
Reserve stock control, 358
Reserve stock rooms, 388
Reservoir concept, 604
Resident buying offices, 310, 314–15, 667–68
Resource file, 304–5
Resources; see Merchandise resources and Vendors
Responsibility center defined, 599
Restricted distribution, 342
Retail advertising; see Advertising, retail
Retail credit and collections, 540–74; see also Collection of credit accounts; Credit; and Credit management
Retail executive; see Executives, retail
Retail Installment Sales Contract, 546
Retail inventory method, 386, 586–92
advantages of, 589–91
averaging method, 591
basic approach to, 586–88
book inventory, 586–87
estimating closing inventory at cost, 587–88
fundamentals of, 586–89
gross margin, 590
large stores' use of, 586
LIFO valuation technique, 586, 595

Retail inventory method—Cont.
limitations of, 591–92
operating statement preparation, 589
summary of steps in, 588–89
Retail labor unions; see Unions
Retail management; see Management
Retail markup, 406
Retail organization; see Organization
Retail policies; see Policies of retailing
Retail research; see Research
Retail sale
customer, 501
fundamental elements in, 500–503
merchandise, 501–2
salesperson, 502–3
store and its policies, 500–501
Retail sales promotion; see Sales Promotion
Retail salespeople; see Salespeople
Retailer-manufacturer joint agreements, 346
Retailers; see also specific topics
basic requirements for successful management, 41–57
buildings, 50; see also Store buildings
central markets, visits to, 312–16
competency of personnel, 55
contrasting features of, 15
direct buying from manufacturers, 308
financial structure, 49
functions of, 15
influences on, 3
initiative to find vendors, 310–16
kinds of, 59
local markets, visits to, 312
loyalty of personnel, 55
markets for, 3–37
number of establishments, 16
organization of; see Organization
physical facilities, 50; see also Fixtures and equipment
policies of, 50–55
sales of, 16–17
structure of; see Organization
Retailing; see also specific topics
careers in, 58–88
defined, 3
employment aspects of, 59–65
influences on, 3
market factors affecting, 4–11
methods of, 15–16
opportunities in, 58–88
policies of, 50–55
technological advances in, 11–12
Retirement pensions, 250, 256
Return on capital investment, 102
Returned goods, 526–29
causes of, 526–28
cost of handling, 526
customer responsibility for, 528

Returned goods—*Cont.*
 faulty store service, 526
 group store approach to, 529
 individual store approach to, 528–29
 minimizing, 528–29
 store policies, 526, 528
 unsatisfactory merchandise, 526
Returns of merchandise to vendors, 345–46
Revolving credit, 547
Robbery, 646–47
Robinson-Patman Act (U.S.), 14, 308 n,
 328–30, 332–36, 341, 386–87
 cost defense, 330
 defenses, 334
ROG (receipt of goods) dating, 337
Routing shipments, 389
Rubber-stamp marking, 383

S

Safety measures, 248
Salaries, 62–64; *see also* Compensation
 accounting and control division, 79
 chain store headquarters' positions, 84
 chain store management trainees, 80
 chain store managers, 82–83
 department stores, 73
 drug chain managers, 83–84
 executive, 63
 merchandising division, 76–77
 nonselling employees, 62
 nonsupervisory workers, 62
 operating division, 77
 publicity division, 77
 salespeople, 62
 service division, 77
 supermarket executives, 83–84
 trainees' initial, 62–63
Sales, 16
 estimating; *see* Forecasting sales
 by kind of business, 16–17
 percent distribution by firm size, 19
Sales checks, 622–24
 electronic equipment, 624–25
Sales-below-cost laws, 433–34
Sales projections, 672; *see also* Forecasting
 sales
Sales promotion; *see also specific topics*
 advertising, retail, 443–75
 display, 443–75
 governmental control, 491
 limitations of, 491
 monthly statement to customer containing material for, 560
 nonpersonal methods of, 443, 476–94
 personal selling, 443, 495–512
 variety in types of, 490–91
Sales registers, 624–26
 receipts and tapes, 622
Sales representatives, 310
Sales standards, 662–63

Sales-supporting employees
 compensation, 238
 training, 224–25
Sales tests, 673–74
Sales transactions control, 617–35
 characteristics of effective system, 620–
 21
 equipment for, 621–22, 624–33; *see also*
 Sales transactions equipment
 objectives, 620–22
 recording sales, 622–24
 requirements of, 620–22
 responsibility for establishing, 617
 sales checks, 622–25
 sales register receipts and tapes, 622
 types of sales transactions, 617–20
Sales transactions equipment
 electronic equipment, 627–29
 electronic fund transfer systems, 631–32
 evaluation of, 621–22
 optical scanner, 629
 optical scanning and industry code
 marking, 630–31
 pneumatic tubes, 624–27
 point-of-sale recorders, 628–29, 632
 sales registers, 624–26
 selection of, 621–22
 traditional, 624–27
Sales volume, planning of; *see* Forecasting
 sales
Salesmanship: *see* Personal selling
Salespeople; *see also* Employees *and*
 Personnel
 carelessness and mistakes of, 522–23,
 650
 compensation, 234–38; *see also* Compensation *and* Salaries
 evaluation of, form for, 499
 floor coverage to deter shoplifting, 640–
 42
 markdowns caused by, 422
 retail sales factor, 502–3
 suggestions as buying information
 source, 295
 training of, 223–24
Satellite cities, 117
Satellite stores, 103
Savings and loan plans, 250
Scattered stores, 108
Scrambled merchandising, 97, 263–64,
 284 n, 285 n
Seasonal dating, 337
Seasonal discounts, 332
Seasonal goods, 413
Seasonal stocks, 422
Secondary shopping districts, 107
Secured transactions, 546
Security, retail, 636–56; *see also specific*
 types of crimes or offenses
 defined, 636

Security Agreement, 546
Security measures, 367–68
Selection of personnel, 217–19
Self-liquidators, 494
Self-selection layout, 164–69; see also
    Self-service layout
Self-service layout, 164–69
    definitions of self-service and self-
        selection, 164–65
    factors essential to success of, 166–
        67
    food stores, 165–66
    future prospects, 168–69
    historical development, 165–66
    limitations of, 167–68
    merits of, 167
    other than food stores, 166
    requirements for, 166–68
Self-service stores, 60
Self-supporting cities, 117
Selling agents, 307
Selling process, 503–8
    approaching and greeting customer, 504
    closing the sale, 506–7
    determining the customer's needs, 504
    goodwill development after sale, 508
    meeting objections of customers, 505–6
    presenting merchandise effectively, 505
    price question, handling of, 506
    steps in, 503
    suggestion selling, 507–8
Semiblind check, 378–79
Senior citizens, 5
Separate store plan, 190
Separate store structure, 201
Service activities for employees, 248–50
    educational, 249
    financial benefit plans, 249–50
    health services, 248–49, 256
    medical services, 248–49, 256
    recreational activities, 249
Service advertising, 445
Service charges, 515–16
Service division, opportunities in, 77–
    78
Service equipment, 138
Service policies, 514–16
    guides to services offered, 514–15
    number and variety of services, 514
    realistic standards, 515
Service standards, 664
Service wholesalers, 305–6
Share of the market, 663
Shelf-displays, 468
Shipping costs, 393
Shop merchandising, 474
Shop within a shop concept, 148
Shopping bag, 518
Shopping calendar, 424

Shopping centers, 108–13, 143
    accessibility, 99–101
    air conditioning, 137
        enclosed malls, 109–10
    common area maintenance charges, 103
    developers of, 109
    enclosed, 31, 109–10
    factors governing location of, 92
    future of, 113
    government objections to restrictive
        leases, 103–4
    growth of, 108–9
    leasing arrangements, 102–4
    malls, 148
        enclosed, 109–10
    multilevel, 110
    nature of, 108–9
    pedestrian traffic, 99–100
    planned, 22
    problems, with, 109–13
    rental charges, 102–3
    rental of space to lower-priced competi-
        tors, 13
    tax escalation clauses in leases, 112
    trends in, 109–13
    vertical, 116–17
Shopping districts
    central, 106–7, 115–17
    secondary, 107
Shopping-news type of publication, 460
Shopping plaza, 108
Shopping report, 245
Shopping service, 479
Shoplifting, 11, 367–68, 638–44
    apprehension for, 642–44
    article surveillance, 640–41
    blister packs, 640
    closed-circuit TV, 640
    community campaigns, 642–43
    control measures, 639–42
    danger signals, 638–39
    defined, 638
    detection devices, 640
    displays and fixtures, 640
    fitting rooms, 639
    floor coverage, 640–42
    L-shaped self-service layout, 639
    packaging deterrence to, 482
    prosecution for, 642–44
    store design and layout, 639–40
    types of shoplifters, 638
    uniformed guards, 642
Shortages; see Stock shortages
Show windows, 130–31
    backgrounds, 131
    visual fronts, 131
Showings, 312, 315
Shrinkage, 637–38
    controllable problem, 637–38

Shrinkage—*Cont.*
  defined, 637
  failure to enforce control systems, 656
  legitimate causes of, 637
  videotape training programs, 654
Simplified selling, 165
Single markup, 409–10
  impracticality of, 410–11
Single price, defined, 436 n
Single-price policy, 398
Single-unit stores, 17–18
Site selection, 97–102
  accessibility, 99
  accuracy of sales estimates, 99
  analogs, use of, 98
  branch stores, 101
  chain stores, 101
  compatibility, 100
  competition and other stores, in rela-
      tion to, 100
  competitive comparisons, 98
  customer buying habits in relation to
      types of goods sold, 99
  detrimental characteristics of, 101
  estimated volume of business, 97–99
  incompatibility, 100
  long-run considerations, 98
  number of potential customers within
      reach, 98
  pedestrian traffic, 99–100
  return on capital investment, 102
Skill tests, 218
Sleepers, 367
SLIM, 281
Slow-moving items, 367, 422
Small Business Loans Act (1960) (Canada),
    72
Small department stores
  organization of, 183–84
  two-function organization charts for,
      183–84
Small stores, 17–18, 111
  accounting knowledge required, 579
  competitive developments, 22–28
  credit account-opening procedures, 553
  defined, 178
  delivery system, 520
  forecasting sales, 268
  limited opportunities as employee, 66
  location problem, neglect of, 92
  merchandise budget form, 267–68
  merchandise budget requisites, 266
  merchandise budget supervision, 279
  merchandise complaints, 294
  opportunities in, 65–72
  organization of, 178–79
  ownership, rewards of, 66–72
  personnel evaluation, 244
  physical inventory, 367

Small stores—*Cont.*
  policies of operation, 50
  receiving merchandise, organization for,
      392
  receiving room layout and equipment,
      373
  stock assortment plan, responsibility for,
      283
Small towns, continued viability of, 104
Social changes, 661
Social events, 64
Social indicators, 664–65
Social responsibility of retailing manage-
    ment, 681–82
Source marking, 386–87
Sources of comparative data, 666–70
Sources of information; *see* Information
    sources for buying
Sources of personnel, 215–17
Sources of supply; *see* Merchandise
    resources *and* Vendors
Special events in sales promotion, 488–89,
    494
Special sales events, 464–65
  planning of, 465
Specialized independent stores, 26
Specialized merchandise lines, 263–64
Specialized nondiscount chains, 26
Specialty discount outlets, 23
Specialty discount stores, 26
Specialty shops, 148
  free-standing, 114
  opportunities in, 72–79
  optical scanning and industry code
      marking, 631
Speculative buying, 293
Sponsor system of training, 213, 223–24
Staff services, 202–3
Standard Merchandise Classification, 355
Standards, 662–65
  defined, 662
  establishment of, 665
  inapplicability of, 665
  types, 662–65
  using, 665
  written, 665
Staple goods
  basic stock list for, 286
  central buying of, 320
  defined, 286
Stationary tables, 373–74
Steering committees, 324
Stock
  assortment plans, 283–301
  average, planning of, 271
  beginning of the month (B.O.M.), 271
  monthly, planning of, 271–73
  planned reductions in, 274–75
  turnover of, 271

Stock-sales ratio method, 273
Stock shortages, 274–75, 282, 367–68, 590
  dishonesty as cause of, 367–68
  errors as cause of, 368
Stockkeeping unit (SKU), 285 n, 286–87
Stockturn rate, 271; see also Turnover of
  stock
Store audit services, 673
Store building, 15, 50, 122–46
  common features, 123–27
  customer entrances, 130
  energy problem, 124–27
  expenditures for, 123
  exterior, 127–31
  front, 127–31
  handicapped persons, needs of, 123–24
  interior, 131–40
  land expenditures, 123
  phased construction techniques, 124
  preparation for occupancy, steps in, 122
  recent changes, 123
  reflective glass exteriors, 124, 130
  selling instrument, 122–27
  show windows, 130–31
Store communication devices, 138
Store development, 141; see also Store
  modernization
Store display; see Display
Store exterior, 127–31
Store front, 127–31
Store hours, 64–65, 531–32
  extended , 403
Store interior, 131–40
  air conditioning, 137–38
  ceilings, 132–33
  color of, 132–33
  color zoning, 132
  fixtures and equipment, 133–34
  floors, 132–33
  layout; see Layout
  lighting of, 134–36
  vertical customer traffic, equipment for
    handling, 136–37
  walls, 132–33
Store Labor and Inventory Management
  system (SLIM), 281
Store layout; see Layout
Store location, 91–121
  basic factors in, 93–104
  changing retail markets, 104–6
  city selection, 93–97
  future trends, 114–18
  importance of, 93
  influence of, 91
  leasing arrangements, 102–4
  megalopolis, 106
  metropolitan area; see Metropolitan
    area
  neglect of problem concerning, 92–93
  problem involving, 91–93

Store location—Cont.
  purchasing arrangements, 102–4
  reevaluation of, 91
  small towns, 104
  specific site selection, 97–102
  study of flow of customers, need for, 92
  suburbanization, 105–6
  trading area selection, 93–97
Store maintenance, 188
Store management division, organization
  of, 188–89
Store management and supervision, opportunities in, 80–83
Store manager's responsibilities, 188–89
Store modernization, 141–43
  defined, 141
  expenditures, 141
  future prospects, 143
  programs for, 142–43
Store ownership
  established business, buying of, 68–70
  failure, 67–68
  financing methods, 69–72
  legal form of organization, 72
  new business, starting of, 68–70
  opportunities for, 66–67
  personal qualities, 68
  profitability, 67–68
  rewards of, 66–72
Store patronage motives, 10–11
Store signs, 469
Store site; see Site selection
Storeless shopping, 117–18
Stores; see specific topics
Storewide sales, 465
Stuffers, advertising by, 477
Style count, 298
Substitute service, 341
Suburban shopping center movement, 6–7
Suburbanization, 7, 9, 105–6
  factors causing, 105–6
Suburbia, 105
Suburbs, urban areas compared with, 7
Sudden illness, 651
Suggested pricing, 433
Suggestion selling, 507–8
"Sun Belt," 6
Sunday openings, 152, 403, 532
Supermarkets, 13, 18, 148
  committee buying, 316
  displays in, 162
  energy problem, 124–27
  enlargement of space, 124
  furniture industry, 25
  hourly wage, 256
  opportunities in, 83
  optical scanning and industry code
    marking, 630–31
  retail inventory method, 586
Superstores, 26

Supervisors, training of, 226–27
Suppliers, selection of; see Merchandise resources and Vendors
Supplies, changes in, 660
Supply sources; see Merchandise resources and Vendors
Systems research, 674

T

Table-top displays, 468
Technological advances, 11–12
Technological changes, 660
Telephone-order business, 15; see also Telephone selling
Telephone selling, 117, 476–81
    customer's viewpoint, 478
    extent of, 476–78
    factors for success of, 481
    future of, 480–81
    growth in, 493
    importance of, 476–78
    limitations of, 479–80
    methods of using, 479
    newspaper advertisements for, 477
    reasons for growth of, 478–79
    retailer's viewpoint, 478–79
    shopping service future, 479
Television, influence of, 9–10
Television advertising, 457, 460–61, 473
Terminations of employment, 246–47
Terms of sale, 325, 327–39; see also Dating and Discounts
Testing laboratories, 298, 380
Tests for job applicants, 218
Theater tickets, 535
Theft; see Crime and Shoplifting
Ticket switching, 644
Tickler systems, 359
Tie-in arrangements, 467, 485
Total debt to tangible net worth ratio, 667
Tracing of delayed shipments, 389
Trade associations, 143, 155, 223, 434, 456, 666, 669
    membership in, 53
Trade discounts, 331–32
    defined, 331
    legality of, 332
Trade-in allowances, 397
Trade papers, 297
Trade publications, 456, 459
Trade tests, 218
Trade unions; see Unions
Trading area selection, 93–97
    buying habits of potential customers, 95
    character of industries, 93–94
    competition, nature and strength of, 96–97
    dispersion of wealth, 95–96
    legislation, state and local, 97
    population factor, 94

Trading area selection—Cont.
    progressiveness of, 95
    purchasing power of population, 95
    type of industries, 93–94
Trading stamps, 486–88, 491, 494
    redemption centers, 25
Traffic department functions, 389
Traffic management, 370–71, 388–89
Traffic manager, 392
Training employees, 221–29
    advanced management programs, 227
    appraising program for, 228–29
    centralized, 221–22
    decentralized, 221–22
    determining extent of program for, 222
    different types of employees, 222–28
    extra workers, 227–28
    follow-up, 225–26
    job training, 225–26
    new experienced employees, 225
    new inexperienced employees, 223–25
    part-time workers, 227–28
    promotional, 226
    regular employees, 225–27
    sales-supporting employees, 224–25
    salespeople, 223–24
    sponsor system, 213, 223–24
    supervisors, 226–27
Training of key executives
    chain store programs, 80–83
    department store program for junior executives, 73–74
Training for key positions, 61–62
    salaries during, 62–63
Transfer of title, 299, 344–46
Transfers of personnel, 246
Transportation terms, 340
Transportation tickets, 535
Trouble-shooting, 227
Truth-in-Lending Act, 563 n, 565, 567–68, 574
Truth-in-Packaging Act, 484
Turnover of capital, 292 n
Turnover in sales, 464
Turnover of stock, 271, 663
    cost method of computation, 291
    definitions, 291–92
    economics of small and large inventories, 291–93
    hand-to-mouth buying, 292
    measurement of, 291–92
    planning for, 289
    rapid, advantages of, 292
    rapid, disadvantages of, 292–93
    retail method of computation, 291
    speculative buying, 293
    units method of computation, 291–92
Turnover rate
    costs of, 211
    employees, 210–11

Turnover rate—*Cont.*
    executives, 211
    formula to measure, 230
Two-functional organization plan, 183–84, 194

U

Unemployment insurance, 209
Unfair advertising, 463–64
Unfair-sales practices acts, 433–34, 437
Unfair-trade practices acts, 433–34
Uniform Consumer Credit Code, 546 n, 567
Unions, 65, 251–54
    aims of, 252–53
    growth of, 251–52
    management reaction to, 253–54
    wage and hour laws, 253
Unit controls, 350, 356–62; *see also* Merchandise control
    benefits of, 359–60
    defined, 352, 356
    instituting system of, 361–62
    reasons for limited use of, 360–61
    selling tool, 360
Unit pricing, 435–36
    defined, 436 n
Universal Vendor Marking (UVM), 631
Universal Product Code (UPC), 380–81, 427, 435, 631
    coupons, 427
    price marking, 435
Urban areas, suburbs compared with, 7
Urban renewal programs, 143
Urbanization, 104

V

Vacations, 65
Variety chains
    opportunities in, 80–83
    organization of, 196
Variety stores, 18, 131
    limited price, 131 n
Vending machines, 117
Vendor displays, 468–70
Vendor-marking, 393
Vendors; *see also* Merchandise resources
    best buys of, 304
    catalogs, 310–11
    central markets, retailers' visits to, 312–16
    concentrating purchase, advantages of, 303
    defined, 296 n
    dividing purchases, advantages of, 303–4
    initiative to find buyers, 309–10
    large, 304
    local markets, retailers' visits to, 312

Vendors—*Cont.*
    number of, 303–4
    price lists, 310
    qualifications, 304
    resource file, 304–5
    retailer initiative to find, 310–16
    sales representatives, 310
    selection of, 303–5
    small, 304
Verbrauchermarkt, 26
Vertical centers, 116–17
Vest-pocket supermarkets, 28
Visual-front stores, 131
Vocational Education Acts of 1963 and 1968, 224
Voluntary chains, 29, 67, 306–7
Voluntary Retail Identification Standard, 631

W

Wage assignments, 565 n
Wage and Hour Law, 253
Wage and Price Guidelines (U.S.), 13–14
Wage-to-sales ratio, 211–12
Wages; *see* Compensation *and* Salaries
Walk-in trade, 99–100
Wall finishes, 132
Want slips, 295
Warehouse control system, 358–59
Warehouse operation, 373
Weeks' supply method, 273
Weighing machines, 138
Wheeler-Lea Act of 1938, 464
Wholesalers, 305–7
Will-call sale, 534, 618–19
Window display, 130–31, 465–67
    image building, 466
    item promotion, 466
    message of, 467
    productive, 466–67
    value of, 467
    vendor-supplied material, 467
Window signs, 469
Window sticker showing price, 434
Windowless stores, 131
Windows
    display of merchandise in, 130–31; *see also* Window display
    size and type, 131
Women
    changing role of, 9
    employment opportunities for, 60–61
Work schedules, 64
Working conditions, retail, 64–65, 247–48
    safety, 248
    working hours, 247; *see also* Store hours
Working hours, 247; *see also* Store hours

Working wives, 9
Workrooms, 189
Wrapping merchandise, 517–19
   arrangements for, 517–18
   central wrap, 518
   clerk wrap, 517
   department wrap, 517–18
   prepackaging, 519

Wrapping merchandise—Cont.
   variations in amount and kind of
     service, 517

Y–Z

Young workers, 210
Youth market, 5
Zero population growth, 4

This book has been set in 10 and 9 point
Optima, leaded 2 points. Part titles are 24 point
(small) Optima and chapter titles are 18 point
Optima Semi Bold. The size of the type page
is 27 by 46½ picas.